Race, Nature, and the Politics of Difference

Race, Nature, and the Politics of Difference

Edited by Donald S. Moore, Jake Kosek, & Anand Pandian

Duke University Press   Durham and London 2003

©2003 Duke University Press   All rights reserved
Printed in the United States of America on acid-free paper ∞
Typeset in Trump Mediaeval by Keystone Typesetting Inc.
Library of Congress Cataloging-in-Publication Data appear
on the last printed page of this book.

Contents

Acknowledgments

Generous funding from the Ford Foundation, the MacArthur Foundation, and the Rockefeller Foundation enabled our contributors to attend a conference we convened at the Institute of International Studies, University of California, Berkeley, in February 2000. Eowyn Greeno, Estee Neuwirth, Dar Rudnyckyj, and Jennifer Sokolove provided crucial assistance for the workshop. Michael Watts took an early interest in the project, and his inspired support remained critical to its completion. Our contributors are appreciated interlocutors whose work is the condition of possibility for this volume. Colleagues in the Departments of Anthropology and Geography at UC Berkeley offered enabling dialogues. We also wish to thank colleagues whose participation in the conference contributed to our collective insights: Iain Boal, Jacqueline Nassy Brown, Lawrence Cohen, Caren Kaplan, Ruthie Gilmore, Allan Pred, Ato Quayson, Helena Ragone, Ajay Skaria, and Steven Small. Funding from the Agrarian Studies Program at Yale University provided crucial support. For their critically constructive comments on previous versions, giving weapons to the weak, we thank Arun Agrawal, Shubhra Gururani, James Scott, and Margaret Sommers. Conversations with Gillian Hart, Barnor Hesse, Orin Starn, Amita Baviskar, Leti Volpp, and Vron Ware helped clarify key moves, taking us beyond the pale. Paul Gilroy and Donna Haraway offered more than small acts and situated knowledges generative to the project; our thanks for their gracious engagement and challenges. We are especially grateful to David Theo Goldberg and Hugh Raffles, whose extensive critical comments sharpened our introduction; their rigorous involvement proved both formidable and formative. At Duke, Ken Wissoker's supportive yet critical editorial savvy and Rebecca Johns-Danes's insights improved the assemblage through a *Latour de force*. Ginger Doll's spirit and generosity engendered insights about race, nature, and difference as well as a politics of the possible. With unwavering love and guidance, Lalitha and Ganesa Pandian have provided the freedom to imagine these themes otherwise. Jon and Margaret Kosek, Julie Greenberg, and the spirit of Adam Kolff have provided critical encouragement and continual inspiration. Our thanks for all these ensouled practices that informed our articulations.

Race, Nature, and the Politics of Difference

INTRODUCTION. The Cultural Politics of
Race and Nature: Terrains of Power and Practice

Donald S. Moore, Anand Pandian, and Jake Kosek

Perhaps it is wrong to speak of [race] at all as a *concept* rather than as a group of contradictory forces, facts, and tendencies.—W. E. B. Du Bois[1]

Employed as a metaphysical concept, which it mainly is in the argument of philosophy, "nature" is the concept through which humanity thinks its difference and specificity. —Kate Soper[2]

Why do ideas of race and nature incite such passion and protest? Pervasive in their reach and forceful in their effects, the two work together in strikingly powerful ways. Images of wild nature animate racial anxieties about crime and poverty in the urban jungle.[3] In the global south, indigenous peoples must often describe themselves as Noble Savages to claim rain forest resources. From Paris to Buenos Aires, medical metaphors of disease and contagion circulate through cultural imaginaries of the dangers posed by racialized foreigners and immigrants. Race and nature work together.[4] And it is their recombinant mutations that so often haunt the cultural politics of identity and difference. Discourses of race and nature provide the resources to express truths, forge identities, and justify inequalities. They form a vast terrain for the exercise of power, spanning the distance from genetic coils to national territories and diasporic communities. *Race, Nature, and the Politics of Difference* explores these landscapes of affect and effect, the busy traffic of nature and culture that articulates racial formations and their contested legacies.

We begin this project with a question: *how do race and nature work as a terrain of power?* The phrasing is deliberate. We argue that these three terms—work, terrain, and power—offer a useful means to illuminate the *cultural politics* of race and nature. We understand cultural politics as an approach that treats culture itself as a site of political struggle, an analytic emphasizing power, process, and practice. Cultural practices bear tangible political effects: they forge communities, reproduce inequalities, and vindicate exclusions. Yet they also provide the means by which those very effects are challenged. Cultural politics insists that such struggles are simultaneously material and symbolic, taking seriously the ties that bind fleeting signs to embodied practices and living bodies. Refusing to accept that race or nature are matters of common sense, we insist that neither keyword is natural.[5] Neither can be taken as a foundational ground beyond the bounds of history and social struggle. We follow instead the means by which such essences of race and nature are fashioned, and we track their echoes and movements through time and space. By attending to the struggles through which races and natures are made and unmade, bound together and pried apart, we actively encourage new ways of imagining these tenacious terms.

With what imaginings do we struggle? Race and nature are often opposed in both popular and technical discourse. Many natural scientists have sought to describe a material world free from human influence. And reciprocally, critics of racism often insist that there is nothing natural about social differences. Their insistence is instructive. The invocations of race with which they struggle rely on ideas of nature. And there are few forms of nature that do not bear the traces of racial exclusion. From eighteenth-century assertions that climate determined racial character, to twentieth-century medical debates concerning the racial dimensions of genetic disease, race and nature meet on a well-worn path. The contributions to this volume underscore what Donna Haraway terms the "traffic between what we have come to know historically as nature and culture."[6] They chart this traffic's routes across diverse sites, moments, and contexts. In so doing, they illuminate the practices, processes, and power relations that articulate race, nature, and the politics of difference.

Nature is not merely the material environment, nor is race merely a problem of social relations. Race and nature are both material and symbolic. They reach across this imagined divide, acting at once through bodies and metaphors. Natural character is written into discourse and expression but is also worked into flesh and landscape. Racialized discourses mark both living beings and geographical territories with the force of their distinctions. We take both race and nature as historical artifacts: assemblages of material, discourse, and practice irreducible to a universal essence. Imagined as an ontological foundation, nature has served as the generative terrain from which assertions of essence emerge. Nature appears to precede history, even as it wipes away the historical traces of its own fashioning.[7] Race has provided mobile markers of identity and difference on this naturalizing ground, rationalizing orders of exclusion as laws of necessity. Race provides a critical medium through which ideas of nature operate, even as racialized forces rework the ground of nature itself. *Working together*, race and nature legitimate particular forms of political representation, reproduce social hierarchies, and authorize violent exclusions—often transforming contingent relations into eternal necessities.

For precisely this reason, we insist on the historical specificity of particular racisms and naturalisms.[8] We agree that racial and natural verities must be rigorously denatured, robbed of their naturalizing power. But this is not enough. Couplings of these two persistent terms gain their specific character on what Gramsci termed "the terrain of the conjunctural."[9] These contingent formations are at times profoundly dangerous but at other moments potentially liberating. They bear contradictions both enabling and disabling. Both fascist Nazis and radical environmentalists have shared a passion for organic bread in twentieth-century Germany. Both Hitler and Black Nationalist LeRoi Jones used the notion of a *lebensraum*—living space—to make racial claims to national territory, as we later discuss. Their sharing of symbols is troubling but does not produce an allied political vision. Arguments for Aryan supremacy in 1930s Germany differ radically from assertions of African American identity in the United States in the 1960s. The political stakes of race and nature lie in the ways they become *articulated* together in particular historical moments.

Here, we have in mind not the clunky, economistic articulation of 1970s structural Marxism and the modes of production debates. Rather, as Stuart Hall notes, articulation carries within it the twin concepts of joining and enunciation.[10] An articulation both brings together disparate elements and, in the process of assemblage, gives that constellation a particular form and potential force. The shape of this *formation*, the effectiveness of the linkages established among its elements, and the impact it will have on cultural, social, and political processes is historically contingent, not able to be "read" off from an underlying structural logic. A critical question becomes how contingent constellations come together in particular historical contexts, the heterogeneity of practices and cultural forms they authorize—in other words, what novel forms emerge from this provisional "unity"—and how these linkages inform political subjectivities and cultural identities.[11]

Thus conceived, articulation offers a means for understanding emergent assemblages of institutions, apparatuses, practices, and discourses. Nodal points of intersection give shape to formations that are reworked through historical agency rather than structurally determined. The distance of this vision from Althusserian structuralism is most clear not simply in the rejection of the economic as the determinative "last instance" but also in the proliferation of sites that constitute subjects. Rather than positing the state as overdetermining subject formation, we see the discursive contours of race and nature as critical to shaping identities enacted through historical struggles and the practices of everyday life. Structural determination is here supplanted by a politics of contingency, open-ended historical processes without guarantees.[12] Within this conceptual framework, we ask: how do race and nature invoke each other, speak through each other, build on each other? Race may work to biologize culture.[13] But cultural difference also may be seized as a means of marking race.[14] These mutual entanglements and relational histories inform one another dialectically, animating the forms of practice, process, and power our contributors explore.

Racial and natural essences are forged in the crucible of cultural politics. How do they claim authority as foundational truths? On the one hand, invocations of race and nature often betray a sense of stable fixity, a settled character beyond the flux of history and politics. On the other hand, these very ideas traverse vast scales—indeed participate in the production of those scales—moving fluidly across radically different historical and geographic contexts: from blood to soil, from courtrooms to laboratories, from national parks to toxic neighborhoods. As race and nature move across time, scale, and context, their "polyvalent mobility" links distinct subjects, artifacts, and environments.[15] Yet there is no paradox in these widely traveling claims to stability. Time and again, race and nature stake claims to commonsensical truth. These verities can be discovered and rediscovered in the most distant of places and the most disparate of times precisely because their essence can be taken for granted. Their sense of universality both makes race and nature continually available for naïve rediscovery and continually obscures the historical conditions that make and remake them. Because race and nature always seem to precede history, they can be taken again and again as the very substrate on which myriad social truths are built.

This volume explores disparate sites where articulations of race and nature work together to powerful effect. We envision the cultural politics of race and nature as an emergent field that cuts across disciplinary divides and established intellectual communities. For this reason, the volume's interdisciplinary contributors employ a variety of theoretical and methodological perspectives. While our approaches are often distinct, they converge in a shared emphasis on the articulated effects of race and nature. In charting this field, we draw especially on the following bodies of work, which we later elaborate, building on established routes while advocating emergent paths to explore novel terrain. Our aim is to signal suggestive genealogies that inform an emergent analytic—the cultural politics of race and nature—without policing the boundaries of an exclusionary field.

Scholars of the "cultural politics of difference" have understood identities and affinities as constructed through social struggle, positioning subjects within multiple matrices of power.[16] Black cultural studies and race critical theories foreground race as both a constitutive feature of modern power and a formative prism shaping lived experience. Stressing the historical specificity of racisms, they have challenged an understanding of race as a transhistorical, universal category.[17] Postcolonial theorists have "provincialized" Europe's claims to universal reason by conceptualizing metropole and colony as mutually constituted, finding global logics of racial exclusion in the "rule of colonial difference."[18] Environmental justice scholars remind us that in both north and south the violence of racial exclusion manifests itself in the drastically heavier burdens of environmental hazard borne by marginalized communities of color.[19]

Political ecologists have also brought the tools of political economy to bear on environmental inequalities. Differential histories of access to natural resources, they argue, shape struggles over social reproduction between state, capital, and community.[20] Environmental historians—insisting that nature too has a history—have tracked the imperial circuits fashioning natural resources into modern objects of science and management. Anthropologists have chronicled myriad livelihood practices in vastly diverse cultural contexts, exploring alternative maps of both human and natural worlds.[21] Their challenges to normative notions of Western nature echo feminist insights that trouble a fixed, stable boundary between the bodily truths of sex and the social relations of gender. As Marilyn Strathern stresses, both anthropologists and feminists share the project of actively interrogating "the 'naturalness' of structures."[22] Feminists illuminate the articulation of multiple modalities of power—notably those of race, class, gender, and sexuality—whose naturalizing effects work relationally and conjuncturally, as social assemblages rather than as isolated essences. In turn, we draw from science studies the insight that nature is at once social construct and material artifact. Much like feminisms, science studies expands the boundaries of the political itself while alerting us to the consequential assemblages of nonhuman actants and human agents.[23]

Taken together, these accumulated insights ground what we have come to understand as *the cultural politics of race and nature*. We hope that readers familiar with each of these fields will find in this volume not only an echo of their own interests but also a compass orienting disparate endeavors toward a common project. Our intent is to encourage recognition of terrain both familiar and unfamiliar in the hope you will find the footing to carve new paths across landscapes entangling nature and culture. In the following pages, we refract our discussion of the cultural politics of race and nature through three conceptual prisms: work, terrain, and power. Our engagement with the fields laid out above motivates our use of these metaphors as critical tools. In turn, it shapes our subsequent discussion of four prominent themes organizing this emergent domain. We conclude by positioning the project in relation to the constitutive exclusions of liberalism and to contemporary forms of liberal multiculturalism—powerful normative discourses that have naturalized particular formations of race and culture. In this new century, violence waged against alterity and cultural difference remains haunted by historical *exclusions* of specific identities, practices, and communities from the fully human. Our hope is that a critical genealogy of the articulation of race and nature may provide both insight and challenge to these forms of social injustice and their affiliated political technologies of violence.

Work

One must start . . . from the concrete historical "work" which racism accomplishes under specific historical conditions—as a set of economic, political and ideological practices, of a distinctive kind, concretely articulated with other practices in a social formation.
—Stuart Hall[24]

One of the great shortcomings—intellectual and political—of modern environmentalism is its failure to grasp how human beings have historically known nature through work.
—Richard White[25]

A bumper sticker sold in the Pacific Northwest sharply poses a trenchant question: "Are you an environmentalist or do you work for a living?"[26] Deeply rooted contrasts oppose the labor of work to the care of nature.

For many environmentalists, work itself—and especially modern industrial labor—requires and sustains the destruction of nature. Memories of Eden haunt such narratives, which echo that catastrophic fall from original natural leisure into the degraded toil of a working world. A similar origin story animates much modern Western discourse on nature and history from the Enlightenment onward. John Locke argued that sovereign individuals gained rights to their share of the primordial commons through labors of improvement: "In the beginning all the World was America," he wrote, evoking the fallow condition of a continent awaiting the redemptive touch of European labor and private property. Karl Marx described a metabolism shared between humanity and the natural world, powered by the act of labor: through their work people develop the "potentialities slumbering within" both the external natural environment and their own material bodies. In accounts such as these, history itself begins with strenuous exertions on a pristine nature.[27]

These propositions yield a difficult double bind for modern developers and environmentalists alike. On the one hand, because play is natural—that is, because bodies in their original state tend to idle dissipation—natural bodies must be trained and taught to do productive work. Visions of wasted lands and their idle inhabitants, for example, authorized violent colonial interventions into both land and livelihood in the name of improvement. On the other hand, because history requires such work, only bodies and landscapes that evade its force qualify as properly natural. Environmental discourse routinely suppresses evidence of the insistent human labor that has shaped and reworked the very terrain to be protected from the corrosive force of history. In Richard White's terms, "We seek the purity of our absence, but everywhere we find our own fingerprints."[28]

What has often vexed Western environmentalists, of course, is that such fingerprints are not their own but those of racialized others. Influential Enlightenment theories of climate, for example, made productive labor into the very index by means of which races were distinguished and natural environments classified. In his 1748 *Natural History*, Buffon argued that the climate of the tropical New World produced an inferior race of peoples, unable to develop nature for the higher purposes of civilization because of their environmentally conditioned indolence. Native plants and peoples in the tropical New World, Buffon believed, shared a nature inferior to Europe's. In the same year, Montesquieu published his *Spirit of the Laws*, finding justification for different human characters and spirits, including slavery, in relation to "the nature of the climate."[29] Hume wove the influence of natural climate on racial character into his infamous assertion of racial inferiority: "I am apt to suspect the negroes and in general all other species . . . to be naturally inferior to the whites." Nature, Hume argued, "made an original distinction between these breeds of men." Kant, too, praised nature's climatic foresight, finding the "strong, fleshy, supple" Negro well suited to his climate, but also finding in this very environment a reason for his "lazy, soft and dawdling" nature.[30]

These ideologies suggest ways in which notions of race and nature themselves *work* as instruments of power. Neither ancestor of nor victim to human toil, nature itself is a means of enacting, expressing, and reproducing the works of humanity. Natures are made and manifest through embodied activity; notions of nature work as discourse and ideology; and natural bodies are sustained through repeated material and symbolic practices. Race works alongside these constructions of nature in a host of related and sometimes contradictory ways, at times providing a means of biologizing the cultural, and at other times racializing the biology of nonhuman species. We call attention in this section to working nature and working race.

A distinction between natural and artificial objects runs deep in the Western imagination, sustaining what Donna Haraway has described as a "productionist logic" that takes nature as the raw material for cultural and capitalist elaboration.[31] Cultural and political ecologists have excavated cultural alterity to unsettle this divide, finding environments saturated by differing understandings and practices of human labor in diverse non-Western contexts.[32] But even within the West, the notion of a working nature has a long and complicated history. As early as 1658, Kenelm Digby conceived the "oeconomy of nature" itself as a working household managed by the hand of God, and this metaphor has reverberated profoundly over the course of modern ecological science.[33] For Marx, the worker made his own human nature by making over that of the world. Foucault upturned this dialectic, finding free man—the very spirit that Marx sought to liberate from the clutches of capital—produced by the disciplinary force of modern power.[34] At stake for both Marx and Foucault was the simultaneous cultivation of labor and the labor of cultivation—the conjoined fashioning of useful workers and profitable environments. Following these thinkers, we suggest that the very substance of nature is made and manifest through material and symbolic practices.[35]

"Cultivation" provides an especially apt metaphor for a working nature.

Stemming from the Latin verb *colere*—to till, tend, or care for—cultivation is a term for social practice rooted in engagements with nonhuman nature. The word surpassed its agrarian connotations in the eighteenth century to gain social, educational, and moral significance. Modern arts of cultivation fabricate manifold natures. Animal breeders, hydraulic engineers, and social planners mold natural bodies to develop their qualities. Landscape architects, park rangers, and forest dwellers fashion the very environments that viewers and visitors take as pristine and natural. Each of these cultivating practices acts simultaneously on worldly environments, bodily capacities, and interior dispositions. The English planted gardens in the New World both to establish rights of possession and to nurture civilized dispositions that would legitimate those claims. And mission gardens in nineteenth-century South Africa cultivated both crops and selves, an ordering of nature in the Lord's fields that produced both commodities for market and souls for salvation.[36]

As soils and selves become fused through work they also produce racial orders of difference. When Billie Holiday sings the haunting words of Abel Meeropol's 1939 song "Strange Fruit," she grafts images of lynching onto harvested crops: "Black bodies swinging in the southern breeze/Strange fruit hanging from the poplar trees." While *Gone With the Wind* played in theaters, the song invoked unnatural aberrations such as "Blood on the leaves and blood at the roots" to critique a brutal history of racialized violence. Black bodies shaped the very landscape yielding slavery's bitter fruit. Cultivated crops and human harvests provide ample means of illuminating what the seeds of racism have sown. Such historical entanglements, in turn, shape the cultivation of racialized subjects whose natures are frequently grafted to metaphors of roots, blood, and soil. In the late 1960s, Martin Luther King Jr. professed that "white America is still poisoned by racism, which is as native to our soil as pine trees, sagebrush and buffalo grass." These powerful images bear witness to the many kinds of work—material, ideological, and sentimental—done by both race and nature.[37]

But as many of the chapters of this volume suggest, notions of nature often function by effacing the very traces of their fabrication through human labor: witness the primordial status ascribed to racial bloodlines, national boundaries, and instinctual behaviors. This naturalization of identities and differences is one of the most powerful means by which race works. Like the Guatemalan images of a *moronga* brain that Diane Nelson describes in chapter 3, racial essences are congealed and hardened by historically specific practices. Popular understandings took Guatemalan political violence first as a problem of class and then as a problem of race at different historical moments. Nelson's discussion echoes longstanding Marxist concerns with the relative autonomy of race and class and the work that each performs in the reproduction of social inequalities. Racialized distinctions have both material and ideological effects that stabilize "race"; these effects must in turn be reproduced to secure enduring hierarchies.[38]

The reassuring stability of race and nature is one of their most powerful fictions. But race and nature often fail to work as they should. Closely managed game animals drop suddenly and precipitously in numbers; indigenous communities lose legal claims to the forests with which they are identified; dark kinky hair in a newborn child betrays the genetic impurities of an Afrikaaner family.[39] Constructions of race and nature are repeatedly challenged by the recalcitrance of the very bodies and groups they define. Like all hegemonies, they have "continually to be renewed, recreated, defended and modified."[40] Manifold and ongoing practices are required to sustain the self-identity of cultivated natures, from the sexual assignation of hermaphroditic infants to the policed boundaries of "native" spatial reserves. A host of agents seeks to keep races and natures as they should be: activists and officials, scientists and tourists, planners and lovers. Their labors combine to maintain both the clarity of nature's differences and the persistence of its inequalities.

Terrain

If landscape carries an unseemly spatiality, it also shuttles through temporal processes of history and memory.—David Matless[41]

You come to situations with a history and the enunciation is always in the light of an existing terrain. . . . There are collective projects and there are therefore collective identities. Those identities are not given forever, but they're hard to shift.—Stuart Hall[42]

The cultural politics of race and nature shape terrain both material and metaphorical. As environmental historian William Cronon argues, "Nature will *always* be contested terrain. We will never stop arguing about its meanings, because it is the very ground on which our debates must occur."[43] Contentious and disputed natures point to the power-laden practices that simultaneously create and unfold on natural sites, idioms, and grounds. Gramsci reminds us that "ideologies . . . organize human masses, and create the terrain on which men [and women] move, acquire consciousness of their position, struggle, etc."[44] Nature as contested terrain both grounds material struggles over environmental resources and refracts racial essences through the discursive prisms of nation, population, and gene. Race and nature reach far beyond biology and ecology, science and state, also crafting interior landscapes of sentiment and selfhood. Our contributors traverse conceptual and material ground from wombs to wilderness. Rather than presume inherent affinities between nature and environment or race and biology, the analytic of terrain calls attention to the historical formation and discursive effects of these powerful grounds for struggle.

The concept of landscape provides a useful means for understanding the workings of natural terrain.[45] John Berger describes landscape as a "way of seeing." Inherently duplicitous, the term "landscape" refers both to this visual perspective and to the geographical territories that are seized by it. Landscapes articulate both culture and nature, seer and scene. But equally at stake in landscape are the embodied practices that transform the objects of a proprietary gaze. A multiplicity of situated practices—of cultivators and pastoralists, slaves and colonists, labor migrants and adventure travelers—shapes both terrain and identity. We thus move beyond Berger's emphasis on the hegemony of vision, stressing also the cultural practices that cultivate both landscapes and subjects. Cultivating practices traverse the interior topographies of body and self as readily as exterior expanses of environment and resources.[46]

Marxists, in particular, have stressed the kinds of historical relationships among perspective, power, and property that landscape both reflects and reproduces.[47] Nature's provenance, for example, differs radically for poacher and proprietor. What Marx termed the "customary rights of the poor" to harvest the "alms of nature" hinged crucially not on nature's inherent properties but rather on the proprietary claims asserted on nature's bounty.[48] Britain's 1723 Black Act criminalized efforts by the poor to provide for themselves as poaching, affirming instead the rightful possession of the countryside by the landed gentry.[49] Such insights do not *reduce* the study of landscapes to class analyses of property and profit but rather remind us of the social orders often reproduced by these perspectival formations of nature. At the same time, they persistently ask about the *work* that landscape does in relation to the work performed upon it. Thinking through landscape invites us to reconsider the relationship between an assumed objective ecology of natural processes and the human, all too human, world of ideology, discourse, and history.[50]

As prominent theorists of colonial discourse have argued, imperial explorers, natural historians, and colonial administrators tended to abstract indigenous people out of landscapes of imperial encounter and contemporaneous history.[51] A widely shared imperial taxonomic impulse assigned aboriginal peoples their presumed proper place in a natural order along with the flora and fauna whose habitat they shared. This placement in a Natural Order of Things was simultaneously a fixing of racial hierarchy and an assertion of essential differences—between natives and their colonizers and among distinct "primitive" groups. Images of "wild men" in Europe and lands both mythical and distant informed racialized perspectives on cultural and phenotypical difference; these envisioned natures and cultures were deeply entangled with understandings of evolution, species classification, and beastly alterity. Linnaeus, whose vision of taxonomic orders shaped the modern imagination of nature, biological being, and racial classification located *homo monstruosus* within the *homo sapien* species. His system of nature was simultaneously a system of race. By 1753, *Systema Naturae* was in its tenth edition, where the "Wild Man" shared a common species, along with the "European," with *Homo africanus*, whose "apelike nose" betrayed an external body reflecting an inferior nature "ruled by authority." Linnaeus's search for savagery in his own Swedish backyard underscores the global routes of natural history, comparative ethnology, and imperial science that converged to map race and nature at "home" and worlds away. He fashioned his "Sami savage," based on his 1732 travels in Lapland, from ethnographic images of American, Indian, and West African peoples as well as those of Inuits and others.[52]

Colonial discourses of savagery and barbarism linked understandings of natural history and racial essence. These formations often defined normative European humanity in relation to an imagined "constitutive outside" that located racialized alterity in bodies and landscapes at once wild, uncultivated, and prehistorical. Conrad's influential exploration of nature, culture, and the savage customs of colonialism in the African interior turns pivotally on the boundary between the human and nonhuman. Rather than finding a "conquered monster" in the Belgian Congo, his narrator is both thrilled and repulsed by a recognition of a common humanity bridging racial divides, reaching back across an imagined passage to prehistory: "what thrilled you was just the thought of their humanity—like yours—the thought of your remote kinship with this wild and passionate uproar."[53] During the rubber boom in the Colombian Amazon, colonial discourses of terror and labor extraction imagined the savage *auca* as an "ethereal mingling of animal and human" in El Oriente's Heart of Darkness.[54] In southern Africa, the South African Defense Force's use of so-called Bushmen as trackers in the service of apartheid's regime of regional rule relied on their constructed proximity to a primitive, instinctual animality.[55]

The circuits of imperial science and colonial legislation mingled from Cuba to the Congo, targeting the conduct of racialized bodies in domestic spaces and regulating mixed-race unions as well as legitimate forms of interracial intimacy such as domestic labor arrangements.[56] Bodies, social and environmental milieux, and their entangled racialized relations became the ground of colonial discipline. Interventions sought to police normative boundaries in defense of dangerous transgressions deemed immoral and repugnant precisely because they challenged the natural and racial order of things. Naturalists followed Darwin's search for "constancy of character" in their taxonomies of race and nature while imperial projects often sought their transformation through management and improvement.[57] Ideologies of "good breeding" found common bedfellows in fears of racial degeneration, the wild passions of lascivious natives in the tropics, and imperial tropes of the prophylaxis of social distance from primitive proximity. The "problem" of mixed-race progeny, of course, attests to the historically gendered patterns of unsafe sex, suffused with power and imperial anxiety.

However, colonial visions of a native proximity to nature made for an "ambivalent primitivism."[58] Rousseau's Noble Savage, living harmoniously as gentle custodian of a bountiful nature, also preyed on wildlife and environmental resources desired exclusively for colonial use. In many cases, colonial constructions of a pristine nature entailed the forced removal of local inhabitants from the landscape. This reorganization of landscapes and livelihoods in the tropics, trafficking in both nature and culture, emerged out of the powerful circuits of imperial science, natural history, and regimes of rule—a formation Richard Grove terms "Green Imperialism."[59] In Africa's white settler colonies, state laws effectively created national parks and game reserves out of racial land designations. Customary practices of African hunting were criminalized as poaching and trespass.[60] Primitive proximity to a nature "before" history helped legitimate these forcible expropriations. At its extreme, in the brutal extermination of the Herero in the 1904 colony of German South West Africa, officials let "nature" finish their project of genocide. The German General Staff's official publication, *Der Kampf*, reported: "like a half-dead animal he was hunted from water-hole to water-hole until he became a lethargic victim of the nature of his own country."[61] Brutal nature here abets the cultural, social, and political practices of genocide.

When these insights from imperial contexts are brought home to the West, they illuminate the racialization of national landscapes often seen as naturally white. National parks in the United States such as Yellowstone, Glacier, and Yosemite were established by forcibly moving Native Americans from the landscapes they inhabited. Mark Spence has chronicled these Native American evictions and "the cultural myopia that allows late-twentieth-century Americans to ignore the fact that national parks enshrine recently dispossessed landscapes."[62] In erasing Native American presence from his own writings on the area, John Muir followed the trail blazed by the capture and removal of Chief Tenaya from Yosemite. In many contexts, the celebratory tenor of white histories is predicated on the removal—both rhetorical and material—of racialized others from natural landscapes protected in the national interest.[63]

Echoes of these racial erasures haunt even emancipatory visions of nature, nation, and history. Raymond Williams's laudatory socialist humanism, critics have noted, neglected the effects of empire on the formation of British nationalism and its racialized landscapes.[64] Ingrid Pollard's photographs of dreadlocked black bodies in the pastoral landscapes of Britain provide a powerful complement to such critique.[65] Pollard's images challenge the notion of a people's proper place in a natural terrain beyond the reach of imperial politics and diasporic migration. Depicting a black woman holding a baseball bat for protection in what appears an otherwise bucolic pastoral scene, she reminds us that geographies of belonging privilege particular subjects' positioning while simultaneously rendering other bodies vulnerable to violence.[66] Race, nation, and subjugation are powerfully entangled in geographies of belonging and exclusion. Bodies, populations, histories, and geographies—understood as contested terrain—converge to illuminate the cultural politics of race and nature.

Power

To dominate is to ignore or attempt to crush the capacity of action of the dominated. But to govern is to recognize that capacity for action and to adjust oneself to it. To govern is to act upon action.—Nikolas Rose[67]

If genocide is indeed the dream of modern powers, this is because of a recent return of the ancient right to kill; it is because power is situated and exercised at the level of life, the species, the race, and the large-scale phenomena of population.—Michel Foucault[68]

Nature too can be politics by other means. Nature, in other words, works as a contested arena and an effective means for the exercise of power. From the victimization of inferior races to the making of national spaces to the replication of inherited differences, natural bodies form the terrain and instruments of power's expression. We suggest that power works on and through nature in several overlapping ways: through violent acts of domination, through the constitution of subjects and truths, and through the maintenance of these identities and differences across time and space. This section elaborates these *repressive* and *productive* operations, arguing that race and nature are constitutive features of modern power.

Many contemporary discussions of the politics of nature take power as a repressive force from which downtrodden natures and cultures must be liberated. Liberal discourses of tolerance, for example, often depict race as a fiction peddled by particular individuals and institutions to obscure the universality of human nature. Studies of rural political ecology often focus on people's legitimate struggles against state and capital over access to and control of natural resources. In these cases, agents find their true nature through concerted action against oppressive structures. These contemporary calls for nature's liberation from social power echo—ironically—an earlier Western understanding of nature itself as a sovereign force constraining the possibilities of human agency. Enlightenment thinkers conceived of nature as a dominating environment that had to be overcome to enable the full development of humanity and its capacities. Freud argued much later that civilization emerged from the renunciation of instinct.[69] We suggest that such understandings of a repressive nature—one that itself demanded repression—form one of the original maps of the structure-agency problematic.

Marx took the model of a repressive nature and used it as a means of challenging the exploitative social conditions of capitalism, precisely by depicting these conditions as the *naturalization* of a human-made order.[70] Insofar as these conditions represented a form of repression, they demanded to be overthrown. But what Marx sought to liberate through this struggle against a hostile environment was itself an essential human nature, realized fully through the exercise of labor. When taken as a problem of structure and agency, then, power is opposed to nature: power represses human nature on the one hand, but nature itself becomes the ground from which struggles *against* power are staged.

Critical histories of nature's repression are embedded in stories of racial bondage, exclusive entitlements, and unequal exposure to environmental hazards. Environmental justice became a means of understanding both the global asymmetries between north and south and the unequal burdens of risk, resource deprivation, and ecological degradation borne by racial minorities in the United States. Bullard's pioneering work, for example, chronicled the location of waste disposal sites in black working-class neighborhoods in the U.S. South.[71] Scholars have more recently mapped environmental hazards and differential resource access onto racialized geographies, showing historical patterns of environmental injustice. Such treatments, while critically insightful, have often treated nature as a given material environment and race as a fixed field of difference. Both are understood through an analytic of repression. We must also consider, however, nature's ongoing formation and reformation in the contested realms of culture, power, and history.

Struggles over resources and territory are simultaneously material and symbolic, as scholarship in the fields of political ecology and environmental politics demonstrates. These perspectives build on and rework Marxian political economy, treating struggles over cultural meanings as *constitutive* of agrarian politics rather than as epiphenomenal trappings to deeper structural truths. For Sara Berry and others, contests over access to land and labor simultaneously call into question the meanings of "custom" and "community."[72] Conflicts over social boundaries provide common ground for debating nature and culture, casting as a cultural problem the very question of what constitutes a "natural" resource. We follow these scholars in connecting agrarian and environmental concerns to questions of gender, cultural politics, and environmental justice. Feminists, for example, have long explored the power-saturated entanglements of gender and nature.[73]

How does nature come to provide a language for the truths of bodies, selves, and landscapes while also becoming a medium for their transformation? First, we call attention to the taxonomic orders through which nature and race are made intelligible as *objects* of knowledge. The truths of difference are recorded in hierarchies of value that oppose and rank particular natures according to endless criteria: skin color, cleanliness, physical and mental capacity, spatial location, historical depth, and so on. Scientific, administrative, and popular classifications often define the essence of both human races and natural landscapes by establishing a boundary between them. Defining a natural site as wilderness, for example, can erase the traces of certain peoples from the places they inhabit. These active erasures powerfully shape struggles for resource and land rights. Second, a host of social technologies also make people into *subjects* of their own nature. Individuals come to recognize themselves as embodiments of racial essences and natives of particular landscapes. Racialized subjects take up their own natures as objects of labor, training their bodies, desires, and dispositions. Foucault himself relied on a term with rural roots to describe such "pastoral" care.[74] Cultivated nature provides both materials for the exercise of power and means for its analysis.

An array of scholars have conceived race and racisms as "formative features of modernity, as deeply embedded in bourgeois liberalism, not as aberrant offshoots of them."[75] Modern technologies of rule have targeted racialized bodies, populations, and territories in the project of "improvement," a theme we later elaborate. The exercise of power has relied on race's mobility across these sites and surfaces, producing discourses of fundamental difference that shuttle across the divide between nature and culture. In many colonial contexts, censuses, surveys, ethnographic maps, and development schemes made "natives" and their natural milieu into the object of racial betterment through administrative management.[76] These instruments of colonial governmentality interpellated subjects both in the metropole and its hinterlands, linking colonizer and colonized through a grid of racial intelligibility. Race was not an afterthought to imperialism but rather constitutive of the colonial encounter itself.[77] Claims of racial superiority— authorized by the laws of nature, legitimating violence, dispossession, and the subjugation of racial alterity—also lurked in Europe. Bauman's germinal study of the Holocaust argues that the modernity of racism required that a "new *naturalness*" had to be "laboriously *constructed*" to fix the racial distinctions that underwrote genocide.[78] Imperialism, the Holocaust, and apartheid are all interwoven from the threads of race and nature. Yet so also are Texas's death row, racial profiling on the New Jersey turnpike, and *adivasi* struggles against massive dams in India. While the powerful work of race and nature shifts across historical, geographical, and cultural contexts, it remains integral to the rule of modernity rather than an exception.

The following sections trace this fabric of violent exclusions and productive techniques through four distinctive articulations of race and nature. The first three describe influential treatments of the nature of race: as a terrain of management and improvement, as a domain of distinction and protection, and as a site of felt attachment. The fourth section attends more closely to the practices of representation through which natures are recognized and races are naturalized. Work, terrain, and power provide critical tools within each thematic section. While contributors differ in their disciplinary perspectives and conceptual frameworks, we all share a commitment to understanding the articulated effects of race and nature. *Race, Nature, and the*

Politics of Difference signals directions for the further development of an emergent field of critical inquiry.

PART ONE. Calculating Improvements

At some future period not very distant as measured in centuries, the civilized races of man will almost certainly exterminate and replace throughout the world the savage races. —Charles Darwin[79]

Racism is a policy first, ideology second. Like all politics, it needs organization, managers and experts.—Zygmunt Baumann[80]

In his 1749 essay "The Oeconomy of Nature," Swedish natural historian Linnaeus suggested that each species was provisioned with adequate food and range thanks to the beneficent foresight of a divine Creator. The word *oeconomy*, used as early as 1530 to describe the art of household management, shares its Greek root *oikos* with "ecology," a neologism proposed by Ernst Haeckel in 1866 to christen the nascent science of nature's households.[81] The invocation of Haeckel's famous adage "politics is applied biology" by Nazi propagandists reminds us of the historical routes connecting ecology and fascist social engineering.[82] Yet invocations of "liberation ecologies," "social ecology," and ecology as a "subversive science" signal alternative political projects also harnessed to Haeckel's household.[83] Across diverse contexts, metaphors like *oikos* call attention to nurtured natures.

Raymond Williams has pointed out that the word "manage" came into English from the Italian *maneggiare:* "to handle, and especially to handle or train horses." The term evokes acts of force and discipline considered necessary for the proper care of natures both human and nonhuman. In the late eighteenth century, Malthus stressed the "fixed laws of our nature" that placed limits on the relationship between population, resources, and wealth. His proposal to abolish the social welfare policies of parish laws was "calculated to increase the mass of happiness among the common people of England" whose care could be managed while improving national wealth and natural resources. At stake is a concern for the welfare of subject populations that Foucault conceived as crucial to modern biopower. This historically specific formation, he argued, brought life itself into the realm of explicit calculation and improvement.[84] Political and social technologies targeted bodies, populations, and environments, seeking to nurture and manage their welfare. Logics of racial difference infuse the workings of such improvement.

Hegel found in Africa a people "wrapped in the dark mantle of night" beyond the Enlightenment's noble glow, their inferior nature effectively removing them from the course of History.[85] Hegel's "universal reason" gained a later corollary in Lewis Henry Morgan's model of social evolution, which assigned each race a particular place in a necessary progression from savagery to barbarism to civilization. In this unilineal teleology, those who occupied the highest rung of civilization held both the moral duty and political right to rule subject races. Victorian discourses of social evolution thereby legitimated the violence of imperial conquest as part and parcel of a civilizing mission. In the 1837 *Natural History of the Negro Race*, Virey asserted: "Negroes cannot be managed, except by captivating *their senses* with pleasures, or striking *their minds* with fear." Because "natural desires" rule the Negro character, Europeans must rule their racial inferiors through forceful subjugation. "Their character being more indolent than active," Virey reasoned, "they seem more fitted *to be ruled, than to govern,* in other words they *were rather born for submission, than dominion.*" Here, racialized differences of culture legitimate the use of force in a project of imperial subjugation, at once authorizing colonial rule and offering a violent blueprint for labor discipline and political control. In colonial contexts, discourses of essential differences in "character," "race," and "culture" all rely on regimes of truth that ground the qualities of colonized alterities in "nature."[86]

Imperial projects of improvement targeted cultural characteristics, seeking their transformation through social and political technologies of rule. In turn, by referencing race and nature as the foundations for cultural alterity, colonial policies invoked the discourse of improvement to legitimate subjugation. Architects of colonial rule such as Lord Frederick Lugard argued that imperial states had the "grave responsibility of . . . 'bringing forth' to a higher plane . . . the backward races." Europeans were responsible for developing "the bounties with which nature has so abundantly endowed the tropics" precisely because subject races were "so pathetically dependent on their guidance."[87] His famous Dual Mandate did double duty: the white man's burden of colonial rule required administration of both nature and natives in the tropics; both were resources to be managed, improved, and developed for the benefit of metropole and colony.

The temporal teleology that underwrote visions of "backward" cultures also invoked a resonant notion of racial inferiority as a justification for European imperial rule. Kipling's infamous 1899 poem "The White Man's Burden" legitimates a project of racial and cultural improvement. He urges imperialists "To serve your captives' need," to attend to their demonic, infantilized nature imagined as "Half devil and half child." We write in the wake of President George Bush's 2001 proclamation of a "Crusade" against terrorism—mapped, in hegemonic political and popular imagination, to a satanic threat envisioned as Islam run amok. Recall that Kipling launched his defense of imperialism amidst fierce debates over U.S. policy in the Philippines. At the time, the term *moros*, derived from the Spanish term for Muslims, fused Western fears of Islam with concerns about robust indigenous political movements in the Philippines. A full century later, such racializations of cultural difference haunt Bush's call for a U.S. crusade.[88]

Entrenched imaginaries of civilizational difference, founded on the radical alterity of enduring essence, have long fused culture and race. The current "clash of civilizations" discourse pits a "traditional" Islam against the "modern" West, normatively Christian but complexly allied with particular formations of Judaism.[89] The teleological trope of "modernizing" the culturally "backward" forces of terrorism does not simply mistake the profoundly modern formations of political Islam in the contemporary world. It mimics imperial discourses of a "civilizing mission" entangled with notions of cultural transformation and racial progress. The Bush administration's feeble attempts to invoke liberal multiculturalism cannot mask the enduring imperial logic of a self-proclaimed Crusade.

Yet we must also consider divergences in such teleological thinking. Consider two prominent formulations of natural history and social evolution that have left enduring legacies: those of Darwin and Lamarck. Darwin attributed a distinct history to the natural world, the laws of which would work on society as an external impetus for change.[90] He held a somber belief in the competitive replacement of inferiors who must be "beaten and supplanted" by their superiors. Progress demanded that "an endless number of lower races" be wiped out by "higher civilized races." Reflecting on the savages of Tierra del Fuego, Darwin notes: "I could not have believed how wide was the difference between savage and civilized man: it is greater than between a wild and domesticated animal, inasmuch as in man there is a greater power of improvement." Like other Victorians, Darwin derived great satisfaction from what Donald Worster terms the "march of improvement" set in motion by Christian missionaries and the British empire, much like Lord Lugard's civilizing burden.[91]

Such improvement worked for Darwin through the violence of extinction. But Lamarck, in contrast, placed a greater degree of faith in the mutability of organic beings. Lamarck understood nature as a historical process linking living beings and their environmental milieu in a dialectical relationship. Organic beings were plastic, responsive, molded by the qualities of their surroundings.[92] Habits stimulated the further development of particular organs and their faculties, acquired characteristics that could then be passed on through reproduction. Habits and habitats were thus bound through projects of social transformation. The Lamarckian milieu provided planners and reformers in both Europe and its colonies a useful metaphor for society itself as a manipulable object of improvement. Latin American scientists and officials, for example, found Lamarck's theory of the "inheritance of acquired characteristics" much more palatable than the blind evolution Darwin proposed, precisely because it promised the possibility of national—and racial—evolution through social reform.[93]

In the United States, Social Darwinism—propelled by Herbert Spencer's dictum "survival of the fittest"—influenced late-nineteenth-century thinking on race and social evolution.[94] Galton's notion of eugenics crossed the Atlantic near the turn of the century to reach U.S. shores along with waves of immigrants. Ideas of racial improvement found common cause with projects of social engineering that would manage the health of the national body, policing the dangers of crime, disease, and moral degradation posed by foreign bodies.[95] There were, of course, regional variations in patterns of eugenic ideology and practice. While Southerners sang the popular hymn, "There is Power in the Blood" in the early twentieth century, many struggled to reconcile eugenics with prevailing norms and forms of family, kinship, and agrarian populism. Poor whites were frequently the targets of class-inflected fears of racial degeneration. H. L. Mencken advocated the sterilization of whites and blacks in the South, fearing that sharecroppers would migrate north, threatening to "swarm like a nest of maggots." During the 1920s, a state mental health official enthusiastically supported proposed legislation in Louisiana requiring the mentally ill to "voluntarily submit to a sterilizing program" in the hopes of promoting "the aristocracy of health."[96] Yet eugenic thinking was not exclusive to the political right. While followers of Weisman and Mendel sought the "pruning out of biological weakness" in society, neo-Lamarckians saw the reduction of social inequalities as another means of biological improvement.[97] Debates contested the appropriate leverage point for reform: should programs target individual bodies, populations, environments, or social arrangements? Answers hinged on placing race in relation to nature and culture.[98]

Such questions turned on the protection of society—and its nature—from those who threatened its well-being. Distinctions of race supported such efforts. Ann Stoler argues that the cultivation of bourgeois civility in the nineteenth century was underpinned by racial discourses reverberating across metropole and colony, cordoning an emerging "European" middle class from the degenerate morals, habits, and desires of creole neighbors, colored servants, the urban poor, Irish peasants, and others. The "crucible of empire" informed the changing contours of racial formations in the wake of European immigration to the United States, including the instability of categories such as White, Black, Jewish, and European.[99] In this context, U.S. debates over Social Darwinism often hinged on the relation between the natural order of things and the social hierarchies of race, class, and sex seen to reflect a universal design. The normative nature of heterosexuality, for instance, has been defended through theories that saw homosexuality as a form of hereditary degeneration but also as a social contagion of modern culture. Whether seen as aberrant nature or culture, deviant bodies were targeted, pathologized, and medicalized in efforts to ensure society's welfare.[100]

In the urban environments of colonial India, miasmatic filth prompted draconian sanitation and public-health measures that put native bodies under the "watchful care" of colonial administration. However, such measures sought mainly to protect resident European bodies from contamination. In colonial metropoles such as Calcutta, urban planners wrote off the noxious and refuse-laden spaces of the native quarters, securing instead the health and sanitation of European neighborhoods. Administrators' seasonal spatial remove from urban centers to British hill stations, colonial officials reasoned, served Europeans' mental and physical health because, as one colonial quipped, "like meat, we keep better there." In South Africa, black miners infected with tuberculosis, attributed by officials to migrants' inability to adjust to urban living conditions, became suffering subjects dumped by state administrators and mining companies into the welcoming pastoral care of rural environs. These rural landscapes and communities—spatially and racially removed from white privilege—were celebrated by officials for their allegedly natural capacities to nurture the afflicted bodies of miners, thus obviating the need for state assistance. Racialized discourses of welfare bound bodies, populations, and landscapes of improvement and decay. These practices killed not with kindness but with pastoral "care," while reproducing the seemingly natural properties of race and the social benefits of segregation.[101]

Such exclusions in both colonial and postcolonial settings have often been described and justified in the purportedly apolitical language of technical management—what James Ferguson terms the "anti-politics machine" of development discourse. State claims to conserve and develop national resources, framed frequently under the rubric of Western science, often disenfranchise marginal communities from the right to steward local environments. In West Africa, for example, the legacies of imperial science and colonial administration continue to pin the blame for forest degradation on local forest users. Powerful outsiders thereby occlude effective management of the landscape by small swidden agriculturalists. One need not assume that "traditional" resource uses are inherently sustainable ecologically. Yet "ecological managerialism" often categorically dismisses such possibilities.[102] Hegel's *geist* still casts a long shadow on the Dark Continent. Primitives, in this logic, cannot represent themselves nor can they represent nature. Powerful outsiders must preserve, protect, and rule them both.[103]

Nationalist politics has often seized the racial elaborations of imperial science for anti-imperialist agendas. Liberatory struggles in the global south, especially during the era of decolonization, turned the very promise of a liberal humanism against its colonial roots. At the Asian-African Conference in Bandung, Indonesia in 1955 President Sukarno envisioned an anti-imperialism "united by a common contestation of racialism."[104] The shared project of opposing the historical alignments of race and nature could thus be marshaled in pursuit of diverse imaginations of nation, community, and belonging.

Competing regimes of truth have linked the cultural politics of race, nature, and nation to social movements waged in the name of democracy, freedom, and liberation. In the early 1960s, with the Civil Rights movement rendering the cultural politics of race highly visible, the American Anthropological Association passed a resolution repudiating statements of racial inferiority: "there is no scientifically established evidence to justify the exclusion of any race from the rights guaranteed by the Constitution of the United States."[105] Such pronouncements echoed the anthropologist and public intellectual Franz Boas's earlier call for democratic nonracialism. Forty years later, at the United Nations' 2001 World Conference Against Racism, Racial Discrimination, Xenophobia, and Related Intolerance in Durban, fierce debates surrounded the specific wording of racial discrimination and the political boundaries of "racism." These contentious disputes pivoted on definitions of "culture" and deployments of difference. Cultural politics, rather than a singular scientific consensus, formatively shaped pronouncements on restitution for transatlantic slavery, on Zionism's relationship to forms of ethnic absolutism, and on Palestinian national determination.

The contentious volatility of these political positions animates recent debates while highlighting the historical salience of competing legacies of race and nation, science and sentiment, managerial expertise and popular democracy. Who is capable of managing what nature on whose behalf? How do these acts of improvement racialize their targets and with what exclusionary effects? Each of the three chapters in this section explores different means by which natures are managed and races nurtured. Paul Gilroy, Zine Magubane, and Diane Nelson each investigate colonial and postcolonial arenas where national welfare has been articulated through idioms of racial progress. Taking in turn the disparate sites of imperial ambitions, colonial Africa, and postwar Guatemala, each chapter describes how notions of natural history make particular racial forms intelligible. The campaigns for national improvement that these authors describe harness racial assessments to dynamic understandings of natural capacity.

In his chapter, Paul Gilroy reflects on the disputed genealogies of antiracist projects, exploring Fanon's radical historicization of racism in colonial relations. Both remind us of the *relational* histories of racialized identities, colonial governmentality, and national territories. Gilroy highlights the imperial dynamics that linked political technologies of rule with bodies, the state, and violence. In the spirit of C. L. R. James, he calls both for a nuanced appreciation of the historical work of racisms in the imperial world and for a revival of neglected traditions of antiracism within black political cultures.[106] Harvesting a counterhistory of modern governmentality while elaborating a vision of cosmopolitan humanism, Gilroy charts an alternative imaginary of community and identity. Crucial to this project of fomenting a "new rebel humanism" is a critical interrogation of many of liberal politics' most naturalized keywords: sovereignty, market, nation, and state.[107]

Zine Magubane describes how colonial sciences of the body placed African natives, simians, and European women in the same position at an earlier moment in evolutionary time. Analogical reasoning, she argues, is crucial to racial regimes of truth and their attempts to establish what Fanon famously termed "the fact of blackness." She eloquently traces the legacy of scientific racism as it crosses from colony to metropole, and shows how race is made intelligible within Europe itself. This naturalizing of social difference not only produced new forms of scientific knowledge but also justified the need for imperial violence. She stresses, however, that this process is not entirely hegemonic, analyzing Xhosa critiques of colonial reason and other African refusals to recognize the logic of European classification. By unpacking the cultural politics of imperial science and colonial governmentality in southern Africa, Magubane reveals racial fact as historical artifact.

Lamarckian grammars of racial improvement animate Diane Nelson's discussion of race wars and blood talk in contemporary Guatemala. Nelson finds multiple metaphors of pure blood and mixed descent at the center of recent political violence in Guatemala. Violence and genocide cannot be explained by recourse to bad faith, duplicity, or a virulent hatred of "otherness," she argues. She probes instead the passionate attachments through which race works, attending to the powerful ways in which the body politic may be imagined as an arena of racial progress. As an anthropologist long involved in solidarity work with Guatemalans, Nelson grapples with the complex cultural politics of representing race within competing grids of intelligibility. In so doing, she raises critical questions about the loyalties and affinities that draw racialized identities together in political struggle.

PART TWO. Landscapes of Purity and Pollution

When do we begin to look? Or does the landscape enter the bloodstream with the milk? —Ronald Blythe[108]

And despotic hands clapping limitations on dawns of brown eyes, America is my song, red blood of native Americans eavesdropping on the heavy sack my mother pulls. This land is my landscape of inherited harvests.—Sterling D. Plumpp[109]

From violent expressions of exclusionary nationalism to the genetic determinations of bodily pathology, race and nature do some of their most powerful work as keys to essential qualities and differences. Hidden away in the blood or expressed directly on the skin, elaborations of racial nature root identity and difference in the unchanging material of bounded bodies. In the annals of the social sciences, to "naturalize" is to assign such stable and intrinsic essences to people, relations, and things. But what practices enable "nature" to name the given? How is nature equipped with its "naturalizing power"?[110] If nature is itself artifactual, as we suggested earlier, how is it made to work as a terrain of immutable identity and difference? At stake in this idea of natural essence, Raymond Williams suggests, is "the fusion of a name for the quality with a name for the things observed."[111] Bodies as wildly dissimilar as blood cells and nations have been subject to the force of such idealism. It is the very possibility of a given, underlying, essential being that enables racial ideologies to "*discover* what other ideologies have to construct."[112]

Where are such essences recorded? Race is often taken as a question of phenotypical variation, colored surfaces expressing biological difference. The racializing gaze, writes Franz Fanon, settles on the epidermal fabric of the black body as the locus of its identity. But essences are drawn just as readily from the depths of a body's being.[113] Labor discipline on the *maquildora* assembly lines along the U.S.-Mexico border, for example, relies on work performed by "naturally" nimble fingers. Mine managers in South Africa used the supposed ethnic qualities of workers, including their bodily capacities and natural dispositions, to legitimate differential compensation in both food and pay, effectively constructing many of the very ethnic differences they attributed to native natures.[114] Recent analysts have called attention to a *nano-politics* that finds difference expressed by the interior coils of the gene. Paul Gilroy sees the shift to the molecular as a displacement of previous hegemonies of vision: "Screens rather than lenses now mediate the pursuit of bodily truths."[115] New genetic and reproductive technologies have indeed reworked relations between power and visibility, between identity and essence.

Novel racial imaginaries such as these, however, must compete with more entrenched popular understandings and a robust array of vernacular forms of recognizing race.[116] Ironically, Gilroy, who has insightfully stressed the dynamism and politics of black popular culture, attends little to the disarticulations between scientific and popular images in his discussion of nano-politics. A key question remains the relationship between new technologies of imaging race and the embodied politics and social relations in bars, buses, and Babylons near and far. In Guatemalan race talk, for example, as Diane Nelson's contribution to this volume sketches, medical markers of blood purity jostle with superficial signs such as the *cara de indio*, the face of the Indian. The vagaries of racial essence bear what W. E. B. Du Bois described as "illogical trends and irreconcilable tendencies." Spatial practice, class relations, and cultural context radically shape the articulation of racialized identities that shift across locations.[117]

These fissures and displacements in racial formations, postcolonial theorists argue, enable emergent discourses of hybridity that further trouble cultural logics of purity. Narratives of national essence often elide the sedimented histories of mongrelization, transcultural processes, and relational routes that challenge nativist myths of origin and roots. Homi Bhabha reserves hybridization to refer to enunciatory processes of appropriation, positioning, and subjectivation within radically asymmetrical fields of power. While his poststructuralism refuses the notion of a sovereign subject authorizing her own identity, his influential vision flirts with the danger of voluntarism, of neglecting the power relations that position subjects in racialized locations not of their choosing.[118] In Central and South America, for instance, discourses of *mestizaje*—mingling metaphors of mixed race, culture, and blood—have been "radically polysemic," deployed for both progressive and reactionary political agendas. Indigenous social movements, transnational activist networks advocating human rights, and also national elites who endorse an imagined community's generative myth have all struggled over the term's meanings and traction. Purity of blood, rooted ethnic essences, gendered normativities, and tropes of authenticity all animate the cultural politics of *mestizaje*. Invocations of creolization and transculturation similarly turn on the *relational routes* of representational forms and embodied practices that infuse cultural imaginaries of identity and difference.[119]

Amidst a world of unequal travel and mobility, attributions of bodily nature help fix racial distinctions to the national order of things. Such adherence has been effected in part by the transformation of cultural difference itself into something of a biological quality.[120] Nation and nature articulate in postwar Britain, argues Gilroy, through a form of "ethnic absolutism" where "culture [is] almost biologized by its proximity to race." These politically charged formations fuse race, nation, ethnicity, and culture in hybrid formations difficult to disentangle. "Biological racism and cultural differentialism," Hall asserts, "constitute not two different systems, but racism's two registers."[121] Recent anti-immigrant rhetoric in Europe differs from older variants of racism in its stress on incommensurable cultural traditions rather than distinctive biological endowments. This assertion of fundamental cultural difference, observes Verena Stolcke, assumes that "because humans are inherently ethnocentric, relations between cultures are by 'nature' hostile."[122] A Hobbesian residue haunts these formations: atavistic individualism scaled up to the "natural" social antagonism among differing cultures. Those who occupy hegemonic positions of race and class privilege do not monopolize such exclusionary cultural logic. Zulu articulations of ethnic nationalism in South Africa follow the contours of an "ethnogeneticism," what Rob Nixon describes as "biology by other means."[123] In instances such as these, culture is grafted to biology as a fact of nature—conceived as fixed, inherent, primordial—and opposed to the malleable contingencies of history and society.

In the early twentieth century, the anarchist formerly known as Prince Kropotkin brushed social theory's engagement with Darwin against the grain. He criticized those who ossified the "struggle for the means of existence" as a universal "law of Nature." Kropotkin sought evidence from animal behavior and comparative ethnology to argue for the importance of "mutual aid" and social cooperation as a factor in evolution, stressing that his research articulated a neglected Darwinian insight.[124] In 1950, UNESCO's First Statement on Race sought to both reflect and shape scientific consensus on the topic, claiming "biological support" for "the ethic of universal brotherhood; for man is born with drives toward co-operation." A number of physical anthropologists and geneticists objected to the implicit Kropotkinian position and the offending passage was removed in UNESCO's revised Statement on Race issued the following year. Yet subsequent statements echoed the initial UNESCO position: "For all practical social purposes, 'race' is not so much a biological phenomenon as a social myth." For this reason, the panel of experts recommended "to drop the term 'race' altogether and speak of ethnic groups."[125] While midcentury debates unyoked biological fact from racial destiny in scientific circles, they failed to capture popular sentiments. In the wake of UNESCO's statements, moreover, exclusionary forms of ethnic absolutism and cultural fundamentalism could sidestep the tag of "racism" by making recourse to the essential differences of culture, custom, and tradition.[126]

Racial logic sustains vast landscapes of inclusion and exclusion. At stake here are the myriad forms of "boundary work" that maintain the self-identity of dominant groups and ideologies: the cultural against the natural, the domestic against the wild, the city against the country, the masculine against the feminine, the West against the Rest.[127] The plastic pink flamingo, Jennifer Price has documented, emerged in the late 1950s on lawns whose owners sought to project particular aesthetics of race, class, and beauty. She traces the cultivation of a class- and race-distinct "taste" for adorning miniscule enclosures of nature to property relations and to vacation circuits linking northern working-class subdivisions to Florida's colorful allure. Class, cultural dispositions toward nature, and spatial transgressions converge in the placement of plastic pink flamingos in "white-trash" trailer parks and John Waters's films.[128]

Cultural politics here turn on how people and nature are positioned as out of place, disturbing the natural and social order. Popular and scientific fascination with "queer animals," for example, reveals a complex fabric of recursivity weaving anxieties about "unnatural acts" into challenges to heteronormative constructions of gender and sexuality. During his bid for the Republican Party's presidential nomination in 1992, Pat Buchanan described AIDS as "nature's retribution," placing unnatural acts of homosexuality beyond the pale of heteronormativity.[129] Hitler's *Mein Kampf* also took recourse to natural ground, yoking race to nation in demands to protect a "racial purity, universally valid in Nature." Significantly, Hitler saw a "spatially delimited state" as the "basis on which alone culture can arise," rooting national destiny in territorial ambitions.[130]

Claims such as these call to mind the germinal arguments of Mary Douglas concerning purity, pollution, and the social order. Douglas suggested that "dirt" finds its own nature through efforts to protect the social order, strategies that define and exclude certain bodies and substances as "matter out of place." Building on these insights, Julia Kristeva argues that subjects too depend on the expulsion of contaminating elements—filth, fluids, decay—for their very identity and integrity.[131] "Geographies of exclusion" thereby segregate both pure and defiled spaces and the kinds of people that are expected to belong naturally to them. State legislation mapped Vancouver's Chinatown, for example, as an exclusive ethnic enclave through discourses of racial hygiene, foreign contagion, and the social and moral degeneration of racial mixing. Discourses of purity have demonized invading aliens—at times weaving exotic plants and abject alterities into a common field of moral panic. Accusations of arson from southern California to southern Africa have targeted foreign invaders who threaten the purity of geobodies of nation and state. Immigrants to Los Angeles—shifting from Oakies to Chicanos in different historical moments—have been targeted as incendiary others in the wake of large-scale fires. During World War II, a Japanese submarine fired incendiary shells into Los Padres National Forest, igniting racialized anxieties around threats to the purity of nation and protection of nature. Smokey the Bear, the guardian of a nation's nature, was born from these ashes. In South Africa, both "non-native" plants and peoples came under fire as "invading aliens" in the wake of a prominent 2000 conflagration in the Western Cape.[132]

The chapters in this section explore the natural and racial politics of exclusive geographies. In each, human bodies and social collectives are united and divided on landscapes of purity and pollution. Racial and spatial divides protect vulnerable bodies from the essentially dangerous. Crossing the borders of these exclusive spaces—national bodies, uninhabited wilds, racialized ghettoes—unsettles natural orders. Spatial transgression itself becomes a deeply political act, demanding repression in the case of Linke, unsettling the naturalized in the case of Braun, and enabling new formulations of place and identity in the case of Di Chiro.

In Uli Linke's account of linguistic nationalism in Germany, projects of language purification are tied to natural symbols of national belonging. A deeply corporeal imaginary links nature and nation, human bodies and the body politic, flows of blood with migrations of people. Excavating historical debates that stretch back for centuries, Linke demonstrates how origin stories of common descent bind linguistic purists in the seventeenth century with anti-immigration sentiments in the 1990s. Building on Adorno's argument that deemed foreign words "the Jews" of the nation, she traces relations between linguistic purification and Nazi racial hygiene. The seventeenth-century project of "landscaping the speech-garden" of nature finds its twentieth-century resonance in exclusionary fantasies of purifying blood, soil, and language. Robert Proctor has described the "organic monumentalism" through which ideologies of Aryan destiny were inscribed into natural spaces such as forests.[133] In a similar vein, Linke finds in linguistic nationalism a means of cultivating nation-loving subjects on landscapes purged of alterity.

Bruce Braun is equally concerned with the spatial consolidation of whiteness, but his essay dwells on a different means by which the color of place is naturalized. Braun focuses on the discursive practices that frame contemporary American narratives of "risk culture" and adventure travel. Black adventurers, he argues, are *illegible* in the pages of magazines such as *Outside*. Like Linke, he suggests that this whitening of the normative adventurer echoes earlier consolidations of racial space, in his case the colonization of the North American frontier. The frontier was a zone of purification, carving out the essence of American and Canadian national identity on the receding threshold of a wild "beyond." The unstated and insidious presence of these very norms in the contemporary annals of adventure travel enables a racializing series of metonymic displacements: from climber to explorer to European to white. Nature, nation, and whiteness find a common body of expression in the heroic adventurer as Braun renders visible the trope of white mobility animating North American cultures of nature.

From the vantage point of Braun's texts, the image of a black voyager charting a tenuous path through the risky terrain of an urban jungle could only be parodic, if possible at all. However, it is this very landscape that Giovanna Di Chiro seizes for her reflections on the promises of "toxic tourism." Environmental justice movements have adopted the "fallen" landscapes and "sacrifice zones" of the urban jungle as their object of struggle, committing themselves to the recovery of polluted space.[134] Unlike the purging of alterity that Linke describes, these activists practice a "borderlands" politics of difference, one that embraces hybridized and situational identities rather than clinging to the vanishing residues of historical essence. Their ventures in toxic tourism transgress the borders dividing racial others from more privileged populations, transforming blackened space into an incendiary force for cooperative organizing. Di Chiro powerfully documents the alternative possibilities for coalition politics afforded by activists and the alliances they forge. Environmental justice struggles hinge crucially, in this vision, on a cultural politics of place and identity that grounds shared projects in specific sites of struggle.

PART THREE. Communities of Blood and Belonging

As I face Africa I ask myself: what is it between us that constitutes a tie which I can feel better than I can explain?—W. E. B. Du Bois[135]

To my compatriots, I have no hesitation in saying that each one of us is as intimately attached to the soil of this beautiful country as are the famous jacaranda trees of Pretoria and the mimosa trees of the bushveld. Each time one of us touches the soil of this land, we feel a sense of personal renewal.—Nelson Mandela[136]

Passions for body and blood, place and community, race and nation: nature makes a powerful terrain of sentimental attachment for its human subjects. Each of the chapters in this section situates the emotional dispositions of individuals and communities in wider topographies of fear and love, suffering and belonging. Trespassing the thin boundary of the skin, these three themes chart workings of identity and affinity that sculpt both interior senses of selfhood and natural environments of nativity. These *landscapes of affect*, as one might call them, enable the simultaneous imagination and fabrication of inner selves, social bodies, and environmental milieux. Race and nature gain their tangible presence in the lived experience of individuals and communities through this play of passionate desires, fears, and faiths.

"As places make sense, senses make place," writes Steven Feld. Selves and environments are fashioned together in a dialectical movement shuttling between physical worlds of experience and psychic dispositions. Landscapes both interior and exterior are made simultaneously.[137] Edouard Glissant argues that self, community, and landscape are "inextricable in the process of creating history." On the one hand, the material practices through which places "make sense" often have profound emotional reverberations. Urban planning regimes that ghettoize impoverished racial minorities, for example, contribute to suburban fear and loathing of the concrete jungle. On the other hand, the sentiments themselves work to fashion the living world of experience. Raymond Williams argues that nature has always served the West as a projection screen for social hopes and anxieties.[138] Whether figured as a hostile terrain to be conquered violently, an indifferent milieu to be survived, or a nurturing cradle for human development, the natural landscape is repeatedly invested with emotional dispositions that both mirror and challenge those of its inhabitants. These "environmental imaginaries"[139] dispose thinking and feeling subjects to undertake particular kinds of creative work on worldly nature, to make certain kinds of places. Images of the tropical Antilles, asserts Derek Walcott, were depicted by "travellers [who] carried with them the infection of their own malaise." The melancholia of their own nostalgia *inscribed* landscapes with lament and desire; these images were then read as reflections of an inherent nature of tropicality, as essential properties of environment, climate, and landscape. *Tristes Tropiques*, for Lévi-Strauss, have a deep structuralist logic. When willows weep, an environmental milieu takes on human sentiments to convey a structure of feeling binding intimate feelings and animate landscapes.[140]

As the hinge of articulation between interior dispositions and exterior environments, bodily nature forms a vital terrain of "passionate attachment." The surface of the skin has often been marked as a measure of racial difference. For Fanon, the white racialized gaze interpellates the Negro through the "epidermalization" of "inferiority." Subjected to this hegemony of colonizing vision, Fanon experiences an exclusionary violence over which he cannot "choose" his blackness. The black subject thus dwells in a "zone of nonbeing," from which self-liberation articulates an alternative to colonial violence and its constitutive dehumanization.[141] In stark contrast, Zora Neale Hurston refuses a sense of feeling "tragically colored," criticizing those "who hold that nature somehow has given them a low-down dirty deal and whose feelings are all hurt about it." Crucially, her liberation from the violent histories of racialization is only afforded by a sovereign subject's *choice* to escape history: "At certain times I have no race, I am *me*. . . . I belong to no race nor time."[142] Political and aesthetic debates around racialization have turned, crucially, on the kind of subject—and related processes of subjection and subjugation—who *experiences* "race."[143] In turn, how these subjects position themselves—and are positioned—in relation to nature, culture, and history remains critical to the practices of identity, analysis, and politics.

The suffering body often provides a living map to chart wider landscapes of emotion and experience. Grappling with the violence of exclusive geographies, Aimé Césaire wrote of a "world map made for my own use, not tinted with the arbitrary map of scholars, but with the geometry of my own blood." Césaire's anti-imperialism broke the shackles of biological destiny, elaborating a pan-Africanist concept of *negritude* that was "no longer a cephalic index, or plasma, or soma, but measured by the compass of suffering." In the 1940s, Senghor lamented his black brothers' "blood that cleansed the nation," only to have their heroic struggles forgotten by imperial France.[144] Sartre too considered the critical geography made by sentiments of *negritude*—what he termed a project of "antiracist racism"—emphasizing its "affective attitude toward the world." *Negritude* wrote suffering onto both bodies and landscapes together, cultivating interior souls by evoking the "mystical geography" of violent imperialism and the remembered transatlantic slave trade.[145]

Pan-Africanist visions mapped imaginative geographies to imagined communities. Du Bois's reflections on the souls of black folk understood a racial identity built around shared experience rather than biological destiny, held by those who "have had a common history; have suffered a common disaster and have one long memory." The political community of African Americans, he expected, would emerge not from their common geographical roots but from their shared history: "the real essence of this kinship is its social heritage of slavery." Historical experience, mediated by the cultural politics of memory, shapes Du Bois's vision of community: routes rather than roots, bondage rather than blood lines, and experience rather than essence articulate "race" to self, soul, and embodied practice. Breaking from the metaphorics of blood, Du Bois links his assertion that "Race is a cultural . . . fact" to a shared notion of group belonging. In *Dusk of Dawn* he explains to a mythical white man that "the black man is a person who must ride 'Jim Crow' in Georgia." Du Bois renders visible the interpellation of a racialized subject, situating both his experience and "race" in history, social relations, and cultural practices.[146]

One of the most profound imaginations of a natural environment of belonging has been, of course, the nation. Indeed, as Benedict Anderson notes, the "profoundly self-sacrificing love" that nations inspire is often expressed through the idioms of home and family.[147] Yet as Liisa Malkki emphasizes, nationalist discourses frequently reveal "the metaphoric slide from harmonious egalitarianism to steeply hierarchical family and gender metaphors." These gendered constructions of national belonging articulate relations among body, kinship, nation, and race. National territories become motherlands or fatherlands, nations claim patrimonies, and a body politic becomes bounded and defended. Violence waged in the name of "ethnic cleansing" has targeted women's bodies, including brutal campaigns of mass rape undertaken to violate purity, honor, and ethnic essence. Militarized masculinities gender the nation-state, mingling with discourses of exclusion that target forms of impermissible differences—cultural, ethnic, or religious—that racialize both domestic and foreign "enemies."[148] When and why are citizens willing to die for their nation? This sacrificial love often relies on a play of identification between the living body of the citizen and the mortal body of the nation.[149] But critical scholarship on the nation has demonstrated that such intimate feelings of belonging are by no means "primordial" bonds of loyalty and affinity.[150] Rather, natural affinities are historical artifacts; natural identifications with native place must themselves be cultivated.

Enlightenment legacies of environmental thinking have provided one powerful means of cultivating such attachments to national place. Friedrich Ratzel's nineteenth-century "anthropogeography" conceived the *Volk* as sharing a historical relationship to common territory, what he described as their *lebensraum*, their living space.[151] Ratzel's notion of living space has found ironic reverberations not only in Hitler's exclusionary soil politics but also in a Black Nationalist vision of community expressed by LeRoi Jones/Amiri Baraka. "Black people are a race, a culture, a nation," he proclaimed, needing "what the Germans call *lebensraum* (living room), literally space in which to exist and develop."[152] The radically different political valences of these two echoes remind us to pay close attention to the concrete *relational histories* of race, nature, and nation. In modern "ecologies of belonging," rooted identities contest with routed ones as histories of migration, diaspora, and displacement transform stable senses of community and places of belonging.[153]

Ironically enough, these very passions for national belonging have traveled in and out of the annals of positivist social science. For example, twentieth-century geographers and cultural ecologists such as Carl Sauer, Alfred Kroeber, and Julian Steward built up the "Culture Area" concept on the foundations laid by German Romantics. By treating the natural properties of place as the template for mapping differences and similarities among cultural traits, these academics further reinforced assumptions about the natural isomorphism of people, place, and culture formulated by Herder. For Kroeber, " 'natural' factors such as climate, soil, and drainage" conditioned but did not determine cultural activities. Sauer argued that " 'natural resources' were in fact cultural appraisals" and that "the history of mankind is a long and diverse series of steps by which he has achieved ecologic dominance." Moreover, his notion of landscape morphology stressed "a strictly geographic way of thinking about culture; namely, as the impress of the works of man upon the area." Following suit, Steward saw ecological adaptation as the motor of cultural history, and the resultant "culture area" became "a construct of behavioral uniformities which occur within an area of environmental uniformities."[154]

If locations of culture travel, so too do geographically uneven racial formations. And as embodied subjects journey through landscapes of differential affect, they encounter disparate forms of racialization. A U.S.-born-and-based "black" anthropologist finds himself hailed as a "gringo" and "white man" on the Nicaraguan coast while a Peruvian anthropologist, constructed as "white" in Cuzco and Lima, finds colleagues positioning her as a "woman of color" in the U.S. academy.[155] The performative possibilities of racial "passing," of course, do not extend equally across hierarchies of difference. Not all passings are created equal. Just as the location of race—in genes, blood, skin, customs, or community—traverses scales and sites, so also racialized subjects move across a geographically differentiated terrain of racial formations that resists homogeneity.

The global traffic of commodities, representations, and cultural practices that have routed through China, an array of scholars have argued, articulate both distinctively national visions of ethnicity and localized imaginations of community and identity. From the racial hierarchies that shaped jazz performances in the early twentieth century, to ethnic minorities enlisted in the production of state-sponsored ethnology, to the performance of ethnicity for tourists: contested moral geographies of belonging link Chinese places to translocal travels.[156] Recent explorations of the influence of Spanish discourses of race in the U.S. Southwest and their relationship to African American and other subaltern histories provide yet another example of a robustly entangled and geographically differentiated history of racialization's competing processes. Neither the location of culture nor of race remain fixed in place. Stuart Hall has famously reflected on how he became "black" only after migrating fom the Caribbean to Britain. Migratory subjects, of course, are not uniformly positioned in relation to other fields of difference—notably class, gender, and sexuality.[157]

The *relational histories* of people, place, and culture—and their *racialized routes*—lead us to ask how people make their homes in communities of belonging. The three chapters in this section probe the sentimental attachments that motivate constructions of place and identity. Keith Wailoo, Donna Haraway, and Robyn Wiegman describe different coagulations of community feeling around blood, gene, and place in contemporary America. Each chapter tracks simultaneous mutations in technobiological nature and senses of belonging, suggesting that a love of one's own guides attachments to a changing nature. The objects of attachment borne by the subjects of each of these studies vary widely. What they do share, however, is a common terrain of biosocial identification that has been radically unsettled by new medical and biological interventions into bodily nature. Normative liberal notions of property and personhood get entangled in webs of technobiopower linking labs, kennels, and courtrooms as well as genes, wombs, and persons. Such cross-fertilizations open up novel ways of imagining race and nature.

Keith Wailoo describes the invention of the "heterozygote" as a category of American personhood in the decades after the Second World War. Echoing Paul Rabinow's discussion of biosociality, Wailoo finds racial communities forming around the biological truths of sickle-cell disease, Tay-Sachs disease, and cystic fibrosis. Rabinow predicted that biosocial communities would soon have "medical specialists, laboratories, narratives, traditions, and a heavy panoply of pastoral keepers to help them experience, share, intervene and 'understand' their fate."[158] Wailoo finds much of this apparatus at work already—albeit in quite different ways—in the case of these three racialized diseases. His contrasts illustrate the distinctive means by which attachments to racial nature may be experienced and expressed. African Americans incorporated biomedical discourse on sickle-cell disease, for example, into historical narratives of community pain and suffering. Ashkenazi Jewish narratives, on the other hand, represented Tay-Sachs as a mark of community survival in the face of oppression.

Wailoo concludes his discussion with the possibility of a genomic eclipse of heterozygotic discourse. Donna Haraway argues that this shift from population to genome has already occurred in the world of North American dog breeding. Tracking racial discourse into the canine world, her chapter charts a series of transformations in the means by which a lovable breed is identified, produced, and protected. Evolutionary understandings of a breeding population, she argues, supplanted Victorian notions of a racial pedigree, only to be superceded in recent years by the manipulable matter of genomic discourse. Foucault himself is disciplined and punished for his "species chauvinism" as dogs are brought into the domain of what Haraway terms technobiopower. These relations of power and affect forge novel bonds of affinity across the boundaries of species and community, drawing unlikely fellows into webs of study, care, and intervention. These "naturalcultural" webs are woven through a diverse spread of places, from pet kennels to scientific society meetings, from neighborhood parks to Internet Web sites.

Robyn Wiegman casts a net just as wide to understand the transformations in American race and kinship wrought by new reproductive technologies, tacking between legal rulings on a mistaken case of in vitro fertilization, contemporary legacies of U.S. slavery, and a recent cinematic representation of multiracial family. Techniques such as in vitro fertilization pry apart biological paternity and paternal feeling, enabling the fulfillment of sentimental hopes for multiracial kinship without the disturbing possibility of interracial sex. Wiegman points to an emerging form of white masculinity founded on a contractual relationship to one's own colored kin. Grappling with the legal constructions of contract and property that inform contemporary American personhood, she suggests that liberal notions of personhood are paradoxically sustained by metaphoric recourse to slavery as a critique of these transactions.[159] Nature itself is being transformed by these new possibilities, Wiegman argues, shifting from the essential ground of racial difference to the sentimental terrain of a nation imagined as Benetton family.

PART FOUR. The Politics of Representation

By being embodied as qualitatively different in their substantial natures—by creating group identities in difference—communities of individuals were placed outside the liberal universe of freedom, equality, and rights. In effect, a theory of politics and rights was transformed into an argument about nature; equality under liberalism was taken to be a matter not of ethics, but of anatomy.—Nancy Leys Stepan[160]

So how are we ever going to achieve some kind of language which will make my experience articulate to you and yours to me?—James Baldwin to Margaret Mead[161]

Reflecting on the political constraints precluding peasants from articulating their class interests in nineteenth-century France, Marx famously declared, "They cannot represent themselves, they must be represented." Significantly, for Marx, the relationship of these peasants to nature constrained their political agency and class consciousness. The small-holding peasants' mode of production, Marx argued, isolated them on self-sufficient farms like "potatoes in a sack." This socioeconomic isolation grounded peasant livelihoods "more through exchange with nature than in intercourse with society." Recognizing peasants through organic metaphors yet denying them status as organic intellectuals, Marx echoes discourses of primitivism, previously discussed, that treat particular subjects' proximity to nature as a negation of their historical agency and political representation.[162] Gayatri Spivak invokes his germinal position to underscore how contemporary theory often falters on the slippage between two senses of representation, a political sense of "speaking for" and a literary sense of re-presentation as "speaking of."[163] The cultural politics of representation revolving around race, nature, and difference frequently hinges on this complex coupling.[164]

Natural objects cannot speak of their own accord: they require a mediator—a proxy, a speaker, and an active subject—to draw them into articulation.[165] The politics of representation reveals a frequent elision of nature and race, as subjects located within historically contingent discourses struggle to position themselves.[166] Indigenous activists asserting their ecologically sustainable resource management practices may voice a fiercely felt sense of localized knowledge, resource rights, and political entitlement. Before his execution by the Nigerian military state, Ken Saro-Wiwa insisted on calling his homeland "Ogoni" rather than Ogoniland: "this is because to the Ogoni, the land and the people are one." Similarly, indigenous movements such as the Huaorani—who opposed the ravages of oil exploration and extraction in Ecuador's El Oriente—have countered the federal state's claims to subsurface mineral rights by invoking cultural identities asserted as essentially grounded in the local environment.[167]

Yet, as they invoke an inherent bond with particular landscapes, indigenous social movements confront the possibility that their asserted proximity to nature may unintentionally enable their own dispossession and exploitation. Enlightenment legacies—enduring discourses of primitivism, evolutionary teleologies, the grounding of cultural differences in nature—prove formidable. Moreover, the political realities of differentiated communities undermine the very metaphor of speaking in a single representative voice. Saro-Wiwa's execution by the Nigerian military regime and armed escorts who accompanied oil executives to visit El Oriente are a stark reminder of the bloody business of petroleum development. Violence, state power, and capital accumulation work *through* the cultural politics of race and nature. Yet so do potentially oppositional social movements.

Consider, for example, the contradictory political possibilities opened by what Michel-Rolph Trouillot has named the "savage slot," a triangular relation between order, utopia, and savagery proposed by Western epistemic traditions.[168] Contrasting images of the "wild man" as guileless native and violent savage have framed radically different reformist interventions into society and nature. "Edenic narratives" echoing Rousseau's pastoral visions have grafted the garden's grace onto the contemporary Amazonian landscape.[169] Transnational environmentalists often use such a "green lens"[170] to buttress their critical claims, while liberals in the north typically find its depictions of "primitive ecological wisdom"[171] much more attractive than the hues of radical red. However, these bucolic representations of the Noble Savage must still compete with more hard-bitten perceptions of primitives locked in a Hobbesian "horrible world of struggle." In France, for example, anti-immigration sentiments of the 1970s and 1980s explicitly invoked images of "l'immigration sauvage," a wild, unruly flow threatening the nation's own race and culture.[172]

Recent debates over the cultural politics of identity and difference hinge, as Diana Fuss underscores, on theorizing the relationship between the social and the natural. We find her cautionary tale especially instructive:

> Too often constructionists presume that the category of the social automatically escapes essentialism, in contradistinction to the way the category of the natural is presupposed to be inevitably entrapped within it. . . . If we are to intervene effectively in the impasse created by the essentialist-constructionist divide, it might be necessary to begin questioning the constructionist assumption that nature and fixity go together (naturally) just as sociality and change go together (naturally). In other words, it may be time to ask whether essences can change and whether constructions can be normative.[173]

We build on Fuss's refusal by emphasizing the *work performed* when identities are rendered as natural and essential, by stressing how these effects unfold differentially in historically specific contexts, and by attending to the ways these articulations bind together particular formations of race and difference. Such a perspective requires an understanding of how race and nature interpellate their subjects and how they come to recognize themselves within its material and discursive formations. Far from false consciousness, the deep attachments many actors may hold to essential identities emerge through a complex cultural politics of difference. As Stuart Hall argues, "identities are the names we give to the different ways we are positioned by, and position ourselves within, the narratives of the past."[174] Our contributors seek to trace the discursive effects of these deployments, the tactics of subjects who make histories while inhabiting identities not entirely of their choosing.[175] Rather than conceive of sovereign subjects who choose and deploy fixed identities, we appreciate how historical agents are positioned within discourses of development, environment, and globalization. Savage slots shift a lot. Yet within this shifting terrain of struggle, subjects acknowledge and engage their relationships to race and nature, acting as agents in provisional fields of political possibility.

Following Fuss, we might spend less energy arguing over the inherently emancipatory or necessarily repressive character of "essence." Instead, as recent debates encourage, we might consider with an open mind the situated struggles waged in particular landscapes. Such mobilizations may turn, crucially, on how identities are articulated in relation to race and place, nature and environment. Apartheid's system of spatial control mapped ethnic identities to fixed territories in the so-called ethnic homelands or Bantustans.[176] But in Latin America today, highly sophisticated indigenous federations are also actively mapping ethnic identity to territory, tactically deploying a "sedentarist metaphysics" to claim deep cultural roots in place.[177] These distinct histories necessarily create different fields of political possibility.

A second implication follows. Judith Butler identifies a recent tendency among some leftists to oppose the "materialist project of Marxism" to the "merely cultural" struggles of new social movements.[178] Here, insights from agrarian studies complement poststructural pyrotechnics focused on the politics of identity in the metropolitan West. In both cases, we emphasize the *simultaneity* of symbolic and material struggles, refusing an assumed distinction between "merely" symbolic recognition and material resource redistribution. The cultural politics of representation, in the two senses we elaborated above, enables us to conceive of how race, nature, and difference simultaneously shape both the very terrain that produces political subjects and the claims that these subjects make to rights, resources, and their redistribution.

Our authors develop these insights, offering ethnographically enlivened instances of the contingent cultural politics of race, nature, and difference. In Steven Gregory's chapter, international tourism and sex work position Dominican women as natural subjects of labor and sexual exploitation. Several complementary notions of nature are at work here: the regulatory norms of heteronormative sexuality; the tropical fantasies of North American male sex tourists; and the "imperial masculinity" that naturalizes racial, class, and geopolitical hierarchies in a global capitalist system. But sex workers also find some room to maneuver on this terrain of radical social and economic inequality, Gregory argues. Insofar as their work provides material resources and access to transnational circuits of production and exchange, women working in the Dominican tourist industry find certain means of negotiating their subaltern position.

Transnational connections also frame two complementary perspectives on indigeneity offered by Alcida Ramos and Tania Li. Both their chapters grapple with a difficult double bind confronting indigenous movements for land and resource rights, one that we described above. Insofar as these peoples are located in and of nature, they are effectively removed from the space of politics and history: they cannot represent themselves, they must be represented. Furthermore, indigenous usage of the idioms of ethnic nationalism may win them territorial concessions, but such strategies also reproduce the sovereignty of the nation-state as the guarantor of their rights to citizenship. Rather than applauding or condemning these paradoxical consequences of "strategic essentialism" outright, both authors search for the implications of such claims in the crucible of cultural politics. "Difference" performs different work in distinct historical and geographic contexts.

In contemporary Brazil, Ramos argues, Indians occupy a "savage slot" that enables the district governor to speak for them at the opening of the very National Indian Museum in which they are depicted. Both popular media and official state policies differentiate Indians from normative Brazilian citizens, recognizing them as dependent wards of the state bearing a "metonymic bond" to untamed nature.[179] Yet indigenous activists also counter the logic of state rationality by appropriating such images of their primordial nature as political resources. Ramos sees indigenous agency in the instrumental uses of cultural essentialism, and she cautions anthropologists and critics against a dismissal of these chosen strategies.[180] She thereby argues forcefully against a universal antiessentialism that is inattentive to the constraints under which specific social movements labor.[181]

Contemporary Indonesian movements for indigenous rights, Tania Li argues, must also contend with identities not of their own making. These structures of recognition and identification are highly contingent, however, less fixed essences than shifting fields of force.[182] Recent Indonesian political reforms and transnational environmental politics have turned the very category of *masyarakat adat,* or indigenous people, into a terrain of cultural struggle. Cultural difference has become the prism through which resource rights may be demanded, binding together the politics of recognition and the politics of redistribution. Li too understands indigenous subjects as produced by powerful agencies such as law and economy, even as they position themselves against the state. She envisions their struggle as a cultural contest waged on the contested terrain of race, nature, and difference. By attending to both the boundaries of this terrain and the maneuver that it enables, Li captures much of the spirit of our collective project.

A Different Politics of Race and Nature

The point is to make a difference in the world, to cast our lot for some ways of life and not others. To do that one must be in the action, be finite and dirty, not transcendent and clean.
—Donna Haraway[183]

Cultural identities provide the very means by which we craft our futures.[184] The politics of the possible is shaped profoundly by the ways in which we imagine our communities of affinity and our places of belonging. Struggles over identity and difference, our contributors underscore, are thoroughly imbued with the cultural politics of race and nature. We have stressed in this introduction that both race and nature are historical artifacts: assemblages of material, discourse, and practice irreducible to a single timeless essence. By charting the ways in which race and nature work together, and by tracing key disruptions in their busy traffic, we emphasize the cultural labors required to maintain them as they are. "The hope of every ideology," writes Stuart Hall, "is to naturalize itself out of History into Nature, and thus to become invisible, to operate unconsciously."[185] Yet one can also hope against ideology.

We write against such naturalisms, but not against "nature." We write against racisms—not against "race" but against the exclusionary effects produced through its invocation, deployment, and reproduction. We have challenged the ways that racisms work, their recourse to essential truths of difference in order to rationalize hierarchies, to reproduce inequalities, and to justify exclusions. But at the same time, we recognize race as a crucial foundation of modern power, a terrain of identity and difference making us all into political subjects. We have argued against forms of naturalism that find in nature both laws for its own management and scripts for social conduct.

Yet we also recognize nature as an inescapable ground of struggle, generating both materials and passions for politics. The contributions to this volume underscore the violence rationalized on the cultural terrain of race and nature. But they also insist that it is on this very terrain that domination may be challenged and undone. While culture is sometimes taken as an immutable kernel of fundamental human difference, it may also provide the malleable means of contesting normative relations of power.[186] As Lani Guinier and Gerald Torres suggest, the present demands a project of envisioning "race as political space" rather than embracing an erasure of race that underestimates the historical sedimentations of racialized regimes of rule and their enduring effects.[187]

These politics emerge in relation to contradictory efforts to treat race in contemporary America not as a problem of bodily biology but as a question of cultural heritage. Liberal multiculturalism often disavows the complex histories of racial violence, domesticating social antagonism through a celebration of cultural diversity. "Color-blind" visions have emerged from a liberalism often blind to its own historical legacies—and contemporary politics—of exclusion. Such writings often echo Franz Boas's celebrated arguments for cultural relativism while neglecting his insistence that in modern times "race antagonism is a fact"—a social reality and historical artifact.[188] Conservative thinkers often concede the social facticity of racial difference but find in such difference an argument for social reform. "What blacks need to do is to 'act white,' " argues Dinesh D'Souza, promising their redemption through a project of cultural improvement and "civilization restoration."[189] D'Souza locates the pathologies of the black underclass in their cultural tendencies rather than their biological being. This is precisely the liberal logic of cultural racism that we discussed previously. As Kimberle Crenshaw notes, discourses of color-blindness that inform contemporary debates about civil rights legislation "legitimise the continuing relations of power between communities of colour and whites under a logic of racial *laissez-faire*-ism. A key feature in this newly emerging paradigm is the re-deployment of culture as a marker for race." In reflecting on the naturalization of this emerging tendency, Patricia Williams asks: "How precisely does the issue of color remain so powerfully determinative of everything from life circumstances to manner of death, in a world that is, by and large, officially 'color-blind'?"[190] Recognizing that race is a social product and cultural construction—not a natural essence—does not dismantle the social, cultural, and political effects and affects of race. Race is a powerful fiction—a constructed cultural artifact—with material, exclusionary effects.

Such insights suggest another way of unsettling the natural relation between racial fact and biological truth. Toni Morrison once described Bill Clinton as "our first black President. Blacker than any actual black person who could ever be elected in our children's lifetime."[191] Her startling imagination of a black Bill Clinton is powerful and challenging. While some may question her literary license, she unsettles the fact of blackness as either naturally fixed or exclusive to any racial identity. D'Souza's vision of black subjects performing white identities presumes that marginalized groups may improve by mimicking their social betters. In his formulation, subjugated actors freely choose to change the racial markers of their cultural identity. Morrison's alternative image also suggests political affinities that cross lines of essential difference. Yet, critically, she recognizes that subjects are positioned within histories of racist exclusions perpetuated in the name of liberal freedom.[192] Morrison's bold political imagination envisions emergent affinities of coalition. At the same time, she is well aware of the contentious legacies of race: the historical sedimentations—the practices, processes, and powers of a naturalized vision of race—that shape the terrain of a politics of the possible.

Morrison's unsettling image reminds us of the historical processes that have made the limits of liberalism itself *appear* natural. Uday Mehta's historical excavation of the circuits of British imperial administration links liberal rule with practices of racial subjugation targeted at inscrutable others. Historically, most forms of liberalism have celebrated what Mehta terms an "anthropological minimum" within which cultural difference can be tolerated: "the limiting point of this perimeter is a form of alterity beyond which differences can no longer be accommodated." This limit—liberalism's constitutive exclusion of intolerable difference—challenges its very foundations, the purported "natural" capacity of humans to live as free and equal citizens.[193] Subjects who can be located beyond the boundary of cultural understanding can more readily be politically excluded, disenfranchized of rights, citizenship, and the very freedoms liberalism vociferously defends.

The terrain of liberal exclusion articulates race and nature in a shifting politics of home and world. *The location of race* emerges from struggles where subjects position themselves, and are positioned, in ecologies of belonging. This dialectic of identity formation, suffused with power, is crucial to appreciating the racialization of political terrain that forcibly excludes and includes. Du Bois's insights of racialized self-understanding emerged from his journeys through a "white environing world" while Fanon experienced colonial spaces as saturated with a violent white gaze.[194] In 1957 Nelson Mandela challenged the racial logic of apartheid that sought to fix ethnic essence in a forceful policy of spatial containment. He outed the violent exclusions of a liberal rhetoric of self-government in the so-called Bantustans of South Africa: "Behind the self-government talks lies a grim programme of mass evictions, political persecution, and police terror." A decade later, in 1967, Muhammad Ali refused induction in the military draft, claiming conscientious objector status. The war, he argued, amounted to "White men sending black men to kill yellow men."[195] In a stinging retort, he articulates domestic and imperial racial subjugation and the violence that targets bodies, populations, and nations. More than thirty years later, popular and official perceptions of citizenship rights in the United States continue to position many people of color as "immigrant," whether as aspirant minorities or dangerous threats to the liberal nation-state.[196]

We write in the wake of a renewed and robust U.S. patriotism fueled by a persistent imagination of fundamentally opposed civilizations. Despite demonstrative disclaimers, both popular and official discourses of national solidarity have fused race, culture, and religion. Polyvalent and mobile racializing technologies have targeted bodies and populations from Afghanistan to airplanes and passengers in the United States. When U.S. Apache helicopters fire on the Occupied Territories in Palestine, their missiles' trail traces the entangled histories of two continents haunted by colonial dispossession and brutal violence waged against culturally marked populations. Noam Chomsky points to the ambivalent tensions within the meaning of "Enduring Freedom," the name for the U.S. military operation that emerged in response to the 2001 hijackings and attacks on the Pentagon and World Trade Center. To endure is to persevere but also to suffer.[197] In the global south and north, many endure freedom and its complex legacies. A critical challenge is to articulate freedom, power, and a cultural politics of social justice in a world where radical alternatives counter complacency and an entrenched naturalization of limits.

A number of contemporary political movements have challenged the naturalized triumphalism of neoliberal orthodoxy. The Zapatistas's call for a global movement *against* neoliberalism and *for* humanity positions a political project on the terrain of the conjunctural. By articulating a common interest *through* political struggle, such visions alert us to alternative practices of justice, freedom, and rights. One crucial move has been to challenge the liberal "rule of law" on its own terms, revealing its forceful exclusions while recognizing the persuasive power of its subjection. This tactic shaped Subcomandante Marcos's letter to Tom Ridge, the Governor of Pennsylvania in 1999: "I do not ask clemency, pardon, nor mercy from you for Mr. Mumia Abu-Jamal. I demand justice. . . . Justice, supposedly, is all that should matter."[198] During our writing of this introduction, in response to the events of September 11, 2001, Tom Ridge has been appointed the point-man for "Homeland Security" while the United States continues to wage its "war against terrorism." In this moment of danger, the so-called Bush Doctrine advocates pre-emptive military action by the United States government against unilaterally declared enemies. These imperial assertions of moral duty and political right echo the "burdens" of colonial history. A discourse of "civilizational" difference continues to shape assertions of supreme sovereignty, governing missions, and naturalized hostilities. The pursuit of justice, we argue, requires among other struggles the reworking of such alignments among race, nature, and difference.

We seek to be accountable to these histories of violence waged in the name of race, culture, nation, and empire. Our contributors chart strategies of racial exclusion and the historical formation of natural differences across diverse contexts, sites, and targets. In so doing, they recover from the wreckage of exclusionary histories ways of practicing race and nature differently. They demonstrate how history and power shape without fully determining cultural identities. Racial subjects, while active agents, are not sovereign selves free to choose any nature as their own. We hope to encourage a double move: to track entrenched genealogies of racism and naturalism while at the same time imagining race and nature otherwise. Those who conceive of such alternatives must also grapple with the brutal legacies of exclusionary politics. Adorno's sobering words echo across the histories of genocide: "The familiar argument of tolerance, that all people and all races are equal, is a boomerang . . . the most compelling anthropological proofs that the Jews are not a race will, in the event of a pogrom, scarcely alter the fact that the totalitarians know full well whom they do and whom they do not intend to murder."[199] It will take much more than an active imagination to challenge the legacies of race's entanglements with nature and culture.

Political coalitions are formed around shared interests, but we recognize, with Gramsci and Hall, that such interests are fashioned through cultural and political struggle and do not inhere in fixed structural locations, natural properties, or essential differences.[200] As a result, class and sexuality politics, race and gender, ethnicity and culture all shape the terrain of contingent struggles without determining their outcomes. Identities and affinities are expressed and bound together through such struggles. Brushing history against the grain may encourage novel articulations, fomenting alternative political possibilities. Forming new affinities across embattled lines of difference may be one means of challenging oppressive forms of racism and naturalism. *Making* race and nature work differently will require both new ways of imagining identity and belonging and the cultivation of new forms of political community. Novel rearticulations of race and nature will require disarticulating them from entrenched discursive formations. These counterhegemonic practices are hard work. *Race, Nature, and the Politics of Difference* hopes to contribute to these efforts.[201] We offer these accounts of race and nature—their making and unmaking together as a terrain of power and difference—as "resources of hope" for alternative politics.[202] Insofar as our readers are all bricoleurs, fashioning found materials into creative futures, we all share the challenge of fomenting emergent possibilities.

Notes

1 Du Bois 1986 [1940]: 651.

2 Soper 1995: 155.

3 Debates over "wilding" that followed brutal sexual attacks in New York's Central Park in the late 1980s fused anxieties around race, sexual violence, and degenerate instinct in the metropole. An incident in which six black youths were accused of beating and raping a young white jogger captured headlines for weeks and became a highly charged site of intense racial tension and anxiety. Particularly troubling in the media coverage and editorial commentaries following the incident were persistent analogies between urban men of color and the predatory instincts of pack animals (see Brasier 1990; Goldman 1989; Davies 1990; Pitt 1989; Will 1990). Five of the young men went to jail though their confessed guilt has been called into question by recent DNA evidence and a confession by a man not originally tied to the incident (see McFadden and Saulny 2002).

4 As our introduction elaborates, we understand both "race" and "nature" as social, historical, and cultural constructs that are materially consequential. We avoid the potentially tiresome use of "scare quotes" throughout the text. Similarly, when we discuss historical formations of race and their allied processes of racialization, we use the adjectives "racial" and "natural" without consistent invocation of our unsettling their historical claims to truth.

5 For an illuminating discussion of the distinction between "common sense" and "good sense" understandings, see Gramsci 1971. Stepan (2001: 15) asserts: "nature is always culture before it is nature," a view she also extends to race in her recent exploration of tropicality.

6 Haraway 1989: 15.

7 Barthes (1972 [1957]: 101) suggests that the very myth of a universal "human 'condition' rests on a very old mystification, which always consists in placing Nature at the bottom of History. . . . Progressive humanism, on the contrary, must always remember to reverse the terms

of this very old imposture, constantly to scour nature, its 'laws' and its 'limits' in order to discover History there, and at last to establish Nature itself as historical." For de Certeau (1988 [1975]: 72), "Historians metamorphose the environment through a series of transformations which change the boundaries and the internal topography of culture. They 'civilize' nature—which has always meant that they 'colonize' and change it." What Chakrabarty terms the "naturalism of historical time" emerges from an entrenched teleological tendency: "History as a code . . . invokes a natural, homogeneous, secular, calendrical time without which the story of human evolution/civilization—a single human history, that is—cannot be told" (2000: 73, 74).

8   See Hall's (1980) germinal essay on race and articulation for the importance of attending to historically specific forms of racism. For thoughtful discussions on the philosophical and political stakes of race, racism, and racialism, see Appiah 1992, Goldberg 1993, Memmi 2000 [1982], and Todorov 1993.

9   Gramsci (1971: 178). Here, we echo Gramsci's insistence that the "terrain of the conjunctural" is the product of historical practices, processes, and power relations and "it is on this terrain that the forces of opposition organise." Such a formulation shares affinities with Foucault's insistence that there is no resistance outside or beyond power. For an elaboration of these affinities, see Moore 1998a. Hall 2002 provides an extremely lucid reflection on the Althusserian, Gramscian, and Foucauldian influences on his formulations of race and articulation in the early 1980s.

10 See Hall 1980, 1986a. Althusser (1977 [1965]: 202) famously asserted structural Marxism's claim to theorize the "unity of a structure articulated in dominance," developing the notions of contradiction and overdetermination to advance his reading of a materialist dialectic. Hall's neo-Gramscian vision broke from this rigid structural determinism and class reductionism, as well as from the state-centric account of subject formation and interpellation elaborated in Althusser 1971 [1969]. Foster-Carter 1978 offers an influential perspective on articulation's paired practice of conjoining and enunciation. Laclau (1977: 70) elaborates a notion of articulation to counter the twinned evils of Althusserianism: taxonomy and formalism. Laclau credits Plato's allegory of the cave as a classical theory of articulation. Yet he deploys a Gramscian analytic to interrogate the "common sense discourse, *doxa*" that he deems crucial to abandoning "the Platonic cave of class reductionism" (7, 12). Crucial to these neo-Gramscian formulations was an emphasis on power relations, political economic forces, and historical sedimentations that shape the terrain of the conjunctural.

Latour extends the participants in articulation to include nonhuman actants and an array of practices, instruments, and objects. Nonhuman entities join human agents in historically specific assemblages that produce new boundary objects and revise old ones: DNA, HIV, "race." Key to this move is Latour's break from the notion of mute facts that "speak for themselves." Rather, he argues, "we have to abandon the division between a speaking human and a mute world" (1999: 140). Thus, for Latour, articulation becomes a constellation where human agents find their practices conjoined with nonhuman actants who are *also* active participants in the process of enunciation. Crucially, articulation and enunciation are not incarcerated in language but rather extend to world making and multivalent "imbroglios of human and nonhumans" (201) whose assemblages are meaningful and material. Pasteur, the laboratory, and lactic acid ferment provide one prominent example of a consequential articulation in Latour's sense. By pulling together the analytics of articulation, assemblage, and actants, we hope to render more visible the boundary work that demarcates the human and nonhuman, race and nature, culture and history.

11 By emphasizing the "formations of modernity" S. Hall (1992: 7) stresses that the former term covers *both* the activities of emergence and their outcomes or results: both process *and* structure. "Formation" thus shares affinities with our emphasis on emergent assemblages, a thematic fruitfully explored in Rabinow 1999.

12 We borrow the phrase "without guarantees" from Hall 1986b. For an alternative perspective on articulation, yet one strongly resonant with Hall's writings on ethnicity and cultural identity, see Barth 1998 [1969]. John Comaroff provides an extremely thoughtful reflection on an Althusserian tendency in "some Leftist academic quarters" to write "the 'native' entirely in the passive voice" and structural Marxist difficulties contending with colonized subjects as cultural agents (Bhabha and Comaroff 2002: 22). See Li 2000 and Moore 1999 for ethnographically grounded elaborations of "articulation" in the cultural politics of environment and development with particular attention to race and nature. Watts 1999 provides an insightful perspectives on articulation within the geographical imaginaries of national development.

13 See, e.g., Appiah 1992: 45, Gilroy 1987. Goldberg 1993 stresses that while all racisms have recourse to nature, not all require a biological basis.

14 Reflecting on the anti-immigration politics of the French Right, Etienne Balibar (1995 [1991]: 22) argues that "*culture can also function like a nature* and it can in particular function as a way of locking individuals and groups a priori into a genealogy, into a determination that is immutable and intangible in origin."

15 See Stoler 1995 for a helpful elaboration of Foucault's notion of "polyvalent mobility." More recently, Stoler (2002: 119) argues that "the porousness we assign to the contemporary concept of race is a fluidity inherent in the concept itself and not a hallmark of our postmodern critique. . . . Genealogies of racisms must reckon with racisms' power to rupture with the past and selectively and strategically recuperate it at the same time."

16 More than a decade ago, Cornel West (1990) coined the "new cultural politics of difference" as an emergent formation constituted by analysts' and activists' historicized attention to contingency, provisionality, and heterogeneity. We are aware of multiple genealogies of "the politics of difference," many informed by feminist formulations of the "simultaneity of oppression" experienced by women of color (e.g., Smith 1983: xxxii). These perspectives emphasize the multiple matrices of socially reproduced inequality shaped by race, class, gender, sexuality, and other modalities of identity and belonging. For more recent elaborations, see Alexander and Mohanty 1993, Sandoval 2000, and Trinh 1989. "The politics of difference" has also been an important theme in political philosophy and social theory that has sought to analyze identity claims, the social exclusions of marginalized groups, and citizenship rights within multicultural societies. See, e.g., I. Young 1990, 2000; Connolly 1991; Seidman 1997. Harvey 1996 is one of the few attempts to explore these themes explicitly in relation to nature.

17 Among a vast literature, see Baker et al. 1996, Bhattacharyya et al. 2001, Dent 1992, Gilroy 1993, Goldberg 1993, Hall 2000, Volpp 1996, Brackette Williams 1989, Ware and Back 2001. We are aware that "critical race theory" will conjure for some readers a field of legal studies— e.g., Delgado and Stefancic 2001—but as should be clear, we envision a much broader field of critical inquiry. We borrow the phrase "race critical theories" from Essed and Goldberg's (2002) excellent collection of writings that contributes to constituting that field.

18 The phrase comes from Chatterjee 1993. For closely related arguments, see Appiah 1992,

Bhabha 1994, Chakrabarty 2000, Cooper and Stoler 1997, Hall 1996a, Mbembe 2001, Olson and Worsham 1999, Prakash 1995, Scott 1999, and Young 2001a. Kant (1978 [1798]: 227) argued that it was the uniquely European habit "to travel in order to learn about people and their national character" that mapped Western taxonomies to universal reason, provincializing the non-West: "this is done by no other people but Europeans, which proves the provinciality in spirit of all others."

19 For a sense of the range of the literature concerning global asymmetries, see Gadgil and Guha 1993; Guha and Martinez-Alier 1997; Cock and Koch 1991; Athanasiou 1996. The relative attention devoted to race varies significantly within this literature. In the United States, Benjamin Chavis Jr., director of the NAACP, put environmental racism on the policy agenda as early as 1983. For a sense of the environmental justice field, with particular emphasis on struggles in the United States, see Bullard 1993, 1994; Cole and Foster 2000; Comacho 1998; Cutter 1995; Kuletz 1998; Pulido 1996a; Peña 1998. Peluso and Watts 2001, Westra and Wenz 1995, and Zerner 2000 offer a less U.S.-centered perspective on environmental justice struggles, examining processes in the global north and south. Pulido 1996b provides a critical review of how environmental racism has been deployed within the environmental justice movement, a theme elaborated in this volume by Di Chiro's contribution.

20 See especially Hecht and Cockburn 1989, Peluso 1992, Peet and Watts 1996, Neumann 1999, Schroeder 1999, Watts 1983, Zimmerer 1996. For recent overviews of the field, see Bebbington and Batterbury 2001 and Peluso and Watts 2001.

21 Wilson 1991 opened up critical questions around the cultural politics of nature's representation, themes more recently pursued in anthropology by Escobar 1999, Leach 1998, Raffles 1999, and Tsing 1999. Raffles 2002 and Braun 2002 attend to the materiality of representations and artifactuality of nature through the prism of cultural politics. For ethnographic perspectives on the cultural politics of environmental struggles, see Brosius 1999a, Li 2000, Moore 1998b, and Crumley 2001.

22 Strathern 1988: 34. Feminist anthropologists, in particular, have long insisted that "what appears a 'natural' fact must yet be understood in social terms—a by-product, as it were, of nonnecessary institutional arrangements that could be addressed through political struggle and, with effort, undermined" (Rosaldo 1980: 397). As Weston (1998: 79) astutely argues, "Attributions of permanence obscure power relations by locating relationships outside of time and therefore beyond social intervention. What exists in perpetuity, like what occurs 'in nature,' appears impossible to contest." Haraway 1989, MacCormack and Strathern 1980, Merchant 1980, and Schiebinger 1993 provide thoughtful historical perspectives on gendered representations of nature. Among those feminist perspectives particularly attentive to race, see Anzaldúa 1987, Carby 1999, Grewal and Kaplan 2001: 53–78, hooks 1992, and P. Williams 1989. For influential feminist statements that have explicitly linked the projects of feminism and antiracism, see Bulkin et al. 1984, A. Davis 1998a, Grewal 1988, Hull et al. 1982, Jordan 1981, Moraga and Anzaldúa 1983, Smith 1983, and Ware 1992.

23 See, e.g., Biagioli 1999, Braun and Castree 1998, Haraway 1997, Latour 1999.

24 Hall 1980: 338.

25 White 1995: x. For a helpful discussion of the differences among environmentalisms, with particular attention to global inequalities, see Guha and Martinez-Alier 1997.

26 White 1996: 171.

27 For memories of Eden, see Slater 1995 and Merchant 1983. For "America," see Locke 1993 [1689]: 139; for metabolism, see Marx 1977: 283. For insightful perspectives on Locke, race, and nature, see Mehta 1992 and Pieterse 1992. Taylor 1989 offers a helpful discussion of "Enlightenment naturalism."

28 White 1995: 173. For a germinal perspective on nature's history, see Williams 1980 [1972].

29 We underscore potential dissonances among influential Enlightenment philosophers to give a sense of the contrapuntal positions that operated within heterogeneous discursive formations of race and nature. See Buffon 1997 [1748] and for helpful commentaries see Glacken (1967: 679–81). Herder, who cites Buffon approvingly, implores his readers "to sympathize with the Negro, but not despise him, since the conditions of his climate could not grant his nobler gifts, and let us honor mother nature, who gives in denying" (1997 [1784]: 183–84). While Herder wrote explicitly against slavery and argued that American Indians' "savagery, passivity, and weakness are responses to [colonial] mistreatment, not innate," he envisioned Indians as occupying a "culturally inferior rank" (Zantrop 1997: 76, her words in quotation marks). Herder insisted that "all mankind is one and the same species upon earth," using this shared "nature" to critique prevailing assumptions of "race." Significantly, he saw nations as distinct cultural communities that shared a common language (Herder 1999 [1784]: 204). Zammito (2002: 345) distinguishes Herder's *cultural* contempt from "Kant's *biological* disqualification of non-Western peoples for self-determination," suggesting that Herder's "thoughts on the physical anthropology of race are, for modern eyes, vastly less painful than Kant's." Montesquieu (1989 [1748]) especially in part 3, elaborates a vision of the relationship between character and climate. He considered it "natural to think that color constitutes the essence of humanity," linking his reflections on the external climate of environments to the inner essence of racial being, both "naturally" determined. Crucially, a Christian god helped legitimate slavery since "One cannot get into one's mind that god, who is a very wise being, should have put a soul, above all a good soul, in a body that was entirely black" (250).

30 For Hume's comment regarding "breeds of men," see Hume (1997 [1748]: 33). For relations between climate and the nature of "the Negro," see Kant (1997a [1775]: 43, 46). This crucial role of climate, Zammito (2002: 302) suggests, stems from "Kant maintain[ing] simultaneously that species were fixed and that varieties arose within species as adaptations to ecological constraints." In the early nineteenth century, Humboldt linked his planned treatise "on the races in South America" to "what hinders civilization in the torrid zone, from the climate to the vegetation" (1995 [1834]: 10). For insightful readings of the racializing effects of the writings of Herder, Kant, and Humboldt, see, in particular, Eze 1997, 2001; Zammito 2002, and Zantrop 1997. For an analysis of Humboldt and race, see Poole 1997. On the linkages between conceptions of climate, nature, and race, see Livingstone 1994 and Orlove 1993. Anderson 2002 offers a recent analysis of medical discourses that envisioned the Australian environment as a significant influence on the mental and physical degradation of a white racial "type."

31 See, e.g., Collingwood 1960: 29, Haraway 1989: 13, and Strathern 1988: 30, 55. As Hall (1992: 277) argues, "'the West' is a *historical,* not a geographical construct." Coronil (2000: 357) asserts that "for Marx *land* stands for *nature* in its socialized materiality rather than in its independent material existence."

32 See, e.g., Lansing 1991, Croll and Parkin 1992, Descola and Palsson 1996.

33 Worster 1977: 37.

34 Foucault 1979a.

35 We also rely here on both the "socialized ecology" proposed by Fairhead and Leach 1996 and the "artifactual" analysis of science's nature undertaken by Latour 1993, 1999. For an overview of the diversity of "contested natures" in academic and policy debates, see Macnaghten and Urry 1998.

36 On cultivation, see Mukerji 1997 and Williams 1976: 92 and, on the linkages between tillage and culture, see Ratzel 1896: 27. Bacon (1999 [1625]: 104) saw, in the cultivation of gardens, "the purest of human pleasures" and evidence of a "civility and elegancy" demonstrating the "greater perfection" of humanity. On gardens in the New World, see Seed (1995: 25–31), who takes pains to differentiate among colonial projects, countering the depiction of a unitary European civilizing mission. Rabasa 1993 offers a complementary perspective on "natural gardens" in the New World with particular attention to Columbian visions of nature and culture. Pollan 1991 provides an insightful examination of the cultural valences of gardening in North America, analyzing discourses of democracy and historical resonances of enclosure, from which the term *garden* derives through a German root. Concerning connections among Christianity, cultivation, and the colonial civilizing mission in South Africa, see Comaroff and Comaroff 1997: 127. Drayton 2000 and Grove 1995 offer illuminating explorations of the relationship between botanical expeditions and imperial rule. See Rodriguez 1994 and Strathern 1992a for analyses of the gendered valences of gardens, domestic space, and national imaginaries; all pivot on embodied practices of cultivation. Bauman (1992: 178–79) provocatively links metaphors of gardening to the political technologies of modern states. Significantly, he emphasizes the usurpation of the right to classify useful and useless plants, and the violence of extermination and exclusion. Candide's injunction "that we must cultivate our own garden" has long been grafted onto imperial exclusions, genocide, and racialized dispossession (see Voltaire 1961 [1759]: 101). For a provocative reflection on the imperial routes haunting these sites of French cultivation, see Senghor's "Gardens of France" (1991: 163). As Patricia Williams (1999: 88) suggests, "hate cannot always be divined by those who are looking only for weeds."

37 Holiday first performed the song by schoolteacher Abel Meeropol, who wrote under the pen name Lewis Allan, in 1939. See A. Davis 1998b and Margolick 2000 for an assessment of the antiracist politics of Holiday's and Meeropol's work. The year before "Strange Fruit" 's debut, a Senegalese soldier reflected on his comrades who died for France, a landscape of violent memory saturated with the blood of race and nation: "Receive this red earth, under a summer sun this soil/Reddened with the blood of white hosts/Receive the salute of your black comrades . . . " (Senghor 1991: 47). For provocative reflections on the relations among fruit, passions, and desire, see Pollan 2001 and Bosch's 2002 collection of poems, "Passion Fruit." Recently, Alice Randall has countered *Gone With the Wind*'s racial imaginary of the U.S. South in *The Wind Done Gone*. Race, blood, intimacy, and identity are rerouted through fictional form. Other, the Scarlett O'Hara refigure, reflects on a refigured Rhett's misrecognition of race: "I had never known him to be ignorant. But he is. He thinks like the others, the common tide. He thinks that the blackness is in the drop of blood, something of the body. I would have thought he knew enough women's bodies to know that that could not be true. And enough blacks and whites to know there is a difference. What did I suck in on Mammy's tit

that made me black, and why did it not darken Other's berry?" (Randall 2001: 162). Thanks to Heike Schmidt for bringing this imagery to our attention. For King's quotation, see Prashad 2000: 86.

38 See Solomos 1986 and Wolpe 1986 for elaborations of Marxist positions. Despite salient differences, both advocate multiple determinations of race and class, refusing a reductive economism. Gilroy 1981 offers an explicit formulation of the relative autonomy of race and class. He has also argued that the crises of postimperial Britain are "lived through a sense of race" Gilroy (1990a: 265), echoing a germinal formulation by Hall (1980: 341): "Race is . . . the modality in which class is 'lived', the medium through which class relations are experienced, the form in which it is appropriated and 'fought through.' " For elaborations, see Hall 1986a and Gregory 1998. For Marxist feminist perspectives with particular attention to antiracist formations, see Davis 1998a: 111–231. Brodkin 2000 provides a recent overview in conceptualizing the relations among race, capitalism, class, and gender while Besteman 1999 offers a historical ethnography of the articulations of race and class that have shaped the contours of political violence in Somalia. Du Bois (1986 [1940]: 563) offers an often-neglected reflection on how the "racial angle" worked through income and ancestry rather than color in positioning Irish and African American in his high school experiences.

39 Swarns 2000: A4. This contemporary controversy echoes Francis Bacon's 1626 assertion that "hairiness" was a key distinguishing feature separating civilized and savage peoples (cited in Comaroff and Comaroff 1999: 32). Boas (1986 [1928]: 42) took pains to differentiate the hair of "domesticated" human races from those of wild mammals.

40 Williams 1977: 112. On the recalcitrance of embodied differences to normative natures, see Terry and Urla 1995.

41 Matless 1998: 13.

42 Hall 1997a: 35.

43 Cronon 1996: 52. For related positions, see Soper 1995 and Ellen and Fukui 1996.

44 Gramsci 1971: 377.

45 See also Feld and Basso 1996, Hirsch and O'Hanlon 1995, and Matless 1998. Competing genealogies of landscape both within and beyond the West raise alternative possibilities for rerouting the traffic between nature and culture. There is an extensive literature on non-Western landscape traditions, which we do not here review. For a sense of its range, see Mignolo 1995, Graphard 1994, and Wigen 1999.

46 For "ways of seeing," see Berger 1972. While this early formation stressed the perspectival enframing of visual techniques and artistic representations, Berger has elsewhere written compellingly about the embodied and ensouled practices of cultivating selves who work and live in rural and urban landscapes. On landscape's duplicity, see Daniels 1989 and Olwig 1996. On landscape and power, see Mitchell 1994.

47 See Cosgrove 1984 and Mitchell 1996.

48 Marx 1975: 232–34.

49 See Thompson 1975.

50 See, e.g., Demeritt 1998; Raffles 2002; and Zimmerer 1994, 2000.

51 See Carter 1989, Greenblatt 1991, McClintock 1995, Noyes 1992, and Pratt 1992. Raffles 2001 provides an elaboration of the critical assemblages of "local" and "traveling" knowledges through the practice of natural history and the circuits of imperial science that have routed

through the Amazon. In so doing, he renders visible critical erasures of non-European labor and expertise. Wilmsen 1996 explicitly links imperial erasure of a "Bushmen" cultural history situated in the southern African landscape to racialized discourses of primitivism. Both, he argues, legitimated colonial practices of racialized dispossession of land, resources, and labor. See Povinelli 1999 and Tuhiwai Smith 1999 for discussions of the complex legacies of these discursive formations that shape contemporary indigenous struggles for cultural citizenship, land rights, and political representation. Kenyatta (1962 [1938]: 306) offers a prescient and politically powerful analysis of colonial dispossession, violence, and the historical formations of "freedom" and "culture" they have engendered.

52 On images of the wild man in Europe with particular attention to discourses of alterity beyond the West, see Bartra 1994 and White 1978. Skaria 1997 connects these European imaginaries with colonial formations of racialized cultural difference in India. For Linneaus on *Homo Africanus*, see Pieterse 1992: 40. For a relevant illustration of Linnaeus's taxonomic system, see Bartra 1994: 157 and for an elaboration of the racialized implications of Linnaeus's work, see Blakey 1999, Eze 2001, and Hannaford 1996. Koerner (1999: 57) suggests that "Linnaeus's own canonical tenth edition of *Systema naturae* (1758) . . . has the dubious honor of pioneering a global race order." For Linnaeus on the "Sami savage," see Koerner 1999: 62. Recall that Linnaeus was a doctor whose classification of diseases and work on diet and nutrition shaped his writings on natural history, botany, and ethnology. While his taxonomic system remains formative in Western epistemes, we are aware of multiple genealogies that we do not here map. See Stuurman 2001 for an illuminating perspective on the influence of Francois Bernier's seventeenth-century system of racial classification on later formations.

53 On the "constitutive outside," see Derrida 1976. For his remarks on the Congo, see Conrad 1995 [1902]: 62. See Hochschild 1998 for an excellent historical treatment of colonial "monstrosity" in the Belgian Congo and Lindqvist 1996 [1992] for an enigmatic reading of Conrad's project. Fabian 2001 provides an insightful discussion of anthropological articulations between human recognition and alterity. Especially relevant is his mapping of the anthropological break from natural history through a trope of coeval recognition—an understanding of anthropological subjects and objects inhabiting a shared temporality and history.

54 Taussig 1987: 99. More than four centuries ago, De las Casas inverted prevailing tropes of savagery and civilization, rebuking the "inhuman barbarity" of Europeans in the New World whose "error and ignorance . . . attribute publicly to the Indians the gravest failings both of nature and conduct" (1992 [1552]: 27, 26). See Kane 1995 for a more recent discussion of how representations of "auca" savagery have shaped indigenous struggles and petroleum politics in the Ecuadorian Oriente. His ironic title echoes De las Casas' inversion.

55 See Gordon 1992 and Skotnes 1996.

56 See Martinez-Alier 1974; Hunt 1999; Schmidt 1992; Stoler 1995; and Verges 1999.

57 On naturalists' desire for "Constancy of character," see Darwin 1981 [1871]: 214.

58 Neumann (1997: 568) relates a colonial administrator's argument, in 1930, for including "primitives" in national parks in Tanganyika (now Tanzania), where "pastoralists are quite literally equated with the fauna as part of the overall spectacle of 'wild' Africa, an analogy repeated by conservationists up until the decade of independence."

59 For "Green Imperialism," see Grove 1995. On empire and nature, see also, Arnold and Guha 1995, Arnold 1996, and MacKenzie 1990. Lohmann 1993, 1999 has developed the notion of

"Green Orientalism" while Sawyer and Agrawal 2000 have elaborated the concept of "Environmental Orientalism."

60 See Carruthers 1995, Neumann 1999, and Ranger 1999.

61 Quoted in Mamdani 2001: 11.

62 Spence 1999: 5. Significantly, Spence historicizes the relationship between Native Americans and wilderness, arguing that antebellum Americans conceived of the two as necessarily fused within the notion of an "Indian Wilderness." Their separation emerges in the late nineteenth century, legitimating twin policies that removed Native Americans from parks to reservations and sought to "preserve" the recently dispossessed landscapes as uninhabited wilderness. For scientific racism's relation to U.S. Indian policy, see Baker 1998 and Michaelsen 1999.

63 Major Savage commanded the Mariposa Brigade, the punitive military expedition deployed to capture Chief Tenaya and the Yosemite Miwok in the wake of the 1851 "Indian War." Solnit 1994 provides an excellent account of Muir, Savage, and Tenaya in Yosemite. Writing in his journal on virtually the spot of Tenaya's capture, Muir marvels at his lakeside camp's pristine isolation, depicting a nature devoid of history: "No foot seems to have neared it" (quoted in Solnit 1994: 220). Churchill 1992 and LaDuke 1999 chronicle environmental racism's effect on contemporary Native American struggles.

64 For critiques of Williams in relation to empire and race, see Gilroy 1991 [1987], Parry 1993, and Viswanathan 1993.

65 See Pollard 1989. Lola Young offers a thoughtful discussion of Pollard's work in the context of landscape and environmental imaginaries within Britain (Young and Pollard 1995). Hall and Sealy 2001 situate Pollard's images in the cultural politics of black representation within Britain.

66 Empire's history routed English rule over landscapes surrounding Dublin in a project of national subjugation in Ireland from the twelfth century. "Beyond the Pale," an expression that travels far from the Green Isle across the Black Atlantic, emerged from a territorialized regime of rule that *positioned* subjects beyond an English-enclaved administration as wild, unruly, and belonging to a culturally inferior nature. Thanks to Vron Ware and Iain Boal for discussions about these processes. A racialized geography of natural belonging frames Kipling's short story "Beyond the Pale": "A Man should, whatever happens, keep to his own caste, race, and breed. Let the White go to the White and the Black to the Black." Apartheid's political logic of rigid spatial segregation and "separate development" relied on a resonant cultural understanding. For an array of perspectives on the changing locations of Jewish "race places," see Goluboff 2001.

67 Rose 1999: 4.

68 Foucault 1990 [1978]: 137.

69 For Francis Bacon, for example, science promised a sort of secular salvation through mastery over nature; see Merchant 1980: 170. For Freud on instinct, see 1961: 36–52.

70 See Hall's 1986b elaboration of "the *naturalization* effect."

71 Bullard 1990.

72 Berry 1993: 13. See also Carney and Watts 1990, Moore 1993, Alonso 1995, and Peters 1994.

73 For influential positions on gender and nature, see Ortner and Whitehead 1981 and Yanagisako and Delaney 1995. On feminist environmentalism, see Agarwal 1992, Di Chiro 1995, and Sturgeon 1997.

74 Foucault 2000: 298–325.

75 Stoler 1995: 9. See also Arendt 1968 [1951], Bauman 1989, Gilroy 1993, Goldberg 1993, S. Hall 1992, Mamdani 2001, Outlaw 1996, and West 1999, especially 55–86. While many have noted Foucault's relative neglect of race and empire within his writings o .odern power, his insights have been generative for this field. Scholars of racialization have found especially helpful his concept of governmentality, the project of constituting governable subjects who regulate their own conduct. See Foucault 1991b, Gregory 1998, Hesse 1997b, and Goldberg 2002.

76 Arendt (1968 [1951]: 65) argues that in the first decades of imperialism two new technologies for political rule emerged: "race as a principle of the body politic" and "bureaucracy as a principle of foreign domination." On the census, see Dirks 2001, Appadurai 1993, and Hannah 2000.

77 See Arendt 1968 [1951] and Frazier 1957 for influential formulations of race and imperialism. Goldberg 2002, Stevens (1999: 172–208), and Stoler 2002 provide recent elaboratic that link contemporary regimes of government to their racialized histories of imperial rule. Nietzsche's imaginatively graphic origin story for the state pivots on relations among race, conquest, and violence: "some pack of blond beasts of prey, a conqueror and master race which, organized for war and with the ability to organize, unhesitatingly lays its terrible claws upon a populace perhaps tremendously superior in numbers but still formless and nomad. That is after all how the 'state' began on earth" (Nietzsche 1967 [1887]: 86).

78 Bauman 1989: 57.

79 Darwin, *The Descent of Man* (1871) quoted in Lindqvist 1997: 107.

80 Baumann 1989: 74.

81 Worster 1977. For an elaboration of the relationship between the emergence of the "economy" as a bounded domain and the discursive terrains of family and *oikos*, both seen as targets of government, see Foucault 1991b and Donzelot 1979. Here, we follow Foucault and Donzelot by stressing the historical emergence of the "social" as a site and means of governmental intervention in the welfare and security of the population, understood as subject to calculating improvements.

82 See, e.g., Gasman 1998, Biehl and Staudenmaier 1995, Gilroy 2000, Linke 1999a. Proctor (1988: 141) reminds us that Haeckel spoke ⸤. anthropology as "the third biology" (after botany and zoology).

83 See Peet and Watts 1996, Guha 1994, and Peña 1998.

84 On managing, see Williams 1976: 92; on laws natural and social, see Malthus 1985 [1798]: 70, 102; on pastoral power, see Foucault 1981: 235.

85 For Hegel on history in the temperate zone, see Hegel (1956 [1899]: 80); on nature, Africa, and savagery see Hegel (1997: 110, 124, 127). See B. Williams 1989 and Harrison 1995, 1998 for reviews of more recent anthropological perspectives on race.

86 Virey 1837: 39. A century later, Lugard introduced Westermann's reflections on "the African" in a text that traveled through administrative circuits in colonial Africa and beyond. Westermann (1949 [1937]: 14) uses race to explain the "innate cheerfulness" and "care-free nature" of Africans. Unsurprisingly, readers learn that during the colonial encounter, Africans "willingly" entered the service ʾuropean employers (34). In his study of colonial power in Egypt, Mitchell (1991 [1988]: 105) argues that disciplinary practices and representational regimes in the late nineteenth century "create[d] the new subject of colonial politics, the individual

character or mentality. Like the more sophisticated ethnographic concepts that would replace it—first 'race' and later 'culture'—the concept of character was to acquire explanatory force by representing the historically moulded 'nature' of both the individuals and the society studied." Kant (1978 [1798]: 246) famously linked human character to nature's purpose unfolding through the only species capable of exercising reason: "the first characteristic of the human species is man's ability, as a rational being, to establish character for himself, as well as for the society into which nature has placed him." Kant (1978 [1798]) elaborated the "character" of sexes, nations, races, and species—all of which reflected nature's purpose and design.

87 Lugard 1926: 66, 68. For recent formulations of tropicality in relation to tropes of race and nature, see Aravamudan 1999 and Arnold 1996. Dirks 1992 explores how colonial rule articulated understandings of subjugating na ˇure and culture.

88 Salman 2001: 60.

89 Samuel Huntington's 1993 Manichean millenarianism, prominently preached in "The Clash of Civilizations," has formed a commonsense fundamentalism of sorts in analyses of the events and antecedents of September 11, 2001. For an excellent critique of this position prior to that moment of danger, see Ong 1999. And for a sharp rebuke to Huntington's cultural logic, see Said 2001. Thongchai 2000 analyzes linkages between tropes of civilization and race in colonial Siam.

90 Malthus's 1985 [1798] proposals for social reform through the abolition of the Poor Laws in eighteenth-century England hinged on the immutable laws of nature that governed the relations among population, resources, and wealth.

91 For Darwin's 1881 letter referring to "lower races" and their need for "improvement," see Worster 1977: 165; for Worster on the Victorian "march of improvement," see 171. Darwin (1981 [1871]: 404–05) closes *The Descent of Man* by preferring his apelike ancestors to his racially distinct savage contemporaries: "I would as soon be descended from that heroic little ⌐ʼonkey, who braved his dreaded enemy in order to save the life of his keeper . . . as from a savage who delights to torture his enemies, offers up bloody sacrifices, practices infanticide without remorse, treats his wives like slaves, knows no decency, and is haunted by the grossest superstitions." Among the many commentaries on Darwin, we find Lewontin et al. 1984, Marks 1995, and Rose 1998 to be especially insightful. Gobineau ˍ ˍnfamous *Essay on the Inequality of the Human Races* (1970 [1853]) also stresses the theme of improvement.

92 For helpful elaborations of these aspects of Lamarck, see Jordanova 1984.

93 On Lamarckian understandings of milieu in relation to the emergence of "the social," see Rabinow (1989: 66). On Latin American Lamarckian legacies, see Stepan 1991.

94 Darwin's famous phrase encapsulating the master narrative of natural selection and evolution was the "struggle for ᵔᵛistence." Spencer (1965 [1892]: 110) morphed this into "the survival of the fittest." For Dₐ   the "struggle for existence" in relation to race and savagery, see 1981 [1871]: 180. Whₙₗₑ we here focus on the United States, Social Darwinism obviously had global routes. Fabian's exploration of colonial travelogues and scientific treatises in Central ∩ᵢrica, for example, argues: "a firm belief in [European's] racial superiority, a kind of social Darwinism, constituted an unshakeable a priori" (Fabian 2000: 214).

95 Among the most prominent critics of such racial thinking was Franz Boas. He challenged the belief that "race consciousness and race antagonisms are instinctive," critiqued the terminology used by immigration authorities, analyzed the conflation of race and nation in Nazi

Germany, and championed the "social adaptability" of immigrants to the United States while attacking racial and religious prejudice (Boas 1945: 21, 22, 14). Boas (1986 [1928]: 84) refuted the "erroneous identification of a race as the true representative of a culture within a nationality," thus interrupting both popular and official perspectives that sought to find a natural logic linking race, culture, and nation.

96 For Mencken's position, see Larson 1995: 156. For Louisiana debates, see 99. Larson discusses regional differences in debates over eugenics and allied social and public health policies.

97 While Francis Galton first used the term "eugenics" in 1883, it was not until the 1901 Huxley Lecture at the British Anthropological Association that his views became widely disseminated. Significantly, the lecture was subsequently published in both *Nature* and *Popular Science Monthly*, thus reaching a range of audiences. See Baker 1998: 90–91. For differences between Weisman's germ-plasm and neo-Lamarckians, see Dubow 1995: 120–23. And see Barkan 1992 for a range of political positions advocated by eugenicists.

98 Breaking from the Lamarckian notion of the inheritance of acquired characteristics was crucial to dismantling a "bridge" enabling the scientific shuttling between race and culture. Like W. E. B. Du Bois, Franz Boas 1982 [1931] located barriers to 'racial' improvement outside of 'nature,' in the social forces of racism rather the biological inferiority of bodies and their capacities. For Boas (1986 [1928]: 60), "it does not matter from which point of view we consider culture, its forms are not dependent upon race." For a discussion of their "bridge," see Stocking 1982: 265. Baker 1998 offers an insightful elaboration of the affinities between Boas and Du Bois; Williams 1996 places Boas' insights in conversation with his African American contemporaries. As Darwin (1981 [1871]: 228) argued, the certitudes of race and evolutionary assumptions have long been "agitated by anthropologists."

99 See Ignatiev 1995, Jacobson 1998, and Stoler 1995. Roediger 1991 provides an influential analysis of relations among race, class, and labor in the United States.

100 See Terry 1999 for a brilliant cultural analysis of the technologies of assemblage surrounding homosexuality in the United States. She is particularly attentive to the cultural politics of race, gender, and class in relation to normative notions of nature. Mosse 1985 and Linke 1999a chart the body politics of race, nation, and sexuality in Germany with attention to the relations between heteronormativity, race, and nature.

101 For hygiene and difference in India, see Prakash 1999, Prashad 1994, and Kenny 1995: 694 for the quip on European preservation. On South African miners and tuberculosis, see Packard 1989. For a formulation of the racial divide between colonizer and colonized, see Chatterjee 1993. On the violence of pastoral care in Indian imperial settings, see Pandian 2001. Bayly 1995 and Beteille 1991 provide overviews of colonial formulations of race and caste in India, and Ghosh 1999, Guha 1998, and Pels 1999 offer compelling illustrations of the racial assumptions of colonial anthropology in India with particular attention to aboriginality.

102 For the "anti-politics machine," see Ferguson 1990. For "ecological managerialism," see Fairhead and Leach 1996 and resonant arguments in Luke 1997.

103 For exclusion of nonwhites from protected natures, see Neumann 1997. For the paramilitarization of antipoaching campaigns, see especially Peluso 1993. For recent debates on Bushmen and their implications for the cultural politics of race and nature, see, in particular, Wilmsen 1989a, 1996a; Gordon 1992; and Skotnes 1996. Neumann 1999 provides resonant pastoralist examples from East Africa, especially regarding the Maasai. Lohmann 1999 offers

an overview of "racist patterns and processes . . . sustained and strengthened through the activists of international environmentalists and developmentalists" in Southeast Asia.

104 Sukarno's 1955 Bandung speech, quoted in Frazier 1957: 338.

105 For a discussion of the resolution and its relationship to Boas, see Bunzel 1986 [1962].

106 See, among many critical articulations, James (1963 [1938], 1994 [1939]).

107 In this sense, Gilroy's project shares resonances with Boas's (1986 [1928]: 98) antiracism, which criticized both the League of Nations and the modern peace movement for being "not sufficiently clear and radical in their demands." Key to this move was countering the assumed "natural" linkage among race, nation, and culture. His explicitly cosmopolitan critique of the exclusionary practices of nationalism proposed a radical humanism celebrating citizenship rights and democratic inclusions grounded in internationalism and sharply critical of a "league of imperialistic nations" (Boas 1945: 152). Boas would appear to be implicitly engaging Kant's influential formulation of human freedom, a cosmopolitan-conceived Universal History (1983 [1784]) and Perpetual Peace (1983 [1795]). Fanon's call for a "new humanism" (1963 [1961]: 246) echoed Frazier's explicitly anti-imperialist and cosmopolitan call (1957: 338) for the emergence of "new cultures" that forged an antiracialist humanism. Both took inspiration from the 1955 Asian-African Conference in Bandung. Recently, Lowe's call to "reclaim utopia" for a Marxism attentive to the politics of difference sharply opposes neocolonial and liberal deployments of "universal rational forms." Strongly resonant with Fanon and Gilroy, she "imagines an alternative public sphere that respects the *human* through the process of bringing into evidence the series of exclusions, disappearances, and unevennesses upon which modern *humanity* has been constituted" (2001a: 16).

108 Ronald Blythe, quoted in Solnit 2001: 193.

109 Plumpp poem invoking a blues song from the Mississippi Delta, cited in Woods 1998: vi.

110 See Yanagisako and Delaney 1995. Ong (1999: 68) offers an illustrative analysis of how "Chinese race, culture, and economic activities" are imagined as "natural" regimes of truth. Polanyi (1957) undermines the notion of natural laws governing social relations. His germinal analysis of the Speenhamland system in England explored how nature, market, and labor relations converged to shape welfare policies—what he glossed as "the right to live," offering a formation interestingly resonant with Foucault's notion of biopower. Class inequalities understood as "natural" were, for Polanyi, economic processes embedded within historically specific social relations. On the naturalization of arbitrariness, see Bourdieu 1977: 164; his analysis draws explicitly on Polanyi.

111 Williams 1980 [1972]: 68.

112 For ideologies of "discovery," see Gilroy 1980: 281, cited in Wade 1993a (emphasis added).

113 On phenotype in the United States, see Wade 1993a; on epidermalization, see Fanon 1967 [1952]. Wagatsuma's (1968: 156) analysis of social perceptions of skin color in Japan traces the valorization of "white" skin to its "*unsuntanned*" status. He weaves notions of class, social distance from the rigors of manual labor, and gendered constructions of beauty into formations of race.

114 For labor discipline in the *maquiladoras*, with particular attention to the naturalization of race, gender, and sexuality, see Wright 1997 and Schmidt Camacho 1999. For South African mining, see Ranger 1985 and Moodie 1994.

115 Gilroy 2000: 37.

116 Wailoo (2001: 24) seeks to distinguish the "clinical and scientific visibility" of racialized diseases from their "social visibility." Since the scientific is necessarily social, we invoke both the contrast as well as resonances among vernacular or popular images of race and their technical, scientific representations. While Fanon, among others, has stressed the visual gaze of racial inscription, Bastide's 1968 research with blind Brazilians suggests a range of sensory markers projected onto racial identities. Malkki (1995: 78–80) offers a detailed analysis of "body maps" among Hutu refugees in Tanzania during the 1990s where distinct body parts bore the weight of ethnic differences. In turn, these perceived distinctions were constructed as signs of "innate moral character" and an essential cultural difference.

117 Du Bois 1986 [1940]: 651. On racial situations and cultural context, see Hartigan 1999.

118 On cultural hybridity and mongrelization, see R. Young 1995 and Hall 1990. Bunche (1968 [1936]: 9) saw "mongrelization" as a necessary challenge to "every possible scheme of racial classification." On hybridization, see Bhabha 1994, 1999: 39. Mitchell 1997 provides a cautionary critique of a tendency to presume emancipatory possibilities as imminent within cultural hybridity. Ifekwunigwe 1999 and Werbner and Modood 1997 argue for contextualizing contemporary debates around cultural hybridity in relation to the discursive formations of racial contamination, degeneration, and the mixing of previously pure racial types. Latour (1993: 1–2) suggests that we are living in a time of the "pr   ation of hybrids" in which "All of nature and all of culture ret churned up again every day." For a generatively provocative discussion of "the conjoining of nature and culture" within the figure of hybrids and its link to contemporary cultural politics, see Strathern 1999, especially 117–35.

119 On discourses of mestizaje, see Hale 1996a: 3. On mestizaje in the Americas, see also Gould 1998, Grandin 2000, Smith 1997, and Wade 1993b. Ortiz (1990 [1947]) coined the term "transculturation." For influential elaborations, see Liu 1995, Mignolo 2000, and Pratt 1992. For creolization, see Burton 1997, Glissant 1997, and Hintzen 1999.

120 For an elaboration of the "national order of things," see Malkki 1992. Recent analysts have identified forms of "new racism," "cultural racism," and "cultural fundamentalism" that ground difference in a cultural terrain of essential race, nature, and nationality. Rattansi 1994: 54–55 points out that there are multiple referents for the term "new racism," referring both to appropriations of sociobiology by the British New Right as well as Balibar and Gilroy's analyses of the culturalist forms of racism in Europe. Barker 1990 offers an analysis of resonant ideologies of "New Racism" in Britain and tenets within sociobiology and ethology. A group he terms the "new instinctivists" turned to natural selection to explain racial animosity, using models of "ritualized aggression" among animals.

121 On the fusion of nation and race, see Gilroy 1990a: 267. On difference, see Gilroy 1991 [1987]: 61. On race's registers, see Hall 2000: 223. Gupta and Ferguson 1992 argue that cultural difference is produced through spatial relations rather than conceiving of it as an inherent property of geographically separate cultural enclaves.

122 Stolcke 1995: 4, 6. See Lentin 2000 for a critical discussion of "culturalist" discourse in contemporary antiracist politics in Europe. Barker 1990 provides an important analysis of how arguments from sociobiology and ethology have been used to defend the "natural" human tendency for hostile exclusion of others. See Hesse 2000, Pred 2000, and Rattansi and Westwood 1994 for accounts of the racial politics of multicultural debates in Western Europe. Barker 1981, whom most credit with coining the term (e.g. Rattansi 1994: 54) "new racism,"

explores the British New Right's appropriations of sociobiology. Cohen 1999, Gilroy 1987, Balibar 1995 [1991], and Stolcke 1995 are among the more prominent accounts of "cultural racism" in Europe. Fanon 1967 [1956] provides an early influential commentary on "cultural racism" in the context of colonialism. Among the sharpest perspectives on articulations of "culture" and "race" in the United States, see Gregory 1998, Hartigan 1999, Lowe 1996, and Volpp 2001. De la Cadena 2000, Hale 1996b, Nelson 1999a and Wade 1999 offer ethnographically informed reflections on cultural racism in Latin America.

123 Nixon 1994: 343. See Hamilton 1998 on deployments of essentialism within Zulu cultural nationalism. M. S. Golwalkar, an early and influential leader of the Hindu militant *Rashtriya Swayamsevak Sangh* In India, found in Nazi Germany a model for his own brand of Hindu "cultural nationalism." In one passage from his *We or Our Nationhood Defined*, Golwalkar writes: "Germany has also shown how well-nigh impossible it is for races and cultures, having differences going to the root, to be assimilated into one united whole, a good lesson for us in Hindustan to learn and profit by" (cited in Basu et al. 1993: 26).

124 Kropotkin 1955 [1902]: ix. He acknowledges his debt to Kessler's influential 1880 lecture on "mutual aid" presented in Russia.

125 Compare the statements in Montagu 1972. For quotations: cooperation (12); "social myth" (10); "ethnic groups" (9). Convened in 1949, the UNESCO panel published the First Statement on Race in 1950; a revised second edition emerged the following year. Interestingly, the 1950 statement quotes Confucius in support of cultural relativism and a commonly shared human nature: "Men's natures are alike; it is their habits that carry them far apart" (Montagu 1972: 9). The same quotation launches Leiris's influential UNESCO publication, *Race and Culture* (1958). For a sense of the range of positions endorsed by UNESCO, see the essays published in Kuper 1975 to mark the international year to combat racism and racial discrimination.

126 See Gilroy 1990b and Visweswaran 1998. There are, of course, alternative genealogies of ethnicity. Among the most helpful, we find a route that runs through Barth's 1998 [1969] germinal formulations of ethnicity as relational, processual, and practiced and Hall's 1991 elaboration of "new ethnicities."

127 "Boundary work" underscores both the social and cultural work required to reproduce and reconfigure boundaries as well as the discursive effects those boundaries produce. See Haraway 1997 for a related discussion of boundary maintenance and Barth 1998 [1969] for a germinal perspective on ethnic boundaries.

128 On pink flamingos, see Price 1999.

129 On queer animals, see Terry 2000; on non-normative sexualities that trouble theories of natural selection, see Roughgarden (forthcoming). While Buchanan echoed the moral valences of Thomas Aquinas's thirteenth-century missionary position, his mapping of nature to nation is confounded by the formative heterosexual vectors of a global epidemic. See Coates 1998: 6 for the links between Buchanan and Aquinas's positions.

130 Hitler 1943 [1927]: 285; 302. Hannah Arendt 1968 [1951] brilliantly demonstrates how this category of "stateless people" contributed to the Holocaust.

131 Douglas 1966: 41 and Kristeva 1982.

132 For "geographies of exclusion," see Sibley 1995 and Cross and Keith 1993; for Chinatown, see Kay Anderson 1991; for exclusionary walls and urban enclaves, see Caldeira 2001. On fires and "incendiary others" in southern California, see M. Davis 1998. Kosek 2002 con-

textualizes Smokey the Bear's relationship to discourses of nation and nature, including perceived threats of foreign invasion such as the Japanese submarine's attack on a U.S. national forest. On invading aliens and fires in South Africa, see Comaroff and Comaroff 2001.

133   Proctor 1999: 264 describes the planting of evergreens within a German deciduous forest in a pattern chillingly visible, from the air, amidst autumnal color. The natural process of seasonal change reveals a seasonal swastika, the sign of racial supremacy organically inscribed in the landscape itself.

134   Kuletz 1998.

135   Du Bois 1986 [1940]: 639.

136   Statement of the President of the African National Congress, Nelson Mandela, at his inauguration as President of the Democratic Republic of South Africa, Union Buildings, Pretoria, 10 May 1994, http://www.anc.org.za/ancdocs/speeches/inaugpta.html. Mandela's rooting of the jacaranda to national soil is especially instructive since the plant is exotic to South Africa and a native of South America. Intentionally or not, his rainbow nation rhetoric weaves transcontinental routes into national roots. In so doing, he unsettles naturalized distinctions in citizenship rights between settler and native.

137   While we here focus on landscapes of affect that map meanings to specific sites, geographical features, and terrain, we distance ourself from the humanistic definition of place implicit within much of the "senses of place" literature. We stress the meaningful valences of human affect related to specific sites yet do *not* endorse the assertion that what *defines* place is the presence of cultural meaning. This humanistic conceptualization of place often operates with an implied contrast with the presumed noncultural category of space; place then becomes defined as space rendered meaningful through cultural signification. For critiques of this position, see Massey 1994, Moore 1998a, and Raffles 1999.

138   Feld 1996: 91; on sentiments in relation to interiority and exteriority, see Moore 1988, Strathern 1992a, Chakrabarty 1994; on inextricability, see Glissant 1989: 105; on nature as a screen of projection, see Williams 1980 [1972].

139   See Conklin and Graham 1995 and Peet and Watts 1996: introduction.

140   For melancholia in the Antilles, see Walcott 1998: 75–76. On tropicality and melancholia, see Lévi-Strauss 1961, Slater 2001, Stepan 2001. On "structures of feeling," see Williams 1973; on the "pathetic fallacy," see Ruskin 1897.

141   Fanon's radical critique of race prejudice and colonial violence (1967 [1956]: 41) analyzed forms of alienation animated by the "life-stream of psycho-affective, economic relations. . . . This culture [of the colonized], abandoned, sloughed off, rejected, despised, becomes for the inferiorized an object of passionate attachment." Butler 1997 elaborates a perspective on "passionate attachment" that shares Fanon's concerns with the psychoaffective dimensions of power, recognition within the process of subject formation, and Hegelian dialectics. Despite these affinities, however, her influential formulation of the "psychic life of power" remains largely silent on race, Fanon, and imperialism. For epidermalization, see Fanon 1967 [1952]: 13; "zone of nonbeing" (10). In a different context, yet one resonating with Fanon's formulation, Geertz suggests: "Foreignness does not start at the water's edge, but at the skin's" (quoted in Ware 1997: 248).

142   For "race pride," see Hurston (1995: 783); for "nature" (827); for "no race nor time" (829).

Significantly, when Hurston "escapes" her racialization, she becomes embodied as "the eternal feminine," existentially invoking gender to trump race.

143　For reflections on the category "experience" and critiques of its deployment as a foundational ground for identity, see Scott 1991 and Mohanty 1992.

144　Césaire 1983 [1939]: 77; Senghor 1991: 68. Renan's influential Paris lecture of 1882 charted a vision of the nation as a "spiritual principle" that endures "in spite of differences of race and language." Crucial to this imagined community was a shared sense of "suffering in common" that "unifies more than joy does" (Renan 1990 [1882]: 18–19). This trope of shared suffering as the moral bond of community and cultural belonging thus had both national and imperial routes. For an insightful use of Renan in relation to memories of violence, nation, and suffering, see Malkki 1995.

145　Sartre 1988 [1949]: 296, 298, 314. Elsewhere, Sartre (1976 [1948]: 10) argued that anti-Semitism is "first of all a passion." While Fanon recognized "the Jew" as "my brother in misery," he criticized Sartre's reflections on negritude and anti-Semitism for forgetting "that the Negro suffers in his body quite differently from the white man" (1967 [1952]: 122, 138). See Diawara 1998 and Young 2001b for a recent reflection on Sartre's relationship to negritude. Brown (2000) offers an enlivened ethnographic perspective on narratives of suffering in relation to constructions of race, locality, and nation in Britain. For influential Caribbean formulations, see Glissant 1989: 231–33 and Scott 1999.

146　On community, kinship, and suffering, see Du Bois: 1986 [1940]: 640. On race as a "cultural fact," see 665; and on Jim Crow designations as constitutive of racial formation, see 666. On Du Bois's shift from a more biologically fixed notion of race as inhering in blood to his emphasis on "the cultural aspects of race," see 628 and more broadly 625–51. For a helpful analysis of Du Bois on race and culture, see Baker 1998.

147　Benedict Anderson 1991 [1983]: 141. See Park 1950: 115 for an earlier elaboration and Chatterjee 1993, Gilroy 1991 [1987]: 44–45, and Ong 1999: 56 for a critique of Anderson's assertions of the role of class and race in the cultural formations of nation. Davis 1992 offers an incisive mapping of the complex affinities and structures of feeling that have animated progressive nationalisms in the United States.

148　Malkki 1994: 51. She shares our concern with the processes through which "the national order of things becomes a natural one—a moral taxonomy so commensensical that it is sometimes almost impossible to see" (62). On gendered formations of nation and idioms of kinship, see Chatterjee 1993, Gilroy 1992, and Kaplan et al. 1999. On rape and ethnicized violence in the context of cultural nationalism, see Das 1995, McClintock 1995, and Nixon 1994. On gender, violence, and nationalism, see Alonso 1995, Aretxaga 1997, and Taylor 1997. Brown 1995 offers a brilliant reading of the gendered assumptions of violence and sexuality that have been foundational to liberal notions of nation-states. For discussions of the relations among race and the "enemy within" the social, see Foucault 1990 [1978] and Stoler 1995.

149　The "geo-body" of modern Thailand, argues Thongchai (1994), inspires both loyal pride and passionate hatred precisely because of its own ability to *suffer* dismemberment. For an elaboration of the gendered politics of bodies, landscapes, and nationalism, see McClintock 1995, Nash 1994, and Schmidt 1995.

150　See Geertz 1973: 255–310 and, for a critique, Wilmsen 1996b. Malkki 1992 places these tendencies within the wider discursive formation of what she terms "sedentarist meta-physics" within anthropology and cultural theory. In particular, she challenges the notion that cultures are rooted in particular territories, thus discouraging an isomorphism of people, place, and culture.

151 Ratzel remains, in our opinion, an extremely underappreciated influence on territoriality, culture, nation, and nature. None less than E. B. Tylor (1896: v) introduced the 1896 translation of Ratzel's mammoth *Volkerkunde (The History of Mankind)*, heralded the work's "indispensable outline sketches of the races of mankind," and praised its map of "mankind as related together in Nature." Du Bois (1986 [1897]: 816) credits Ratzel, along with Huxley, for appreciating the "intermingling of the blood" within any "race." Ratzel distinguished "natural races," which were "in bondage to Nature," from "cultured races," which were "less dependent on accidents of her being," thus emphasizing a commonality of human dependence on nature (1896: book one, 15; see also 9). He took pains to distance himself from evolutionism, arguing that with "natural" races, "we must not assign them a place at the root of the human family-tree, nor regard their condition as that of a primitive race, or of child-hood." He hastened to add that they were not cultureless (Ratzel 1896: 22). Bassin (1987: 480) stresses that, for Ratzel, the idea of the people as a nation of *Volk* was a shared historical relationship to territory and "not an *a priori* ethnic or racial kinship." This did not, however, prevent Hitler from recasting Ratzel's notion of *lebensraum* (living space) into *Bodenpolitik* (soil politics) and the active exclusion of biologically inferior races. While he derived his notion of *lebensraum* from biogeography—and specifically, the territorial requirements for organisms to survive—Ratzel was an outspoken critic of this sort of "chauvinistic racism" (Bassin 477). See Ratzel (1988 [1876]) for an elaboration of the relationships among nature, culture, and national history. In his classic study of anti-Semitism, *Are the Jews a Race?*, Kautsky (1972 [1926]) explored terrain where "a race may pass beyond the geographical boundaries set up by nature," envisioning natural processes of racial mixture. Kautsky's conceptualization of animal and human races is replete with organic metaphors of roots, growth, and domestication.

152 LeRoi Jones 1966: 248.

153 Gilroy (2000: 55) develops a notion of "ecologies of belonging," building on the work of William Connolly. Geschiere and Nyamnjoh 2000 argue that contemporary processes of neoliberal globalization in Cameroon have fomented a cultural politics of belonging that hinges on autochthony. Key to their analysis is an appreciation for the historical emergence, through transnational routes, of the political mobilization of autochthony as a rooted identity.

154 The quotations are from Kroeber 1969 [1939]: 350; Sauer 1952: 2–3; Sauer 1963 [1925]: 326; and Steward 1955: 35. Kroeber's emphasis on environmental possibilism—the constraining yet not determining influence of nature on culture—opened up space for the formation of a cultural ecology reliant on notions of diffusion, multilineal evolution, and the importance of subsistence activities for defining a "cultural core." This twentieth-century formation also emphasized adaptation to geographically differentiated ecologies, the diffusion of technologies, and a materialist conception of subsistence as the linchpins of the historical relationship between nature and culture. For critical reflections on the presumed isomorphism between people, place, and culture within cultural theory and anthropology, see Gupta and Ferguson 1992 and Malkki 1992.

64   Moore, Pandian, and Kosek

155 See Gordon 1998, de la Cadena 2000.

156 For jazz, see Jones 2001; for ethnology, see Litzinger 1999; for ethnic tourism, see Oakes 2000, Schein 2000; on ethnic minorities, moral geographies, and national belonging, see Litzinger 1999 and Mueggler 2001.

157 For articulations of Native American, African American, and Latin American routes of race and nation, see, in particular, Forbes 1993, Lewis 2000, Menchaca 2001, and Strong 1996. For blackness and migratory routes, see Hall 1985, 1999.

158 Rabinow 1996. On cultures of expertise, see Rose 1999. For an exemplary analysis of the production of race through biomedical discursive practices, see Fullwiley 1998. Terry 1999 offers a related history of the scientific expertise that informed discourses of homosexual- ity—and hence normative and deviant natures and cultures—in the United States.

159 Wiegman 1995 explores at length the specificity of North American histories of slavery and their legacies for racialized discourses of personhood, patrimony, and property. For related formulations that emphasize the legacies of slavery inscribed in the contemporary cultural politics of personhood, see Spillers 1987 and Patricia Williams 1991. We certainly do not propose a singular "North American" racial formation.

160 Stepan 1998: 29–30. Warwick Anderson 2002, Arnold 1996, and Stepan 2001 sketch histor- ical formations specific to tropicality, while Slater 2001 explores Amazonian imaginaries of nature and culture.

161 Mead and Baldwin 1971: 168.

162 Marx 1963 [1869]: 124, 123. Marx's nuanced analysis, of course, recognized both revolution- ary and conservative peasants. Hence he did not see their mode of production as determining each subject's political agency as much as a constraint on their collective realization of a unified class consciousness.

163 Spivak 1988: 275.

164 For insightful analyses of representation within the context of black cultural politics, see, e.g., Carby 1999, Dent 1992, Mercer 1994, and Wallace 1990.

165 Latour (1999: 142) envisions articulation as a process in which nonhuman actants can partici- pate. He stresses that "articulation is no way limited to language and may be applied not only to words but also to gestures, papers, settings, instruments, sites, trials." In this sense, the materiality of nature and of nonhuman actants is consequential for politics insofar as it shapes assemblages that inform cultural, social, and hence power-laden practices.

166 The cultural politics of representation abounds with spatial metaphors of location (Mohanty 1992), positioned subjects (Rosaldo 1989), and situated knowledge (Haraway 1988).

167 For the Ogoni struggle, see Saro-Wiwa 1995: 2. For Huaorani constructions of identity and resources in the context of multinational petroleum politics, see Kane 1995.

168 Crucial in Trouillot's 1991 formulation is his insistence on the relational quality of multiple others rather than a singular, universal dialectic between self and other. Gikandi 1997 makes a resonant argument in his mapping of British constructions of African identity. Both argu- ments rely crucially on Fabian's 1983 germinal formulation of anthropology and alterity. See Cooper and Stoler 1997 and Catherine Hall 1992 for the mutually constitutive histories of metropole and colony.

169 For images of the "wild man," see Bartra 1994, Dudley and Novak 1972, Taussig 1987, and White 1978. For "edenic narratives," see Slater 1995; Merchant, 1995; Greenblatt, 1991.

170 See Keck 1995 and Zerner 1994.

171 See Milton 1996, Willems-Braun 1997, Li 2000, Churchill 1992, and LaDuke 1999.

172 See Guillaumin 1995: 108–15. She translates *l'immigration sauvage* as "wildcat immigration," tracing semantic links to its "uncontrolled" denotation and the connotations of wildness and savagery. For reflections on racialized constructions of "foreigners" in France, see Derrida 2000; Jelloun 1999a, 1999b; and Todorov 1993.

173 Fuss 1989: 6.

174 Hall 1990: 225.

175 Provocatively, de Certeau suggests that strategy is best reserved for "the calculus of force-relationships which becomes possible when a subject of will and power . . . can be isolated from an 'environment' " (de Certeau 1984: xix). Tactical maneuvers, he suggests, seize opportunities in force-fields of power by insinuating themselves into spaces frequently controlled by political, economic, and scientific rationality. Without endorsing an absolute distinction between tactics and strategies—indeed, they are necessarily relational concepts, and the same practice may be simultaneously strategic and tactical within different fields of power—de Certeau's insight might inform contemporary struggles over identity and nature.

176 See, in particular, Mandela 1965 (1959), Mamdani 1996, Nixon 1994, and Robinson 1996.

177 Among the many illustrations of these processes, see the examination of indigenous social movements in Alvarez, Dagnino, Escobar 1998 and Ramos 1998.

178 Significantly, Butler adds that leftists then "construe this cultural politics as factionalizing, identitarian, and particularistic" (1998: 33).

179 See Neumann 1997 for a discussion of "ambivalent primitivism"; Trouillot 1991 for the "savage slot" and Taussig 1987 for a related instance in Colombia of racialized subjects' powerful associations with both magic and danger. Conklin 1997 offers an ethnographic perspective on icons of indigenous authenticity. Hanchard 1999b provides a helpful contextualization of the racial politics surrounding citizenship struggles in contemporary Brazil.

180 See Fusco (1994: 27), referring to Gayatri Spivak's 1988 notion of "strategic essentialism," which Spivak herself has subsequently qualified. See also Pulido 1996a, Sturgeon 1997, Baviskar 1997, and Di Chiro 1997 for thoughtful reflections on strategic essentialism in the context of environmental politics. Radhakrishnan 2000 emphasizes the importance of historicizing and locating both "essence" and "essentialism" in uneven geographies of power. For an early discussion of identity politics, see Hull et al. 1982, especially chapter 2.

181 See Brosius 1999a, Jackson 1999, Li 2000, Nelson 1999a, Ramos 1998, Turner 1991, and Warren 1998 for broader explorations of the relationship between anthropological representation and indigenous peoples.

182 Taylor 1994 locates the "politics of recognition" at the heart of identity struggles in contemporary debates surrounding multiculturalism. Iris Young (2000: 86) critiques commonsensical understandings of "identity politics," preferring to emphasize the "politics of difference" that animates social movements whose members do not share uniform interests, values, and political ideologies, let alone common understandings of a unitary cultural identity. She critiques Taylor's formulation for its privileging of symbolic recognition over material resource claims in the context of structural inequalities (105). Butler 1998 and Fraser 1997 offer an illuminating exchange over the analytical and political stakes of the cultural politics of recognition. Chatterjee 2002, Fabian 2001, and Povinelli 2002 offer helpful elaborations of these stakes where discourses of alterity beyond "the West" figure prominently.

183 Haraway 1997: 36. We strongly endorse her echo of Marx's Eleventh Thesis on Feuerbach, penned in 1845.

184 In Ang's (2000: 1) terms, cultural identities are "the very subjective instruments, or discursive conduits, through which we may shape and construct our futures."

185 Hall 1988b: 8. For an elaboration of race and the representational strategy of naturalization, see Hall 1997b: 245.

186 Reflecting on the racial formation of Asian Americans in contemporary debates surrounding U.S. immigration and citizenship, Lisa Lowe (1996: 22) suggests that it is "only through culture that we conceive and enact new subjects and practices in antagonism to the regulatory *locus* of the citizen-subject," and it is "by way of culture that we can question those modes of government."

187 See Guinier and Torres 2002, especially chapter 3.

188 Boas 1982 [1931]: 14. Boas decried the "absurd falsity" of "undemocratic prejudices," including those held by the Nazis, that "ignore the elementary facts of anthropology." At the same time, in the fresh wake of World War II, he noted "the rising tide of race prejudice and of anti-Semitism and anti-Catholicism" in the United States (1945: 13–14). Democratic principles of citizenship and national development, Boas argued, require political commitments—to anti-racisms and against social prejudices—grounded in the "facts" of anthropological science. On a resonant chord, Donald and Rattansi (1992: 3) argue, "the fictional or metaphorical status of the category 'race' in no way undermines its symbolic and social effectuality." For a related formulation, see Baker 1998: 227.

189 D'Souza 1995: 556. For sharp critiques of D'Souza's argument, see Goldberg 1997 and Prashad 2000. D'Souza's position echoes Ronald Reagan's 1984 remarks that the only barrier to blacks was "within" themselves (see Takaki 1990: 304).

190 Crenshaw 2000: 68; Patricia Williams 1997: 15. For a related argument, see Baker 1998: 227.

191 The political disenfranchisement of particular racially marked voters who traveled to the polls in the 2000 U.S. presidential election and the disproportionate incarceration of African Americans in the U.S. prison-industrial complex remind us that "even though a biological category of race is meaningless, the social category of race is very real, meaningful, and still dictates life chances and opportunities" (Baker 1998: 227). For Morrison's quote, see Cose 2001: 29. Clinton's location of a post–White House office in Harlem provoked both supportive affirmation and derisive denunciations by African Americans and other urban residents. Chants of "We love Bill" mingled with "Slave Master" and "Go Home." This clearly complicates any uncritically celebratory image of Clinton's "racial" mobility. See Waldman 2001 for coverage of Clinton's arrival in Harlem. See Reagon 1983 and Davis and Martinez 1994 for influential formulation of coalition politics and Haraway 1992 for an illuminating discussion of affinities.

192 Fanon's humanism envisioned "reciprocal recognition" as critical to the "battle for the creation of a human world," a necessary struggle in his vision of selves emancipated from colonialism (1967 [1952]: 218). See Gilroy's chapter in this volume for an elaboration. On the constitutive exclusions of liberalism, see Brown 2001, Hanchard 1999a, Lowe 2001a, Mehta 1999, Okihiro 2001, Rose 1999, and Sartre 2001 [1956].

193 Mehta 1999: 67. As Mehta convincingly argues, classical formulations of liberalism such as those of Locke and Mill mobilize culture as a means for reconciling a universal human nature

with the practices of subjugation and rule. "Liberal exclusion works by modulating the distance between the interstices of human capacities and the conditions for their political effectivity" (49). On Locke's reflections on the "natural" capacities of freedom, see Mehta 1992 and McClure 1996. Williams 1990 offers an illuminating discussion of "Indian capacities" in the context of Native American conquest and dispossession. For sharp reflections on the "limits" of liberal multiculturalism, see Hall 2000.

194 Du Bois (1986 [1940]: 653). Here, we wish to remind readers of the "polyvalent mobility" of race we previously discussed and underscore the unfixed and often mobile locations of race. Interestingly, a number of accounts that stage formative sites of racialization invoke journeys. Du Bois, Fanon, and Patricia Williams, for example, have all used the interpellation of bodies on trains to stage discussions of racialized subjection. This move does much to challenge emancipatory invocations of travel that neglect exclusionary processes at work. These mobile terrains of subject formation are at once existential journeys and embodied movement. Trains are also "public" spaces where the close physical proximity of bodies engenders both a sociality of relative intimacy and encounters that often highlight the marked differences of race, class, and gender, among others. These traveling sites are at once interstitial—moving between other sites—and themselves a context of encounter, intimacy, and power.

195 Mandela 1965 [1959]: 79. Apartheid, literally "apartness," proposed an official policy of "separate development" for distinct races. Apartheid was simultaneously a discourse of multiculturalism and of racialism. Robinson 1996 and Hart 2002 provide overviews of the spatial politics of racialized rule under apartheid. Ali's remarks were reported on National Public Radio: 19 December 2001 *Morning Edition* interview with Juan Williams. The quotation attributed to Ali shares an uncanny resonance with Spivak's (1988: 296) formula for struggles over gendered and racialized bodies in colonial India during debates surrounding *sati:* "White men are saving brown women from brown men."

196 See, among an extensive literature, Lowe 1996, Prashad 2000, and Volpp 2001. Lowe 2001b stresses both the distinct yet related patterns of racial formation that have interpellated different "immigrants" to the United States as well as their affiliate. constructions of gender and sexuality.

197 An engagement with the moment of danger following "9/11" is beyond the scope of this introduction, which we conceived and initially drafted long before September 2001. We wish, however, to emphasize the linkage between a civilizational discourse demonizing cultural alterity abroad and a resurgence of racial profiling "at home." Samuel Huntington's 1993 "clash of civilizations" argument has been extremely influentia' 'n framing debate. Various media and the U.S. administration's repeated imagery of Taliban and al Qaeda forces hiding in "caves" foregrounded the natural features of Afghanistan, downplaying the histories of U.S. and other foreign interventions that had long fortified such "natural" spaces. In November 2001 many pondered the question: can the subterranean speak? Secretary of Defense Donald Rumsfeld married the neoliberal logic of market triumphalism and the promise of Enduring Freedom in the hopes of ferreting out subterranean dwellers in Afghanistan: "we have large rewards out, and our hope is that the incentive—the dual incentive of helping to free that country from a very repressive regime and to get the foreigners in the al Qaeda out of there, coupled with substantial monetary rewards, will incentivize, through the great principle of University of Chicago economics . . . incentivize a large number of people to begin

crawling through those tunnels and caves, looking for the bad folks." See Defense Department Briefing, 19 November 2001, online at http://embajadausa.org.ve/wwwh1207.html. For a compelling analysis of post-9/11 discourses of racialization and their relationship to the ˙tics of difference, see Bacchetta et al. 2001. On enduring freedom, see Chomsky 2001.

198 .e might do well to remember one of Marcos's inspirations, the lyrics of a song by S⁺ ⁻hen Stills. By invoking a "white" male icon of popular U.S. music from the 1970s, Marcos taps into a four-way street of race, class, gender, and ethnicity. He might just have easily invoked Gil Scott-Heron's song "Work for Peace," from the 1994 album *Spirits*; the lyrics resonate sharply with Kant's 1795 essay "To Perpetual Peace." For Marcos 2001 on neoliberalism, see 109 and 260. For his 1999 letter to Tom Ridge, see 192. For Marcos's invocation of Stephen Stills, see 297. Behind the black mask, Marcos has invoked an affinity of interests united in a commonly articulated humanity and in opposition to processes of neoliberalism that cut across class, color, nation, and cultural difference: "Behind we are the same simple and ordinary men and women, who are repeated in all races, painted in all colors, speak in all languages and live in all places. The same forgotten men and women. The same excluded, the same untolerated, the same persecuted" (111). In his opening remarks at the 1996 First Intercontinental Encuentro for Humanity and Against Neoliberalism, Marcos (2001: 122) called for a "network of voices that resist the war Power wages on them." Wary of the dangers of romanticizing resistar˙e, we argue that oppositional movements are never waged from a site outside or beyond power, a critical perspective echoed by our contributors.

199 Mamdani 2001 builds on and reworks both Arendt and Fanon in his reflections on genocide and racialized violence in Central ˙frica. He looks to the geographical, historical, and cultural practices of race, state, and nation that shaped the administration of "subject races" in the crucible of colonial power. For reflections on pogroms, see Adorno 2000 [1951]: 102. The prominent anti-Semite Wilhelm Marr wrote confidently of the inferior "cultural level" of blacks and based his arguments in the 1870s on the "question of race." This chain of signification, locking inferior cultures in the abject qualities of natural races, emerged through Marr's historical claim that "the Jew is a White Negro" (quoted in Lindqvist 1997 [1995]: 83). As we go to press, Adorno's sobering reminder might well be directed against Israeli state violence against Palestinian targets in the Occupied Territories. The crucial project of supporting Palestinian rights for self-determination requires disarticulating anti-Zionism from anti-Semitism, two discourses that have become powerfully (con)fused in many contemporary accounts of violence and political loyalties in the Middle East. Part of this work, we argue, requires attending to ˙.e histor   ˙xclusions and violent ˙ ˙cupations perpetuated in the name of race, nation, and culture—as well as their articulation to civilizational discourses of fundamental difference.

200 Hall 1988a offers a compelling analysis of Gramsci's insight that interests are formed through political struggle. This move is crucial to what Hall 1986b terms a politics "without guarantees." For this reason, Hall and Sealy (2001: 35) conceive of "black" as "a politically, historically and culturally constructed category; a contested idea, whose ultimate destination remains unsettled." For recent elaborations of the political and theoretical legacies of Hall's germinal cultural politics, see Gilroy, Grossberg, and McRobbie 2000.

201 On the twin tasks of articulation and disarticulation in relation to race, see Hall 1999. As Wiegman 1999 cautions in her critical review of whiteness studies, the political project of

rendering race visible should not be a point of final arrival but rather part of a much wider fabric of antiracist politics and representation. Ware and Back 2001 offer a complementary perspective.

202 We draw "resources of hope" from Raymond Williams (1989). In so doing, we also echo an aphorism Gramsci (1990 [1920]: 188) took from Romain Rolland and popularized in *L'Ordine Nuovo:* "pessimism of the intellect, optimism of the will."

PART ONE. Calculating Improvements

1. After the Great White Error . . . the Great Black Mirage

Paul Gilroy

The Negro is not. Any more than the white man.—Frantz Fanon

The horrors of the twentieth century brought "races" to political life more vividly and naturalistically than imperial conquest had done. Postcolonial time reverberates with the catastrophes that resulted from their militarized agency and their unprecedented victimization. Those events have been left behind, but contemporary analysis of racisms and their morbidities still belongs emphatically to that unhappy period.

I want to begin this chapter by endorsing the suggestion that critical analysis of racisms needs self-consciously and deliberately to be updated. Few new ways of thinking "race" and its relationship to economics, politics, and power have emerged since the era of national liberation struggles to guide the continuing pursuit of a world free of racial hierarchies. If we are now seeking means to revive that worthy aspiration, of making it sound less banal, more attractive and more political by showing where it touched and still transforms modern dreams of s 'nstantive democracy and authentic justice, we will need to reconstruct the history of "race" in modernity, offering multiple genealogies of racial discourse that can explain h' v the brutal, dualistic opposition between black and white became entrenched and has retained its grip on a world in which racial and ethnic identities have been anything but stable or fixed.

That worthy goal introduces a conflict between the obligation to pay attention to local and conjunctural factors and the lingering desire for a totalizing theory that can explain the attachment to "race" and ethnicity under all conditions. The former is demanded by a subversive commitment to the relocalization of a networked world, the latter is animated by the troubling fantasy of controlling that world by reducing it to a set of elegant categories. This attempt to reconcile the irreconcilable claims of abstraction and immediacy involves returning in a systematic and historical fashion to the interpretations of racism and racial hierarchy that were produced during the Cold War, which emerged from the critical theorists of national liberation struggles and which flowed from the confrontation with a variety of differing incarnations of fascism not all of which appealed openly or consistently to the metaphysics of "race."[1]

Along this path we will be obliged to consider the fate of the libertarian and cosmopolitan left during the twentieth century and to ask why there have been so few successor projects capable of articulating antiracist hope in anything other than its negative moment: as creative conjuring with the possibility of better worlds rather than embattled criticism of this disenchanted one.

Though they were addressed to a very different context, Adorno's challenging words on the relationship between nationality, ethnicity, and forms of intellectual freedom can be borrowed here. They communicate something of the specific problem that arises from dissenting contemplation of the mystified, alienated world in which racial truths and biocultural ontologies have supplied indices of realness as well as key markers of sensible social policy, mature political thought, and good scholarly habits: "The person who interprets instead of accepting what is given and classifying it is marked with the yellow star of one who squanders his intelligence in impotent speculation, reading things in where there is nothing to interpret."[2] Transposed in this way, his observation points firstly to the way in which "race" is obstructively invested with common sense. It might also suggest that the signs of "race" do not speak for themselves and that the difficult work of interpreting the system of meaning they create is always likely to appear illegitimate, "politically incorrect," sometimes treasonable, and usually speculative in the most dismissive sense of that term. Adorno reminds us that while the political order of "race" endures, the character of racial and ethnic groups is already at stake in attempts to transform a mode of exploitation and domination that is not merely comfortable with the phenomena of racialized differences but has amplified and projected them in order to remain intelligible, habitable, and productive.

This opportunity to consider relations between "race," nature, and the politics of difference provides a welcome chance to defend another orientation toward "race" in the political field. It emphasizes the currently un-fashionable values of critical speculation and interpretative work and is therefore likely to offend black and white proponents of "identity politics" in equal measure. I should emphasize that I know opposing racism in practice does not always permit these varieties of reflection, but I think antiracism's practical political maneuverings are weaker and less convincing as a result of that shortcoming. The alternative stance I want to outline here aims initially to consolidate the creativity and insight displayed by brave mid-twentieth-century thinkers in whose work confrontations with Nazism, the possibility of armed anticolonial resistance, and commitments to civil and human rights struggles combined to produce a new analysis of "race" and its political dimensions in several different places—not all of them obviously colonial in character. The imaginative scope of this political project typically spanned the overdeveloped and developing worlds. Today it is best conceptualized as a self-conscious successor to the translocal interpretations of "race," racism, culture, belonging, and identity that were first laid out in the complex and forbidding work of Frantz Fanon, which has recently been so poorly served by its growing legion of scholastic fans.[3]

This pursuit of a history of the present can be guided by the irreverent spirit evident in Fanon's youthful flirtations with existentialism. In that frame of mind we have to be prepared to ask what antiracism should become in the future?[4] I suggest that it will have to be more than either a fading footnote to the injustices of colonial domination or a strategic maneuver designed to maintain elite control over divided and confused collectivities that fall back on the imaginary bonds of "race" as a cheap but nonetheless effective surrogate for the political solidarity they think they need if they are to defend themselves.[5]

The willingness to invent political cultures capable of ending racism demands real creative and prophetic work. A decisive "refusal to accept the present as definitive" is not as easy as Fanon made it sound in 1952 when the failures of Western European civilization were apparent to everyone and the destructive potency of race-thinking was impossible to ignore.[6] The reconstructive labor signaled in these transgressions is most useful when it is directed not into the well-intentioned but utterly mistaken task of pumping up the phenomena of racial differences into a full-blown phenomenology[7] but when it turns against the political anthropology of "race" that *always* precedes the identification of that order of difference.

The youthful Fanon trumpeted his decisionistic escape from the constraints of inherited circumstance but was still operating in a conceptual framework informed by substantial elements of historical materialism. Anticolonial solidarity and his professional sense of the depth of the human subject made him essentially sympathetic to arguments made by Sartre, who had emphasized that it was the anti-Semite who created the Jew, and those of de Beauvoir who, to cut a long story short, argued under the same constellation that Woman was made rather than born.[8] In this distinctive "constructionist" problematic, which grows in importance as we grasp its ethically grounded refusals of scholastic protocol, Fanon stripped not only the Negro but "race" itself of the ontological claims that removed it from history and delivered it instead to the unnatural realm of what he called "timeless truths" and "ultimate radiances."[9] Today this radical approach refers us to the processes he identified as "sociogeny,"[10] a valuable but oddly neglected concept that opens a difficult angle of vision on racialized politics and promotes the disturbing conviction that racial divisions have no given, necessary, or automatic effects and can therefore be made to serve various ends.

Fanon's combative stance is readily compatible with an approach to raciology that identifies "race" as a precarious discursive construction rather than the achievement of primordial or biocultural emanations. He encompasses but also moves beyond a radical historicizing of racism that encourages alertness to its changing forms and functions. He allows for the possibility that "time lags" or "differences of rhythm" can arise in the systematic flow of racialized mentalities and identifications. Symbolic constructs, imaginary representations, and political meanings that derive from discrete phases in the history of "races" can coexist, interact, and combine. For example, the brutal biopolitical force of the colonial order was supplemented but never completely erased by the culturalist, anthropologically minded race-thinking of the 1950s when, in the bloody penumbra of the Third Reich, innocent culture took over from raw natural hierarchy as the favored medium through which racial differences would become apparent. We must note that both are still latent within more recent genomic innovations adding their weight to the density of multiply accented racial signs that serve the interests of corporate multiculturalism. We must also entertain the possibility that the simplifying and solidarizing effects of racial discourse may thrive and be enhanced in situations where the fundamental or ultimate meanings of "race" are muddled or deferred. Anyone who would oppose racisms must be no less careful than Fanon was not to confuse these strands of discourse. Their conspicuous perlocutionary power means that success in opposing racisms may depend on not mistaking one for the other.

The recent emergence of genomic theories of "race" has left those older constructions—culture and biology—in a residual condition, but, like abandoned munitions under an old battlefield, though they may be obsolete they are nonetheless powerful. Indeed, the passage of time may have added to their volatility even as the rigid hierarchy they created has lost many of its attractions. It offers no plausible therapy capable of salving the visceral anxieties and largely prepolitical concerns that now testify to the currency of "race" and absolute ethnicity not only in the lives of subordinate groups, gilding their traditional badges of inferiority, but in the increasing fears of those who feel themselves to be superior but find that the postcolonial world withholds automatic assent to that historic a priori.

In these circumstances, to approach the problem of racialized political cultures via the dualistic system of ideas that gives us blackness and whiteness may already be to have conceded too much ground to raciality's accumulated common sense. The Manichaean opposition of those color-coded aggregates is a fatal one. It erases earlier patterns of intermixture and combination through a simplifying mechanism that is the very instantiation of the colonial order. All its original violence is concentrated there in a condensed, and suspended, but nonetheless traumatic form. Today it tells us that relation—complex, tangled, profane, inconvenient interdependency— must supply the starting point for inquiries into the making and projection of racialized bodies.[11]

Before we can deal with the historical specificities that shaped localized racial identities and made them translocal, bringing those pure and irreconcilable entities into being and then baptizing them repeatedly in warm blood, we must address the principles of solidarity and collectivity that produced black-ness and white-ness as totalities governed by distinctive arrangements that are inseparable from the political rules and ontological foundations of national states. This requires a lengthy detour through the political philosophies of modernity, which can then be reconsidered in the light of their colonial and imperial provenance. It is not just that theories and concepts, notions of history and culture, government and statecraft are found to have been implicated in the workings of European domination that they subsequently rationalized and legitimated. Without lapsing into an idealist approach to the history of these raciological ideas, we can recognize the discourses of "race" and nation as having had a larger, world-historic significance than most historians of imperial power have so far been willing to grant.

Once the rational irrationalities of raciology are factored in as a driving element central to the development of modern political theory, this line of inquiry can be used to dispute conventional conceptions of the relationship between metropolitan state and colonial outpost, between core and periphery.[12] It takes us instead toward a view of the colony as rather more than an extractive commercial operation. No longer merely a settlement, an adventure, an opportunity, a place for self-creation and a space of death, it becomes a laboratory, a location for experiment and innovation that transformed the exercise of governmental powers at home and configured the institutionalization of imperial knowledge: judicial, medical, anthropological.

These are enormous topics that have been the subject of substantial absorbing volumes.[13] Here I want to concentrate briefly on the central problem of what we use to identify the distinctive political and juridical dynamics of colonial power. This involves asking how those relations may have been shaped by the articulation of racial discourse and the belief in racial difference and how the pattern of political relations that lay at the heart of the old imperial systems was transformed as a result of a sometimes murderous enthusiasm for the racial ordering of the world. This historic shift was initiated long before Europe's colonies began to export living labor as well as commodities and raw materials, thereby beginning a new kind of link to imperial power through having to manage and contain colonial enclaves at home. From this unorthodox angle, the colony can be recognized as a special kind of place. Its necessary reliance on divisions within humankind, for example, demanded and institutionalized the abolition of all conceptions of citizenship as universal entitlement. This might also represent the end or limit of politics as it had been previously understood. The racial ordering of the colonial world inaugurated novel patterns of statecraft the consequences of which are still to be understood.

Though many able and committed scholars have followed in the pathbreaking footsteps of Fanon, Foucault, and Elias, the story of how modern *political* cultures linked the body, the state, and violence is not usually told on a scale that encompasses these distinctive imperial and colonial dynamics. This academic resistance is significant in itself and cannot be explained away by issues of historical probity or disciplinary duty that have made empire, when it is considered at all, principally into a matter of history and economics rather than culture and politics.[14]

The nature of cultural and ethical connections between colonial and metropolitan life became central to the political and moral agenda set by national liberation movements of the twentieth century. Their core questions included asking whether the Nazi genocide could have had colonial precedents, whether Europe's continuing colonial empires reproduced or converged with the raciology that had lent its logic to the Third Reich's crimes, whether Europe could recover, and whether capitalism could be divested of its historic attachment to racial divisions. This provocative inventory is still unresolved. It will remain so while the impact of governmental techniques and technologies that derived from colonial imperatives is considered unworthy of scholarly investigation even in the most obvious fields: planning, medicine, policing, killing, propaganda, communications technology, and population control.[15] Important links have certainly been identified between the development of modern social policy and the life of imperial systems. But outside of interesting material drawn from the analysis of sexuality and consumer cultures, they remain significantly underexplored.[16]

As far as the history of Western statecraft is concerned, problems like the disappearance of public torture are often understood to identify a significant stage in the development of a new type of power: capilliary, biopolitical, and primarily directed toward the management of population. This is only one institutional element in the larger history of modern government that would have to be explained quite differently if colonial conflicts and their distinctive legal ordering were fully taken into account.[17] The history of colonial power overflows with evidence that suggests a particular relation to military power and martial law that must have changed the workings of institutional complexes like the army and medical practice as well as the professional thinking of administrators, planners, managers, and rulers alike.[18] Time and again we are required to face up to the differences that raciology made to the administration of justice and the organization of legitimate violence.

Focusing on basic institutional components of state power—sovereignty, territory, population, and government itself—raises numerous issues that complicate and can even overturn orthodox accounts of how modern political authority was secured and transmitted. This worthwhile corrective exercise does not merely yield an amended account of the institution of biopolitics, which is seen differently when it is approached from imperial angles. A fuller appreciation of the specifically colonial input into national statecraft promises an altogether different sense of where biopolitical procedures and anthropological hierarchies fit into the history of modernity. Understanding of the telling balance between normal and exceptional deployments of governmental violence is transformed by accounts that can operate on this scale. Finally, modernity itself becomes a different sort of geopolitical project when the colonial extensions and outposts that remain peripheral within narrowly Europe-centered accounts are shown to have been intimately and complexly associated with its core domestic activities in ways that move beyond their valuable role as a stimulus for the development of critical comment and oppositional consciousness.

The significance of this conceptual adjustment can only increase if colonial modernity can be shown to rely on its various investments in the idea of racial hierarchy both at home and abroad. However, as I have said, most commentators on these dynamic threads of planetary history have failed to mention "race" specifically or to entertain the possibility that histories of racism and of raciology might be productively associated with the genealogies of political anatomy and biopower that culminated in the ideal of the apartheid state and furnished Western modernity with the important governmental laboratory in which the political technologies of separate development could be refined. After all, under the sign of "race," that is the only form of development available.

The desacralization of the body has rightly become a major issue in accounting for the transition toward modern political authority. It provides an important way to explore the new range of analytical possibilities that emerges from this change of focus. The role of race-thinking in rendering the bodies of natives, slaves, and other infrahumans expendable is a pivotal issue in specifying how the racialization of governmental practice impacted on the exercise of power. Though he is clearly uninterested in the analysis of colonial relations, there is something profound to learn from Giorgio Agamben's recent attempts to reconcile the complicated legacies of Arendt and Foucault. He has made a dense but intellectually invigorating study of sovereign power centered on the politically ambivalent and juridically marginal figure of the person who can be killed with impunity and the reduction to the infrahuman condition of "bare life" that sanctions his or her death.[19] Though it is limited by a frustrating Europe-centeredness, this important work raises the hope that integrating genealogies of governmentality with histories of race-thinking will eventually be an especially stimulating and productive combination. Colonial power contributed to the manifestation of bare life in historically unprecedented quantities and circumstances under the supervision of administrative and managerial systems that operated by the rules of raciology.[20]

It is not only that rationally applied terror routinely became colonial administration but also that the critical figure of the person who could be killed with impunity moved out of the liminal position to which it had been allocated by the unruffled workings of the national state and merged with those of the infrahuman natives and the racial slaves. At that fateful but very familiar point, the colonial project manifests a new kind of political space and fills it with a new cast of characters. This development can contribute directly to our understanding of how the state of emergency associated with the spatial and juridical institution of colonial power has contributed to the normal functioning of postindustrial and postcolonial societies where inequality is increasing, mass incarceration has become systematic, and other forms of confinement delimit the lives of racialized minorities.[21] The lowly life-forms that populate this zone or quarter exhibit the full shocking depth of their infrahuman character only when their bare lives are contrasted with the healthier modes of being enjoyed by the settler population. These different types or castes were products of a colonial enterprise that mandated the reduction of the native to the status of an animal in order to operate properly. The native, always closer to the condition of scarcity, stood at the epicenter of governmental action, placed there by the imperatives of exploitation and kept there by progressively more elaborate racial anthropologies that, however potent they appeared to be, could never, according to Fanon anyway, completely "mask the human realities" involved. This verdict seems to be endorsed by his conviction that colonialism triggered mental illnesses in which the guilt-ridden recognition of this human equivalence must have played a part.

Fanon describes the process through which colonial subjects are rendered vulnerable to the forms of rationality, violence, and legality that can be routinely visited on the paradoxical conditions of social death and exclusionary inclusion that Agamben identifies with bare life. He contrasts the practical morality that guides native resistance against this downward pressure with the overly abstract forms of universalism that are more likely to be found at the other end of the imperial chain. The key to grasping this important difference in ethical outlooks lies in the natives' pursuit of a concrete and immediate dignity. This reaction is a response to the dehumanization involved in the institution of race hierarchy. Humanity can only be recovered, he continues, through a new relation to the land that "will bring them bread and, above all, dignity." Territory thus supplies an "essential value" in the economy of colonial reparations that inevitably also includes the counterviolence and resentment of the natives, the slaves, and unfree.

These geopolitical and spatial aspects of power are intrinsic to Fanon's analysis of the colonial order of "race," its nomos. As is well known, he presents apartheid as the paradigm case of this arrangement and reveals how the reduction of the native, unfree worker, or slave to infrahumanity becomes inseparable from the foundational opposition between blackness and whiteness. Those terms of racialized identity are values but they are also places *and* cultures in the older sense of the term preserved by the English words "agriculture" and "horticulture." The warring totalities to which they refer promote and identify ecologies of belonging saturated with the mythologies and metaphysics of race-thinking that are always close at hand.

We should remember that for Fanon this arrangement was not a matter of politics. Instead, the emergence of color-coded, Manichaeistic duality marked the suspension of political relations and fostered their replacement by a rather different set of technologies and procedures. They have helped to make a special brutality—seemingly anachronistic by mid-twentieth-century European standards—into the engine of a colonial power so chronically absurd and so total in its infiltration of everyday life that it has parceled up the earth itself along racial lines. Needless to say, this was done in ways that explicitly confounded Marxian distinctions between base and superstructure and posed difficult questions to movements that looked only to economic progress as the means to deliver a raceless world.[22]

Though it is fed by a sacred belief in racial hierarchy, the violence that inaugurated the motionless world in which blackness and whiteness confronted each other is not only a symptom of the fact that racial code has been engaged as both governmental terror and technique. For Fanon, colonial power is Manichaean in its nature. The same ruthless simplifying logic places blackness and whiteness in mutually antagonistic relation. They are separated spatially, geopolitically; but conceptually, their common reliance on racialization ensures that they are bound to each other so tightly that each is unthinkable without the proximity and hostility of the other. The distinctive geometry of colonial power pushes cultural questions to the fore,[23] but we should also pause to identify other related issues that can be highlighted through an acknowledgment of Carl Schmitt's deeply problematic theory of politics as the practical expression of elemental distinctions between friend and enemy.[24] This increasingly popular and influential approach can be interpreted as an attempt to incorporate a damaging Manichaean code into a universal theory of the political and to rewrite the tradition of modern political reflection according to the ultranationalist and race-friendly rules that make all political relations conform to the deadly exigencies of imperial foreign affairs. Few commentators on Schmitt's work have thought that it might be worth asking whether this might have been related either to his sense of Germany as an imperial power in need of "raum" or to the racialized opposition between itinerant Jews and rooted Christians.[25]

Fanon shared this geopolitical and philosophical interest in the living room that colonial power won for the settler and denied to the native. He saw whiteness and blackness as among the first and most durable products of territorial expropriation. Their coupling and separation was central to his account of the political arrangements that characterized colonial rule. There, as we have seen, he placed a heavy emphasis on the spatial configuration of these two great camps—totalities that could synthesize unity and plurality into the distinctive patterns associated with the lives of "races." Color-coded duality specifies the transmutation of sameness and plurality into racial identities. Those great "encampments" were permeated with neurosis and a "dual narcissism." Their opposition draws us toward the primal problem of difference if not to the essential features of monotheistic systems and their genocidal successors. This, perversely, was also his route to universality and perhaps, eventually, to the evasive new humanism about which he wrote so much.

The Sartrean emphasis that Fanon placed on Manichaeism shows how the relationship between blackness and whiteness denies any possibility of a comforting dialectical resolution. The omnipresent violence of colonial administration creates the colony as a frozen, immobile world of statues that is not in teleological or progressive motion toward freer, healthier, or more comfortable arrangements. The split character of that militarized colonial world allows it to be inhabited, in effect, by different species each of which nourishes itself inadequately with the fantasy of its unanimity. Fanon underlines that the breakup of the colonial world "does not mean that . . . lines of communication will be set up between the two zones. The destruction of the colonial world is no more and no less than the abolition of one zone, its burial in the depths of the earth or its expulsion from the country."[26] Though many of his interpreters overlook it, this is not the end of Fanon's colonial tale. The issue of blackness and whiteness as both political values and cultural cues recurs in his critique of bourgeois nationalism and his unsettling account of the postrevolutionary transition. The original Manichaeism of the settler—which, as we have seen, culminated in the transformation of the native into either an animal or the quintessence of evil—has by this time been destroyed. However, an inverted but essentially similar mentality has taken root in the other encampment: among the natives. In his optimistic scheme, this second, transitional formation yields finally to a wider consciousness that can break with the alienated logic of epidermalization and open this oppositional and for the first time fully hu. ı consciousness to a wider range of ethical and political sensibilities. But this happy outcome, which is not the third term in a dialectical movement, is also flecked with blood. It provides a reminder that the association of blackness and whiteness is not just a site of ontological obstacles to the emergence of disalienated human consciousness among blacks (which is Fanon's primary concern). Blackness and whiteness identify the depths of alienation itself. Their symptomatic pairing is especially unhelpful when it can be misread as precipitating a system of ethnic or racial equivalences that would produce whiteness as a straightforward effect of the racialization of humankind pure and simple. On the other hand, it becomes usefu hen it helps to question the ridiculous notion that "race" is somehow the innate or particular property of its black subjects, something that is assigned to them alone.

Fanon recognizes that whiteness can carry its own wounds even if they are still veiled in postcolonial melancholy and colonial privilege. He is again instructive in viewing this as an amputation. But abstract whiteness is never a parallel or complementary "white" version of the culture, history, and consciousness that previously produced abject blackness as the object of anthropological knowledge, colonial exploitation, and racialized power. The precious postrevolutionary stage, which marks the end of "race," may also prove to be the starting point for a new version of class analysis prompted by postcolonial varieties of exploitation and authority. This insight arises amidst a moment of the gravest danger in which the revolutionary project can be hijacked and disenchanted people are offered back their racial and ethnic difference in exchange for their human freedom. His disturbing point is clear even in translation. I would like to quote . at length: "The people must be taught to cry 'stop thief!' . . . the people must also give up their too-simple conception of their overlords. The species 's breaking up under before their very eyes. . . . The barriers of blood and race-prejudice are broken down on both sides. In the same way, not every Negro or Moslem is issued automatically a hall-mark of genuineness; and the gun or the knife is not inevitably reached for when a settler makes his appearance. Consciousness slowly dawns upon truths that are only partial, limited and unstable. As we may surmise, all this is very difficult."[27]

If we follow Fanon's inspiring example and work toward creative possibilities that are too easily dismissed as utopian, our moral and political compass

might profitably be reset by acts of imagination and invention that are adequate to the depth of our postcolonial predicament. This comm ment is part
of an approach that has several additional virtues. It can be readily linked to
that diminishing and invaluable commodity: hope. And it can be connected
to a vibrant political and ethical (prise that carries antiracist dissidence
into a deeper confrontation with the history and philosophy of modernity—
understood here, following the eloquent and compelling arguments developed by Enrique Dussel as the process in which Europe ruthlessly instituted
itself as the center of planetary development *and* the critical responses to
that development.[28]

The innovative emphasis Fanon placed on the sociogenesis of racial mentalities originally licensed his humanist and existential ventures and marked
his departure from the psychologism of his professional training. It seems to
have been shaped by his growing conviction that "Marxist analysis should
always be slightly stretched every time we have to do with the colonial
problem"[29] and still offends attractively against all economically deterministic accounts of "race" and racism. Today, his scurrilous : culations also
underline the benefits of turning away from the list of dull priorities established by purely scholastic reflection on the rational irrationalities of "race"
and racism. The limits of that polite labor were reached long ago.[30] Its
fruits should certainly be disseminated, but contemporary political strategies must involve more than simply chanting them indefinitely in the optimistic expectation that one day they will be heard by power.

The more negative and reflexive orientation I favor is part of restoring
moral credibility to antiracist critique and exploring the rehabilitation of a
humanist voice.[31] In drawing energy from Fanon's dete ination to make
"race" historical and above all social, it assigns racisms to the past and can
ther fore help to make antiracism more than just a jumbled collection of
political instruments and techniques. The necessary element of negation
endows today's project of liberation from "race" with an unsettling ethical
character.[32] Even though this has gone out of fashion recently, it has long
been apparent and constitutes a noble if muted presence in the buried, disreputable lineage of antiracist action and commentary that has shadowed modern race-thinking since its inception. Withou the crude injustices of racial
slavery and colonial conquest to orient us, we are now obliged to know even
more comprehensively than in the past precisely what we are against and
why. But, as far as the order of racialized differences is concerned, our political imaginations are inclined to falter or become blocked at the point of

maximum defensive solidarity. That is where we are certain of what we are against but cannot say what we are *for* with the same degree of clarity and conviction. The debate in contemporary South Africa over how to evaluate the historic, insurrectionary commitment to nonracialism in the face of racial government would seem to bear this out.

This hesitancy is associated with the inability to explain how people become intimidated by and resigned to the mystifications of raciality and its narcissism of minor differences; how they try to make the refusal to see beyond reified racial categories into a measure of their political virtue; and how, while usually according racial difference a routine and empty measure of recognition as a social and historical construction, they are only too happy to lose the capacity to imagine its unmaking, its deconstruction, its transcendence, or even the possibility of its eventual descent into irrelevance. These problems have been compounded by a voguish reluctance to trespass on the imagined communities of oppressed groups who may have seized the discursive categories through which their subordination has been transacted or imposed and then lodged them in the centers of their "wounded" solidarity and the carnival of identities that it supports.[33] This compensatory commitment to unanimity cannot succeed for long. The inevitable appearance of differences within the favored collective creates grave disappointment with the group's lack of spontaneous fellow feeling and mutual regard. Here the idea of "race" damages us by feeding expectations of being together that are impossibly high. As Cornelius Castoriadis controversially pointed out, there is also a degree of self-hatred to be reckoned with.[34]

I am not suggesting that the utopian-sounding procedures involved in seeing, thinking, and acting beyond race hierarchy can be divorced from practical confrontations with the immediate manifestations of racism. Indeed, I would argue that the precious ability to imagine political, economic, and social systems in which "race" makes no sense is an essential, though woefully underdeveloped, part of articulating a credible antiracism as well as an invaluable transitional exercise. However, that useful capacity has fallen into disrepute. In this area, the long-idealized unity of theory and practice has given way to the dominance of practice in ways that are a convenient measure of the defeats, weakness, and marginality of antiracist critique. At best, we have no time to think critically because we are always on the move from one funeral, detention center, or police station to the next. At worst, cheap if heartfelt assertions of absolute ethnicity and unbridgeable racial difference can provide a convenient means to postpone any confrontation with racism. The narcissism of minor differences takes over and engulfs any critical aspirations or creative impulses.

The inability to deal with this situation has been compounded by the retreat of Marxian anticapitalism. That strand of analysis promoted not only a distinctive critique of ideology that could explain racism away as mirage and mystification but an attachment to labor as a race-transcending abstraction. It was inevitably tied to the existence of an alternative developmental project that fed Western dissidence and anticolonial movements in numerous ways. However dreadful the fate of racialized and ethnic minority populations inside the communist systems, their outward-looking governments were alert to the fact that the moral authority of capitalist states would be compromised where capitalism was seen to be too cheerfully compatible with racism. Combined with new communicative technologies, this development brought assessments of racial antagonism into the field of Cold-War politics and was an essential feature of the planetary discourse of human rights in its mid-twentieth-century form.[35] The moralization of remote spectatorship became part of the technocultural complex through which some asymmetrical invitations into antiracist solidarity were extended.[36] People became present to one another in new and significant ways even at the risk of an aestheticized response to remote suffering. The immortal celebrity of figures like Malcolm X, Muhammad Ali, and Nelson Mandela is one obvious illustration of that stage in the unfolding of global or rather translocal connections. In reply to their sometimes rash but always exciting promises of revolution, a pallid, official antiracism emerged close to the memory of the Third Reich and as a result of anticolonial and African American freedom struggles. It was a minor but inescapable part of the liberal democratic project of cold-war governance.

We've seen that today's continuing difficulties in the face of racism reveal a discrepancy between where we are and the tools that are available to us to make sense of our postcolonial predicaments. At worst, we drift back into scholastic eighteenth-century concepts and outmoded nineteenth-century biological imaginings to make sense of a political and moral topography around "race" that is completely different from the Darwinian landscape in which the natural imperatives of culture, nation, and empire were first braided into the political ontologies of European domination and imperial rule.

Under the spell of Marxism for too long, critical thinking about "race" consoled itself with the wish that racialized attachments and collectivities could be disposed of by being shown to be unreal, insubstantial, invented, and ideological in character. We must all be familiar with arguments of that type, which can be far more sophisticated than I've allowed them to sound. They invite us to wave the magic wand of rationality toward forces that cannot possibly acknowledge its power. Against that vain attempt stands another popular option. It says that however they may motivate, bite, corrode, and inspire, racial identities are a misplaced and rearticulated form of something else. This something may be economic relations, gender attachments, class solidarities, religious, regional, or primordial aesthetic distaste, but the question of why they require the particular language and symbols of racialized difference as a cloak cannot be considered. Now, I agree that we need to see the virtual realities of "race" in their complex and profane patterns and that we must be able to possess them, analyze them, and criticize them in relation to other dynamics of power and dimensions of hierarchy including those of gender and class.

This is a nice neat formula that has energized some interesting and important work, but it offers little when tactical choices have to be made and contributes even less when the question of double standards gets raised and would-be antiracists are required to say how the invocation of absolute "race" or ethnicity by the exploited and the oppressed and their more fortunate descendants differs from the ways it has been solicited and traded by their oppressors. Faced with that uncomfortable situation, it is easier to respond by recycling the interpretative habits with which earlier political generations had struggled to make sense of "race." The other safe options are easily identifiable. We can defer to ethnic absolutism and ignore its fascistic poetics. We can overlook the self-interested antics of the group Fanon dismissed as the native petite bourgeoisie. Where racial difference boils down to lifestyle, consumer choice, management theory, or new-age biooccultism, the resuscitation of a vulgar Marxism that subordinates "race" absolutely to class does not seem quite so bad. In this scenario, antiracism is finally silenced by resurgent corporate trading in "race"; by the manipulation of absolute ethnicity by those who have been its victims and cannot now be measured by the same moral standards as everybody else; and lastly by the exercise of racialized power in patterns that do not conform to the binary logic of "Manichaeism delerium."

I would like us to ask if our hesitations and inhibitions in the face of these developments are connected to the dominance of antihumanism in what is left of left thinking? This pattern of responses needs to be interpreted as a reaction against the articulation of liberalism and humanism in Cold-War discourse as well as a symptom of the scientific pretensions that accompanied the retreat of Marxism and its accompanying scholastic turn. The hesitation that characteristically freezes us in our encounters with "race" and the increasingly assertive voice of corporate multiculturalism might also result from the Trojan horse represented by the malign influence of figures like Schmitt and Heidegger in framing political ontologies and, more recently, in moving oppositional commentaries beyond the limits of Marx's Europe-centered conceptions of political freedom and onto solid elemental ground.[37] Giving antiracism a cosmopolitan history and endowing it with a philosophical skeleton that is not reducible to recent, vaguely Marxist or feminist commitments helps not only to undermine Heidegger's growing authority over these important matters but to answer the apprehensions of those who do not want to accept that it is racism that has made "race" into a burden—on individuals, on polities, and on democracy itself.

Everybody knows that conceptual innovations cannot bring racism to an end. But they can highlight how sharply scholastic theories diverge from the commonsense world through which we walk to find our way home after sessions like the one that produced this publication. There, the life-threatening jeopardy provoked by being racialized as different is undiminished and may even have increased now that "race" and its certainties claim to heal or at least calm the anxieties over identity that have been precipitated by globalization and the multiple insecurities and yawning inequalities of what is sniggeringly referred to as "turbo capitalism." The academic tribunes of globalization do not usually include the end of formal empires or the wars of decolonization in their contentious genealogies of our planet's commercial and political integration. They are mostly a complacent bunch more content with pondering the enigmas of weightless economic development than the violence that seems to be proliferating in the borderlands around it. In Britain, anyway, they are disinclined to acknowledge the fact that they live in an environment that has been shaped over a long period of time by colonial relationships and by what I've come to identify as melancholic responses to the loss of imperial privilege and position. Even after the debacle of the Stephen Lawrence episode,[38] they are unlikely to see action against racisms as something that can shape the life of their own polity for the better, enriching popular understanding of justice, fairness, and rights or assisting in the reform of legal procedures that can impact on the lives of all citizens.

This unhealthy situation has redirected attention to the uncomfortably flimsy boundaries placed around racial and ethnic identity by fading national states and their desperate political leaders, who will try anything to locate the populist pulse of the ailing body politic. Once the postcolonial subjects move in close by, the colonial hierarchy that previously specified the proper relation of blackness to whiteness breaks down and yields to a different—usually commercial and resolutely antipolitical—understanding of what "races" are and how they may differ from themselves and each other. The previously separated worlds of blackness and whiteness can then be made to leak, to bleed risk, pleasure, and excitement into one another as part of selling things and accumulating capital. The magic of these freshly racialized markets means that it is important to recognize and affirm that blackness and whiteness—those interdependent homogenous magnitudes bequeathed to us by metaphysical dualism—are nothing but transient symptoms of an alienated and dying order. In the meantime, that insight brings little comfort. It does not help us know what antiracism should be *for.*

If there is still a good side to today's unwitting and anachronistic borrowings from the racial theory of the eighteenth and nineteenth centuries, it is that they underline the extent to which Enlightenment agendas and problems remain pending in our translocal, worlded modernity. We can also see that those approaches are outmoded for a number of urgent economic, political, and cultural reasons. They are incapable of addressing the political and moral shifts provoked by the revolution in biotechnology, biocolonialism, and informatics that completes the privatization of nature begun in the seventeenth century. These changes are, of course, bound to a larger process of technological and economic acceleration that is having a profound impact on our relations with ourselves, our bodies, and our natures. If the nature within is under assault, the nature outside our bodies is also being assailed by an environmental catastrophe that exceeds the power of national states to resolve. This crisis of the biosphere is a global problem but it is experienced locally and with a radical unevenness that can only feed the righteous hunger for relocalization.

It bears repeating that all this necessitates producing a better history not only of our own planetary movement but of the political dimensions of racial discourses that were not peripheral or decorative ideological motifs appended to colonial adventures. They shaped the intimate, essential workings of imperial power in ways that confound any oversimple split between material embodiment on the one hand and culture, ideology, and discourse on the other. The history of political struggle that we construct through them does not conform to any neat sociological dichotomy between recognition and redistribution.

We need to see where and how the experiences of slave descendants, conquered and postcolonial peoples worldwide have fit into the wider historical processes that we understand via the political, philosophical, and sociological notions of democracy and modernity. We need to understand and be able to intervene in contemporary debates over globalization and translocal justice, to find some new ways to orient ourselves in the fields that those debates are struggling to identify via conceptions of humankind that have not as yet fully registered the necessary break with humanity's liberal and Cold-War specifications.

At this point, colonial and postcolonial folks acquire a distinctive mission: our special modern history as the descendants of people who were themselves commodified for sale on an international market or deemed expendable within the larger racial logic of Europe-centered historical processes gives us ready access to a fund of knowledge that we can make useful in a number of areas. These insights are not ours alone but will belong to anybody who is prepared to make use of them. This history is not intellectual property and we are not defenders of cultural and experiential copyrights. The first task is to contribute to a post-Marxist critique of market relations that is tied to the memory of human commodification. A second immediate project relates to the fraught issue of what, if anything, distinguishes human beings and therefore what any irreverent new humanism must include. We need to try and take any lessons that can be found in the histories of suffering and resistance that have shaped us and make them into resources for the future of this planet. Those lessons do not, of course, aim to redeem past suffering or make it worthwhile. Their very failure to be productive in this way helps to specify that they should be available to anybody who dares, in good faith, to try and set them to work in pursuit of justice. Lastly, it seems imperative to try to revive and sustain those elements in earlier phases of black political culture that are tolerant, humane, pluralistic, and cosmopolitan in outlook. Those elements are still present in diminishing quantities but they are somewhat muted these days. They have had to take a back seat behind other simpler, noisier, and, for many, more attractive options that are in step if not always in tune with the mainstream sentiments of consumer capitalism and have the additional virtue of echoing a seductive nationalist agenda set elsewhere.

Nationalism is no longer the correct name to be given to our pursuit of solidarity and hope for a future in which we work to synchronize our translocal agency and act in concert. It retains the aspiration toward sovereignty and propriety just as we are being moved into a very different era in which the definition of private property in terms of personal ownership has been superceded. New issues of privatization, access, and entitlement that are central to the ambitions of governmental and corporate power are reconceptualizing the relationship between peoples and resources.

We cannot be content with the casual proposition that authoritarianism, coercion, and militaristic hierarchy have privileged claims on that world of blackness. We are also entitled to ask why our antiracist movement has so often been content to build its alternative conceptions of the world from simple inversions of the powers that confront us rather than altogether different conceptions guided by another political morality.

The guiding terms of this Fanonian project—humanism, justice, cosmopolitanism—are all contested. We should be wary of them because they resonate most strongly in the traditions of liberal political thought that have descended from European Enlightenment writings. Those attempts to see the lives of individuals and nations in broader contexts supplied by a subversively shifting sense of scale, above all by a sense of the earth as but one small and insignificant location in an infinite and only partially knowable space, are by no means the only forms of cosmopolitical thinking in circulation. The black thinkers of the Western hemisphere have sometimes been alive to the destiny involved in understanding their own distinct positions relative to the fate of Africa from which their distant ancestors were kidnapped and sold. The antiracism that drew its energies from pan-Africanism and lent them to worldwide anticolonial movements did not descend to the present through the temperate landscape of liberal pieties. It comes to us via disreputable abolitionism and histories of anti-imperial activism that was allied with the insurrectionary practice of those who, though legally held in bondage, were subject to the larger immoralities of a race-friendly system of domination and brutality.

Du Bois, James, Fanon, Senghor, and company have already shown that there is a whole counterhistory of modern government to be written from the genealogy of these neglected political formations. They contributed vitality and hope to dissident democratic formations that derived their moral confidence and many of their political dreams from confrontations with the evil and immorality they discovered in the operations of colonial domination. This opposition confronted and undermined the codes of Western liberalism at several significant points. Its principal value is that it can still embarrass and contest the overly innocent versions of liberal thinking that are still in circulation. It highlights their failures in the face of raciology and their refusals to admit the humanity of the racial Other. If we are going to interrupt the romance of blackness and whiteness at last, we will need to find an explanation for how that telling blockage has damaged the planetary movement we should probably no longer refer to minimally and apologetically as antiracism. In recognition of the need for more assertive and wholeheartedly political moods and tactics, we should become prepared to acknowledge the extreme difficulty of moral and political enterprises that require the systematic denaturing of "race" as part of their confrontations with the alienated modern sociality that drowns out the cries of those who suffer.

The well-to-do New England town where I am revising this essay sits in the shadow of New Haven, a black city, currently the third-poorest in America. Under any rational system of administration these communities would be part of the same financial and governmental apparatus. Instead they are divided by the fortifications of American apartheid. A short bus ride apart, they are economically and culturally consigned to different postindustrial galaxies. The pyschological and emotional convergence that has resulted from the terrorist assault of September 11, 2001, is raising questions about the future of these traditional divisions and the status of racial divisions in the new geopolitical circumstances we inhabit.

Both places are within commuting distance of Manhattan. The small-town world of monolithic whiteness is tinted only by the Latin Americans who collect the rubbish and sweep up the brilliantly colored leaves at this time of year. They can't be easily mistaken for Arabs and so far they have been safe from the resentful violence of those who want to purge and homogenize the country. Plenty of Pleasantville residents are now decked out in red, white, and blue. They look forward to their President "opening a can of whup ass" on Osama bin Laden. My son tells me that when the county fair came through last weekend they cheerfully took aim at targets emblazoned with the enemy's swarthy devilish face.

Their patriotism is a more brittle thing than it might appear from afar. Depression and a palpable anxiety are in the air. The infowar is underway. We're told that gun sales are up and biological and chemical attacks are in the cards. Many people who seldom went to the next town and certainly never went anywhere near New York now fear that they may become victims of the next terrorist onslaught. The local gyms are offering various special deals to anyone who wants to get buffed up for the impending fray. No payments necessary for the next thirty days.

More significant is the distinct impression that young people are not as keen as their parents on the prospect of this new war. Families in which any communication across generational lines was a rarity are now hosting intense conflicts over the wisdom and morality of calling Arabs towel-heads and sand-niggers. The MTV generation raised on the consumerist conceits of global shows like *Real World* and *Road Rules* is talking back and struggling to understand whether a desire for peace and the belief that potentially the whole world is theirs can be compatible with patriotic feelings.

For me, the chickens of corporate multiculturalism came home to roost in the disturbing image of a silent Chris Rock tentatively swaying next to the manic, superannuated figure of Neil Young on the TV gala. That odd scene, coupled with the widely publicized news that Dr. Dre—the man who gave you Eminem—has already pledged a million dollars to the relief effort, raises new issues about the predicament of African Americans in this new national mood. A new crop of Bush fans has been discovered in the black barbershop on Whalley Avenue.

This week Nelly's gangsta anthem "#1" has captured the spirit of the moment and spontaneously mutated into a hymn to American preeminence. The answer to his insistent question "What does it take to be #1?" is echoed in other currently popular rap tunes by DMX and Pdiddy. While debating the desirability of a move from the ghetto to the 'burbs, these heavily rotated songs have also voiced a new African American bid to belong: "we ain't going nowhere" they announce, "we right here."

For the old-school nationalists, Minister Farrakhan's response was characteristically vain and overlong. However, it would be impossible to deny that his careful blend of condemnation for the attacks and respectful questioning of his government was also sensitive and judicious. Almost alone among black America's voices of leadership, he seems to have resisted the pressure to fall back on an old script first articulated by W. E. B. Du Bois in an opportunistic and mistaken response to the country's entry into the First World War. When American society closed ranks, it was argued, blacks won a new chance to be recognized as worthwhile members of the expanded national family.

Confirmation that Du Bois's patriotic aspirations remain overly optimistic and that the country's appetite for justice is still rather unevenly developed came last Tuesday when a Cincinnati judge acquitted Stephen Roach, a police officer charged with the "negligent homicide" of Timothy Thomas. The unarmed nineteen-year-old African American was considered to have invited his own death by making a sudden movement while being chased.

The same depressing feeling of a drift back toward business as usual came to me while sitting in a university "speak out" convened to consider the possibility of political responses to the national crisis. A diverse group of students seemed hungry for something more specific than shallow demands for peace or restraint that can sound bland and generic. The organizers' intentions were noble yet speaker after speaker turned away from the tasks involved in measuring this geopolitical reordering of the world. Instead, they found comfort in a sequence of minutely detailed, almost therapeutic commentaries on their own feelings and experiences. Of course, self-scrutiny will have a place in the healing process that is now underway, but it seemed absolutely wrong that it should become what seemed an easy substitute for engaging in the practical, difficult tasks of historical explanation and democratic watchfulness. As the peace rallies proliferate, the campus left will have to tear down the tofu curtain and dig itself out from underneath the wreckage of an identity politics so narcissistic and short-sighted that it reproduces the political solipsism and imperialistic indifference that are more usually associated with power and privilege.

Whether the multiethnic diversity of those who died and who dug in New York will be able to update middle America's portrait of itself remains to be seen. The upsurge in "hate crimes" and "bias attacks" suggests otherwise. We may have to wait to see the same rainbow nation laid out in body bags before that particular penny drops. While the leaders of the USA are having to reconsider their commitment to unilateral action and their folly in imagining they could withdraw easily from the international system, the cultural adjustments involved in that variety of reflection seems like too much of a stretch. Locally, both black and white Americans have a lot more work to do before they can place their national sufferings in a planetary context and imagine interacting with strange and distant people in any role other than that of Sergeant Major. Fanon, it seems, was right: blackness and whiteness are the bond between them as much as the favored rationalization for their conflicts and their separation.

Notes

1   Some breadth of the literature involved in this last part of the task is provided by Roger Griffin's indispensable reader *Fascism* (1995).

2   T. W. Adorno "The Essay as Form," in *Notes to Literature,* vol. 1 (1991): 1.

3   The delicate and insightful interpretation offered by Ato Sekyi-Otu in *Frantz Fanon's Dialectic of Experience* (1996) stands out from the crop of recent commentators on Fanon's writing. See also Robert J. C. Young's introduction to Jean Paul Sartre's *Colonialism and Neocolonialism* (2001).

4   "The problem considered here is one of time. Those Negroes and white men will be disalienated who refuse to let themselves be sealed away in the materialised Tower of the past. For many other Negroes, in other ways, disalienation will come into being through their refusal to accept the present as definitive." Fanon, *Black Skin, White Masks,* 226.

5   In a thoughtful and interesting piece, Zimitri Erasmus has argued that this "strategic essentialism" can be extremely effective as a means of political mobilization. See Barnor Hesse, ed., *Unsettling Multiculturalisms* (2001). Following Fanon, my response to this would be to say firstly that politics ceases at the point where "race" rules, secondly that once racial "essentialism" receives an intellectual imprimatur there is nothing strategic about it, and thirdly that there is no reason to suppose that the solidarities "race" creates will remain receptive to regulation by intellectuals or academics.

6   Look, for example, at the opening chapter of W. E. B. Du Bois's *The World and Africa* (1946).

7   For another view, see the carefully nuanced arguments of Linda Martin Alcoff, "Towards a Phenomenology of Racial Embodiment" (1999).

8   "Let us recall that antisemitism is a conception of the Manichaean and primitive world in which hatred for the Jew arises as a great explanatory myth." *Anti-Semite and Jew* (1948), 148. See de Beauvoir 1953 [1952].

9   *Black Skin, White Masks,* 9.

10 I am grateful to Sylvia Wynter for underlining the importance of this concept.

11 "Ontology—once it is finally admitted as leaving existence by the wayside—does not permit us to understand the being of the black man. For not only must the black man be black; he must be black in relation to the white man. Some critics will take it on themselves to remind us that this proposition has a converse. I say this is false. The black man has no ontological resistance in the eyes of the white man." *Black Skin, White Masks,* 110.

12 Susan Buck-Morss, "Hegel and Haiti," *Critical Inquiry* 26, no. 4 (summer 2000).

13 Richard Drayton, *Nature's Government: Science, Imperial Britain, and the "Improvement" of the World* (2000); James R. Ryan, *Picturing Empire* (1997); Nancy Leys Stepan, *Picturing Tropical Nature* (2001); Megan Vaughan, *Curing Their Ills* (1991).

14 The work of Edward Said is of course an honorable exception to this disabling tendency.

15 Peter Linebaugh and Marcus Rediker's *The Many-Headed Hydra* (2000) is a recent notable and dazzling exception to this pattern which treats the eighteenth century. Robert Proctor is one historian of Nazi racial science who has seen their eugenic aspirations in the context of German colonial anthropology. See his "From Anthropologie to Rassenkunde in the German Anthropological Tradition," in George Stocking, ed., *Bones, Bodies, Behavior* (1988). E. M. Spiers, "The Use of the Dum Dum Bullet and Colonial Warfare," *Journal of Imperial and Commonwealth History* 4 (1975).

16 Anna Davin, "Imperialism and Motherhood," *History Workshop Journal* 5 (spring 1978); Megan Vaughan, *Curing Their Ills*; Kenneth Ballhatchet, *Race, Sex, and Class Under the Raj* (1980); David Howes, ed., *Cross Cultural Consumption* (1996).

17 Sir John William Kaye, *A History of the Sepoy War in India: 1857–58* (1864).

18 Jock McCulloch, *Black Peril, White Virtue* (2000); Robin Evelegh, *Peace-Keeping in a Demo-cratic Society* (1978); see also Daniel Moran, *Wars of National Liberation* (2001); Douglas Porch, *Wars of Empire* (2000).

19 Giorgio Agamben, *Homo Sacer* (1998).

20 "Out on the plain . . . the Maxims chattered vindictively. Under such fearful punishment no troops in the world could have stood their ground. It was not a battle but a massacre. Hadow, manning one of Norfolk's Maxims, wrote to his mother that night, 'I got so sick of the slaugh-ter that I ceased to fire, though the general's order was to make as big a bag as possible.'" P. Flemming, *Bayonets to Lhasa* (1961), 151, as quoted by John Ellis, *The Social History of the Machine Gun* (1975), 99. See also Clive Turnbull, *Black War*, and from a more recent phase of colonial warfare, Lewis M. Simons, "Free Fire Zones," in Roy Gutman and David Reiff, eds., *Crimes of War* (1999). Douglas Porch, *Wars of Empire* (2000), and Ian Hernon's two-volume study of the "forgotten wars of the nineteenth century," *Massacre and Retribution* (1998) and *The Savage Empire* (2000). If the "performance" of bare life in military campaigns is not to your taste, think of Haffkine's opportunities to study the development of cholera in Indian bodies, of Robert Knox's earlier pursuit of colonial corpses, or Carothers's contributions to the study of racial personality in the asylums that were annexes of the colonial prison system. See Jock McCulloch, *Colonial Psychiatry and the African Mind* (1995).

21 Loïc Wacquant, "Deadly Symbiosis," *Punishment and Society* 3, no. 1 (January 2001); William Boelhower, "Open Secrets: African American Testimony and the Paradigm of the camp"; Jon M. Bridgeman, *Revolt of the Herero* (1981), 128–29.

22 Fanon, *Wretched of the Earth*, 40.

23 Amilcar Cabral, "National Liberation and Culture," in *Return to the Source* (1973).

24 Carl Schmitt, *The Concept of the Political* (1996), and *Land and Sea* (1997). *Der Nomos der Erde im Volkerecht des Jus Publicum Europaeum* (1950).

25 Gopal Balakrishnan, *The Enemy* (2000), especially chapter 17, "Diaspora, Utopia Katechon."

26 *Wretched of the Earth*, 41.

27 *Wretched of the Earth*, 145–46.

28 Enrique Dussel, *The Underside of Modernity* (1998), 133; and *The Invention of the Americas* (1995).

29 *Wretched of the Earth*, 40.

30 The hollow pieties of so much recent political theory on the topic of multiculturalism seem to fall into this category. The extraordinary rich and insightful contribution made by Kwame Anthony Appiah's various works stands out as the most rigorous and patient consideration of these political and ethical problems from a liberal angle of vision. See most recently "Liberal-ism, Individuality, Identity," in *Critical Inquiry* 27, no. 2 (winter 2001).

31 Think, for example, of these powerful words spoken by Frederick Douglass in 1889, which though they are masculinist in their conceptualization of political freedoms lose nothing of their revolutionary character by being articulated together with his Christianity. "My senti-ments at this point originate not in my color, but in a sense of justice common to all right minded men. It is not because I am a Negro but because I am a man. . . . When a colored man is charged with want of race pride he may well ask, What race? for a large percentage of the colored race are related in some degree to more than one race. But the whole assumption of

race pride is ridiculous. Let us have done with complexional superiorities and inferiorities, complexional pride or shame. I want no better basis for my activities and affinities than the broad foundation laid by the bible itself, that 'God has made one blood of all nations of men to dwell on all the face of the earth.' This comprehends the fatherhood of God and the brotherhood of man." "The Nation's Problem," in *African-American Social and Political Thought, 1850–1920*, ed. Howard Brotz (1992), 317.

32 Pierre Bourdieu, *The Political Ontology of Martin Heidegger* (1991); Dipesh Chakrabarty, *Provincializing Europe* (2000); Achille Mbembe, *On the Postcolony* (2001).

33 Wendy Brown, *States of Injury* (1995).

34 Cornelius Castoriadis, "Reflections on Racism," *Thesis 11*, no. 32 (1992).

35 I am reminded here of Dave Hendley's poignant 1978 photograph of Burning Spear (Winston Rodney) standing next to a wall that bears the slogan "Human Rights Rasta Dread Lion." See Dave Hendley, "Black Disciple: An Interview with Winston Rodney—The Burning Spear," *Blues and Soul* nos. 239–40 (October 1978).

36 Luc Boltanski's discussion of the politics of pity does not include "race" and its association with human rights but his thoughtful framework can be hijacked here and made to serve our purposes: *Distant Suffering* (1999).

37 The racial dimensions of Heidegger's philosophical project are a scary and intimidating topic that has been skirted by most appropriators of his work. Valuable exceptions to this from both sides of the political spectrum are Julian Young's *Heidegger, Philosophy, Nazism* (1997) and Alan Milchman and Alan Rosenberg's edited volume, *Martin Heidegger and the Holocaust* (1996).

38 Brian Cathcart, *The Case of Stephen Lawrence* (1999).

2. Simians, Savages, Skulls, and Sex

Science and Colonial Militarism in

Nineteenth-Century South Africa

Zine Magubane

In a provocative turn of phrase, Frederick Cooper and Ann Stoler (1997: 5) have christened the colonies "laboratories of modernity." The image of a laboratory is meant to evoke a number of associations. Laboratories are popularly understood as places where knowledge is constructed, uncovered, and invented. Laboratories are places where experiments, designed to produce new knowledge, are carried out. Laboratories are also places where standardized procedures exist for turning our existing prejudices about the world into incontrovertible facts—assuming that the existing rules for marshaling, testing, and evaluating evidence are followed. The image of a laboratory is thus compelling on a number of different levels. If laboratories are as Latour described them, places where facts that "represent nature as it is" can be created out of whole cloth, then colonies are a particularly fascinating type of laboratory. For, as Cooper and Stoler point out, these laboratories produce very many things. They produce geographical conceptions of the world like the "Orient" and the "West." They helped to produce something Cooper and Stoler called the "bourgeois self." They also, as I will demonstrate below, helped to produce large-scale, seemingly stable aggregates of matter called "races" and "sexes."

In a fascinating article on the role of analogies in scientific research, Nancy Stepan (1990: 38) argues that analogies do much more than represent the world. Rather, she explains, they actively work to create it, thereby playing a critical role in the creation of new knowledge. "Similarity," she writes, "is not something one finds but something one must establish." The project of establishing similarity is solidly linked to the project of calibration and measurement. Bruno Latour describes how acts of calibration and measurement function in ways not unlike those of analogies. They, too, work to construct a world of commensurable objects that did not exist before the act of measurement called them into being. The emergence of a science of race and sex in South Africa during the nineteenth century provides a fascinating glimpse into the conjoined workings of analogical reasoning, technologies of calibration and measurement, and the mobilization of nature in the service of politics. Looking at concurrent struggles over how to establish what constellation of physical characteristics established racial difference and the struggles over the ownership of capital and labor superbly illustrates Latour's point that the invention of nature and the invention of citizens are mutually enabling processes. The simultaneous emergence of racial science in Britain and South Africa, an export trade in wool between the two countries, and the expansion of colonial militarism effectively challenges what Latour (1993: 29) terms the invented separation "between the scientific power charged with representing things and the political power charged with representing subjects."

The Fact of Blackness?

Between 1800 and 1830 Southern Africa was host to a number of travelers, many of them naturalists, who took it upon themselves to make careful records of everything they saw—birds, beasts, rocks, trees, fish, and people—with the aim of eventually classifying them. One thing they looked for and didn't find, however, was "Africans" or "Negroes." John Barrow (1968 [1801]: 168–69) saw people (the Xhosa) whom he variously described as being "nearly black" and having skins that were "dark glossy brown verging on black." He also noted that these people had "short curling hair" (169). Nevertheless, after observing their teeth, which he described as "beautifully white and regular," and the contours of their faces and heads, which he pronounced to be "as well formed as those of Europeans," he declared them to have few of the features of what he termed "Africans in general" (168). He thus concluded, "Though black, or very nearly so, they have not one line of the African negro in the composition of their persons. The comparative anatomist might be a little perplexed in placing the skull of a Kaffer[1] in the chain, so ingeniously put together by him, comprehending the links from the most perfect European to the Ourang-Outang, and thence all through the monkey tribe" (205). Barrow's opinions did not place him in the minority.

George Thompson (1827: 194) declared that whatever Barrow's other ethnographic errors might have been, he "had not exaggerated the fine qualities of these people." Thomas Pringle, who also described the Xhosa as being "dark brown" and having "wooly hair," declared that the Xhosa had features that "approached the European or Asiatic model" (1966 [1835]: 14). Like sentiments can be found in the writings of Henry Lichtenstein, who described the Xhosa as "brown" in color and having hair that was "black and wooly" but concluded that "their countenances have a character peculiar to themselves and which do not permit their being included in any of the races of mankind" (1928 [1812]: 301). Although unable categorically to assign the Xhosa to a race, Lichtenstein indicated that he felt they bore "a great resemblance to Europeans." Indeed, based on his observations of "the bones of the face and the form of the skull," he surmised that the Xhosa had "more resemblance to [Europeans] than to either Negroes or Hottentots" (303). Travelers John Campbell (1815) and William Burchell (1822) also expressed similar views.

A notable feature of these early travelers' reports is the physical parameters used to establish racial similarity and difference. Most of these early writers seem to have adhered to Barrow's adage that the head and face were the key sites for determining what Uday Mehta (1997) was later to term the "anthropological capacities" of the individual. Barrow wrote that "The ancients were of the opinion that the face was always the index of the mind. Modern physiognomists have gone a step farther and say that a fine form, perfect in all its parts, cannot contain a crooked or an imperfect mind" (207). Thus, although all of the writers made detailed accounts of African bodies, the bodies of Africans and Europeans were almost never subject to comparison. Barrow, for example, found Xhosa men to be possessed of "the finest figures . . . tall, robust, and muscular" (169). However, he compared them to Greek statues rather than live Europeans. John Campbell (1974 [1815]: 11) also remarked on the superior physical attributes of the Xhosa but went only so far as to compare them with "other tribes of that quarter of the globe." Likewise, Lichtenstein, Burchell, and Pringle all limited their physical comparisons of Europeans and Africans to those features located above the neck.

It is also important to pay some attention to the differences that mark how males and females were described and evaluated in these early accounts. Women, like their male counterparts, were generally evaluated favorably. Lichtenstein described them as "no less handsome" than their male counterparts, possessed of "sleek soft skin, beautiful teeth, and pleasing features"

(309). Thompson described them as being "of the middle stature" with "fine figures" (485). Barrow concurred that they were "very strong-limbed and particularly muscular in the leg" (169). What is striking about these descriptions is the fact that women's heads and skulls are rarely described. In the rare instances that they are, comparisons are never drawn between them and those of European men or women. Indeed, at that time, relatively few of the early travel writers deemed it necessary to draw any *physical* comparisons between European and African women.

Neither, it seems, did these incipient naturalists find any salient points of comparison between Xhosa men and European women. Indeed, the possibility of making such a comparison most likely never entered their minds. The one thing that they all seemed to agree on was that Xhosa men's masculinity was unsurpassed. Barrow described the Xhosa men as "manly" in their deportment (198). He compared them much more favorably to other indigenous groups in the same region, describing the Khoisan, for example, as having bodies that were as "delicately formed as that of a woman" (157). Pringle, likewise, described the Xhosa as "frank, cheerful, and manly" (413). Campbell also agreed that the Xhosa were "infinitely superior in physical energies and in manly appearance" (11).

The points of comparison that organized the observations and perceptions of the first cohort of travel writers (all of whom wrote between 1790 and 1830) become even more interesting when they are compared to what was to become the received scientific wisdom by the end of the nineteenth century. As Londa Schiebinger (1993: 158) explains, by 1850 "women and Africans were seen as sharing similar deficiencies." Nancy Stepan (1990: 40) also argues that by the turn of the century most scientists accepted without question the adage that the "lower races represented the 'female' type of the human species." Given the near complete absence of such thinking for at least a third of the century, this rather radical shift in scientific paradigms merits explanation. First, however, we should briefly consider the role that early primate studies played in forging connections between nature, physiology, and politics.

Simian Similarity and the Production of Scientific Knowledge

Donna Haraway (1991: 11) has argued that a "physiological politics based on domination" has always been central to animal sociology. She identifies primate studies as having been particularly important sites for mobilizing nature in the service of politics. During the seventeenth and eighteenth centuries, for example, the behavioral tendencies of female primates were singled out for close scrutiny. The ongoing effort to naturalize social conventions by projecting them onto primates was made manifest in studies of female primate behavior. The assumption that underwrote these studies was that females, whether human or beast, were by nature modest and retiring. "Beginning in the second half of the seventeenth century," Schiebinger explains, "modesty became a key attribute of the female ape. In this, naturalists followed newly emerging ideals for middle-class European women" (99). Schiebinger's observations about the importance of the ideal of female modesty in organizing scientists' perceptions of the world is particularly interesting when we consider the ways in which Xhosa women are described in early travelers' reports. As I mentioned above, naturalists rarely drew *physical* comparisons between Xhosa and European women. However, they very often drew behavioral comparisons. The idea of modesty as a universal feminine attribute was frequently reiterated. Burchell, for example, described Xhosa women as having "modest manners" (1953 [1822]: 291). Pringle also attributed to them "feelings of womanly modesty and decorum" (304). Barrow concurred that Xhosa women's behavior indicated that they were "modest without reserve" and "sportive without the least shadow of being lascivious" (168). Thus it appears that Xhosa women of the late eighteenth and early nineteenth centuries, like female apes of the seventeenth and eighteenth centuries, were believed to exemplify a universal female standard that was behaviorally defined. It was only in the nineteenth century that the physiological branch of primate studies really took off. And it was then that male apes displaced females as the objects of scientific research. As Schiebinger explains, "skulls, and indeed male skulls, remained the central icon of racial difference until craniometry was replaced by intelligence testing in the late nineteenth and early twentieth centuries" (156).

Thus, although apes have long functioned as objects that connected nature to political economy, the manner in which these connections have been forged has shown a marked degree of variation over time. Because apes were critical to the project of mobilizing science in the service of the social order, political considerations have profoundly influenced which aspects of primate societies—physical, mental, or behavioral—naturalists focused on. The change in focus from the behavioral characteristics of primates to their physiological ones over the course of the nineteenth century is yet another shift in scientific paradigms that we must document and explain.

Simians, Skulls, and Savages

How we organize our perceptions of the world has long interested philosophers. Given the infinite variety that is our world, how do we come to decide which objects are similar enough to be grouped together? How do we determine which features of the object merit consideration? When the objects in question are human beings who, in addition to having potentially classifiable physical characteristics, have mental, emotional, and cultural ones too, the issue becomes that much more complicated. Living in the twenty-first century, where what Fanon (1967) called the "fact of blackness" appears so incontrovertible, it might appear that skin color has always presented itself as a stable truth—an anomaly so striking that it easily enabled the project of establishing similarity and difference. My close examination of the writings of early travelers was done, in part, to unsettle this very notion. As the writings of Barrow, Lichtenstein, and Pringle demonstrate, the shape of the head could override the color of the skin or the curl of the hair as the essential marker of racial similarity. It is clear from these early writings that the "truth" of racial difference was not self-evident, rather it had to be actively *created*. I devote the remainder of this essay, therefore, to exploring the ways in which the inchoate and unstable world of human bodies of infinite variety was transformed into a seemingly stable set of racial "truths."

As noted above, the head and skull had long been considered key sites for guiding and grounding the project of racial classification. John Barrow, for example, made reference to physiognomy and phrenology, the twin "sciences of character analysis." While both were based on the idea that a person's inner character could be divined through examination of his or her external appearance, the former concentrated on the shape of the head and face, the latter on the measurement of "organs" or "humps" on the exterior skull. Two assumptions underwrote these methods of scientific practice. The first was that human types could be arranged along a hierarchy of lowest to highest in terms of intelligence and moral capacity, provided that the right characteristics were identified. The second was that the characteristics so identified were permanent and unchanging—utterly indifferent to social engineering. As methods of scientific practice, phrenology and physiognomy were always closely aligned with issues of dominance. J. G. Spurzheim, one of the founders of phrenology, argued that it would "exercise a great influence in indicating clearly . . . the relations between individuals to each other in general, and between those who govern and those who are governed in particular" (1830: 312).

The popularity of phrenology among settler populations in South Africa cannot be separated from issues of colonial governmentality. English merchants who settled in the eastern Cape, and whose livelihoods depended on the export trade in wool, were its strongest proponents. Their enthusiasm for phrenology, and their aggressive and avaricious attitudes toward the Xhosa, frequently brought them into conflict with nonconformist Protestant missionaries, many of whom were employed by the London Missionary Society, who saw themselves as the "saviors" of "Afric's benighted sons." Phrenology came to play an extremely important role for English colonialists involved in the wool trade because the issue of who would rule and who would be ruled was still being actively contested and because they had the legacy of scientism in Britain to draw on. The Afrikaans-speaking bourgeoisie, although they too were involved in the wool trade and sought mastery of the Xhosa, had strikingly little interest in phrenology. As Bank (1996: 395) explains, "notwithstanding the predominantly anti-liberal racial ideology of the established settler community, there is no evidence whatever of any support for theories of scientific racism among the Cape Dutch in this period."

This contest for mastery on the colonial frontier was intimately connected to the contest over the control of nature, the specific contest being over whether nature (specifically defined as land) would be transformed into a capitalist commodity. When Marx (1967 [1867]: 733) wrote that the bourgeoisie committed acts of "reckless terrorism" when they "conquered the field for capitalistic agriculture, made the soil part and parcel of capital, and created for the town industries the necessary supply of a 'free' and outlawed proletariat," he could easily have been writing about the eastern Cape during the 1840s. Wool was the principle export of the Cape Colony, and after 1840 wealthy immigrants began to arrive from Britain with capital to invest in sheep farms. By the mid-1840s practically all of the productive, viable farming land in the Cape Colony had been granted by the government to private owners. Therefore, acquisitive British settlers developed a strong interest in expropriating territory that lay outside the boundaries of the colony and was occupied by Xhosa communities who had yet to come under colonial rule. As John Mitford Bowker, a wealthy landowner, stated in his famed "Springbok Speech" of 1847:

> The day was when our plains were covered with tens of thousands of springboks; they are gone now, and who regrets it? Their place is occupied with tens of thousands of merino sheep, whose fleeces find employment to tens of thousands of industrious men. . . . And I begin to

think that [the Kaffir] as well as the springbok, must give place, and why not? Is it just that a few thousands of ruthless, worthless, savages are to sit like a nightmare upon a land that would support millions of civilized men happily? Nay, heaven forbids it. (Bowker 1962 [1864]: 123)

Reading Bowker, one might be led to believe that there were no Xhosa people living within the bounds of the colony, but actually, by the 1840s there were significant numbers of Xhosa people there, most of whom were in service to the eastern frontier farmers. As early as 1826, the labor shortage in the colony had led the colonial government to allow orphans and abandoned children of the Xhosa to be "rendered useful to the colony" (Newton-King 1980: 75). There were also communities of Xhosa people, such as the Gqunukhwebe on whom the Wesleyan missionaries had focused their efforts, who had become enthusiastic converts to Christianity. One of the most famous converts was Chief Kama, "the first Xhosa chief to incline towards deference to the social values of outsiders" (Mostert 1992: 599). Hence, the Xhosa communities that Bowker and his fellow wool merchants were intent on expropriating were primarily the Ngqika Xhosa, who still lived in their traditional manner in the area between the Fish and Kei rivers and had not converted to Christianity.

The expropriation of the Ngqika Xhosa required concerted action on two interrelated fronts, the military and the ideological. The settlers were interested in a military solution to their problems for two reasons: first, because they assumed that war was the quickest and most effective way to remove the Xhosa; and second, because they stood to make enormous profits from the military endeavor itself. As Timothy Keegan (1996: 156) explains, a strong military presence meant "a large market for all kinds of produce and services, a climate of confidence and security for investors, and upward pressure on land values. It meant state investment in infrastructure and public works."

However, wars of imperial expansion were extremely expensive endeavors and imperial governments were notorious for their reluctance to finance them. The following speech to parliament made by a Mr. Molesworth is typical:

We all know that, ever since the New World was discovered it has been the unceasing desire of England to plant that New World with New England's. It was the ardent wish of this country that its children should occupy the uninhabited portions of the earth's surface and carry along with them to their new homes the laws, institutions, and feelings of Englishmen. That they should there become bold, energetic, and self reliant men capable and willing to aid their parent in times of need, and not weak, pulling infants, ever crying to their mother for assistance and emptying her purse. (Great Britain 1851a: 1373).

The onus was on the settlers not only to demonstrate that military action was worth the financial expense but that military action was even necessary at all. For it was widely believed that aboriginal peoples simply melted away in the wake of more advanced civilizations. Although they agreed on relatively few things, this was one belief held by humanitarians and imperialists alike. A Mr. Roebuck argued before parliament that since the eventual triumph of civilized over primitive peoples was a foregone conclusion, time and patience could take the place of financial support. English colonists, he argued, "cannot be placed in South Africa without the inevitable consequence of annihilating the aborigines. That is what has been done in New Zealand, in Australia, in North America, in all our colonies. And this is what will be done in South Africa" (Great Britain 1851b: 275). The preponderance of this belief meant that the settlers had to become astute propagandists, as it was commonly held that the unwillingness of the colonial office to free up resources for colonial expansion could be directly traced to "those misrepresentations of the dispositions, habits, and character of the tribes beyond the colonial boundary, which have been published to the world by mistaken or designing writers" (*Grahamstown Journal*, 27 June 1845). Therefore, the project of primitive accumulation in South Africa required, in the words of one editorialist in the *Grahamstown Journal* of 22 May 1845, that "the actual merits of the Kaffir Question are properly understood in those quarters where it is of most importance that they should not be mistaken."

Racial science and technologies of measurement were seized on as being of utmost importance for providing an alternative account of the "dispositions, habits, and characters" of the Xhosa. But calibration and measurement, in and of themselves, were not enough. Barrow, Pringle, and a host of others had employed the elementary principles of phrenology and physiognomy in their discussions of the Xhosa. Their rudimentary forays into science led them to conclude that the Xhosa, if not yet on par with Europeans, could certainly rise to their level. Barrow, for example, wrote that if one were to evaluate the Xhosa by the principles of physiognomy, they "could not be judged deficient in talent" (208). Accordingly, settlers who wanted to harness these types of arguments had to do so in ways that precluded potentially destabilizing uses.

It was important to attempt to control the range of "facts" that could potentially be produced.

One way this was attempted was through drawing analogies and associations between the Xhosa and other categories of persons whose inferiority was more firmly established. It is here that we see the first attempts being made to draw close associations between African males and European females. The project of naturalizing the "patriarchal division of authority" in the family and the body politic in England was of longer duration and, thus, relatively stable compared to that of naturalizing the rule of the "lighter races" over the "darker" around the globe (Haraway 1991). As Anne McClintock (1995: 45) explains, "because the subordination of woman to man and child to adult were deemed natural facts, other forms of social hierarchy could be depicted in familial terms to guarantee social *difference* as a category of nature." However, as I demonstrate above, these associations between African men and European women had precious little to recommend them in the way of historical precedent. More than one observer had remarked on the impressive masculine air of the Xhosa. Indeed, even the settlers' own descriptions of the Xhosa seemed to suggest that they had more in common (psychologically speaking, at least) with the manly and martial European races than with weak and retiring aboriginal ones. Essays and editorials expressing real fear that the Xhosa might prove too intractable for the British appeared frequently in the settler press. One settler wrote to the *Grahamstown Journal* of 3 July 1852 that it was entirely possible "the natives will expel civilized man from the African soil." Another writer remarked that the very sight of the Xhosa was "sufficient to inspire the bravest with dread, for such encounters cannot be considered fair fights between man and man" (Ward 1851: 100). In response to events in South Africa, the 17 November 1851 edition of the *Times of London* printed an editorial that expressed much the same sentiment: "*The Kaffir is the most intractable savage with whom Europeans have ever been brought into contact.* Less brutal and stolid than the New Zealander or the Negro, he is not on that account more amenable to management. . . . He had never been taught to love the white man and he has long ceased to fear him. He is too clever to be cajoled." Thus, efforts to reconcile assigning the Xhosa to the role of female in the "family of man" required that a very selective group of attributes be singled out as important for fixing racial and gender essences. Outward physical appearance, as it related to issues of size and strength, was clearly unsatisfactory. Matters of behavior and disposition seemed equally irreconcilable. Few Englishmen would have agreed that the average English woman had "all the cunning of the wild beast" (Ward 1851: 100). Nor would most have agreed that "rapine and murder were in all [her] thoughts" (Bowker 1962 (1864): 9). Yet this is how the Xhosa were generally characterized. Establishing the truth of the similarity of African men and European women initially required going beyond issues of gross anatomical characteristics or even behavior and disposition and engaging with a more ephemeral (but ultimately more consequential) shared feature—the capacity (or lack thereof) for reason.

Liberal universals, Uday Mehta (1997: 61) has shown, are founded on a set of "anthropological capacities" that systematically authorize acts of exclusion. "Behind the capacities ascribed to all human beings there exist a thicker set of social credentials that constitute the real bases of political inclusion. The universalistic reach of liberalism derives from the capacities it identifies with human nature and from the presumption, which it encourages, that these capacities are sufficient and not merely necessary for an individual's political inclusion." The "anthropological minimum" for attaining moral personhood is the capacity to reason. Self-commanding reason, David Goldberg (1993: 18) explains, "defines in large part modernity's conception of the self." Reason is, then, the "philosophical basis of this broad human identity." Those deemed incapable of exercising reason may be governed without their consent. Further, once the capacity for reason is thrown into question, the status of an individual as even *human* is no longer guaranteed.

The attempt to stabilize the truth of the essential similarity of African men and European women precipitated a shift in the ethnographic gaze of science from the behavioral attributes of female apes to the physiological attributes of male apes. Central to the quest to determine what distinguished apes from humans was ascertaining to what extent they had the capacity to reason. According to Schiebinger, until late in the Enlightenment "apes were rarely seen as completely devoid of moral and intellectual capacities" (81). The interest in studying the faculty of reason brought to the fore the study of skulls. And because reason had long been considered a masculine trait, the skulls of male apes took center stage. "Female apes rarely figured in these reveries of simian potential" (Schiebinger 1993: 112). Like their human counterparts, the possibility of their exercising the capacity for reason was dismissed a priori. The standard by which these skulls were measured was always the same, that of the European male whose capacity for reason was unquestioned. The male simian skull was measured along a variety of axes. Measurements of the face were made to determine the angle of "prognathism," or forward jutting of the jaw. Craniometric measurements were taken of the skull. And phrenological investigations were made into the "organs" or humps on their heads. Efforts to measure the capacity for reason (a notoriously difficult faculty to measure, particularly in the era before IQ tests) fixated on the size and shape of the skull as a proxy for measuring intellect. Gradually, however, the skull soon came to be less a proxy than an absolute indicator of reason (or lack thereof) itself.

Ultimately the idea that apes had the capacity to reason was dismissed. However, the motivations and methods for studying and ranking skulls remained, because the corollary to the question of whether apes had the capacity to reason was whether they could be enfranchised. Although most of the debates about ape enfranchisement were posed in satirical form, behind them lurked the decidedly serious issue of how widely the rights of citizenship should be extended. Could they be extended to women, propertyless Europeans, slaves, or colonized Africans or Indians? These questions remained of pressing importance and the skull retained its emblematic status as the ultimate arbitrator of moral personhood.

Hence, in South Africa, when settler Thomas Baines posed the question of whether "the black man should ever regain possession of any part of South Africa which has been occupied by the white," he pointed to the deficiencies of the African skull by way of answer. Having felt the head of chief Sandile, he pronounced him to be "insipid," and "idiotic" (Kennedy 1961: 39). H. E. Macartney, author of the pamphlet *A Plain and Easy Way to Settle the Frontier Question*, which advocated the removal and gradual extermination of the Xhosa, based his arguments on his phrenological examinations of "some Kaffir skulls lately received" (1840). Phrenological examinations "proved" that the Xhosa utterly lacked the faculty of reason and authorized their complete subordination. At the same time, their purported lack of reason also authorized making the "aggressive" and "bellicose" Xhosa (who had proven to be formidable opponents on the battlefield) occupy the subordinate position of woman in the family of man. Thus, it was the transition from the study of the behavioral attributes of female apes to the physiological ones of males that ultimately authorized the linking of African men and European women, two seemingly unlike categories of persons, by demonstrating their shared incapacity to exercise reason. And it was the linking of Africans to apes, a category of subhumans, which exempted them from the protections offered to European females and ultimately justified the genocidal acts of aggression that were directed against them. As the *Eastern Province Herald* of 14 June 1851 editorialized, "Home newspaper writers and politicians may denounce in language of the strongest condemnation such a system of extension of all that is British in South Africa. . . . Yet the spread of the civilized and more powerful man goes on; *for the movement is not South African but universal—is not of today, but is as ancient as the history of our race.*"

Mobile Discourses and Traveling Skulls: Colonial Militarism and Metropolitan Scientific Practice

Because it was taken as self-evident that women were deficient in their capacity to reason, far fewer studies were made of their skulls and there was less urgency to actively demonstrate the similarity between their skulls and those of apes. When these studies were undertaken, they inevitably showed that women had low facial angles, suffered from pronounced prognathism, and had heads of inferior size and shape. More important than their potential for confirming existing prejudices, however, was the potential that these findings had for opening up new areas for metropolitan research. The skull provided a seemingly incontrovertible measure of the most fundamental attribute of personhood. For this reason it was considered as the ideal empirical basis for making comparisons across groups. Because the essential similarity of Africans, apes, and European women had been established by means of skull measurement, it appeared that the possibilities for drawing even more associations were infinite. The fact that colonial militarism was a continual source of research materials should not be overlooked as a significant factor contributing to the dominance of cranial studies. As Adele Clarke (1995: 183) observes, "in order to observe or produce the phenomena they study, all working scientists must obtain and manage research materials." South Africa's many frontier wars (nine in all) were particularly important and steady sources of raw data. Indeed, the traffic in skulls between Britain and South Africa began in the 1820s. The Royal College of Surgeons in London, for example, listed in its catalogue of specimens a number of skulls of Xhosa men that were taken from battlefields (Bank 1996). Indeed, one of the founding texts of scientific racism owes its genesis to South Africa's long and bloody military history. Dr. Robert Knox, whom Philip Curtin (1964: 378) described as "one of the key figures in the general Western movement toward a dogmatic pseudo-scientific racism," served as an army surgeon in South Africa from 1817 to 1820. His interest in the anatomy of the indigenous peoples of South Africa led him to begin thinking about the role of race in history as it provided him with the skulls and skeletons that would form the basis for his research.

Two decades after leaving South Africa Knox published *The Races of Man*, a thoroughly racial view of history. Although it would be inappropriate to reduce racial thinking to a few explicit scientific expressions, it is important to recognize the far-reaching effects of Knox's work—both intellectually and in terms of actual policies. The idea that colonial warfare should have, as its ultimate goal, to "civilize" colonized people off the face of the earth is a direct legacy of Knoxian thinking. When Disraeli argued against the wisdom of having emancipated the West Indian slaves, he, too, did so in "Knoxian" terms (Eldridge 1996). Ideas that Knox popularized, likewise, justified the dispossession of the Irish by the English.

What is notable about Knox's book, aside from its obnoxious racial characterizations, is the freedom with which Knox drew associations between different groups based on their crania. Because of his experiences with and strong support for British colonial efforts in Southern Africa and Ireland, Knox was particularly interested in studying the indigenous people in both places. He had, Cheng (1995: 29) observes, "a particular phobia about the Irish races." He described the Celts as "the lowest form of civilized man" and likened them to the Xhosa because of their "love of war and disorder and hatred for order and patient industry" (Knox 1850: 26). Knox also described the Irish as suffering from prognathism and on that basis pronounced them as having a particular affinity with apes. The absence of the capacity for reason among the Irish, he argued, could definitively be shown by virtue of their simian characteristics. When arguing against the rights of the Irish to self-determination, Knox also attributed their inability to reason to their "feminine" natures. And as was the case with the Xhosa, his logic inevitably led to justifications for refusing the Irish the right of self-government. Knox wrote that, as a member of the Anglo-Saxon race, he generally abjured dynasties, monarchies, and other nonrepresentative forms of government. However, he concluded that based on their physical and mental characteristics, despotic governments were "the only ones suitable for the Celtic man" (27). His prescriptions for the eventual annihilation of the Irish closely echo the writings of the eastern Cape settlers about the Xhosa. "The Irish race," he wrote, "must be forced from the soil. . . . England's safety requires it" (253).

After the publication of *The Races of Man* it was quite common to see European women being compared to Africans, Africans being compared to apes, and the Irish being compared to all three. Racial science so influenced "ways of seeing" that the flaxen-haired and fair-skinned Irish were frequently tested for the evidence of residual melanin in their skin. John Beddoe's "Index of Nigriscence," which was designed to measure the ratio of "blackness" in any fair-haired or -skinned person, is perhaps the best example. Beddoe's index "served to confirm the impressions of many Victorians that the Celtic portions of the population in Wales, Cornwall, Scotland, and Ireland were considerably darker or more melanous than those descended from Saxon and Scandinavian forebears" (Curtis 1997: 20).

Sometimes these types of associations were based on actual anatomical comparisons. However, the widespread dissemination of these ideas made it increasingly easy for nonscientists to make such pronouncements as a matter of course. The missionary George Brown, for example, described chief Sandile as "effeminate," and "full of vanity" (Brown 1855: 155). The Reverend Calderwood (1858: 21) similarly pronounced Sandile to be "weak in intellect" and "a promoter of the greatest sensuality amongst the people." The characterization of the Irish as a feminine race of people likewise entered the realm of taken-for-granted fact. According to Perry Curtis, "there was a curiously persistent and revealing label attached to the Irish, namely their characterization as a feminine race of people. The theme of Celtic femininity appears repeatedly" (1968: 61).

As a result of their being so frequently compared to colonial populations, European women began to be investigated by anthropological societies with the kind of ethnographic curiosity previously reserved for aboriginal people. Intellectual societies like the London Anthropological and Ethnological Society (to which George Grey, the governor of the Cape, belonged) devoted themselves not only to classifying racial types and debating issues of empire but also to establishing the differences between English men and women. The founder of the London Anthropological Society, Paul Broca, devoted most of his time to devising a method whereby he could rank the human races. However, the rapidity with which women were organizing social reform groups, speaking on public platforms, publishing new journals, and trying to reform education made him decide that it was incumbent on men of science to turn their attentions to "the woman question." As an article titled "On the Real Differences in the Minds of Men and Women," which appeared in the *Journal of the Anthropological Society* of 1869, put it this way: "The assertions and claims put forward under the term 'Woman's Rights', are a challenge to anthropologists to consider the scientific question of women's mental, moral, and physical qualities, her nature and normal conditions relative to man. Nowhere can this question be more appropriately and profitably discussed than in the Anthropological Society" (quoted in Fee 1979: 416).

The power of analogical reasoning to create new knowledge is nowhere better evidenced than in Victorian racial science. The "truth" of the analogies the Victorians drew appeared so incontrovertible that scientists began to search for evidence of still more anatomical features that could prove beyond a doubt the essential similarity of subhuman populations. As Stephen J. Gould (1996: 135) observed, "inferior groups are interchangeable in the general theory of biological determinism. They are continually juxtaposed, and one is made to serve as a surrogate for all—for the general proposition holds that society follows nature, and that social rank reflects innate worth." Analogical reasoning helped to shape the reality it appeared to describe by guiding research priorities, constituting new objects of inquiry, determining what types of measurements would be taken, and deciding what types of data would be collected. What had begun as a relatively limited project of measuring the faculty of reason in a few select groups helped to give rise to entirely new subfields and disciplines such as criminal anthropology and criminology. These new disciplines, in turn, worked to delimit new classes of persons such as "Criminal Man." Criminals were measured for prognathism and subject to phrenological investigations to determine the development of their organs of acquisitiveness and destructiveness as well as to see if they possessed the so-called murder bump. The criminal type was characterized as having "ferocious instincts of primitive humanity" (Leps 1992: 27). These instincts were explained anatomically by the shape of their jaws, hands, and ears. Criminals were widely believed to have the atavistic features that were also characteristic of "savage" people and apes. Phrenological examination showed prostitutes (preeminent examples of "Criminal Women") to suffer from similar signs of atavism. Consequently, they were characterized as having low facial angles, misshapen heads, and malformed skulls. Their genitals were likewise examined for evidence of their primitive characters. Measures were also developed to assess the relative placement of the foramen magnum (the hole at the base of the skull), the length of the arm, the size of the ear, the roundness of the stomach, and the size of the pelvis. It was believed that these measures, when taken with the standard craniometric measurements of the face and skull, could establish the common physical attributes that linked criminals, prostitutes, colonized people, and women (Gilman 1985; Leps 1992).

Colonial science thus profoundly influenced metropolitan understandings of domestic social problems and their possible solutions. Scientism transformed economic and social problems into medical ones that could be dealt with effectively without disturbing extant authority structures. Representing social and political unrest as simply the societal manifestations of individual or group personality defects, and crime as a problem of genetics and morality, worked to efface the role that structural inequality played in producing Britain's social crises at home and abroad. Representations of "Criminal Woman" or "Criminal Man" that stressed their physical atavism provoked mental associations with "savage" races. This, in turn, legitimized viewing criminals as primitive and degenerate members of a separate race, which required strict social control and segregation.

The deep connections between colonial expansion and metropolitan science—whether we are speaking of the transfer of skulls and skeletons, finance capital, or ideologies about and images of people—support Anne McClintock's (1995: 61) suggestion that the formative categories of imperial modernity are articulated categories. In other words, they "came into being in historical relation to each other and emerged only in dynamic, shifting, and intimate interdependence."

The Critique of White Supremacy and the Emergence of a Counterhegemonic Xhosa Worldview

One of colonial modernity's least stable yet most enduring myths is that of the naturalness of white supremacy. The myth of the omnipotence of the modern subject rests on the fact that this subject alone possesses the power to "criticize and unveil" (Latour 1993: 36). The power that accrues to those who control the direction of the gaze was, as Fanon (1967) recognized, intimately connected to the power that accrued from the control of capital or instruments of war. The dialectic of dominance and dependence that marked the relationship between the colonizer and the colonized was encapsulated in the struggle over the control of the gaze. For the dominated were required not only to supply their labor power, to surrender their land, and to facilitate the transformation of living labor into capital; they were also required to supply the dominator with recognition. As Fanon (1967: 212) explained, the colonizer tries "to read admiration in the eyes of the other." Colonized people functioned as objects and colonizers "do not wish to experience the impact of the object. Contact with the object means conflict. I am narcissus, and what I want to see in the eyes of the others is a reflection that pleases me." Given this fact, no analysis of science and colonial governmentality would be complete without thinking about the ways in which Xhosa people attempted to challenge British pretensions toward what Frances Hutchins (1967) called "the illusion of permanence." The history of any struggle, no matter how one-sided it appears, is incomplete absent the perspectives of all the social agents who shaped it.

As was discussed above, one of the ways that science was put to work in the service of colonial dominance was by means of the authority scientific discourse gave to "experts" to construct the very world they purported to describe. Accordingly, an important element of the counterdiscourse that came from Xhosa communities was the articulation of an alternative world-view and the appeal to forms of expertise other than the scientific. Xhosa leaders frequently likened the settlers' aspirations toward global dominance to English attempts to assume even greater powers than those of God—the same God whose world the English were purportedly bringing to the heathen. As Sandile told George Brown (1855: 155), "God made me the chief. The white men now say that I cannot be a chief. How do these men think to undo the word of God?" While another chief informed the Reverend Renton that "the Queen did not make him a chief. She could make great men. She could even make a governor, but God had made him a chief. God had given the white man England and he had given the Coloured men Kaffirland. Why then [did] the English wish to undo what God has done?"[2]

The hubris that marked British encounters with the Xhosa emanated from their confidence that they were representatives of the most rational, advanced, and powerful society in the world. The *Eastern Province Herald* of 15 June 1852 published a leading article titled "The Progress of the Anglo-Saxon Race" giving typical expression of these views: "In 1851 it [the Anglo-Saxon race] was ahead of every civilized race in the world. Of all the races which are now striving for the mastery of the world, to impress on the future of society and civilization the stamp of its own character and genius, to make its laws, religion, manners, and government prevail. The Anglo-Saxon is now unquestionably the most numerous, powerful, and active." It is not surprising, therefore, that this view of British as the "master race" was subject to vigorous interrogation. Even as the Xhosa were, in the words of a writer to the *Cape Frontier Times* of 23 February 1847, "being taught to feel the hopelessness of a contest with the Government," they were engaging in a process of challenging English claims to power—stripping them of their seeming omnipotence. Chief Sandile, shortly before the outbreak of the Seventh Frontier War, expressed this quite strongly when he remarked that formerly the Xhosa "thought white men could not be killed but we see they are only like us, they can also be killed."[3] Chief Umkai expressed a similar sentiment when he warned the government that the Xhosa would "rise unless some measures, or chance, prevent it. Kaffirs do not see that the English are so strong in power."[4] What these pronouncements amounted to were declarations that despite British attempts to prove the contrary, they had no greater claims to personhood. However many skulls they measured or how strongly they proclaimed their superiority, they could never be completely invulnerable. Mortality is the great equalizer.

This process of questioning the omnipotence of the power of the English led the Xhosa to search for and draw inspiration from other instances where the English suffered military defeat. When the Russians killed a former governor of the Cape[5] during the Crimean War, the word quickly spread among the Xhosa. It was widely believed that Lynx, Ngqika, and Mlanjeni (three deceased Xhosa leaders) were across the sea fighting against the English in the Crimean War. As one informant told Governor George Grey, "They say it is a lie, which has been told about the Russians being a White nation. The opinion is that they are all blacks, and were formerly Kaffir warriors who have died or have been killed in the various wars against the colony."[6] In 1856 the Xhosa people, particularly those who lived within the Ngqika district whose cattle had been hit by lung sickness, acted on the prophesies of a young girl, Nongqawuse. They slaughtered their cattle and ceased planting crops in the belief that these deeds would lead to the resurrection of their ancestors, the expulsion of the British, and the return to a precolonial idyll (Peires 1989). Mhlakaza, one of the principal interpreters of the cattle-killing prophesies, reported that he was visited by Russian spirits and figures who came from fighting against the English and were now able to help the Xhosa (Brownlee 1977 [1896]: 129).

Implicit in the above statements are several important challenges to the hegemony of the British worldview, the most obvious being their refusal to accept English metaphysics of life and death. Beyond this, proposing that the Russians were African rather than European was a powerful reversal of the hierarchy whereby the more powers a nation possessed, the more it was said to approximate the European standard. The British had long ascribed "European" traits to indigenous groups whose abilities did not conform to the stereotype of the hapless native. Thus, the suggestion that the Russians were an African nation demonstrated that the Xhosa did not accept the idea that white-skinned people were destined to rule the world. Indeed, this is why the Indian Mutiny of 1857 was also widely talked about among the Xhosa. The activity was such that Grey expressed concern that the chiefs were using news of the mutiny to revive the desire for war against the colony (Weldon 1984: 67). For, in the words of Chief Maqoma's son, who studied for seven years in England, "England has no more right to our country than we have to take England. It is merely a question of might against right" (Adams 1941 [1884]: 275).

The brutality with which the British dealt with the Xhosa was meant not only to rob them of their country but also to make them accept the myth of their own inferiority. In this way the British would dismantle Xhosa society from within as they attacked it from without. As a writer to the *Cape Frontier Times* of 19 January 1847 explained, "the native communities must be made to feel that they are *subjects* and not masters . . . and thus by degrees out of wild and savage races will be formed communities of men . . . who will be British subjects not only in name, but also in practice—in their sentiment and thoughts, their wants and wishes." Making the colonized see themselves as the colonizer sees them, and thus to aspire to be more like their oppressors rather than oppose them, has always been integral to the exercise of colonial rule. As Fanon explained:

> It is of course obvious that the Malagasy can perfectly well tolerate the fact of not being a white man. A Malagasy is a Malagasy; or, rather, no, not he *is* a Malagasy but, rather, in an absolute sense he "lives" his Malagasyhood. If he is a Malagasy, it is because a white man has come, and if at a certain stage he has been led to ask himself whether he is indeed a man, it is because his reality as a man has been challenged. In other words, I begin to suffer from not being a white man to the degree that the white man imposes discrimination on me, makes me a colonized native, robs me of all worth, all individuality, tells me that I am a parasite on the world, that I must bring myself as quickly as possible into step with the white world. (1967: 98)

The fact that the British were failing in their project of making the Xhosa see themselves as the English saw them, and thus aspire to become like them, is evidenced by the remarks of Renton, a missionary, who observed that the Xhosa were "very acute in marking the inconsistencies and bad conduct of Englishmen."[7] The British were known by various epithets, including "scum of the sea" (Godlonton 1965 [1852]: 176). The Xhosa also compared the English quite unfavorably to their arch nemesis, the Afrikaners. John Fairbairn, testifying before the Select Committee on the Kaffir Tribes (1851: 85), reflected that "the natives consider the Dutch natives like themselves and they consider the English as intruders who have come to take their country from them." Missionary John Green agreed that "the Natives hold the Dutch in far higher estimation than the English." Testifying before the Select Committee former governor of the Cape Colony Peregrine Maitland (1847) confirmed that the Xhosa had sent messages to the Boers to ask them "why did the Boers not join the Kaffirs to drive the English away from the country?" The Xhosa also sent messages to the Dutch asking "why they [did] not stand aside so that they [the Xhosa] may drive the English into the sea."[8] These statements clearly indicate that many Xhosa people did not aspire to "become British in their sentiments, thoughts, wants, and wishes." Comparing the British unfavorably to the Dutch was a particularly strong indication of their rejection of the hierarchy the British constructed to delineate civilization from savagery. For the Afrikaners (or Boers, as they were known at the time) were widely considered by the English to occupy an even *lower* rung on the ladder of civilization than did many Africans. As J. M. Coetzee (1988: 29) explains, "The harshest remarks of the nineteenth century commentators were reserved for the Boers of the frontier . . . a refrain taken up by every traveller who penetrated into the back country and encountered farmers living in mean dwellings set on vast tracts, barely literate, rudely clad, surrounded by slaves and servants with too little employment, disdainful of manual labour, content to carry on subsistence farming in a land of plenty."

The Xhosa's refusal to surrender to the British the power to delimit the boundaries of the human, to have their essence reduced to a handful of measurements, and to see the world as their oppressors saw it was a powerful challenge to the English quest for global mastery. To borrow a phrase from Martin Luther King Jr., they were not about to let the *English* man be "the measure of all things" (Walvin 1986). Although it is not overtly stated, one can read an implicit critique of Western scientific practice in Xhosa remonstrance of British hegemony and white supremacy. Donna Haraway (1991: 43) could easily have been describing science, conquest, and colonial militarism in Southern Africa when she wrote: "Science is about knowledge and power. In our time natural science defines the human being's place in nature and history and provides the instruments of domination of the body and the community. By constructing the category nature, natural science imposes limits on history and self-formation. So science is part of the struggle over the nature of our lives." Thus, in refusing to adopt the British worldview as their own, the Xhosa posed a powerful challenge to one of the foundational axioms of Western scientific practice—that certain "facts" are transhistorical givens. Their resistance to the British in the form of an articulation of a counterhegemonic worldview illustrates that all "facts"—even those about nature and science—are historically mediated and, thus, are not the same for all human beings in all places and times.

Conclusion

No study of racism, classism, and sexism is complete that does not consider their ideological dimensions. As ways of thinking, they have been deeply indebted to one another. Greedy capitalists, seeking to further dehumanize and objectify their workers, found racism superbly good to think with. Racists, on the other hand, found sexism equally satisfying to think with. Exploring the important role that analogical reasoning played in reinforcing colonial governmentality provides a unique avenue of entry for understanding the points of intersection between language, action, and the reproduction of social systems. Understanding the social structures and processes of representation and signification that work to produce collective ideas about races, classes, and genders requires going far beyond simply recognizing that discourses about powerless and dispossessed groups frequently can and do resonate for one another. Rather, we must, in the words of Paul Gilroy, "highlight the elasticity and the emptiness of racial signifiers as well as the ideological work which has to be done in order to turn them into signifiers in the first place" (1991 [1987]: 39). Any analytical attempt to understand race, class, and gender as systems of oppression must, therefore, look at the multiple dimensions that constitute their interconnections. It is imperative that social scientists move beyond sterile debates over which form of oppression is more "foundational" and instead embrace theoretical models that allow not only for theorizing these interconnections but also for thinking through their global dimensions.

In the book *We Have Never Been Modern* Bruno Latour (1993: 26) critiques the conventional wisdom of a sociology of science that argues that there is a macrosocial context "out there" that impacts scientific practice. He calls for a sociology of science that is not constructivist where nature is concerned and realist where society is concerned but, rather, problematizes both by exploring the ways in which they operate as "double artifacts." My analysis here has attempted to historicize and deconstruct the collection of activities we call "science" and the collection of activities we call "politics," not simply to understand how the latter impacts the former but, more importantly, to understand the processes whereby we come to naturalize their bifurcation. Latour's admonition that "we cannot change the social order without modifying the natural order and vice versa" (42) is writ large in the history of South Africa. If we refuse to accept that some facts, by their nature, are "political" while others are "scientific," we open the door to exposing the processes whereby both "science" and "politics" are produced as seemingly stable, separable, and autonomous entities.

Notes

I would like to thank Emily Ignacio for providing valuable research materials that greatly assisted me in completing this essay. I would also like to thank the Center for Advanced Study, University of Illinois, Urbana-Champaign, where I was a fellow during the completion of this essay.

1 Kaffir (sometimes spelled Kaffer, Kafir, or Caffer) is an Arab word meaning infidel that came to function as a racial epithet similar to "nigger" in American parlance.

2 Select Committee on the Kaffir Tribes (London: 1851), 437.

3 Irish University Press Series of British Parliamentary Papers, *Correspondence with the Cape Governor Regarding the Kaffir Tribes, 1837–47* July, vol. 21 (Ireland: Shannon, 1971), 451.

4 Ibid., 507.

5 Sir George Cathcart (1852–1854).

6 Command Paper [2002], vol. X. Grey to Labouchere, sub enclosure 1 in no. 1.

7 *Kaffir Tribes*, 436.

8 *Kaffir Tribes*, 356.

3. "The More You Kill the More You Will Live"

The Maya, "Race," and Biopolitical Hopes for Peace in Guatemala

Diane M. Nelson

There is here a chance to break away from the dangerous and destructive patterns that were established when the rational absurdity of "race" was elevated into an essential concept and endowed with a unique power to both determine history and explain its selective unfolding. If we are tempted to be too celebratory in assessing the positive possibilities created by these changes in race-thinking and the resulting confusion that has enveloped raciology, we need only remind ourselves that the effects of racial discourses have become more unpredictable as the quality of their claims upon the world have become more desperate. This is a delicate situation, and "race" remains fissile material.—Paul Gilroy

The CEH concludes that agents of the State of Guatemala, within the framework of counterinsurgency operations carried out between 1981 and 1983, committed acts of genocide against groups of Mayan people. . . . This conclusion is based on the evidence that, in light of Article II of the Convention on the Prevention and Punishment of the Crime of Genocide, the killing of members of Mayan groups occurred; serious bodily or mental harm was inflicted; and the group was deliberately subjected to living conditions calculated to bring about its physical destruction in whole or in part . . . —United Nations Commission for Historical Clarification (CEH)

We were between two armies. This war was not ours. 99 percent of the violence was brought on us by ladinos,[1] those who benefit from national racism. Maya people were killed by both the left and the right, but both were ladino.—Otilia Lux, Guatemalan truth commissioner

The anthropologist is in a ludicrous position, Bronislaw Malinowski suggests, attempting to seize hold of something at the very moment it melts away.[2] She attempts to fix—in the sense of hold still—complex, fluid, contingent entities. Mesoamerican anthropology done by North Americans might be characterized as a series of efforts to document the Indian before "he" disappears, assimilated into mestizo nationalist modernity.[3] My essay is likewise concerned with disappearance—the legacy of decades of "antiracist" assimilation policies and of mass murder of indigenous and other people in Guatemala's civil war. Assimilation discourses are mobile and they trouble understandings of race, which are intent on fixing, holding people still. But to fix also means to repair, and I focus on a few of the complex relations between attempts to fix the pressing problems of poverty, injustice, and endemic violence that the majority of Guatemalans (and many North Americans) confront, and the ways these apparent solutions simultaneously (and often unconsciously) fix humans into raciological positions.[4]

I feel a bit ludicrous, or absurd, fixing my gaze on race and "genocidal" civil war in Guatemala,[5] because they are quite mobile entities. For example, memory in the struggles to assign meaning to the loss, violence, and pain of thirty-five years of war is very unstable as people try to answer the questions of why did people kill and why did they die? Second, I review the changing ways "race" (or some sense of "genos") figures in those meanings. Since 1985, when I first started working with Guatemalans, stories told about the civil way have changed. In my interviews, in the influential United Nations Truth Commission report (CEH), in public statements, and in media coverage, race increasingly explains what the war was about. In broad strokes, what in the 1980s was a class war with an ethnic component (left versus right, society versus the state, poor versus rich—with most indigenous people being poor) is, in the early twenty-first century, a race war. As Otilia Lux describes it, left and right are ladino and both killed indigenous people.[6] Rather than suffering as "peasants" or "subversives" many people now seem to believe that the Maya were repressed for *being* indigenous. And yet discussion of racism is also considered taboo (Arenas Bianchi et al. 1999) because "race does not exist in Guatemala," as I was often told.

In this essay I briefly explore some forms of race-thinking—including charges of racism in a nation supposedly without race—and the stakes of both antiracist and raciological readings of the civil war. In exploring hopes for peace, I am curious about the role of "nature" as expressed in discourses about the body, blood, and descent and in the appeal and productivity of race and eugenics discourses. What is it that articulates particular understandings of race, nature, and politics to hope and the desperate commitments to fix or repair untenable lifeways?

Race is hard to hold on to. Biologists, anthropologists, UNESCO bureaucrats, even U.S. pop culture figures like Tiger Woods repeatedly tell us that race doesn't matter. And yet scandals in the United States over police profiling and state murder based on particular phenotypes suggest that race—an instantaneously visible physiognomic mark of an internal essence such as criminality or *being* a menace to society—does matter in crucial ways. And yet U.S. history is full of certain people "becoming white" or leaving race behind to become an ethnic group.

Similarly, in symptoms of Latin American race-thinking like Tschudi's 1847 table delineating Peruvian "mongrelity," signs of "nature" such as visible differences in pigment or "frizzlyness" of hair mix with more obviously "cultural" judgments as "beautiful" and "miserable" (Young 1995: 176). Such Latin American diagrams fixed twenty-three (or more) "races" visible to experienced observers, and yet in Guatemala at the opening of the second Christian millennium I hear constant expressions of anxiety about the inability to tell an "Indian" from a "ladino" (nonindigenous). In trying to fix race we find that the way we have *learned* to see is not so natural but instead historically specific. Bodies become less obvious and more meshed in stories and power relations that *make* them meaningful, actively *racialize* them.[7] And yet it is compelling for many people (including myself) to explain the ferocity and horror of the violence of Guatemala's war through the idiom of genocide, positing an existing raciologically marked people who are viciously repressed, victims of a racist state. And yet a number of indigenous activists are working through that very state to fix and repair the wounds of the last thirty-five years of war and five hundred years of colonization.

In this project I address work to fix or repair the damaged lives of victims by reading across these unfixed series of "and yets"—or what Paul Gilroy calls "the pious ritual in which we always agree that 'race' is invented but are then required . . . to accept that the demand for justice requires us nevertheless innocently to enter the political arenas it helps to mark out" (2000: 52). While it is difficult to say where North America ends and Latin America begins, I am also reading across the U.S. "one-drop rule" and Latin American mestiz@[8] understandings in ways that I hope illuminate and un/fix both.[9]

The mobile memory of war is produced by both Guatemalans and North Americans as we think about and through Guatemala's grid of race and politics. I want to understand the possibilities for the future, the conceptions of a common good that lie embryonically within these discourses. This essay is meant to work in solidarity with hopes for a more just and equitable future in Guatemala. However, it, like many of those projects, may assume fixed identities. As I wonder about the move from stories of class to race war in

Guatemala, I am also curious about the grid of intelligibility in recent North American thinking (my own included) in which, in otherwise careful and important works, all the ladin@s are racist, the state and all the left are ladin@, but we will speak for the authentic Maya (Carlson 1997, Fischer 2001, Green 1999, Garzon et al. 1998, Stoll 1999, Warren 1998, Zur 1998). The idea of a fundamental divide between victim and perpetrator in some recent ethnography may reflect developments on the ground in Guatemala, and it is a time-honored way to invoke the political action necessary to fix injustice and resist repression. But I am called out by Michel Foucault to explore the productivity of "racism," and by Paul Gilroy and other antiracist activists to question the "allure" of basic mythologies of racial difference. To do this I will try to keep my own situated, diffracting knowledge in view.

The Guatemalan Civil War

Briefly, most accounts of the civil war fix its start in 1962 when disgruntled army officers formed a revolutionary guerrilla movement. Their anger can be traced to the 1954 CIA-backed coup against the elected reformist Colonel Jacobo Arbenz, linking the war to Guatemala's violent relation to transnational capital and U.S. foreign policy. The United Nations truth commission (CEH) also attributes the war to an ongoing history of colonial relations and an "anti-democratic . . . political tradition [with] roots in an economic structure which is marked by the concentration of productive wealth in the hands of a minority" (CEH Summary 1999: 7). Until 1996—when a peace treaty was signed between the guerrillas (the URNG, Guatemalan National Revolutionary Unity) and the government—over 200,000 people were killed, many of them victims of large-scale massacres. Hundreds of villages were destroyed during scorched-earth counterinsurgency, and at least one-eighth of the total population was displaced, with hundreds of thousands becoming refugees. The CEH found that state forces were responsible for 93 percent of the violations they investigated.

The war waxed in the mid-1960s, culminating in U.S. Green Berets aiding in a brutal counterinsurgency campaign in the eastern part of the country inhabited primarily by people who identify as ladin@. Through the late 1960s to the mid 1970s the guerrillas and the military governments were regrouping and violence waned, picking up again after 1976, this time in the western highland areas, with a heavy indigenous population. It is here that scorched-earth tactics were used, including the destruction of hundreds of villages and every living thing in them. The CEH concentrates on four indigenous areas to make its case for genocide. After 1983 and the worst of the massacres, overt state violence against the population became more selective and guerrilla possibilities for taking state power seemed quite limited, although armed activities continued throughout the country. Negotiations over a peace treaty dragged on for almost a decade after a return to civilian rule (with military backing) in 1986. Selective human rights abuses, including disappearance, torture, and murder, continued against both indigenous and ladin@ people, as they do to this day (González 2000).

In the late 1980s a pan-Mayan movement, decades in the making, emerged to organize for cultural and political rights (Bastos and Camus 1993, 1995, Cojtí Cuxil 1991, 1995, Fischer and Brown 1996, Warren 1998). The response of leftists and what became known as the *popular* indigenous rights groups is ambivalent (as I'll explore below). After 1992, a watershed in hemispheric indigenous organizing around the Columbus Quincentennial, more and more indigenous cadres abandoned the guerrilla to work with the *culturales*, as the pan-Mayanists are often called. These Maya have been successful in passing international conventions for indigenous rights, lobbying for state funding for education projects, and representing the population through ministerial positions in the government. The Coordination of Organizations of the Pueblo Maya of Guatemala (COPMAGUA) was established to implement the portions of the peace treaty dealing with indigenous issues and brings together *populares* and *culturales*. The Maya demand recognition for their specific experiences of colonialism and racism, which, they insist, cannot be subsumed into the fact that most Maya are poor (it's not just class). Some claim that confronting racism within the revolutionary and radical grassroots movements led them to begin organizing differently, around indigenous identity. (The fact that many Mayan activists are funded by foreign NGOs or work for the Guatemalan government has led some former allies to accuse them of selling out.) They in turn have been accused of racism for excluding ladin@s from their plans for the future.

Blood and Identity

What is an Indian? A ladino with no money.

What blood type is Rigoberta Menchú? URNG positive.—Jokes told in Guatemala

The only solution for Guatemala is to improve the race, to bring in Aryan seeds to improve it. On my finca I had a German administrator for many years and for every *india* he got pregnant, I would pay him an extra fifty dollars.—Ladino plantation owner (in Casaus Arzú)

Do you know how to make *moronga* (blood sausage), Diana? Well, you take a mess of blood and boil it and boil it and boil it until it hardens into sausage. That's what's happened to Guatemalans. All the suffering, the blood spilled in the violence and then the boiling and boiling of the decades of war, the counterinsurgency, we have a hard time thinking new thoughts because our brains have become hard like *moronga.*—Guatemalan ladino

These epigraphs are about blood and the many ways it can signify. In the first joke blood is unimportant in defining what an Indian is—identity is about money, or class, not about anything inborn. In the second, a political position—membership in the revolutionary URNG—is seen as inborn, carried in the blood. The third calculates an economy of "race improvement" through "mixing" or *mestizaje* across the borders of a global racial hierarchy, a "solution" meant, perhaps, to overcome the deep divisions that led to thirty-five years of civil war. Finally, my friend's explanation of *"moronga* brain" suggests the problems of "fixing," holding something still, when there's so much to "fix," or repair. He points to the deep frustration, expressed in a blood idiom, among many Guatemalans at the current state of affairs—their own limited imaginations, impunity for war crimes, stalled peace-treaty implementation, and the rise of popular authoritarianism.[10]

In February 1999 the CEH concluded, after four years of archival and interview work, that the Maya as a group have suffered genocidal violence. While the 1948 UN Convention calls genocide the intent to destroy a "national, ethnic, racial, or religious group," the etymology of the term suggests a certain fixity to the identity of the victims (Kiernan 1998). Genocide is degree zero of racism as a repressive system. Part of what is intriguing about this important resolution is that the term "Maya," used to refer to living indigenous people in Guatemala, is associated with the indigenous cultural rights movement and has only been widely used for about fifteen years. In turn, the Guatemalan army does not deny that it committed massacres in the 1980s. However, it says it was killing subversives primarily, and "Indians" only secondarily, in the interest of "national security" (Schirmer 1998). Otilia Lux was one of three UN commissioners on the CEH. At the biannual Maya Studies Conference in August 1999 she said, "We were between two armies. This war was not ours. 99 percent of the violence was brought on us by ladinos, those who benefit from national racism." She was heavily applauded. Her words, however, may reflect army counterinsurgency strategy, which was to place indigenous villagers between two armies, destroying any neutral ground. They also echo North American anthropologist David Stoll (1993, 1999), who criticizes Nobel Laureate Rigoberta Menchú Tum for supporting the guerrillas when, he claims, they used Maya as cannon fodder. Later Ms. Lux, describing a "paradigmatic case" in the CEH report of a guerrilla massacre of indigenous villagers, argued that Maya were killed by both the left and the right, but both were ladin@. However, historically, most foot soldiers in both the army and the guerrilla have been indigenous.

Blood (and "nature") mingle with race (and politics) in these simultaneous and contradictory understandings of why people kill, of war horrors, identity, and the different political projects they animate. And these understandings are transfused with the spilled blood of the war and continuing abuses.[11] Blood and the folk genetics that underlie racial categories are, as David Schneider (1968) reminds us, metaphors for identity, for links between the individual and the species, between present and future generations. Race-thinking, tied to notions of descent of type, informs genocidal practices of killing children and pregnant women as well as adults. In Guatemala's context of massive death, race-thinking of any kind appears unquestionably repressive. The CEH report (and the enthusiastic reception of Ms. Lux's comments) represents a nodal moment in struggles to co/memorate the war, fixing an account of repressive racism in hopes of fixing, or healing, an exclusionary national body politic.

However, alternative strategies for fixing Guatemala's body politic point to race-thinking itself as the problem. Many Guatemalans and gring@s who consider themselves progressive or revolutionary antiracists hope to transcend, or at least mitigate, racism through nation-building, class solidarity, mestizaje, "intercultural education," and/or by arguing that there is no race in Guatemala. But many Maya respond that these forms of unification are essentially exclusionary and repressive of Mayan existence. This is Stoll's critique of the Guatemalan left, suggesting that the URNG actually caused the genocide. "At bottom rural guerrilla struggles are an urban romance, a myth propounded by middle-class radicals who dream of finding true solidarity in the countryside" (1999: 282).

How are we to analyze the proliferation and vacillation of race meanings in even the brief examples deployed here? Did the people who killed during the civil war do so because they wanted a group of people, racialized into infrahumanity, to disappear? Does racism (a virulent hatred of "otherness") explain the genocidal actions of the millions of people (including indigenous soldiers, civil patrollers, and spies) involved in the revolution and in the counterinsurgency war? How do we explain thirty-five years of ladin@ and indigenous alliance aboveground and in guerrilla struggles against impossible odds? What could antiracism look like in postwar Guatemala?

I address these questions in the next section by tracing blood and race discourses of phenotype and blood purity (which are supposed to naturally fix identity, hold it still) and of mixing (*mestizaje*) and eugenics (which promise to fix or improve not only one generation but, through raciological notions of descent, to launch hope into the future). I want to explore some of these blood and race discourses to see how "racism is a grid of intelligibility, it instills a sense of righteousness through the struggle for a common good" (Stoler 1995: 69). In other words, I think it is vital to address biopolitics, the way life and productive power, and not only repression, incited the war and impact its aftermath.

Some Vacillations in the Grid of Intelligibility

"Indian" and "Ladin@"

Most introductions to Guatemala (anthropological, touristic, even business literature) start by describing the large indigenous population (estimated at 40 to 70 percent, depending on who is counting). The rest are *ladin@s* (nonindigenous) with a small sprinkling of Garífunas (people of African descent) and "others." While the identity categories of "ladin@" and "Indian" tend to disappear if looked at too closely, they are deeply salient as binary oppositions (Fischer and Brown 1996, Hawkins 1984, Rojas Lima 1990, Rosada Granados 1987, Smith 1990, Watanabe 1990, 1992).

"Indian" (*indio*), like most terms used to designate less powerful people, comes heavily charged with racist history (and geographical confusion, given its coining by Columbus). On closer inspection it dissolves into some twenty ethnic-linguistic groups (K'iche', Q'eqchi, Mam, etc.), identities strongly linked to particular towns and landscapes, lineages, production methods, older terms like *natural*, and the newer term Maya, usually meaning people active in the cultural rights movement. Not all "Indians" identify as Maya, either because they're not in the loop, or they suspect the emphasis on culture to be apolitical, or even racist.

To add to the confusion, geography, networks, even the availability of spare time influence the identity terms used. When I interviewed the *Alcalde Indígena* (indigenous mayor) in an area singled out by the CEH as a site of genocide, he complained about ladin@s in the area who called him an "indio" because "these were people who lived here a long time ago . . . naked, without schooling. Now there are schools in all the hamlets. There are only *naturales* here." I asked if there were any Maya. "Like in a museum?" he asked. "Here there aren't any of those, like from before. But there is an organization in Guatemala City. People who have their degrees. . . . There is a Grupo Maya here. . . . They talk about how we can all be united, how to come together. . . . When I leave here [retire] I'm going to become a Maya."

The word "ladin@" also may be taken as an insult, depending on context, and decomposes under the pressure of analysis into myriad terms that mark class, distinction, color, and history, like *criollo, gente decente* (decent people), *blancos* (whites), or elite, who in turn are differentiated from the *cachimbiros, gente común, gentuza, chusma* (commoners), etc. Ladin@, as the other to Indian, is "inherently relational, context-sensitive, and thus blurry and unstable" (de la Cadena 1996: 117). It may be difficult to find anyone in Guatemala who identifies themselves as mestiz@, ladin@ or indi@, but everyone assumes they know what the words mean and what the bodies look like.

Identity Is "Racial": Blood Purity and the Cara de Indio

In everyday life, in the city and the country, folk knowledges understand the differences between indigenous and ladin@ to be real, marked physically, and discernible in blood types and genes.[12] What often goes without saying is that there "are" explicit racial differences between indigenous and non-Indians—understandings that lean on tropes of blood purity and "objective" phenotypic marks of difference like the *cara de indio,* face of the Indian (Hale 1996a: 44). In an important ethnography of upper-class ladin@ race-thinking, the Guatemalan anthropologist Marta Elena Casaus Arzú argues that purity of blood was and is a central concern in the identities of the elite. In matters of identification, bodies matter as "proof" of authenticity, of purity. When asked to define their ethnic background, many say, "white and with no mixing of Indian blood." One family insisted they "do not have even a drop of Indian blood. This is proved by our certificate of blood purity (*limpieza*) and the fact that all of us have blood-type O negative" (Casaus Arzú 1992: 118).[13] In my own interviews (see also González Ponciano 1991, 1997), when ladin@s were asked to describe an "Indian," *physical* attributes—the color of the skin, height, facial features, and even smell—were central to their definitions. What are apparently nonphenotypical stereotypes of Indians as lazy, traditional, conformist, and submissive are also held by many ladin@s to be passed down in the blood, to be genetic traits. A number of people mentioned the ultimate bodily proof: "the Mongolian spot"—a birthmark on the lower back—which would prove that someone was an Indian "even if it didn't show up in their genealogy." Even attitudes are thought to be related to blood. Alvaro Colóm, who ran the government development agency FONAPAZ (Peace Fund) and was the presidential candidate for the URNG political party in 1999, told me, "We need to create a way for Indians to participate in decision making in this country. I don't have Indian blood, but I believe this anyway."

The complex intersection of "beliefs" with blood, sex, and reproduction came up at the Mayan Studies Conference in August 1999. Although they denounce racism, I have found very few Mayan activists who make race (i.e., essentialist) claims for indigenous identity. With little history of blood quantum in Guatemala, Mayan activists emphasize language, clothing, and choice as central to identity (Cojtí Cuxil 1991, 1995, 1999; Sam Colop 1996; Raxche' 1996; Otzoy 1996). However, several Mayan organizers expressed great consternation after a paper (Velásquez Nimatuj 1999) that described how many economically successful indigenous men chose ladinas as wives. "I am proud of my K'iche' blood," said one man during the discussion, "but I am very worried by what the compañera describes. There is a lot of mestizaje. We as the *Pueblo Maya* have our own history we must protect."

Identity Is "Cultural": Dressing "Up"

These notions of genotypic and phenotypic difference exist simultaneously with often contradictory understandings of identity as *cultural,* based on self-definition, family history, language use, clothing, cosmovision, etc. In simultaneous understandings, a ladin@ is someone who speaks Spanish, wears "Western" clothing, is Christian or secular, and modern. Mayas can (and have traditionally been expected to want to) *become* ladin@ by learning Spanish and dressing "up." *Ladinization*—the decision to take up these cultural markers—is seen as a major threat to Mayan identity and has been one strand in the state's historic project of assimilationist nation-building. Many people I interviewed assume that five hundred years of mestizaje have erased phenotypic (sight-specific) difference. All Guatemalan bodies and blood are the same and this mestiz@ body promises to fix the nation, to liberate people from the horrors of essentialist racial difference, to heal the wounds of Conquest, and to provide a unity that sublates—acknowledges yet transcends—difference (Casaus Arzú 1992, Hale 1996b, C. Smith 1996; see also Anzaldúa 1987, Klor de Alva 1995, Mallon 1996).[14] Mestizaje is usually defined as "racial and/or cultural mixing" and in Guatemala it is a concept with great power, assumed as an identity, weighted with desires for a better future, and denounced as state-supported ethnocide. In this way it resembles many identity categories, like nation, gender, ethnicity, or its own supposed building blocks, race and culture.[15]

Embedded in Guatemalan discourses of mestizaje and "blood" mixing is the possibility of "whitening" or "improving" the race, a sense that is counterintuitive for many North Americans whose racist tradition has considered someone with even 1/99th part "black" "blood" to be black (B. Williams 1989) (paralleling the "not a drop" fantasies of elite Guatemalans). In Guatemala and much of Latin America, despite the sense that a lineage can be stained by mixing blood, it is widely held that an influx of whiter blood can *improve* a "lower" race. Robert Stutzman describes this process, known as *blanquemiento,* as "a putative lightening or 'whitening' of the population in both the biogenetic and cultural-behavioral senses of the term *blanco.* The cultural goals, the society, and even the physical characteristics of the dominant class are taken by members of that class to be the objective of all cultural, social, and biological movement and change" (1981: 49). This belief informs the practice of encouraging immigration from Northern European countries. Supposedly the backwardness of the Indian, and thus of Guatemala, can be combated through importing superior races. These understandings deeply inform both ladin@ and indigenous senses of self and life choices. In turn, the Mayan movement is a major challenge to this hierarchical calculus.

Identity Is Political: Reversing Ladinization,
Reverse Racism, Mestizaje

Although indigenous rights activities have been going on for some four hundred years (Grandin 2000, Martínez Peláez 1985), in the late 1980s and early 1990s Guatemala experienced an explosion in organizing around what began then to be called Mayan cultural rights. This was partly a way of working differently from the revolutionary movement (in order to organize without being killed), partly the result of a political economic shift that created a critical mass of educated indigenous men and women, and partly the incitements of the Columbus Quincentennial (Cojtí Cuxil 1991, 1995, Menchú Tum 1998, Raxche' 1996). One need only glance at the peace treaty signed in December 1996 and its Accord on Indigenous Rights and Identity, stop by the busy offices of COPMAGUA, which is implementing those accords, or walk down the street in Guatemala City full of Mayan women proudly wearing *traje* (traditional Mayan clothing) to get a sense of the effectiveness of Mayan identity politics in the past few years. Recent U.S. scholarship on Guatemala reinforces this view. It is not always clear from our work that Guatemala is at least half ladin@. One aspect of Mayan struggles is to prove that ladinization is reversible. Even if you exhibit the cultural marks of "being" a ladin@— business suit, Spanish-speaking, white-collar worker, etc.—you can still choose to *be* Maya.[16] And, even if you "really are" ladin@, you can acknowledge your Mayan heritage as "Maya-ladin@." Although most state functions and the means of production remain in the hands of wealthy ladinos, one ladino friend calls the Mayan movement "the Reconquest."

While he is joking, it is not hard to find resentment and defensiveness in many ladin@ reactions: "It is a finger in the wound," "it will lead to race war, the Yugoslavization of Guatemala," are comments I've heard. Similarly, Charlie Hale documents a growing trend of ladino@s accusing the Maya of "reverse racism" (1999c). In 1998 the ex-guerrilla commander Pablo Monsanto publicly warned of an impending "race war," paralleling comments from state and army officials. In May 1999 the referendum on whether to add specific indigenous rights to the constitution raised similar fears. Vast amounts of money, air time, print space, pulpit sermonizing, and gossip hours were spent convincing ladin@s and Maya that a "yes" vote would bring the war back, encourage Indian men to sleep with white women, and make lynch-mob justice the law of the land. The "no" vote won, but the fact that the "yes" won in all the highland indigenous areas highlighted the very geographic and ethnic (or is it racial?) divisions many ladin@s fear (Warren 2002).

The response of many thoughtful progressive and revolutionary ladin@s (in and out of the state) is to encourage identification with the mestiz@, a category of biological origin, but socially understood to lie *between* the Indian and the ladin@—bridging that gap (Morales 1999). Mestizaje resists the oligarchic racializing of the indigenous body by relying on an undifferentiatable body and encourages the acceptance of one's indigenous heritage (both "blood" or genetic, as well as cultural). Casaus Arzú describes the ladin@s who so vehemently reject their (obvious, by looking at them) indigenous blood, as lacking an identity of their own, as being defined only through negativity. In contrast, she finds that among those who call themselves "mestizo" "their identity seems more consolidated and their consciousness of being mestizo is fully assumed" (Casaus Arzú 1992: 216).

This mestiz@ pragmatism is voiced in many sectors, from former radicals writing in the national press to social scientists and government officials. In fact, the newly elected president, representing the party associated with genocide in the early 1980s, deploys the mestiz@ discourse and claims to have been a sympathizer with the URNG. The race-thinking of mestizaje resonates with the modernization narrative, as well as with U.S. anthropology on Guatemala—which has insisted since the 1940s that there are no races (Smith 1999)—and with the notion that the "real" divide in Guatemala is elsewhere, between classes, for example. As a progressive response to genocidal violence, mestiz@ discourse reacts against ancient race prejudice, which continues to weigh on the minds of the living, but can be shucked off in favor of more "modern" sensibilities. In this sense the categories of ladin@ versus mestiz@ take on a temporal aspect. The ladin@ is a mestiz@ who still refuses to acknowledge he or she is mixed with, rather than non-, indigenous. Thus ladin@ is an older, less efficient mode of being in the world, caught up in an outmoded "symbolics of blood"—believing in the Mongolian spot or the "improving" qualities of white blood in the calculus of "blanquemiento." The mestiz@ is more modern, flexible on personal choice, maximizing economic networks, and rational regarding romantic entanglements, more in the mode of an "analytics of sexuality."

Andrés Cus, a Mayan activist, told me that Mayan men tend to disappear into the ladino population. "Without these markers—*caites* (sandals), the belt, the hat, even a little piece of *traje*—you don't even see that they are Maya." The joke in the epigraph about the difficulty of distinguishing between ladino and Indian is similar: "What is an Indian? A ladino with no money." The "fact" that raciological optics fail in Guatemala is used as proof for the mestiz@ antiracist alternative promulgated by many modernizing, progressive activists, as well as by nationalists, state officials, and U.S. academics like myself desirous of rescuing the racially marked body from genocide. As a gringa haunted by the seemingly insuperable blood-base of U.S. race-thinking, I find the unfixedness of this discourse—identity as cultural, political, agency, full rather than constitutional, a priori, essential—to be appealing. But *is* raciological thinking left behind by these discourses? Or is it preserved, and is its allure central to the differently configured hopes for peace in postwar Guatemala?

On the one hand, a "race" hierarchy *is* maintained in mestiz@ discourse, as Wahneema Lubiano reminds me (personal communication). Its antiracist allure presupposes mestizaje, not Mayanness, as the goal. While some ladin@ may claim to think like a Maya even though they don't have indigenous blood, I have not found many willing to accept the Mayan invitation of reverse ladinization.[17] Mestizaje's "fix" of antiracism still fixes a certain fundamental divide.

And yet mestizaje within Guatemala pivots on a cross-cutting fundamental divide at the global level. Latin American nationalist and revolutionary discourses have traditionally deployed a notion of mestizaje in order to differentiate themselves as peoples of color against *white* aggressors, including internal elites and external (read gring@) interventions. Given Guatemala's extremely disadvantageous position in the world system and its history of external intervention (including the promised package of one billion dollars now that the peace agreement is signed), I find an analysis that highlights this antagonism in order to empower resistance and fix it to be a good thing. This forms one link between the state and revolutionary discourses, which I'd like to continue to read through notions of race as productive, not only repressive. In the next section I turn from the ludicrous (laughable from incongruity), melting work I've been doing here, of trying to fix "race" and the politics of difference, to another war over "nature." Is she Lamarckian or Darwinian?

Remarks on Lamarck: State Power over Death and Life

The Guatemalan state clearly has enormous power over death, killing and disappearing over 200,000 people since the early 1960s. The war has been denounced as genocidal and ethnocidal against "the Maya," although I'm arguing we have to think carefully about what we assume to be the *genos* (race, species, kind, origin) or *ethnos* (people, nation) under attack. Are we positing an already existing solid identification with a presumed biological component? Or has something like "subversion" taken on biological characteristics in the mind of the military state? The war targeted primarily ladin@s in the 1960s and both ladin@s and indigenous people in the 1970s and 80s, attempting to purify "down to the last seed" according to army officials (Falla 1984). Repeatedly army spokespeople insist that the army's plan was not genocide (unless "communism" is considered a genotype). The fundamental division may have been between "subversives" and decent people, but drawing on a biological lexicon. In this sense, racism is not necessarily about (although sometimes it is) ladin@s or Indians but is "woven into the weft of the social body" (Stoler 1995: 69). This is the creepy raciology of the joke about Rigoberta Menchú's blood type being URNG+.

But the Guatemalan state also wields power over life. Even at the height of the state repression in the early 1980s, horrific violence was wedded to "pastoral power," and the current Guatemalan government deploys a huge range of funds, development projects, support for Maya cultural rights, and other forms of both co-opting and supporting "life" (see Nelson 1999a, Wilson 1995). I first started thinking about this "biopower" of the Guatemalan state (which I had previously viewed only through the repressive hypothesis) when I was conducting interviews at the Ministry of Culture and Sports in 1992. A number of state workers there railed against the "unnatural" pairing of sports with "culture" (which was supposed to include both "high culchah" such as ballet and orchestras and "anthropological" forms such as folk and indigenous culture). In trying to understand this apparent anomaly I found what may be precisely what Foucault urges we look for in racial coding: how racial discourses are righteous because they profess the common good and disqualified accounts. One such account is early-twentieth-century neo-Lamarckian eugenics, which may resurface in the Culture Ministry and in other state attempts to repair the body politic.[18]

Nancy Leys Stepan suggests that early-twentieth-century biology in Latin America tended to be neo-Lamarckian, that is, acquired traits are inherited. To explain the giraffe's long neck Lamarckians say that the individual endeavor of stretching in one generation is passed on, leading, after several generations, to the giraffe of today. In junior high biology I was taught to giggle at this explanation and to prefer the random workings of natural selection. While discarded for Darwinian theory in Euro-America, Stepan suggests that Latin American neo-Lamarckians saw progressive possibilities denied by social Darwinism, which sees poverty, criminality, and other forms of "degeneration" as genetically determined, racially fixed. Neo-Lamarckianism was linked to hopes for progress through *state intervention* in sanitation, hygiene, and family and reproductive health. The doctors, activists, and state officials involved in the "hour of eugenics" linked "general hygiene, anti-alcohol campaigns, sports education [aha!], a minimum-wage law, and a reduction in the cost of living" (1991: 100) to improving the miserable conditions of their nation's citizens.

Neo-Lamarckian eugenics discourses are biopolitical in Foucault's sense, contending that the collective body should manage life. They are also raciological in their reliance on notions of descent. They legitimate interventions that improve social conditions and strengthen both individual and social bodies, since advances are passed on through the blood, improving the national body politic as a whole. In Guatemala the state has played a major role in this struggle for the common good against both internal and external enemies. External aggression takes the form of military, political, and economic intervention, but it also attacks through aesthetico-scientific criteria. Euro-American Social Darwinism blamed Latin American "backwardness" on the degeneracy caused by mixed unions or "miscegenation" (Young 1995). "As evidence that 'halfbreeds' could not produce a high civilization, anthropologists pointed to Latin Americans who, they claimed, were now 'paying for their racial liberality' . . . the 'promiscuous' crossings . . . had produced a degenerate, unstable people incapable of progressive development" (Stepan 1991: 45). The eugenics developed in Latin America in response to these racist dismissals emphasized nurture rather than nature (or maybe a different nature), and the importance of a collective antidote.

The Guatemalan state suffers a legitimation crisis, riddled with impunity, accused of genocide, rife with corruption, abuse, and deadly force. And yet it plays the legitimizing neo-Lamarckian role of intervening in social life, responsible (despite neoliberal pressures) for health, food, education, sports, development work, and general improvements in the individual and collective body.[19] Enfolded here is a promise of future improvement because this work is tied not only to "politics" or "culture" (and sports) but to type (although for Lamarckians "nature" is malleable and improveable) and to descent.

So how do these policies in favor of life bring so much death? Perhaps it is the unfixed, pivoting position of the state on two fundamental divides: the internal and the external. If developing the national body politic is understood to depend on free trade, direct foreign investment, loans, or credit ratings (for example, if a minimum-wage law conflicts with attracting global capital through promises of cheap labor) then perhaps "subversion" and instability are seen as a threat to the life of the whole.[20] Racism, Foucault argues, should be understood as the constant war against threats to the health and happiness of the body politic, and it promises a common good. "It establishes a *positive* relation between the right to kill and the assurance of life. It posits that 'the more you kill . . . the more you will live'" (Stoler 1995: 84). Perhaps this is why people were convinced to participate in counterinsurgency. In part they were forced, through the implacable violence of scorched earth and mass murder, but they were *also* convinced, through the contradictory pastoral actions of a state that could allow them to think they were acting for the common good. It is a bigger project than this essay to think about this simultaneity and contradiction, but we must try to diffract these actions through the preserved possibilities, the refolded surfaces that join state biopower with lived experience, rather than fix a fundamental divide between victim and perpetrator.

The postwar Guatemalan state is increasingly a site and stake of struggle for many Maya and former revolutionaries, and I think neo-Lamarckianism is a "preserved possibility" that animates people to turn to it, to struggle over it, and to kill for it. Current struggles over implementing the peace accords might be seen as a raciology, not necessarily targeted against Indians, but as a productive technique.

Re: Marx on Lamarck

"Race has not always been what we might assume, a discourse forged by those in power, but on the contrary, a counter-narrative, embraced by those contesting sovereign notions of power and right, by those unmasking the fiction of natural and legitimate rule . . . for Foucault this polyvalent mobility . . . critically accounts for the nature of modern racism and the sustained power invested in it"—Ann Laura Stoler

Revolutionary discourse may also draw on neo-Lamarckian raciology, biopolitically promising a common good and joining the life (and death) of the individual to the life of the nation and the species. The left (Maya and ladin@) also refuses to view misery and poverty as genetically determined, and the guerrilla struggle seems transfused with a grammar of race in Foucault's sense, which provided the moral authority to defend the social body. This is not racism as unthinking abjection of a phenotypically marked body, it is a grammar of folding and vacillating differentiations, a discursive tactic that can map onto social classes and nations, as well as "races." In all those divisions it "establishes a *positive* relation between the right to kill and the assurance of life" (Stoler 1995: 84). Here again Guatemala's internal divide pivots on the global fission between "underdeveloped" (brown) Guatemala and (white) first-world privilege. And again the simultaneous and contradictory raciology of progressive discourses of mestizaje comes into play.

Mestizaje promises antiracist unification at the same time that uneven development and dependency theory (Amin 1974, Cardoso and Faletto 1979, Gunder Frank 1967) challenge capitalist assumptions of national development once internal differences are assimilated. Instead, relations of dependency hemorrhage off the vital components necessary for integral development. These theories powerfully legitimate revolutionary organizing by showing that the body politic will not naturally mature and that poverty is not the result of some inherent weakness (like degeneracy based on interbreeding). Instead, "backwardness" is caused by Guatemala's unnatural insertion into the world system of unequal exchange, a relation that can be changed through struggle. The revolutionary conviction that it's about class and the global divide, not race, offers a very powerful "cultural" and political promise in response to genocide and the complexities of ethnic and national identification. It may also be animated by "subjugated knowledges" similar to the Lamarckian eugenics that fold into mestizaje discourse and state pastoral policies so powerfully. Antidependency praxis acknowledges that the body politic is wounded, not simply immature, and promises to heal it through unifying mass struggle. This "antiracist" denial of racial difference and racism, in support of class (and incipient national) unity draws on deep-rooted lexicons of progress and modernization.

However, Carol Smith (1992) suggests that while they reject liberal modernization theory, many Guatemalan leftists retain its notion of stages: the Maya must unify with poor ladin@s (proletarianize) before Guatemala can successfully resist dependency. This may explain the deep antipathy many progressives feel when Mayan cultural rights activists resist their invitation to class-based (and race via "mixing") unity. The Maya appear divisionary, blind to the links of poverty and mestizaje that unite the majority of Guatemalans, and all this just in the name of some esoteric "feathers and flourishes" cultural effluvia (B. Williams 1989: 435) rapidly becoming extinct in any case.

The lack of indigenous commanders in the URNG, the murder of indigenous villagers, as the CEH report remarked (and to which the U.S. press gave ample coverage), and the story, growing in popularity among some Mayan activists, that they were caught between two armies bolster Mayan and other critiques that the left is ladin@ and racist. In turn, it's hard for a gringa like me, with friends and investments in the left *and* the Mayan movement, to hear members of the URNG accusing the Maya of being racist. It's depressing to hear the comandantes warn of race war and to watch the left's political party self-destruct, in part over the participation of the Maya (a 1999 split left the fissioned parties woefully short of the votes needed for continued existence). How can I explain how these brave, thoughtful people, ladin@ and Maya, came to such straits, developed such *moronga* brains, even as they are struggling for life?

Re-Marking the Maya

The Mayan movement also refuses to accept that "backwardness" is inborn, and as such may fold in strands of neo-Lamarckian thinking. The robust and eloquent denunciations of neocolonialism and continuing racism in Guatemala are undergirded by horror at their effects on the Mayan body politic and its future. Mayan activists struggle against the loss of potential as children work grinding hours on the plantations, are denied education in their language, and are forced to amputate a part of themselves by wearing nontraditional clothes in order to attend schools. Language valorization, the right to culturally sensitive education, and to freedom from violence are about improving individual bodies and lives in the moment, but the larger goal, often clearly stated, is to revitalize a large entity, the Pueblo Maya. Much of the discourse around the Quincentennial focused on five hundred years of survival with the implied temporal dimension that, with struggle, this body politic would survive, healthy and happy, for many more rounds of the *katun* (the long count Mayan cyclical calendar).

There was already a division between *populares*—Mayan guerrillas and those working in alliance with popular organizations around labor, land, and human rights issues—and *culturales*—Mayans pushing for cultural rights like state support of indigenous languages, etc. (Bastos and Camus 1993, 1995) in the early 1990s. But the years of peace-treaty implementation have seen the widening of a "fundamental divide." In this rereading by Mayas, gring@s, and ladin@s, shared histories are erased and indigenous *populares* are often ignored, to leave all the leftists as ladin@ and all the ladin@s as racist, as Ms. Lux expressed. At the same congress where she was applauded, however, Juan Tinay, leader of the "popular" Maya organization CONIC (National Indigenous and Campesino Coordination) said, "Brother Mayans, make this struggle your own! Our divisions are terrible! Some Maya do not invite certain people to their meetings because they say, 'they're not Maya, they're *popular.*' But who has bled with the people? We have a reason for this struggle. We are risking our lives in a full-on struggle. The Maya are not at the margin of the class war!"

"Creating 'Biologized' Enemies Against Whom Society Must Defend Itself"

The theme of social war articulated in biopower provides the overarching principle that subsumes both *la lutte des races* and *la lutte des classes.*—Ann Laura Stoler

OK, I've regaled you with a range of "race" thinking in Guatemala, which is contradictory and often exists simultaneously in the same person. Clearly, in Guatemala as elsewhere (people's beliefs to the contrary), there's no such thing as "race" as a fixed visible marker of an unchanging essential identity.

Most Guatemalans, if pushed, seem pretty Boasian, acknowledging that identity is fluid and can change in a generation or two or "simply" through making certain choices.

I feel ludicrous as a gringa trying to understand race (whether one-drop rules or race improvement), because it tends to melt away. Yet the understanding that society is divided and fixed into ladin@ and indigenous and/or rich and poor and/or decent people and subversives and/or racist and antiracist, has *both* inspired struggles to fix injustice *and* had horrific material effects for which, at some level, genocide seems an adequate term. Just as the state seems to read subversive and "decent" as "biological" traits, so too the divisions between the poor and the elite or third world vs. imperial late capital may harden *moronga*-like into racism in Foucault's sense. The terms may vacillate but a fundamental division between those who may live and those who must die retains. Counterinsurgency war *and* revolutionary struggle may be animated by *unconscious* Lamarckian biopolitics—to improve the "blood" by taking the state and improving living conditions for the greater good of all.

So, was it a race war? or a class war? Both and neither. The war was and is *raciological*. The apparent fundamental divide—between race and class or between "there is race" and "there is no race" or between race and culture—itself *produces* "race-thinking." While I have been poking like a finger in the wound at what race "is" (for Guatemalans or gring@s), I have also tried to diffract rather than reflect it, by asking what "race" *does*. Swerving through Foucault's sense of biopolitical racism and neo-Lamarckian preserved possibilities for the common good, I see "race" offering fixes of hope for postwar Guatemala through notions of nature, blood, and descent into the future.

Gilroy reminds us that, even as we try to break away from it, " 'race' remains fissile material" (2000: 14). Foucault suggests that racism is not "an *effect* but a *tactic* in the internal fission of society into binary oppositions, a means of creating 'biologized' internal enemies against whom society must defend itself" (Stoler 1995: 59). Racism is not just the assignment of hierarchical value to a range of phenotypic expressions (hair, skin color, nose shape, etc.) but a grid of intelligibility, a grammar that is not necessarily about any particular group of people but a more generalized division within a body politic. Racism is not simply a negative or repressive discourse. "It establishes a *positive* relation between the right to kill and the assurance of life. It posits that 'the more you kill [and] . . . let die, the more you will live' " (Stoler 1995: 84, emphasis in original).[21]

A Modest Conclusion

Please don't misread this attempt to diffract Guatemalan race-thinking as simple relativism: well, since everyone who committed heinous crimes in Guatemala *thought* they were contributing to the common good, what else is there to say? This wouldn't bring us any closer to an analysis that tries to honor the struggles over memory and hope in postwar Guatemala. It would also hardly explain the continuing power of racism despite the reams of paper expended on obliterating it (Visweswaran 1998). Antiracism activists can argue till we're blue in the face that bodies, blood (including "blue blood"), populations, genes, etc. are all metaphors. The *cara de indio* or certificate of blood purity based on the O-negative type is no more "real" than blood type URNG+ or the claim that Indianness depends on your bank account. Yet how do we fix the real material effects of raciology on bodies and minds? Supplanting race with "culture," ethnicity, politics, or a neo-Lamarckian notion of "nature" as mobile and changeable, or smashing the irrational symbolics of blood with scientific truths, cannot resist the constantly morphing power of racism. In turn, reading racism as only negative and repressive easily turns into scapegoating bad people while I remain less tainted.

Here I return to the sense of reproach embedded in the ludicrous anthropological position that haunts me and Malinowski. The necessity for those of us in privileged positions to side with oppressed peoples can slip too easily into being redeemed by those peoples. This is an important caution David Stoll (1999) makes (then ignores). No one is outside racism's grid of intelligibility, and racism's terrifying power comes in part from people's sense that they are working *for* life. Without this understanding I am too often writing morality tales that *reflect* what I am trying to understand: reinscribing a fundamental divide in which only one heroic side deserves to live. While all subject formation comes from complex relations with otherness, I have to be careful that hopes of being part of a solution or fix don't fix or harden, *moronga*-like, into a raciology that is part of the problem. Struggles in Guatemala over memories of the war are deeply enmeshed in a global relation that includes anthropology. Without overestimating the impact of gring@s or social science, my writing and my "choice" of allies in Guatemala do change things. As the Mayan anthropologist Irma Velasquez Nimatuj (2000) asks, how much of the shift in Guatemala to seeing the conflict as a race war is related to gring@ anthropology and its raciology?

And I am left with another question. I have struggled to see the mechanisms of how subjugated knowledges make racial discourses righteous, even for the violent (but biopolitical) state. I have tried to expose the historic continuity of social war, of a fundamental divide that vacillates mightily (class, race, subversion, third world) over who is considered worthy of life and death. And yet this means that as I confront the overarching principle that articulates the war of races (which I abhor) I see that it is the same principle that articulates the war of classes and the late capitalist anti-imperial struggle (which I support). And here's the rub, of course. Like the Maya, the Guatemalan state, and the revolutionary left, and to the horror I'm sure of my junior high biology teacher, I think I'm a little neo-Lamarckian myself. If that means believing in improving everyone's life chances now through adequate nutrition, a comfortable home, safe and hygienic streets, and the chance to fully develop the mind and body. And I think I see "real" divisions in the world[22] (articulated in Seattle and Genoa more, I hope, than at the World Trade Center and Pentagon), which block these improvements to life. How do we fight this "full-on struggle" (as the Mayan activist Juan Tinay calls it) against the powers of death without it folding back onto grids of exclusion that can so easily vacillate into struggles against those who should be allies? I try, with these allies, to deracialize and denaturalize the politics of difference through "culture," *mestizaje*, class unity, etc., but are these cures actually pharmakons, poisonously retaining the sense of "social war," the fission into two parts, one of which must die (if only metaphorically)?

I wish I had an answer adequate to millennial new times. To work toward such a politics of difference we must keep in mind the productiveness and not just the repressiveness of power and remember that the self, as much as the sites and stakes of struggles, is a moving target. The word "ludicrous" means to play as well as to reproach (to get back to sports!) and what better time to switch our losing games?

Notes

Fieldwork for this paper was made possible through the generous support of Stanford University, the National Science Foundation, and Lewis and Clark College. I want to thank the audiences at the AAA session, UC-Irvine, Duke University, and CIRMA, where earlier versions were presented, especially Abigail Adams, Tani Adams, Carmen Alvarez, Teresa Caldeira, Marta Casaus Arzú, Marisol de la Cadena, Marcial Godoy-Anativia, Greg Grandin, Charlie Hale, Sarah Hill, Rodolfo Keffler, Wahneema Lubiano, Louis Herns Marcelin, Bill Maurer, Amanda Pop, Carol Smith, Luis Solano, Irma Velasquez Nimatuj, Kay Warren, Ken Wissoker, and the two anonymous reviewers for Duke Press. Thanks also to José Fernando Lara, Marcie Mersky, Ramón González Ponciano, Liz Oglesby, and Paula Worby, and profound gratitude to Avery Gordon. Special thanks to all the participants in the workshop on "Race,

Nature, and the Politics of Difference," especially Jake Kosek and Anand Pandian. The thanks owed to Donald Moore for his labors of love on many terrains are off the scale. Mark Driscoll always helps me think and he makes me live more—thanks!

1   In Guatemala and Southern Mexico the term "ladino" refers to nonindigenous people. The term "mestizo" may also be used.

2   "Ludicrous" can mean "laughably absurd," "to play," and "to rebuke."

3   Carol Smith argues that much of this anthropology sees itself as antiracist by insisting that neither races nor racism exist in Guatemala (1999).

4   I follow Paul Gilroy in using the term "raciology" to emphasize the *process* of racializing. I realize that the terms for this process are as fissionable and wobbly as their object, and I do not mean to disregard the range of critical positions developed elsewhere. Also, as Gilroy points out (but doesn't really fixate on), where there is race thinking, there is sex, and where there is mestizaje (race mixing) there is usually violence against women, especially women of color, as the plantation owner quoted below makes clear. This will not, unfortunately, be the focus of this paper (see Nelson 1999b, also Mallon 1996, de la Cadena 1996, Stoler 1995, Smith 1996, 1999).

5   Since 1985 I have spent close to five years in Guatemala investigating the causes and effects of the war.

6   There may be global parallels as primordial ethnic "hatreds," "terrorism," or the "clash of civilizations" replace the "Communist menace" as putative threats to Euro-American security and as justifications for punitive policing (Gordon and Newfield 1996) and aerial massacre.

7   I was reminded of the way "race" (social categories) influences how "nature" (physiognomy, anatomy, color, etc.) works during an exercise on the first day of my Introduction to Anthropology class. I asked the students what race they thought I was and most said "white." When I asked them how they knew this they threw out phenotypic marks like skin color and hair as well as my language and position of authority as a teacher. When I said, "What if I told you I have Native American heritage?" there was a wave of exclamations—"Of course!" "I knew it!" "You don't really look white." "I can see it now." When I said that this Native American blood is a Nelson family myth, confusion enveloped raciology.

8   I am borrowing from the feminist movement in Guatemala to use the gender-neutral @ rather than ladino/mestizo (masculine) or ladina/mestiza (feminine), gringo or gringa, where appropriate.

9   It is beyond the scope of this essay to trace the long history of postcolonial dialectics concerning race through the Euro-Americas (see Arenas Bianchi 1999, Graham 1990, Wright 1990). The notion that race is about black and white while brown is an ethnicity is clearly linked to plantation histories based on African slavery in some areas and indigenous and mestizo labor in others (González Ponciano 1997), but I don't know if this explains how "brown" is also racialized into a fundamental divide in Guatemala. The Atlantic Coast Garífuna inhabit a strange liminal space in the Guatemalan national imaginary due in part to their minority status and geographical isolation. Through struggle they were included in the Quincentennial protests and in COPMAGUA (see below). How are we to understand the scary metonymies of post–September 11 profiling that endanger all "Arab-looking" people, from "Caucasian" Turks, to Sikhs, South Asians, and Mexicans and allow the mass murder of Afghani civilians with almost no outcry in the United States?

10   In November 1999 the political party led by General Efraín Ríos Montt, accused of the worst human rights abuses of the war, was voted into power. While the general could not run for president of the nation, he won a congressional seat and serves as leader of the legislature. Of course, gring@s also face the uncanny return of murderous '80s regimes.

11   These include the murder of Bishop Juan Gerardi in April 1998 just days after he released the Catholic Church's truth commission report. Three army officials were found guilty of the murder in the spring of 2001.

12   New genetic technologies are trickling into folk knowledges through news coverage of their use in forensic anthropology—primarily to identify massacre victims.

13   This suggests a fundamental divide between those who identify themselves as white and an undifferentiated mass of mestiz@s, ladin@s, and indi@s. The former seem to cleave to a U.S.-style one-drop rule in which whiteness is threatened by miniscule menaces.

14   This is the weirdly utopic finish to a film I otherwise enjoyed, Warren Beatty's *Bulworth*. Although it enumerates the economic and political limits on African Americans' life chances, it ends with a booty call, encouraging such exuberant "miscegenation" that within a few years everyone will look alike and racism will have to disappear (he clearly hasn't been to Brazil!). In the film Beatty's character called this "affirmative racial deconstruction." Of course, it's an age-old story of a fifty-plus white dude getting it on with the nubile black babe at least twenty years his junior (hooks 1981).

15   Deborah Poole describes the visual economy of race in the Andean world (1997) in ways that resonate with the situation in Guatemala. Hale, too, describes mestizaje carrying "dauntingly multiple meanings . . . as elite ideology, subaltern identity, historical process, and theoretically-licensed banner of resistance (to name a few)" (1996a: 3).

16   Of course, this brings up all the sharp questions unsympathetic ladin@s raise: so what IS a Maya? Without a blood quantum tradition and with material goods at stake given the peace accords and international treaties that acknowledge collective rights, is it just a mystic sense of belonging? I explore elsewhere (2001) how these questions place enormous pressure on Mayan women to *be* traditional, cultural preservers, a link to the pre-Conquest past, precisely in order to legitimate these claims.

17   As I explore elsewhere (Nelson 1999a, 2001), in Guatemala a temporal bias also links Maya with tradition and the past and ladin@ with modernity and the nation's future. While this mix of race, time, and the other may seem a familiar and banal expression of supremacist thinking, I urge care with a too-quick dismissal of these attempts.

18   Gilroy also addresses the importance of sport in raciology. On my first research trips to Guatemala in 1985 and 1986 I spent time in the army-run resettlement areas called "model villages" where captured internal refugees were held. Part of the infrastructure that starving internees were forced to build if they wanted to receive U.S.-supplied food aid were playgrounds and soccer fields. Ladin@ army and government officials stationed there told me that one of their tasks was to teach the indigenous children how to play.

19   In Nelson 1999a I describe this as the "piñata effect"—everyone hits the state, but everyone expects it to give them treats.

20   The infamous 1994 Citicorps demand that the Chiapas rebels be liquidated if Mexico wanted to preserve financial stability undergirded by international "confidence" left the Mexican state pivoting between the demands for life made by the Zapatistas and those made by its insertion into transnational governmentality and discipline.

21 According to Stoler, Foucault is concerned with a general racial grammar, "what he carefully labels as a racial 'coding' that provided an "instrumental space, at once discursive and political' in which each group could infuse a shared vocabulary with different political meaning (DS: 77). . . . Second, he identifies not the end of one discourse and the emergence of another, but rather the refolded surfaces that join the two. Third . . . race is a discourse of vacillations. It operates at different levels and moves not only between different political projects but seizes upon *different* elements of earlier discourses reworded for new political ends. Fourth, the discourses of class and revolution are not opposed to the discourse of social war but constituted by it . . . The 'economic struggle of classes' and the 'natural fight of races' [are not] the two prominent 'ideologies' of the nineteenth century, for Foucault they are neither independently derived ideologies nor alternate 'persuasive views'; their etymology is one and the same" (Stoler 1995: 72–73).

22 *The Nation*'s alternative history of the century reminds us that in 1999 "census figures reveal that benefits of years of economic growth and booming stock market have accrued mainly to the richest 5 percent of the population, producing one of the highest levels of inequality of income and wealth in American history" (33).

PART TWO. Landscapes of Purity and Pollution

4. "There is a Land where Everything is Pure"

Linguistic Nationalism and Identity Politics in Germany[1]

Uli Linke

The theme of this chapter is linguistic nationalism. My analytic gaze is drawn to a particular phenomenon: German language politics. After political unification, the projected frontiers of the German nation, internal and external borders, the lines dividing the native from the foreign, are mapped through the medium of language. In a united Germany, identity politics has become language politics, a terrain marked by a fear of linguistic estrangement and a public preoccupation with preserving an authentic national interior: the *nation* is configured as a speech community of ethnic Germans. Central to my analysis is the political production of linguistic nationalism, a "nation form,"[2] which tends to legitimate itself through corporal metaphors.

Linguistic nationalism is embedded in quasi-mythic notions of the German nation as a language body—a closed linguistic corpus. An early metaphor of this national idiom is blood. In this chapter, I examine the cultural politics of a linguistic corporality, which defines that which is "German" as organic, natural, and pure. Language purism, which aims to preserve the integrity of an ethnoracial linguistic organism, is located on an imaginary landscape of intensely charged concepts: nation, nature, and race. My ethnographic evidence is drawn from a diversity of political fields: the citizenship debates, immigration policies, German language reform, and the formation of German literary societies, which render visible the phantasm of language purity and the fear of linguistic "otherness," themes I also examine historically.

Problematizing the National Imaginary

The formation of a united Germany posed a profound challenge: the creation of a single nation-state. Such a historical production of unity and sovereignty must anticipate, if not accommodate, the transformation of legal subjects into nationals (Linke 1997a). There are, however, different ways of "becoming national" (Eley and Suny 1996). But in all instances, as Etienne Balibar points out, the "individuals destined to perceive themselves" as nationals—as "members of a single nation"—have to be "brought mutually to recognize one another" within a national frontier (1995: 94). The process of German unification entailed the reinvention of a political community: the fabrication of a national imaginary—the articulation of a specific ideological form with ideal signifiers that could be transposed to and implanted at the threshold of the state (Anderson 1983). By what means could such a nation form be produced? And more importantly, as noted by Balibar (1995: 96), "how can it be produced in such a way that it does not appear as fiction"—an audacious fabrication—but as inevitable, "as the most *natural*" of processes? The production of nationhood, and the making of nationals, as in the case of German unification, required "ways of rooting" historically diverse "populations in a fact of 'nature'" (ibid.: 96–97). According to Balibar, there are two complementary routes to this: by language and by race. On occasion, these terms "operate together, for only their complementarity makes it possible for the 'people'"—the *nation*—"to be represented as an absolutely autonomous unit" (96). Moreover, "both express the idea that the national character . . . is immanent in the people"; both relativize and subordinate diversity in such a way that "the symbolic difference" between Germans and foreigners prevails and "is lived as irreducible" (96, 94). In other words, the *external* frontiers of the German state had to become *internal* frontiers, imagined both "as a projection and protection of an internal collective," enabling Germans as a people—as a nation—"to inhabit the space of the state" (95). The formation of a united Germany necessitated alternative ways of *thinking* the nation (Malkki 1995), whether by the "mere inculcation of political values" or the "sublimation of [an] ideal nation" (Balibar 1995: 94, 96). But, at the same time, this very process of nation-building ushered in a "naturalization of belonging,"[3] instilling among all legal subjects an irrevocable sense of allegiance to a natural community of kin.

German unification was accompanied by profound changes, including a resurgence of anti-Semitism, xenophobia, and racist nationalism. Although the collapse of the socialist regime in the German Democratic Republic and the opening of the Berlin Wall in 1989 were supported internationally, "the rapid unification of East and West Germany brought ambivalent reactions, especially from Germany's European neighbors" (Kurthen, Bergmann, and Erb 1997: 3). Western visions of an expansive German state evoked an apprehensive uneasiness on three fronts: (1) a growing fear of "the emergence of a new sense of nationalism" that would threaten Western democracies and promote a new era of "German assertiveness"; (2) concerns about "the political and economic dominance of a united Germany in the center of Europe"; and (3) "recollections of the devastating consequences of German national unification movements of the past" (ibid.). When a surge of violence against asylum seekers began in 1991 with pogromlike actions in eastern Germany, accompanied by media reports of neo-Nazi marches and a revival of right-wing solidarities, these "events were regarded as symptoms of dangerous developments" (ibid.: 4; see also Husbands 1991). Antirefugee riots, anti-immigrant street violence, the destruction of synagogues and Jewish cemeteries, the arson murders of Turkish and other immigrant families, and the firebombings of refugee housing all "seemed to confirm warnings of the political consequences of German unification" (Kurthen et al. 1997: 4): of revisionist history, anti-Semitism, racial violence, *völkisch* cultural traditions, and nationalist identity rhetoric.

The intensity of antiforeign sentiments after unification articulated a perceived threat to German ethnic identity and racial homogeneity (Jaschke 1993; Bergmann and Erb 1994; Rommelspacher 1997; Linke 1999a: 115–51; Linke 2001). The goal among some segments of the German population was to "reaffirm a supposedly ethnocultural homogeneity—as expressed in the slogan 'Germany for Germans' and the often repeated mantra 'Germany is not an immigration society' " (Kurthen et al. 1997: 5–6), thereby promoting an ethnoracial concept of nationhood and identity (Martin 1998: 36; Linke 1995). The anxieties of everyday life (the strain and cost of unification, a deepening economic recession, inflation, rising taxes, unemployment, and housing shortages) have excavated collective mentalities and memories of a national community of ethnic Germans.

What were the political responses to this crisis of identity formation? Preoccupied with gatekeeping, border guarding, and national armament, the German government failed to "reform not only the asylum law but also citizenship, naturalization, and immigration" (Erb 1997: 215). German politicians were persistent in their refusal to "improve the protection of minorities through detailed anti-discrimination legislation" (ibid.; see also Kurthen and Minkenberg 1995: 175). The political response to the challenges of immigration took form through counterproductive government campaigns "against the perceived abuse of the liberal right of asylum by so-called economic refugees" (Erb 1997: 215; see also Linke 1997b). Instead of changing structural inequities, applicants for political refugee status were criminalized (Mattson 1995). Portrayed as parasites, freeloaders, and welfare spongers, ethnic minorities were treated as a threat to the nation (Linke 2001: 416–22; Jäger 1993; Chavez 2001). The political instrumentalization of antiforeign sentiments by mainstream democratic parties promoted an ethnic fortress mentality: the closing of national borders, the reduction of the resident alien population, and the limiting of immigration, in particular that of refugees in 1994 (Sen 1999; Martin 1998). A political climate that encouraged a renaissance of nationalism, ethnicization, and racism effectively impeded the implementation of programs designed to safeguard the legal status of foreign nationals and their offspring born in Germany. Since unification, there have been no significant changes in social or legal policy to offset the increasing marginalization of foreign residents: immigrants and refugees are forced to the fringes of society through stigmatization, ethnic violence, stringent administrative controls, cumbersome bureaucratic practices, and a repressive system of civil justice.[4]

In a world characterized by increasingly flexible markets, mobile populations, global economies, and supranational alliances, "the problematic concept of *nation* has been used to deny immigrants the right of full political participation and easy access to citizenship" (Erb 1997: 215; see also Hoffmann 1994: 46–47). Nurtured by an understanding of nationhood as a homogenous community based on common descent (*Abstammungsgemeinschaft*), the formation of a united Germany was complicated by a corporal imaginary. German perceptions of the "national order of things" (Malkki 1995) rest on metaphors of the human organism and the body. Among the potent metaphors for the national community is blood (Brubaker 1992). German nationality is imagined as "the flow of blood"—a unity of substance (Linke 1999b, 2001; Williams 1995). Such metaphors are thought to "denote something to which one is naturally tied" (Anderson 1983: 131). Thinking about the German nation takes the form of origins, ancestries, and racial lines, which are *naturalizing* images: a genealogical form of thought.

Apparently exempt from critical reflection in political debates, the judicial field of German nationality has rendered *normal* a modern conception of race. The citizenship law of the Federal Republic of Germany determines national membership through the idiom of descent, as expressed by the Latin term *ius sanguinis*, "power/law of blood" (Basic Law, article 116a; Senders

1996; DeSoto and Plett 1995). Enacted in 1913—and still in effect today—the German citizenship law permits, and even encourages, the "nation's racial closure" (Frankenberg 1999: 11). In other words, immigrants born in Germany do not automatically acquire citizenship status. German nationality is configured by an understanding of a community of blood/descent, shaped by an "ethnonational" perception of statehood (Brubaker 1992). Deeply embedded in Germany's imperial history, this blood-principle of citizenship is defined by racial premises, which were established at the turn of the twentieth century to exclude colonial subjects from inheritance and voting rights (Wildenthal 1994, 1997). In the Weimar Republic, just after the First World War, the blood-right of citizenship was to protect the German nation from "the radical invasiveness of 'Turkish' ethnics" (Frankenberg 1999: 11).

Beginning in the early 1920s, German media campaigns amplified the political discourse against outsiders: protofascist military phantasms of a communist insurgence were synchronized with popular anti-Semitic sentiments. By tapping into the national imaginary of blood, Jewish refugees and immigrants from Eastern Europe were perpetually described as an "inundating flood," a "surging tide," an "amalgamating danger," a "teeming mass," a "deluge of blood" that threatened the survival of the nation (Gerhard 1994: 138–44; Maurer 1986). German politicians wanted to implement defensive measures by a closure of borders: by shutting "the floodgate" against Eastern Jews; by "slowly expunging Jewish blood" from the indigenous German population; and by "purging the national body from the blood of foreign Jews," because it "contaminated and poisoned," "festering and feeding" on "the living body of German cities" (Gerhard 1994: 140, 141). The symbolic coding of Jewish immigrants as liquid contagion produced a public imaginary that promoted the erasure of difference. Once adopted as law, the idea of the modern German nation as "a reservoir of blood" was rendered uncontestable (Bloch 1990: 90). But such a concept of nationality, which "enunciates the proposition" that all citizens are interrelated by blood or "should constitute a circle of extended kinship," promotes a logic of racial ethnicity (Balibar 1995: 100). The population politics of the Third Reich document how this logic of heredity and blood was operationalized in the program of racial hygiene and genocide.

Nationality and Language: Citizenship as a Flexible Commodity

How can immigrants become German citizens when nationality is rooted in descent by blood? In 1998 this question became a much-contested issue, when the leftist coalition government made a concerted effort to reform the country's naturalization practices: Chancellor Schröder wanted "to create an open society, with flexible borders, to make Germans capable of joining the European Union" (Darnstädt 1999: 30). The nation's racial closure was perceived as incompatible with the requirements of global economic systems, shifting markets, mobile populations, and transnational political alliances. Nevertheless, this attempt to reform the German citizenship law by eliminating the blood-principle of nationality proved unsuccessful (Böckelmann 1998: 49; Böhm 1999: 13–16). A subsequent proposal, introduced by liberal democrats (FDP) under the heading "dual citizenship for children," seemed more palatable, because it accentuated the foreignness of foreigners (Hommel 1998; Darnstädt 1999: 30–32; Bischoff 1999: 1). Dual citizenship or binationality was to create a hyphenated identity for young immigrants by appending German citizenship to that of national origin.

The proposal affirmed the privileged status of native-born Germans. As citizens by hereditary sanguinity, German nationals retained their membership in an ethnoracial community of blood. But immigrants, perceived as transient bodies in geopolitical space, merely gained an identity supplement. Dual citizenship, acquired by *ius soli* (territory/residence), was read as a signifier of alterity, marking a life course of displacement and uprootedness. The legal reform instituted a two-tiered, caste-like system of national belonging: by blood (descent) and by space (residence). One native-German, based on consanguinity, which is presumed natural, authentic, and permanent; the other foreign-German, based on territorial affinity, which is deemed artificial, inauthentic, contractual, and impermanent. Given the underlying racial paradigm, it seemed only logical that the citizenship status of immigrant children be temporary: in its current form, German nationality can be abrogated on the child's entry into adulthood (Bischoff 1999). Under the impact of globalization, the hyphenated citizen is treated as a *flexible* commodity: German nationality is issued on loan; the German passport is granted to immigrants as a revocable entitlement.

Such a regime of flexibility, as it pertains to borders, bodies, and markets, has been termed the modus operandi of late capitalism (Harvey 1989; Jameson 1981; Martin 1994; Basch et al. 1994; Clifford 1997; Appadurai 1996). Moreover, in response to globalization, as Aihwa Ong observed, "governments [like Germany] develop a flexible notion of citizenship and sovereignty as strategies" for accumulating "capital and power," albeit within "particular structures of meaning" that tend to impose cultural "limits to such flexible productions and subjectivities" (1999: 6, 18). In the German

154   Uli Linke

case, the concept of citizenship is patterned by a cultural logic of blood and race: sentiments of allegiance and identity are fashioned by organic modalities, and not by a politics of space. Genealogical imaginaries are deterritorialized political formations. Under the impact of global capitalism, such machinations of citizenship persist as a stronghold against the perceived effacement of borders and the failure of the territorially bounded state to restrict immigration. German nationality, which affirms the cultural logic of a *natural* community by blood, stands opposed to a "flexible notion of citizenship" (Ong 1999), which bolsters the judicial logic of space in the case of foreign subjects. In a united Germany, *natural* citizenship enshrines claims of allegiance to a community of blood; "*flexible* citizenship,"[5] which is treated as a counterfeit form, accommodates claims of state sovereignty over territories, markets, and borders. The disjuncture between these imaginaries of citizenship bears the imprint of competing routes to governing under global capitalism: state-making and nation-building.

In a united Germany the struggle between such disparate modes of governance had a decisive impact on border matters, resulting in ever more drastic restrictions on access to citizenship. In response to the mandates of unification, and in seeking to reconcile the uneven recruitment of subjects by regimes of blood and of space, German politicians began to redefine the frontiers of the nation-state in terms of linguistic practices. Issues of sovereignty and nationhood were recast by visions of the German body politic as a discrete community of native-language speakers. This premise of linguistic unity was transferred to the threshold of nationality: Germanness and citizenship were to be configured through the idiom of language. The transformation of political subjects into nationals should now require an act of performance: speaking German. Such a formation of linguistic nationality, although intended to promote inclusion, became a mechanism of segregation and exclusion.

In the accompanying public debates, the criteria of eligibility for "naturalization" (*Einbürgerung*) were linked to language: the immigrants' knowledge of German. Conservative Christian Democrats insisted that applicants for citizenship status needed to document their "integration into German society" by having achieved an "attestable level of language fluency" (FAZ 1999: 6). Potential immigrants, according to this proposal, were expected to enroll in mandatory German-language courses, preferably in their home countries; after completing a minimum of 720 hours of language training, the applicant's linguistic competence was to be certified by means of a final examination (Ruf 2000). The working draft of the dual-citizenship proposal likewise insisted on "sufficient familiarity with the German language" as a prerequisite for naturalization (*Tagblatt* 1999a: 1; Finke 1999: 1). The primary aim was to "promote the integration of foreigners by offering German-language courses. Foreigners completing such courses could receive 'integration certificates' that entitled them to receive unlimited . . . work permits" (Martin 1998: 36–37). Both the left and the right regarded a formal evaluation of the applicants' "mastery of German" as indispensable. Liberal Social Democrats wanted to test the linguistic competence of resident aliens. According to Ekkehard Wienholtz, interior minister of Schleswig-Holstein, a written examination to determine whether foreigners had acquired "sufficient mastery of German" was to be mandatory (*Tagblatt* 1999b: 2). Otto Schilly, federal minister of domestic affairs, suggested in his original draft proposal that foreigners should be denied German citizenship if "communication with them proved impossible" and "if they were unable to make themselves understood in German" (*Tagblatt:* 1999b: 2; John 1999). The conservative state of Bavaria demanded a "written spelling test" for citizenship applicants (*Tagblatt* 1999c: 2; Guyton 1999: 2). In its final form, as ratified by Germany's parliament, the legal provision defines "German language fluency" as an imperative for naturalization (*Tagblatt* 1999d: 1).

This emphasis on linguistic nationality might explain why German lawmakers agreed to extend the right of citizenship only to children: second-generation immigrants can "inhabit the national language and through it the nation itself" (Balibar 1995: 99). The linguistic construction of national identity "possesses a strange plasticity," for a language community "is by definition *open*": ideally it "assimilates anyone, but holds no one"; and although it continuously absorbs new members, it "produces the feeling that it has always existed" (ibid: 98, 99). Linguistic nationality fabricates "a collective memory which perpetuates itself at the cost of an individual forgetting of 'origins'" (ibid.: 99). This formative power of linguistic systems, which provides centralized regimes with the capacity to absorb and assimilate a diversity of subjects, seems to exhibit a democratic propensity. But such a making of nationals is inherently coercive: through the medium of language, and its strategic deployment in citizenship and immigration politics, the nation-state engrafts a hegemonic memory of Germanness.

Linguistic Ethnicization:
Language Competence and Racial Hierarchies

Language politics in a united Germany seeks to reinvigorate a fictive ethnicity of Germanness: the community instituted by the nation-state, that is, the population included by and dominated within its projected frontiers, is ethnicized through language. By imagining the German nation-form as a linguistic unity, social or political disparities can be "expressed and relativized as different ways of speaking the national language, which supposes a common code and even a common norm" (Balibar 1995: 97). The fact of this articulation of a predominantly linguistic ethnicity has obvious political consequences.

As diverse populations are nationalized, political ideology engrafts ethnic identity "in advance in a sense of [national] belonging," making it possible for "a preexisting unity to be seen in the state": it is one way, writes Etienne Balibar, "of rooting a historical population in a fact of 'nature' " (1995: 96–97). Thereby, the unity of a linguistic community appears naturally predestined: "The ideal of a common origin, projected back beyond learning processes and specialist forms of usage" (ibid.: 98), emerges as a metaphor for a common national sentiment: a fabricated linguistic nationalism.

But the problematic of German unification shows that a language community is not sufficient to produce ethnicity. Its historical specificity is affixed to a multitude of similar political institutions. Under certain circumstances, as in the case of a divided Germany, the same language may be used by different nations (Reiher and Läzer 1996; Ammon 1995, 1996). For language "to be tied down to the frontiers of a particular" national form, it requires "an extra degree of particularity": a "principle of closure, of exclusion" (Balibar 1995: 99). This principle is evident in the racialization of language.

The ability of foreign-born individuals to increase the range of their linguistic competence, and to thereby become German nationals, is guarded by a racial imaginary of segregation and prohibition. Access to language learning is severely restricted. Language politics in a unified Germany is marked by a resurgence of hypernationalism: racial ethnicity produces a fortress mentality that seeks to reduce membership by a closure of linguistic borders. Public language programs for immigrants are offered, but the eligibility for enrollment is determined by origin and residence status, thereby inducing "a terribly constraining ethnic memory" (Balibar 1995: 98): former labor migrants with their families and offspring, recognized political refugees, naturalized immigrants, resident aliens, and ethnic German resettlers are treated differentially. The categories of foreignness and ethnic difference are constructed by variable degrees of linguistic access. For instance, applicants for political asylum, even recognized refugees, are officially forbidden to take German classes: "No public efforts must be made to promote the assimilation or integration of individuals, whose long-term presence in Germany has not been confirmed" (Kabis-Alamba 1999: 18). Certain foreign populations are to remain culturally excluded and linguistically isolated (Geiger 1991; Bade 1992). This policy of linguistic segregation for refugees stands in stark contrast to the nation-state's treatment of other foreign-born individuals. Ethnic German resettlers from Russia or Eastern Europe are granted unconditional language access: legally defined as nationals, based on the principles of filiation and *ius sanguinis,* the blood-right of extended kinship, their linguistic integration is supported by a multitude of separate government budgets. Resident aliens or naturalized immigrants, however, can enroll in German-language courses only if they meet certain conditions. The decisive factor is their national origin: citizens of the European Union states or former German contract-states (Turkey, Yugoslavia, Morocco, Tunisia, the Philippines, Angola, Mozambique, and Vietnam) are permitted to enhance their German language competence (Kabis-Alamba 1999: 18). But even in these cases, the training is restrictive: the duration and intensity of language programs varies with each category of the ethnic register.

The "openness of the linguistic community is an ideal openness" (Balibar 1995: 103): its permeability is in reality controlled by the official German phantasm of hereditary ethnic substance. And the greater the state's intervention in the foreigners' access to German, "the more do differences in linguistic . . . competence function as 'caste' differences, assigning different 'social destinies' to individuals" (Balibar 1995: 103–4). Under those conditions, strategies of linguistic exclusion come to be associated with "forms of a *corporal* habitus" (Bourdieu 1984) that "confer on the act of speaking," in its particular, idiosyncratic traits, "the function of a racial or quasi-racial mark" (Balibar 1995: 104): "'foreign' accents," degrees of language competence ("broken" German), unaccustomed and nonstandard "styles of speech, language 'errors' or, conversely, ostentatious 'correctness'" instantly designate a nonnative speaker as "belonging to a particular population and are spontaneously interpreted as reflecting a specific origin" and a judicial or "hereditary" status (104). The production of Germanness thus also entails, following Balibar, a "racialization of language" and a "verbalization of race."

Linguistic Nationalism:
Foreign Words as "the Jews" of Language

In the 1990s, an era marked not only by the forging of a united Germany but also the constitution of the European Union (with its sublimation of borders, common currency, and integrated market economy), the sense of belonging to a linguistic community reemerged as a symbol of Germanness, invigorated by the myth of ethnic unity through language purity. German ethnic racialization is driven by a purging of language.

Since German unification, during the last decade of the twentieth century, a diversity of literary societies have come into existence to reclaim and fortify the nation's linguistic boundaries: under the impact of global capitalism and European integration, which gave rise to hybrid forms of multilingual communication, Anglicization, and traffic in foreign vocabularies, the survival of the German language is deemed threatened (Janich 1997; Ammon 1997; Trabold 1993). The rapid formation of literary societies attests to the reinvigoration of a popular nationalism committed to the closure of linguistic frontiers: a desire to purge the national idiom—the "beloved mother tongue"—of contaminating foreign influences.

Most prominent is the "German Language Society" (*Verein Deutsche Sprache*): founded in 1997, it recruited over 16,000 dues-paying members in less than four years. The members, drawn from a broad social spectrum, stand united as "citizens for the preservation and cultivation of German" (*Verein* 1999). According to the society's official charter, the members are bound "to defend the self-esteem and dignity of all human beings, whose native tongue is German"; "to combat the amalgamation of German" and its "excessive inundation" by foreign words; and to protect the "cultural distinctness" and "survival of the German language" (*Verein* 2001a, 2001b). The movement's publicity campaigns, via the Internet, newspapers, and television, seek to implant in public consciousness a sense of linguistic ruin: the adulteration and corruption of the "national character" of German by the infiltration of foreign idioms (*Verein* 1999, 2001a). Media headlines, in both local and national papers, articulate the movement's concerns: "Battling Against Word Heretics"; "Safeguarding the German Language"; "Language Purification"; "We Speak German, Not English"; "The Shambles of Language"; "Against Language Trash"; "The Corruption of the German Language"; "Fighters for the Purity of German"; "Storm of Protest Against Foreign Words"; "The Foreign Subversion of Language Is Shameful"; "Language Abuse: A Society Fights Against the Flood of English Words"; "Against Language Colonisation"; "Protection Against Language Dirt"; "How French and English Expressions Are Seeping into the German Language"; "Bitter Resistance Against Foreign Words"; "Language Purging Instead of Stomach Ulcer": "The Flood of Plastic Words, Emptied of Meaning, Is a Danger"; "United in the Battle Against the Flash Flood of Superfluous Anglicisms"; "The Murder of Language"; "Pro German" (see *Zeitungsartikel* 1999; *Verein:* 1997, 1998, 1999, 2000, 2001).

In an effort to sustain media coverage and public support, the German Language Society has launched a series of initiatives: the establishment of local and regional chapters; the creation of a nationwide language forum; the production of Germanized glossaries and dictionaries; the bestowal of literary prizes and awards; and the administration of language tests. Moreover, in trying to gain recognition as a public-service advocate, the German Language Society has inaugurated a "linguistic consumer protection" program. Under this rubric, the language habits of major service sectors are scrutinized for potential assaults on the national idiom: the use of foreign words, especially Anglicisms, is rendered a public offense. The targets of inspection include the postal service, hospitals, funeral homes, airlines, train companies, and "German health insurance providers, German TV guides, German political parties, German travel agencies, German utilities, and German mail order companies" (*Verein* 2001d). The furor of the publicity scandals provoked by such language tests and linguistic consumer protection surveys has effectively placed an entire society on language probation: national allegiance is enforced by linguistic censorship; nationalization proceeds by the erasure of non-German vocabularies.

The ethnicization of language is enforced by other publicity campaigns. Since 1997, this movement of "language warriors" or linguistic purists regularly conducts nationwide media contests in search of "the most un-German word [*Unwort*] of the year," the "language heretic [*Sprachhunzer*] of the month," and "the language adulterer [*Sprachpanscher*] of the year" (Janich 1997: 81–82; *Tagblatt* 1999e: 1, 2000: 2; *Verein* 2001e).[6] The finalists, typically businesses, institutions, or public figures, are chosen on the basis of nationwide opinion polls; the protagonists are then put at the pillory to be publicly ridiculed or shamed on charges of language defilement (*Verein* 2001c, 2001e; Steinhoff 1999a: 56–60, 1999b; Nölkensmeier 1999). The fabrication of an ethnic Germanness invokes "the myth of a pure Ur-idiom" or linguistic Urform, "the ideal of the internally coherent and organic nature of language" (Levin 1985: 116). Linguistic nationalism supplants history and memory by recourse to organic images of a natural speech-community of Germans.

The sociologist Theodor W. Adorno, in a series of essays published in the sixties and seventies, subjected this notion of an organic language to critical analysis. His critique is unequivocal: "No language, not even the ancient folk-idiom [*Volkssprache*], is that into which restorative doctrines want to transform it, something organic, seemingly natural" (1961: 114). But for Adorno, the linguistic medium, the Germanness of language, remained an imperative of critical reflection. In an essay from 1969, titled *On the Question: "What is German?,"* Adorno's answer is: language. His answer "recast[s] . . . the question of nationality as a question of language and linguistic nationality" (Levin 1985: 111). Such a transposition of the problematic of nationhood into a query about "what is (the) German (language)?" successfully disentangles a critical discourse on language from the uncanny anathema of national character. Adorno's starting point is the decision to return to Germany after years of exile in the United States. "The decision," writes Adorno, "was hardly motivated simply by a subjective need, by homesickness. . . . There was also an objective factor. It is the language [and] characterizes more generally the relation of anyone's native tongue to a foreign language" (1985: 129, 130; 1969: 110, 111). The essay sets the stage for a prolonged analysis of Germanness and the linguistic boundaries that are fabricated to separate the foreign (*fremd*) from the native (*eigen*).

In Adorno's work, "the question of the *Fremdwort* [foreign word] is tied to the question of linguistic nationality . . . from the very start" (Levin 1985: 115). In his discussions about these words from foreign lands, "Adorno recounts how, as a child, he delighted in [their] 'exterritorial and aggressive' character which provided a refuge from the increasingly unavoidable German chauvinism of the period" (ibid; Adorno 1961: 115). For him, foreign words were verbal missiles—"arrows"—which he hurled at "assiduous patriots" and their programmatic concern with language purity: "Foreign words," Adorno recalls, "formed tiny cells of resistance against the nationalism of the First World War" (1961: 112).[7] Such a rebellious use of language became a means of reflexive disentanglement from German nationalist culture by a detour to the faraway worlds of other linguistic systems. But Adorno remembers these tactical ventures across a nation's linguistic borders not merely as an "index of alienation" (1974: 643). The tensive "distance between the *Fremdwort* [foreign word] and its [new] linguistic context" (Levin 1985: 115) can also be read as a sensual encounter, a source of pleasure: linguistic difference produces an enticing emotional charge. According to Adorno, this logic of feelings is enmeshed with the erotic appeal, the seductive allure of the foreign: "The early passion for non-German words resembles the desire for foreign, possibly exotic girls; the lure of an exogamy of language" (1961: 112). The public outrage against any entanglement with linguistic aliens seemed to be fueled by "this very love" and a "language that, in its words, was erotically charged" (ibid.). The sanguine nationalism of the period supplied the German idiom with a libidinous corporeality, thereby fastening the ideal of an immanently closed, organic language to the emotional fabric of a sexual and moral imaginary. Acts of linguistic border-crossing came to be seen as shameful and embarrassing: "Foreign words induced blushing, just like the mention of a beloved name kept secret. This emotion is treated with abhorrence by those national communities [*Volksgemeinschaften*] that long for a single-dish stew even in language" (Adorno: ibid.). Once placed within the affective domain of erotic taboos and phantasies, the use of foreign words evoked the same response as unpermitted acts of sexual transgression: the promiscuous, indecent, and lewd. Linguistic patriotism, forged by the moral commitment to an endogamous community of nationals, was successfully incorporated into the emotional censure-system of every German subject. During this process of inculcation, "becoming national" (Eley and Suny 1996) took on an ethnoracial charge. The mandate of linguistic purity was modeled on the political management of German bodies: a racist body politic that eventually "criminalized 'interbreeding'" and "the mixing of populations" (Balibar 1995: 103).

Adorno's primary interest, however, was focused on the "explosive power" (*Sprengkraft*) of alien words: their ability "to shatter the stultifying incarceration of human beings in the prisonhouse of preconstituted language" (1974: 640, 643). Words from foreign lands, Adorno emphasized, were tensive "vehicles of dissonance": they acted as tools, as weapons, that could be deployed in the battle against the presumed naturalness of language (1969: 116).[8] A "strategically placed" foreign word, through a shift in meaning and sound, could help destabilize, estrange, or "*specify* a semantic field. . . . In all these cases, it is the 'otherness' of the foreign word which enables it to perform in ways unavailable to any 'native' word" (Levin 1985: 115). According to Adorno, "Its crassness and contours, all that, which moves it out of the normal stream of language continuity, serves to bring forth precisely that . . . which is obscured by the inadequacies of habitual language use" (1961: 115). The German resentment toward linguistic aliens seems to be directed against this semantic potential of disclosure: the unwelcome exposure of the performative inadequacies of the national idiom.

The use of foreign words is provocative, estranging, and dangerous: in everyday speech, "unassimilated foreign words stand out" and provide the linguistic medium with an "affective tension," "a tendency toward a doubling of meaning" that breaks open and exposes the seemingly natural stratigraphy of language (Adorno 1961: 113). Through the relativizing radicality of such linguistic "otherness," writes Adorno, "the discrepancy between the foreign word and language can be enlisted in the service of truth" (115).[9] Through the use of the linguistically alien—which is a performance of untranslatability—the myth of a pure Ur-idiom can be unmasked. The foreign word "destroys the facade of naturalness in historical language": "Of this we are reminded by foreign words in German" (Adorno 1961: 116, 114). The German purist movement, with its relentless insistence on the organic nature of language, labors against this potential act of semantic violence, which is transported with the use of foreign words.

The fear of (hidden) linguistic aliens is conveyed by the distinction made in German between "foreign words" (*Fremdwörter*) and "loan words" (*Lehnwörter*). The loan word is "defined as a borrowed word of foreign origin which has become so assimilated in the course of time that its foreignness is known only to experts" (Levin 1985: 118). In this context, linguistic assimilation is regarded as a natural process of language incorporation whereby the distinctively alien phonetic morphologies are muted. Based on the presuppositions of the Romantic ideal of an organic history of language, German words are called "loan words" (*Lehnworte*) when the acoustic or rhythmic trace of their foreign origin is no longer apparent: these are "naturalized" (*eingebürgerte*) immigrant words, which "have obediently inserted themselves into the language body [*Sprachleib*] without seam and scar" (Adorno 1974: 640). According to the logic of this organic paradigm, the progressive continuity of language would take hold of even the "genuine foreign words" to steadily assimilate them to the prevailing linguistic conventions. But what are the consequences, Adorno asks, when "foreign words persevere in the linguistic space of speech," "where they, as foreign organisms [*Fremdkörper*], besiege the body of language?" (ibid.: 642, 643). The recognizable foreignness of the foreign word (*Fremdwort*) "raises the question as to whether other words might not be *Lehnwörter*" (loan words) or assimilated aliens, that is, linguistic strangers "in disguise," "and thereby casts aspersions on the 'purity' of the most seemingly 'native' words" (Levin 1985: 118). Those naturalized words of foreign origin or assimilated immigrants "appear with no indication of their foreignness and, for that reason, are all the more dangerous. The Nazis, not surprisingly, systematically eliminated foreign words from their literature and pedagogy from the very start" (ibid.). The practice of racial hygiene, as carried out by the Third Reich, was also applied to the linguistic medium. Debates about this campaign to purify language "began as early as May 1933" (ibid.). At a conference of state ministers, the "bastardization" of German was thematized by Wilhelm Frick, federal minister of domestic affairs, who saw in the use of "superfluous foreign words" a threat that "plainly endangered" the German language—"our mother tongue"—this "precious treasure," which was to be passed down from generation to generation "pure and unadulterated" (Noakes and Pridham 1974: 352; Michaelis 1964: 445–46).[10] In this context, we can begin to understand Adorno's chilling claim in *Minima Moralia*: "Foreign words," he wrote, "are the Jews of language" (1951: 141).[11]

The campaigns of racial hygiene and language purism were inextricably enmeshed under the reign of the Third Reich. But the dual emphasis on body boundaries and language barriers first emerged in conjunction with the heightened fervor of German national consciousness during World War I. In the preceding years, during the first decade of the twentieth century, there continued to appear a scatter of linguistic studies authored by researchers "for whom foreign words [were] not harmful invaders, who [had] to be deported at all cost, but useful guests to whom we are indebted with a sense of gratitude and who, in any case, have a right to be treated with decency" (Michel 1911: 431–32). Such explicit appeals for linguistic tolerance, however, also carried an ominous note. The protection of foreign words in their perceived role as "useful guests" or migrant laborers was highly opportunistic. Their asylum status was made contingent on the shifting currents of Germany's national interests and the prospects of cultural gain: the ability to harvest from the linguistic productivity of others a surplus of semantic value. Such acts of expropriation, according to modern economic principles, enhanced the symbolic capital of language, endowing the German speech community with the performative signs of the sophisticated, cosmopolitan, and civilized. In short, foreign words, exploited as a temporary labor force, were deemed instrumental in a global arena of commodity exchange and national distinction. The rise of German linguistic patriotism, fueled by the onset of the war in 1914, negated this postulate of capital gain by an emphasis on the self-worth of indigenous language: a new German subjectivity, fabricated by purging foreign signifiers, was to be nurtured and preserved.

The subject of linguistic otherness continued to capture Adorno's attention, and he supplemented his observations in further essays from the 1970s. Thus *On the Use of Foreign Words* is a critical discussion, in which Adorno emphasizes the "negative, dangerous . . . power" of foreign words (1974:

646). In language practice, Adorno writes, the use of foreign words is akin to a surgical operation: the alien word is inserted into the language body like a prosthesis, "a silver rib" (Benjamin 1972: 131). According to Adorno, this linguistic implant or prosthetic supplement is "necessary for the survival of the linguistic corpus [*Sprachleib*] which was dying of organic causes" (Adorno 1961: 113–14, 1974: 645).[12] The Nazis' vehement resistance against linguistic/physiognomic otherness uncovered the provocative power of foreign words and "revealed very clearly, as violent resistance often does, what is at stake: the possibility of linguistic nationalism" (Levin 1985: 118–19), a nationalism forged by the racial phantasm of an idealized language organism. "In every foreign word, there resides the dynamite of enlightenment; in its controlled usage lies the knowledge that the immediate cannot be expressed immediately, but only through extended reflection and mediation" (Adorno 1961: 116).[13] In its insistence on the historicity of even the most "natural" and seemingly "organic" folk-idiom (*Volkssprache*), the use of foreign words challenges our own mastery over language: "What one resents in the foreign word," comments Adorno, "is, not least, that it reveals the condition of all words: that language once again imprisons those who use it and actually fails as their very own medium" (116).[14] Therefore, "what is so disturbing" about the linguistically alien is that "as a paradigmatic encounter of the foreign (*fremd*) and the native (*eigen*), as a performance of untranslatability, it simultaneously constitutes the specificity of a national idiom and destroys the myth of its 'natural' or 'organic' status by exposing its limits" (Levin 1985: 117). The strategic deployment of foreign words, the unsettling presence of these linguistic border-crossers, always contains a political momentum: that of demythification.

Language Physiognomy and Nationhood: The German Reformation of the Linguistic Medium

When was the German nation form first envisioned as an organic speech community? And what circumstances contributed to the inception of these racial phantasms? Although the idea of a national linguistic corpus was promulgated by the literary elites of the Romantic period (Herder 1772 [1975], 1778/79; Humboldt 1818–35 [1963]; Iggers 1971; Trabant 1985, 1990), the corporal metaphor of language unity had its beginnings much earlier. The vision of a *linguistic physiognomy of German nationhood* was first crafted in the early seventeenth century. As a product of the contemporary political imagination, it was a vision that nurtured the novel image of the German-speaking population as a *single human body* and its language as *blood* that passed through and vivified this national corpus.

Such blood and body metaphors were mobilized as organizing emblems by the German literary societies in the early seventeenth century. Initially established as loose confederations of writers and poets, these associations promoted the use of German in literature, education, and government (Bircher 1970, 1971). The aim was language reform: the cultivation of linguistic patriotism by creating a common German vernacular purged of foreign signifiers (Anhalt-Köthen 1622, 1646 [1971]; Hille 1647 [1970]). The nationalization of language, promoted through medical metaphors and blood images, served as a means to implant a sense of Germanness in popular consciousness. As a result of the literary societies' educational and moralizing efforts, the use of German was intensely politicized: language reform became a pedagogical tool in a process of national unification.

What was the historical impetus for such a programmatic? Linguistic nationalism in Germany came into being as a revolutionary force, an emancipatory movement. At first a literary movement of cultural protest, German language reformers promoted the creation of a genuine speech community. The movement's nationalistic concerns were directed at transforming the realities of political rule. Seventeenth-century imperial Germany, which embraced an enormous land mass in the center of Europe, consisted of a loosely organized confederation of some 250 sovereign territories. Austria, Bavaria, Prussia, and Saxony were the most important of the eight electoral states. Additional territories belonged to twenty-seven spiritual members of the College of Princes, thirty-seven lay princes, ninety-five imperial counts, forty-two imperial founders, and fifty free or imperial towns (Bendix 1978: 379). These German territories, represented by the hereditary imperial crown of the Habsburg family, were governed with little structural cohesiveness: "crisscrossed by countless political, cultural, economic, and religious dividing lines" (Wehler 1987: 47). Every region, even if governed by the same sovereign, possessed its own administration and judiciary. Commercial and economic institutions were decentralized, religious practices localized. "One, 'Germany,'" writes Hans-Ulrich Wehler (1987), "existed neither as a state nor as a distinct geographic entity, even less so as a nation. . . . [A] plurality of German states coexisted side by side in central Europe. To these belonged the loyalty of its inhabitants but not to some nebulous 'Germany'" (44). By the onset of the Thirty Year War, in 1618, the German empire was already an intensely volatile construct (Langen 1952: 1080).

The political fragmentation of the imperial state was mirrored in Germany's linguistic heterogeneity: adjacent sovereign territories lacked a common language. A plurality of German and Dutch dialect forms existed side by side in their own right well into the modern age: a tangle of territorially differentiated speech forms, ranging from the common and distinguished courtly standards to the latinized German used by monks as well as a "confusing assortment of specialized language constructs, an immensely complex simultaneity and blending of linguistic strata and forms" (Moser 1952: 946). Language pluralism was a distinctive characteristic of a fragmented imperial state.

In the history of German language politics two issues were of special relevance for the seventeenth century: the colonizing influence of foreign languages and the absence of a standard written language (see Langen 1952). Germany's increasing political and cultural dependence on other lands gave rise to the foreign-word problem: the Thirty Year War intensified this predicament. Complaints about linguistic alienation resounded in the late sixteenth century, when large segments of the population had abandoned their native tongue in favor of foreign models of refinement. As a language of distinction, French was spoken by the nobility, the higher societal classes, and the reformed Calvinist courts (Bendix 1978: 391–96). Latin dominated in schools and universities, the sciences, the state, the administration, jurisprudence, law, and the church (Langen 1952: 1078). All areas of public life, from the arts to the army, were infused by foreign vocabularies: French, Latin, Spanish, and Italian (Langen 1952: 1079, 1082). In this context, an era marked by linguistic heterogeneity, political decentralization, and a prolonged war, the German literary societies came into existence as an emancipatory movement.

We encounter attempts at language reform before the seventeenth century. The Protestant Reformation initiated this movement. Martin Luther's translation of the bible into a German vernacular set into motion this reform process (Anderson 1983). While Latin was displaced as a sacred script, German becomes, via the battles of Reformation, for the first time an ideological weapon in the promulgation of religious truths: a written language with sacred significance. But the seventeenth-century editions of the Luther bible are relevant for additional reasons. In these baroque editions, the need to develop a common written standard was for the first time publicly debated (Stammler 1954). In these early issues of Luther's bible, we observe phonetic, inflectional, and syntactic changes that normalize German writing over the course of only three generations (ibid: 1954: 39–43). Initiated by the Protestant Reformation, and driven by the requirements of "print capitalism" (Anderson 1983), a standard German script emerged, which assumed nationwide validity and became binding for all social groups. Although such battles against the idiosyncratic use of vernacular forms began in the second half of the sixteenth century, the very ideal of an orthographic standard first appeared in the seventeenth century for national reasons (Moser 1952: 954). Such a systematizing of written German emerged, during this era of the Thirty Year War, with a heightened articulation of national consciousness.

Reforming the Linguistic Corpus: Cultivating, Breeding, and Purging

National unification was the basic programmatic of the German literary societies. In the early seventeenth century, these reform societies came into being to propagate mythic visions of an ethnonational body of language. During this era, marked by the onset of the Great War, and through the attempts at linguistic reform, the nation—the political community—was for the first time imagined as a single political body. Building on the traumatic experiences of military violence and prolonged foreign occupation, German language reformers mobilized nationalistic sentiments as a weapon against the external threat, agitated feelings of Germanness through a negative discourse of linguistic estrangement, and implanted in cultural memory their vision of nationhood as an organic speech community.

Among the language associations, the Fruitful Society (*Die Fruchtbring-ende Gesellschaft*), founded by Prince Ludwig of Anhalt in 1617, was the first and most important. By 1650 it consisted of more than five hundred members: court scribes, poetic theorists, linguists, grammatologists, historical record-keepers, and translators who were united in their commitment to cultivate language: the task of transforming German into the national idiom. "Their pedagogical mission [was] language cleansing, language standardization, language censure and language breeding" (Schirokauer 1952: 1074–75).[15] The society's political aim, as mandated by a statutory directive, was to nationalize the "widely honored High German mother tongue" (Anhalt-Köthen 1646 [1971]: ii) by purging it from foreign signifiers. This project was legitimated by an emphasis on the antiquity of German, which involved the fabrication of a phantasmatic linguistic genealogy: "Our German mother tongue is so noble that one needs not be ashamed of it/before emperor/king and prince . . . among other main languages [Greek and Latin] not the lowest, but the most magnificent, the nearest indeed to Hebrew [the oldest and first language since the creation of the world] (Hille 1647 [1970]: 78).

Within this symbolic universe of linguistic emergence, German was presented as a primary and ancient language: equipped with a Hebrew-German stem vocabulary (ibid: 77–87), it was defined as equal to Latin and Greek. With the tools of etymology—a novel science—French was demoted in rank: through a historical fluke, it had come into being as a "peculiar" aberration of Latin (83). The eulogist of German, the club member Justus Georg Schottel, one of the most learned linguists of his time, summarized the advantages of his mother tongue as follows: she was "not a mish-mash mingle," "not an offshoot or progeny" (like French), and "not a patchwork" (Langen 1952: 1083). Based on these convictions, the reformers' battle against linguistic estrangement and their attempt to "breed" (züchten) German back to its source had begun.

The society's primary task was to restore German, an autonomous stem-language—this "noble ancient High German mother tongue" (Neumark 1668 [1970]: 15)—to its original form: "Even if German is no longer spoken in the same manner as it was 800 years ago, it endures in its stem vocabulary in pristine form . . . an eternal duration" (Hille 1647 [1971]: 73, 76). The quest for a genuine linguistic nationality was propagated by a demand for language purity: the cleansing of verbal repertoires from any contaminating foreign influences. The promotion of German nativism was to be accomplished by a purging of language.

The society's explicit goal was to create a setting, a symbolic space "in which everyone could speak [and] write in good pure German" in order to "elevate the mother tongue" (Anhalt-Köthen 1646 [1971]: ii) and to "preserve standard high German to the utmost and in the most feasible manner in its correct essence and status, without the intermixing of strange foreign words, and to cultivate the best pronounciation in speech and the purest form in writing and poetic verse" (ibid: iii). The creation of German as a national idiom, a proclaimed natural duty in the "service for the fatherland," was based on a commitment to language purity:

> The highly commendable task of the Fruitful Society is firstly based on that which should serve to promote the German language; namely that one should preserve the same in utmost purity, without recourse to foreign words, [and] write and compose in purest form; [and] for this reason remove and discontinue use of all foreign mingled words, which have currently come into such popular misuse" (Hille 1647 [1971]: 75).

The project of linguistic purity was envisioned through natural symbols. According to the code of the society, every initiate had to choose a membership name and emblem. Interestingly, the written statues of the association, which first appeared in 1621, restricted this choice to vegetative signifiers: "plants, trees, flowers, herbs or the like, grown from the earth or having come into being therefrom" (Anhalt-Köthen 1646 [1971]: iii). The emergence of a national language was equated with the cultivation of nature. Language reform, an act of political intervention, was articulated through a system of natural and organic metaphors. According to the association's written codex, the society's political project was defined as "fruitful" or "fruit-bearing": a harvest of words. The cultivation of German was an attempt at "landscaping" the "speech-garden" (*Sprachgarten*) of nature (Neumark 1668 [1970]: 180; Hille 1647 [1970]: 73). Such linguistic tropes were based on idealized images of domesticated nature:

> This beautiful *garden culture* . . .
> Paints the purest ornamental miracle of *our language:* has for its
> Gardening care *highest aristocratic hand* (Hille 1647 [1970]: 74).

According to the aims of the literary society, the "corrupted mother tongue" was to be restored to its original beauty: newly replanted, without savage linguistic growth, with the ill weeds of "foreign words uprooted," and the "word heretics," with their "popular misuse of foreign mish-mash words" weeded (Neumark 1668 [1970]: 15, 16). The German "language garden," an achievement of artistic splendor, was to be stocked only with useful and ornamental plants.

Phantasms of Blood:
The Symbolics of the Language Organism

The society's iconographic vision, with its invocation of a domesticated, useful nature, appeared in a variety of published texts. A first illustrated edition of the list of members was issued in 1629. The last edition, revised and expanded, was published in 1668 with a comprehensive illustrated register. On numerous pages of these multivolume works we can make out villages, castles, or gardens in the background. These rural matrices are dwarfed by the iconographic ensemble of names and emblems in the foreground of these graphic illustrations: the images of flowers, trees, herbs, or roots are framed by poetic narratives. Remarkable in these texts is the recurrent emphasis on the medicinal properties of plant emblems. It is this healing power that the members of the literary society seek to appropriate symbolically. Examples include: *The Purger of Heavy Blood* (no. 140); *The Engorger of Veins* (no. 151); *The Cleanser of Impure Blood* (no. 239); *The Queller of All That Bleeds* (no. 400); *The Monthly Purger of Blood* (no. 394); *The Relentless Blood Stopper* (no. 189) (e.g., Anhalt-Köthen 1646 [1971]). The members' choices of emblems was justified in poetic form. In these rhymed narratives, the writer commented on the curative power of his emblem, thereby justifying his nominal appropriation of the plant's potency. For example:

> *The Engorger of Veins*
> The noble liver herb replenishes our veins with good, pure blood, and it cools down the liver and opens there whatever is congested, and quells all accidental ills: I am called the "engorger" and summon the power of the herb. (Joachim Johann Georg von der Schulenburg, No. 151)

In these narratives, the reformers' principal aim was articulated through medicinal metaphors and a symbolics of blood: "corrupted" by the "misuse of foreign words," German was equated with polluted, weakened, putrid, and congested blood. This is a discourse of bodily pathologies: a vision of the wounded, unhealthy, and poisoned German-language organism. The restoration of linguistic health required the curative intervention of special plants: "The wound herb heals all hurt," "with its healing power benefits the wounds," "the herb is medicinal," it "purges the heavy blood," "restores the human body back to health," "heals the body from all poisons," and "brakes coagulated blood," "a cure for many ailments in body and blood and stomach wounds," "flushes out the body's heavy [thickened] blood," and "cleanses its polluted blood" (Anhalt-Köthen 1646 [1971]: XXVII, XLVI, XLVII, XLVIII, LVII, LIX, No. 237, No. 357).

In several of the earlier texts, this symbolism of healing, cleansing, and deliverance is fused with eschatological visions: the death of Christ, whose "red blood redeems our sins," a "medicine for our souls" (Anhalt-Köthen 1646 [1971]: XLVII, L, LI). The national promise of salvation, as granted by German language reform, was coupled with religious metaphors: "through his healing blood, Christ has overcome hell, sin and death, so that we can become pure" (Anhalt-Köthen 1646 [1971], no. 63). But in such eschatological poems the Christian longing for deliverance was tied to a linguistic programmatic: the redemption of German through the blood-cleansing intervention of nature. The association members, through their emblematic use of the curative attributes of plants, present themselves as language healers, the purgers, the redeemers of a sanguine essence—the German language—the blood of the nation. The convalescence of linguistic discourse was imagined through images of blood that pulsed freely, unhampered, through the body's arteries:

> [The aim of our society is] firstly that one bears in mind the good codex for the preservation and propagation of the German language, and always insist on this, with such passion that, as a result, with the aid of the Fruitful Society, god be praised, the well-spring of veins, the pure High German language, is opened: the same should not be plugged and covered up again through negligence, but from time to time be more purely drawn out" (Hille 1647 [1970]: 76).

The promulgation of such organic/vegetative images of language reform was linked to the rise of nationalist ideology. The German literary societies came into being as a logical extension of nation-building, a process in which the standardization and preservation of language was deemed essential for the formation of a new political community: the modern German nation-state.

Contemplating the Future:
National Language Politics in a United Europe

German nationhood "accorded a privileged place to the symbol of language in its own initial process of formation: it bound political unity closely to linguistic uniformity" (Balibar 1995: 104) and linked national unification to the ethnicization of language. Movements of language reform, language cultivation, language breeding, and language purging have always been an integral part of German national ideology (Straßner 1995). But the symbolic coding of linguistic nativism was radically transposed "at the end of the nineteenth century, [when] colonization on the one hand, and an intensification of the importation of labor and the segregation of manual workers by means of their ethnic origin on the other, led to the constitution of the phantasm of the '[German] race'" (Balibar 1995: 104). In the twentieth century, linguistic nationalism, with its tropes of blood and nature, was remade and refurbished by racial regimes.

Such historical formations, as Balibar points out, "in no sense impose any necessary outcome"; rather, they are, in the present as in the past, "the stuff of political struggles" (104–05). Nevertheless, linguistic racism does profoundly alter the conditions under which issues of immigration, citizenship, and national sovereignty are brought to light in public debates. "One might seriously wonder," Balibar suggests, "how the formation of a 'United Europe'—insofar as functions and symbols of the nation-state are transferred to the level of the 'Community'—might affect the future production of fictive ethnicity and linguistic racism" (1998: 128–29). Or, stated differently, "will the community of European states favor the establishment of a European colingualism (and if so, adopting which languages) or lean toward the idealization of a European demographic identity, conceived mainly in opposition to the 'southern populations,' that is, Turks, Arabs, Blacks" (Balibar 1995: 105). Furthermore, we might ask whether the political, administrative, and educational institutions of a united Europe will adopt Arabic, Turkish, and other "immigrant" Asian or African languages on equal terms with English, French, and German?[16] Or will these languages be excluded as foreign?

Every nation-state that has been forged by a process of linguistic ethnicization is forced today, under the impact of globalization, to seek the means of going beyond exclusivism or racial ideology. Will Germans be compelled to find in the transformation of the European polity the means to abandon their national phantasms of blood, body, and language, "in order to communicate with the individuals of other peoples with which [they] share the same interests and, to some extent, the same future" (Balibar 1995: 105)? Although the machinations of global capitalism produce ruptures, disparities, and paradoxes that may serve as an impetus for linguistic transformation, such currents of change are always culturally mediated: systems of meaning, memory, and politics impose limits on the flexibility of national imaginaries. And while the fate of a multilingual Europe still remains uncertain, the question of linguistic sovereignty has a decisive impact on the political future of a United Germany.

Notes

1   The quoted essay title is a fragment of a stanza from Richard Strauss, *Ariadne auf Naxos: Oper in einem Aufzuge nebst einem Vorspiel von Hugo von Hofmannsthal*, op. 60 (London: Fürstner, Boosey, and Hawkes, 1943 [1916]). I am indebted for this reference to Professor Michael Geyer, who captioned his reflections on catastrophic nationalism during World War II (in *Sacrifice and National Belonging*, edited by Greg Eghigian et al., 2002) with a longer version of this narrative excerpt. My essay was first presented at the interdisciplinary conference "Berlin, Beijing, and Beyond: Cultural Politics since 1989" at Cornell University, 12–13 November 1999. I thank Jonathan Monroe and Leslie Adelson for their constructive commentary.

2 This term was coined by Etienne Balibar (1995). His writings on the interrelation between language, race, and nationalism greatly influenced my thinking in this chapter.

3 This is a phrase from Balibar (1995: 94).

4 In response to economic market pressures, German federal labor laws were revised in 2000: refugees are permitted to seek employment. But in reality local bureaucracies stifle this process. Applications for work permits by refugees are categorically rejected. Local labor offices justify such discriminatory practices by reference to statewide unemployment figures, which show a surplus of job-seeking German citizens. In local demographic terms, this is a statistical fiction that is strategically deployed against foreign nationals.

5 This term was coined by Aihwa Ong (1999).

6 The first of the above media contests, ushered in by a Frankfurt linguist, wants to censure "the irresponsible or discriminating use of public language" (Janich 1997: 82). The annual campaign produces a form of ethnopolitical correctness by a focus on the semantic "misuse" of words: language "errors" are rendered as "Un-German speaking violations." Such a censure of speech acts seeks to create a common standard of proper "German" thinking through the policing of language.

7 English translation adopted from Levin (1985: 115).

8 Here see *Language Is a Weapon* by the German cultural critic Kurt Tucholsky (1989). In this biting historical account of language politics during the Weimar Republic, Tucholsky provides us with sarcastic insight on the ongoing "battle for language purity" and the ensuing campaign against the "naturalized" "misuses of German."

9 English translation adopted from Levin (1985: 117).

10 Also quoted more extensively in Levin (1985: 118, n. 12).

11 See Levin (1985: 119).

12 English translation adopted from Levin (1985: 118).

13 English translation adopted from Levin (1985: 118–19).

14 Also see Levin (1985: 117).

15 See the commentated collection of original texts by language reformers and language purists between 1478 and 1750 (Jones 1995).

16 This is my paraphrasing of Balibar (1995: 106, n. 21).

5. "On the Raggedy Edge of Risk"

Articulations of Race and Nature After Biology

Bruce Braun

It is a commonplace today that race has no basis in nature. There are no races, only racisms. This insight is not new: Franz Boas mobilized population biology in the 1930s to question the phylogenetic trees that were used to establish race as a system of biological difference, arguing that there was as much genetic variation within groups as between groups. In the decades that followed, research in biochemistry, molecular biology, and quantitative genetics further separated race from nature, such that by the 1990s it could be widely argued that the concept of biological race had been "thoroughly dismantled," and the American Anthropological Association could declare that "any attempt to establish lines of division among biological populations [is] arbitrary and subjective" (Graves 2001).[1]

This does not mean that race has lost its significance. While it may merely be an effect of signification—a "floating signifier," as Anne McClintock (1995) puts it—it hardens into social categories and has real effects in social and political life. Further, biological notions of race may have been challenged only to be supplanted by notions of cultural difference in which ethnicity, character, and habit constitute an equally immutable order analogous to the previous phylogenetic schema. Indeed, the popularity and controversy surrounding books like *The Bell Curve* and concepts in sociology such as the underclass thesis attest to the continued hold of a metaphysics of race that assumes racial difference to be a real "thing" that exists in the world.

To the extent that the separation of race from biological nature has been achieved, then, it may merely have been shadowed by the naturalization of culture. But there are *other* ways that race remains tied to nature too, for while the "dismantling" of biological racism in the United States may have gone some way toward separating race from *corporeal* nature, *external* nature continues to be a remarkably potent site for the articulation of racialized identities.[2] I refer here to the many ways in which "encountering nature" in the United States is entangled with cultural and political economies of difference, from the technological and institutional spaces of the laboratory, to the discursive spaces and imaginative geographies of physical culture. The latter will be our concern here, for at few sites has the articulation of race and nature been more evident in recent years than in the discursive and spatial practices of extreme sport and adventure travel, two rapidly growing industries that have gained immense popularity among some sectors of American society. An interrogation of these phenomena—what I will abbreviate as "risk culture"—may enable us to see how nature continues to be a material and discursive site through which effects of race are produced and naturalized even after the apparent dismantling of biological racism.

The Return of Adventure

Adventure has a long history in the United States, but it returned with renewed vigor in the last decades of the twentieth century. This was evident not only in the explosive growth of the adventure and extreme sport industries but in the widespread dissemination of images of "risk taking" in mainstream media and popular culture. On billboards, network television, and local newspapers, all manner of commodities were marketed through association with cliff-jumping snowboarders, Moab-bound mountain bikers, and toned and tanned rock climbers. Books like Sebastian Junger's *The Perfect Storm* and Jon Krakauer's *Into Thin Air* remained on bestseller lists for months, even years. Adventure travel magazines like *Outside* and *Men's Journal* were joined by countless others, such as *National Geographic Adventure* and *Ecotraveller*, as adventure publishing expanded beyond the niche markets it occupied in the 1970s and 1980s. Even established magazines and newspapers like *Vanity Fair, Atlantic Monthly,* and the usually staid *New York Times* leaped onboard, publishing gripping stories of adventure and, occasionally, grisly accounts of death.

The pursuit of adventure was given new life too. It had never disappeared, of course: the quest for adventure has been a constant, if shifting, element in discourses of gender, race, and nation in the United States for more than a century, although often thought to have attained its highest popularity at the last fin-de-siécle, when the "frontier" and encounters with "raw nature" were depicted in Jack London novels, symbolized in public figures such as John Muir and Teddy Roosevelt, and made into a popular pursuit among the middle classes (see Haraway 1989; Seltzer 1992; Jasen 1995; Phillips 1997). A century later, adventure was again on the agenda, as a burgeoning adventure-travel industry produced "risk taking" as a key site of desire, and as state tourism and land-management agencies promoted specific landscapes as "adventure zones." Indeed, if adventure named an ideology, it found its subjects by the tens of thousands, reflected in exploding markets for specialized adventure gear and in increased pressure in rural areas to restrict traditional resource industries in favor of a "new economy" of risk.

It is equally true, however, that not all subjects properly fit risk culture's ideological frames. This was evident in the demographics of adventure travel, which during the period remained the preserve of white, middle-class travellers. It was also evident in *representations* of adventure, and in how and where images of risk taking circulated. Marked differences existed between how advertisers, photographers, writers, and editors portrayed encounters with nature in magazines that targeted middle-class whites, and those aimed at black or Latina readers.[3] Outdoor sport magazines like *Outside, National Geographic Adventure,* and *Men's Journal,* which defined adventure for middle America, had few if any comparable publications within the African American and Latina media. Where encounters with nature appeared at all in the latter, "risk taking" was rarely, if ever, highlighted.[4]

Such differences can be read in various ways. Appeals to identity would suggest that the absence of the black or Latina adventurer has its basis in *cultural difference:* a nation divided by race, each with its own cultural traditions and practices. A second explanation would locate this absence in the workings of *class.* By this view, the paucity of black and Latina adventurers—both as practitioners and in adventure travel's discursive fields— merely reflects a racialized social and economic order, in which the opportunity to engage in adventure travel and extreme sport is determined by one's social location. Accordingly, the lack of images of nonwhite adventurers should not surprise us, because the adventure travel industry knows well that there is little to be gained by catering to a constituency that cannot afford what it sells. Such strategies no doubt exist and serve to remind us that the present social order in the United States can be productively analyzed in terms of those who have the resources and security to *take* risks, and those who are instead continuously positioned *at* risk (or imagined to be so). In contrast to explanations that point to cultural difference, then, this explanation would suggest that the absence of the nonwhite adventurer has less to do with taste and subculture than with property, economy, and law.

To discuss the absence of the black or Latina adventurer in terms of identity or social location, however, is to make two related and problematic assumptions: that race exists as a category of analysis and thus has an ontological priority; and that what is significant about risk culture lies elsewhere than in its practices, since it merely expresses or reflects an underlying social reality to which it contributes nothing of its own. The freedom to take risks in nature is undoubtedly a white, middle-class privilege. But arguably risk culture—a phrase I use to call attention to the cultural and representational practices that produce risk as culturally meaningful—is in part *constitutive* of white middle-class identities, for it consists of an important set of discursive practices through which race, class, and gender differences are articulated and temporarily sutured. In what follows I take the absent figure of the "nonwhite" adventurer as a point of departure to trace itineraries of race, nature, and power in risk culture's discursive fields.[5] I will suggest that the absence of this figure is not only, or even primarily, an economic or sociological matter but an ideological matter: within the discursive terrain of "adventure" in the United States today, the figure of the black or Latina adventurer *has no proper place.* Why this is so and why it is significant, are the questions this chapter seeks to answer.

Three remarks are necessary before I proceed. First, the phrase "risk culture" suggests both a proximity and a distance from "risk society." The latter, coined by German sociologist Ulrich Beck, names a stage of modernization characterized by the *generalization* of social and environmental risk (as byproducts of science, technology, and capitalist development). Beck (1991) argues that this has given rise to new forms of social organization and politics, as well as new roles for (and suspicion of) expert science, as communities and states struggle over definitions of, and solutions to, the proliferation of social and environmental problems. Quite apart from Beck's thesis that we now live in a "reflexive modernity," what must be stressed is that while risks may now be generalized (as in global warming), who lives *most* at risk in the United States remains quite specific, overdetermined by capitalist development, racialization, and the social production of space, place, and nature. In the context of risk society's uneven social and environmental geographies, *risk culture* names a specific set of discursive operations around risk and risk taking that help constitute, and render natural, risk society's racial and class formations. The proximity of risk culture to risk society, then, calls attention to an irreducible *cultural* or *discursive* aspect of risk society, something not examined by Beck or his numerous commentators.

Second, my intention is not to *denounce* risk culture but instead to understand it as a site of cultural politics. Some might wish to retain or even celebrate aspects of risk culture, albeit with caution and in a critical fashion. Advocates have suggested that its value lies in its displacement of some of the normalizing and rationalizing aspects of modernity, and in particular workplace regimen and cultural conformity. Such a position is taken by *Outside* magazine editor-at-large Tim Cahill, who, in a characteristically colloquial statement, suggests that there is much value to be found in letting things hang out "in the raggedy edge of risk." Echoing these sentiments, *Outside*'s editors introduced their twentieth-anniversary issue by declaring that adventure travelers were those who "refuse to be bound by convention." By this view risk culture is about limit-experiences that challenge social and cultural norms, about refusing the disciplinary regimes of modern society and global capitalism, and about pursuing *embodied* rather than *virtual* experiences.[6] Others have described adventure travel as a thoroughly postmodern phenomenon, involving the loss or reinvention of the self, either in nature or other cultures (see Beezer 1993). Risk culture is thus seen to have an explicitly *ethical* dimension, involving a care of self that involves physical and mental tests, and demands an almost ascetic bodily discipline.[7] Finally, parallels can be drawn between readings of risk culture as antinormative and recent efforts by radical ecologists to replace the notion of wilderness, commonly understood as "origin" and "home," with *wildness* as a rhetorical figure signifying capitalist modernity's inappropriate/d others—that excess that cannot be fully incorporated within capitalism's imperative to normalize and rationalize external and internal nature (cf. Rothenberg 1995). Yet such recuperations must be tentative and cautious, for the celebration of risk culture's antinormative gestures often elides its cultural politics. If we wish to retain something of risk culture's edginess, then, its racial and class economies must be thoroughly acknowledged and interrogated.[8]

Finally, this essay contributes to the urgent project of examining the relation between environmentalisms and cultural difference in the United States today. Cultures of nature are rarely, if ever, innocent (Wilson 1991; Braun 2002). This extends beyond analyzing who participates in different environmental practices, or counting the number of people of color among the directors of mainstream environmental groups, or even calling attention to the invisibility of the concerns of poor, racialized communities in the agendas of environmental groups. Other stories must be added, about not only the ways in which environmental discourses and practices reflect difference but how they constitute it (see Di Chiro 1995; Sturgeon 1997).

Figuring the Adventurer

With the inclusion of a sixteen-page supplement dedicated to adventure sports in the 11 March 1998 issue of the *New York Times*, risk culture arguably came of age, jumping from the pages of speciality magazines like *Outside* to the newspaper that has long sought to define the nation's cultural tastes. Indeed, not long after its appearance a backlash emerged among self-styled purists, who found this apparent mainstreaming of adventure a threat to its value, dismissing what the adventure-travel industry offered as "frontierland" (Greenfield 1999) and "pasteurized adventure" (Randolph 1999). Others, invested in maintaining a *distance* between adventure and class privilege, looked askance at the ability of the most rich to buy their risky accomplishments by purchasing the skills of expert guides, thus emptying risk from adventure and remaking it as leisure, a criticism which only dissembled the class basis of risk culture more generally.[9]

While class—and its anxious disavowal—could be clearly traced in the pages of the *New York Times* supplement, the supplement also provides a point of departure for an analysis of risk culture's racial economies.[10] In one respect these racial dynamics were obvious: story after story related the adventures of white travelers, picturing them in action in exotic natural locations, battling natural elements, or testing their mettle against raw nature. Persons of color were entirely absent, not only in the subject material or as article writers but also in advertisements, the one place where nonwhites might be expected to appear, given the commodity value of multiculturalism. This absence extended to *Outside, National Geographic Adventure, Men's Journal*, and other popular publications of risk culture. However, as noted above, reading this absence only as an expression of economic class would miss a crucial point, for far from designating a set of cultural practices that people of color do not have *access to*, risk culture designates a discursive order in which they have no *proper* place.

We can begin to understand the *illegibility* of our fictional nonwhite adventurer by comparing two images taken from the twentieth-anniversary issue

Figure 1. Acts of adventure. Advertisement from *Outside*.

of *Outside* magazine. The first depicts a heavily laden mountain climber clawing his way up a steep rock face (figure 1). He climbs in the most adverse conditions. Wind whips at his body. Water streams from his clothes and gear. A gritty determination is etched on his face, as he searches the rock for the next secure hand- or foothold. In some respects this is an unremarkable image, following well-worn conventions for establishing the status of an act as "adventure." Like many adventure-travel images (especially those used in advertising), the photo shows a solitary individual engaged in tests of strength and mettle. Whether climbing, running, jumping, or plunging, it is the *encounter* and the *challenge* that matter. The climber exerts great effort and determination. Any lapse in attention may result in injury, maiming, or death. Here is the consummate image of courage and skill—heroic efforts and great fortitude in the face of nature's raw forces.

Much more could be said about this image: how it individualizes the encounter with nature, envelops it within a discourse of courage and conquest, and sutures an anxious middle-class masculinity. What might go unnoticed at first, however, is that the image's possible meanings are also structured by, and help constitute, a discourse of race. At first glance this appears not to be the case: no effort has been made to present the climber as a *racial* subject, and as readers we are invited to contemplate the *act* of adventure, not the

Figure 2. Skin/fitness: fixing racialized bodies. Advertisement from *Outside.*

adventurer himself. The face of the climber is partially turned away from the camera, focusing on the task at hand. We take it in only as we scan the image for its more important details, evaluating the actions and situation of the climber, his physical and mental strain, and the wind, rock, and rain. Crucially, viewers are not asked to inspect the body for signs of difference; at most they are invited to consider the climber's effort or his fatigue, or, even more likely, to put themselves *in the climber's place.*[11]

Contrast this with a second image found a few pages earlier, one of the few places in the entire issue where a person of color appears, or, more correctly, where readers are asked to view an individual in explicitly *racial* terms. Again, the image is drawn from advertising copy, in this case a men's fragrance (figure 2). Dominating this advertisement is an African American man, stripped to his athletic briefs, holding a black ball at right angles to his body. Here race structures the image's meanings, and it does so explicitly. In contrast to the image of the climber, it is the model's *body*, not his *activity*, that is the center of attention. The viewer is invited—one might say obliged—to focus on the model himself, on his muscular frame, on the darkness of his skin. What action there is—holding the ball—does not belong to the model in the same way that the action of the climber—ascending the mountain—belongs to the climber. It is prescribed *to* the model, so as to fully display his body. The gaze focuses on skin, muscle, sinew. Significantly, in contrast to the previous image, *Outside*'s readers are *not* invited to place themselves in the frame in an act of identification; instead, they are invited to view the subject from a distance and as an object.

What can be learned from these images? Clearly, they are open to a plurality of interpretations, and these would almost certainly vary between persons and across reading publics. It is also important to note that like most advertising copy, these images were not specific to *Outside*, although it is significant that they appear in its pages. Indeed, it is crucial to think about these images both in terms of the reading public—white, middle-class—that *Outside* actively solicits and in terms of the visual and semiotic codes that govern risk culture more generally, of which these images and others like them are in part constitutive. To admit a plurality of interpretation, then, does not foreclose attending to bell hooks's (1996) demand that we recognize entrenched patterns of representing race, class, and sexuality in American culture, nor David Roediger's (1997: 45) caution that how race is portrayed in popular culture draws on "deep and long patterns of seeing."

We can continue our investigation into our fictional but absent nonwhite adventurer by noting that the cultural intelligibility of these images is in part an effect of citationality (Butler 1993); images are invariably viewed with other images and narratives in mind. In the case of the first image, we might suggest that its legibility lies at least in part in its unstated invocation of histories of European exploration and adventure. The image of the climber makes sense because readers can readily draw on *other* images of climbers— George Leigh Mallory, Edmund Hillary, Reinhold Messner—even if they are not known by name. Other aspects of risk culture invoke different persons and activities: Amundsen, Scott, Shackleton, Peary, Lewis and Clark, Muir, Roosevelt. I will return to this matter later, although it merits noting that citationality does not refer to the repetition of history "as it really happened," but instead to the reiteration of statements, images, and narratives that have achieved a sort of hegemonic or commonsense status through their continuous repetition and circulation. As Lisa Bloom (1993) has shown, adventure has not always been the preserve of "white" explorers. Other narratives of adventure exist, but they are not readily available. Despite numerous attempts to reinsert the presence of Sherpa climbers in histories of Himalayan mountaineering, for instance, few people can name the Nepalese mountaineer who scaled Everest with Edmund Hillary.[12] For most readers of *Outside* the whiteness of the climber needs no mention because it would be assumed.

As we will see, this is not simply the default category that kicks in when the adventurer is not clearly racialized. Rather, in the representational economies of adventure, no *other* identities are fully sanctioned.

Let me return to the second image. Like the first image, it too is citational. But it recalls a different history, and a different visual archive. Indeed, the image is all too familiar. The emphasis on the racialized, "black" body recalls the visual economies of slavery. The reference here is the auction block, the black body shackled and stripped (cf. hooks 1996).[13] If the previous image conjoined exploration and whiteness through an act of *identification*, this image links property with whiteness through the production of a *distance* from which one identifies and objectifies. In representing the racialized "black" body as a commodity, the viewer is positioned in terms of a white look that "invests" in the racialized other (economically and psychically), evaluating the body of the other in terms of quality and value.

Despite the advances of the civil-rights era, such a look remains prevalent (even pervasive) in certain sectors of American culture, although it is not without a certain ambivalence.[14] Often, as in the case here, it is a look that links race and sexuality, an insight that has received the attention of numerous critics. As Hall (1996) explains, the binary white/black is cross-cut by a phantasmatic binary of fear and desire. The "white look" is, accordingly, a *sexualized* look, constructing black masculinity as threat, something hooks (1990) has described as an obsession in the mainstream media. In the image in question, the returned gaze of the model achieves precisely this, evoking the threat of sexual predation within a discourse that links black male sexuality with the rape of white women. Again, this hardly needs mention since the image of the predatory black male is so thoroughly ingrained in U.S. race politics, underlining the ways that racism and sexism are articulated discourses.

For my purposes, what is most interesting about the second image is its difference from the first. The two figures are separated by a yawning gap. They are not substitutable, nor the figures in them. This pattern of staging race and nature is repeated throughout *Outside*'s twentieth-anniversary issue. Where nonwhite subjects appear, they appear only in guises other than the adventurer: as "entertainers" (jazz musicians), as "local color" in stories of overseas adventure (exotic culture), or, as honorable "third world environmentalists" (a figure bequeathed by Romanticism). From the hundreds of images of active travelers and athletes in the issue, only three might be said to trouble the association of adventure with whiteness. In one, an African

American mountain biker is shown posing for the camera (significantly, the biker is not "in action" like our climber, but posing beside his bike). In another, a clothing advertisement, the Japanese climber Isammu Tatsuma is pictured on the summit of a mountain (revealing risk culture's racial schema to be more complicated than a simple white/black binary). The third is a now-dated photo of the Cuban American marathoner Rosie Ruiz, who, as the editors take pains to remind us, was famously shown to be a fraud. To be sure, *Outside* magazine does not exhaust possibilities for staging encounters with external nature, nor should the apparent illegibility of the "nonwhite" adventure traveler be equated with the impossibility of such a subject (after all, blacks go camping too!). A different point needs emphasis: in the visual economies of risk culture, the adventuring subject cannot properly be a *racialized* subject—the appearance of such a subject would be a disruptive presence and thus effect a kind of crisis in risk culture's discursive order.

In the remainder of this essay I delve further into these discursive orders and their temporal and spatial aspects. I first extend my discussion of risk culture's citationality to show how adventure travel takes recourse to particular historical narratives and discursive conventions. I then turn to the imaginative geographies that inform how encounters with risk culture are understood. Finally, I draw out the ideological or political effects of risk culture by positioning it within the social relations of *risk society*. As we will see, risk culture cannot admit the presence of the nonwhite adventurer without at the same time introducing a problem for arguments about the "naturalness" of risk society's race and class divisions.

In the Tracks of Whiteness: Risk Culture and Citationality

Performativity is thus not a singular "act," for it is always a reiteration of a norm or set of norms, and to the extent that it acquires an act-like status in the present, it conceals or dissimulates the conventions of which it is a repetition.—Judith Butler, *Bodies That Matter*

As mentioned above, discourses of adventure are not produced in the present from whole cloth but instead operate through a kind of citationality; they attain their meanings through the iteration of already established norms and conventions that are grafted into, and grafted together, within new cultural and political contexts.[15] This can be explored further, keeping two points in mind: first, that if meaning necessarily operates through a kind of repetition, race must be seen not only as an effect of its signification but also an effect of the *sedimentation* of a set of discourses that constitute and regulate differ-ence in terms of certain norms; and, second, that for this very reason the stabilization of race within systems of cultural difference is always incom-plete and thus open to the possibility of resignification or dissolution.

Consider a recent story in *National Geographic Adventure,* a magazine which began publication in 1999. Its second issue contained a lengthy story on sea-kayaking in the Haida Gwaii, a small set of islands located seventy kilometers off the coast of British Columbia (Brandt 1999). For the most part, the story follows established protocols of adventure-travel writing. The site is established as wild and remote: "you are nearly a hundred miles from the nearest telephone pole, TV set, Dodge Ram, or flush toilet." Physical exer-tion, climatic inconveniences, and unpredictable natural forces are empha-sized. We are told that the region is famous for its continuous stream of fierce north Pacific storms—nicknamed Earl—that lash the islands with vicious winds and pelting rains. Travel is clearly an effort. Members of the expedi-tion are constantly wet and even when the sun shines they wear two sets of rain gear in anticipation of "Earl's" inevitable return. The author notes that the previous year a kayaker, overcome by wind and waves, lost her life in the same waters. During the day wind renders waters dangerous, even impass-able. At night gales lash at expedition members' tents, disrupting sleep. Even before the group embarks, a local old-timer offers prophetic words of advice: "The sea rules. Forget your schedule." On cue, the expedition misses its return date, delayed by a howling Pacific storm.

In one respect we know that this is adventure because it draws on a system of differences that distinguishes this way of encountering nature from other, less adventurous ways (gardening, sight-seeing, work). Adventure may be an activity, but like all acts it is intelligible only within a system of signs. It trades, for instance, on that enduring distinction between travel and tourism by which bourgeois travelers in the 1800s differentiated *their* mode of travel from the "mere pleasure seeking" of working-class tourists (Buzard 1993). It is a moment where one's mettle is tested; it is about character, about step-ping off the beaten path in order to struggle against, experience, and over-come nature's raw forces.

That we recognize this act as adventure, then, cannot be explained by the act itself, but only by how this meaning is secured within a differential system of signs. But here we need to complicate the story. If we accept Der-rida's (1988) critique of Austin's speech act theory, no statement or act at-tains its meanings fully within the present context, but rather through re-peating a prior act or statement. To use Derrida's example, smashing a bottle of champagne against a ship signifies "launching" because it conforms to an iterable model. It is a *legible* act because it repeats a previous action (or an earlier statement: "I christen"). The notion of citationality, then, calls attention to this basic point: meanings do not come into the world fully formed, nor can they be explained solely through reference to the intention of the subject who speaks or acts. Rather, they operate through repetition (but, as we will see, not without the possibility of difference).

To say that risk culture is citational does not mean that it explicitly connects the present act or statement to a prior one, but only that it conforms to iterable norms. In the act of launching a ship, after all, one doesn't directly refer to an earlier event through a direct statement of reference: one simply smashes the bottle. The same might be said for adventure travel: its meanings require no *explicit* reference to an earlier act but instead turn on the sedimentation of a *discourse* of adventure by which acts in the present—or their representation—are readily understood as conforming to an established model. As we will see shortly, this is also why meaning drifts, for statements or acts in the present can be related to—or be articulated in terms of—different acts and statements and can be grafted into new contexts in which the terms are transformed.

The citationality of risk culture can be illustrated by returning to the article on sea-kayaking. As previously noted, this article was published in one of the first issues of *National Geographic Adventure.* Like much travel writing, it focused on the itinerary of the writer and his fellow-travelers, tracing their path and noting the various events and sights along the way. On the last page of the issue, entirely separate from the article, the editors of the magazine reproduced two pages from the dog-eared journal of Newton H. Chittenden, an American explorer-for-hire who led a six-month expedition to the Haida Gwaii for the British Columbia government in 1884, accompanied by the photographer Richard Maynard (figure 3). Pasted in Chittenden's journal were two photographs: the first, a photograph of the lodge of Haida chief Edenshaw, including the impressive totem pole that stood beside the main doorway; the second, an image of the two explorers. In the latter, Maynard stands holding a rifle while Chittenden sits at his side, holding an artifact purchased (or stolen) from the Haida. Scrawled beneath the former photograph is a note in Chittenden's handwriting: "Maynard was a man of remarkable courage. An Indian thinking he was pointing a dangerous weapon toward his village crept up and knocked him down with a club. But instead of running, Maynard beat off the native and took the photograph desired."

What makes this example noteworthy is not the curious content of the

Journal N

EWTON H. CHITTENDEN
was an explorer-for-hire. In 1884, Chittenden (seated) and his photographer, Richard Maynard, led a six-month expedition for the British Columbian government to explore and map the Queen Charlotte Islands in the remote Canadian Pacific Northwest (see also "Dodging Earl in the Ghost Islands," page 86). That April, Chittenden wrote, they feasted with Haida chieftain Edensaw in his village (right), while "investigating the meaning and purpose of [their] remarkable carved totem columns…covered with representations of all animal life known to them, and many grotesque creatures of their imagination."

Figure 3. Adventure travel's racial unconscious. From
National Geographic Adventure, 1999, vol. 1, no. 2.

caption but that the editors of the magazine apparently felt no need to explain why they included this image at the end of the issue. After all, at no point does the story about sea-kayaking in the Haida Gwaii make any reference to Chittenden, Maynard, or the journal. Nor is there any effort by the editors to link these images with the *contents* of the story in the middle (beyond a small heading beneath the photo that invites readers to turn to the story on kayaking). It is simply assumed that the reader does not *need* to be told what relation exists between a kayak trip into the "wilds" of the Haida Gwaii in 1998 and the journey of an American mercenary and Canadian photographer in 1884, since, within a discourse of "European exploration" (the terms of which are in part secured by the reproduction of the image and others like it), adventure today is understood to be the *same* as, or *continuous with*, acts of European exploration set in the past. Accordingly, we are told nothing about Chittenden and Maynard or their journeys, and do not need to be, since the general outline of the story is already known. Borrowing from Judith Butler, adventure today is governed by regulatory norms that operate even in the absence of their explicit articulation.

This does not mean that other articles do not make the connection to historical examples of exploration by Europeans in a more direct fashion. A recent article in *American Heritage*, for instance, juxtaposes in a one-to-one ratio photographs of present-day adventure travelers with nineteenth-century explorers. Accordingly, pictures of white-water rafters on Idaho's Lochsa River today are placed alongside photos of boatsmen navigating rapids in New York in the 1880s (Brandt 2001). But here several remarks are necessary. First, while the presence of these historical referents calls attention to the existence of regulatory norms that govern risk culture meanings (which is why *this* connection is made, and not another), the presence of these referents is not necessary for those norms to operate. Indeed, it is precisely when these referents are *not* present that the norms may be most fully at work (in the same way that norms of heterosexuality operate implicitly). Hence, the images do not produce the norm so much as call attention to its operation. Moreover, the presence of historical references like these reminds us that the meanings that adventure holds today, and the links between adventure and whiteness, can never be finally fixed, since other kinds of grafting could possibly occur that would introduce a certain drift to risk culture's meanings.

A second remark concerns the status of the historical referent in risk culture. As mentioned earlier, risk culture is citational not because it recalls an objective historical event (what "actually" happened in the past) but instead because it repeats a norm, the normativity of which is secured in part by a historical narrative ("European exploration"). That we are on the terrain of narrative and not history is made clear from the images of Chittenden and Maynard, the historical details of which matter little. The importance of these figures lies in the narrative and the meanings they are asked, and able, to bear. In this sense the magazine's choice is entirely arbitrary, for the editors could just as easily have substituted an image of George Dawson, who visited the Haida Gwaii in 1878, six years earlier. What is invoked in these articles, then, is a *mythological* past whose truth is an effect of its representation (and its repetition). Third, to understand the invocation of these historical figures as a kind of nostalgia for an earlier, lost moment of European exploration is misleading, since it elides the way that exploration has come to be *understood* as a European activity through the erasure or displacement of non-European actors. That is, to say that risk culture "repeats" the past is wrong on two accounts, since it gives the past an undue transparency (it assumes that there is a "real" past that it repeats) and since it assumes that what is repeated is the *history*, rather than the norm.

It is now possible to recognize the provisional and precarious nature of adventure's racial meanings, for repetition is not without difference. When Derrida writes of iteration, he writes of a "grafting" that is in important respects arbitrary, in the sense that words or concepts can take on new meanings, and in the sense that there is no limit to what *sort* of graftings can occur. This suggests a crucial difference between the *American Heritage* and *National Geographic Adventure* articles. In contrast to the latter, in which the historical referent was largely assumed, in the former the referent is made explicit, which attests not to the fixity of a discourse that links adventure and whiteness, but to a certain uncertainty over its terms, which must be continuously secured.

In passing, this suggests added significance to the writing of history and to debates over how the history of the U.S. West should be understood. Given the common understanding of exploration as a "white" activity, and the prominent place of the U.S. West in risk culture's imaginative geographies, this is no small matter. Beginning in the 1980s with the work of a loosely knit group known as the New Western Historians, an understanding of the U.S. West has emerged that is considerably more complex than the mythological West found in American popular culture. Leaving aside internal debates over whether the West names a place or a process (see Lansing, in press), what is significant about this work is that it provides a picture of the West's historical geographies that can no longer be contained with a singular story of Euro-American westward expansion. What was formerly viewed as a single "frontier" has come to be fractured into multiple contact zones each suffused with multiple relations of difference, and each shaped by political, economic, and social relations that tied these zones to wider geographical networks. For New Western Historians, telling these stories has meant reading historical records with *other* subjects in mind and attending to the erasure of nonwhite actors from official accounts of exploration and settlement. It has also involved calling attention to the social, political, and economic conditions of the post-Reconstruction era, which enabled the mobility of whites while restricting the mobility of former slaves. Ultimately, it has meant refusing to understand the West in terms of a single teleology centered on the expansionary logic of European society, or in terms of a limiting white-native binary that declared that particular drama the only game in town.

If the West in American history (and a Canadian West annexed by American popular culture) has routinely been depicted as a space of white ingenuity, fortitude, and morality, then New Western Historians remind us that this version of the West is not simply there waiting to be found in the historical record but is instead called forth through a series of cognitive failures. These have now been given names: the erasure of Native American agency, the invisibility of African Americans in stories of settlement, the staging of the West as untracked land, the whitening of the cowboy in Hollywood films, the construction of the U.S. West as an "American" space despite centuries of Spanish/Mexican influence.[16] Downplayed in white historiography, both in the United States and Canada, have been the complexity and plurality of the continent's social and cultural landscapes, or the fact that extensive routes of communication and forms of travel long predated the arrival of European travelers.

To return to the *National Geographic Adventure* story recounted above, explorers like Chittenden, who traveled the long sea journey from Victoria to the Haida Gwaii (over 450 miles), regularly met the boats of Haida traders making similar journeys in the *other* direction, much as they had done for hundreds of years. The actors in the image can be reversed, although they rarely, if ever, are speaking to the hold of a "sedentarist metaphysics" (Malkki 1997) that posits the racialized other as fixed in place. Hence, the significance of Dan Clayton's (1999) recent reading of historical documents and oral histories surrounding Captain James Cook's arrival on the coast in 1779, somewhat farther to the south, in which he argues that Cook found himself immediately enmeshed in a confusing array of trading networks and political relations that stretched across hundreds of miles of coast and penetrated deep into the continent's interior. Although Cook had immense difficulty grasping the full import of these networks, his journals and those of his crew, along with oral histories of the "Nootka," provide ample evidence that the peoples he met were neither isolated, primitive, nor sedentary. Similarly,

Lewis and Clark followed familiar and heavily traveled routes, relying extensively on native informants and guides (White 1995). In the Arctic Peary traveled to the North Pole with Matthew Henson, an African American, although Hensen was subsequently erased from official accounts (Bloom 1993). These revisionist histories may not (yet) have effected discursive displacements on a scale that would challenge the hegemony of historical narratives of white, European exploration, nor do they escape the pull of empiricism and its ontologizing of difference as an analytical category. Yet, they help underline the provisional—and precarious—nature of the discursive norms that underwrite risk culture's cultural and racial economies.

Risk Culture, Imaginative Geographies, and the Racialization of Space

We are all, in some sense, mountaineers, and going to the mountains is going home.
—John Muir, "Summer Days at Mount Shasta"

Risk culture is marked not only by temporality (iteration), it is inherently spatial. It involves movement—into nature, away from the city, across space— and thus traverses imaginative geographies that give meaning to movement and significance to place.[17]

This can be understood by extending the previous discussion of the West, and in particular the frontier. That risk culture turns on this spatial trope is evident in its emphasis on boundary crossing, on moving from a pacified world to one that is wild, untamed, and unknown. But this demands that we refine our understanding of this imaginative space, for in American political and cultural thought the frontier appears in more than one guise. Most Americans are familiar with frontier ideologies from the early writings of Frederick Jackson Turner, for whom the frontier was a site of moral, cultural, and political regeneration. This belief was deeply indebted to primitivism, and the assumption that "the best antidote to the ills of an overly refined and civilized world was a return to simpler, more primitive living" (Cronon 1996: 76).

Such sentiments had already found strong expression a half-century before Turner in the writings of Henry Thoreau, and in the musings of Turner's contemporary, John Muir. But these writers—especially Muir—also understood the frontier somewhat differently. Henry Nash Smith's (1950) more complicated and ambivalent reading provides a starting point. For Smith, representations of the frontier in the second half of the nineteenth century were not always, nor unambiguously, primitivist. In contrast to William

Cronon's recent gloss on Turner, Smith argued that the frontier was not uniformly set *against* civilization; rather, it was often represented as the *outpost* of that very civilization, the first step in the civilizing of the West (or, in Thoreau's words, the inevitable "becoming East" of the "West").[18] Clearly, this contains elements of Turner's evolutionary model of development (nature—agriculture—metropolis), but whereas Turner celebrated the ever-advancing frontier as the site of moral regeneration, Smith identified in certain writers a desire to *elude* this ever-encroaching civilization altogether. Daniel Boone, for instance, was mythologized not because he settled on the frontier, thereby domesticating difference (nature), but because he kept moving. In his readings of stories about Boone, Kit Carson, and characters like Leatherstocking, Smith notes that the salient distinction was not frontier/civilization but rather the frontier and that which lay *beyond* the frontier. The real heroes in these novels and biographies were not Turner's farmers, ranchers, and townfolk but instead hunters, trappers, and explorers: "For Americans . . . there were two quite distinct Wests: the commonplace domesticated area within the agricultural frontier, and the Wild West beyond it. The agricultural West was tedious; its inhabitants belonged to a despised social class. The Wild West was by contrast an exhilarating region of adventure and comradeship in the open air" (1950: 52). Smith argues that in nineteenth-century literature the frontier was often portrayed as the site of the "already domesticated." The line that divided the "frontier" and the "West beyond the frontier" was precisely the line between savagery/ civilization, wild/domesticated, known/unknown, nature/culture and, of course, risk/safety. Crucially, in the stories Smith analyzed, one did not flee *from* the frontier to reach safe ground; one returned *to* the frontier, since danger lay in those areas beyond the line of settlement. Real adventure involved crossing from the frontier to the "beyond." The frontier represented less an escape from civilization than the incursion of civilization into a domain previously beyond its reach; thus, to arrive and settle at the frontier was to have already arrived too late.

If in the pages of *Outside* and *National Geographic Adventure* risk culture recalls the frontier, what it recalls is decidedly not Turner's agrarian idyll but instead Smith's notion of the frontier as threshold. Frontier, then, is understood in terms of boundary or dividing line, rather than as place or region. Further, if we retain Smith's notion of the frontier as an anxiously policed line between the beyond and the civilized (or the different and the same), it becomes evident that central to its meanings—and to risk culture today—is the matter of wilderness. To journey beyond the frontier was to journey into a domain ruled by natural forces. In the case of our intrepid mountain climber, this takes the form of rock, wind, and rain. For sea-kayakers in the Haida Gwaii, it is the unpredictable fury of Pacific storms ("Earl"). As evident in both examples, adventure turns on crossing a great divide between culture and wild nature; it is about physical and moral tests that the encounter with *unmediated* nature provides (hence, adventure travel's emphasis on self-propelled transportation is not only a nostalgia for earlier modes of travel, it is also about stripping away the most obvious source of alienation from nature—modern technology). It should come as little surprise that the article on sea-kayaking begins with the statement "Try to imagine North America before the car . . . ", or that it goes on to describe adventure lodges "in the boonies of British Columbia" as "not some hoity-toity, glassine-wrapped spas." The language may be colloquial, but it is an anxious one that seeks to establish and sustain the space of adventure as one of unmediated encounters with nature's wildness.

As evident in the words of John Muir, this boundary crossing was simultaneously a spatial and ideological move *away* from unnatural humanity (culture) and *to* humanity's true home (nature).[19] To go to the mountains was to go home. This merits further discussion. Clearly, this imaginative geography of wild nature is gendered (and sexualized), although perhaps in a more complex manner than the familiar binaries of nature as feminine and culture as masculine. That wilderness can be considered men's true home alerts us to the workings of a different binary—domesticated/wild—in which the "domesticated" home (the frontier, the place of one's wife), is contrasted with a "true" home (wilderness, the mistress who excites and whom one masters). For Smith the frontier was "tedious." That which lay beyond was "exhilerating" (and the site of "comradeship"). Likewise, for Muir civilization was enervating, while nature was a site of excitement and regeneration.

Second, the journey into external nature is consistently troped as a journey into the (inner) self. It brings the individual in touch with that *primal* self that has been lost in humanity's "descent" into modernity. Thus, entirely consistent with Muir's claim that the mountains are our home, a recent advertising campaign by Canada's Yukon Territories shows a group of wilderness explorers gazing down on a pristine valley from atop a high mountain ridge, with a predictable slogan: "Down there is your soul."[20] Here I am less interested in risk culture's pervasive primitivist tropes—and its view of modernity as alienation—than in the unstated racial text at work in them. The point that must be stressed is that the staging of nature-as-origin, or nature as "home," first requires an understanding of humanity as separate from, and alienated from, nature. Thus, from the outset, the act of going home to nature is articulated with other ideas, not only about gender, but also race, civilization, and progress. This argument has been developed at some length by others and requires only a cursory summary here (see Haraway 1989, Cosgrove 1995, Cronon 1996, Di Chiro 1995, Slater 1995, DeLuca 1999). Kevin DeLuca states the case most baldly, arguing that dominant constructions of wild nature in North America invariably posit a "white" nature, rooted in European cultural histories, and traceable to Judeo-Christian traditions, which he claims both externalize nature and establish it as a privileged site of spiritual renewal and testing.[21] For DeLuca, this tradition underlabors for Romanticism and supports ideologies of the sublime, both historically and today (see also Cronon 1996). Thus, he suggests, what Henry Thoreau and John Muir celebrated as a universal human need—the encounter with external nature—must be rethought in terms of understandings of nature, self, and modernity that emerged from European cultural traditions, or "white culture."[22]

Denis Cosgrove (1995) comes to a similar conclusion but by way of a somewhat different path. The notion of primal nature, he argues, gains its cultural intelligibility not only in relation to civilization or the city but more directly in relation to European expansion. Thus wilderness, especially in North America, referred to those places as yet untouched by the *European imperium*. Further, this teleological narrative allowed an equivalence to be drawn between nonhuman nature and non-Europeans, since both were thought to occupy a similar site outside, or prior to, a modern, transformative European culture (see also Haraway 1989, Di Chiro 1995, McClintock 1995). Similar views persist, as evident in the advertising of adventure travel companies like Vancouver-based Ecosummer Expeditions, in which journeys into "pristine nature" are placed cheek-by-jowl with journeys to "primitive cultures," or as is often the case in its catalogue, conflated into single "journeys of discovery."

Here we can return to an earlier argument—that in risk culture the "black adventurer" has no proper place. Although we might question aspects of Cosgrove's and De Luca's arguments, they call attention to the ways in which the primitivism of historical figures like Muir—and adventure travelers today—involves much more than an escape from the city and a hankering after a more direct experience of, and physical tests in, nature. Such a primitivism was also, almost by definition, bound up with understandings of racial difference. It assumed a world divided in two: a European modernity alienated from nature, and a non-European premodernity peopled by natural cultures.

The search for nature (as a return to origins) was something that only Europeans needed to participate in because it was only they whose advanced development had opened an almost unbridgeable gulf between a cultural present and a natural or biological past. Returns to nature were unnecessary for non-European others, since they were by definition closer to nature in the first place (see Di Chiro 1995; Slater 1995). What primitivism assumed, then, was not just a distinction between civilization and nature, or between the modern and premodern, but also a racial hierarchy established through a discourse of progress. Thus, within the racial text of primitivist discourse, the figure of the Indian *seeking* danger or the "black adventurer" wishing to *return* to nature becomes absurd, even comical. When John Muir asserted that the journey into nature was a universal human need, he did not have in mind non-Europeans: *they were already there.*[23]

Frontier ideologies were not the only way that wild nature was constituted as a performative space of whiteness at the last fin de siécle. These imaginative geographies ran alongside, and were entangled with, other representations of space that turned on racialized discourses of danger and purity and binary oppositions between city and country. This has been noted by several historians and cultural critics, who understand the turn to nature in that period among white, middle-class Americans as a response to changes in the nation's social fabric. Donna Haraway (1989) argues that in this period the experience of nature served as a prophylactic against racial degeneracy. At issue was not only massive increases in immigration but the *type* of immigrant that was arriving, including Italians, Jews, and Slavs, who were thought to be separate races, inferior to Anglo-Saxons. For instance, while Anglo-Saxons were thought to delight in open spaces, it was commonly thought that others found perverse pleasure crowded into the tight spaces of the city. In turn, anxieties over the reproductive capacities of immigrant women, as well as the threat of "urban diseases," led to widespread fears of "race-suicide," a term popularized by Teddy Roosevelt. For Denis Cosgrove, appeals to wild nature, and the system of nature reserves set in place in the period, were suffused by these histories of racism and white nationalism.

In such a context, the great surge of wilderness preservation in the first decade of the new century (so often attributed to the individual charisma of men such as John Muir and Teddy Roosevelt) should perhaps be reassessed. The open spaces of the West were as far removed geographically, culturally, and experientially from the crowded immigrant cities of New

York, Philadelphia, Pittsburgh, or Chicago as they could be. Patrons of the wild came overwhelmingly from "old stock" and the middle classes; many had been as strongly committed to the introduction of urban parks modeled upon the English picturesque tradition (a style often opposed by newer immigrants, who favored playgrounds and baseball diamonds to lakes, trees, and flower beds) . . . National parks represented . . . the kind of environment in which earlier—and racially purer—immigrants were believed to have forged American national identity. (1995: 35)

Consistent with a discourse that linked nonwhites with degeneracy and associated both with the city, nature was troped as a site of moral and racial purity: the true foundation of the nation, and the true home of its original settlers. Moreover, since it was assumed that the moral character of (white) American culture came in part from immersion in nature, the experience of nature could be held out as a means of both racial and national regeneration. The journey into nature was in part how whiteness was constituted (conversely, the city became the place of darkening, where one risked moral, if not genetic, decline). Nature, then, served as a purification machine, a place where people became white, where the racial and hereditary habits of immigrants could be overcome. In short, the journey *into* nature was just as much a journey *away* from something else, and that something else was race.[24]

Many of today's ideologies of nature, Cosgrove argues, retain these "hidden attachments." There are disturbing reasons to believe that he is correct. The almost reverent invocation of figures like Muir—who sought regeneration through the encounter with "wild" nature—continues to tie mainstream environmentalism, as well as risk culture's "journey in," to a political and intellectual tradition that includes nineteenth-century nature advocates and their vision of nature as a salve for a degenerating society.[25] Admittedly, Muir's somewhat transcendental bent seems quaint today, especially after the macho (and often explicitly racist) environmentalisms of Edward Abbey and Dave Foreman, whose libertarian strains are in some respects more direct precursors to risk culture today than Muir's more philosophical and contemplative writings. Yet the "white nature" that Muir represents, and which Abbey and Foreman updated during the Reagan years, remains dominant, despite efforts by grassroots environmental groups and the environmental justice movement to articulate other cultures of nature that do not rehearse the same race and class assumptions (Di Chiro 1995).[26]

Further, representations of city and country today share many of the same assumptions as those found at the end of the last century. As Mike Davis noted in *City of Quartz* (1990), urban spaces like central Los Angeles are increasingly racialized. This is true not only in terms of the production of racialized landscapes through linked processes of racialization and class formation (see Pulido et al. 1996) but also in terms of a white middle-class imagination that sees the city through a "demonological lens" (Davis 1990).[27] Arguably the war on drugs, the criminalization of African American males (i.e., as "gang members"), and the spatial incarceration of impoverished and racialized workers has over the past decade had the effect of intensifying understandings of the city that conjoin race, place, and degeneracy. Media representations and Hollywood films have intensified these racial and spatial semiotics. As Andrew Light (1999) notes, films such as *Falling Down*, which tracked the degeneration of a recently laid-off middle-class professional (played by Michael Douglas) as he journeyed through the inner city, drew equivalences between racialized inner-city communities and Joseph Conrad's "dark continent," contrasting the suburb as a space of reason and order and the inner city as a primitive space of chaos and violence. To travel "into" the city is thus figured as a sort of moral descent. Traveling "out" from the city appears as its opposite, a journey into a more refined state.[28]

Risk Taking Within Risk Society:
Naturalizing White, Middle-Class Privilege

In these stories of space, race, and risk only white subjects move. All others are spatially incarcerated—fixed in place within a social imaginary that assumes the whiteness of the adventurous individual.

We are now in a position to do more than consider the illegibility of the "black" adventurer; we can consider the immense ideological work performed by risk culture within risk society. What made Michael Douglas's character so disturbing to white audiences was not simply his descent into the dark continent of the city but that, as a white middle-class professional, he did not belong in a place where risk was thought to be an ontological condition rather than a personal choice. Within mainstream American culture, *taking* risks is understood as an individuating activity associated with whiteness. One takes risks when one chooses to. Being *at* risk is commonly viewed as a property that belongs to someone else, the *racial* subject. It is associated not with agency or choice but with a kind of passivity, helplessness, or deviance.[29]

This observation returns us to the at risk/taking risk binary with which I began and makes explicit the ideological effects of images of rock climbers and sea-kayakers. Over the past decade a large body of scholarship has explored the uneven distribution of risk in American society. While within risk society all people live "at risk," who it is that is most at risk and who it is that is most able to distance him- or herself from risk is in part the outcome of a politics of race and class. Middle-class whites face risks like everyone else, but they constitute themselves as middle-class and white precisely through the *externalization* of as many risks as possible (locating socially undesirable land uses elsewhere or sending children to private schools) and through *barricading* themselves from many others (through gated communities or purchasing insurance). Hence, if you are white and middle class, "risk" is something you take on voluntarily, not something you are subject to.

The significance of risk culture, then, lies not only in the impossibility of the black or Latina adventurer within its discursive order but also in its *naturalization* of risk society's racial and class orders. This is captured brilliantly, if unintentionally, in a recent Moosehead Beer ad ("Nature's Corporate Ladder," figure 4*). For many readers it would be disturbing—even shocking—to substitute a black or Latina person in this image. This is true in part because, as I have shown, in risk culture's discursive formations the racialized subject can not properly be the "risk-taking" subject, but also because his or her presence would disrupt a myth of the present that understands the unequal distribution of wealth in American society in terms of a kind of natural order. Climbing the corporate ladder is akin to climbing a mountain: it is about skill, ability, and ambition, not politics, economy, or power. It is presented as something innate in the person (although apparently less innate in the woman who follows) but also as a property that belongs to the physically *superior* specimen whose superiority is deserved (through training and diet, for instance).[30] The absent figure in this final image—but whose absence is precisely that which allows it to carry the meanings it has— is the figure bequeathed by workfare advocates and culture-of-poverty theorists: the poor black whose degeneracy is a guarantee of his social position, whose natural proclivity is to watch TV, eat junk food, and take drugs, who has no work ethic, is overweight, unhealthy, and unmotivated. The black subject simply can't be this "active" climber. He or she is unable to "heed the call." To place the black or Latina subject in the frame, *as* the adventurer, would produce a kind of crisis within the ideological fields of the present social order, in which the absence of the entrepreneurial, risk-taking black is solely a fault of his or her own.

*I thank Kristin Sziarto for drawing this image to my attention.

Figure 4. Nature's corporate ladder: naturalizing white privilege.
Advertisement from *Backpacker*.

Risk culture does not reflect "realities" of class and race. In its assumption of the whiteness of the adventurer, it proclaims a racial and economic order as natural; it reminds us we deserve our situation in life. In its encounters with nature, it teaches us again that races have their proper places. While racial subjects have no proper place in risk culture's discursive economies they most certainly *do* have a place in today's risk society: as the subject who can never be the "risk-taking" subject, the subject who must always be "at risk," the subject who, naturally, can never climb nature's corporate ladder. In an age "after biology," race and nature have perhaps never been so tightly bound together.

Notes

Versions of this paper were presented at Dartmouth College and at the University of Minnesota's Center for Advanced Feminist Studies. My discussion of risk culture and the naturalization of class owes a great deal to Lisa Disch. Michael Dorsey, Caren Kaplan, Michael Lansing, and the editors of this volume provided helpful comments on earlier versions. All remaining errors are my responsibility. Finally, many thanks to Gwen McCrea, who tirelessly tracked images of adventure and risk in American popular culture.

1   That the AAA felt obligated to make such a pronouncement only reveals that the debate continues, not that it has been finally closed.

2   External nature is a discursive site, not a physical one (see Smith 1984; Haraway 1992; Latour 1993).

3   I use "Latina" in this essay as gender neutral. It is important to emphasize that magazines actively *constitute* their audiences in racial terms, and thus that the "reading publics" that they target are, in important ways, produced by the publications themselves.

4   Activities set in natural environments were depicted in media targeting black and Latina readers, but most commonly in terms of recreation, not risk or adventure.

5   I posit the figure of the absent nonwhite adventurer to enable a reading, not as a historical subject to be searched for and recovered.

6   As Kirshenblatt-Gimblett (1998) explains, the distinction between "embodied" and "virtual" cannot be sustained; like all modes of travel and tourism, adventure travel is virtual "all the way down." More significant, the distinction "embodied" and "virtual" traces a racial discourse where adventure travel is the proper domain of white subjects (figured as active risk takers) while the "virtual" belongs properly to the poor, racialized subject whose relation to the world is thought to be completely mediated, passive, and lazy. I take up these issues in the concluding section.

7   For insight into the ascetic dimensions of risk culture, see Krakauer 1996.

8   There are countless examples of the disavowal of race and class in adventure travel. A recent ad by Woolrich in *National Geographic Adventure*, for instance, shows a fit, middle-aged white male climbing a rocky ridge, with the slogan "think outside the importance of knowing where you're going." At once gesturing to the rationalization of time and space in capitalist

modernity, it disavows the system of property and privilege that determines who is able to "think outside."

9 The fact that early Everest climbers like Mallory and Hillary "bought" their accomplishments through extracting the labor of Sherpa guides and porters seems lost on these critics.

10 It is possible to read this supplement as conforming to Derrida's notion of *supplementarity:* in this case, risk culture, with its normalizing of racial ideologies through staging encounters with nature, becomes one of the supplemental terms that is "added to" the present American socioeconomic and discursive order in order to stabilize its class and race characteristic.

11 Clearly not all individuals will be successfully "hailed" by the image. Here it is crucial to keep in mind that *Outside* does not only target a white audience, it actively constitutes its readers *as* white.

12 It was Tenzing Norgay. It came as no surprise that I could find Hillary but not Norgay in the "biographical names" section of my dictionary.

13 One might object that the visibility of the body is a necessary function of the product advertised—a fragrance and skin-care line—but as we know, *use value* is rarely what advertising portrays. Moreover, this only further highlights the question of why it is the racialized *black* body, rather than any other.

14 While it is important to caution that this is not the *only* way that the black body is represented within present-day visual cultures, it is surprisingly prevalent. Perhaps the most notable site of black male visibility in the 1990s (apart from "crimebuster" shows on TV) was professional sports, especially basketball. While an important arena for expressions of black male identity (Dennis Rodman, for example), it too did not entirely escape dominant representations of "blackness" in American popular culture. Black male participation in professional sports may be sanctioned, even promoted, but it remains white owners who obtain profits from the same strong, young, black, and expendable bodies that fed slavery. As bell hooks notes in her discussion of *Hoop Dreams,* the visibility of black male athletes speaks to "the reality that . . . institutionalized racism and white supremacist attitudes in everyday American life actively prohibit black male participation in diverse cultural arenas and spheres of employment while presenting sports as the 'one' location where recognition, success and material reward can be attained. . . . Just as the bodies of African-American slaves were expendable, the bodies of black male ballplayers cease to matter if they are not able to deliver the described product" (see hooks 1996: 79, 80).

15 My discussion of citationality is indebted to Derrida (1988) and Butler (1993).

16 Much of this work occurred in the early 1990s. See Limerick et al. 1991; Cronon et al. 1992; Deutsch 1992; Faragher 1992. More recently, ecocritics have started to rethink frontier literature in similar ways. See Comer 1999.

17 I borrow the phrase "imaginative geographies" from Edward Said (1994). See also Derek Gregory (1995).

18 Smith (1950) also notes that for some of these writers the frontier was not viewed as a site of values and virtue but only as *inadequately* civilized.

19 Of course, the West "beyond" the frontier was *also* a cultural landscape and could be understood as natural only by collapsing Indians into nature.

20 I discuss this further in Braun 2002.

21 See also White 1967. DeLuca problematically reduces the externalization of nature to a single dynamic: Judeo-Christian theology. Others have suggested that Judeo-Christian traditions are

somewhat more ambivalent, while still others have suggested that notions of "external" nature attained dominance only with two related developments: the scientific revolution (with its nature/culture dualism) and the rise of capitalist production (with its commodification and externalization of nature).

22 Although important, DeLuca's analysis falls short on two counts. First, his assumption that the externalization of nature is *unique* to European cultures is no doubt overstated. Second, his notion of "white nature" risks falling into a kind of identity politics based on essential cultural differences.

23 Romanticism and primitivism are profoundly ambivalent discourses: at the same time as they assert European superiority, this superiority is also found to be the cause of a lack that must be resolved by recovering links with a natural past.

24 Likewise, the Scouts and Woodcraft youth—with their emphasis on nature and adventure—come to be about much more than recovering the emotions and experiences of primitive ancestors or the cultivation of a (lost) primitive vitality. In the face of an emerging eugenicism, these movements can also be read as centrally about the *purification* of (the white) race (Seltzer 1992). As Cosgrove (1995: 36) notes, the "cult of childhood" that these movements represented merged with two different developments: on the one hand, the "cult of strenuous exercise" as a route to the recovery of unrepressed emotions and an imaginative life, and, on the other hand, the emergence of ideas of racial purity.

25 Although a number of critics have noted the nostalgic invocation of figures like Muir today, few note that Muir himself was *already* articulating a nostalgic vision that imagined a "purity" to nature (and the nation) that had never actually existed.

26 This was all too evident in debates among radical ecologists in the late 1990s over whether immigration to the United States should be restricted in order to preserve wilderness. Critics saw in this a veiled racism, most evident in the view that (nonwhite) immigrants *threatened* wilderness in part because they were not thought to hold the right/white attitude to, or appreciation for, nature.

27 This is a somewhat more complex discourse than I present here. In some senses the "inner-city" itself becomes scripted as "nature"—albeit "jungle" rather than "wilderness"—and the line between "white" space and "racial" space in the city takes on the form of a new urban frontier (it was precisely this frontier that was commodified by realtors and developers in the 1980s and early 1990s; see Smith 1996).

28 It is worth noting that journeys away from the suburb in *both* directions—to the city and into wilderness—are associated with risk taking and whiteness: the former, as a journey into the "urban jungle" and the latter as the journey into "raw nature."

29 The black subject can also be a risk-taking subject, but the activity is often understood to be *pathological* (i.e., drug use, gang violence).

30 It is noteworthy that white women *are* permitted within the visual and discursive orders of risk culture, although, again, their presence does a certain amount of ideological work. In this case, the presence of white women figures enables a self-congratulatory story of progress, introducing an enlightened present where women can now do what men do (even if when men and women are shown together, a natural gender hierarchy is reasserted). This merely reinforces the striking absence of the black subject in risk culture's visual frames, for whereas the "white women adventurer" is permitted in it, the "black adventurer" is not.

6. Beyond Ecoliberal "Common Futures"

Environmental Justice, Toxic Touring, and

a Transcommunal Politics of Place

Giovanna Di Chiro

If you're willing to fight, willing to accept your struggle, then you can make a difference. This big [environmental] issue that we've had to deal with has renewed our faith in a great many things. One is that we found out that environmentalists are not just tree-huggers and we found out that they are caring people, you know. And that they care about the very same things that we as a union care about. At heart, we're all environmentalists.—Darnell Dunn, President U.S. Steelworkers Local 8394, Baton Rouge, Louisiana, 1997

We've got only one planet to take care of, one planet floating out here in the air. . . . We've only got one air that we breathe: we all breathe the same air all around this globe. In other words, everything is the same. There's no difference in the air over here and the air over there. There's no difference in the water, there's no difference anywhere for anything on Mother Earth.—Corbin Harney, Spiritual Leader of the Western Shoshone Nation, 1995

The idea that we must recognize our "common future," ecologically speaking, did not originate with the declarations calling for "limits to growth" and "sustainable development" in the pages of the Bruntland Commission Report that came out of the United Nations Conference on the Human Environment held in Stockholm in 1972. For centuries, the cultural politics of the Quechuan and Aymara peoples of the Andes, for example, was negotiated within a conceptual framework known as *Aruskipaxidcajananakasakipunirakispawa*, or the necessity that "we communicate with each other, face to face, our feet rooted in the earth, with which we also must communicate, if we are to live" (Childs 1998: 165). Since the advent of nuclear testing in the desert sacrifice zones of the southwestern United States in the 1950s, members of the Western Shoshone have "come out from behind the bush" and invoked their spirituality as an intercultural style of politics enjoining "we, the people today, everywhere across Mother Earth . . . to unite together, no matter what color we are, no matter what 'lango' we speak" to prevent future environmental and social devastation (Harney 1995: xxii). Although mainstream environmentalists portray the United Nations gathering in Stockholm as having ushered in the era of global environmental politics and the conviction that global (particularly north/south) cooperation was now vitally important to stave off certain ecological catastrophe due to the excesses of industrial capitalism, these insights are common knowledge in many communities across the globe that have long suffered from the externalities of modernity.

This ecological discourse of unity and interconnectedness is emerging from very different environmental predicaments, however. The popular, modern environmental imagination—one born of a perception of crisis potentially at the doorstep of the privileged and promulgated through expressions like "spaceship earth," "international heritage sites," "thinking globally/acting locally," or "the global commons"—evokes rhetorics of universality, one-worldism, and common fate. Another modern environmental imagination, born of communities' firsthand experiences of poisoned rivers, depleted soils, over-logged forests, polluted air, and environmental illnesses, also calls on the idea of "one water, one air, one earth" and the necessity for common struggle among all peoples for environmental health. But how are these discourses of unity, commonality, and one-world community differently constituted? What kinds of languages of a "global commons" are being produced in these very differently situated political, ecological, and cultural landscapes?

This notion of the necessity of articulating a discourse of commonality, communication, and cooperation across racial/ethnic, class, geographic, or national divisions is a politics of difference deploying the central metaphor of the commons. One commons discourse—peddled by mainstream environmentalists and the architects of the world-historical sustainable development project, the so-called Worldwatchers (World Bank, GEF, UNCED, NAFTA, WTO)—wants to whitewash the differential social and environmental impacts of globalization and to proclaim that "we're all in the same boat now." Spaceship earth, on which "we" all depend for our survival (akin to a lifeboat), is imperiled; and so we must put our differences behind us (and stop creating havoc, such as overbreeding, or slashing and burning the rain forest, which threatens to swamp the lifeboat) so that the international class of enviro-experts can get down to the business of saving nature and, consequently, "our" economic prospects. In the Worldwatchers' narrative, diversity lies in the international division of labor as is spelled out in the economic doctrine of comparative advantage: everyone doing their part, in the manner that is best suited to their cultural differences and productive capacities, to ensure the long-term equilibrium of the spaceship. This expression of the global commons signifies a neoliberal environmentalism reasserting cultural difference in the terms of making the world environmentally secure for unrestrained capitalist accumulation on a planet of finite resources and limited ecosystemic resilience (in the name of "sustainable development"). Ecoliberalism, in this sense, is about constructing an ideology of the "global commons" (a concept and entity one "cannot not want," to paraphrase Gayatri Spivak) in order to justify the enclosure of, and guarantee ongoing access to, more and more of the world's dwindling resources by multinational corporations and the national regimes that underwrite them. Situated squarely within the doctrine of globalization, ecoliberalism encompasses the neoliberal paradigm of the effectiveness of the free marketplace benevolently to solve all social and environmental woes, while specifically emphasizing the necessity of winning the war of ideas regarding the global nature of "our" problems. Now, economic security and power is dependent on wrestling control over the global commons (in the name of "preserving" it) to ensure open access to the planet's natural wealth remaining in the hands of the rich (in the name of helping the world's poor).

Another "global commons" discourse, that which is articulated by members of communities identifying themselves as part of a worldwide network of movements for environmental justice (EJM), also engages in an ecological narrative of universal nature/human connections, but with a twist. As an antiracist movement, the EJM aims to reduce the disproportionate impacts of environmental problems on people of color and poor people and simultaneously attempts to create multicultural alliances among people of different racial/ethnic, national, and class backgrounds. For many activists, this move toward common cause is grounded in the concept that environmental problems are the ultimate equalizers. Although people of color and low-income communities are the most poisoned populations, EJM activists argue we all live in one world and the poison and despoliation eventually travel, even to the most elite locales. The metaphor of "one worldism" emerges as analytically and strategically powerful for people of color and low-income communities fighting to reclaim and sharpen the ecological commons debate and to improve their environmental conditions. It becomes a counterhegemonic move to proclaim, as does steelworker Darnell Dunn, that "at heart, we're all environmentalists."

What analytical/political tools can we design, to support livable social/

ecological futures in the twenty-first century? I suggest that the grassroots organizing strategies of the EJM, and other movements around the world relinking communities and environments, provide important clues. Many EJM activists build alliances and common ground across differences that are not based on an abstract, ecoliberal "we are the world" model but on *situational pragmatism:* we know what is happening to the natural world because we are experiencing it firsthand. Can we fashion nonimperializing formulations of the global commons—those that retain its "gathering together" impulse without obscuring real differences in livelihood and survivability, power, and environmental consequences? In this chapter I argue that the ecological discourse of the global commons, while carrying with it a new set of justifications for social/environmental control (over land, natural resources, environmental expertise) by environmental-science authorities and political-economic elites, also provides opportunities that create new political spaces and identities for environmental change. First, I discuss the different versions of the "global commons" that argue we now live with parallel, if not equivalent, environmental predicaments. I then concentrate on different ways that environmental justice activists construct a politics of difference grounded in an ecological discourse of interconnectedness and common ground. These include the creation of multiracial/ethnic, oppositional political networks that build linkages and create communities of action resisting destructive modes of production and in support of environmental justice. In the final section I discuss "toxic tourism," an organizing strategy using a tourism model to bring together communities of color struggling to improve highly polluted living and working conditions and "outsider" tourist visitors. The hope is that this uncommon tourist exchange will encourage people from diverse and unequal backgrounds to perceive that "we're all environmentalists" and therefore should work together collectively to combat all environmental injustices.

The Global Commons and the Ecoliberal "Agenda for the Twenty-first Century"

[UNCED] is a once-in-a-generation opportunity for the one-world community.—Gus Speth, President, World Resources Institute, 1992

The historical consciousness that humans are all inhabitants of a global environment has today become commonplace, even though the scale of worldly visions and the concept of the global reach are not new political, economic, technological, or ideological phenomena (Schaeffer 1997, Feather-stone 1990). However, since the late 1960s and early 1970s, a new global vision has been invented through the apparati of socioeconomic reproduction of primarily northern political elites, corporate heads, and environmental professionals, based on the notion that international cooperation is now required to prevent the "tragedy of the commons" from overwhelming earth's carrying capacities and ecosystem services to humankind. This relatively new version of globalization foregrounds industrialized countries' anxieties about an "earth out of balance" and the real social, economic, and ecological threats that such disequilibrium portends.

The contours of *Our Common Future*[1] were shaped and codified in the documents produced from the United Nations Conference on the Human Environment convened in Stockholm in 1972. The Stockholm conference was the first international effort to discusss the fate of the earth in comprehensive terms and it introduced the ideas that there are inherent limits to growth and consumption patterns facing the international economy, which, if left unchecked, would result in a collective tragedy of the commons and would eventually produce widespread ecological collapse.[2] This newly articulated global vision, popularized in the late 1960s with the Apollo Space Program's whole-earth image, created an imperial "we" who would locate responsibility for the environmental scarcity brought on by the commons tragedy in the public sphere and on an international scale. The notion of "us" as a human community in peril if we don't change our ways emerged in full force, papering over the very different agents responsible for unbridled growth and the very different social and physical consequences of disregarding the ecological limits of nature. Murray Bookchin conveys well the analytical problem of the new commons authorities invoking a unified humanity to save the world:

> A mythic "Humanity" is created—irrespective of whether we are talking about oppressed ethnic minorities, women, Third World people, or people in the First World—in which everyone is brought into complicity with powerful corporate elites in producing environmental dislocations. In this way, the social roots of ecological problems are shrewdly obscured. A new kind of biological "original sin" is created in which a vague group of animals called "Humanity" is turned into a destructive force that threatens the survival of the living world. (1990: 9–10)

The argument of common cause and common fate, however, was not unequivocally convincing to the nations of the south. The attempt by the new commons architects calling for "limits to growth" and for all of us to pull together to prevent the commons tragedy was looked on as politically suspicious by government representatives and activists from the developing nations, who argued that this call for a global policy on environment and development cast a blind eye to the differences in roles and responsibilities in the environmental crisis the planet was now facing. At the Stockholm conference, the Brazilian ambassador to the United States, João Augusto de Araujo Castro, argued for the need for a politics of difference in the emergent discourse of globalization because the north's "limits to growth" proposal functioned to socialize responsibility for the problems when the benefits reaped from environmental exploitation have long been privatized. Invoking the familiar spaceship earth metaphor, he chided the UN conferees for their apparent inability to appreciate fully the existence of "different classes of passengers on the spaceship" (1998: 34).

According to de Araujo Castro, although the nations of the south had never spoken with one voice on issues of economic and social change, there was broad agreement on the point that the success of global cooperation in solving environmental problems would necessitate first the recognition by the north of the very different histories and patterns of development among the spaceship's unequal passengers. Moreover, representatives from the south argued that environmental problems brought on by poverty and survival-based resource depletion differ substantively from those luxury-based problems associated with affluence, as do the responses crafted to solve them.

Twenty years later in 1992 the United Nations Conference on Environment and Development (UNCED) took place in Rio de Janeiro, an international spectacle resurrecting the codes of "one world community" and "our common future" but adopting different strategies for global environmental crisis management. Global managerialism would now be grounded in a scientific expert class, proffering the authority of objectivity in policy making. But the work of promoting global "sustainability" would not simply be left to the scientifically and politically select few. Drawing on worldwide concern about the health of the environment and the threat to peoples' livelihoods, UNCED encouraged increased NGO participation at many of the official assemblies. In contrast to the Stockholm UN conference, the so-called Earth Summit was convened in the "optimistic afterglow of the end of the Cold War, amid a general sense of new opportunities for global cooperation" (Conca and Dabelko 1998: 6). For twelve days in Rio, political elites from 178 nations, over 8,000 journalists, and activists from close to 1,500 NGOs gathered to fashion a new global consciousness and set of guidelines for action that would irrefutably represent environmental unanimity in the years leading up to the twenty-first century.

The official conference deliberations produced the *Rio Declaration*, a set of general principles on environment and development, and *Agenda 21*, an eight-hundred page, wide-ranging document prioritizing environmental problems and outlining action plans to solve them on a worldwide scale.[3] The Earth Summit also created the foundations for global environmental governance: the UN's new Commission on Sustainable Development and the Global Environmental Facility (GEF), the multilateral lending body overseen by the World Bank and committed "to funding environmental projects that are of 'global'—rather than 'local'—significance, and which would therefore be of benefit to the world at large" (Hildyard 1993: 33). The primary message that materialized from these official documents was that we "must seek mutual accommodation. The new wisdom is that we want economic progress, but we also want to live in harmony with nature."[4] Probing the underlying intentions of the new global commons/global responsibility project, the editors of the British journal *The Ecologist* published the book *Whose Common Future?* in 1993, critically questioning the twenty-year globalization drive that began with the Bruntland report's optimistic *Our Common Future* and was culminating at Rio in the triumphalism of the composing of an "Earth Charter" (Finger 1993: 37).

Many argue that this restructuring of the global commons effectively amounted to a new enclosure policy or a privatizing of nature that simply reflected a shrewd containment move by political and economic power holders to secure control of those components of the global environment—the atmosphere, the oceans, the genetic wealth of biodiversity—that are necessary to the "continued throughput of resources in the global economy" (Hildyard 1993: 34).[5] The newly established global institutions, such as the GEF, by designating the earth's atmosphere and genetic diversity as global commons, intended to "override the local claims of those who rely on local commons and effectively assert that everyone has a right of access to them, that local people have no more claim to them than a corporation based on the other side of the globe" (ibid.). The *local*, in terms of local environments and local communities, becomes expunged from this universalizing discourse focusing on *global* ecology, and the real needs of peoples and lands become subordinated to the imperatives of global capitalism, now dressed in the mantle of "sustainable development." This new global green regime represents ecoliberalism at its finest.

The ecoliberal project highlighted at Stockholm and Rio, which is embodied in the new global commons discourse, emerges, according to many critics, as a discursive and material restructuring of economic development at the moment when elite financial and social planners recognize that neglecting the ecological services of nature threatens the reproduction of capital.[6] The problem of the commons tragedy, as Garrett Hardin (1968) put it, was that locals/commoners, with their soaring fertility rates, were rapidly becoming the primary threat to the future of the global commons, and so they and the local ecosystems on which they depend would need to be managed effectively. The response at UNCED was to put scientifically trained "global resource managers," equipped with their technologies of monitoring, measuring, and modeling global environmental change, at the center of a new global ecosystem management scheme.[7] Challenges to this position argue that it was simply a mechanism to bring the emergent development studies and environmental sciences into the service of promoting the "global logic of the market" as the instrument to revitalize the (recently perceived) threatened resources of the global environment (Goldman 1998: 45–46). According to Michael Goldman, the establishment of a new regime of global environmental managers supposes that "the crisis of the commons must be universally tackled and rationalized by well-trained teams of international experts" (1998: 42). The new global commons management doctrine conforms to an ecoliberal political philosophy shored up with professional expertise.

Clearly, the identity of the "global citizen," which first appeared in Stockholm and was reinvented in Rio, did not stand for the unitary environmental subject worldwide. Not all global citizens would be equally empowered to identify what counted as global environmental problems, nor would they be similarly authorized as active agents to solve them.[8] Like the gathering at the Stockholm conference, the "we are the world" fest in Rio was not monovocal. The significant appearance of activists and NGOs at the Earth Summit reflected a marked difference from the character of participation at the Stockholm conference two decades earlier—a presence that contested the attempt by "nation-states and their governments to rehabilitate themselves as pertinent and legitimate actors in the eyes of their citizens" (Finger 1993: 39). When I speak of NGOs in this context, I am referring to those organizations representing marginalized communities/nations and that challenge dominant forms of environmentalism. Mainstream NGOs, like the World Wildlife Fund and the International Union for the Conservation of Nature, essentially adopted the global-commons discourse and political intentions of the elites and, accordingly, figured prominently in the drafting of *Agenda 21*.

The preparatory meetings held by NGOs in 1991 also drew on the universalizing symbolism of the "global citizen" and the need for global cooperation, but not in the interest of preserving the global commons for the free-flowing capital circuits needed to sustain business as usual and for keeping intact northern standards of living. For example, a network of hundreds of activists from around the world met in Paris in December 1991 to draft an NGO statement on the Earth Summit titled "Agenda Ya Wananchi: Citizens' Action Plan for the 1990s." *Ya Wananchi*, which is Swahili for "children of the earth," reveals a "startling degree of consensus" hard won in many hours of "difficult international conversation" (Athanasiou 1998: 9). A significant part of the international NGO consensus was focused on eliminating persistent global inequities creating radically different livelihood and health options that militate against any easy proclamation of a "common future." Other presentations, events, and documents that emerged during and after UNCED also exposed the ecoliberal underpinnings of the Earth Summit and its calls for uncritically embracing the global community and being interpellated as global citizens. These include, for example, the cluster of tents located many miles away from the official convention hall in Rio housing the NGO gatherings known as the "Global Forum," and even farther away was the "Earth Parliament," a global summit of indigenous peoples (Athanasiou 1998). Kenyan activist Wangari Maathai, the founder of the Greenbelt Movement, addressed the official UNCED plenary by clearly mapping out the "issues vital to building environmentally sound and socially equitable societies" for the new global community being forged at Rio.[9] These issues included, among other things, "eliminating poverty, internalization of the environmental and social costs of natural resource flows, fair and environmentally sound trade, and democratization of local, national, and international political institutions and decision-making structures" (Athanasiou 1998: 11). Again the global environmental politics outlined in these demands was hammered out by the challenger NGOs, not the mainstream ones.

The NGO challenges to the framing of the global commons that appeared at the Earth Summit reveal the globalization-from-above agenda of political, scientific, and corporate elites' global ecological policies and mainstream environmental NGOs' assertion that "we're all environmentalists now." The uncommon NGO activists at Rio also appropriated the discourse of global visions and insisted that we are in fact all "children of the earth"; however, their use of the commons metaphor helps to illuminate the differences in the social and ecological conditions of those offspring. Although some critics, such as Chatterjee and Finger (1994), are more skeptical about the achievements of the NGO participation at Rio and suggest that they functioned primarily to "[feed] the peoples into the Green Machine" and to do what the "UNCED establishment wanted them to do, i.e., mobilize for UNCED" (89), I am arguing that the activist presence made it impossible to sustain the seamless narrative of a unified planet and, moreover, widened the discursive and political spaces for the production of a global politics of difference seeking a common, equitable ecological future. More recently, the environmental justice movement is also grappling with the hegemony of environmental and global-commons politics. Although not always acting on the international stage, the EJM appropriates the vocabularies of commonality and community in its framing of a politics of social and ecological difference.

Imagining Communities Through the Lens of Environmental Justice: Shaping New Political Spaces and Identities

How can we imagine and practice a politics of difference in a world of "one water, one air, one Mother Earth"? For activists in the environmental justice movement, this is a central question and a political dilemma calling for a rigorous and dynamic cultural politics of the environment. Environmental justice activists appropriate discourses of both "differential impact" and "common interests" in their community/global visions of equitable, healthy, and environmentally sound futures. This requires the production of an identity politics that is not totalizing and does not posit a timeless, essentialized, homogeneous notion of culture, tradition, or community from which to launch its socioenvironmental change program.[10]

The question of identity and community, and the social meanings associated with them, as representing essential factors constituting a unifying political force is not an unproblematic formulation, as many scholars and activists have clearly illuminated (Massey 1994, Anner 1996, Penrose and Jackson 1994). Critical scholarship has revealed that, in many instances, claims on behalf of the local, the community, cultural traditions, innate ecological wisdom, or earth-based spiritual values may in fact be well-crafted political screens obscuring discriminatory social relations and relegating a particular "race," "gender," "community," or "nation" to a prediscursive, static, often infantilized social category that may be subject to various authoritarian or fascist structures of state intervention including disciplining, regulating, monitoring, co-optation, or, worse, ethnic cleansing. The trope of community can also be deployed to denote natural or native rights, which can deteriorate into violently racialized ethnic/religious communalisms and fundamentalisms. However, it is also important for critics of all stripes to avoid what I would argue is a reflexive allergic reaction to discursive constructions of the spatial and temporal associations of culture, place, traditional values, and the commons, when they are used strategically or "situationally" by activists in the many transnational networks fighting for environmental justice. This view of community activism raises the questions: Can the race/nature/landscape nexus be appropriated (or rehabilitated) for socially and environmentally just purposes, especially in the present historical moment when the actual landscapes and ecosystems that make up the global commons are deteriorating at an unprecedented pace? And whose and which assertions of environmental expertise, ecological wisdom, epistemological certainty, and organizational strategy should be embraced in the framing of a just green politics?

Reimagined Identities and Communities for Environmental Change: Globalizing a Sense of Place

A political ecology rooted in environmental justice poses the question of how geographies are encoded with or stripped of racial and sexual markers and, furthermore, asks what would be the social meanings and political consequences of this process. I explore the ways that environmental justice activists recode these historically constructed profiles of landscapes and their inhabitants and imbue these identities with representations and meanings that are useful for political empowerment and environmental change. For activists and communities participating in the U.S. environmental justice movement, this necessitates engaging in the difficult work of intercultural politics; a labor-intensive task, they argue, that is essential for their survival.

Environmental historians have argued persuasively that the meanings ascribed to the North American landscape have alternated between those representing a fallen/defiled nature and those representing an edenic nature depending, in part, on the racial, gender, and class make-up of the people who inhabit these places, resulting in the partitioning of U.S. landscapes into either "geographies of sacrifice" *or* endangered and invaluable ecosystems

(Merchant 1980, Cronon 1996, Spence 1999). This cultural and institutional labeling of different landscapes continues to influence significantly the development of racially discriminatory environmental policies—if the rural land or the urban area is coded as a sacrifice zone, as barren and unpeopled, or as already tainted (either with pollution or "inferior" people), it becomes a rational geographic decision to select these locations to bury high-level nuclear waste, to test nuclear bombs, or to incinerate large quantities of toxic sludge shipped in from other more desirable places (Bullard 1994, Pulido 1996c, Kuletz 1998, Camacho 1998).

A geography of environmental inequality produced by the communities that are suffering these injustices inspires a reconstructed sense of place, in fact, a *global* sense of place that embraces an intercultural understanding of common struggles and shared futures. Grassroots activists in the EJM offer a set of theories and practices for an ecologically grounded politics of place that reshapes the universalizing tendencies of ecoliberal "one-worldism." This cultural work requires a politics of recognition of *both* environmental/geographic specificity *and* ecological unity.

*Culture, Community, and Panracial Politics
in the Environmental Justice Movement*

The U.S. EJM emerged with a strong politics of place opposing the disproportionate siting of industrial facilities emitting environmental toxins and hazardous wastes in communities of color and thus focused on the geographic specificity of pollution. This historical process of the unequal spatial distribution of hazardous exposure and the consequent unequal protection of poor and minority communities within the state regulatory apparatus was identified by activists as "environmental racism" and since the mid-1980s has been a galvanizing force energizing the oppositional politics of the EJM (Mohai and Bryant 1992, Hofrichter 1993, Bullard 1999).

A number of scholar/activists have written supportive yet critical analyses of the pitfalls inherent in the use of the environmental racism frame by the EJM and caution activists that a legalistic notion of race and what constitutes racist acts (i.e., racism can be judged by applying the intent standard) suggests that "racism is a specific thing whose effects can be neatly isolated" (Pulido 1996a: 149).[11] Moreover, by limiting the opposition to environmental racism to the elimination of specific "measurable discriminatory acts" rather than exposing it as a deeply embedded ideology shaping culture, politics, and economic structures, the EJM contributes to a partial understanding of how racism works and ultimately "disadvantages nonwhites, as it recognizes racism as only a limited sphere of actions and thought" (ibid.: 150–51). Arguing in support of a "political economy of environmental racism" (Cole and Foster 2001: 15) and against a unitary and fixed notion of environmental racism, supportive critics urge EJM activists and scholars to "clarify the ways that different racial/ethnic groups are constituted" because "the conversation necessary to move towards a multiethnic movement . . . not torn asunder by competition, ethnic tension and prejudice" requires that a more complex construction of race and racism be used. Laura Pulido explains:

> There is sparse acknowledgement of the fragmented and multifaceted nature of racism. Yet, there is a difference in the racism experienced by, say, Asian women in corporate America and that experienced by undocumented Mexican immigrants. . . . Thus it is entirely plausible that the racism at work in the placement of an incinerator in a black, rural community is different from the racism which causes Latinos to face severe occupational hazards. While it may be temporarily strategic to categorize all forms of disproportionate exposure as "environmental racism," it is uncertain how effective an antiracist frame can be in uniting diverse constituencies. (1996a: 152)

While critics admonish environmental justice scholars for promoting a "liberal antiracism" that ignores other forms of oppression, they also recognize the political utility of the construction of the unifying identity "people of color" to fight the damaging consequences of environmental racism in local communities and to organize in solidarity with similarly impacted communities around the globe (Pulido 1996b, Foster 1998, Cole and Foster 2001). The articulation by activists of the concept "environmental racism" called for an identity politics of the environment that gathers together as a commons the communities of color whose neighborhoods, workplaces, playgrounds, schools, fishing streams, gardens, and bodies are all at risk for increased environmental contamination. The politics of identity that the environmental racism frame engendered was one that was based on the establishment of a set of actual or mythic commonalities—"some anchored in material conditions (poverty, racism, environmental degradation) and some in a selective appropriation of ideological elements (cultural similarities, harmonious ecological relations)" (Pulido 1996b: 159). This identity-building process, institutionalized in events such as the 1991 People of Color

Environmental Leadership Summit, generated an international, multiracial network of grassroots groups promoting environmental justice that simultaneously constructs a unitary identity to bolster political solidarity *and* recognizes and values racial/ethnic differences.

Antiracism has been the central mobilization tool for the EJM, at least in its early stages, and this forging of a political identity for people of color as agents for environmental change necessitated the construction of a positive "environmentalist" identity and a reimagining of the fallen, neglected, poisoned, or bombed landscapes in which many activists live as places worth restoring, preserving, and fighting for. For many people of color in the United States, the coincidence of their communities/cultures and these discarded, "lost to nature" (Pollan 1991: 188) landscapes (in contrast to the pristine landscapes of "wilderness") has meant being linked perceptually to images of filth, disease, poverty, and chaos.

Part of the reimagined self contained in the "people of color" environmental justice identity emerges through the production of new racialized meanings of nature/culture relationships—the idea that their cultures represent a different, and more harmonious, relationship of humans to nature. Environmental justice activists attribute these more ecologically balanced relationships to, on the one hand, strongly held "traditional" cultural values or, alternatively, as the outcome of their experience of long-term political and economic marginalization. For example, EJM activists claim that they inhabit the moral high ground in the environmental debate because, as oppressed people, they were not responsible for the widespread pollution and ecological degradation that are symptoms of the historical and present-day exploitation of both nature and people. Furthermore, the position of many EJM activists, and especially American Indians, Native Hawaiians, and Chicanos, is that their cultural values and practices, which are rooted in earth-based spirituality, are more ecologically sound and less domineering than those of the dominant white culture.[12] This positive ecological identity serves to reverse the negative, racist stereotypes that are personally and politically debilitating and also asserts an ecological expertise, grounded in the historical experience of environmental injustice, that mainstream culture (especially environmentalists) could learn from. Although the imagining of an ecologically harmonious people of color identity has constructed a unitary political subject in the EJM, particularly when engaging in actions at the national level such as confronting the Environmental Protection Agency (EPA), "the fact that it is unitary but not totalizing may be one of the keys to the movement's success" (Pulido 1996a: 172). The panracial commons/community discourse used by EJM activists to mobilize effectively against the state or corporate polluters and in support of environmental justice does not rely on a liberal universalism. In the inner workings of their organizational and leadership structures, activists inhabit a double consciousness and value and create space for racial/ethnic, gender, and cultural diversity (Di Chiro 1992, Taylor 1997, Pulido 1996b).

The colonial, neocolonial, and postcolonial situation of American Indians, and their particular relationships to the North American continent, create a unique set of issues for environmental justice organizing. On the basis of their histories of oppression, displacement from ancestral lands located on what is now U.S. territory, and their ongoing legal battles with the U.S. government, Indians mobilize around the notion of sovereignty rather than on their citizenship rights to make claims on the democratic state (Westra 1999). Native peoples in the EJM invoke a pan-Indian spiritual identity, one that is respected and honored within the movement, and one that avows a very special ecological consciousness that is a universal part of Indian cultures. Corbin Harney writes, "I don't see any other way we can change the world, except by the people coming together, praying for the Earth, and then waking up the rest of us. A long time ago, the elders said that there would come a time when the Native people would have to lead everyone else out of this mess, so that's what we're trying to do now" (1995: 161). Although Harney's language rhetorically invokes a return to a romanticized past and makes an essentialist assertion that Indians are inherently suited to lead the way, it should be understood as a postcolonial argument averring self-determination, not evidence of a nativist appeal to preexisting ontological essences.[13] American Indian EJM activists identify themselves complexly and adopt a situational, postcolonial, multicultural identity—as culturally unique tribes/nations, as members of an international network of indigenous peoples, as people of color suffering from environmental racism, and as the "Red Man" who, in alliance with all peoples, including whites, will lead the way toward global peace and a clean, healthy earth. Therefore, like other EJM activists, Native American activists also construct hybridized identities, even while they stake out sovereignty claims on native rights to particular landscapes/homelands. They are situated on the borderlands spatially and culturally, in the "interstitial zone of displacement and deterritorialization" (Gupta and Ferguson 1992: 18) and produce an intermingled politics of difference and ecological unity.

From "Sacrificed" Landscapes to Socially and Ecologically Sustainable Communities

For EJM activists, solving environmental problems means building trans-local alliances to contest the destruction and repudiation of the places where they live, work, and play. Therefore, the industrial or military sacrifice zones that are overwhelmingly located in or near communities of color are reconstructed, even naturalized by activists as "home," the places that must be fiercely defended. Some EJM activists have even likened themselves to "endangered species" whose habitats are under threat (Martinez 1991). A politics of place, for many communities of color in the EJM, very often means fighting to protect environments in cities or rural areas that have been abandoned, neglected, contaminated, used as dumping grounds for all manner of waste, and written off as wastelands by government and corporate officials. Most environmental justice activists do not have easy access to mobility out of a contaminated neighborhood, nor do they automatically expect the state or corporate sector to relocate them in the unlikely event of successful legal action. Moreover, many communities do not necessarily want to be relocated, as in the case of some Native American or Chicano communities' historical ties to the land, or the connection to the places of residence that some African Americans feel as descendants of the freed slaves who had built these communities from the ground up. Many community activists in the EJM stay where they are and reclaim their landscapes in positive terms. The neighborhoods, rural towns, city-centers, and the people who live there who have been perceived as "fallen" by the dominant society are places and people who deserve to be protected and valued (Anthony 1995).

A good example of this environmental justice dilemma in which the identities of both people and land must be reinvented to bring about socioenvironmental change is in the remediation and redevelopment of so-called brownfields.[14] A brownfield is the name given to any "abandoned, idled, or underused industrial and commercial facilities or properties where expansion or redevelopment is complicated by real or perceived contamination."[15] These abandoned and contaminated facilities, which include factories, steel mills, refineries, warehouses, gas stations, and dry cleaning businesses, are strewn on primarily urban landscapes and are the result of historically profit-driven land-use patterns and economic development decisions (Hernández 1999, Healy 1997, Davies 1999, Lerner 1996). The spatial arrangements of U.S. industrial cities followed racial discrimination patterns in the work-place and in housing and zoning regulations, and by the end of World War II most communities adjacent to noxious facilities were composed of people of color and poor and low-income whites (Hurley 1995). Consequently, the postwar socioeconomic transformations of suburban sprawl and a retooled version of global capitalism that sent large manufacturing plants "racing to the bottom" in the interest of cost minimization and environmental regulatory leniency resulted in the abandoned, often highly contaminated facilities becoming visible features of the environments in which many urbandwelling, low-income people of color reside.

For many EJM activists who live in cities like San Francisco, Baton Rouge, Chicago, Baltimore, and New York, these brownfield sites have emerged as places of possibility for "creating a strong community vision" that is "reflective of the diverse needs and cultures of the neighborhood" (Hernández 1999: 66). In the San Francisco Bay area, for example, multicultural, cross-class alliances have developed around revitalizing the 3,412 registered brownfields in the city of San Francisco, and others in the cities of Oakland, North Richmond, and East Palo Alto. To set in motion a socially and ecologically beneficial form of sustainable economic development, environmental justice activists have organized multicultural community/professional assemblages in the brownfield remediation process, committed to the methods of community-based participation and linking members of impacted communities with urban planners, environmental engineers, developers, landowners, state and federal regulators, and city government officials. The reclamation of these poisoned, discarded landscapes is not just about efficient economic development; it is also about a revitalization of the community to awaken a sense of pride and awareness "of the beauty that's around you and the beauty of the people around you" (Anthony 1995: 276).

Brownfields are postindustrial borderlands that, as new political and ecological entities, enable us to learn from the past and reinvent a more sustainable future. This is a challenge to the ecoliberal framing of sustainable development that arose out of the UN's environment and development conferences from Stockholm to Rio; sustainability is not about protecting far into the future the economic prospects of corporate and political elites under the universalizing rubric of safekeeping the global commons. Brownfield revitalization, from the perspective of environmental justice, envisions a sustainable, "green" community in the terms of social equity and ecological interconnectedness.

The environmental justice construction of the community or the global commons relies on what John Brown Childs (1998) has called "transcommunality." For Childs, transcommunal relationship "is a way to maintain particularistic rooted affiliations, while creating broad constellations of inclusive cooperation that draw from multitudes of distinctly rooted perspectives" (145). This approach borrows from the intercultural communication practices embedded in the longhouse confederate structure developed by the Haudenosaunee (Iroquois) peoples and from Child's work to build bridges of cooperation among teenage gangs in California. Transcommunal cooperation is a method that entails face-to-face contact and mutual trust that is built up through "shared practical action" in which people from different "emplacements of affiliation" can work together around common goals.

This describes the negotiation of a political borderland, one that is sometimes painfully contested in environmental justice organizations that aim to create multiracial alliances—multiracial does not always include "white," and "people of color" does not always include all racial/ethnic groups recognized as "nonwhite" (Pulido et al. 1996). Transcommunal dialogue from the margins generates a form of solidarity and connectedness that moves beyond the homogenizing unity of the UN's global commons discourse yet also resists the ever-fragmenting relativism of postmodern notions of diversity. Transcommunality is what Childs and others argue is the cross-cultural communication technology necessary to forge genuine socioenvironmental sustainability.

The final section of this chapter presents an analysis of "toxic tourism," a transcommunal political strategy developed by the EJM to facilitate communication, understanding, and collaborative action among communities whose environmental predicaments are vastly different. By inviting visitors to "tour" their neighborhoods to witness the polluted environments in which they live, EJM activists hope to create the conditions for transcommunal cooperation leading to environmental change.

Bearing Witness or Taking Action?: Rethinking a Politics of Place for Environmental Justice

Leading a "toxic tour" of Newtown, Georgia, an African American community located fifty-five miles north of Atlanta, Rose Johnson speaks gravely about the "high rates of throat and mouth cancers, excessive cases of the immune system disease, lupus, and a variety of respiratory ailments" that have afflicted the residents of this small southern town (Spears 1998: 3). "Too many people have died" is the message that comes through her portable microphone as she directs the visitors along a somber route. Moving door to door, neighbor to neighbor, Johnson visually maps the terrible trail of pain by respectfully placing black ribbons on the homes of residents who were ill or who had died of cancer, lupus, or from chemically induced heart disease. The several dozen guests participating in this toxic tour, first organized in 1993 and repeated many times since, consisted of city and state officials and members of the National Council of Churches who wanted to experience "firsthand the sharp contrast between the Newtown environment—where the acrid odor of toxic industry and scrap yards presses in on the little park and well-tended homes—and the flourishing green lawns and flowering trees of Longwood Park and the generous houses on the north side of town where most whites live" (Spears 1998: 2).

Traveling in an old yellow school bus and on foot, visitors to Newtown follow an itinerary charted on a community-generated "toxic" map that traces the location of thirteen industrial sites and numerous hazardous waste generators surrounding the residential area of town. Johnson's toxic profile map helps her navigate this guided tour, which demonstrates the spatial relationships between industrial facilities and serious health problems. Visitors from other cities and towns begin to envision a scene of environmental catastrophe; this is not the usual fare offered up on an ordinary tourist excursion.

Rose Johnson is a member of the Newtown Florist Club, a community organization founded in the 1950s by local women to generate the funds to provide flowers for funerals and "to care for the sick and comfort the families as they buried their dead" (Spears 1998: 4). More recently, the club has turned its attention to the health of the entire community and organizes against the environmental injustices perpetrated by numerous toxic polluters that have long imperiled the community. Activists such as Johnson organize the toxic tours to provide unassailable physical evidence that Newtown residents are suffering from a disproportionate impact of hazardous pollutants. As they lead their tour groups from one site to the next, they enable their visitors to see for themselves what is graphically documented on the toxic profile map— the high density of industrial facilities located in and around exclusively black communities. Guests to Newtown can "sightsee" the close proximity of schools, playgrounds, and houses to toxics-emitting facilities such as the Leece-Neville machine plant, which discharges annually thousands of pounds of xylene and 1,1,1-trichloroethane into the local soil, air, and water.

The final stop on Rose Johnson's tour is the Bethel African Methodist

Episcopal church, where tour participants disembark, "feeling the weight of evidence of life in a toxic zone" (Spears 1998: 6). This is the environmental reality for the predominantly African American residents of Newtown—a reality that has been briefly and poignantly experienced on this day by a group of outsiders, most of whom are white. Many visitors attending these uncommon tours avow it is the closest they have ever come to witnessing firsthand the consequences of what activists have long contended is overt environmental racism. The toxic tour has succeeded in illuminating the historically invisible components of the Newtown landscape—the devastating effects of the externalities of industrial development on the land and the people who live on it. Providing the opportunity for this firsthand, "authentic" experience of environmental injustice partly underlies Johnson's and the club's use of toxic tourism in their strategy for social and environmental change. The act of seeing with one's own eyes is not intended to be the only experience, however. Their aim is to take action to change what the eyes witness.

Ecotourism with a Twist

Toxic tourism is situated in the broader socioeconomic phenomenon known as ecotourism. Like all tourism, ecotourism aims to provide direct access into another's world, to gain a deeper involvement with other peoples and other places (MacCannell 1989: 15, Urry 1990). Ecotourists set out on journeys to faraway places to escape the anxieties and alienation that have accompanied rapid industrialization and urbanization in modern, Western societies. The primarily Western, middle- to upper-middle-class tourists are not interested simply in gawking, however, but in asking questions and in finding answers—how did we get ourselves into this ecological conundrum, and how can we unite with others to create solutions? Ecotour packages promote the idea that you can do something to protect the environment while on vacation, maybe even "join a local grassroots conservation group."[16]

Another alternative form of tourism, also emphasizing the interrelationships between the environment and local cultures, is *toxic* tourism. The toxic tours led by the women activists of the Newtown Florist Club can be interpreted as environmentally based tours, or *ecotours*, but in this case they highlight the not-so-scenic sites scattered on the landscape and cast a very different light on the neoliberal assertion that a compatible relationship can exist between capitalism as we know it and the health of humans and the environment. The "reality" that is uncovered in the toxic-tourism experience is often disheartening; toxic tours are not "feel good" vacations. What are some of the benefits and problems of the politics of place embedded in toxic tourism as environmental justice strategy?

In this section I argue that the growing popularity of the ecotourism industry is the historical context in which toxic tourism has emerged and which has opened up potentially innovative political spaces for environmental justice organizing. I present the argument that toxic tourism is a spatial politics that foregrounds racial/ethnic and community difference yet is rooted in a politics of ecological commonality. I examine two versions of toxic tourism used by a variety of environmental justice organizations:[17] first, the "reality tour," a theme-driven low-cost guided expedition to geographical sites (polluting facilities, toxic-damaged neighborhoods, sludge-filled rivers) that are indicative of specific environmental problems highlighted on the tour. Reality tours aim to introduce tourists to people whose social and environmental predicaments are very different from their own.

The second kind of toxic tour I discuss is the model used by the women of the Newtown Florist Club. Undertaken by communities who are *themselves* suffering from the effects of environmental injustice, these tours seek to build political and economic support with members of other communities or with sympathetic allies in government and the private sector.

Vacations with a Message for a Changing World:
Global Exchange's Reality Tours

After attending one of many "Reality Tour" excursions sponsored by the San Francisco–based nonprofit organization Global Exchange, tourists comment on their experiences: "This was a real fact-finding tour. I could watch, touch, listen and converse using my eyes, ears, hands and skin." "I've been all over the world, yet this trip affected me more than any other. It was hands-on, not theory or ideology . . . but talking with and looking into the faces of real people."[18] The desire for the unmediated rub with "reality" features heavily in tourists' reflections, even if that reality is not about contact with the sites of spectacular nature that draw millions of people into the ecotourism industry each year. The itinerary of a California-based reality tour, for example, might include a stop at an East Bay oil refinery to see its impact on neighboring communities, or a strawberry farm in central California to learn about the impact of the soil fumigant methyl bromide on farmworkers and their families.

Reality tours are "dedicated to promoting people-to-people ties between the North and the South"[19] and to building personal contact through productive partnerships at local, national, and international scales—what Childs refers to as "shared practical action" through transcommunal exchange. For instance, an urban professional from Los Angeles might get the chance to meet with government officials in Haiti, or to talk with young women union organizers working at a maquiladora factory at the U.S.-Mexico border. According to tour leaders, using a socially responsible form of ecotourism to build linkages based on understanding between people from different cultures, classes, and geographical locations is a first step toward constructing a strong grassroots base supporting environmental justice. Reality tour organizers argue that they are challenging top-down tourism and the problems associated with the positionality of the tourist gaze from afar. Appropriating the tourism model has its drawbacks, however, as one reality tour organizer acknowledged: "sometimes a tourist's curiosity can mutate into prurient interest, something like, come see the poor people, come see the toxic sludge oozing out of the ground." This tour guide explained that "selling the ugly side of industrial development is not the point—selling the solution side is."[20]

In April 1998 Global Exchange hosted a customized reality tour called "What do you mean, Free Trade?" for a high school student group from Atherton, an elite community bordering Silicon Valley. On this tour, students were taken on a six-day spring break expedition that investigated the environmental and human rights effects of the North American Free Trade Agreement (NAFTA) on local communities close to home and those living in border towns in Mexico. The students were introduced to a host of community organizations, such as the Silicon Valley Toxics Coalition, where they heard about the dismal labor practices and lenient environmental standards pervasive in the computer industry—the industry in which most of their parents have made successful careers.

Loaded into tour vans, the students traveled to Tijuana, where they met with maquiladora workers, some of whom are teenagers like themselves. Adjacent to the shiny new factory buildings the high school students see the dilapidated shacks built from wooden shipping pallets housing several families, and they smell the acrid odors of sulfuric acid fumes or sewage runoff from one or another processing plant. What is it that tour organizers expect these young people will gain from the information and the experiences that they get on this toxic tour? César Luna, an environmental lawyer with the San Diego–based Environmental Health Coalition and director of the Border Justice Campaign, thinks most students are challenged and moved by what they see and learn on the tour.[21] Other students, however, become over-whelmed with guilt and respond defensively: "It's not [my] fault [I] live in an upper-middle-class family in a first-world country" (Dowling 1998: 86).

Referring to the toxic tour as a political "tool" for change that should benefit the host communities, Luna warns that it must be used cautiously; it should not "turn the communities into parks" that tour groups are peren-nially passing through. Furthermore, he argues, the issues of who controls the agenda and whose interests are being served are paramount; visitors have a certain responsibility to give something back to the community. He and other activists are wary about the virtue of touring to distant locales as a strategy to promote change in the first place. For example, Luna responded to a young high school student's anxieties about whether she would need to go to a third-world country to help save the world: "You may be able to make a bigger change if you stay home than if you come here to Mexico. Staying put has its advantages."[22]

Toxic Tours and Community Action:
Practicing Environmental Justice

Toxic tours are one educational and political tool that many community organizations use to tell their stories and promote face-to-face, personal con-nections. Environmental justice activists hope that these brief snapshots of the daily realities of people struggling with the devastation of toxic pollution will move beyond simply "opening one's eyes" and toward positive action to help change the unjust social and environmental conditions witnessed on the tour.

The locally initiated toxic tours are designed to show outside groups, whether school children, official EPA delegations, or skeptical environmen-tal scientists, the complex realities of the community's circumstances. This may include scenes of a deteriorating housing stock with unsafe lead levels or a Texaco oil refinery abutting an elementary school attended by low-income African American and Latino students. However, guests would also be conveyed to local sites that make the community distinctive, such as an architectural landmark or a thriving community garden, in addition to meeting with community groups who are actively working to improve their environments.

The West County Toxics Coalition (WCTC) in Richmond, California has been organizing toxic tours for many years. Henry Clark, director of the

WCTC, says of his organization's interest in leading the tours, "We've taken classes from UC Berkeley, Stanford, Berkeley High, and Richmond High. We show them the work that we're involved in so that they get some firsthand sense of the issues and the territory that the WCTC organizes in. The toxic tours certainly are helpful in terms of environmental education and whatever contacts we might make that may be useful in our work."[23] Some tourgoers have returned as interns, volunteers, or doctoral researchers, all of whom help in the day-to-day activities of the organization. For example, student researchers use their skills to help document the evidence of noncompliance with environmental emissions regulations that is consistently charged against the Chevron oil refinery and the Chevron Partho-Chemical Company, the two major toxic facilities located in this primarily African American community. Although Clark applauds the benefits of the WCTC bringing outsiders into the community to see what's happening with their own eyes or listening to residents with their own ears, he argues that just witnessing the outcomes of environmental injustice in communities of color is not always enough to bring about change. He advocates the need for strengthening strategic political organizing to generate grassroots pressure on a particular agency, company, or decision-maker.

The visual, embodied experience of the East Bay community-led toxic tours produces reactions from tourists that vary from "giving me inspiration to do something with my life" to feeling "thankful for what I have."[24] Environmental justice activists like Clark admit that this method of organizing may result in wildly divergent responses, so his organization tries to create the conditions for a transcommunal exchange on the tour that may develop into sustained political action. He acknowledges that sometimes it's successful, sometimes not; the toxic tour strategy represents a politics without guarantees.[25]

Highlighting the transborder components of environmental injustice, activists Teresa Leal and Rose Marie Augustine, both from the Southwest Network for Environmental and Economic Justice (SNEEJ), organize a toxic tour traversing the "biological and social corridor along the Santa Cruz River"[26] that flows north from Nogales, Mexico, to Tucson, Arizona. On a tour that Leal and Augustine organized for academics attending the American Society for Environmental History (ASEH) annual conference in April 1999, guests were transported in a plush air-conditioned bus following a route that first visited the downtown Tucson Barrio El Agujero and the Connie Chambers Public Housing Project—neighborhoods that are both dealing with toxic assaults from nearby polluting facilities. Speaking in clear, commanding voices into the P.A. system on the bus, the women recounted appalling statistics of unusually high incidences of neurological disease, miscarriage, and birth defects suffered by the low-income Latino residents of these Tucson communities. The tour's final destination was Nogales, Sonora, a stop providing tourists the opportunity to see the social and environmental impacts of the maquiladora production system on the Mexican side of the border. Tour-goers witnessed the shantytown *colonias* lining the highway into the Mexican "free trade zone" and the neon green and rust-colored effluent being discharged from one or another assembly or manufacturing plant—Sony, Canon, General Motors, Guess?—into the dry riverbed of the Santa Cruz. At the end of the long trip, the tour leaders confessed to being exhausted from having to relive the memory of a child's death or their own or a relative's experience with cancer. However, they explain, "this is a history that has to be told, and we decided that since this was a group of historians who might tell the story, it was worth it."[27]

One of the central uses of the toxic tour by environmental justice groups across the country is to educate and lobby government officials, journalists, and decision-makers from the public and private sectors. In July 1998, the EPA's NEJAC delegation went to the Philadelphia area for a toxic ecotour of Chester, a city of primarily African American residents who sued the Pennsylvania Department of Environmental Protection, charging environmental racism for granting five low- and high-level waste site permits in this community of 40,000 poor and low-income people of color (Nussbaum 1998). Local organizer Zulene Mayfield, from the environmental justice group Chester Residents Concerned for Quality Living (CRCQL), led the delegates along a charted route that followed the "smells and noise" from multiple waste incinerators dispersed throughout the neighborhoods and a steady stream of tractor-trailers with full cargoes of medical waste, garbage, and toxic materials from all over the state heading toward the various dump sites. For a stunning visual contrast, Mayfield took the group of official visitors to Swarthmore, a neighboring affluent college community overflowing with elegant homes and well-manicured, verdant landscapes. This sensory comparison enhances the visitors' opportunity to experience momentarily life in an "industrial sacrifice zone."

Clark's, Leal's, Augustine's, and Mayfield's toxic tours engage in a politics of place that provides indisputable physical and visual evidence of uneven environmental circumstances. The material and perceptual borderlines separating contaminated neighborhoods and landscapes from their privileged counterparts are marked with the histories of racial and class injustice. Yet, these activists emphasize, traversing the boundaries on a toxic tour may help participants to "see with *one* set of eyes" and, perhaps, as Rose Johnson from the Newtown Florist Club envisages, "join us and share our struggle" (Spears 1998: 1).

Ecotourism Gets a Reality Check

The explosion of general interest in preserving the environment and its human inhabitants, as evidenced in the popularity of ecotourism worldwide, presents activists with an opportune climate to develop creative environmental justice strategies. Exploiting modern Western societies' appetite for touring to gain direct, unmediated experience of the world, environmental justice organizations make use of the tour as one of the many potentially effective social change strategies in their organizing toolkits. Toxic tourism can be understood as a species of ecotourism, even though it is not a money-making venture, because of its focus on the relationship between environmental degradation and social problems, and the belief that firsthand experience through transcommunal exchange may result in environmental action.

Why do environmental justice activists organize toxic tours even though they are time- and resource-consumptive and, furthermore, even though they embody a politics "without guarantees"? I think there are several reasons: one is to increase outsiders' knowledge about the externalities of production and disposal and to challenge the assumption of the "purity" of consumption. The point of consumption is generally understood as an act of individual choice guaranteed by a free market society—an act that is, however, disarticulated from the material aftereffects of its stages and places of production and disposal. Visitors on the toxic tour learn that their consumer choices are not always based on possessing full information about the life cycle of particular products—there are very real consequences of their consumer actions on the health and quality of life of other peoples and environments. The toxic tour aims to construct what I have argued is a globalized sense of place, that is, it demonstrates how the toxic-damaged place witnessed or experienced by the tourist is connected to the "home" from which the tourist has departed. These fetishized places of contamination and "fallen nature," be they the "inner city," the U.S.-Mexico "border," or the "wastelands" of the desert southwest, are in fact produced within a complex set of interlocking, nonlocal processes that actually implicate travelers in the scene they are witnessing on the tour.

A second purpose of the toxic tour is to create environmental "contact zones" (Pratt 1992), bringing together guests and hosts so that people who do not live in the contaminated communities are able, at least temporarily, to see, feel, hear, smell, and experience what residents live with every day—an experience that activists hope accentuates the otherwise concealed life cycle of production, consumption, and disposal. This heightened awareness of interconnectedness may create political alliances or "contentious coalitions" of different sorts. The contact zone strategy of toxic tourism engages in what Raymond Williams (1989) terms "militant particularism": showcasing the specific environmental predicaments of local communities, while at the same time encouraging the recognition of collective ecological fates.

Toxic tourism is an EJM strategy that addresses critically the cultural and historical construction of a "sense of place" and works within a political framework emphasizing the recognition of differential environmental impact and supporting transcommunal dialogue. Toxic tourism is rooted in the conviction that where one lives, works, and plays makes a difference, environmentally speaking. In this chapter, I have argued that activists in the EJM are constructing a politics of environmental *difference* while acknowledging our mutual dependence on a planet of "one water, one air, one earth." The *differences* among communities, however, through the labor of transcommunal cooperation, and in a contact zone experience—perhaps on a community-led toxic tour—can become resources for tilling common ground and for promoting environmentally just futures.

Notes

Many thanks to Anne Wibiralske, Bruce Braun, Ruth Wilson Gilmore, Richard Hofrichter, and the anthology editors, Donald Moore, Jake Kosek, and Anand Pandian, for extremely helpful comments and suggestions on early drafts of this essay.

1   World Commission on Environment and Development, *Our Common Future* (Oxford: Oxford University Press, 1987).

2   For a more detailed analysis of this history, see Conca and Dabelko 1998.

3   The UNCED participants also drafted—and many, but not all, governments signed on to—a set of international agreements on biodiversity protection, climate change reduction, the halting of desertification, and the promotion of sustainable forestry, all based on the new techno-sciences available from the so-called planetary sciences (climatology, atmospheric chemistry and hydrology, oceanography, terrestrial ecology).

4   Tommy Koh, Singaporean diplomat, quoted in Conca and Dabelko (1998: 164).

5   For discussions on the Earth Summit's discourse on world community as a screen for re-inscribing elite control over resources and global economic governance, also see Chatterjee and Finger 1994, *The Ecologist* (1993), Brecher et al. 1993, Karliner 1997, Luke 1997, Goldman 1998.

6   For a cogent analysis of the resurgence of neoliberalism within the environmental movement in the United States, see Faber 1998: 27–59.

7   For a discussion of the emergence of the global environmental expert see Taylor and Buttel 1992.

8   For a discussion of different formulations of the global "environmental expert," see Di Chiro 1997.

9   Wangari Maathai, speech on behalf of the environment and development NGOs at the UNCED Plenary (11 June 1992) quoted in Athanasiou 1998: 10.

10 For excellent discussions of the dangers inherent in adopting an unreflective and hegemonic construction of community, cultural tradition, and identity, particularly in the context of Third World "community-based environmental management" initiatives, see Li 1996, Watts 1998, Moore 1998b, Brosius et al. 1998.

11 Also see Foster 1993, 1998; Tesh and Williams 1996.

12 People of Color Environmental Leadership Summit, *People of Color and the Struggle for Environmental Justice* (Washington, D.C.: United Church of Christ Commission on Racial Justice, 1991).

13 Valerie Kuletz, "Appropriate Technology, Cultural Revival, and Environmental Activism: A Native American Case Study," in Jennifer Croissant, Giovanna Di Chiro, Ron Eglash, and Rayvon Fouché, eds., *Appropriating Technology: Vernacular Science and Social Power* (Minneapolis: University of Minnesota Press, in press).

14 The term "brownfield" itself is a problematic formulation, according to EJM activists. Coined by developers and the EPA's community-based sustainable development initiative in the 1980s, the brownfield is the "lost to nature" landscape that is perceptually and physically contrasted to the "greenfield," a place of edenic integrity. The racialized coding of these two potential development spaces is unmistakable. Not surprisingly, big commercial developers, like Wal-Mart, prefer to snatch up greenfields (buying up arable farmland, cutting down a forest, or draining wetlands) rather than renovating brownfields.

15 U.S. Environmental Protection Agency, *Brownfields Action Agenda* (1995). EPA Brownfields Homepage, http://www.epa.gov/swerosps/bf/index.html.

16 "How Green Can You Get?" *Economist* 346 (8050) (10 January 1998): s16.

17 In an earlier version of this section on "toxic tourism," I discuss a third genre of these environmental justice tours, which I call the "toxic tour as political protest," and I examine the "Cancer Industry Awareness Tour" organized by the San Francisco–based Toxic Links Coalition. This type of tour directs participants on a predesignated protest march with the intention of engaging them in political opposition against the particular toxic offenders who have business offices or corporate buildings located at each tour stop along the way (see Di Chiro 2000). For a discussion of toxic touring focusing on women's activism against breast cancer treatment policy, see Klawiter 1999.

18 Reality tour publicity brochure, Global Exchange, 2017 Mission St. #303, San Francisco, CA. 94110.

19   From Global Exchange's promotional literature.

20   Author's interview with Lisa Russ, Global Exchange, San Francisco, California (27 April 1998).

21   Author's phone interview with César Luna, Environmental Health Coalition, San Diego, California (22 June 1998).

22   Luna interview.

23   Author's interview with Henry Clark, West County Toxics Coalition, Richmond, California (1 May 1998).

24   Responses by University of California, Santa Cruz college students to a Contra Costa County toxic tour led by Yin Ling Leung from the Asian Pacific Environmental Network (January 1999).

25   Borrowing from Stuart Hall's critique of rigid structural determinacy in political theorizing of the Marxist sort.

26   From "Environmental Justice Tour Itinerary," Teresa Leal and Rose Marie Augustine (April 1999).

27   Author's interview with Teresa Leal and Rose Marie Augustine, SNEEJ, Tucson, Arizona (16 April 1999).

PART THREE. Communities of Blood and Belonging

7. Inventing the Heterozygote

Molecular Biology, Racial Identity, and the Narratives
of Sickle Cell Disease, Tay-Sachs, and Cystic Fibrosis

Keith Wailoo

Historians of medicine have been interested for some time in how, where, and by whom diseases are defined (and where disease resides).[1] They have considered, for example, the historical construction of such "diseases" as homosexuality and hysteria, as well as the historical evolution of anorexia nervosa, occupational diseases such as venereal disease, silicosis, tuberculosis, and numerous others.[2]

Many of us also have been particularly interested in the ways in which the discourse of the medical and biological sciences shape, and are shaped by, national politics and by the politics of identity—and these issues are particularly relevant in the era of debates over research funding for AIDS and breast cancer. In our time we have seen how the biomedical sciences and the diagnostic technologies they produce—such as the HIV test—give rise to entirely new categories of persons—the HIV-positive person, an individual not yet clinically diseased. Once designated, this individual has become a social, clinical, and political problem. The status of the HIV-positive person—is he or she a public danger, or "at risk" for losing health insurance, etc.—is defined by a range of moral, social, and political debates of our time. This question— the dynamic relationship between new biological disciplines and their technologies and forms of social identity—is the subject of this chapter.

I consider aspects of racial, ethnic, and religious identity in post–World War II America.[3] This chapter offers a partial history of three "racial" diseases, of the ways in which technology and questions of identity defined these diseases, and of the very different meanings of race that emerged in each case. In the process, I argue that the term "biopolitics" is, perhaps, an inadequate formulation in our attempts to understand the interaction of biological knowledge and identity. Where other scholars have suggested that the new genetic technologies of the mid- to late-twentieth century radically reconfigured questions of race, nature, and identity, this chapter offers an alternative conception of the historical interaction of biological knowledge and identity, one in which genetics provides a new template of cultural understanding on which novel interpretations of historically defined identities might be developed.[4] As we will see, the "racial diseases" at issue in these pages are not so much new inventions of the science of genetics; they are, rather, reinterpretations that draw on particular notions of group history, identity, and memory (in addition to modern genetic technology) in order to flourish and to achieve their reality.

One disease is sickle-cell disease—since the second decade of the twentieth century labeled a disease "of Negro blood," and since the 1940s described in medicine as a characteristically "black disease"—because its incidence in African Americans is one per every 400 births. The second disease is cystic fibrosis, since the 1950s labeled a "white disease," or (according to one observer) "the most common lethal or semi-lethal genetic disease in Caucasians of [northern and] Central European origin."[5] Cystic fibrosis has a frequency among Anglo-Americans comparable to that of sickle-cell disease in African Americans and occurs approximately once per 2,000 births across all ethnic groups. The third disorder is Tay-Sachs disease, often characterized as "a disorder prevalent among Ashkenazi Jews." Its incidence is recorded as 1 per 3,600 births to Ashkenazi Jewish parents.

In the 1940s and 1950s, it became clear to clinicians and medical scientists that in all of these disorders, sufferers had inherited a trait from both of their parents—neither of whom had shown any outward sign of ill health. Because mechanisms of inheritance from parents to child appeared to be similar, the three diseases have often been linked in the minds of geneticists, physicians, policy makers, and others as autosomal recessive diseases. That is, children with these diseases are said to have inherited a "double dose" of the recessive trait—alleles from both parents. The parents, in the terminology of twentieth-century human genetics and public health, were labeled "heterozygotes" or (somewhat more ominously) "carriers." Not themselves sick, the parents were however responsible—jointly—for the sickness of their child. (Of course the concept of disease carriers—like the symptomless "Typhoid Mary" of the early twentieth century—was brought into popular consciousness with the advent of the laboratory revolution in medicine. In particular, the use of bacteriological identification in medicine and public health helped detect the presence of virulent organisms in the absence of disease symptoms.) The concept of the carrier highlights how new technologies gave rise to new forms of identity, and to widespread anxieties about social interaction and new methods of surveillance.

This chapter (a history of a very different person than Typhoid Mary) might be called a history of the heterozygote, and particularly of the scientific discourse about these individuals and their social status in the United States in the late 1960s to the late 1970s. In that period significant public controversies first emerged over practices of genetic counseling, genetic testing, and mass screening for hereditary disease, with, concomitantly, an intense national refocusing on hereditary disease. Historians have variously decried and praised these developments—for their eugenic overtones, or for the aggressiveness with which national and state legislatures promoted mass screening.[6] I will compare how particular actors in this drama (first, physicians and biological researchers; then legislators; and finally disease advocates who claimed to speak for patients themselves) portrayed the heterozygote, in cystic fibrosis (CF), Tay-Sachs disease (TSD), and sickle-cell disease (SCD). I am interested here in how biological stories of the heterozygote emerged from evolutionary biology, and how they were intertwined with then-contemporary narratives and anxieties about the fate of ethnic identity and racial identity. I am interested as well in how the story of the heterozygote sheds light on the changing social relations of genetics and medicine, and how in each disease the heterozygote becomes the site of community, memory, and the making of bodies.

In what follows, I will highlight particular aspects of the biological and social definition of the heterozygote in TSD and the other disorders. Both within biology and in larger communities, the heterozygote became part of discussions of group identity. The heterozygote raised questions of social surveillance. The heterozygote became the basis for discussions of the ethics of group membership—and so, for example, I will consider the role of TSD in religious rituals within Orthodox Judaism. I am also interested in the ways in which the heterozygote became a key reference point in the historical definition of race—highlighting specific historical experiences that defined group membership and defined the responsibility of group membership. These histories of the heterozygote provide, then, an important backdrop for understanding the appeal of genetic explanations of disease and the debate about ethnic difference in twenty-first-century American society. As we will see in the case of TSD, for example, the history of the heterozygote has become a key reference point in later discussions about a range of new "Jewish diseases" and in the "racialization" of Ashkenazi Jewish identity in our time.

Technology and Disease Identity

There is an important therapeutic backdrop to these diseases. All of them were obscure in the early twentieth century but became increasingly central to medical, public health, and public discourse in the last half of the century. All were discovered in the late nineteenth or the early twentieth centuries, but several factors explain their rising significance after World War II. One was the decline of other childhood infectious diseases, for as tuberculosis, diphtheria, pneumonia, and other disorders disappeared, these other maladies became more visible. Particularly important in their rising visibility was the advent of penicillin (made available in World War II for soldiers and civilians); antibiotics treated the infections that often killed children with CF, SCD, and TSD. Effective antibacterial agents often treated the infections in these children, revealing their "true underlying disease" in the aftermath.

Technologies other than drugs played a role in the rising prominence of these diseases. In the 1940s and 1950s, for example, both CF and SCD were characterized as "great masqueraders," highlighting their ability to mimic other disorders. But at the same time, new diagnostic techniques migrated into clinical practice from the field of molecular biology. The growing use of electrophoresis (a late 1930s invention for chemical analysis of the composition of large molecules) in clinical diagnosis was particularly crucial to the identification of SCD and CF.

The following decades saw the increasing social prominence of these disorders. With identification and antibacterial therapy (in the case of SCD and CF) came an enlargement of the population of patients, and their growing numbers would parallel the slow transformation of disease in America—from a focus on acute infectious disorders to the brighter spotlight on chronic disease. And with longer life and the focus on chronic illness came also the focus on illness as lived experience. The Civil Rights movement in particular helped put the spotlight on SCD, which exemplified a disease of "pain and suffering" that had long been ignored in America.

It was precisely in these decades of the 1960s and 1970s that hereditary diseases (these three and others like Cooley's anemia, a disorder not unlike sickle-cell disease but prevalent in Greek and Italian Americans) became newly visible and ethnically politicized. An article in an issue of *Science* in 1972, titled "Special Treatment for Another Ethnic Disease," focused on Cooley's anemia legislation being considered by Congress and called readers' attention to "the process of transforming an obscure ethnic disease . . . into the target of a national program of research and screening." So here were newly visible diseases—partly because of new technology but also because of what these diseases symbolized for the group to which they "belonged," what they meant for group aspirations, and to social ideals.

The late 1960s and early 1970s saw the emergence of a new national politics of disease in American biomedicine. The '60s had witnessed the rising influence of particular patient constituencies (from the elderly to the CF Foundation to SCD advocacy groups) and of consumer advocacy in matters of health. These groups saw diseases not merely as biopathological entities but as reflections of their political pursuit of rights and of their particular social concerns. Legislators and civic leaders responded to these social movements, even as they shaped ideas about disease to fit their own interests.[7] A wide range of disease-specific legislation was passed in this era—from research funding for cardiovascular disease to kidney dialysis legislation, from the Sickle Cell Anemia Control Act of 1972 to the Cooley's Anemia Act later that same year, to the Genetic Disease Act of 1976.

One thing is clear. Amidst the transformation of these diseases, tensions over the allocation of research dollars, and a national politics revolving around national health insurance and health consumption, a relatively new individual emerged in public health discourse—the heterozygote.

Inventing the Heterozygote: Sickle Cell Disease

It was molecular biologists, evolutionary biologists, and human geneticists (and their tools) that played a leading role in characterizing the problem of hereditary disease. These scientists believed that the detection of heterozygotes was one of the most obvious and rational methods of disease control. Often (in the 1940s and 1950s) the detection of these heterozygotes or carriers occurred retrospectively. That is, after the disease CF or SCD was diagnosed in their children, only then could parents be said to be heterozygotes. But increasingly in the 1960s the production and use of electrophoresis and other diagnostic tools (coming from disciplines including molecular biology and human genetics) rendered their status "knowable" before illness appeared in their children.[8]

The reason for creating such diagnostic tools seemed obvious to biological researchers—to estimate the supposed burden of heterozygotes on society, possibly to restrict their reproduction, and thereby to control the prevalence of disease.[9] This was perceived as a form of preventive therapy. As many historians have written, these tools fit neatly into what many molecular biologists saw as a "new eugenics"—not, they said, anything like the coercive program of involuntary sterilization of the early twentieth century, or like efforts to eradicate the "unfit." This "new eugenics" was a medical service in the form of genetic screening and counseling for consumers. It emphasized a large degree of individual, family, and community control.[10] These diagnostic tools provided the basis for the invention of a new identity and brought narratives from evolutionary biology directly into public debates over health policy and social policy. The question emerging in the aftermath of identification of heterozygotes was simple—what to do about these people and about the hereditary diseases they might cause?

What was known about these diseases? Beginning in the late 1940s, TSD, SCD, CF, and other clinical disorders became an important area of medical focus. Clinicians observed that children diagnosed with SCD, TSD, and CF had many different clinical problems but also had a common family dilemma. The diseases were quite different, clinically speaking. SCD was a disorder characterized by sickled blood cells, joint pains, frequent infections, and high likelihood of childhood mortality. CF was characterized by severe pulmonary congestion, digestive and gastrointestinal problems, frequent infection, and (also) a high likelihood of childhood mortality. The third, TSD, was a rapidly degenerative disease of early childhood, stemming from the accumulation of lipids (fatty molecules) in particular brain cells, resulting in neurological and cognitive decline, mental retardation, cerebral seizures, loss of vision and motor control, and death between the ages of two and six. By the 1960s it was (unlike the others) almost uniformly fatal in early childhood, rather than a chronic disease with an expanding population of sufferers.

According to the rules of Mendelian inheritance, however, all three disorders had the same hereditary mechanisms. This was confirmed as clinicians took up the tools of molecular biology in the 1950s and 1960s. In all three disorders, the mating of two heterozygotes subjected their offspring to predictable odds for inheriting the disease. If such a pairing of two heterozygotes produced a child, then (if the odds played out as expected) each child had a one in four chance of inheriting the disease, a two in four (50 percent) chance of inheriting only one allele and becoming (like their parents) heterozygotes, and a one in four chance of inheriting the trait from neither parent.[11] These mechanisms suggested the specific intervention. Molecular biologists, public health advocates, and clinicians in the 1960s and 1970s (in a time of increasing interest in the use of technologies to control reproduction) saw the heterozygote parent as a key point of intervention against disease. They spoke of these disorders, accordingly, as "hereditary diseases," emphasizing their links to family inheritance and hereditary probabilities. They did not speak of them as "genetic diseases"—a term which, at the time, implied a disorder originating in the DNA, possibly because of a mutation, possibly because of inborn errors, but not necessarily inherited.

But there were significant differences in the ways in which medical experts discussed and portrayed the heterozygote in CF, TSD, and SCD. In what follows, I move back and forth between these characterizations, exploring these differences. These stories give us insight into the convergence of biological narratives (coming out of evolutionary biology and human genetics, ascendant disciplines at the time) and the politics of racial identity, ethnic heritage, group survival, and racial pride.

One finds an intense preoccupation with these themes in discussions of the sickle-cell heterozygote, and (given the similarities among diseases) a relative lack of interest in constructing parallel racial stories about cystic fibrosis. Yet, for these experts, the female CF heterozygote did hold particular interest. In the case of Tay-Sachs disease, this disorder took on a social image intricately intertwined with the problem of Jewish survival and preservation—and this unquestionably influenced images of the heterozygote. Indeed, historians and policy makers still puzzle over the question of why heterozygote screening was such a "success" in the case of TSD (embraced by American Jewish communities) and such a controversial undertaking (seen as a form of reproductive control and even "genocide") and even a failure in the case of SCD. The answer to such puzzles, I argue, resides in the meanings of the heterozygote.

The key question about the heterozygote's status were these: If heterozygotes could be detected, should they be prevented from marrying other heterozygotes? Could mass screening of "at-risk" populations be carried out economically?[12] Would it reduce the prevalence of the disease in the long term? How should this "hidden" identity be presented to these individuals, and to the public?[13] Such questions were debated in scientific journals, public health meetings, religious groups, and state and national legislative hear-

ings. Some argued that heterozygotes were not to be considered social burdens but should be understood as special individuals, to be cherished because
of their difference. Whatever their character, clearly these individuals represented broader problems in family health, ethnicity, racial identity, and national character.

The prevailing view of the SCD heterozygote was that he or she was the by-
product of an historical and evolutionary process. According to a study by
British scientist A. C. Allison in the mid-1950s, these heterozygotes were
found in high frequency in certain parts of Africa, and they seemed (based on
Allison's small study and a handful of studies carried out since) to have a
slight but statistically significant resistance to a strain of falciparum malaria.[14] Allison proclaimed that the heterozygote had a "helpful defect." This
speculation was handed down from one generation of researchers to another,
tested only by small studies. In passing the trait to their children, African
heterozygotes were said to grant their offspring a competitive advantage for
survival in those regions where falciparum malaria was endemic.[15] Where
others succumbed to malaria, the sickle-cell heterozygote thrived, increasing their numbers relative to the larger African population. But if both parents passed this trait to their child, the advantage became a grave clinical
problem—a disease producing high mortality in childhood. As one observer
noted, "the gene causing sickle cell trait [i.e., heterozygote status] helps to
defend against malaria, but when there is no malaria [as in many urban and
industrial settings], it has no use and is only disadvantageous."[16] The disease
therefore told the story of a population uniquely adapted to its native, indigenous, or original environment. But when removed from that environment,
the heterozygote's favorable adaptation became a maladaptation.

By the late 1960s some physical and cultural anthropologists extended and
fleshed out this biological argument. To Frank Livingstone and other anthropologists, for example, the emergence of malaria needed further scrutiny.
Malaria was itself a product of African cultural evolution, Livingstone argued. He speculated that the movement from hunter-gatherer cultures to
agricultural societies in certain regions resulted in the clearing of land and
the creation of stagnant pools of water where mosquitoes bred and increased
their population. Mosquitoes were crucial vectors for the passage of malaria
to humans, and so the transformation of this entire ecosystem set the stage
for the competitive advantages of the heterozygote.

As one anthropologist noted, "the new agricultural system allows expansion . . . of the population and, at the same time, is the ultimate cause of an

increase in malarial parasitism."[17] Only after malaria was thus established could the heterozygote thrive. Thus, for anthropologists the disease and the heterozygote were deeply embedded in African cultural history, their existence showing "how the rising prevalence of malaria, resulting from changes in agricultural practice, has caused a potentially harmful characteristic to become selectively advantageous."[18] The very genetic identity of the heterozygotes, these anthropologists argued, was shaped by the history of their culture and their human-made context.

For evolutionary biologists, the importance of SCD was due not to this cultural history but to its exemplary role as a balance polymorphism, a trait whose stability owed much to its ecological utility. By the 1960s the study of the sickle-cell heterozygote was (for molecular biologists, anthropologists, historians, and physicians) also a case in point in the nature-nurture debate, the debate over whether genes or environment were more responsible for shaping identity. Together, these experts had (by the late 1960s) constructed a rich, proud, and textured historical narrative of the heterozygote and African heritage. The SCD case became an exemplary in these disciplines—a disease that established a framework for thinking about other hereditary disorders.

The Heterozygote and Ethnic Identity:
Tay Sachs Disease and Cystic Fibrosis

Tay-Sachs disease highlighted a very different set of associations. It was discovered in the late nineteenth century and entered the twentieth century as a mental disorder labeled as "familial idiocy" prevalent among Jews.[19] Early on, the disease was regarded by Sachs (a Jewish physician working among a large Jewish population in New York City) as "almost exclusively observed among Hebrews."[20] But in the 1940s the disorder was increasingly redefined in biochemical terms—as a lipid storage disorder of the brain with severe cognitive effects.[21] Relative to the cases of SCD and CF, the identification of the molecular origins of this disorder came late. In the late 1960s researchers isolated the key enzyme defect (a hexosaminidase A deficiency) that resulted in the inability to remove fat from the brain. These developments from the 1940s through the 1960s led to the identification of presymptomatic cases, the possibility of widespread testing, and the possibility of heterozygote testing.

In TSD, explaining the prevalence of the disease among Ashkenazi Jews in this era brought out theories of genetic drift (which I cannot elaborate here, except to say that these theories revolved around speculation about small numbers of Jewish communities in Eastern Europe in the thirteenth and fourteenth centuries and the movement of their gene pools).[22] Other theorists pointed to population isolation and inbreeding as key mechanisms of transmission. But others went the route of speculating about heterozygote advantage—that is, the existence of selective forces that may have encouraged the heterozygote's survival and the gene's successful transmission through many generations. These theories can best be understood as different historical narratives of group formation.

Among theories of heterozygote advantage, some speculated that large populations of Jews have lived in cities longer than most other ethnic groups. The crucial selective environment, therefore, could be the preindustrial and industrial town, where "crowd diseases" like tuberculosis were more prevalent.[23] Perhaps, these theories ran, the heterozygote was a survivor of adverse disease conditions and had developed increased resistance to such crowd diseases.[24] Or were there historical circumstances that had taken their toll on the heterozygote, reducing their incidence in certain populations? Such theories give insight into the historical consciousness of biological scientists (many of whom themselves identified as Jewish). But these theories also highlight their awareness of social and religious structures. Some suggested, for example, that mental ability and intelligence might explain the survival of the heterozygote. The idea here was that the scholar and the rabbi in Eastern European Jewish communities tended to marry the most desirable women and to have more children than did other men. "If true," noted one author—one of the premier authors on Jewish genetic diseases, Richard Goodman—"this would have resulted in selection for a type of rational intelligence." In this telling of the tale of heterozygote advantage, it was the rabbis who were responsible for the disorder.

Turning to the case of CF—and to the more amorphous group of "Caucasians" associated with the disease—we note some obvious contrasts. CF had only appeared as a prominent urban medical concern in the 1930s and 1940s, and by the 1950s it had gained the attention of a handful of academic specialists. Most observers argued that "the disease is rare both in Negro and Mongolian populations," but they admitted that "no survey figures in such populations are known."[25] Gradually, diagnoses of the disease established its relatively high frequency in Americans of Central European descent. But there were those who objected to the "racialization" of CF, noting that such a focus distracted clinicians from sound medical practice. One Washington, D.C., physician believed that "the failure to identify blacks with CF is not surprising since the disease was first studied in centers largely serving whites."[26] By contrast, in the late 1960s there was no such rich academic discussion of the identity and ethnic heritage of the heterozygote in cystic fibrosis—researchers seemed uninterested in this dimension of the disease. There was speculation, for example, about increased resistance to influenza and cholera. But this discussion was sparse by comparison with discussions of SCD and TSD. There was, however, significant interest in heterozygote women and their fertility. Researchers reasoned that there was good reason to believe that "a heterozygote advantage may exist in CF" and they looked to the heterozygote women for explanation.[27]

Into the late 1960s there was, then, a certain asymmetry in the construction of a racial profile for the heterozygote in each disease. In CF, some studied what seemed to be abnormal levels of salt in CF heterozygote women and speculated that this feature may have made them more fertile, because their salt levels were more biologically welcoming to the spermatazoa.[28] Others suggested that perhaps heterozygotes had "a greater urge to reproduce"—implying that heterozygotes "understood," on some deeper psychological level, the likelihood of having sick offspring and sought to compensate by enhanced reproduction.[29] One physician noted that "numerous candidates for the selective agent have been proposed ranging . . . including "the 'agreeable personality' of the mothers . . . but these proposals have generally not been supported."[30] Speculating among themselves and using the evolutionary framework created by sickle-cell disease, biologists looked at CF (the disease) with a puzzled expression—and they constructed a problematic CF heterozygote mother to explain it. They admitted, however, that there was no valid consensus on her health status, identity, or personality.

Only in British journals like the *Lancet* (in a few articles written by a South African researcher) and in the South African *Medical Journal*—perhaps not surprisingly in a country where "white" did evoke deeply ingrained anxieties about minority-group status—could one find richly detailed, historical, regional, and race-conscious narratives linking the CF heterozygote to historical events. One author observed that while CF was very common among white Afrikaners (in South-West Africa, now Namibia), it had not been found in great numbers among descendants of the Angola Boers. The researcher speculated that the difference between the two groups stemmed from the heroic and historical treks made by the Angola Boers from 1875 to 1905, across the Kalahari Desert, during which many died of thirst. "I suggest," he wrote, "that heterozygotes for CF, because of their impaired electrolyte regulation, died more readily during these treks, thus reducing the frequency of the deleterious gene among their descendants."[31] There was little evidence to support such claims; nevertheless, for this author, speculations on CF heterozygotes were important primarily because they fed into questions of (or confirmed beliefs about) regional identity, ethnic heritage and pride, and distinctive, defining historical experiences—just as in the case of the sickle-cell heterozygote in the United States.

What are we to make of these highly speculative, evolutionary biological stories of the heterozygote? In sickle-cell anemia and in cystic fibrosis, we have seen how molecular biologists, clinicians, and medical experts shaped not merely scientific observations but historical narratives about the status and identity of these ambiguous persons. This was not merely idle theorizing. To understand why, let us turn to the uses of these narratives by politicians, community leaders, and heterozygotes themselves in reinforcing the sense of self, and in preserving an embattled group identity.

Heterozygotes and Social Policy

In the United States, these narratives had particular symbolic and political importance. Let me focus here on congressional hearings surrounding sickle-cell anemia in 1971. To many grassroots critics of screening policies, it was clear that the heterozygote was not the root of the disease problem. One representative of the Black Athlete's Foundation for Research in Sickle-Cell Disease noted that "the problems of the trait carrier [i.e., the heterozygote] are mild in comparison to the agonizing pain and the terror that the sickle cell anemia victim endures."[32] Tennessee congressman Dan Kuykendall agreed. He noted that focusing on the trait has skewed public debate. "The word 'carrier' brings to all of us the image of 'Typhoid Mary,' " he noted, and he urged "that the words 'disease' and 'carrier' be stricken from our vocabularies when we are talking about the trait (the heterozygote)."[33]

This white Southern Republican congressman preferred a more proud historical portrait of the heterozygote, believing that "when we talk about selling the sickle cell anemia screening program, we must emphasize the positive aspect of being a heterozygote." The heterozygote, he argued, should be a symbol of black pride. "An individual who has the sickle cell trait is stronger [in Africa] than other people are, and I wonder why we do not use some of the strengths and the positive aspects of the trait instead of emphasizing the 'disease'?" "Being a carrier," he concluded, "is not a weakness. Actually it is a historical strength . . . historically a protection from malaria."[34] Such views echoed biological speculation, and would (in turn) be echoed by genetic counselors in later years. Others (including many black health care experts) remained skeptical about the possibility of controlling this positive message (and of transforming the stigma associated with screening and counseling into racial pride).[35]

How widely had stories of the heterozygote of sickle-cell anemia spread? One noted black researcher stated that "the ignorance even among experts [about the status of the heterozygote] is appalling." He juxtaposed this ignorance against his own story of the heterozygote—a story of feats of national heroism carried out by the heterozygote. He noted that "some athletes who have represented their country at the Olympic Games in Mexico (at a height of more than 7,000 feet where sicklers [heterozygotes] are supposed to flake out) and [who] beat the world, went back to their country to be found to be sicklers on mass screening campaigns and were promptly labelled sick."[36] In this telling, heterozygotes were national heroes, stigmatized by the screening programs of their own country; they were real achievers on the international stage, relegated to second-class status at home.[37] Stories of the sickle-cell heterozygote had also permeated popular culture in the early 1970s, in the form of Hollywood films and made-for-TV movies.[38]

Again, in contrast, in the case of CF, molecular biologists, counselors, geneticists, and pulmonologists watched the story of sickle-cell anemia attentively. They saw it as a paradigmatic case, drew lessons from it, but did not develop similarly complex narratives of identity, achievement, and status, at least until some years later. Most scientists and policy makers suggested that the social burden of the CF heterozygote was minimal.[39] Only in the aftermath of sickle-cell anemia legislation (and in a sense as a backlash against this racially preferential disease legislation) did CF researchers forcefully begin to make the argument that "their" disease was "the most common inherited disease among Caucasians"—and in this atmosphere, their argument was translated into enhanced funding.[40]

In the period from 1965 to 1975, however, an asymmetrical controversy swirled around the status of the sickle-cell heterozygote. The U.S. Air Force instituted a ban on SCD heterozygotes as pilots in the early 1970s (a policy that was repealed in the early 1980s). Of course, at the same time, there were many who celebrated and praised the achievements of heterozygotes (in both sickle-cell anemia and cystic fibrosis), noting that "parents who are concerned at either being carriers, or of their healthy children being carriers, can be assured that they are as fit, if not fitter, than average, and that they have no responsibility to reduce the number of carriers." Such celebrators of biological diversity railed against the very foundations and charities that thought they were doing a public service by educating the public: "further posters by charities about the high frequency of carriers should be more carefully worded in order to avoid the leprous connotation which is so easily conveyed. . . . Heterozygote advantage is difficult to explain but unwise to destroy."[41] By 1975 there was no scientific consensus on the social status of the heterozygote in CF and SCD. There were, indeed, many competing stories of "hereditary disease" (most of them based on biological speculation), generated by molecular biologists and human geneticists, many of them based on their concerns about parenthood, maternity, heritage, personality, regional identity, and racial identity.

Conclusion: From Hereditary Disease to Genetic Disease

Implicit in the history of the heterozygote or the genetic "carrier" of disease, then, are a host of residual questions regarding the constantly negotiated meanings of "race," the ways in which the biological sciences imagine "nature," and the politics of disease and difference among American ethnicities in post–World War II society. These case studies of "racial diseases," at the very least, should move us beyond Fanon's assertion about the powerful effects of a racialized gaze where skin and phenotypic surfaces of the body become privileged sites for the articulation of "race."[42] Clearly, as the history of the heterozygote suggests, the epidermis does not constitute the only (or even the primary) site at which identities are "fixed" within the body. The case of the heterozygote suggests that, with the rise of genetic technologies, different kinds of internal bioanalyses are at work in the processes by which racial identities are "assigned." At the same time, however, this study suggests that these new racial formations in biology are themselves modified, and altered by, group memories, community experiences, and constantly shifting cultural idioms and identities. As such, the heterozygote—whose origins stem from the technologies of modern genetics—becomes a cultural "work in progress." Disease identities become complex assemblages of technologies, practitioners' ideologies, and social relations. Medical technologies may help to generate historically specific forms of identity, but those technologies are always altered and reinterpreted by the users—whose notions of self, identity, suffering, memory, and cultural difference give new meanings to the technological finding.

Briefly, let me compare the discourse of "hereditary" disease that I've been describing to the discourse of "genetic" disease today. Hereditary disease was a construction that framed and informed pressing social concerns and policies, about the heterozygote, family inheritance, and in some cases gender and racial identity and the health of society. The language of "hereditary" disease (and this is how these diseases were labeled) focused on what parents handed to their offspring, what they owed to their social group, to society at large, and on the government's interest in their reproduction. In an era that saw the rise of genetic counseling and screening, this was the most "natural" way to describe these diseases. But this natural description was the byproduct of programs, social debates, the language and status of particular disciplines, and their constructions of disease and patient identity.

Neither of these diseases—SCD and CF—have changed their manifestations, but they are now much more frequently subsumed today under the rubric of "genetic" disease. Just as "hereditary" disease discourse reflected particular interests—those scientists, legislators, and federal agencies who sought to create and legitimate counseling programs—so too does the "genetic" disease label reflect the influence of the Human Genome Project, a new NIH funding philosophy, and a contemporary politics of disease today.

Today, genetic disease narratives are constructed not by evolutionary biologists and human geneticists but by clinical-minded medical geneticists (doctors interested in treating individual patients). In other words, those biologists who sought (earlier) to translate hereditary measurement into counseling and screening programs had their own definition of disease. They believed that controlling disease involved family intervention and attention to population analysis, social origins, nationality, and that it often necessitated discussing the history of race and identity. The concept of "genetic" disease relegates those concerns to a secondary status, in favor of a refocusing on the patient, an individualistic focus. "Genetic" disease also has a kind of futuristic appeal in an era when tests can be imagined to locate genes that someday, in the future, will produce disease, like the gene for Alzheimer's disease.

Our contemporary notion of "genetic" disease is, then, also a construct, the new label reflecting a new politics, a response to new technologies of genetic testing, gene therapy, and debates about their use and their meaning for identity. In many instances, this new conception is seldom environmentally and geographically contingent, never historically nuanced, and much more deterministic than suggested by the complex history of the heterozygote. And yet, as recent scholarship has suggested, genetics offers a great deal of room for maneuvering and countless possibilities for individuals, communities, and the state to reshape and redefine biological findings into potent cultural idioms about race, nature, and the politics of difference.[43]

Notes

1 See, for example, Daniel Fox and Elizabeth Fee, eds., *AIDS: The Burden of History* (1990); Charles Rosenberg and Janet Golden, eds., *Framing Disease: Studies in Cultural History* (1992).

2 See for example, Allan Brandt, *No Magic Bullet: A Social History of Venereal Disease in the United States Since 1880* (1985); Joan Brumberg, *Fasting Girls: The Emergence of Anorexia Nervosa as a Modern Disease* (1988); David Rosner and Gerald Markowitz, *Deadly Dust: Silicosis and the Politics of Occupational Disease in Twentieth Century America* (1991); Barbara Bates, *Bargaining for Life: A Social History of Tuberculosis, 1876–1938* (1992); and Ronald Bayer, *Homosexuality and American Psychiatry: The Politics of Diagnosis* (1987). See also Keith Wailoo, *Dying in the City of the Blues: Sickle-Cell Anemia and the Politics of Race and Health* (2001).

3 My own work has focused in part on the role of technology in such interactions: *Drawing Blood: Technology and Disease Identity in Twentieth-Century Medicine* (1997). I have been interested in the ways in which tests and technologies construct ambiguous identities, and the ways in which physicians, patients, and others debate the status of these constructed identities. Such interactions among technology, politics, and identity have been characteristic of twentieth-century medicine.

4 See, for example, Donna Haraway, "Universal Donors in a Vampire Culture," in William Cronon, ed., *Uncommon Ground: Rethinking the Human Place in Nature* (1996); and Paul Rabinow, "Artificiality and Enlightenment: From Sociobiology to Biosociality," in his *Essays in the Anthropology of Reason* (1996).

5 W. T. Shier, "Increased Resistance to Influenza as a Possible Source of Heterozygote Advantage in Cystic Fibrosis," *Medical Hypotheses* 5 (1979): 661.

6 See, for example, the essays in Dan Kevles and LeRoy Hood, eds., *The Code of Codes* (1992) op. cit.; see also Congress at the United States, Office of Technology Assessment, *Cystic Fibrosis and DNA Tests: Implications for Carrier Screening* OTA-BA-532 (Washington, D.C.: GPO, August 1992); see also Appendix B: "Case Studies of Other Carrier Screening Programs," *AGAP Conference Reports: Psychosocial Aspects of Heterozygote Detection in Cystic Fibrosis* (14–15 May 1974).

7 The year 1972 saw passage of the Sickle-Cell Anemia Control Act. For the Nixon Administration, largely disinterested and even hostile to civil rights legislation and the plight of African Americans, its focus on sickle-cell anemia demonstrated the continuing influence of powerful

grassroots and legislative pressures. In the same year legislation passed Congress providing Medicare coverage for renal dialysis for all patients in kidney failure. In addition, the 1972 National Heart, Lung, and Blood Act announced the special importance of cardiovascular diseases and lung diseases as national manpower concerns. For the U.S. Congress and for the Administration, targeting specific diseases became a vehicle toward fiscally responsible research that reduced overall expenditures, and public reassurance of the government's true commitment to focused and socially meaningful disease research. See Steven Peitzman, "From Bright's Disease to End-Stage-Renal-Disease," in Rosenberg and Golden, eds., *Framing Disease.* See also Alonzo Plough, *Borrowed Time: Artificial Organs and the Politics of Extending Lives* (1986). On 30 October 1972 (P.L. 92-603), the Congress "amended Title XVIII of the Social Security Act (Medicare) to provide full Medicare coverage for at least six months to all individuals, regardless of age, who were diagnosed as having ESRD" (119).

8   Electrophoresis in sickle-cell anemia is generally accepted. In CF, questions continue to be raised about the reliability of various testing methods. John Thomas, A. Merritt, and M. E. Hodes, "Electrophoretic Analysis of Serum Proteins in Cystic Fibrosis," *Pediatrics Research* 11 (1977): 1148–54.

9   In the late 1960s most geneticists believed that the detection of heterozygotic identity meant "warning them against marrying each other." Carter, "Genetic Aspects of Cystic Fibrosis of the Pancreas," *Biblioteca Paediatrica* 10 (86): 378.

10 Robert Sinsheimer, molecular biologist at California Institute of Technology, quoted in Daniel Kevles, *In the Name of Eugenics* (1995), 267.

11 These are called autosomal recessive traits. Lowe, May, and Reed, "Fibrosis of the Pancreas in Infants and Children," *American Journal of the Disease of Children* 78 (1949): 349; for discussion of this issue, see P. A. di Sant Agnese, "Research in Cystic Fibrosis," *New England Journal of Medicine* 277 (1976): 481.

12 For a discussion of the history of molecular biology and human genetics after World War II, see Evelyn Fox-Keller, "Nature, Nurture, and the Human Genome Project," in Kevles and Hood, eds., *The Code of Codes* (1992), 281–99.

13 The racial character of sickle-cell anemia had been firmly established by the 1920s—so firmly, in fact, that for decades when cases of sickle cells were found in apparently white patients and in the parents of white children, physicians frequently insisted that these individuals had Negro blood in them. See, for example, S. Rosenfeld and J. Pincus, "The Occurrence of Sicklemia in the White Race," *American Journal of Medical Science* 184 (1932): 674–82; Russell Haden and Ferris Evans, "Sickle-Cell Anemias in the White Race," *Archives of Internal Medicine* 60 (July 1937): 133–42; and "Sickle-Cell Anemia, a Race-Specific Disease," *Journal of the American Medical Association* 133 (4 January 1947): 33–34. These issues are discussed in Wailoo, *Drawing Blood.*

14 A. C. Allison, "Protection by the Sickle-Cell Trait Against Sub-Tertian Malaria Infection," *British Medical Journal* 1 (1954): 290; A. C. Allison, "Sickle-Cell Anemia and Evolution," *Scientific American* 185 (August 1956): 87–88.

15 Ibid. Bentley Glass, "Malaria and Sickle-Cell Anemia," *Science* (5 October 1956); see also J. V. Neel, "Data Pertaining to Population Dynamics of Sickle-Cell Disease," *American Journal of Human Genetics* 5 (1953): 154.

16 Lionel Penrose, *Outline of Human Genetics* (1959), 124.

17 Steven Weisenfeld, "African Agricultural Patterns and Sickle-Cell Anemia," *Science* 157 (1967): 1134; Frank Livingstone, "The Origins of the Sickle-Cell Gene," in Gabel and Bennett, eds., *Reconstructing African Culture* (1967), 139–66.

18 Alfred Hexter, "Selective Advantage of the Sickle-Cell Trait," *Science* 160 (26 April 1968): 436.

19 Sachs, "A Family Form of Idiocy." See also D. Slome, "The Genetic Basis of Amaurotic Family Idiocy," *Journal of Genetics* 27 (1933): 363–72. Because of the disease's slow degeneration, Sachs attached the label "amaurotic familial idiocy" to the disorder, and that descriptor persisted well into the twentieth century.

20 Quoted in P. R. Evans, "Tay-Sachs Disease: A Centennary," *Archives of Disease in Childhood* 62 (1987): 1056–59.

21 E. Klenk, "Beitrage zur chemie der lipodosen (3 mitteilung): Niemann-Picksche krankheit und amaurotische idiote," *Hoppe-Seylers Z Physiol Chem* 262 (1939–1940): 128–43; and E. Klenk, "Uber die ganglioside des gehirns bei der infantilen amaurotischen idiotie vom typus Tay-Sachs," *Ber Dtsch Chem Ges* 75 (1942): 1632–36.

22 Josie Glausiusz, "Unfortunate Drift," *Discover* (June 1995): 34–35. On expansion of other Jewish genetic diseases, see Rick Weiss, "Discovery of 'Jewish' Cancer Gene Raises Fears of More than Disease," *Washington Post* (3 September 1997): section A, 1; Karen Rafinski, "Early Warning," *Chicago Tribune* (5 June 1997): 2; and Gina Kolata, "Breast Cancer Gene in 1% of U.S. Jews," *New York Times* (29 September 1995): section A, 24.

23 Jared Diamond, "Curse and Blessing of the Ghetto," *Discover* (March 1991): 60–65.

24 C. Anderson et al. 1967. As in sickle-cell anemia, CF researchers also looked to history to explain the CF heterozygote. Did events like the plague, smallpox epidemics, and other infectious diseases explain why these heterozygotes may have survived when such ravages had wiped out the less hardy, thus multiplying their numbers?

25 C. O. Carter, "Genetical Aspects of Cystic Fibrosis of the Pancreas," 374.

26 Lucas Kulczyki and Victoria Schauf, "Cystic Fibrosis in Blacks in Washington, D.C., *American Journal of the Diseases of Children* 127 (January 1974): 64; see also Kulczycki, Guin, and Mann, "Cystic Fibrosis in Negro Children," *Clinical Pediatrics* 3 (1964): 692–705.

27 C. Anderson, J. Allan, and P. Johansen, "Comments on the Possible Existence and Nature of a Heterozygote Advantage in Cystic Fibrosis," *Biblioteca Paediatrica* 381.

28 "Does the Heterozygote Possess a Better Mucus-Salt Relationship at Ovulation or for a Longer Time Before and After Ovulation?" Anderson et al., 1967, 385.

29 Anderson et al., 1967, 384.

30 D. Gairdner, "Heterozygote Advantage in Cystic Fibrosis, *Lancet* 1 (1975): 279; M. D. Crawfurd, "A Genetic Study, Including Evidence for Heterosis, of Cystic Fibrosis of the Pancreas, *Heredity* 29 (1972): 126.

31 M. Super, "Letter: Heterozygote Disadvantage in Cystic Fibrosis," *Lancet* 2 (17 December 1977): 1288.

32 John Henry Johnson, statement in "Bills to Provide for the Prevention of Sickle Cell Anemia," *Committee on Interstate and Foreign Commerce, U.S. House of Representatives. Subcommittee on Public Health and Environment. 92d Congress, first session. 12 November 1971. Serial no. 92–57, 86.

33 Dan Kuykendall, statement in "Bills to Provide for the Prevention of Sickle Cell Anemia," 1971. Ibid., 46.

34 Ibid., 48.

35 See, for example, Doris Wilkinson, "Politics and Sickle-Cell Anemia," *Black Scholar* 5 (May 1974): 26; see also R. E. Jackson, "A Perspective on the National Sickle-Cell Disease Program," *Archives of Internal Medicine* 183 (April 1974): 533.

36 Felix I. D. Konotney-Ahulu, *Medical Considerations for Legalizing Voluntary Sterilization: Sickle-Cell Disease as a Case in Point* (1973); and Felix I. D. Konotney-Ahulu, "Sickle-Cell Trait and Altitude," *British Medical Journal* 1 (1972): 177–78.

37 This story repeats, of course, frequently told stories of black achievement in the American military in World War I and World War II. See Mary Frances Berry and John Blassingame, "Military Service and the Paradox of Loyalty," chapter 9 in *Long Memory: The Black Experience in America* (1982).

38 This was highlighted by the 1973 Hollywood film *A Warm December*, starring Sidney Poitier as a doctor who falls in love with an African woman stricken with sickle-cell anemia, and by the 1972 made-for-TV movie *To All My Friends on Shore*, featuring Bill Cosby as a family man who discovers that his son has sickle-cell anemia.

39 Statement of Guilio Barbero, director, National Cystic Fibrosis Research Foundation, 1972.

40 P. M. Conneally, A. D. Merritt, and P. Yu, "Cystic Fibrosis: Population Genetics," *Texas Reports on Biology and Medicine* 31 (1973): 639; and M. J. Polley and A. G. Bearn, "Cystic Fibrosis: Current Concepts," *Journal of Medical Genetics* 11 (1974): 249.

41 J. H. Edwards, "Heterozygote Advantage," *Archives of Disease in Childhood* 52 (1977): 344.

42 Franz Fanon, *Black Skin/White Masks* (1967).

43 Susan Lindee and Dorothy Nelkin, *The DNA Mystique: The Gene as Cultural Icon* (1995); Kaja Finkler, *Experiencing the New Genetics: Family and Kinship on the Medical Frontier* (2000).

8. For the Love of a Good Dog

Webs of Action in the World of Dog Genetics

Donna Haraway

To put this in more enthusiastic terms, the dog is a veritable genetic gold mine.

—Scott and Fuller, *Genetics and the Social Behavior of the Dog*

Prehistories

Story: A Political Awakening

Born in 1944, I grew up in Denver in the 1950s. McCarthyism passed me by, but the new leash law really got my attention. While my adult peers were once red-diaper babies radicalized by black lists, my earliest political passions were of a lower order on the great chain of chromatic consciousness. When I had to fence my "intact" male Dalmation-cross mutt—despite getting every adult I knew to promise to vote against the leash law—my political soul came of age. The adults lied, the law passed, the dog was restricted, and my notions of nature and culture got their first rude reworking. That lesson in cross-species democracy, mendacity, freedom, and authority is my key for this chapter.

What happens when the mongrel fields of the biological and cultural anthropology of genetics are approached through the genome of "man's best friend" instead of "man"? My goals are modest. I am at the beginning of a project that promises to require all the cartographical resources I can learn to deploy. But here, I will draw a low-resolution linkage map. I want to suggest how large and rich the world of the dog genome is, how many kinds of investment—emotional, intellectual, ethical, communal, institutional, narratival, financial, and political—are made in canine genetics, how full of fascinating actors these companion-animal genetic worlds are, and how some vexing questions in science studies and anthropology might be approached with a canine eye. In particular, this chapter will develop the notion of an apparatus of naturalcultural production, through which the subject-making object called the dog genome collects up the passions and skills of a mangy crowd of human and nonhuman actors. I am interested in the ways that trading zones and boundary objects are constructed to facilitate traffic among scientific professionals and lay people, commercial and academic sites, conservation biologists and dog-breed club members, magazine writers and population biologists, and so on. Not least in such a list must be attention to how the traffic between popular stories and scientific theories ties together historically specific dogs and humans over the species-life of both sorts of genetically diverse social mammals.

Institution of the Kennel Clubs:
The Galapagos Islands of Canine Evolution

What is a dog breed? And what does a nineteenth-century object like a "breed" have to do with a postmodern marvel like the "genome"? Accompanied by their equally weedy companion species, *Homo sapiens,* dogs are globally distributed. Both species appear at first glance to be highly diverse, or "polytypic," as the comparative anatomists and anthropologists say. Interestingly, however, for dogs as for humans this phenotypic diversity seems to rest on modest genetic diversity compared to other widespread large-bodied mammals. From the remarkably consistent genetic evidence (including comparisons of mtDNA, Y-chromosome DNA, and nuclear gene DNA), dogs and humans appear to have breeding habits that keep the genes flowing back and forth through evolutionary time (say 50,000 to 100,000 years)— yielding what geneticists call a "trellis model" (Templeton 1999) instead of a divergent "tree model" for their patterns of genetic relatedness. There's lots of traffic in genes in a trellis, yielding populations that regularly show more intrapopulation heterozygosity for genes of interest than interpopulation divergence in the repertoire of available alleles. Populations do differ genetically, with difference being a function of greater or lesser geographical distance. Both natural and cultural selection and genetic drift operate in dogs, as in people, producing some important genetic difference among populations; but enough back and forth gene mixing has characterized the history of both species, who keep close company with each other, to render them strikingly genetically unified—swimming pretty promiscuously in the same global gene pools. As a consequence, the measured genetic distances fall *far* below values that, to a biologist, would allow one to talk about "races" in people or "subspecies" in dogs.[1]

Distinct kinds of dogs, linked by various rates of partly human-controlled gene exchange, have existed for a very long time all over the world; but the institutionalized breed has a recent pedigree. Controlled by hundreds of breed clubs throughout the industrialized world, and organized into national kennel clubs, the purebred dog is the population geneticist's and evolutionary biologist's nightmare for the dangerous drama of genetic drift and evolutionary bottlenecks. Purebred dogs belong to bounded populations, whose members are registered in a closed studbook and whose breeding stars are selected by interpretations of a closely guarded written standard. Even if the numbers of a breed total in the tens of thousands, the effective population size in the evolutionary biologist's sense might be very few, even fewer than a dozen animals for some breeds. If the original group of registered dogs was already more or less related, only a few of those founders were used much for breeding, some male dogs were wildly popular as studs, and various forms of inbreeding were regarded as the best ways to fix desired types and stabilize an identity for kennels and strains, the current dogs in a numerous breed might go back to a tiny ancestral population. A breed numbering in the thousands *could* be as inbred as modern cheetahs; they could almost be a clone.[2]

The studbook, the written standard, the breed club, and the dog show constitute an historically specific genetic technology for the production of dogs in urban industrial society. It is a technology that has reshaped dogs across all landscapes, urban and rural, and across all canine jobs in these societies. If dogs are perhaps the chief agents of their own original domestication from their wolf forebears, as we will see in the second part of this chapter, modern breeds are most certainly a social invention for which particular sorts of humans call the shots. And ironically, as breed-club controlled dogs in the last hundred years or so have become textbook lessons in the loss of intrabreed genetic diversity through genetic drift, the breeds consequently come to differ from each other by higher values of genetic distance. Of course, breeds differ from each other in genes that are deliberately selected for or against in breeding programs, but the troubling story for genetic diversity comes from another aspect of those breeding practices—namely, the unintentional and random loss of alleles at unselected loci. The very *random* loss of alleles that *necessarily* characterizes fixed small populations over time means that different breeds lose *different* alleles. That is, genetic diversity is increased between breeds (populations) in a perverse—but mathematically correct—sense of no longer sharing the same range of alleles at more and more loci. At the same time, genetic diversity within breeds is decreased, producing homozygosity at more and more loci, to the point of causing an international research and regulatory emergency, not to mention canine suffering and human grief. The old trellis is morphing into a young tree bearing genetically dangerous fruit.

The institutionalized dog breed came into the world branded with typological thinking about race, quality, purity, and progress. Harriet Ritvo (1987) told this story in exquisite detail for English dogs in the nineteenth century. Her narrative highlights the developing urban business and professional classes, for which the ideology of social position based on competitive merit was fundamental. Unlike aristocratic cultivation of prize cattle and horses, breeding dogs demanded only modest means and offered an excellent avenue to demonstrate the merit of their breeders. Ritvo traces the tangled threads of symbolic action in the class stakes in various dog breeds in the Victorian world of pets and show dogs during the late nineteenth-century institutionalization of the "dog fancy" in the kennel club, breed clubs, dog shows, and stud books.

The nonisomorphic codes of "individual merit" and "pure blood" were written into the script for the ideal dog. Urban middle-class Victorians celebrated the power to manipulate the raw material of breeding dogs to "invent" a breed with standards divorced from the utilitarian. Such power reinforced discourses of instrumentalism, progress, earned wealth, and meritorious leisure. The current commercial technophiliac celebration of the "invention" of genetically engineered organisms has an ancestral tie to Victorian middle-class adulation of its control over nature. The power to mold dog flesh symbolically destabilized rank and status based on nature; added weight to the appreciation of the achieved status of the business and professional classes; and *at the same time* reinforced the nexus tying together race, blood, genealogy, merit, and purity in "good breeding." This contradictory brew was stabilized by blending the arbitrary standard and instrumentalism with hierarchical merit fairly judged and purity of lines assiduously maintained. This solution jelled in the ideal types that molded modern purebred dogs.

It would be an error, however, to stop the story of "purebred dogs" here. If my participation in the Internet discussion lists of dog breeders, owners, and biological professionals; prowling through the canine newsletter, magazine, training manual, and scholarly and popular book literatures; researching the breed and applying for a purebred Australian Shepherd puppy produced from working lines; living with an adult Australian Shepherd-Chow mix from a ranching family; and talking to breeders, trainers, hunters, service dog handlers, conformation show competitors, dog sport participants, rescue activists, and other contemporary dog people has taught me nothing else, it has taught me to eschew ideological—or academic—reductionism about these cross-species communities. Very few of these canines and humans, both the heroes and the villains, breathe the rarefied air provided by a purely critical analysis of the institution of the modern breed.

My best information so far comes from communities committed to Australian Shepherds, Border Collies, Golden Retrievers, Basenjis, and Great Pyrenees. These dogs do different jobs and must respond with often specialized skill and judgment to all sorts of people, other dogs, equipment and machinery, and varied species and landscapes. For a quick glimpse of practices, including interpretations of written breed standards that are neither arbitrary nor reducible to class symbolic action, consider the many self-critical, ethical breeders of sport or working dogs. They tend to raise one or two litters a year for sale, and they work assiduously to produce dogs who can perform physically and mentally with good health for many years. They care about temperament, physical qualities (including "conformation"), both context-specific trainability and independent judgment by the dogs, and working drive and skill. The best among these breeders evaluate dogs carefully and place them in pet, show, and working homes only after a process of evaluating the people as well.

These breeders keep lifelong tabs on their dogs. They insist on sale contracts for dogs that should not be bred (or people that should not be breeders) that specify spay-neuter arrangements in an effort to keep the dogs out of ignorant breeding practices in homes or, worse, in commercial puppy mills. Breeders sometimes promise lifelong willingness to take back a dog in order to keep their dogs out of shelters. These people and their friends often spend money and time—lots of it—rescuing abandoned or abused members of their breed from puppy mills and shelters.

These breeders are caught up nonetheless in the dilemmas of the claims about increasing incidence of genetic disease and the increased surveillance of canine health. Activists among them set up health and genetics committees in their breed clubs and work to reform kennel clubs, their own breed club, and their own breeding practices. These activists, mostly self-educated in science, ask hard questions about the adequacy of data that strike at the heart of knowledge production in technoscientific worlds. There is a lot of symbolic action in all of this, but the story of class crucial to Ritvo's valuable narrative is at best a thread in the tapestry of the apparatus of production of purebred dogs in the late twentieth century.

My larger project must ask multilayered questions about the material-semiotic practice of "love of the breed" that permeates dog worlds. The story of these practices is not fenced in by the arguments Ritvo erected in *The Animal Estate*. For now, I rest uneasily with the specter she helped me raise of the "type" and go fearlessly into another ghostly narrative, that of the "population." My destination is the "genome" and its associated discourses of health and diversity.

The Origin of Dog Behavioral Genetics Research

In short, the dog may be a genetic pilot experiment for the human race.
—Scott and Fuller, *Genetics and the Social Behavior of the Dog*

In 1945, shortly after the end of World War II, Dr. Alan Gregg, director of the Rockefeller Foundation's Division for the Medical Sciences, lunched with Dr. C. C. Little, founder and director of the Roscoe B. Jackson Memorial Laboratory in Bar Harbor, Maine (Scott and Fuller 1965: v). Their conversation was the spark for a long-range research project that became known as "Genetics and Social Behavior of Mammals." The Rockefeller Foundation had funded the Bar Harbor lab from the start in 1929, including Little's research on cancer in mice. Gregg and Little's topic in 1945 was the Rockefeller Foundation's desire to stimulate research on the relations of heredity and behavior in the context of the "sciences of man" that guided the Foundation's post-1928 reorientation of priorities and research styles, including its early funding of molecular biology through the Division of Natural Sciences under Warren Weaver and the sponsorship of medical genetics through the Division of Medical Sciences headed by Gregg (Paul 1998: 53–79). Gregg and Little had been classmates at Harvard, and Little's father was a Boston dog fancier. Little himself served as a judge at dog shows. Besides his cancer work, Little studied the Mendelian genetics of coat color in dogs. He was also a strong eugenicist, an "advocate for race betterment" who advanced controversial opinions on delicate subjects, including divorce and birth control, which had forced his resignation from the presidency of the University of Michigan in 1929. Little and Gregg were well connected men who saw themselves as shapers of a more rational, scientific future.

It would be hard to overestimate the importance of the Jackson Laboratory in the development of animal models for the study of genetics. It would also be hard to overestimate the importance of the Rockefeller Foundation's joining of genetics, the physical and chemical sciences, and the behavioral sciences, including psychiatry and sociology, into a research program that took shape from the mid-1930s to the 1950s. This program energized the emerging technohumanist doctrines that shaped the relations of humans and other animals in technoscientific apparatuses of cultural production in the United States in the last half of the twentieth century. The origin story of the study of canine behavioral genetics is right in the middle of this large drama.

A strong believer in the genetic determination of mental health and mental talent, in 1941 Gregg, in response to a grant application from Little to breed a strain of dogs for cancer experiments, initiated discussion about the possibility of a study of behavioral genetics in dogs (Paul 1998: 68). With one eye Gregg had the market for friendly and bright pets in view; with the other he saw visions of convincing the American public that genetics underlies mental performance, so that taxpayers would not waste money on misguided social reforms. Much better than the geneticists' rodents, dogs could soften the public's mind in relation to *post*–World War II hereditarian doctrines. Encouraged by the English geneticist and eugenicist R. A. Fisher, a founder of mathematical population biology, Gregg continued to mull over the value of demonstrating the heritability of intelligence in dogs and to encourage Little in the same notions. Historian Diane Paul quotes Gregg, "My point of departure is a conviction that one of the constant afflictions of educators is their ignorance of the hereditary equipment of their pupils." If an animal could be bred that was "conspicuously intelligent and satisfactory as a pet, I believe the inference would be almost inescapable that in human beings also intelligence is affected by heredity and that the limitations of education in certain instances are clearly coming from genetic rather than pedagogic sources" (Gregg to Little, 3 January 1944, quoted in Paul 1998: 69).

Little hardly needed convincing. In 1937 he had applied to the Rockefeller Foundation to fund an Institute of Social Biology and Medicine, linking "population problems," eugenics, human psychology, sex and reproduction, medical genetics, and other topics (Paul 1998: 58). This proposal was not funded, but Paul details how the lack of enthusiasm for applied eugenics in the post–1928 Rockefeller Foundation did not apply to that holy grail within scientific worldviews—pure research. More than physiological disease, medical genetics tended to mean primarily the genetics of mental health and function—i.e., intelligence—even in the post–World War II period (Paul 1998: 64). Human medical genetics has deep roots in the ties of the old eugenics to assessments of mentality. Such ties are abundant in pronouncements by leaders of the Human Genome Project, even while they denounce the "old" eugenics; and those ties were evident in the turn to dogs at Bar Harbor in 1945.[3] Canine behavioral genetics was to be a research science in the best modernizing sense.

That modern touch included courting the news media, even while proclaiming commitment to the purest of research and disdain for the eugenic excesses of yesteryear. The planning conference in 1946 for the "Genetics and Social Behavior" research at Bar Harbor included not only leading advocates of psychobiology but also journalists from the *New York Times* and the Hearst papers (Paul 1998: 72). These men constituted the "Committee on Social Interpretation," which stood ready to publicize the results of the pure science of the genetics of behavior to the American pet buyer and taxpayer. But the story, which never got written, did not turn out as planned. Negative results make lousy press and muted careers, if great history of science.

In those negative results (from Little's and Gregg's points of view), canine behavioral genetics became an important bridge between the discourses of the breed and of the population. Recruited to head the dog behavioral project at the Jackson Laboratory was the thirty-five-year-old Dr. John Paul Scott, who had studied genetics at the University of Chicago under one of the architects of the evolutionary synthesis, Sewell Wright. Scott earned his Ph.D. in 1935 for a study of the embryology of the guinea pig. Wright had also published on the guinea pig, in one of the few studies of developmental genetics undertaken by a founder of the evolutionary synthesis. Wright was the only mathematically savvy contributor to Darwinian evolutionary theory and population genetics before the recent past to study the "role of specific genes in growth processes and pattern formation and the implication of such manifestations for evolution" (Hamburger 1980: 99).

Scott's and his colleague John Fuller's, as well as many other collaborators', thirteen-year study of the behavioral genetics of dogs was a centerpiece at Bar Harbor. The Rockefeller Foundation funded eleven of those years, to a total of $632,000—a very big project for the period. From the start, Scott and Fuller adopted a developmental approach within the context of Mendelian genetics linked to the biometrical tradition that Wright had so fruitfully transformed in his mathematical treatment of the theory of natural selection. Jackson Lab's Biometrical Service processed the massive dog data on about 500 animals from five breeds and a set of breed crosses and back crosses.

Crucial to these calculations was the discursive object called the population. Scott and Fuller missed no opportunity to show that their theoretical and methodological edifice depended on antitypological formulations of genetically heterogeneous populations, diverse individuals, and varying alleles. In their hands, the typological notion of the breed mutated and recombined with a populationist entity integrated into the evolutionary synthesis. That genetic recombination was central to the integration of the dog study into the biological humanism that the Rockefeller Foundation, UNESCO, the World Health Organization, Millbank Memorial Fund, Macy Foundation, and many others promoted so assiduously after World War II. In the process, the funders' expectations had to mutate. At Bar Harbor, "man's best friend" was a guide dog into less genetically determinist modernist utopian realms than Gregg and Little imagined.[4]

Scott and Fuller chose dogs for their investigations in order to probe the influence of "breed" on behavior.[5] Throughout, they emphasized that a "breed is not defined by conformity to type, but by common ancestry and absence of outbreeding" (Scott and Fuller 1965: 389). They insisted that each of the breeds they studied (Basenjis, Cocker Spaniels, Fox Terriers, Shetland Sheep Dogs, and Beagles) maintained genetic morphological and behavioral flexibility, even within the conditions of the Bar Harbor experimental breeding program. They argued that the capacities of breeds are broader than most people, who are committed to typological descriptions, recognize. Nonetheless, Scott and Fuller also found considerable inherited breed specialization in "behavior and physique, and even in the development of social relationships" (385).

Within a Mendelian and population genetics framework, the approach taken in the Bar Harbor studies was straightforward—if labor-intensive for dogs and people, expensive, densely structured by "built metaphors" in concepts and equipment, and so essentially unrepeatable in the way sustained studies of sizable mammals must always be. A breeding pair for each breed was the foundation of the lab populations, which were multiplied by inbreeding. Two breeds as different from each other as possible—namely, Cocker Spaniels and Basenjis—were selected for hybrid crossing to get F_1s, F_2s, and back crosses in order to test Mendelian hypotheses about segregation of alleles and modes of inheritance for traits. All the puppies were tested at numerous points in their development from birth to the age of one year. Tests probed such things as emotional and motivational reactions like fear or confidence, problem-solving abilities and performance in ingeniously designed situations, physical development, trainability, and intraspecific social interactions (especially dominance).

The researchers' practices of category formation and test design make a fascinating study. For example, what exactly is a "behavior pattern" or a "trait"? What are the practices that link such putatively visible things to invisible entities called genes? What kinds of interactions among dogs, humans, and environments make such crucial discursive objects come into focus? But that thread cannot be pursued here. The behavior of the humans and the physical environments for the pooches were standardized as much as possible (no small trick over thirteen years with social animals kept in fairly rich circumstances). Thus, the dogs could vary to their genes' content; and the researchers could make crosses, calculate heritabilities, do comparisons of performances across different tests based on handy tools like the stanine scoring system, and figure out modes of inheritance (single gene, multiple genes, recessive, dominant, etc.) to their hearts' content.

The most striking impression made by the Scott and Fuller study on a reader steeped in the debates about breeds, specialization and flexibility, genetic diseases, and genetic diversity in dogs after the 1990s is that most of the arguments and many of the data were in place by 1965, at least within the research community in which the Jackson Lab participated. For example, Scott and Fuller note the problem of fixing double recessives with inbreeding; the genetic costs of overuse of popular studs; the phenomenon of hybrid vigor in their F_1 Cocker Spaniel–Basenji crosses; and the problem of polygenic conditions like hip dysplasia that also have a strong developmental and environmental component. They were critical of regular outbreeding because double recessives would show up less and make deleterious genes harder to eliminate. By default, they supported at least line breeding. Despite the internal contradictions, sounding like the critics of the 1990s Scott and Fuller argued that "the current dog breeding practices can be described as an ideal system for the spread and preservation of injurious recessive genes" (405).

What is fundamentally different is the vast apparatus of cultural production of gene discourse that has hypertrophied since Gregg and Little had lunch at John D. Rockefeller's expense. Popular eugenics transformed for post–World War II pure science was nothing compared to the new millennium's geneticism under the sign of the double helix. Also different is that, for all their emphasis on genetic variation, nowhere do Scott and Fuller talk about diversity being "endangered." Notions of dog breeds analogous to endangered species and a biodiversity deficit threatening life itself are products of post-1980s genetic, immunological, environmental, and economic discourses. Absent is discussion of the advantages of heterozygosity across the genome, especially in relation to genes affecting the immune system. "Diversity" has resonances in the 1990s that could not be in the word as it was used at the Jackson Lab in the 1950s and 1960s.

Genetics and the Social Behavior of the Dog made several notable arguments. The research established critical periods in puppy development, especially the sensitive windows for both same-species and cross-species socialization. Also prominent was the book's insistence that genes act throughout a lifetime in whole organisms and social and physical environments. Puppies are adapted to infantile conditions of life, as other-age dogs are adapted to corresponding internal and external worlds. Scott and Fuller worked against simplistic and typological notions of the gene and the organism at individual and group levels. This aspect of their behavioral genetic discourse is striking in view of the frequently simplistic genetic ideologies of 1990s technoscientific culture. Their conclusions are also striking in view of their patrons' expectations. "Pure science" must not be underestimated; it can lead where its practitioners do not want to go. That is its enduring and precious potency.

Scott and Fuller had a comparative eye on human beings in their dog studies, and this was nowhere more evident than in the way they pursued the question of "intelligence." They used their data on the many specialized behavioral capacities and approaches to puzzles relating to the experimental situations that Bar Harbor dogs found themselves in to argue *against* a general intelligence factor. Like other comparative psychologists of the period, they defined problem solving as a process of adaptation. They saw no reason to reduce the complexity of such processes and multiple capacities, no matter whether the heritability values were high or low, to a general factor like that often associated with intelligence testing in humans. With dogs as their guides, Scott and Fuller seemed less than convinced by the human intelligence testers. The dog researchers were also much more impressed by differences in emotional and motivational aspects of performance than by differences in puzzle-solving intellect. A dog might be able to solve a problem, but would he or she want to do so? Under what terms? Breed and individual differences might have much more to do with motivation than with what the testers' meant, and mean, by intelligence. Any dog person, including a behavioral genetics researcher, must meet dogs this way if their knowledge is to be persuasive in cross-species communities of practice. Human psychological test subjects, alas, have proved more docile than even the average Beagle.

Scott and Fuller's skepticism infused the way they approached the dog-human comparison on matters like the consequences of lowered intensity of natural selective pressure in civilized conditions and the possibility of breeding for a "superior" human or dog. They emphasized the diversity in dog and human populations. Changed selection pressures would result in different genetic equilibria in a population, but in no case would an individual dog or human embody a perfected "type." Arguing from evolutionary populationist principles, they insisted that a "developed human society" is biologically feasible, but not a "superman" or other figures of fascist eugenic imaginations. Scott and Fuller imagined that "scientific breeding" might well belong in a good human future; but they kept close to the populationist doctrines of flexibility and diversity of the whole as being the *scientific* goal. That became the core of the post–World War II biological technohumanist liberal discourse.

Just as Ritvo's class arguments in *The Animal Estate* turned out to be a very partial guide to understanding love of the breed in the dog worlds I have begun to inhabit, Little and Gregg's hopes for docile, smart pets and "pure-science" demonstrations of the hegemony of genes for mental capacity turned out to lead somewhere else. As Diane Paul reported, Scott and Fuller never tired in pointing out what they saw to be the implications of their research on differences in dog individuals and breeds: "The behavior traits do not appear to be organized by heredity. Rather a dog inherits a number of abilities which can be organized in different ways to meet different situations. . . . This means, in terms of human behavior, that the best sort of social environment is one which permits a large degree of individual freedom of behavior. Most individuals can reach desired goals if they are allowed sufficient freedom in the ways they reach those goals" (Scott and Fuller 1956: 23, quoted in Paul 1998: 73–74). And adequate school budgets, housing, employment, medical care, and robust public culture. . . . The last word is not in on the genetics of complex, specialized canine behavior. Hardly the first word is in, and the *New York Times* will have to wait for its lead.

Birth of the Kennel

Story: Overhearing Prozac

Toward the end of her sixteen-year life, my half–Labrador Retriever, Sojourner, and I frequented her vet's office. I had read Michel Foucault, and I knew all about biopower and the proliferative powers of biological discourses. I knew modern power was productive above all else. I knew how important it was to have a body pumped up, petted, and managed by the apparatuses of medicine, psychology, and pedagogy. I knew modern subjects had such bodies, and that the rich got them before the laboring classes. I was prepared for a modest extension of my clinical privileges to any sentient being and some insentient ones. I had read *Birth of the Clinic* and *The History of Sexuality*, and I had written about the technobiopolitics of cyborgs. I felt I could not be surprised by anything. But I was wrong. I had been fooled by Foucault's own species chauvinism into forgetting that dogs too might live in the domains of technobiopower. The *Birth of the Kennel* might be the book I need to write.

While Sojourner and I waited to be seen, a lovely Afghan hound pranced around at the checkout desk while his human discussed recommended treatments. The dog had a difficult problem—obsessive self-wounding when his human was off making a living, or engaging in less justifiable nondog activities, for several hours a day. The afflicted dog had a nasty open sore on his hind leg. The vet recommended that the dog take Prozac. I had read *Listening to Prozac;* so I knew this was the drug that promised, or threatened, to give its recipient a new self in place of the drab, depressive, obsessive one that had proved so lucrative for the nonpharmaceutical branches of the psychological professions. For years, I had insisted that dogs and people were much alike, and that other animals had complex minds and social lives, as well as physiologies and genomes largely shared with humans. Why did hearing that a pooch should take Prozac warp my sense of reality in the way that makes one see what was hidden before? Surely, Saul on the way to Damascus had more to his turn-around than a Prozac prescription for his neighbor's ass!

The Afghan's human was as nonplussed as I was. She chose instead to put a large cone around her dog's head so that he couldn't reach his favorite licking spot to suck out his unhappiness. I was even more shocked by that choice— what, I fumed internally, can't you get more time to exercise and play with your dog and solve this problem without chemicals or restraints? I remained deaf to the human's defensively explaining to the vet that her health policy covered her own Prozac, but the pills were too expensive for her dog. In truth, I was hooked into the mechanisms of proliferating discourse that Foucault should have prepared me for. Drugs, restraints, exercise, retraining, altered schedules, searching for improper puppy socialization, scrutinizing the genetic background of the dog for evidence of canine familial obsessions, wondering about psychological or physical abuse, finding an unethical breeder who turns out inbred dogs without regard to temperament, getting a good toy that would occupy the dog's attention when the human was gone, accusations about the workaholic and stress-filled human lives that are out of tune with the more natural dog rhythms of ceaseless demands for human attention: all these discursive moves and more filled my enlightened mind.

I was on the road to the fully embodied modern dog-human relationship. There could be no end to the search for ways to relieve the psychophysiological suffering of dogs, and more, to help them achieve their full canine potential. Furthermore, I am convinced that is the ethical obligation of the human who lives with a member of a companion species. I can no longer make myself feel surprise that a dog might need Prozac and should get it.

Neither can the author of *The Dog Who Loved Too Much*, Dr. Nicholas Dodman (1996), who explained the psychopharmacological treatment of canine behavior disorders in his popular advice book. That thread led to a wealth of canine advice literature; and browsing any good Internet book site or perusing a hardcopy pet catalogue—or stopping off at a PetsMart™ supermall—lets me survey a vast array of materials that could improve canine lives.

I soon realized that the positive-training pedagogical doctrines current for dogs resemble those experienced by my godson at his progressive preschool. As I should have realized from the matrix tying together liberal humanist and caninist discourses in the Scott and Fuller study, the history of pedagogical discourses for the two species is eerily similar. The no-punishment disciplinary technology to shape modern subjects of whatever species through structuring their formative worlds, such that they more or less spontaneously do what the educator wants, makes the Marine-style police and war dog training a thing of repressed memories. Anger management is not just in the high schools. Surreptitiously, buoyed up by success with my mutt, I tried dried liver treats on my then five-year-old godson. This ruse lasted until his cultural anthropologist mother too sang the praises of the species similarities that my Darwinian-Foucauldian soul breathes in with oxygen. The searcher for canine educational approaches can choose among new-age methods, operant-conditioning texts, and many more. We learn how much dog-training techniques owe to dolphins and those training them for the military and film and marine park entertainment industries.

A committed dog companion can get fun-and-games workbooks (including a lesson for multispecies dunking for apples—points get deducted for tooth marks or half-eaten apples) to teach dogs and humans to play together, in neighborhood communities or in the privacy of their homes. I gave such a book to my husband for his birthday, and we began training all the members of our household to have a good time together. It all starts with a lot of mouth massage. The more high-culture types among us can subscribe to an excellent literary newsprint magazine, *The Bark*, published in Berkeley (www. thebark.com). Resemblances to the Berkeley *Barb* are deliberate. *The Bark* no. 7 (1999) took a look at "Dogs in the Visual Arts." Some of my humanist-scholar colleagues aren't ready for this.

Health manuals and self-help literatures abound, and those wishing to avoid the supposedly toxic foods and overvaccination doctrines of the evil official profit-making dog world will not lack for a text named something like *Our Dogs, Ourselves.*[6] Others can find guidance for evaluating a scientific amino acid balance from the Ralston Purina Web site, which also gives information for puppy raising and a link to the latest in genetic research. Those responsible about dental health will do more than get their pooch's teeth cleaned annually—tooth-healthy chew toys are on the market. Sports enthusiasts can find clubs, manufacturers, Internet build-it-yourself sites, and county fairground practice days. We belong to the NBA (Nothin' But Agility, www.users.aol.com/nbagility). Conspiracy theories, government cover-ups, scientific progress, elaborate commodity culture, the war between animal-rights and animal-welfare discourses, team sports, grief groups, adoption bureaucracies, fetal and uterine-contraction monitors belted to a bitch and equipped with a remote modem tied into twenty-four-hour computer data analysis for problem pregnancies,[7] a dog cloning project promoted and closely followed on the Internet, abuse recovery therapies: nothing is lacking in contemporary dog natureculture.

To drive the point home, consider my colleague, Professor Angela Davis, whose impeccable red-diaper credentials extend to an honorary degree from Lenin University, Tashkent, Uzbekistan, in 1972. She certainly noticed Mc-Carthyism, not to mention race, gender, class, and sexuality oppression, in Cold-War America. As adults, Angela and I share more than an antiracist feminist theory commitment to intersectional analyses of inequalities. She gives me names of dog acupuncture practitioners and training consultants to help along faltering child-dog friendships. She purchased a special back-leg wheeled cart to help her aged dog walk in her last months. And, healing in a leg cast from injuries sustained running with her young dogs, she admitted wistfully from behind piles of dissertation chapters that in her alter ego, she imagines herself a dog breeder.

There are also several series of murder mysteries[8] with dog-human co-sleuths. The gene holds sway here too. In Laurien Berenson's 1995 *A Pedigree to Die For*, the plot turns on the discovery of a genetic fraud. Single mother and dog neophyte Melanie Travis is the detective. The Standard Poodle, Beau, disappears the night his owner Max dies under suspicious circumstances. Max's wife and fellow poodle breeder is Peg, Melanie's aunt. The plot treats the hunt for Beau and the ultimate discovery that he carries a genetic defect, which has been hidden from the show poodle community so far (even while his owners Max and Peg were quietly retiring him from stud because they knew about the genetic problem—still, Melanie's aunt did not quickly inform the buyers of his previous puppies or the owners of the bitches). Max and Peg had had punch skin biopsies done on all their poodles the spring before the supposed theft and suspicious death—Beau alone had failed. Beau was quite a popular stud before his genetic fall from grace—bred monthly until the closely guarded bad genetic news. It turned out Beau wasn't stolen after all. Max had sold him at quite a price to an enemy without telling about the genetic problem in order to ruin the man once he found out what he had bought. The gene was for SA, sebaceous adenitis (an autosomal recessive condition in the poodle; see Padgett 1998: 212, 231), a skin problem that could be managed but disqualified a dog as good breeding stock. Max was indeed murdered, however, by a dog show judge being investigated by the AKC for taking bribes to shape his judgments.

These are glimpses of the natureculture in which the dog genome flourishes as practice and culture on technical and popular levels in the United States, and in many other places as well. It is past time to scratch some Hot Spots summarizing key aspects of the apparatus of naturalcultural production of dog genomics in the 1990s.

Dog Days in the Genome: Hot Spots

The following lists are irritatingly raw. Still, several themes leap out at the science studies and cultural studies analyst. Many social worlds traffic in dog genes as the boundary objects tying them together. Actors in these worlds frequently wear several hats. Love, professional and nonprofessional expertise, and activism are in close touch in canine knowledge-producing practices. Familiar from analyses of human genomics, cross-connections stand out among actors. Consider, for example, the ties linking varieties of researchers; industry people; lay and professional activists; national and international regulators and standardizers (e.g., for DNA markers and for pet-welfare legal conventions); breed clubs and their often contentious committees; kennel clubs with their disputed control of breeding and show culture; and veterinarians, trainers, writers, and other sorts of people making their living with dogs.

Dog genomics, like human genomics, is an international endeavor. Witness the three major dog gene-mapping projects and the many labs articulated through such research, including labs whose focus is comparative gene mapping (e.g., mouse/human/dog). The first dog genetics mapping project to achieve high enough resolution, with markers associated with cheap enough testing to facilitate capturing a big enough market, will decide whether crucial parts of the dog genome are privately owned or in the international public domain.

The Internet culture is rich and important. Cindy Tittle Moore compiled dog-related email sites from 1995–99 (http://www.k9web.com/dog-faqs/lists/email-list.html). My twelve-point, Times Roman, single-spaced printout of her copyrighted list required forty-three pages; and, inescapably, important sites are missing. The wired dog world mediates international and local exchanges among actors that either could not occur without the Internet or would occur more slowly and less publicly. Play among metastatic commercialism, thick research cultures, and animated professional-lay exchanges characterize dog gene links. Freelance writers for *DogWorld* (especially Susan Thorpe-Vargas, a Samoyed breeder and Ph.D. in immunology, John Cargill, an Akita person and statistician, and D. Caroline Coile, a Saluki breeder and doctorate in neuroscience and behavior) seed the popular canine knowledge terrain with publications on genetic health and diversity. *DogWorld* has published at least eighteen articles on genetics in relation to health and breeding since 1996 (e.g., Cargill and Thorpe-Vargas 1996, 1998, 2000; Coile 1997; Padgett 1996–97). Older registries for databasing inherited conditions face extensive changes in their practice from the revolution in molecular biology and dog politics. Consumer culture permeates genetic culture and vice versa. The scramble for dog genes is a scramble to survive for competing biotechnology companies. Meanwhile, a giant in the commercial revolution that defined middle-class dog culture after World War II—the dog food company Ralston Purina—is a mover and shaker in the genetics revolution. New kinds of surveillance—epitomized in mandatory DNA-testing for litters to verify pedigrees and in proliferating gene tests for inherited conditions—discipline the lives of dogs and people.[9] Biosociality is the fluid in which dog and human subjects gestate, as they meet at the Progressive Retinal Atrophy gene-test apparatus at national specialty shows.

Contesting for the meanings of genetics has become an obsession in dog worlds. The sense of a state of emergency pervades much of the discourse. In the face of ongoing inbreeding practices that would curl an evolutionary biologist's hair—and in the face of levels of denial that ensure good incomes to therapists into the future—dog-gene discourse is volatile. Millennarian thematics borrow from the rhetorics of endangered species, planetary biodiversity loss, and postcolonial criticisms of typological racism. Like much in technoscientific culture, the discourse is simultaneously practical and apocalyptic—and compelling in both registers. One controversial critic and breeder who ceased to have anything to do with official kennel club registries, the Canadian Jeffrey Bragg, claims that dog breeders have become so overwhelmed by the need to select their crosses in recognition of multiple genetic diseases and the constant loss of genetic diversity in their breeds that they can hardly select anymore to improve the breed in temperament, function, and conformation. Providing a plan of action for radically different breed-creating and sustaining genetic practices focused on the concept of "evolving breeds" rather than "breed types," he writes about a "new millennium" and a "canine revolution" where "there are no soft options left" ("Purebred Dogs into the Twenty-first Century," Canine Diversity Project Web site).

On the listservs, some breeders feel attacked when population genetics is the topic. Others (or the same people in another mood) energetically try to learn what for them is a new language written in the ciphers of statistics, along with the language of molecular genetics written in the technical and commercial codes of DNA. Both of these languages carry major implications for the breeders' practice of "love of the breed." On CANGEN-L, the Canine Genetics Discussion Group, "lay people" and "professionals" vigorously work to educate each other about their realities, and perhaps to shape a better shared reality in the process. "Lay people" welcome "expert" discussions, but not without interrupting and demanding translations of jargon and verbal explanations of equations. And not without contesting the data, models, and theories. Geneticists seek "lay people" as their collaborators in research projects, and vice versa. And "lay people" can be impressively literate in the languages and practices of genetics, while genetics professionals can be amateurs and seekers in dog worlds. Dog natureculture has been a cross-generic symbiosis from the start, and perhaps more now than ever.

Hot Spots: A Listing Obsession

Organizations Relating to Canine Health and Genetics

Canine Eye Registry Foundation (CERF), Dept. of Veterinary Clinical Service, Purdue University. A closed registry and voluntary diagnostic service. www. vet.purdue.edu/~yshen/cerf.html

Canine Molecular Genetics Resource, 3728 Plaza Dr., Suite 1, Ann Arbor, MI 48108

GeneSearch, LLC. http://www.genesearch.net/dogs4dna.html

Institute for Genetic Disease Control in Animals (GDC), Davis, CA. Founded 1990, modeled after the Swedish Kennel Club's open registry. GDC is an open registry for orthopedic and soft-tissue diseases. Listing suspected carriers and affected animals, GDC issues KinReport™s to individuals with a valid reason for inquiring. www.vetmed.ucdavis.edu/gdc/gdc.html

International Society for Animal Genetics. Sponsors DogMap, one of several canine gene mapping efforts. If the ISAG project's microsatellite markers are accepted by breed and kennel clubs first as the international standard, then the key DNA regions will remain in the public domain. If the commercial efforts to corner the market for parentage testing succeed, then microsatellite markers will be proprietary and require license fees for use by others. In 1999 there were several competing and incompatible sets of microsatellite markers for parentage testing used by several companies and vet school laboratories. Lack of standardization of markers and breed genetics/ health registries is a rich context for studying technoscientific canine cultures. www.wisc.edu/animalsci/isag/index.html

Orthopedic Foundation for Animals (OFA), Columbia, MO, www.offa.org Founded 1966, originally focused on canine hip dysplasia; recently expanded to a range of genetic diseases. A closed registry and voluntary diagnostic service.

PennHIP™, Synbiotics, San Diego, CA. www.synbiotics.com

University of California at Davis, with the Veterinary Genetics Laboratory (VGL: www.vgl.ucdavis.edu/), which is affiliated with the School of Veterinary Medicine (www.vetmed.ucdavis.edu/). VGL works with the International Society for Animal Genetics (ISAG) microsatellite markers, which are in the public domain. A "high-resolution" dog genetic map was available through ISAG in August 1998. But ISAG had fewer markers than did VetGen, UM and MSU's Canine Molecular Genetics Resource™ (CMGR™). In early 1999, VGL charged $40/dog for parentage DNA testing. VGL began in 1950 with blood typing for establishing parentage. Much of the VGL genetics research is funded by fees from their DNA-testing services. VGL maintains a links page for overall sites dealing with dog genetics: www.vgl.ucdavis.edu/research/canine/

Many other universities and vet schools, especially, in the United States, Cornell, Pennsylvania, Michigan.

American Kennel Club Health Foundation, New York City. www.akcchf.org/

American Veterinary Medical Association (AVMA)

The first two U.S. open registries for genetic diseases were the PRA (progressive retinal atrophy) Data (started by Georgia Gooch, a Lab Retriever breeder, in 1989) and the West Highland Anomaly Task Council (WatcH), started in 1989 and registering three diseases by 1997. There were no whole dog registries with searchable pedigrees in the United States in 1999. Breed activists argue for open registries with searchable pedigrees showing linkages to dogs with genetic disease.

Commercial Organizations Involved with Dog
Molecular Genetics (1999 prices)

AnSci Products. Canine DNA parentage testing. GENMARK® Genetic testing kits ($39/sample). https://www.ansciproducts.com

ImmGen, Inc. A red blood cell and DNA-typing and research laboratory providing parentage verification and genetic trait detection services to cattle, goat, swine, and dog breed associations. Located near the Texas A&M University campus, the company was started in 1983 by Dr. Jerry Caldwell as a cattle blood typing laboratory providing parentage verification services to cattle breed associations. In 1991 ImmGen doubled its size and added a DNA-typing service and research laboratory. Services include parentage testing, pedigree problem solving, freemartin determination, long-term sample storage, and electronic data management. ImmGen is a member of the International Society for Animal Genetics, which promotes the standardization of parentage testing and cooperation between laboratories worldwide. ImmGen is developing DNA markers for dog, swine, and cattle parentage testing and plans to provide parentage testing and other genetic diagnostic services for a wide spectrum of species. Has the contract with the Australian Shepherd Club of America (ASCA) for parentage DNA testing ($28/sample). http://www.immgen.com/html/Inside-ImmGen.html

Optigen, LLC. Located in the Cornell Business and Technology Park, this start-up company was established in 1998 by Cornell College of Veterinary Medicine researchers Gregory Acland, Gustavo Aguirre, and Kunal Ray to provide DNA-based diagnoses and information about inherited diseases (especially those affecting vision) in purebred dogs. OptiGen emerged from a 1997–98 Technology Development Fund grant administered through the Cornell Office for Technology Access and Business Assistance and the Cornell Office of Economic Development. Extensive cooperation with breed clubs is the lifeblood of companies like OptiGen. http://www.optigen.com

PE Zoogen, 1756 Picasso Ave., Davis, CA 95616. The former Perkin-Elmer Corporation sold off its instrument-making division and emerged in 1998 as PE Corporation, a pure genome business. One major division is J. Craig Venter's Celera Corp., which is engaged in private human genome mapping in competition with the NIH Human Genome Project. email: PEZoogen. perkin-elmer.com

Ralston Purina, with links to the Dog Genome Project at UCB, Cornell, and FHCRC. R-P is the site of the Canine Reference Family DNA Distribution Center, which, as of January 1999, is managed by a committee of researchers from the FHCRC, Ralston Purina, Cornell, and the National Cancer Institute. Collections will be transferred to the new Center from Cornell. DNA from the sixteen to eighteen starting reference families will be made available worldwide. R-P will develop a Web page devoted to canine genetics research. www.purina.com/dogs/index.html

VetGen, Ann Arbor, MI. Identification and pedigree testing, disease genetic markers, ten-year DNA storage (blood samples). VetGen was established in 1995 to optimize the value of research by moving it fast from the university laboratory to the commercial marketplace. VetGen works closely with Michigan State University and University of Michigan labs. Together VetGen, UM and MSU licensed the Canine Molecular Genetics Resource™, with about 625 markers in 1998, then the most comprehensive marker database internationally. Royalties are shared among the three. Product list in early 1999 lists tests for fourteen diseases involving fourteen breeds (The "same" disease in different breeds may involve different loci). Parentage-verification DNA testing cost $60/dog, with special pricing for litters. A test for von Willebrand's Disease cost $140 per sample. The UM (Brewer, Department of Human Genetics) and MSU (School of Veterinary Medicine) collaboration on dog molecular genetics dates from 1988. Catherine Ineson, Vet-Gen's research coordinator, participates in the CANGEN-L canine diversity discussion list. Part of her job is to encourage owner and breeder participation in VetGen research and testing. www.vetgen.com

U.S. Funding Organizations Dealing with Canine Genetics

(Note the paucity of funding for canine genetics compared to agriculturally important species and human medical genetics.)

AKC Canine Health Foundation. The AKCCHF had about sixty active grants (many at UC Davis) in March 1999, not all for genetics, but genetics is a major foundation target ("to identify and sponsor research and education programs, with particular emphasis on canine genetics," Web site homepage). The research is driven by two priorities: (1) parentage verification to correct fraud in pedigrees, and (2) disease-gene identification for diagnosis useful in breeders' decisions and perhaps eventual therapies. No grants bore on genome diversity issues in a conservation biology or population genetics sense. This lack extended to all other sources of funding I have so far identified. www.akcchf.org

Morris Animal Foundation. Founded 1948. MAF funds animal health studies at vet schools in the United States and worldwide. Funds about eighty studies annually with a budget of about $1.7 million. Between 1948 and early 1999 the MAF had dispensed over $18 million for 795 animal health projects (over $9 million for dogs; over $3.5 million for 100+ studies of inherited conditions, including cancer and hip dysplasia). Grants average about $21,000 over two to three years. Cosponsorship of a research project (a fundraising mechanism) costs $2,500 or more. Breed clubs can raise that kind of money. The MAF founder was a practicing vet in New Jersey in the late 1930s. His work on a diet to control kidney failure in a guide dog for a blind client led to a tie-in with the Hill Packing Company and eventually to Prescription Diet® foods marketed through vet clinics and, thus, significant money to fund animal research. The Hill royalty ended in 1968, when the MFA received an endowment gift and started modern fund-raising efforts. Hill's Pet Nutrition, Inc., separately funds animal health studies. The MAF also funds health projects for wildlife. See especially its Mountain Gorilla Health Monitoring and Veterinary Project. www.MorrisAnimalFoundation.org

National Institutes of Health. Dog genes provide models for the study of human genetic diseases.

Ralston Purina, in-house and extramural

Individual breed clubs fund a significant amount of disease genetics research.

Dog Genome Projects

The Canine Genome Project. UC Berkeley, University of Oregon, and the Fred Hutchinson Cancer Research Center. Has long-term aims for behavioral as well as genetic disease gene identification. Data are made available world wide on the Internet. Collaborations tie together researchers at the University of Oregon, UCB (Jasper Rine), FHCRC (Elaine Ostrander), Cornell (Gustavo Aguirre, GM Acland), and others. The second generation map in spring 1998 had 277 markers. Studies of the canine Major Histocompatibility Complex (MHC) are noteworthy for future canine genomic diversity research. In early 1999, Ralston Purina joined this project through agreeing to serve as the independent repository for canine reference families and DNA registries and to set up a publicly accessible Web site for the data. For UCB: http://mendel.berkeley.edu/dog.html. For Fred Hutchinson CRC: www.fhcrc.org/science/dog_genome/dog.html

The Canine Radiation Mapping Project. CNRS, Paris. Aims to identify genes involved in phenotypic, behavioral, and pathological traits. In early 1999 had a map with about 550 markers. www-recomgen.univ-rennes1.fr/doggy.html

DogMap. An international collaboration involving forty-three labs from twenty-one countries, under the auspices of the International Society for Animal Genetics. "Participation in this collaboration is unrestricted as long as it is understood that all data generated within this collaboration belong to the public domain. . . . DogMap emphasizes setting up an internationally accessible database for handling mapping data." http://ubeclu.unibe.ch/itz/dogmap.html

Internet Sites, Magazines, and Other Organs
for Canine Genetic Discourse

AcmePet Canine Genetic Resource. The site has a six-part series of articles on canine hip dysplasia. Commercial, educational, and general pet interests links. www.acmepet.com/canine/genetic/

Australian National Genomic Information Service. Lists journal articles for 300+ conditions in the dog. www.angis.su.oz.au/

Canine Genetic Resource. Popular site with question and answer forum, bulletin board, background information. www.acmepet.com/index.html

Canine Genetics and Dog Health Homepage. www.teleport.com/~gback/cghp.html

Canine Diversity Project, Web site developed by John Armstrong, University of Ottawa, Canada. www.magma.ca/~kaitlin/diverse.html

CANGEN-L listserv (Canine Genetics Discussion Group), John Armstrong, List Administrator, University of Ottawa, Canada. For breeders, geneticists, and evolutionary biologists, and others with a serious interest. CANGEN-L was set up to provide a safe place for the deeper and more controversial discussions of genetic diversity in dogs that were unwelcome on the K9GENES Web site. email: jbarm@uottawa.ca

Cornell University Internet-based canine genetics courses for breeders and other interested lay people, beginning 1999. www.ansci.cornell.edu/disted/canine/genetics/course1/

K9GENES, a listserv for discussing modes of inheritance, basic genetics, etc. Given to endless discussions of the genetics of coat color in dogs.

UC Davis Vet School links to canine genetics sites. www.vgl.ucdavis.edu/research/canine/

Online Mendelian Inheritance in Animals, Dept. of Animal Science, University of Sydney, Australia. www.angis.su.oz.au/Databases/BIRX/omia/

breed-based listservs, e.g., four separate listserv discussion groups for Australian Shepherds.

AKC Gazette and other kennel club and breed club magazines

DogWorld

Double Helix Network News. For Australian Shepherd breeders, privately published by C. A. Sharp, Fresno, CA

Important Sites of Action Outside the United States

Australia

Canada (Jeffrey Bragg, expert on Siberian Huskies and on population genetics applied to dogs, writes and agitates in *Dogs in Canada* and elsewhere; CANGEN-L, initiated by John Armstrong and hosted by the University of Ottawa.)

European Union (The Council of the EU passed the European Convention on pet animal welfare in 1995 that advocates a reduction of breed traits that appear to compromise health and well being, such as excessively short muzzles and legs, bowed legs, extremes in size, and so on. Reduction in extremes is to be achieved by changes in judging standards at shows and rewriting breed standards. A ban on breeding, exhibiting, and selling could follow if voluntary measures prove insufficient. Such direct government banning of specific breeds is the hope/fear for various actors in Europe and the United States)

Germany

Japan

Sweden (Sweden is the most active country in trying to comply with the 1995 Convention on pet animal welfare. See *Hundsport*, the magazine of the Swedish Kennel Club.)

The Netherlands

UK

Dog Cloning Project

Missyplicity Project (www.missyplicity.com/M2.Pages/M2.welcome.html), began in 1998 with a $2.3 million grant for the first two years, from a wealthy elderly heterosexual and heterodox couple, to three senior researchers at Texas A&M University and their collaborators from several institutions. The project has an elaborate Web site, with comments from the public, stories about the mixed-breed dog, Missy, who is to be cloned, a list of research objectives, and a state-of-the-art code of bioethics. Stories abound. My version: The human man, John (writing an autobiography called *The Accidental CEO*), grew up poor, made lots of money, and fell in love with a most interesting woman and then a dog of uncertain ancestry. The human woman donor, Candida, had herself been through a powerful identity-remaking technology in the form of a complete identity change (from witness protection? from having been underground? my informant, a graduate student in my department, did not know) many years ago. My informant had been in a creative writing workshop in the San Francisco Bay Area with Candida until recently and had personally met Missy. Missy flew to Texas for her tissue biopsies. Candida and John live separately and are not married. John was much involved in Biosphere II. Candida is very low tech, says my informant. Her Internet stories about how Missy came to her are wonderful additions to dog literature. Associated with the Missyplicity Project is the cryopreservation tissue and gene bank, The Savings and Clone Company, near Texas A&M. See www.savingsandclone.com. Other cryopreservation banks with an eye also on future pet dog cloning are Lazaron BioTechnologies (whose March 2000 *DogWorld* ad tell us about our chance "to save a genetic life") and The Canine Cryobank. Some participants in one of the dog lists that I follow, themselves self-reflective and ethical breeders of "purebreds," condemned cloning as "eugenics." Mark Derr (environmental historian, dog writer, and acerbic critic of breed and kennel club genetics practices [Derr 1997]), argued that the Missyplicity Project is "intent on cheating death, on going the taxidermist one better by creating a biological sculpture" ("Missyplicity," *The Bark*, no. 6 [Fall 1998]: 11]. Arguments for dog cloning in the interests of preserving genetic diversity are in Cargill and Thorpe-Vargas 2000. Technophilia, not to mention love of money, abounds in Charles Graeber, "How Much Is That Doggy in the Vitro?" *Wired*, March 2000, 220–29.

Agents in Their Own Story

Dogs are agents in cross-species worlds. They "motivate" their humans, even as their humans learn to draw from new bait bags to move their dogs to perform desired actions. This fundamental point can be illustrated in many ways, but I will content myself here with a return to scientific-origin stories. The origin of dogs might be a humbling chapter in the story of *Homo sapiens*, one that allows for a deeper sense of co-evolution and cohabitation and a reduced exercise of hominid hubris in shaping canine natureculture. Even as Man the Hunter was retired from the ecological theater and the evolutionary play a couple of decades ago (try not to notice his distressing radioactive half-life into the "new" millennium), the noble dog-wolf as hunting companion to this mythic hominid personage has a shit-eating grin for more reasons than one.

Accounts of the relations of dogs and wolves proliferate, and molecular biologists tell some of the most convincing versions. Robert Wayne and his colleagues at UCLA studied mitochondrial DNA (mtDNA) from 162 North American, European, Asian, and Arabian wolves and from 140 dogs representing 67 breeds, plus a few jackals and coyotes (Vilá, et al. 1997). Their analysis of mtDNA control regions concluded that dogs emerged uniquely from wolves—and did so much earlier than scenarios based on archaeological data. The amount of sequence divergence and the organization of the data into clades support the emergence of dogs more than 100,000 years ago, with few separate domestication events. Three-quarters of modern dogs belong to one clade; i.e., they belong to a single maternal lineage. The early dates give *Canis familiaris* and *Homo sapiens sapiens* roughly the same calendar, so folks walking out of Africa soon met a wolf bitch who would give birth to man's best friends. Building a genetic trellis as they went, dogs and people walked back into Africa too. These have been species more given to multidirectional traveling and consorting than to conquering and replacing, never to return to their old haunts again. No wonder dogs and people share the distinction of being the most well-mixed and widely geographically distributed large-bodied mammals. They shaped each over a long time.

In a story familiar from the post–World War II studies of human-population gene frequencies that were so important to the early 1950s antiracist UNESCO statements and to reforms of physical anthropology and genetics teaching, dog mtDNA haplotypes did not sort out by breed, indicating that breeds have diverse doggish ancestries. "Pure" breeds are an institutional fiction, if one that threatens the health of animals regulated by the story. Variations within breed sometimes exceeded variations between populations of dogs and wolves. And, in another lab's study, "greater mtDNA differences appeared within the single breeds of Doberman pinscher or poodle than between dogs and wolves," even while "there is less mtDNA difference between dogs, wolves and coyotes than there is between various ethnic groups of human beings" (Coppinger and Schneider 1995: 33). Genetic difference studies are a high stakes game, and emphases on similarity or divergence shift with the theoretical bets laid.

Findings from Wayne's lab have been controversial, partly because the mtDNA clock doesn't measure up to the accuracy demanded by Swiss watchmakers. At an International Council for Archaeozoology symposium in 1998 at the University of Victoria, controversy waxed over Wayne's arguments. Relevant to this chapter are implications for thinking about agency in dog-human interactions. Wayne argued that to domesticate dogs took a lot of skill, or it would have happened more often. His story bears the scent of the anatomically wolfish hunting dog, and this dog is a manmade hunting tool/weapon. In this version, morphologically differentiated dogs did not show up in the fossil or archaeology record until 12,000 to 14,000 years ago because their jobs in settled post–hunter-gatherer, paleoagricultural communities did not develop until then; so they got physically reshaped late in the relationship. People call the shots in a story that makes "domestication" a one-sided human "social invention." But archaeozoological expert Susan Crockford, who organized the Victoria symposium, disagreed. She argued that human settlements provided a species-making resource for would-be dogs in the form of garbage middens and—we might add—human bodily waste. If wolves could calm their well-justified fear of *Homo sapiens*, they could feast in ways familiar to modern dog people. "Crockford theorizes that in a sense, wild canids domesticated themselves" (Weidensaul 1999: 57).

Crockford's argument turns on genes that control rates in early development and on consequent paedomorphogenesis, and so we return to Scott and Fuller's sensitive periods for inter- and intraspecies socialization. Both the anatomical and psychological changes in domesticated animals compared to their wild relatives can be tied to a single potent molecule with stunning effects in early development and in adult life—thyroxine. Those wolves with lower rates of thyroxine production, and so lower titres of the fright/flight adrenaline cocktail regulated by thyroid secretions, could get a good meal near human habitations. If they were really calm, they might even den nearby. The pups who were the most tolerant of their two-legged neighbors might make use of the caloric bonanza and have their own puppies nearby as well. A few generations of this could produce a being remarkably like current dogs, complete with curled tails, a range of jaw types, considerable size variation, doggish coat patterns, floppy ears, and—above all—the capacity to stick around people and forgive almost anything. People would surely figure out how to relate to these handy sanitary engineers and encourage them to join in tasks, like herding, hunting, watching kids, and comforting people. In a few decades, wolves-become-dogs would have changed, and that interval is too short for archaeologists to find intermediate forms.

Crockford made use of the forty-year continuing studies of Russian fur foxes, beginning in the 1950s, which have been in the recent popular science news (Weidensaul 1999; Trut 1999; Browne 1999; Belyaev 1969). Unlike domesticated animals, wild farmed foxes object to their captivity, including their slaughter. In what were originally experiments designed to select tamer foxes for the convenience of the Soviet fur industry, geneticists at the Siberian Institute of Cytology and Genetics found that by breeding the tamest kits from each fox generation—and selecting for nothing else—they quickly got doglike animals, complete with nonfox attitudes like preferential affectional bonding with human beings and phenotypes like those of Border Collies.[10] By analogy, wolves on their way to becoming dogs might have selected themselves for tameness.

With a wink and a nod to problems with my argument, I think it is possible to hybridize Wayne's and Crockford's evolutionary accounts and so shamelessly save my favorite parts of each—an early coevolution, human-canine accommodation at more than one point in the story, and lots of dog agency in the drama of genetics and cohabitation.[11] First, I imagine that many domestication sequences left no progeny, or offspring blended back into wolf populations outside the range of current scientific sensors. Marginally fearless wolfish dogs could have accompanied hunter-gatherers on their rounds and gotten more than one good meal for their troubles. Denning near seasonally moving humans who follow regular food-getting migration routes seems no odder than denning near year-round settlements. People might have gotten their own fear/aggression endocrine systems to quell murderous impulses toward the nearby canine predators who did garbage detail and refrained from threatening. Paleolithic people stayed in one place longer than wolf litters need to mature, and both humans and wolves reuse their seasonal sites. People might have learned to take things further than the canines bargained for and bring wolf-dog reproduction under considerable human sway. This radical switch in the biopolitics of reproduction might have been in the interests of raising some lineages to accompany humans on group hunts or perform useful tasks for hunter-gatherers besides eating the shit. Paleo-agricultural settlement could have been the occasion for much more radical accommodation between the canids and hominids on the questions of tameness, mutual trust, and trainability.

And, above all, on the question of reproduction. It's on this matter that the distinction between dogs and wolves really hinges; molecular genetics may never show enough species-defining DNA differences. Rather, the subtle genetic and developmental biobehavioral changes through which dogs got people to provision their pups might be the heart of the drama of cohabitation. Human baby sitters, not Man-the-Hunter, are the heroes from doggish points of view. Wolves can reproduce independently of humans; dogs cannot. Even Italian feral dogs still need at least a garbage dump (Boitani et al. 1995).[12] Coppinger and Schneider summarized the case: "In canids with a long maturation period, growth and development are limited by the provisioning capacity of the mother. . . . Wolves and African hunting dogs solved the pup-feeding problem with packing behavior, in coyotes the male helps, and jackal pairs are assisted by the 'maiden aunt.' The tremendous success of the domestic dog is based on its ability to get people to raise its pups" (1995: 36). People are part of dogs' extended phenotype in their Darwinian, behavioral ecological, reproductive strategies. It might prove to be a bad bargain; for the cost of puppy sitting is high with the AKC, Whelp Wise™, and Perkin-Elmer in the loop, but surely not as high as that paid by the remaining wolves in relation to the depredations of the two-legged planetary social mammal.

Accounting for Genes: C. A. Sharp and the *Double Helix Network News*

With narrative agency secured to the dogs, and maybe more than that, it is time to conclude with the story of a remarkable dog person, C. A. Sharp, whose practice is a microcosm of the themes of this chapter.[13]

The Australian Shepherd Club of America (ASCA) had a genetics commit-tee from the late 1970s until 1986, when the board eliminated the committee in a controversial and poorly explained move. Sharp had been on that com-mittee; and since its demise, she continued to be consulted about genetics by breeders who had nowhere to go for advice. In the winter of 1993 she began writing and distributing the *Double Helix Network News*. By 1999 about 150 people—mostly breeders, a few dog-research professionals, and one or two ringers like me—subscribed. Learning desktop publishing, Sharp emphasized networking, sharing information, educating each other, dealing with what she called the "ostrich syndrome" among breeders about genetic disease, and practicing "love of the breed" through responsible genetics. She has func-tioned as a clearinghouse for genetic data in her breed; performed pedigree analyses for specific conditions; and taught breeders the rudiments of Men-delian, molecular, and population genetics and the practical steps that both show- and working-dog breeders can and should take to detect and reduce genetic disease in their lines.

The first issue of the *DHNN* described itself as a "kitchen-table" enterprise. Sharp coauthored a paper in the early 1990s with the veterinary ophthal-mologist L. F. Rubin on the mode of inheritance in Aussies of an eye defect (CEA) and is again engaged in collaborative research, on the relation of lon-gevity with coefficients of inbreeding in Aussies with Dr. John Armstrong of the University of Ottawa. Nonetheless, with a B.A. in Radio, TV, and Cinema from Fresno State University and a job as an accountant, Sharp has never claimed scientific "insider" status. She properly claims *expert* status of a rich kind, however; and she is regarded as an expert in both the breeder and professional scientific communities. Hers is not an expertise legitimated by official degrees. Rather, she has developed the power of a mediating position among communities of practice from her location as a self-educated, prac-tically experienced, savvy activist who is willing and able to express contro-versial opinions within linked social worlds. These are worlds to which she has contributed and within which she has taken risks since showing dogs and then breeding her own first litter in the late 1970s. As a retired breeder since about 1990, Sharp knows the material, intellectual, moral, and emo-tional demands of the culture to which the *DHNN* is directed.

The *Double Helix Network News* comes out four times a year. Each eight-page issue puts an important issue on the front page, like news about cata-racts or epilepsy in Aussies; develops an article on the inside pages, such as those on test breeding for Collie Eye Anomaly (CEA) or on the consequences of breeding from too small a gene pool; surveys general science news; recommends reading or Web sites; and presents Aussie health and genetics short items. The newsletter describes the services Sharp offers in genetic disease data collection and CEA pedigree analysis. For expenses only, she offers full-day seminars and shorter presentations on genetics and hereditary disease in Aussies. Her travel schedule for this practice of "love of the breed" is daunting.

Two chapters from Sharp's history must suffice to suggest ways of seeing the stakes in the contemporary naturalcultural worlds of genetics. First, I will explore her involvement in determining the mode of inheritance of an eye disorder in her breed to show how "lay" agency can work in canine genetics research and publishing. Next, bringing her to late 1999, I follow her to the Canine Genetics Discussion listserv, CANGEN-L, to map a mutation in her intellectual and moral field in changing emphasis from disease-linked genes to genetic diversity in the context of widespread turn-of-the-millennium attention to evolution, ecology, biodiversity, and conservation.

Sharp's interest in the genetic basis of eye disorders dated to 1975, when her first bitch was a puppy. She went to an All Breed Fun Match near Paso Robles, which turned out to have an eye clinic. Sharp asked what it was about and had her dog checked. "I just got interested and started educating myself." She made it a point afterward to get her dogs' eyes checked, which meant going annually to a clinic at the local Cocker Spaniel club, or else hauling dogs a few hours away to Stanford to a veterinary ophthalmologist. She started reading in genetics, guided by an Aussie person named Phil Wild-hagen—"who is quite literally a rocket scientist, by the way," Sharp laughs gleefully. About 1983, the Genetics Committee of ASCA put out a call for people to assist it in gathering data. "One thing led to another, and I was on the committee." This was the period when the Genetics Committee was shifting its attention from coat color, which had been of particular interest during the 1970s when what counted as an Aussie was codified in the written Standard, to the more controversial topic of genetic disease. A breeder gave the Genetics Committee two puppies affected with Collie Eye Anomaly, a condition Aussies were not supposed to have. This breeder also went public with the fact of CEA in her dogs and was vilified for her disclosure by Aussie people terrified of this kind of bad news in the breed. Sharp began writing a regular column in the *Aussie Times* for the Genetics Committee (Sharp 1998).

Starting with the original donated pair, the committee conducted a series of test matings to determine the mode of inheritance. Involving a couple dozen dogs and their pups, these crosses were conducted in the kennels of two committee members, including Sharp, at their own expense, which amounted to several thousand dollars. Most of the affected test puppies were placed in pet homes, with advice to spay or neuter. Some were placed in a university for further research work. The committee collected pedigree data and CERF (Canine Eye Registry Foundation) exam sheets on their test matings and on dogs brought to their attention by a growing number of interested Aussie breeders touched by the *Times* column and word-of-mouth. The pattern of inheritance indicated an autosomal recessive gene. It was now *technically* possible to take action to reduce the incidence of the condition.[14] But *real* possibility is another matter.

First, it was more than Aussie breeders who denied the existence of CEA in these dogs. Simply put, "Collie Eye Anomaly in Aussies wasn't 'real' when we started working with it." For example, Sharp brought a couple of puppies from test matings to an eye clinic at a show in Fresno, only to be told by the ophthalmologist that Aussies did not have the condition. Sharp got the exam by mobilizing her technical vocabulary—a familiar move for lay activists in AIDS advocacy, breast cancer politics, or technoscience in general. "Their mother has an optic discoloboma; [another relative] has choroidal hyperplasia; please check these dogs. . . . Grumble, grumble, then he checked the puppies." Sharp recalled breeders around the country telling her about attempting to get genetic advice from vets who told them to relax—Aussies don't have CEA; it's not in the literature. Finally, armed with "nearly 40 pedigrees with varying degrees of relationships, plus the test-mating data, I went in search of an ACVO vet who might be interested in what I had" (Sharp 1998). Sharp emphasized that she could not make CEA "real" on her own—"certainly not with a B.A. in Radio, Television, and Cinema." The data had to be published in the right place by the right person. "It's not recessive until someone out there says it is; then it's recessive." "Out there" meant "inside" institutionalized science. No science studies scholar is surprised by this social history of truth, or by the recognition of it by a savvy "lay" knowledge producer working within a "clerical" culture.

The popular but controversial ASCA Genetics Committee had ceased to be; so Sharp began looking for a collaborator to legitimate the data and analysis she already had. She talked to several likely scientists, but they had other priorities. Frustrated, Sharp recalls insisting, "Look, until one of you people writes it up, it isn't real." Effective corrective action depended on the reality of the fact. The chain finally led to Dr. Lionel Rubin at the University of

Pennsylvania, who was in the process of publishing his book on inherited eye disease in dogs (Rubin 1989). The book was already in galleys, so the Aussie story did not make that publication. Sharp assembled the data and did the genealogy charts from the committee's crosses and turned that over to Rubin, who hired a professional pedigree analyst for the final charts. From the time Rubin began working with Sharp, publication took two years (Rubin, Nelson, and Sharp 1991). With a proper pedigree at last, CEA in Aussies as an autosomal recessive condition was on its way to becoming a fact.[15]

But the reality of the fact remained tenuous. Sharp notes that the demand for independently replicated experiments seems to have kept the "fact" out of the Aussie section of the handbook of the American College of Veterinary Ophthalmology that came out after 1991. Sharp emphasizes that such expensive, ethically fraught research on a large companion animal is unlikely to be replicated. "It wouldn't have happened the first time if those of us out here in the trenches had not been interested enough to gather the data." But, she argues, "Why can't the ACVO say it's *probably* recessive?" She adds, "At least when someone out there asks me now, I can send them a copy of the paper." The newest bible of inherited dog problems does include the fact Sharp's network made real (Padgett 1998: 194, 239). Not surprisingly, Sharp had consulted George Padgett, of Michigan State University, an important institution in the apparatus of dog genetics natureculture, when she designed her pedigree analysis service and data system for Aussie breeders once the first phase of the research indicated the mode of inheritance. Padgett confirmed that her approach was scientifically sound, and Sharp put the service in place a year or so before she started the *Double Helix Network News.* Sharp relates with pride that the veterinary ophthalmologist Greg Acland at Cornell told her that the Aussie CEA study provided one of the most impressive data sets on the mode of inheritance of a single-gene trait anywhere in the dog literature. The CEA recessive gene "fact" is stronger in a robust network that includes Rubin, Padgett, Acland, and Sharp's expert lay practices. This is no surprise to a reader of *Science in Action* (Latour 1987). This is the stuff of objectivity as a precious, situated achievement (Haraway 1988). This is also the stuff of "science for the people"—and for the dogs. Mendelian genetics is hardly a new science in the late twentieth century, but sustaining and extending its knowledge-production apparatus still takes work.

But making the fact hold "inside" official science was not enough. "Inside" the Aussie breed communities is just as crucial a location for this fact to get real, and so potentially effective. Denial here takes a different form from that in the scientific communities, and so the material-semiotic rhetorics for persuading the fact into hard reality have to be different. Sharp's practices in the DHNN are part of the picture. While she set up her pedigree analysis service, a group of committed breeders in Northern California took an extraordinary step. They developed a test-breeding program and forms to document the breedings. Most important, they went public about the results. "As a group, they purchased a full-page ad in the breed magazine admitting they had produced CEA and listing the names of their carrier dogs. In a subsequent ad they told about the test-breeding they had done to clear their related stock" (Sharp 1998). Their group action forestalled the kind of attack that had been made on the donor of the first pair of affected puppies given to the Genetics Committee. This time, the grumblers were relegated to the underground, and the test breeders reshaped the explicit community standard of practice. The standard might not always be followed, but the reversal of what is secret and what is public in principle was achieved.

One final bit helped stabilize CEA as a fact in the Aussie world: emotional support for people who find the disease in their lines. Dog people tend to see any "defect" in their dogs as a "defect" in themselves. This kind of matter is fundamental to the apparatus of situated medical knowledges in both inter- and intraspecies contexts, if usually skirted in orthodox accounts of the care and feeding of biomedical facts. Genetic disease is stigmatizing to the flesh and the soul. Dogs and people are companions in that drama. Sharp could not be the emotional support person in the Aussie genetic disease world. "When people call me about genetic problems in their Aussies, I'm the 'expert,' not a kindred spirit" (Sharp 1998). Thus, Sharp asked the Northern Californians who went public with their dogs' and their own names to function as a support group to which Sharp referred quite literally grieving breeders.[16] Biosociality is everywhere.

In 1999 Sharp received far fewer reports of CEA in Aussies than she did seven or eight years earlier. Getting puppies checked through CERF is now standard ethical practice, and serious breeders do not breed affected dogs. Puppy buyers from such breeders get a copy of the CERF report right along with their new dog, as well as strict instructions about checking eyes of breeding stock annually if the new pup does not come with a spay/neuter contract. Facts matter.[17]

The world of disease-linked genes is, however, only one component of the story of dog genetics, especially in this era of biodiversity discourse. No matter how extensive the DNA-testing apparatus becomes, or how full the computerized and internationally available Ralston-Purina genetic family registry gets, or how successful the canine genetic mapping projects are, or how effective action is to keep crucial genetic markers in the public domain, or how earnest breeders get about open inherited-disease registries and carefully chosen matings, disease-related genes are not the right port of entry to a universe of consequential facts for dog people practicing love of the breed. Enhancing and preserving genetic diversity is not the same thing as avoiding and reducing genetically linked illness. The discourses touch in many places, but their divergences are reshaping the intellectual and moral worlds of many dog people. Sharp's story is again instructive.

Sharp was a subscriber to an Internet discussion group called K9GENES. On that listserv, the population geneticist and rare dog breed activist Dr. Robert Jay Russell, president of the Coton de Tulear Club of America, criticized breeding practices that reduce genetic diversity in dog breeds and the AKC structure that keeps such practices in place, whether or not the kennel club funds genetic disease research and mandates DNA-based parentage testing. Russell's controversial postings were blocked from the list several times, prompting him to log on under a different email account and reveal the censorship.

These events led to the founding in 1997 of the Canine Diversity Discussion Group, CANGEN-L, moderated by Dr. John Armstrong at the University of Ottawa, to allow free genetics discussion among breeders and scientists. Armstrong also maintains the Canine Diversity Project Web site, where one can get an elementary education in population genetics, read about conservation projects for endangered canids, consider activist positions on dog breeding operating outside the kennel clubs, and follow links to related matters. Concepts like effective population size, genetic drift, and loss of genetic diversity structure the moral, emotional, and intellectual terrain. CANGEN-L is an impressive site, where it is possible both to observe and interact with other dog people learning how to alter their thinking—and possibly their actions—in response to each other. Acrimonious controversies have surfaced on CANGEN, and some participants complain that threads get ignored. Breeders periodically express a sense of disrespect for some scientists (not to mention vice versa). Of course, breeders and scientists are neither exhaustive nor mutually exclusive categories on CANGEN. Subscribers, scientists or not, occasionally leave the list in a huff or in frustration. A few dogmatists dedicated to the Truth as revealed to themselves cut a wide swath from time to time.

All that said, in my opinion, CANGEN remains a rich site of discussion among diverse actors. The list started with thirty members, and Armstrong expected it to reach one hundred. Taxing its computer resources at the University of Ottawa, in spring 2000, CANGEN had three hundred subscribers, including writers, various sorts of geneticists, veterinarians, physicians, dog biotech industry representatives, breeders of many kinds of dogs, dog people from a dozen countries, dog historians, one acknowledged science studies academic, and trainers. Judged by facility in composing posts and apparent grasp of arguments, levels of formal education, self-education, and ease with math and writing vary enormously. Let us follow Sharp as she went from endless discussions of coat color on K9GENES to the headier atmosphere of CANGEN.

Sharp welcomed the higher level of scientific discourse and the emphasis on evolutionary population genetics on CANGEN. She felt challenged by the statistical arguments and wanted to explore the practical consequences for the kind of breeding advice she gives in the DHNN. With the summer 1998 issue, the newsletter shifted direction. She began with an article explaining the doleful effects of the "popular sire syndrome" on genetic diversity and made clear that line breeding is a form of inbreeding. In fall 1998 she explored how severe selection against disease-linked genes can worsen the problem of the loss of genetic diversity in a closed population. She cited with approval the success of the Basenji club in getting AKC approval for importing African-born dogs outside the studbook—a move necessitated in part by Basenji breeders' successful efforts to reduce the frequency of a fatal inherited anemia (pyruvate kinase deficient hemolytic anemia) by eliminating not only affected dogs but also carriers from the breeding population with the help of a screening test. The new genetic technology, coupled with a zeal to improve breed health, contributed to severe genetic damage to the population, expressed by increased incidence of other inherited diseases. Other breed clubs faced similar lessons. The work required to get the AKC to accept animals outside the studbook is daunting, and for many breeds the option does not exist. Population size, structure, and history come to be concepts needing to figure in the mating decisions of ethical breeders. This is no simple matter in everyday practice.

Both CANGEN-L and the Canine Diversity Project Web site are places where breeders can follow how those notions guide species recovery plans in zoos and in wildlife management. Sharp's winter 1999 DHNN feature article was introduced by a quotation from a fellow CANGEN member who has been especially outspoken, Dr. Hellmuth Wachtel, Free Collaborator of the Australian Kennel Club and member of the Scientific Council of the Vienna Schenbrunn Zoo. Sharp explained genetic load, lethal equivalents, population bottlenecks, genetic drift, coefficients of inbreeding, and fragmented gene pools. The lesson of the importance of genetic material from fresh sources—for dog breeds, from phenotypically similar but genetically distantly related animals, possibly from outside the studbooks—was plain. In the spring 1999 DHNN Sharp published "Speaking Heresy: A Dispassionate Consideration of Outcrossing"—an article she expected to make "the excretory material hit the circulatory apparatus." Love of the breed is messy. Each subsequent issue continues to hammer home the controversial implications of taking genetic diversity, and just genetic disease, seriously. No virgin to controversy in breed politics and no dogmatist about the finality of the science in hand, Sharp sees herself in the fray for the long haul.

Biodiversity and conservation discourses are hardly panaceas, either scientifically or politically. Simply tracking the dates, contexts, and authorship of major publications on biodiversity, sustainability, and First-World neoliberal formulae for global solutions would be enough to cause dyspepsia in those allergic to mutated versions of colonial discourse. None of that makes the issues of the destruction of genetic diversity, and other kinds of biological richness all over the world, go away. When I asked Sharp what she thought breeders, geneticists, dog magazine writers, and other might be learning from each other on CANGEN or other places, she zeroed in on the rapid and deep transformations in genetics over the last decades. The new genetics is not an abstraction in dog worlds, whether one considers the politics of owning microsatellite markers, the details of a commercial gene test, the problem of funding research, competing narratives of origin and behavior, the pain of watching a dog suffer genetic illness, the personally felt controversies in dog clubs over breeding practices, or the cross-cutting social worlds that tie different kinds of expertise together. Still, Sharp felt that her growth in genetic knowledge over the years, including her ability to handle the whole apparatus of molecular genetics, was natural and continuous—until she got on CANGEN. "The only epiphany sort of thing I've been through was when I got on CANGEN and started reading all the posts from the professionals. . . . I knew there were problems with inbreeding, but I didn't have a grasp about what the whole problem was until I started learning about population genetics." At that point, the analogies with wildlife conservation and biodiversity loss hit home—and she made the connection between her dog work and her volunteering as a docent at her local zoo. Citizenship across species ties many knots.

Coda

My epiphany in this shaggy dog story about webs of action is that anthropology in the age of genetics is about an old symbiosis—that among knowledge, love, and responsibility. Like human genetics, dog genetics is a social network as much as a biotechnical one. Neither microsatellite markers nor thirty-generation pedigrees fall from the sky; they are the fruit of historically located, naturalcultural work. Breed standards, dog genomes, and canine populations are material-semiotic objects that shape lives across species in historically specific ways. This chapter has asked how heterogeneous sorts of expertise and caring are required to craft and sustain scientific knowledge. If the story of C. A. Sharp shows the linkages of lay and professional work, the lists of Hot Spots illuminate how trading zones link science, capital, and diverse human and nonhuman agencies in producing historical dogs and humans as companion species. The account of the origin of canine behavioral genetics reminds us that genetics, as all of biology, is about emergent complexities that do not sit easily with reductionisms or ideological manipulations. At Bar Harbor, the intentions of planners got thwarted by real dogs allied with gutsy researchers. Dogs appear more than once in this chapter as lively actors. We also saw how the trellis rather than tree shape of genetic flows in dogs and humans has implications for meanings of species and race, how origin stories remain potent in scientific culture, how molecular "high technology" can be mobilized to sustain ideas of diversity and conservation, how mutations in Cold War politics make tame Russian foxes speak to Anglo breed-club dogs, how Internet sociality shapes alliances and controversies in dog worlds, and how popular and commercial practices infuse technical and professional worlds and vice versa.

None of this is breaking news in science studies, but all of it holds my attention as a scholar and a dog person. Interested in the symbioses of companion species of both organic and inorganic kinds, I end with fusions. The passage of the leash law enclosed the commons of my childhood dog-human world. The proprietary regimes and DNA-testing surveillance mechanisms at the turn of the millennium map and enclose the commons of the genome and mandate new kinds of relations among breeders, researchers, and dogs. Local and global crises of the depletion of cultural and biological diversity lead to novel kinds of enclosure of lands and bodies in zoos, museums, parks, and nations. No wonder that I am looking in the story of dogs and people for another sense of a common life and future. And so this chapter ends where the sticky threads of DNA wind into the frayed planetary fibers of human and nonhuman naturalcultural diversity so crucial to cross-species cohabitation.

Notes

With special thanks to Susan Caudill, Angela Davis, Sarah Franklin, Val Hartouni, Nancy Hartsock, Rusten Hogness, Gary Lease, Karen McNally, C. A. Sharp, and Linda Weisser—plus General Spots, Alexander, Sojourner, Roland, Cayenne, Hieronymous, Willem, and Bubbles.

1 There are several ways to measure "genetic distance," and the precise measure chosen can affect the conclusion of an argument. However, for humans, all the measures agree. Dogs are less studied. I have not found comparative data on genetic distances separating dog populations around the world. Human geneticist Alan Templeton (1999: 4) uses genetic distance to mean "the extent of genetic differentiation between two populations in terms of the alleles that are unique to each population and the extent to which shared alleles have different frequencies." Referring to people, Templeton (6) stresses, "Indeed it is hard to find any widespread species that shows so little genetic differentiation among its populations as humans." I suspect he would find humanity's peer in dogs. Coppinger and Schneider (1995: 32–34) summarize data from dog molecular genetics to conclude that "there is less mtDNA difference between dogs, wolves, and coyotes than there is between the various ethnic groups of human beings" (33). Vilá et al. (1997, 1999) find no way to separate dog breeds from each other with mtDNA data. These authors provide a context of species biology for debates about genetic diversity and the genetic basis of breed behavioral and structural specialization. Dogs have long been subject to systematic selection by people for specialized behavioral and morphological features; there is no parallel to this kind of selection in *Homo sapiens'* evolutionary history. Thus, we should expect genetic specialization in dogs for behavior, even in the context of a trellis shape to their population genetic history. Still, dogs, not to mention people, likely remain potentially generalists to a high degree. This point is worth remembering in the face of the differences in appearance (height, shape, etc.) that dogs and people show, as individuals and as populations.

2 Jeffrey Bragg (1996) argues that the registered Siberian Huskies of Canada and the United States are in this dangerous genetic condition. The solution of importing unregistered dogs into breeding programs from the "landraces" of Russian Siberian huskies has met fierce resistance from the Canadian Kennel Club. Living in the Yukon Territory and chair of the Working Canine Association of Canada, the controversial Bragg writes about Siberian Huskies and breeds Seppala Siberian Sleddogs. See the Canine Diversity Project (www.magma.ca/~kaitlin/diverse.html). Not all breeds are in such straits. Breeds can have significant numbers of founder animals and effective population sizes, as well as breeders who emphasize moderation and versatility in the interpretation of the standard and in judging in both conformation and performance. Even so, the argument that all registered breeds continue to suffer genetic damage built into their apparatus of naturalcultural production is gaining a hearing among dog

people. But few dog people are fluent in population genetics and biodiversity discourses. Asking how and if these people become influential in their breed clubs, and how and if they change their own and others' breeding and purchasing practices—and make demands on veterinarians, biotechnical food and pharmaceutical companies, kennel clubs, university research apparatuses, funding organizations, and geneticists—is central to my research.

3   The Canine Genome Project initiated by Jasper Rine, Elaine Ostrander, and George Sprague around 1991 also placed its hope to understand the molecular genetics of complex behavior high on the agenda (Ostrander 1992). But published reports and the Web sites for the project do not foreground that aspect, in part because the technical possibility of such a genetic understanding of interesting behavior—like the striking specializations shown by herders compared to livestock guardians—is a long way off, even if one heavily discounts developmental effects and nurture in the shaping of differences among specialized dog breeds' behavior.

4   Scott coined the word *sociobiology* around 1950. The modernist technobiological humanism of sociobiology got some puppy training in the kennels at Bar Harbor. Continental ethology was one strand of the international revival of interest in the relation of heredity and behavior in the 1950s. In 1963 two International Congresses on genetics and psychology took place, and in the early 1960s the U.S. Social Science Research Council established a behavior genetics committee. At a symposium sponsored by the American Psychiatric Society, "one-fourth of the papers were directly concerned with behavior genetics and eight of the thirty-one authors had some direct association with the Jackson Laboratory" (Scott and Fuller 1965: vi–vii; Bliss 1962). Fuller coauthored a textbook in behavior genetics (Fuller and Thompson 1960). The work at Bar Harbor was integrated with comparative psychology, with its ties to embryology and developmental biology, embodied in workers like Frank Beach (who worked on dogs) and C. R. Carpenter (a founder of primate behavior studies) (Haraway 1989). Scott and Beach (1947) coedited the minutes from the conference that sketched the plan for the dog behavior genetics work. Robert Yerkes, who had held numerous positions promoting the biobehavioral sciences for the health of American society (e.g., the Rockefeller Foundation–funded National Research Council's Committee for Research on Problems of Sex), chaired the Bar Harbor dog research planning conference. Yerkes founded the Yale University Laboratories of Primate Biology (Haraway 1989: 59–83). Ties of Jackson Lab scientists to psychological test design practices, with their roots in behaviorism and comparative psychology, were thick. Psychological testing apparatuses and principles of training and measurement developed for the dog study were ingenious; their offspring showed up in training protocols my dogs and I experienced decades later. Jackson Lab dog behavioral geneticists published extensively in the context of human development and mental health (e.g., Scott 1952).

5   The Bar Harbor work was preceded by the Fortunate Fields studies on German Shepherds, which aimed to produce superior guide dogs and police dogs (Humphrey and Warner 1934). Swedish Army dog-breeding programs in the 1960s consulted systematically with population geneticists at Stockholm University (Willis 1989: 260–62).

6   See the dust jacket of Frost and Lightmark (1997), with gorgeous Australian Shepherds sitting around a St. Francis–type figure of a youngish middle-aged white woman teaching in a clearing in sunlight-dappled green woods. Thanks to Val Hartouni and the Siberian Husky Grace. For "natural dog care and training," see the *Whole Dog Journal* (soy ink, recycled paper, email address, but no Web site and no advertising—thanks to Nancy Hartsock.

The World of Dog Genetics   293

7   Check out Whelp Wise™ on http://members.aol.com/wlpwise. Cheri Coley, clinical director and developer of patented methodologies for detection and management of uterine activity and fetal heart rates in veterinary obstetrics for Biomedical Systems Veterinary Division, tells how the technology can help solve genetic and other medical problems in modern breeds. For example, because of fetal heads too large for uterine passage, some modern breeds cannot give birth without Cesarian sections. But even if one holds that such breeds are inherently unhealthy and should be subjected to selection for "natural birthing," "high technology" for whelping bitches has a place within the very discourses closest to biodiversity preservation and wildlife conservation. Many dog breeds have small gene pools and few founder animals and face population bottlenecks. The management of small gene pools is a speciality of zoo and wildlife conservation biologists. Some dog breeders are borrowing from the practices of the conservators of wildlife species whose genetic diversity is threatened. Breeding older females to slow down generation time to delay further loss of alleles through random genetic drift, as well as to observe the genetic health of the breeding individuals well into potential reproductive life, results in birthing animals who require more intervention. Ask older human would-be mothers in advanced industrial societies trying to conceive and carry a pregnancy.

8   Besides Laurien Berenson (Standard Poodles), see Susan Conant (Malamutes), Carol Lea Benjamin (Pit Bull), Virginia Lanier (Bloodhounds), Melissa Cleary (retired police dog), Karen Ann Wilson (staring vet tech Samantha Holt), and Joseph Wambaugh (terriers).

9   If the breeders' main response is not to breed carriers, the affordable tests for disease-causing genes may worsen the genetic diversity crisis in some breeds. Dog worlds are not immune from the American passion for forging market-oriented, technical fixes. Preferring assortative mating over line breeding, as well as participating in *open* health and disease registries, would be a much more comprehensive change in breeder culture than using commercial DNA tests.

10 Like much in the former USSR, this trickster drama of worker safety, industrial efficiency, and evolutionary theory and genetics in the far north devolved in the post–Cold War economic order. Since the salaries of the scientists at the Genetics Institute have not been paid, much of the breeding stock of tame foxes has been destroyed. The scientists scramble to save the rest— and fund their research—by marketing them in the West as pets with characteristics between dogs and cats. A sad irony is that if the geneticists and their foxes succeed in surviving in this enterprise culture, the population of remaining animals bred for the international pet trade will have been genetically depleted by the slaughter necessitated by the rigors of post-Soviet capitalism and commercializing the animals not for fur coats but as pets.

11 Thanks to Sarah Franklin for the British Channel 4 TV program on the Australian Dr. David Paxton's thesis on wolf agency in dog domestication, which stresses advantages accruing to *H. sapiens sapiens* from the early association, including the evolution of speech.

12 Australian Dingoes and New Guinea Singing Dogs are another matter, not discussed here.

13 Thanks to Sharp for an interview, Fresno, California 14 March 1999, and for permission to quote. Unless indicated, quotes in this section are from this interview.

14 For principles of test breeding and CEA pedigree analysis, see *DHNN*, summer/spring 1993.

15 CEA can have other modes of inheritance, and its mode of inheritance is unknown in several breeds in which the symptoms occur. The "same" condition does not necessarily relate to the "same" alleles or even loci in different breeds (or mixes). Sharp is attempting to get Aussie people to cooperate with Acland at Cornell and OptiGen in his effort to develop breed-specific

CEA gene tests. Collies and Border Collies will soon have their test, but Aussies will be left without if inaction persists. Similarly, VetGen is attempting to develop breed-specific DNA tests for certain kinds of epilepsy, and Sharp's efforts to get Aussie people to open up about their epileptic dogs and provide pedigrees and samples for research have not been successful. Her files on epilepsy in Aussies grow thick, but this breed's culture does not seem ready for an open registry and activist research on the problem. VetGen will discontinue its work on epilepsy in Aussies unless data are forthcoming. Lay cooperation here is a fundamental part of scientific knowledge production.

16 "The CEA 'support group,' always informal, does not really exist anymore. Over the years folks have wandered out of the breed or on to other things, but it was helpful at the time." C. A. Sharp, personal communication, 13 April 1999.

17 With about 1 percent of Aussies affected with CEA, CERF reports indicate that the gene frequency is fairly steady; 10 to 15 percent of Aussies may be carriers. Sharp, personal communication, 13 April 1999. Detecting carriers will require a gene test.

9. Intimate Publics

Race, Property, and Personhood

Robyn Wiegman

On 24 April 1998 Donna Fasano, a white woman, and Deborah Rogers, a black woman, underwent in vitro fertilization at a fertility clinic in midtown Manhattan.[1] Six weeks later they both learned of the mistake made that day: while each woman received her own fertilized eggs, Donna was given Deborah's eggs as well. Only Donna became pregnant, and in December 1998 she gave birth to two boys, one of whom, DNA tests showed, was not genetically hers. As the media declared, Donna Fasano had delivered "twins," "one white, one black," but the status of her motherhood was challenged as Deborah and her husband Robert filed for custody of their genetic child.[2] In March 1999 the couples reached an agreement: the Fasanos would give "Joseph" to the Rogerses if the twins would be raised as brothers. "We're giving him up because we love him," Donna Fasano explained to reporters.[3] In May 1999, one day after Mother's Day, as the *Washington Post* duly noted, the Fasanos relinquished the child to the Rogerses, who renamed him Akiel.[4]

The pact between the couples was short lived, however, and in June 1999 they went to court. The Fasanos claimed that the Rogerses had broken the custody agreement by refusing to allow Akiel to spend a weekend at their home; the Rogerses cited a failure of trust between the couples, based in part on an incident that occurred during a scheduled visit. According to Deborah Rogers, Donna Fasano had referred to herself as Akiel's mother, encouraging him to "Come to Mommy" and comforting him that his "mommy is here."[5] David Cohen, the Fasano attorney, explained the white couple's perspective: "The Fasanos don't see [Joseph] as someone else's black baby; they see him as their baby."[6] Or in Donna Fasano's words, "He has two mothers. I am his mother and Mrs. Rogers definitely is his genetic mother."[7] Rudolph Silas, attorney for the Rogerses, countered, "The child can only have one mother, and on that we're very adamant."[8] By the end of summer, the court moved to settle the dispute once and for all by declaring Deborah Rogers the biological (and hence legal) mother.

While earlier court cases involving reproductive technologies raised similar issues about the authoritative status of genetics versus gestation, the Fasano-Rogers case is importantly unique in the history of assisted conception in the United States: it features the first woman, Donna Fasano, to be defined as both genetic mother (to the white child) and gestational surrogate (to the black child) in the same live birth.[9] In addition, there is Deborah Rogers, an infertile black woman, whose very infertility is culturally illegible in a dominant imaginary overwritten by notions of hyperreproductive and socially vampiristic black maternity.[10] How she secures her claim to natural maternity is a story of twin contracts: with the fertility clinic that offered technological assistance for genetic reproduction and with the state that sanctioned and naturalized, via the patriarchal marriage contract, her (hetero)sexual activity and the procreative property it might beget. At work in both of these contract relations is the property logic of liberal personhood, by which I mean the formation of social subjects within a modern state apparatus that recognizes and confers personhood on the basis of contractual relations—on the ability to enter into and stand as a responsible agent in a contract obligation to both the state (as citizen) and to other citizens (as transactors of labor and property ownership on one hand and as recognized heteronormative married subjects on the other). These domains of contract obligation—of citizen, spouse, and laborer/owner—have operated historically as powerful technologies for the production and excision of "proper national subjects," mediating the relationship between the seemingly private world of personal affect, intimacy, and reproduction and the public realm of social exchange, itself evinced by the birth certificate, the voting card, the draft card, and the marriage license. From within the dynamics of liberal personhood, then, the Rogerses win their claim as natural parents, an infrequent event in the racialized discourse of reproduction in the United States.

My contribution to this collection operates as a series of critical meditations on the cultural problematics raised by the Rogers-Fasano story. My goal is to make legible the messiness of affect, personhood, property, and kinship that thinking about race in the context of reproductive technology forces us, analytically speaking, to confront. Early on, my deliberations will stray from the Fasanos and Rogerses as I look at the precedent-setting case, *Anna J. v. Mark C.*, in which genetics and gestation were first defined in a hierarchical relation to one another and in such a way that the black gestational mother lost her claim on the white-Filipino child she bore for a wealthy interracial couple. This case is interesting to me for two primary reasons. First, the scholarly archive, like the media discourse on the case, has insisted on categorizing the contested child as white, which raises a series of questions about the ways in which we can and cannot understand the new reproductive technologies within the racial discourse of property and reproduction set into play by slavery. Second, by considering the critical consequences of the racial dualism of black/white mobilized to discuss *Anna J. v. Mark C.*, I read the story of white paternity differently, not as the repetition of the desire for racial homogeneity but rather as a desire for multiracial kinship—a desire that also animates the Fasanos who regard both of the twins as theirs. To track these stories in ways that pay attention to the generic terms of white paternity's sentimental romance with multiraciality, I turn to the national imaginary of popular culture (specifically the 1993 film *Made in America*) to think about how discourses of multiracial kinship function as a social pedagogy to redefine the affective dimensions of normative white masculinity at the beginning of the twenty-first century. This redefinition is critical to understanding how the present contestations around notions of race and kinship speak in relation to multiple histories and processes of racialization and bear an intimacy with the privileges and subjugations of gender, sexuality, and class.

In making an argument about how multiracial kinship functions to remake white masculinity, I am extending deliberations begun elsewhere on the power of "liberal whiteness" to reconfigure the substance and scope of white subjectivity in the popular imaginary in the postsegregationist era.[11] In doing so, I hope to be able to define how the absence of interracial sexuality in the Rogers-Fasano case is critically important to the presence of white multiracial desire, and hence to explore how the new reproductive technologies can quite literally provide the technological assistance for narrating kinship relations that do not require interracial sex as their originating, "procreative" moment. This distinction between multiraciality (itself the precondition of multiculturalism) and interraciality allows for a hegemonic move toward a kind of panethnicity that hopes to sacrifice little in the way of white masculine power by bearing none of the horror that founding U.S.

culture on the actual act of interracial generative (hetero)sex would imply.[12] How, then, does the story of Donna Fasano and Deborah Perry-Rogers speak in, through, and even against, the histories of both racialized maternity and paternity in the United States? What claim, if any, does Donna Fasano have on the "child" she bore whose genetic material—the fertilized egg—was not her own? By what strategy or cultural logic can the babies be said to be "brothers"? If the Rogerses are Akiel's "parents," as the courts have affirmed, what assumption bans them from kinship with their child's white "twin"? What critical understanding, in short, begins to map the complexity of this "family" tree?

As my use of quotation marks makes clear, new reproductive technologies bring with them a crisis of signification, pressuring the naturalized assumptions that have enabled the most common of kinship terms—family, mother, father, brother—to operate as if they require no critical attention to their social constitution.[13] Indeed, in their reconfiguration of U.S. culture's language for and critical conception of the embodied relationship between heterosexual acts and human reproduction, new reproductive technologies raise knowledge questions about the meaning and origins of both persons and life.[14] While I believe it is too sweeping a statement to say that new reproductive technologies represent an epistemic shift in cultural understandings of kinship (in part because the United States cannot be understood as epistemically coherent), it is certainly the case that they have become a cultural site for the negotiation of contradictions raised by the racial-national discourse of "blood tie" and a scientific worldview that has been radically reconfigured in the late twentieth century by the gene as the informational sign, in Sarah Franklin's words, "of life."[15]

But how, you might ask, can I plan to make so much of what begins, in the story of the Rogerses and Fasanos, as a clinical mistake? This is, after all, kinship by accident not design; as such, my critical analysis bears none of the assurances that a humanist project that tracks individual or collective intention might yield. Hence, my interest in the category of liberal personhood as the domain of a certain kind of abstraction works to divorce my analysis from the calculus of lived experience, which various methodological approaches would seek to make palpably real. As such, what conclusions can be drawn about the very frames of reference—liberal personhood, the national imaginary, multiracial desire, interracial sex, the subject and the state—that I will use to call my arguments into being? These questions raise the methodological and disciplinary stakes of my analysis and draw our attention to some of the enduring problems of any cultural criticism that makes no overt *methodological* claim to knowledge. By foregrounding this chapter's methodological failure to make an evidentiary link between law and culture—or to center human experience—I want to stage the increasing tension between rhetorical critical approaches and methodological ones, tensions that underlie contemporary disciplinary organizations of knowledge and that pose important challenges for interdisciplinary critique itself. At the same time, my unmethodological linkage of disparate discursive sites, subjects, and formations offers its own demonstration of the ways in which race is today performed within a highly mobile and radically inconsistent discourse of embodied nature. In this mobile inconsistency, the "mistake" as the origin of my critical deliberation on race, nature, and kinship emerges as a productive interruption in those processes of normalization that otherwise function to settle the incoherencies and failures of the white supremacist racial project in the United States. To read the "mistake" is thus an attempt to understand the inability of the grammar of race to find its normative production in a stabilized nature.

Maternity

When the court gave Deborah Rogers legal maternity, it departed from an unstable but nonetheless standard legal stance in the United States, where, in every state except California, the gestational mother holds legal status.[16] This standard, like nearly all court rulings that deal with the social intricacies of new reproductive technologies, has been applied inconsistently, often betraying the class, race, and heterosexual assumptions about "proper" maternity and "good" family that coalesce in the naturalization of the white patriarchal nuclear family as the state's normative ideal. In a much-discussed case, *Anna J. v. Mark C.* (1991), for instance, Anne Johnson, an African American woman, challenged her surrogacy contract with the Calverts, a white and Filipina American couple, in order to seek legal custody of the child she bore.[17] Johnson, herself a single mother, was found to have no legal claim on the child in part because she was not its genetic mother. For feminists analyzing the case, the construction of Anna Johnson's body as a surrogate in the most mechanical sense has served as a profound indictment of the gendered and racial politics of the new reproductive technologies, which operate to privilege on one hand the contractual relationship that defines genetic material and new persons as property *and* to reinforce, on the other hand, a cultural imaginary in which black women can give birth only to black children. As Deborah Grayson notes, the very idea that Anna Johnson might be the child's "natural mother," as the court referenced her surrogacy challenge, meant "that the court would have to make [the child] black."[18] On appeal, a higher court denied Johnson's petition by relying on the Calverts' *intention* to raise a child genetically theirs.[19]

As the first instance in the United States in which a surrogate who was not genetically related to the child fought for legal custody, the case reveals the legal distinction that reproductive technologies in the 1990s began to yield: that biology as the epistemological foundation for the naturalness of human reproduction could be hierarchized, with gestation and genetics vying for priority in determinations of legal maternity. Since 1991, surrogacy has witnessed a taxonomic division into "traditional" and "nontraditional" forms. "Traditional" references a contractual situation in which a surrogate performs, through artificial insemination, the role of both gestational and genetic motherhood. Nontraditional—what Sarah Franklin calls "total surrogacy"[20]—identifies the less frequent situation in which the gestational and genetic roles are not embodied in a single individual. In the total surrogacy relations of both *Anna J. v. Mark C.* and the Rogers-Fasano cases, it is the distinction between genetics and gestation that operates to define custody. As such, these cases form symbolic bookends for a decade popularly overwritten by advances and scandals in the world of technological reproduction. From the planet's first sextuplets to Dolly, the cloned sheep, to the final DNA detection of Thomas Jefferson's enslaved children, we have witnessed the growing incoherence of reproduction as a natural embodied process and a profound reconfiguration of the way property and personhood commingle in the commodification of bodily life. But the racialization of this commodification, much like the commodification of race, is difficult to read in any kind of comprehensive scope. Therefore, I want to look more closely at *Anna J. v. Mark C.* in order, first, to chart the path of nineteenth-century slavery and its property logics of kin as it moves through—configuring and undergoing reconfiguration—this case of contract-based conception; and second, to identify how reproductive technologies operate within the postsegregationist cultural imaginary, providing the means for reimagining white paternity in the context of multiculturalism.

Let's begin, then, with what both the media and scholars have found insignificant about the *Anna J. v. Mark C.* case: that the child Johnson bore was—to use the commonsense language of race—racially mixed. Dorothy Roberts, for instance, interprets the case as a concerted effort on the part of the U.S. courts to guarantee white racial reproduction. "By relying on the genetic tie to determine legal parenthood," she writes, "the courts in the Johnson case ensured that a Black woman would not be the 'natural mother' of a white child."[21] While Roberts notes that Crispina Calvert was not white, "the press," she emphasizes, "paid far more attention to Anna Johnson's race than to that of Crispina Calvert. It also portrayed the baby as white." Deborah Grayson similarly reiterates the media presentation of the case when she defines Crispina Calvert as an "honorary white" by pointing to the cultural stereotype of Asian Americans as the "model minority."[22] In this consolidation of a triangle of race into a dualism between black and white, Grayson and Roberts both struggle to establish *Anna J. v. Mark C.* within the property logics of race and (non)personhood that governed nineteenth-century slave culture. Writes Grayson, "The continuing legacy of miscegenation laws that used . . . the 'one drop rule' to maintain distinctions and separations among groups of people place a high value on white skin—white blood—because those who can have it are strictly limited and monitored. . . . To say that Johnson could be a mother to baby Christopher would be to indicate a willingness on the part of the courts and the public to relinquish or, at minimum, to blur racial-familial boundaries."[23] And, states Roberts, "The vision of Black women's wombs in the service of white men conjures up images from slavery. . . . In fact, Anna Johnson's lawyer likened the arrangement Johnson made with the Calverts to a 'slave contract' " (282).

In constructing the notion of a "slave contract," Johnson's lawyer was no doubt hoping to mobilize the history of enforced kinship and state control over black women's reproduction as a discursive tool in arguing against the wealth and marital status that conferred privilege to the Calverts. But to the extent that critics reiterate the analogy between slavery and surrogacy, they fail to distinguish between these two forms of human property relations, overlooking at least two crucial issues: (1) that being married to a white man does not make Crispina Calvert white nor does it make her children unambiguously white; and (2) that Anna Johnson is not a slave woman; she has access to the liberal rights of personhood that enabled her to enter into the contractual relation with the Calverts in the first place. While such contractual rights do not enable Johnson to enter either the court or the media on par with Mark Calvert, it is important to articulate the specificities of racialization through which Johnson is disempowered here. As Saidiya Hartman discusses, the transformation from slavery to contractual personhood that took place in the Reconstruction era (and that has been furthered with the demise of official segregation as a national policy) did not "liberate the former slave from his or her bonds but rather sought to replace the whip with the compulsory contract . . . Liberal notions of responsibility modeled on contractual obligation, calculated reciprocity, and most important, indebtedness . . . played a central role in the creation of the servile, blameworthy, and guilty individual."[24] From this perspective, it is Johnson's status as an indebted liberal subject that explicates the mode of racial subjection operating here where her responsibility to the social world that recognizes her as worthy of universal inclusion makes her guilty—guilty of the failure of honoring the contract, a failure that is made manifest in the media discourse by representing her as a former welfare cheat.

None of this is to say that the history of slavery has no significant bearing on *Anna J. v. Mark C.*; far from it. But its bearing is less analogical than discursive, which is to say that the case transmutes the ideology of the racialized system it fails to fully reenact through the descriptions of Johnson as a default queen, the one who risks social chaos by discarding her responsibility to fulfill the obligations of the social, borne through contract. This is, then, a historical trace of the transformations that black maternity in the United States has been forced to yield: where, first, reproduction in the slave economy writes black women as naturally hyperproductive (and thereby increases productivity in fulfillment of the property logic of accumulation), and where, second, freedom engenders a palpable fear about monstrous reproductivity in the context of a cultural discourse about native black social irresponsibility.[25] Anna Johnson's value, we might say, arises from her obligation to contractual personhood and its twentieth-century reformulations of racialized servitude. Thus, while the media representation of *Anna J. v. Mark C.* ignored Crispina Calvert's racial specificity in order to privilege the white father's paternity over both the genetic and gestational mothers, the subsequent reinstallation of such an analytic in feminist discussions of the case disables our ability to render historically palpable racialization as a multiply scripted cultural and historical process, on one hand, and the status of contract as a means of securing the liberal entitlements of personhood, on the other. It also critically negates the significance of the marital contract between Mark and Crispina Calvert, which, while offering a state sanction to interracial sexuality, places their sex fully within the law as a disciplinary practice for normative heterosexuality and monogamous reproduction. The Calverts' desire for a child that "looked like them" repeats, ideologically, the fantasy of merger that the romance narrative of heterosexuality repeatedly effects, naturalizing the equation between the founding of culture and the act of heteroprocreative sex.[26] But importantly, that naturalization is not materially realized in this case, as reproductive technology begets a multiracial child who is decidedly not the consequence of interracial sex. This is a point I will return to below.

The analytic adopted by Grayson and Roberts is not unfamiliar to those reading the feminist archive on reproductive technology, as it works to counter the patriarchal political economy of surrogacy (which, as in the Baby M case, gave priority to the contractual father[27]) with a moral and/or political clarity about the material labor of the gestating body. While giving birth to a child that the law refuses to name as legally one's own does repeat the theft of the body that slavery enacted, reproductive technologies in assisted conception produce the contract as a form of social mediation that differentially commodifies the relation between bodies and life. In this new economy of the body, the contract serves to secure the ideology of liberal personhood as that which, precisely, differentiates the past from the future. It is this differentiation that functions to place liberal personhood within the progress narrative of modernity, transforming the violence of "bodily theft" under slavery into the seemingly benign social relations of autonomy and choice that the contract is made to speak. This does not mean that for Anna Johnson the contract was not coercive; but it does differentiate among forms of coercion that enable us to examine and anatomize the racializing apparatus of the state after slavery's official dissolution and that underwrite, as we will see, the deployment of various naturalizing discourses of race in the context of reproductive technology today.

More to the point, the contract logic of liberal personhood is central to understanding the racial complications of the Rogers-Fasano case, where genetics replaces gestation as the foundational language of property-as-life, and maternal affect is rerouted in the language of the law from the discourse of the body to the property life of the gene. For the Rogerses, this is the dream of liberal personhood from its other side where the contract obligation borne by the fertility clinic and its manipulation of bodily material enables the nonreproductive black woman to succeed in attaining legal maternity. The theft of the body that characterized slavery—in which maternal affect was unrecognizable as either human or real—and that wrote the gestating black body out of maternity is replaced by capital's authority to mediate two mistakes: nature's "mistake" of infertility and the clinic's mistake of improper property implantation. In paying for a service that promises to give nature-as-reproduction "back" to the province of the body, the Rogerses can guarantee their right to liberal personhood through the contract. In this way, Deborah Perry Rogers comes to own the labor of another woman's gestation, as the property logic of personhood extends itself to the level of the gene.

And what of Donna Fasano, a white woman who gave birth to a black child she hoped to legally claim as her own? As the beneficiary of the mistake, she inherits property that is not, legally speaking, her own; and hence she is, as a white subject in the United States, emblematically "pregnant with history"—a history of improper property acquisition. This is nothing new, to be sure, as the social construction of whiteness in both the nineteenth and twentieth centuries has borne an intimate relation to property of all kinds: corporeal, private, and public—and such intimacy has been repeatedly conditioned on both social and personal disavowals of property theft.[28] From this perspective, Donna Fasano's attempt to privatize her own reproduction, to make her body speak the authority of gestation—of labor and belonging—was both a form of defense against her symbolic historical positioning and a kind of historical repetition of the property logic of race. But it was also not simply a repetition, in the sense that her desire to authorize white maternity of a black child, to have her body recognized as the agency of black life, placed her in the realm of what I call *multiracial desire*, a desire enabled by and in this case quite contingent on the fertility clinic's "mistake." Through the mistake, multiracial kinship, *for the white subject,* was disarticulated from the material lineage of coercion and cultural disavowal that has governed, quite literally, interracial sex and reproduction in the United States. Donna Fasano could embrace the idea of her maternity, in short, without encountering the specter of her own participation in sexual miscegenation. As epistemology, then, the mistake makes legible for us a compelling distinction, wrought by reproductive technologies and the cultural imaginaries they inaugurate, between interracial sex and multiracial desire, allowing us to understand on one hand the historical complexity of the maternal affect that Donna Fasano asked the court to recognize and, on the other hand, the sheer force that the gene as propertied personhood now culturally encodes.

The distinction between interracial and multiracial runs along a number of critical axes and in the next section of this chapter I want to demonstrate how it performs itself in contemporary U.S. life by thinking about and through popular culture. But before I do this, I want to meditate further on the complexity of cross-racial feeling, which underlies the Fasano's claim to

Joseph and their insistence that the boys be raised as "brothers." Let's return to the disturbing language of race and belonging used by their lawyer: They "don't see [Joseph] as someone's else's black baby; they see him as their baby" (Grunwald, "In Vitro, in Error" A01). On the face of it, this quote suggests a kind of radical deracialization of the child Donna bore, such that the baby is marked "black" only at the scene of his potential genetic ownership by Deborah and Robert Rogers; in the structure of the Fasano family, he appears, then, as simply "their baby." But is this the only possible reading? After all, the Fasanos have to make their claim to the child through the discourse of gestation, which means that they must privilege relationality over property and hence kinship through the body over racial categorization as a naturalized mode of familial belonging. As such, seeing Joseph as their baby—not as someone else's black baby—is not in any simple way a negation of racial difference but a means to subvert the gene's ability to naturalize race as property, which functions here to undermine the Fasanos' ability to claim cross-racial kinship. To see him as "their baby" is not, then, a definitive refusal to see the child as black; rather it is a refusal to index his blackness as that which would naturally locate his belonging elsewhere.

In this complex structure, Joseph's blackness—as a pure description of his category of social person—is that which gives him back to the property logic of the gene and hence that which annuls the affective economy of gestation and birth within which the Fasanos make their claim to parenthood (an economy overdetermined, as I will discuss below, by the gender structure of patriarchal marriage and its legislation of reproduction via the contract by the state). In the televisual coverage of the case (both 20/20 and *Dateline* ran segments), the Fasanos talk about the social challenge of raising a black child in a white family. Images of the family in their home show that they assembled a collection of toys for the boys that included figures in both black and white. In this way, the Fasanos claim Joseph as "their baby" not to deny racial difference but to incorporate that difference into the language of family, as evinced by their emphasis on the boys as both "twins" and "brothers." Most crucially, this brotherhood is grounded in the idea (and ideal) that the boys shared the same environment and life force from conception to birth. It is this simultaneously social and familial bond, bred in and itself naturalized by the womb, that makes possible a kinship formation that translates the clinic's "mistake" into cross-racial feeling. For the Rogerses, of course, the imposition of kinship with a white couple has both a structural and historical horror and in interviews they repeatedly refused the idea that the boys could be brothers. For them, brotherhood required a relation of genetic kinship with a shared parent; hence the boys were twins because of their life in the uterus but they were not and could not be "brothers." The war established here between conceptions of race that naturalize it in two ways—as genetic/propertied and as familial/affective—is an important feature of the contemporary terrain of reproductive technologies and the cultural imaginaries they beget. Most crucially for my argument, this war in which race is naturalized by the body in openly contested ways is central to the affective and political articulation of white multiracial desire, as I hope to explain below.

Paternity

If feminist histories of racialized maternity are brought into critical reconsideration by the issues that lead up to and involve the Rogerses and Fasanos, it is not yet clear how the distinctions I have been forging—between the property logics of slavery and those of liberal personhood on one hand, and between interracial and multiracial on the other—shape paternity, which has historically vied with gestation as the lingua franca of natural reproduction. In the case of *Anna J. v. Mark C.*, as elsewhere in the world of racialized technological reproduction, white paternity goes up directly against black gestational maternity and wins the day, as the contribution of genetic material and the contract take priority in a contest bound to commerce and property. This is the case, under different conditions of racialization, for Robert and Deborah Rogers, whose contract with the fertility clinic underwrites their final legal claim to Akiel. But what of Richard Fasano's claim to Joseph's paternity? The Fasanos, as I have discussed, "don't see [Joseph] as someone's else's black baby; they see him as their baby." And this is the case even though the couple learned six weeks into the pregnancy that Donna was carrying a fetus that was not genetically hers. The pedagogic power of gestation and birth to make visible what conception itself has been socially written to mean—as normatively and romantically the life merger between husband and wife—functions here in the absence of the couple's ability to retrospectively construct an originary procreative moment of mutually embodied experience. The marital contract is thus the only vehicle for Richard Fasano to enter into this story as a legal player, and it is precisely that contract that renders his paternity coextensive (at the very least) with Donna's gestational claim.

For Richard Fasano, then, paternity is indicated in the "old fashioned" way, based on the marital contract that legitimates his right to the reproductive consequences of his wife's womb, regardless of his actual status as genetic father. What strikes me as particularly important here is the ideological work that the detachment of sex from birth performs in the cultural imaginary of race. Richard Fasano can imagine himself Joseph's father without encountering any of the historically defined "horror" of miscegenation, as his wife's birthing of a black child bears none of the affect of extramarital interracial sex. For a white man to claim the obligation of kinship to the black child his wife bore is more than a far cry from the kinship structures engendered by slavery, which consecrated, through the hierarchical arrangements of property and (non)personhood, the cultural disavowal of violently extracted interracial reproduction. This claim is, it seems to me, a symbolic rearticulation of white paternity, avowing the formerly disavowed and reconfiguring the romance narrative of implicitly homogeneous heterosexuality into a sentimental form that nurtures cross-racial feeling, made safe by the eradication of sex itself.

This last point is the one I want to pursue in this section by looking at how the development of a multiracial national imaginary in the post–Civil Rights era has worked to reconfigure the popular discourse on race and sexuality, forging what I think of as an increasingly sentimentalized white masculinity that rewrites its centrality to the nation by embracing new modes of cross-racial feeling. These modes stand in stark contrast to public discourses of separation, segregation, and violence that have marked earlier dominant forms of white supremacy in which white masculinity was culturally legible as racial affect through its legal, psychic, and epistemological disavowal of interracial sex. It is my contention here that, by refusing such forms of white supremacy that sought, violently, to preserve the unpreservable (racial purity), the new sentimental white masculinity participates in the project of liberal whiteness by incorporating—as a standard of inclusion and political expansion—multiracial desire as its dominant cultural affect. To make this claim in the context of new reproductive technologies and the cases this chapter examines entails, at the very least, interpreting Richard Fasano's paternity claim to a black child in its historical transformation of white masculinity's grammar of racial affect, emphasizing, as I have above, the force of the heterosexual contract and its propertied relation to the labor of the wife's gestating body as a vehicle for the production of cross-racial feeling. It means as well understanding how, in the Calvert-Johnson case, Mark

Calvert's whiteness was not deployed to ensure its unambiguous racial reproduction but to claim a mixed-race child. In these forms of what I want to think of as "progressive multiracialism" we can understand how the cultural imaginary in which white masculinity today takes shape has undergone its own pedagogical reconstruction.[29] That this multiculturalism is often set against blackness, as in the Calvert case, or deployed to renaturalize race into a corporeal logic is one of the crueler aspects of liberal whiteness: its dream of pan-ethnicity is materially bolstered by the persistent status of white patriarchal authority as the arbitrator of ethnic hierarchies on one hand and as the standard of responsible contractual citizenship on the other.

Nowhere in the popular imaginary have these issues been more cogently portrayed than in the 1993 film *Made in America* (dir. Richard Benjamin). This film was no box office hit, to be sure, but it represents one of the first attempts to explore in popular cinema the new reproductive technologies as an arena for cultural rearticulations of race, kinship, and national belonging. Starring Whoopi Goldberg as Sarah Matthews and Ted Danson as Hal Jackson (and writing their very public affair of the early nineties into the cinematic history), the film is, narratively speaking, a paternity plot. It opens in biology class where Sarah's daughter Zora (Nia Long) and her friend Tea Cake (Will Smith) complete an assignment to determine their personal blood type. What Zora learns sends her on a quest that culminates in a twin discovery: that artificial insemination was her conception's sexless primal scene and that her biological father, Hal Jackson, is white. What strikes me as particularly important about this film is the ideological work that reproductive technology performs in the cultural imaginary of race, engineering a liberal fantasy about the origin and existence of multiracial families that detaches reproduction from interracial sex.

Made in America accomplishes precisely this detachment of interracial sex from the reproduction of multiracial families and persons that I take to be a central symbolic reconfiguration of white masculinity in the contemporary era.[30] It does this through the initial narrative focus on artificial insemination as the origin point of cross-racial alliance, thereby crafting the multiracial family as possible without the procreative enactment of literal interracial sex. And yet, even this disembodied reproduction is not in the end ideologically safe enough. So anxious, in fact, is the film about the specter of interracial sexual reproduction that its final discovery must reverse its inaugurating one: Hal is not Zora's biological father after all. The fertility clinic's records, it turns out, were woefully scrambled when it sent its handwritten documents "overseas" for translation to computer. This last small detail seems hardly worth repeating, except that it provides an ideologically salient displacement: the origin of confused racial origins is external to the nation, that is, it happened "overseas." The plot thus refuses by its end the technological compromise it seemed initially willing to accept, settling instead on the ideologically normative representation of reproduction as a monoracial domain. In this, *Made in America* makes sure that both racial *and national* categories maintain their biogenetic distinction; Hal has not fathered a black woman's daughter; Zora is not a white man's child; the fertility clinic's records have been miscegenated by unseen forces "overseas." If interracial union, then, is disavowed through the focus on artificial insemination and artificial insemination as a vehicle for biracial reproduction is ultimately rendered impossible, how precisely does the film manage to produce a multiracial family as the cultural destination for a distinctly new American kinship relation?

It does this by offering up the proposition that white acceptance of the idea of interracial kinship is itself a healing pedagogical power, both for individuals and for the nation. When Hal consents emotionally to the possibility of his paternity to a black child, he is transformed from a neoliberal-racist bachelor who lives in a white mansion on a hill to a member of a black family, indeed its new father/husband figure.[31] The construction of the scene that marks his affective conversion is crucial to understanding the national discourse that reverberates throughout *Made in America* (the title, displayed in the opening credits in red-white-and-blue script, certainly makes no effort to conceal its national dedication). Sitting alone drinking beer and watching television, Hal becomes emotionally transfixed by the triumphant final scene of *The Little Princess* in which Shirley Temple, that icon of white American girlhood, is reunited with her soldier father and the two embrace. In a wistful identification with this father-daughter reunion, set against the backdrop of melodramatic nationalism, Hal sentimentally accepts Zora as his daughter. The pedagogy of this moment of white liberalism is life transformative; embracing the idea of his parentage of a black woman's child, Hal quits a whole range of bad habits, including his emotionally empty attachment to his girlfriend. The film thus mobilizes the idea of multiracial kinship as a pedagogical lesson in soulful living, thereby rescuing the white man from the very dangerousness that he has come to inflict on himself (through drinking, smoking, reckless driving, and emotional detachment). This lesson is so successful that Hal becomes dejected when he learns that Zora is not his biological daughter. But since the pedagogical lesson requires finally *only the acceptance of the idea of white paternity of a black child* and not its literalization, Hal's sense of loss is recuperated in the final scene as Zora calls him "my father." Through these plot maneuvers, *Made in America* transforms the specter of interracial procreative sexuality into nonprogenitive multiracialism, as the multiracial family form emerges, distinctly, through something other than sexed means.

To a certain extent, one could argue that this last fact demonstrates the film's own understanding of the anthropological distinction between social and biological parenting, as the narrative works to denaturalize the cultural insistence that genetic relatedness founds the affective economy that generates the social ties of kin. The film's ideology of family pivots, after all, on the idea that acknowledging the possibility of fathering a biracial child provides the proper feeling to maintain the psychological link otherwise thought to be initiated by blood. But while the escape from kinship's biological grounding is ideologically enticing—and while the clarity about human interrelations as aftereffects of kinship formations is intellectually exciting—even the social constructionist reading lacks the power to fully rehabilitate the film's invested desire in sentimental feeling as itself a natural domain for the multiracial family's national belonging. For in the translation of Hal's paternity from a biological claim to a symbolically patriotic one that arises from sentimental feeling, the film does not relinquish the discourse of nature, it simply relocates it, and in the process of this relocation, it manages to leave intact the fantasy of distinct bioracial lines. To be sure, *Made in America* does not bar interracial sexuality on the whole, for the romance narrative between Hal and Sarah is quite classically one defined by bodily desire, even if of the PG-rating kind. But their status as a (nearly) postreproductive couple disengages sexual activity from procreative activity. It is for this reason, I believe, that the film labors through a potential sex scene with Zora and Diego, a Latino who works at Hal's dealership. By raising the specter of *this* interracial activity, which is by age definition also potentially procreative, *Made in America* confirms its narrative refusal to challenge U.S. ideologies about the naturalness of race at the level of its most intimate and threatening.

Zora's date with Diego functions in a second important way: it demonstrates that while the film's primary couple-form, via Sarah and Hal, is black/white, its racial imaginary is not uniformly fixed on this binary configuration. Indeed, the secondary cast of characters affirms a representational multiracialism, with named Latino, Asian American, and African American bit players. But while Hal Jackson's world is peopled with racial "diversity," it is significant that the film offers no other named white male character, which means that the crisis of subjectivity being explored in *Made in America* is precisely that of a now singular white masculinity facing the possibility of its own erasure. Hal's sentimentality is ultimately the means by which the film manages this subjective crisis, and it is in the nature of his kinship feeling that he comes to be rescued from a vacuous, dead-white life. While such a narrative in which black people give soul to whiteness is nothing new, its reiteration here rewrites the threat of white subjective disintegration in the context of a liberal multicultural public discourse that defines racial diversity and inclusion as coextensive with national democratic achievement. That the film offers as cultural difference only a commodified representation of Afrocentrism (via Sarah's ownership of "African Queen," a book- and novelty store) is less a contradiction than a strategic redeployment of all signs of "difference" into the discourse of class and consumption. And it is this redeployment, in which the political economy of historical processes of racialization are rendered secondary to the property forms of contemporary identity discourse, that functions to make "equality" the founding sensibility of the language (and ledger) of personhood characteristic of the multicultural national imaginary.[32]

In the narrative movement that I have now charted—where the initial specter of sexual coupling is denounced in favor of a discourse of cross-racial feeling—we witness the film's ambivalence about the genre conventions of romance that it seems to reiterate: the couple-form here must struggle to define itself outside the very conventions of embodied intimacy that found romance as a narrative discourse about the origins of kinship. In *Made in America*, the ambivalence arises precisely from the potential violation of romance's unspoken affiliation with racial sameness—an affiliation that becomes apparent by noticing how narratives of interracial love are more often organized under the genre terms of tragedy or sentiment than of romance itself. Tragedy witnesses the inability of interraciality to sustain itself, often in narratives that feature passing characters whose "real" blood identity is ultimately discovered and the lovers must part. Sentimentalism, on the other hand, negotiates the consequences of interracial sexuality by emphasizing not sexual but familial love and founding that love in a broader discourse about moral and national responsibility. In popular texts of the nineteenth century, including some of the most canonical slave narratives, for instance, sentimental discourse defines family and equality as coextensive in order to link black humanity to blood ties and rewrite slavery as the horror of enslaving one's own kin. While sentimental rhetoric was less a challenge to the economic structure of slavery than to its affective economy, it worked by naturalizing, as a form of feeling, the familial discourse that underwrote the monogenetic Christian belief in the total unity of man. Its strategy was a powerful, if not unproblematical, counter to the slavocracy's legal armature, which substituted property for personhood and repeatedly consigned the slave woman's reproduction to accumulation as a desexualizing and de-familializing economic end. And yet, precisely because of its tie to the violence of slavery, sentimental discourse in the nineteenth century turned to cross-racial feeling not to inaugurate a national discourse about multiracialism as the essence, if you will, of national identity, but rather to right the wrong of slavery, understood primarily through the specter of interraciality as the domain of violation and violence.[33]

Made in America both lives up to this description of sentimental narrative and departs significantly from it. On one hand, its narrative trajectory is aimed toward establishing cross-racial feeling and a sense of the implicit kinship between racially differentiated groups of persons. On the other hand, it works to obviate altogether the possibilities that interracial sexuality might serve as the foundation for inculcating the affective economy of kinship. In this contradictory dynamic between biogenetic and social relatedness, it works to extradite Hal, as the emblem of white masculinity, from the history of racialized property relations while simultaneously ensconcing him in the domain of sentimental feeling. These narrative moves are made possible by the presence of new reproductive technologies which enable a vision of social reproduction that is not dependent on the biogenetic encounter that has come to be written as the originating moment of both nation and culture in sex. We are left, then, with a discourse of cross-racial feeling that sanitizes affect from embodiment, and thereby rewrites the nineteenth-century sentimental tradition from a recognition of inequality and violence into nonsexual romantic comedy, which is to say that *Made in America* achieves the multiracial feeling necessary to the liberal consciousness of multiculturalism itself. In doing so, the film repeats what the legal cases of artificial insemination and accidental in vitro fertilization seem to assume with all the confidence that DNA provides for anchoring the truth of blood and nature: that racial categories are distinct. As the newspaper reports of the Rogers-Fasano case attest, one baby was unquestionably white and the other black.

Critical Kinship

This chapter has used the Rogers-Fasano story as the occasion for considering the messiness of affect, personhood, property, and kinship that disorganizes the racialization of reproduction in contemporary U.S. culture today. My archive was eclectic, even idiosyncratic; and my argument was less comprehensive than mosaic; it proceeded by exploring three points: (1) how the feminist archive has failed to render a nuanced reading of the racial politics of contemporary reproduction by insisting on an analogy between surrogacy and slavery as its chief analytic; (2) how this insistence ignores the contract that serves as the defining feature not only for new reproductive kinship relations but of liberal personhood as the dominant subject formation within which racialization now takes place; and (3) how in the popular imaginary new reproductive technologies provide the technical assistance to imagine multiracial families without engaging the "living horror" of miscegenation as the fleshiness of interracial sex. In all of this, I have been concerned with the way new reproductive technologies raise knowledge questions about the meaning and origins of both persons and life and simultaneously reiterate and reconfigure the naturalized assumptions that have enabled the most common of kinship terms—family, mother, father, brother—to operate as if they require no critical attention to their social constitution.

At the same time, I have tried not to place the issue of reproductive technologies in the context of temporal historical progress, as if the discursive operations of culture enable the seemingly new ever to replace without a living trace the old. Instead, I have used the Rogers and Fasano case to read the realm of reproductive technologies as an incoherent primal scene where embodied relatedness mingles with the genetic scientific imaginary that has now set "nature" in conflict with "life" and remapped the body as an engine of replication (the gene) and not reproduction (gestation). In this primal scene, the scientific worldview struggles to establish its legal authority, already consecrated in academic knowledge regimes, over everyday life. Understood, then, as contestatory knowledge projects, new reproductive technologies function at the "incoherent" intersection of various cultural discourses and domains and make possible, in their articulation in and through cultural imaginaries, our consideration of how race is being reanimated *as nature* in thoroughly contradictory ways in the United States today.

In making this claim for reading reproductive technologies as implicated in contestatory knowledge projects about race and nature, I do not mean to suggest that such technologies are more troublesome objects of study than those we otherwise encounter in critical work. But I am interested in how their analysis across the disparate domains of law, popular culture, and academic feminist criticism fails to identify with precision a consistent or paradigmatic operation for understanding contemporary racialization in the context of assisted conception. This is the case, in part, because racialization, as I noted at the outset, is itself an incoherent process. And it has been for *this* reason that I have made no critical claim to provide an analytically consistent or methodologically coherent linkage of the discursive sites that I have assembled. In this failure to commit to the epistemological optimism (otherwise known as closure) provided by method and secured through a disciplinary apparatus that can claim for itself critical comprehension, I have tried to inhabit what I think of as the antidisciplinary productivity of an interdisciplinary study of race, which is constituted not by making a claim for the radical particularity of my critical sites (and hence for a critical practice borne of the objects of study under consideration), but by trying to resist the normalizing effects of humanistic knowledge production that are secured by reproducing the individual as historical subject.

Such resistance is of course never complete, never more than a failed attempt, if for no other reason than that our critical act cannot *not* be invested in understanding *something* about the specificity of the human in the making and unmaking of culture. How, after all, can I not want to account for the affective complexity, not to mention historical and political strangeness, of the images of maternity that the Rogers-Fasano case offers us: the theft of the body that Deborah Rogers experiences in the presence of the white woman who nurtured and birthed her genetic son; the embodied maternity that Donna Fasano powerfully feels as she who quite literally nurtured the "mistake" of misbegotten property. But it is precisely because agency is so fully awry in this case and the legal apparatus of liberal personhood called on to correct it so completely unable to bring reproduction back into the authority of embodied heteronormativity that one cannot turn to humanistic inquiry's desire for the individual's self-reflective articulation to settle the cultural implications and historical determinations raised by the "case." There can be no justice, to put it in the language of political obligation so familiar in feminist knowledge production, for either the Fasanos or Rogerses here, no account in this critical act that can render their implication in the contestations of race and nature individual in the sense that we might partake comprehensively in the knowledge of the experiential pain that the mistake inaugurated for them. What, after all, do we want *that* knowledge for? Critical kinship with the objects we study?

This is perhaps a long and rather complicated way to explain my own resistance to any critical project that seeks kinship with its objects of study through the promise of methodological knowledge production. Instead, I have tried to demonstrate how the recursivity and relationality among my disparate discursive sites performs the cultural work of "nature" in the absence of knowing human subjects who can constitute themselves as such, even—indeed especially—in the context of liberal personhood's ideological pretensions to the contrary. By reading the technological "nature" of reproduction as it seeks to anchor itself as the contemporary epistemological foundation of both culture and bodies, and by linking this to heteronormativity; liberal notions of law, personhood, and property; contractual entitlements; maternal affect; white masculine sentiment; and national belonging in a multiracial cultural imaginary, I have tried to say something about the powerful effects and contradictory knowledge projects that attend the unstable regimes of naturalized race and racialized nature as they are articulated in and through reproductive technologies in the United States today.

Notes

In writing the initial draft of this paper, I benefited from conversations with a number of thoughtful colleagues, including Brian Carr, Elena Glasberg, and Laura Hyun Yi Kang. To Tom Boellstorff and Bill Maurer, anthropologists-at-large, my thanks for the valiant attempt to school the anthropologically unschooled in the historical debates about kinship. And to the editors of this volume, my appreciation for insights too numerous to name.

1 I am drawing my information on this case from four newspaper sources: Jim Yardley, "Health Officials Investigating to Determine How Woman Got the Embryo of Another," *New York Times* (31 March 1999): B3; Michael Grunwald, "In Vitro, in Error—and Now, In Court: White Mother Given Black Couple's Embryos Will Give One 'Twin' Back," *Washington Post* (31 March 1999): A01; Jim Yardley, "Sharing Baby Proves Rough on 2 Mothers," *New York Times* (30 June 1999): B1; David Rohde, "Biological Parents Win in Implant Case," *New York Times* (17 July 1999), late ed.: B3.

2 In various newspaper accounts, reporters simultaneously use and euphemize the word "twin," putting it in scare quotes and defining the boys as unambiguously black and white. While the dictionary understanding of the word "twin" indicates the emergence of two new persons in a single birth, it is important to chart how the new reproductive technologies are making legible the naturalized assumptions about kinship and social relation on which twinship (and other terms) have long depended.

3 Grunwald, "In Vitro, in Error," A01.

4 Throughout this chapter I use both Akiel and Joseph to refer to the contested child, depending on the family scenario I am discussing at the time.

5 Yardley, "Sharing Baby Proves Rough on 2 Mothers," B1.

6 Grunwald, "In Vitro, in Error," A01.

7 Yardley, "Sharing Baby Proves Rough on 2 Mothers," B1.

8 Ibid.

9 She is not, however, the first white woman to give birth to two children genetically classified as racially different. In 1995 a Dutch fertility clinic mistakenly fertilized a woman's eggs with the sperm of both her white husband and a black man. She gave birth to twin boys and the white couple is now raising both of them. See Dorinda Elliot and Friso Endt, "Twins—with Two Fathers; The Netherlands: A Fertility Clinic's Startling Error," *Newsweek* (3 July 1995): 38. The case is also referenced by Yardley, "Health Officials Investigating to Determine How Woman Got the Embryo of Another," B3, and discussed briefly by Dorothy Roberts, *Killing the Black Body: Race, Reproduction, and the Meaning of Liberty* (1997), 252.

10 On the figure of the vampire as it relates to race and reproduction, see Donna Haraway, "RACE: Universal Donors in a Vampire Culture," *Modest Witness @ Second Millennium, FemaleMan© Meets OncoMouse: Feminism and Technoscience* (New York: Routledge, 1997), 213–65.

11 See "Whiteness Studies and the Paradox of Particularity," *boundary 2* 26.3 (fall 1999): 115–50.

12 Because this chapter was written in the context of a larger project on liberal whiteness, my focus in its latter stages tends to emphasize the racial affect of the Fasanos and their symbolic occupation of what I want to define as white multiracial desire. Readers more interested in the complexity of the Rogers's response will, I hope, understand the analytic purchase this chapter seeks.

13 I have decided not to "scare quote" my usage of parent, mother, father, brother, even reproduction and the human in this paper, in part because such quotes cannot unwrite the power of these terms to renaturalize themselves even in the context of critical attempts at rendering their social construction.

14 Scholarship on new reproductive technologies is by now too lengthy to list comprehensively. Some of the most widely cited studies include: Jeanette Edwards, Sarah Franklin, Eric Hirsch, Frances Price, and Marilyn Strathern, *Technologies of Procreation: Kinship in the Age of Assisted Conception*, 2d ed. (1999); Sarah Franklin, *Embodied Progress: A Cultural Account of Assisted Conception* (1997); Sarah Franklin and Helen Ragone, eds., *Reproducing Reproduction: Kinship, Power and Technological Innovation* (1998); Valerie Hartouni, *Cultural Conceptions: On Reproductive Technologies and the Remaking of Life* (1997); Maureen McNeil, Ian Varcoc, and Steven Yearley, eds., *The New Reproductive Technologies* (1990); Michelle Stansworth, ed., *Reproductive Technologies: Gender, Motherhood and Medicine* (1987); and Marilyn Strathern, *Reproducing the Future: Anthropology, Kinship, and the New Reproductive Technologies* (1992).

15 Sarah Franklin, "Romancing the Helix: Nature and Scientific Discovery," in *Romance Revisited*, ed. Lynne Pearce and Jackie Stacy (1995), 64.

16 Cited from George Annas, a professor of health law at Boston University, in Grunwald, "In Vitro, in Error." This standard seems to be one that has arisen in relation to surrogacy cases in which the gestational mother and the biogenetic mother are the same.

17 *Anna J. v. Mark C. et al.* 286 Cal. Rptr., 372 (Cal.App.4 Dist. 1991) and *Johnson v. Calvert*, 19 Cal. Rptr.2d, 506–18 (Cal.1993); cert. Denied, 113 S.Ct 206 (1993). For critical conversation

about this case, see Deborah Grayson, "Mediating Intimacy: Black Surrogate Mothers and the Law," *Critical Inquiry* 24 (winter 1998): 525–46; Valerie Hartouni, "Breached Birth: Reflections on Race, Gender, and Reproductive Discourse in the 1980s," *Configurations* 1(1994): 73–88; Randy Frances Kandel, "Which Came First: The Mother or the Egg? A Kinship Solution to Gestational Surrogacy," *Rutgers Law Review* 47 (fall 1994): 165–239; and Mark Rose, "Mothers and Authors: *Johnson v. Calvert* and the New Children of Our Imaginations," *Critical Inquiry* 22 (summer 1996): 613–33.

18 Grayson, "Mediating Intimacy," 538.

19 In arguing that natural motherhood resided with the woman whose intention to donate the ova and to raise the child had initiated the surrogacy contract in the first place, the court made a distinction between what Laura Doyle examines as a familiar racial trope, the "ruling 'head' and the laboring 'body'" (*Bordering on the Body: The Racial Matrix of Modern Fiction and Culture* [1994], 21). The lone dissenting opinion by Justice Joyce Kennard argued that the use of "intention" to ground the majority decision suffered from a problematical equation between children and intellectual property (*Johnson v. Calvert*, 514). See also Grayson, "Mediating Intimacy," 534–36.

20 Franklin, "Romancing the Helix," 70.

21 Roberts, *Killing the Black Body*, 281.

22 Grayson, "Mediating Intimacy," 529 n.10. Significantly, the "model minority" label is itself unevenly distributed within the many ethnicities that coalesce under the sign "Asian American," with Japanese and Chinese taking cultural precedence over Southeast Asians and Pacific Islanders, including Filipino/as. In fact, in a recent assessment of education in the state of California, Filipino/as were found to be more on par (which is to say similarly economically and racially oppressed) with Latinos than with several of the ethnic groups within "Asian American." At the University of California-Irvine, as elsewhere in the state, there is currently a move to detach Filipino/a from Asian American, a move with politically controversial implications for Asian American Studies as a program and field.

23 "Mediating Intimacy," 545. This comment is preceded in the article by Grayson's deliberation on Crispina Calvert's statement, quoted routinely in the press, that the baby "looks just like us." Grayson interprets this statement as indicating not only "rights to parentage" but also "as a sign for blood—for the closed, racialized membership of family and race" (545). Here, again, is the condensation of the interraciality of the Calverts into a discourse of white racial homogeneity, one that functions in Grayson's text as the vehicle for rendering temporal continuity between the practices of slave culture and those of reproductive technologies.

24 Hartman, *Scenes of Subjection: Terror, Slavery, and Self-Making in Nineteenth-Century America* (1997), 9. Focusing on the official transformation from slavery to freedom, Hartman argues that "the vision of equality forged in the law naturalized racial subordination while attempting to prevent discrimination based on race or former condition of servitude" (9). In doing so, she "illuminates the double bind of equality and exclusion that distinguishes modern state racism from its antebellum predecessor" (9).

25 In writing this teleology, I do not mean to suggest that in the antebellum period black hyperproductivity raised no fear for the white national imaginary. The point is rather that while slavery structured a racialized division between persons and things, legal enfranchisement marked a process of reordering that offered little conscious or material reward for whites to value the reproduction of black persons.

26 See David Schneider, *American Kinship: A Cultural Account* (1968), and Sylvia Yanagisako and Carol Delaney, eds., *Naturalizing Power: Essays in Feminist Cultural Analysis* (1995).

27 In the "Baby M" case, the court awarded legal custody to the contractual father/sperm provider, giving the birth mother, who was also the biogenetic mother, visitation rights. See Anita Allen, "Privacy, Surrogacy, and the Baby M Case," *Georgetown Law Journal* 76 (1988): 1759–92.

28 See George Lipsitz, *The Possessive Investment in Whiteness: How White People Profit from Identity Politics* (1998).

29 It is perhaps not coincidental that the major cultural text I read in "Whiteness Studies and the Paradox of Particularity" is the popular 1994 film *Forrest Gump*, which, while set in the South and in some ways overdetermined by the historical racial discourse of slavery, nonetheless pairs a white male and an Asian American woman as the model for a nonviolent, multicultural future. This alignment has a great deal to do with the film's articulation of a compensatory narrative concerning U.S. involvement in Vietnam, but it is a significant aspect of contemporary racial discourse that the power of whiteness does not secure itself through a segregation discourse or representational imaginary, as was clearly the case in the slave South. Rather, the fantasy that white supremacy ended with the official disestablishment of segregation is anxiously and hence repeatedly reproduced in images of interracial solidarity and (increasingly) sexuality. That Asian American female subjectivity mediates the racial dynamic of black/white is an important critical component to rendering the intersecting dynamics of racialization.

30 I am not claiming that the sentimentalizing of white masculinity is the only way in which liberal whiteness currently operates as a representational project in the national imaginary. Indeed, the national imaginary is not itself unitary, as the contestation between the far right and the multicultural left, to use the inadequate language of the public sphere, might best indicate.

31 Significantly, Hal's reconstruction is accompanied by financial success (commercials that inadvertently feature Sarah generate boom times at his car dealership). This is of course the ultimate liberal fantasy, that personal transformation is materially advantageous as well.

32 To trace various assessments about the radical and recuperated aspects of multiculturalism's deployment in the public sphere, see David Theo Goldberg, ed., *Multiculturalism: A Critical Reader* (1994); Avery Gordon and Christopher Newfield, eds., *Mapping Multiculturalism* (1996); Amy Gutmann, ed., *Multiculturalism: Examining the Politics of Recognition* (1994); Jeff Escoffier, "The Limits of Multiculturalism," *Socialist Review* 21 (3/4): 61–73; Gayatri Spivak and Sneja Gunew, "Questions of Multiculturalism," *The Cultural Studies Reader*, ed. Simon During (1993), 193–202; and Henry A. Giroux and Peter McLaren, eds., *Between Borders: Pedagogy and the Politics of Cultural Studies* (1994).

33 As a literary/cultural critic whose primary training focused on U.S. narrative traditions, I am well versed in the family romance plot and its reworking in sentimental discourse. But rarely in the literary archive is the social constructionist analytic sustained in rigorous enough terms to yield an interrogation of sexual reproduction as the founding act of humanity and culture. For this reason, Yanagisako and Delaney's edited collection, *Naturalizing Power*, provides an important set of critical models for historicizing the family plot's ideological origins at modernity's intersections of industrialization, secular humanism, scientific nature, and liberal personhood.

PART FOUR. The Politics of Representation

10. Men in Paradise

Sex Tourism and the Political Economy of Masculinity

Steven Gregory

Jimmy's Bar and Grill sits back about twenty yards from the beach in Boca Chica, a tourist resort area on the south coast of the Dominican Republic. Jimmy Ryan, an American expatriate from Boston, owns the small, wooden beach house, nestled among young palms. Over the years, Jimmy's Bar has become a meeting place for male North American tourists who travel to the island to meet Dominican women. On any given day, two dozen or so men stop at the beach bar to drink, socialize with other Americans, or to ask Jimmy's advice about hotels, car rentals, and other traveler's concerns. Jimmy's Bar is also a gathering place for Dominican women who are looking for male clients for services such as manicures, massages, and sex. Many of these women live in the neighboring town of Andrés, a poor community where many who work in Boca Chica's tourist economy live. In recent years, Jimmy's Bar has gained considerable notoriety through *tsmtravel.com*, a California-based, Internet Web site dedicated to "travel and the single male." TSM provides its paid subscribers with up-to-date information and travel reports relating to prostitution around the world. Advertised as a "TSM-friendly" place, Jimmy's Bar attracts first-time and well-traveled male tourists from the United States, Canada, and to a lesser extent Europe.

One night, just before closing, three regulars at Jimmy's place began a conversation about the nature of Dominican people. Bill, a tall, lanky expatriate in his late fifties from Chicago, began the conversation by declaring that Dominicans lacked ambition and had no respect for education. An article on public-school reform that had appeared in *Listin Diario*, a Dominican newspaper, provoked his remarks. The two other men in the bar that night, in addition to Jimmy and me, were both North American tourists. Frank had been visiting the Dominican Republic for eight years and had a steady Dominican girlfriend in Boca Chica whom he supported with a monthly allowance. A New York–based computer programmer in his mid-thirties, Frank visited Boca Chica each month for about a week. Mike, a middle-aged merchant marine, had been visiting the Dominican Republic for about three years, staying for as long as six weeks each trip.

Storytelling dominated the conversation as each man provided an account of an experience that illustrated Dominican ignorance, corruption, and lack of ambition. Jimmy, a taciturn man in his sixties, listened to the stories from behind the bar, nodding his head in agreement and, every so often, offering an interpretation of their significance based on his experience in the country. When Frank had finished one such story, Jimmy turned to Bill, bemused.

"Bill, how many years have you lived in this country? As long as I've known you, I've never heard you speak a word of Spanish." The others looked to Bill, expecting to hear an outrageous response. Jimmy reached for a bottle of Havana Club and filled everyone's glasses.

"You know why I never learned Spanish," Bill declared, "after eleven years in this fuckin' country?" He took a swig of rum and rose to his feet. "I'll tell you why," he continued, jabbing his wiry finger into the air. "Because they don't understand what you're saying anyway. It's like talkin' to a fuckin' brick wall. All the Dominican knows is *money*."

"You're right about that," Jimmy said flatly.

"Let me tell you what happened just the other day," Bill continued. "I took my car to the mechanic to get some work done on the brakes. Now, what the guy did was buy used parts, put them in the car, and then he wants to charge me for *new* parts. I said, 'No way Jose! Show me the receipt. I wanna see the fuckin' receipt for those parts.' So he shows me the receipt. And what the dumb bastard did was change the '1' to a '2' so that he could charge me 22 hundred pesos instead of 12 hundred for the parts. You believe that? Well I paid him the fuckin' money and I told him, 'You wait and see. I'll be back.'

"So I went down to the police station and told them that this fuck had just ripped me off. And those dumb bastards are just sitting there, grinning. They're not gonna do nothing. And do you know why? Because '*no hablo Ingles*.' That's what that sergeant . . ."

"Reyes," Jimmy proffered.

"Right, Reyes. That's what he tells me. So I said, 'OK, you *no hablo Ingles*? Then I'm gonna see if you speak Spanish.' So I called my wife and told her to come down to the station."

Bill turned to me and explained. "My wife is Dominican and her whole family is police—father, brothers, cousins, everybody. They're all high up in the police.

"So my wife comes down to the police station and gets right on the phone and starts talking in Spanish like a fuckin' machine gun—*badadadada!* And when those fucks heard her say 'General Lopez,' they started shittin' in their pants. You see," he continued, looking to me and jabbing his finger, "the only time a Dominican does anything fast is when they think they're gonna get fucked. And those guys were gonna get *fucked*, I shit you not."

Jimmy interrupted, "Now hold it, Bill. You put them in a car and they drive like fuckin' lunatics." He smiled and waited for Bill to respond through the rum.

"That's right, they drive like fuckin' nuts."

"Let him finish the story," Mike protested.

Drunk and distracted, Bill took a few moments to collect his thoughts and then continued. "Anyway, the next day at 9:00 in the morning, somebody rings my bell and it turns out that it's the brother of the prick that ripped me off. He gives me my money back, every fuckin' peso, and he tells me that the police have his brother in jail. And he wants *me* to go down there and tell the police to let him go." Jimmy raised his eyebrows in triumph and peered at me. "See, they're not gonna let that prick out of jail unless *I* tell them to."

"So did you go?" Mike asked.

"Yeah, I went. You should have seen 'em. 'Oh, Señor Bill, I'm sorry about what happened, we made a big mistake . . .' Apologies up the kazoo. And do you know what? They were all speaking *English*, every last one of them. I shit you not."

Like many of the stories that these men tell each other, Bill's story narrates the mastering of social differences—cultural, linguistic, political, and so on—through the exercise of control over women. In Bill's account, it is his Dominican wife (or more accurately, his putative control over her) that empowers him to expose the nature of Dominican people and put them in their place in the global order of things. And Bill is not alone. Each year, tens of thousands of white North American and European men travel to the Dominican Republic in search of women over whom they can exercise sexual and domestic discipline as potential husbands, "boyfriends," or as clients in the sex tourism industry.[1] Through the social practice of this form of heteronormative masculinity, what I will call "imperial masculinity," these men collectively construct and naturalize ideologies of racial, class, ethnic, and sex/gender difference that both register and reinscribe the sociospatial hierarchies of the global economy.

In this chapter I examine the social forms and practices through which heterosexual male sex tourists construct and exercise these masculine gender identities. I argue that, for these men, the real and fantasized subordination of women provides the imagined prototype and concrete field of social practices through which they interpret, naturalize, and eroticize social distinctions and hierarchies (O'Connell Davidson and Sanchez Taylor 1999). In the minds of these men, as Anne McClintock noted of their Enlightenment predecessors, "the imperial conquest of the globe [finds] both its shaping figure and its political sanction in the prior subordination of women as a category of nature" (1995: 24).

I am not arguing that gender asymmetry is necessarily primary in either a historical, political, or psychological sense when considered in relation to other ideologies and structures of social inequality. The issue that I raise and consider here concerns the manner and extent to which the symbolic coherence and practical articulation of complex and increasingly global social hierarchies rely on imagining and exercising this heteronormative model of masculinity. For I would like to suggest that it is the *eroticization* of these social distinctions, on the model of sexual control and discipline, that contributes to their durability, flexibility, and perceived naturalness within hierarchical social systems. One might say that, within the cult of imperial masculinity, hierarchy *feels* good. "You see," to recall Bill's words, uttered with no small amount of satisfaction and glee, "the only time a Dominican does anything fast is when they think they're gonna get fucked. And those guys were gonna get *fucked*, I shit you not."

On the other hand, I highlight and examine the ways in which women who participate in sex work transgress and rework class-inflected gender norms and expectations regarding their labor power and economic futures, while disrupting the heterosexual norms and relations desired by male tourists. Against approaches that treat sex work as principally a "survival strategy" and then assess the degree to which it is coercive or disempowering to women, I direct attention to the cultural practices through which women violate social norms and institutions implicated in regulating and disciplining their gender identity, sexuality, and class position within Dominican society and the wider global economy. In Boca Chica, sex work is neither reducible to "sex" nor to "work" but instead embraces a heterogeneous array of practices through which women negotiate and contest social hierarchies that are secured *simultaneously* in terms of gender, sex, race, and class.[2]

The question of the relationship between sex and gender asymmetries and the structuring of hierarchical social systems has been at the center of feminist research and theory building in anthropology and in other disciplines (e.g., Rubin 1975; Collier and Rosaldo 1981; MacKinnon 1989). Feminist scholars have argued that the widespread if not "universal asymmetry" in how the sexes are culturally evaluated can neither be understood as a necessary consequence of biology—for example, women defined as *natural* childbearers—nor as secondary effects of other social processes, such as capitalist class formation (Rosaldo 1974: 17). Instead, researchers have argued that, since sex and gender relations are implicated in the structuring and reproduction of all social systems, women's subordination must be analyzed in relation to wider, yet context-specific processes of social organization and stratification (Collier and Rosaldo 1981).

In her landmark essay "The Traffic in Women: Notes on the 'Political Economy' of Sex," Gayle Rubin defined the scope of this task: "A fullbodied analysis of women in a single society, or throughout history, must take *everything* into account: the evolution of commodity forms in women, systems of land tenure, political arrangements, subsistence technology, etc. *Equally important,* economic and political analyses are incomplete if they do not consider women, marriage, and sexuality" (1975: 210; emphasis added).

It is to the "equally important" segment of Rubin's exhortation that I direct attention here. For although feminist and, more recently, Queer theorists have taken up the challenge to analyze systemic arrangements of power in relation to sex and gender relations, other students of social inequality have been less disposed to reworking their analyses of social hierarchies in light of the structural implications of sex/gender systems.[3] For example, although it is recognized that elites in stratified social systems typically exclude women or assign them subordinate status, sex/gender and, more to my point here, masculinity is seldom treated as a critical, if not indispensable, condition of possibility for the mobilization and exercise of male power.[4] And though it may be begging the question to point out that in the vast majority of stratified societies studied by anthropologists, men exercise the lion's share of formal political power, the fact that they are men, a politically constituted and exercised category, deserves critical analysis. As Catharine MacKinnon put it in a related context, "The question is, what are they?" (1997: 160).

A central premise of this essay is that heteronormative masculinity (that is, what heterosexual men believe themselves to be, possess, and represent) is a power-laden, social, and semiotic architecture within which men fashion, interpret, and negotiate their relations with each other and the social world. Furthermore, this currency of male sociality, comprising culturally constituted beliefs, values, and structures of feeling, as well as concrete social powers and prerogatives, plays a critical role in mobilizing, coordinating, and "naturalizing" male power in hierarchical social systems. Masculinity, to quote Foucault in a related context, can be viewed as a "moving substrate of force relations which, by virtue of their inequality, constantly engender states of power" (1990 [1978]: 92). From this perspective, masculinity, as practiced ideology, is always already available to lend structural meaning and support to systems of social hierarchy.

To what degree do systems of inequality based on such social differences as race, class, ethnicity, and national identity (or some combination of them all) depend on, if not presuppose, the symbolic as well as political organization of male social power; that is, a sex/gender system that not only privileges but must also reiterate and mobilize heteronormative masculinity? Put differently, to what degree do the political articulation and reproduction of social inequality require the mobilization of heterosexual men *as such*? By investigating the question of masculinity as such, I direct attention to the discourses, practices, and structures of male sociality that serve to model, shore up, and naturalize relations of inequality, such as those being articulated through contemporary processes of global restructuring.

To be sure, the relationship between global economic restructuring and sex/gender hierarchies stretches well beyond the frontiers of tourist enclaves such as Boca Chica. In the Dominican Republic, neoliberal economic development policies, monitored and enforced by the World Bank, International Monetary Fund, and other financial institutions, have given rise to development strategies that rely heavily on the naturalization of gender as well as other social differences (Safa 1995, 1999; see also Ong 1991). Over the past three decades, the Dominican economy has shifted from one based on agricultural production and manufacturing for domestic consumption toward a political economy based on tourism and the labor-intensive processing of exports within "Free Trade Zones." Both the tourist and export-processing sectors of the Dominican economy rely heavily on the participation and exploitation of women in the labor force and, consequently, have set in motion social forces, both structural and ideological, that provide key macroeconomic context for the rise of the sex tourism industry in Boca Chica and the exercise of imperial masculinity.

Docile Bodies and Eroticized Powers

I am a single mother with a 12-month baby. I work in the Zona Franca operating a sewing machine. I have beautiful ideas and dreams of my future. I am a very unlucky lady. I fell in love and I thought that he loved me. But I was deceived, abandoned and left pregnant. I would like to find a man who will truly love me. He can be up to 50 years old. It is all right if he is divorced and has children. My only crime is that I am poor.—Yesenia, 22 years old. Ad placed with an Internet-based bride service.

Beginning in the late 1960s, the Dominican Republic initiated fundamental changes in economic development strategies and policies. Spurred in part by a long-term decline in the value of primary produce exports, such as sugar, coffee, cacao, and tobacco, and by the failure of export substitution strategies to generate a viable domestic manufacturing sector, the Dominican Republic embarked on a course of economic restructuring that emphasized tourism, agribusiness, and the labor-intensive processing of exports in Free Trade Zones, or FTZs (Safa 1999).

Tourism was aggressively promoted by the World Bank, the World Trade Organization, and the United Nations as an economic panacea for the Third World, which would generate foreign exchange by transferring wealth from visiting "guests" of the developed world to their "hosts" in developing nations. As Malcolm Crick observed, "Tourism was represented as an easy option for development because it relied largely on natural resources already in place—e.g., sand, sun, friendly people—and therefore required no vast capital outlays for infrastructure" (1989: 315). Supporters of this strategy argued that tourism would also stimulate job creation and infrastructure development and facilitate technology and skills transfers to developing nations.

In the 1970s, the Dominican government created INFRATUR, a public agency charged with promoting the development of infrastructure for the tourist industry, and offered tax abatements and other incentives to foreign investors. This phase of tourism promotion followed an earlier, though largely unsuccessful, attempt to stimulate tourism under the regime of Rafael Trujillo (1931–1961) when government-financed hotels were built to take advantage of the collapse of the Cuban tourism industry in the late 1950s (Meyer-Arendt et al. 1992). By 1985, tourism accounted for 26.2 percent of all foreign exchange earnings and, by the end of that decade, the Dominican Republic boasted more hotel rooms than any other Caribbean destination. In 1994, tourism accounted for 64.1 percent of all export revenues and, with a labor force estimated at 150,000, had become the largest source of employment (Cabezas 1998).

The rapid growth of the tourism industry has depended on the mobilization and reconfiguration of social hierarchies and ideologies based on gender, class, and racial distinctions. As many researchers have pointed out, the international tourism industry constructs, commodifies, and markets exoticized and deeply gendered images of non-European host societies that stress the passivity, servility, and the enduring "otherness" of their peoples (Enloe 1989; Mullings 1999; O'Connell Davidson and Sanchez Taylor 1999). These representations, rooted in the centuries-old fantasies of European male travelers and colonizers, construct tourist destinations such as the Dominican Republic as sites of hedonistic license and consumption that recapitulate the historic prerogatives of imperial elites among colonized peoples (Kempadoo 1999).

This gendered iconography of space constructs non-European host societies as yielding, submissive, and erotically feminine and finds structural expression in the sexual division of labor within the tourism industry. As Kinnaird, Kothari, and Hall have noted, women hold the majority of tourism-related jobs—typically low-skill and low-wage jobs such as chambermaids, kitchen staff, and other service personnel (1994; Kempadoo 1999). This gendered division of labor reflects both the international tourism industry's conflation of pleasure-producing services with women's labor and dominant gender norms within host societies that relegate women to domestic, "housekeeping-like" service occupations. Thus the tourism industry not only constructs the tourist experience in gendered and racialized terms—as an encounter with a docile, obliging, and feminized other—it also mobilizes, affirms, and reconfigures patriarchal ideologies and power relations within host societies to fashion a division of labor that accentuates wealth and power differentials between "hosts" and "guests" (cf. Mullings 1999). In the Dominican Republic, these patriarchal and racialized discourses and practices, operating at the national and transnational levels, enable and lend meaning to the social practices of masculinity among male tourists.

A second major development associated with economic restructuring policies in the Dominican Republic has been the meteoric growth of export-processing industries in Free Trade Zones. These export-processing zones are industrial enclaves, or estates, that offer investors the duty free import and export of goods and a variety of tax and regulatory incentives that facilitate labor-intensive assembly operations. Typically, FTZs are self-contained, spatial enclaves that are dominated by foreign investment and produce goods designed for export that require high inputs of cheap labor. In 1970, the Dominican Republic opened its first free trade zone with the objectives of generating foreign exchange and jobs. By 1992, promoted by the United States Caribbean Basin Initiative and by World Bank and IMF structural adjustment demands, 403 companies, employing over 100,000 workers, were doing business in 31 free trade zones, all heavily subsidized by the Dominican government (Sagawe 1996).

The rapid expansion of the export-processing sector in the Dominican Republic has led to profound changes in the social and spatial organization of the labor force and in the sexual division of labor (Safa 1999). On the one hand, as Laura Raynolds has pointed out, "Fully 80 percent of export processing jobs and firms are located in the greater Santo Domingo metropolitan area or in the provincial capital cities of Santiago, San Pedro de Macorís, and La Romana" (1998: 163). This location pattern has produced a concentrated pattern of urban job growth and stimulated rapid rural-to-urban migration. For example, the population of San Pedro de Macorís, a city just east of Boca Chica, almost doubled, from 42,000 to 80,000, in the decade following the establishment of its FTZ.

On the other hand, the expansion of export-processing industries has led to a rapid and unprecedented incorporation of women into the labor force in low-paying and labor intensive manufacturing jobs in FTZ industries. Between 1970 and 1994, female participation in the Dominican labor force increased from 25.3 to 36.4 percent. By 1994, women accounted for 58 percent of the labor force in the export-processing sector, and 65 percent of all women working in FTZs were employed by garment and textile companies (Raynolds 1998). Work in the nonunionized export-processing industries tends to be poorly paid and unskilled, requiring compulsory overtime and few, if any, benefits. The average monthly wage paid by FTZ industries to new workers in 1995 was $1,678.69 pesos (U.S.$130.41). Representing an hourly rate of 34 cents, this amounted to about a third of the wage level required to stay above the poverty line, defined by the Dominican government at RD $4,743.33 per month.

The expansion of this low-waged female labor force is the result of gender-biased practices and ideologies that devalue and exploit women's labor within both Dominican society and the globally oriented export-processing sector. Companies profit from Dominican patriarchal traditions, Raynolds writes, that limit women's alternatives and make them disproportionately responsible for home and family. Women's restricted employment ensures that they will accept low-waged and unconventional jobs, particularly if this work permits them to forgo migration and remain near their families (1998: 161). Managers of FTZ industries typically exclude women from administrative and supervisory positions and assign them instead to repetitive and fast-paced assembly-line tasks on the grounds that women are better suited *by nature* for work that requires patience, manual dexterity, and acquiescence to highly regimented working conditions (cf. Freeman 2000).

Thus the rapid development of the tourism and export-processing industries has both shaped and been shaped by practices of gender subordination that situate Dominican women within the global economy as "natural" subjects of labor and sex/gender exploitation. Whereas the export-processing sector appeals to the natural qualities of women in order to mobilize and devalue their labor, the tourism industry produces experiences of consumption and pleasure that depend, symbolically and structurally, on power and wealth differentials that are figured in gendered and racialized terms. In order to illuminate the relationship between this deeply gendered process of economic restructuring and the rise of sex tourism, I turn to my research in Boca Chica. For Boca Chica, like other tourist enclaves in the Dominican Republic, is a nodal point in the global political economy where these complex practices of gender subordination enable the exercise of imperial masculinity.

Tourism in Boca Chica

Boca Chica is located on the south coast of the Dominican Republic, thirty kilometers east of the capital city of Santo Domingo. The town is said to have been founded at the beginning of the twentieth century by Juan Bautista Viccini, a wealthy businessman of Italian descent who owned much of the property in the area. The adjoining town of Andrés, founded as a fishing community, expanded when an American investor constructed the *Ingenio Boca Chica*, or sugar processing factory, there in 1916 (Cabrera 2001). During the 1940s, while Andrés took shape as a company town, or *batey*, for sugar workers, Vincini's waterfront property in Boca Chica was developed as a resort area for wealthy Dominicans in the capital, who built summer homes along the shore. In 1952, the state under President Rafael Trujillo constructed the Hotel Hamaca, the first of Boca Chica's luxury hotels. During the 1970s tourism initiative, the Hamaca was renovated and expanded and other hotels were constructed with the support of foreign investors.

Today, Boca Chica's two largest hotels, the Boca Chica Beach Resort and the Hotel Hamaca, anchor the western and eastern ends of the beach respectively and define the limits of the tourist zone. A third large and all-inclusive hotel, the Don Juan, is owned by the Vicini family and located midway along the beach near the town center. Walking east along the beach from the Boca Chica Resort toward the Hotel Hamaca, one passes an assortment of bars and restaurants that cater to daytime beachgoers. European and North American expatriates own the majority of these beachfront businesses. A few small mid-priced and budget hotels are also located on the beach. A small church and town plaza define the town center, where Boca Chica's municipal offices, gift shops, and currency exchange and telecommunications businesses are concentrated.

After dark, activities in Boca Chica shift from the beach to Calle Duarte, the town's main commercial street that runs parallel to the shore. About two kilometers in length, Calle Duarte is lined with restaurants, bars, discothèques, and other businesses that cater primarily to male sex tourists. Mid-priced hotels line the cross streets extending north to the main highway. Beginning at about 8:00 P.M., women from Andrés, Santo Domingo, and other nearby areas begin arriving at the bars and discothèques on Calle Duarte to socialize with male tourists. Numbering as many as 200 on weekends, the majority of these women are sex workers and receive anywhere from RD $400 to $800 for sex from male clients. With the exception of the three major resorts noted above, hotels in Boca Chica allow male guests to bring women to their rooms, provided that the latter possess *cedulas*, or government-issued identification cards.

Although researchers have directed attention to male sex workers in the Caribbean (e.g., de Moya et al. 1992; Pruitt and Lafont 1995; Brennan 1998), few men in Boca Chica are socially recognized or self-identified as sex workers. This is due, in part, to the fact that Boca Chica is not a popular destination for single, female tourists. But equally important, men who do work with female tourists, sometimes providing sex for money, are able to claim an identity (such as "tourist guide," or *guía*) that stretches beyond the narrow and stigmatized work identity reserved for female sex workers (cf. Kempadoo 1999). And although same-sex sex tourism exists in Boca Chica, it is clandestine and repressed by local authorities and hotel managers. Many hotels prohibit tourists from having local same-sex guests in their rooms. In short, the privileging of heteronormative masculinity, locally and within the international tourist industry, constructs sex work as female and heterosexual.[5]

Female sex workers constitute a large portion of the wider, tourism-based informal economy, which provides income for poor Dominicans and Haitian immigrants in the surrounding area. In the Dominican Republic, as in other areas of Latin America, the expansion of this informal economy has been a consequence of high unemployment rates (15.5 percent overall and 26.5 percent for women in 1994) and low wages in sectors of the economy that have been subject to IMF and World Bank structural adjustment and privatization policies (Portes and Schauffler 1993). Helen Safa reported that self-employed Dominican workers in the informal sector accounted for more than one third of the active labor force in 1991 (1999). Many residents of Andrés, who lost jobs when the town's state-owned sugar *central* closed in the late 1990s, today work as vendors on the beach, selling handicrafts, garments, and other products to tourists. Local women provide body-care services, such as hair braiding, massages, and manicures, catering largely to the guests of the resort hotels. Many men work as motorcycle taxi operators, or *motoconchos*, providing cheap local transportation to residents and tourists. Although government authorities license most of these occupations, few can afford the RD $3,500 needed to purchase a *carnet*, or license. Consequently, many who work in tourism-related jobs do so illegally and are subject to arrest by the police and stiff fines.

Prostitution is not illegal in the Dominican Republic and authorities in Boca Chica tolerate it.[6] Although there is no system for licensing sex workers, they are required to carry state-issued identification cards that confirm their identity, residence, and age. Local authorities describe their policing strategies as targeting women who are "criminals" or minors, under the age of eighteen. Periodically, units of the tourism police conduct sweeps of Calle Duarte, checking identity cards and arresting women without them. Police and hotel managers also prohibit sex workers from soliciting clients on the beach and near the major resort hotels. These hotels are expensive, "all inclusive" resorts that include food, liquor, and entertainment in their package price. All three complexes are surrounded by walls and policed by private security guards. Guests, identified by hotel-issued, plastic wristbands, are cautioned by hotel employees against leaving the resort compound on the grounds that they will be harassed, cheated, or robbed. These policies, which ensure that guests spend their money within the compounds, are a source of bitter contention for Dominican vendors and business owners, some of whom maintain that their lack of access to resort guests forces them to cater to, if not promote, sex tourism.

Technologies of Masculinity: Sex Tourism and the Internet

Many of the men I met in the Dominican Republic became aware of the sex tourism industry there through Internet Web sites that cater to male travelers interested in prostitution. Although there are a variety of Web sites devoted to sex tourism, *tsmtravel.com*, short for "Travel and the Single Male," is by far the most popular and sophisticated North American site. Based in California and boasting 6,000 paid subscribers, TSM offers travel reports about prostitution around the world, message boards, and "adult entertainment" photographs and video clips submitted by subscribers.

The development and social uses of Web sites such as TSM highlight the role that new technologies are playing in the mediation and articulation of transnational social hierarchies and identities within the global economy. TSM provides its members with communicative resources to identify economically vulnerable populations across the globe and to exploit that vulnerability through the naturalized and pleasure-seeking economy of heteronormative masculinity. Like pornography, sex tourism Web sites secure the conflation of desire with domination.

A popular feature of *tsmtravel* is its detailed travel reports, often accompanied by photographs and maps. These reports, submitted by TSM subscribers, provide up-to-date information on sex tourism destinations, such as Thailand, the Philippines, and Brazil, and include data on transportation, hotels, sex-worker venues and prices, and on social and economic conditions. For example, a July 1999 travel report alerted TSM subscribers to the favorable exchange rate in Quito Ecuador:

> During my recent trip to Quito, the big news was the exchange rate: over 11,000 Ecuadorian *sucres* to the dollar. Quito is now undoubtedly one of the better TSM values in the Western Hemisphere. . . . I made one discovery not mentioned in previous posts. There is a bar/brothel located about a one-minute walk from the Hotel Embassy at Almagro 208 @ Pinto in what appears (from the outside) to be a residential house. . . . The price there for 15 minutes of sex is only 30,000 *sucres* (less than $2.75).

TSM also maintains message boards and real-time chat rooms that permit members to communicate with each other and post queries concerning travel destinations, such as brothel locations in Manaus, Brazil, or airfares between Bangkok and Manila. Subscribers using screen names such as "Miami Pete" and "Badboy" also use the message boards to announce travel plans and organize meetings with other members at predesignated places and times.

The adult entertainment photo section is divided between images culled from Internet pornography sites and photographs taken by TSM members during their visits to sex tourism destinations. Frequently, the photographs are incorporated into travel narratives and captioned. TSM's galleries highlight the relationship between the production and consumption of pornography and the practice of sex tourism; they also underscore the fact that both are implicated in the collective construction of heteronormative masculinity through the exercise of control, "scopic" as much as physical, over the bodies and sexualities of women (cf. Dworkin 1981). Significantly, male sex tourists are playing an increasingly prominent role in producing and distributing pornography through Internet Web sites in general and through personal Web pages dedicated to single male travel.

Web sites such as TSM not only provide men with up-to-date information about the relative vulnerability of women around the world but also enable the formation of technologically mediated structures of male sociality, focused on the "self-imagining" of heteronormative masculinity on a global scale (Appadurai 1996). In sum, male sex tourism must be understood within processes of globalization that not only position women, socially and economically, as subjects of gender-based labor exploitation but also figure them within an electronically mediated masculine imaginary as eroticized subjects of sexual control and consumption. As Julia O'Connell Davidson and Jacqueline Sanchez Taylor put it, "their sexual taste for 'Others' reflects not so much a wish to engage in any specific sexual practice as a desire for an extraordinarily high degree of control over the management of self and others as sexual, racialized and engendered beings. This desire, and the Western sex tourists power to satiate it, can only be explained through reference to power relations and popular discourses that are simultaneously gendered, racialized and economic" (1999: 37). And it is in places such as Boca Chica that we observe the relationship between these institutionalized structures of masculinity and their everyday practice most sharply.

Masculinity and Performance

It was 7:30 in the evening when I arrived at Delmonte's, an American-owned restaurant, not far from the Hamaca Hotel. I had earlier scheduled an interview with its owner, Kenny Bruno, a plumbing contractor from Boston who had married a Dominican woman and settled in Boca Chica. In addition to his restaurant, Kenny also operated a lucrative mail-order cigar business.

Delmonte's sits on a terrace overlooking the beach. Steps from the terrace lead down to the sand where an additional dining area services daytime customers.

I sat at one of the white plastic tables on the terrace and asked the waiter for Kenny. He told me that Kenny had gone to Cuba, where he often went to buy cigars for his business. I decided to stay and have dinner. It was a warm, clear night and there was enough moonlight to make out the figures of Dominican teenagers playing in the water below. Three boys were taking turns jumping off each others' shoulders into the waist-deep water to the delight of a group of girls who watched from the beach, laughing and shouting encouragement.

Save for four middle-aged white men who were sitting at a table on the other side of the terrace, the restaurant was empty. The men were dressed in summer, golf-style clothing and were wearing the red plastic identity bracelets for guests at the Hamaca. They talked quietly over their beer about baseball, sailboats, and Fort Worth, Texas, where two of the men had lived. Every so often, one of the men glanced expectantly toward the bar inside.

As I was giving my order, a cheerful and chubby Dominican man arrived with two young girls. His keys rattled in his hand as he waved to the Americans. He was wearing the pale green shirt worn by tourist taxi drivers. When he darted for the table, the girls paused and looked at each other before following. The four men twisted in their chairs to watch the girls approach, grinning pop-eyed at one another as the driver sat the girls at the table. The driver introduced the two girls as Belkis and Maria. The men grinned and greeted them but did not introduce themselves.

Both girls appeared to be teenagers. Maria was dark-skinned and petite and was wearing a white miniskirt, red tank top, and white platform sneakers. Her hair was pulled back tightly into a ponytail. Belkis was light-skinned and tall and wearing a low-cut shiny blue dress that clung to her full figure. When one of the men gawked theatrically at her exposed thigh, she laughed nervously and covered her mouth.

"Hey Stu," a second man blurted. "Ain't she too young for you?"

"I'm drinkin' beer, Bob, I don't give a shit," he replied with a southern drawl. Stu pointed to Bob's empty beer bottle. "Hey, you gettin' behind there, big boy."

The cabdriver laughed, slapped his knee, and signaled to the waiter to bring more beer. The two girls quietly ordered Cokes.

Stu leaned toward Belkis and placed his hand on her thigh. "And how old are *you*, young lady?" He grinned and cut his eyes to his friends. Belkis didn't understand. She covered her mouth, laughed quietly, and then looked to the taxi driver for help. The driver questioned her and reported, "She has sixteen years old."

"*Woowee!*" Stu blurted. "Ain't this some place? You can't beat this."

A third man sitting next to Maria joined in. "Hey Stu, you gotta speak the lingo if you want to get anywhere down here." He turned to Maria, "*Qué e-dad* [age] you got, honey?"

The table erupted in laughter. The cabdriver clapped his hands with glee, "Very good!" Confused, Maria looked to Belkis, grinned, and then clapped her hands as well.

For the next twenty minutes, the four men and the driver talked among themselves while the girls sipped their drinks in silence. When they had finished their Cokes, the driver handed Belkis a bag that he had been storing under the table and the two girls disappeared into the restaurant. Ten minutes later, they returned in bikinis.

Their reappearance was greeted with whoops and hollers from the table. Stu got up from the table and wrapped one arm around each of the girls. "Hey big boy, you gotta get a picture of this. Get out your camera!"

Bob unpacked his camera and each of the men took turns posing with the girls. When the picture taking was over, Belkis and Maria stood awkwardly beside the table unsure of what to do next. The cabdriver talked for a moment to Belkis and then announced to the Americans that the girls wanted to go swimming.

"Sure, why not." Stu replied. "I can handle a wet bikini!" The table laughed again as Belkis and Maria, holding hands, scurried down the steps to the beach below. The men stood, whooped and hollered once more, and then angled to get a better view of the disappearing figures. "Boy that Maria's got a nice bottom," Stu muttered.

"Ain't this paradise?" Bob asked.

"Well, if it ain't, I sure don't know what is," came the response.

I got my check and left. The next day, Kenny returned from Cuba and I went back to do the interview. The Americans from the night before had also returned and were sitting inside the restaurant with Belkis, Maria, and two other women. I asked Kenny about them.

"Who, those guys?" he asked, half waving and half pointing to their table. They waved back. "They're the highest-ranking military officers in the D.R. They come here all the time."

"Why?" I asked.

He was distracted. The restaurant was filling up quickly. Kenny caught the waiter's eye and then pointed to a table of impatient-looking German men.

"No, I mean, what are they doing in the D.R.?"

"They're here to monitor Cuba. You know, the situation there."

As the above example suggests, sex acts occupy a small portion of the time that male tourists spend in Boca Chica. Indeed, male tourists spend more time interacting with each other than they do with women—a fact that highlights the degree to which masculine self-identification relies on male-centered cultural practices and forms of sociality (Sedgwick 1985; O'Connell Davidson and Sanchez Taylor 1999). Striking in the above case, as in many of the ritualized interactions between tourists and sex workers, is the general lack of interest, an almost studied indifference, on the part of most men in the women they have come to meet. During the two hours or so that I watched the Americans at Kenny's restaurant, they spoke few words to Belkis and Maria and made eye contact with them only furtively. Their interactions with the women (groping and gazing at their bodies, asking their ages, and posing for photographs) were all theatrically performed in a manner so as to incite the *collective* participation of the men (through laughter, whooping and hollering, and catching each other's eyes) and enable the alignment of a common male gaze; a gaze whose conditions of possibility rest on the very real, yet contested, economic power of male tourists to position Dominican women as docile bodies within the global political and sexual economy.[7]

Teresa de Lauretis's observations concerning the "nonbeing of woman" capture very well the subject positions assigned to Belkis and Maria in this ritual of masculinity: "The paradox of a being that is at once captive and absent in discourse, constantly spoken of but of itself inaudible or inexpressible, displayed as spectacle and still unrepresented or unrepresentable, invisible yet constituted as the object and the guarantee of vision; a being whose existence and specificity are simultaneously asserted and denied, negated and controlled" (quoted in Kutzinski 1993: 164).

It is this imagined and, indeed, paradoxical state of nonbeing that is the elusive target of the masculine gaze as it is constituted and exercised through the practices of male sociality. Male socializing in Boca Chica revolves around a set of ritualized spectacles through which men fantasize the nonbeing of women and, in turn, imagine themselves to be all-powerful subjects. Much of this socializing occurs at night in the many restaurants, bars, and clubs that line Calle Duarte. For example, by 10:00 P.M., the Zanzibar Cafe and Bar is usually packed with male tourists, expatriates, and Dominican women, some employees and others not.

Like other bars and clubs in Boca Chica, the Zanzibar employs attractive young women to serve as hostesses. The women are provided with photo ID cards that protect them from police sweeps that target women, often under-age, who do not have government-issued identification cards. For the women, employment as a hostess confers the status of workers (*trabajadora*), in contrast to streetwalker (*mujer de la calle*). These hostesses are not paid wages but receive tips from customers. In addition, many of the hostesses also "leave with tourists" (*salir con touristas*) after work for "short-time" paid sex or for longer liaisons. For cafe and bar owners, the hostesses attract and retain male customers by dancing provocatively and by striking up conversations and erotic poses that parody and poke fun at the fantasies held by tourists concerning the "natural" qualities of Dominican women.

I sat at the Zanzibar's high mahogany bar next to Divina, a twenty-two-year-old woman who had begun working as a hostess the week before. Divina was from San Pedro de Macorís and had come to Boca Chica to find work to support her newborn son. She was living with her brother, who worked as a *motoconcho* and rented a small house in Andrés. Previously, Divina and her widowed mother had worked in a textile factory in the San Pedro FTZ. However, with the birth of her son, their combined wages were no longer enough to support the family.

Divina was leaning against the bar, watching the tables outside. In contrast to the other hostesses, she dressed casually, often wearing blue jeans, sandals, and a neatly pressed tee shirt. Serious in demeanor, Divina did not dance or flirt to attract customers but was otherwise very conscientious about doing her job.

I greeted her and asked how things were. Divina made a sour face and said that she was not making any money. She told me that her mother had called that morning to tell her that her baby had a fever. She was worried that the infant might have a virulent strain of the flu that people were calling the "Kosovo flu." She needed money to buy medicine. I asked her how much she had earned the night before. She replied that she had made 150 pesos (U.S. $10) in tips for ten hours work. "*Mucho trabajo, poco dinero,*" she added dryly. There was a flurry of activity outside and Divina left to attend to a group of young Italian men.

The bar was now full and the sound system was blasting Merengue star Elvis Crespo's latest record, *Suavamente*. Hostesses in skin-tight miniskirts filtered through the crowd, shaking their hips and singing along with the record. The extra tables that had been set up in front of the Zanzibar, partially blocking the street, were fully occupied by groups of North American and European men. *Motoconcho* taxis whizzed by, engines roaring, shuttling women back and forth between their homes in Andrés and places along Calle Duarte.

Divina was now sitting at a table with six Italian men dressed in jeans, polo shirts, and Nike sneakers. She appeared livelier than before and was talking to a thin man with gold-rimmed glasses and a pockmarked face. While the others looked on, he questioned her and then translated her replies into Italian for his friends. Each response was greeted by excited laughter and rapid cross-talking. As I approached, I heard the man ask her in Spanish, "Which men are the best in bed—the strongest?" He clenched his fist and raised it into the air like a trophy. The others grinned and gaped at her expectantly. "*Italianos!*" one blurted. The men laughed, looked at each other, and then to Divina for a response.

Divina laughed. "I don't know," she replied. "I don't have that experience. All men are the same." There was a pause for translation and then laughter as the men protested her reply.

I sat down at a table with three middle-aged American men, whom I had met earlier at Jimmy's Bar and Grill. For Rubin, a recently divorced lawyer from Manhattan, this was his third trip to Boca Chica in the past year. He had learned about Boca Chica through TSM's Web site. On this trip, he had brought along Martin, an old friend from Harvard Law School who lived in Los Angeles. They had met the third man, Roger, in Boca Chica. They were sitting with Ana Maria and Gladys, two sisters whom the lawyers had met the night before at a casino in Santo Domingo. The two women talked quietly to each other, musing on the spectacle around them.

Rubin spoke some Spanish and presented himself as an expert on Dominican women and culture. "That's the one I want," he said, grinning widely and watching Divina. He caught her eye and she approached the table, thinking that he wanted to order drinks. The Italians watched with interest. Rubin put his arm around Divina's waist and then looked to us, as if to make sure that we were paying attention. "This is the best girl in Boca Chica," he pronounced. "Look at her!" he added, eyeing her figure. "I want you to be my girlfriend," he told her in broken Spanish. Divina laughed and pulled away.

Another hostess intervened, laughing and shaking her forefinger in Rubin's face. "No, America," she said in Spanish. "She is not for you. She does not leave with tourists." Divina left and the other hostess remained.

"I like this one better," Martin commented, putting his arm around the woman's waist. "She's got bigger tits." The hostess sat on his lap.

"You're nuts," Rubin replied, making a face. "She's hard-core. All she wants is your money. Let me tell you, I know this country. The best girls are in the *campo* [i.e., the countryside.] The women here in Boca Chica are all hardcore whores.

"But that one," Rubin continued, eyeing Divina, "you could marry her. She's not corrupted yet. She'll cook and clean for you, and never give you any trouble as long as you take care of her. That's the way Dominican women are—the good ones."

"But why the countryside?" I asked. "What's the difference?"

"Because life there is simple," Rubin explained. "Everything is natural—the air, the food, the lifestyle, everything," he continued with enthusiasm. "They grow their own food and they don't need money to spend on fancy clothes, and makeup, and all that bullshit. And the Dominican believes in strong families. That's why you see them all with babies."

Martin joined in. "The countryside is about survival for these people. And if they meet an American and they like him, they'll do anything for you. They won't look at another guy. Because these girls hate Dominican men. A lot of guys who come here don't know that. The girls don't want to be with them. They call them *tigres* [tigers] because the Dominican guys treat their women like shit."[8]

Rubin knew that I was an anthropologist and that I intended to write a book. He looked at me and continued. "That's why me, personally, I like the dark-skinned girls here the best. I'm not prejudiced like some of the guys who come down here and don't know anything." He kissed Ana Maria on the cheek. "See, they're not as corrupted with the consumer mentality and the fast life. Most of them are originally from the *campo*." Ana Maria smiled and asked Rubin for another rum and Coke.

Like Rubin, many male tourists imagine *el campo* to be a place bereft of the troubling complexities of modernity and, above all, feminism, and uncorrupted by capitalist commodities—a place where everything is natural and people are good and simple. Like the imagined heart of darkness in Africanist discourse, *el campo* exists for these men as an "impossible nullity," a void where, as Christopher Miller put it, "the head, the voice—the logos, if you will—is missing" (1985: 27). In this racialized fantasy, women from the countryside make good wives and mothers because, living closer to nature, *their* nature, they lack logos and, thus, agency. It is this impossible nullity, this nonbeing of woman that is the elusive focus of the practices of male sex tourists as they collectively work to fashion and inscribe masculinity within the imagined void of the natural women.

"Which men are the best in bed?" the Italian asked, raising his fist like a phallus. "*Italianos!*" another had confirmed triumphantly. Divina's response was moot since this had been a conversation among men in which Divina was positioned as a prop or, better, a *tabula rasa* upon which to both fantasize and inscribe phallic power and agency.

Similarly, Rubin's performance relied on the collective, though putative power of men to situate and, indeed, bond women within this masculine imaginary, enabling him to construct and enunciate the fantastic distinction between the Dominican "whore" who possesses agency and the docile and domesticated woman of the *campo* who is the ideal wife and mother. Within the imagined frontiers of *el campo*, blackness, poverty, and marginality appear to these men as natural differences that both signify and facilitate male power over women.[9] Through their efforts to situate Dominican women as silent and docile bodies, subjects of sexual control and domestic discipline, these men construct and, more to the point, *perform* male gender identities that index and articulate constructions of racial, class, and geopolitical difference (Butler 1993).

In this sense, Boca Chica is a stage, a theme park where men dramatize and reiterate the privileges of economic, racial, and geopolitical power within the eroticized fantasies and rituals of gender subordination. A number of male tourists have remarked to me that Boca Chica reminds them of Disneyland, an observation that registers, for loss of a better word, the "boyish" attitudes of adventure, risk, and competition that men cultivate through sex tourism and the thematic structures of the masculinities they work to create.[10] For example, bars and restaurants, such as the German-owned Austria and Madhouse bars, the Dutch-owned Route 66, and Kenny's American-style restaurant, cultivate a customer base of tourists and expatriates on the basis of national and linguistic identities. Such businesses are typically marked with national flags and offer specialty menu items (e.g., Philadelphia steak sandwiches and schnitzel) and imported beverages that appeal to men as subjects of nation-states. A travel report posted by a TSM member on the group's Web site captures both this nationalistic sentiment and the puerile sense of adventure and competition that men commemorate through sex tourism:

The Italians [in Boca Chica] were retreating to their homeland, with their supplies running out, and they knew that the Americans were cumming [*sic*] in force with big American guns and plenty of ammo. They did not want to be there when our reinforcements rolled into town. So in came such TSMers as Jody, Irving, NY Guy, Omega, Allan F., Worm, Joker, Canuck, Newt, Parrot Head, Ricky, Freddy (he's Danish but we let him hang out with us anyway). . . . There were others but I cannot remember their names. (TSM trip report, 10 September 1999)

This excerpt, replete with militarized sexual euphemisms, not only suggests the degree to which the practice of masculine gender identity implicates an evaluation of national identities and power differentials—at once phallic, economic, and geopolitical—but also underscores the homosocial, if not *homoerotic,* character of the social practices themselves, both on the Internet and in the field. "We are," as Sedgwick observed, "in the presence of male heterosexual desire, in the form of a desire to consolidate partnership with authoritative males in and through the bodies of females" (1985: 38; cf. Mosse 1985). In Boca Chica, men prop up and exercise their nationalisms through the real and imagined subordination of women and, in the process, cultivate a "platoonlike" form of camaraderie.

Women who do sex work ignore, parody, and disrupt these practices of homosociality as well as the attempts of male tourists to render them docile "nonbeings." In social gatherings, for example, women typically carry on parallel conversations among themselves in Spanish, which critically evaluate and often ridicule the actions, conversations, and, indeed, sexual prowess of male tourists. I witnessed an incident that well illustrates this point. Three Canadian men were sitting with their Dominican girlfriends in a restaurant in Boca Chica when one began to complain that his girlfriend was asking him to buy things for her baby. Unbeknownst to him, his girlfriend was following the conversation and translating it, along with caustic commentary, for the two other women. Provoked to action by her friends, the woman reached into her purse, pulled out a bottle of pills, and threw it at the man. "You can buy Viagra but you can't help my baby!" she shouted in Spanish. "Go to hell!" She stormed out of the restaurant, leaving the man red faced and Spanish-speakers in the restaurant bent over in laughter. (Apparently, he had sent her to the pharmacy to buy the pills.)

Moreover, women often perform displays of sexuality that disrupt naturalized stereotypes of their own sex and gender identities and parody the sexual pretensions of male tourists. For example, I once witnessed a hostess circulate among the tables at Zanzibar Cafe holding an imaginary penis, which she lashed at dumbfounded tourists to the delight of her coworkers. In this and other performative venues, hostesses and other sex workers often perform same-sex acts, such as kissing and fondling, which, directed in part at male tourists, violate heterosexual norms. Some women openly acknowledge their bi- or homosexuality, and there is considerable discussion among those who work in tourist-related jobs about sexual identity. Solange, a Haitian hostess at the Zanzibar Cafe, once confronted an American tourist for not leaving a tip. When he rudely dismissed her request, she slapped him in the face and set on him, restrained only by her coworkers. A second hostess, known to be the offended woman's lover, approached the bewildered tourist, laughing. "Do not mess with her, America," she told him in English, "she is a lesbian. You better give her her money." The tourist paid the tip and left, pursued by the jeers and laughter of the hostesses.

Here, I would like to shift the focus of discussion from sex tourists to women who do sex work and consider how the latter interpret and negotiate their own interests and positions as women and as workers within the political economy of masculinity. I want to show that sex workers not only contest the real and imagined prerogatives of male tourists; equally important, through their struggles to make ends meet, they also call into question the gendered structures, norms, and expectations that undergird the wider economy. To develop this perspective, I discuss the experiences of one woman whom I came to know in Boca Chica, Yanira Polanco.

"Luchando por la Vida": Struggling for Life in the Global Economy

Yanira was born in a small town near Santiago and orphaned at an early age. Her maternal grandmother raised her, along with five siblings, and the family eked out a living growing yucca and other produce. At the age of twenty-six, while visiting a sister in Boca Chica, Yanira met a Dominican man who convinced her to move there with her two children. When the relationship ended, Yanira began working as a hostess in Boca Chica and doing sex work to support her family. When I met her in 1998, Yanira was working at the Zanzibar Cafe as a hostess and renting a small house, or *casita*, in Boca Chica.

When I returned to Boca Chica in the summer of 1999, Yanira told me that she was getting married to an Italian man whom she had met two years before. Paolo was fifty-four years old and a factory worker in Milan. He had been sending her money each month to help pay her rent of 3,500 pesos (U.S. $235) and other living expenses, which amounted to about 3,000 pesos per month. I interviewed her on the day that Paolo was scheduled to arrive in Boca Chica. Later in the week, the couple would go to the capital to apply for a three-month marriage visa for Yanira. I asked her how she felt about leaving her country and moving to Italy.

"In this country there is nothing," she replied. "You have to leave here to help yourself. I just have to go because I can't work like this all the time. One day, they'll replace me. I can't go on struggling all the time, here, in the streets, walking home at night at 4:00 in the morning. It's not possible. If I find a man who wants to marry me and live in peace, I will not tell him no."

Paolo had told her that he would get her a job at the factory where he worked, which, Yanira told me, would pay much more than the factories in the FTZs where she had once worked. She also had discussed moving to Italy with a girlfriend who had married an Italian and was living in Genoa. Her friend had reassured her that the schools and healthcare system in Italy were good and that her two children would benefit.

"Sure, I'm afraid," Yanira continued, "but since I am not the first or the last to go, I have to get myself together and go. One must struggle with life. I already know this country. I want to know other countries to see how life is there. I believe that if I go to Italy for those three or four months, I will know better if I like it there. I want to see how they treat me. If they don't treat me well, I will return to my country, the Dominican Republic."

I went back to the Zanzibar Cafe later that evening. Yanira was sitting at a table with Paolo and her two children, whom I had not seen before. She was wearing her ID card but not working. She was a customer. The other hostesses fawned over them and served the children hamburgers, which they had bought with their tips at a nearby food stall. Yanira caught my eye and smiled. Paolo waved.

Yanira did not go to Italy. Two weeks later, she told me that Paolo had become jealous and possessive after she had received her visa. Once in Italy, she reasoned, she would be at his mercy. "Maybe he won't find me a job at his factory. And maybe he won't send for my children." Shortly thereafter, Paolo left and she returned to her job at the Zanzibar Cafe.

Yanira's decision not to migrate to Italy was rooted in the credible fear that Paolo, by exploiting her visa status, might hold her hostage in his household by not allowing her to pursue *paid* work and provide for her children.

The fear of migrating abroad only to be disciplined as a *ama de casa,* or housewife, stands behind the decision of many women not to marry foreigners even when it might improve their standard of living. Stories abound of women whose insecure visa status reduced them to virtual prisoners of their husbands. In short, few, if any, sex workers share the domestic fantasies of male tourists.

Moreover, Yanira's decision also ensured that she would remain relatively free to pursue alternative strategies for socioeconomic mobility. For example, she had enrolled her fourteen-year-old daughter in a school to learn English, which, she believed, would prepare her for a front-desk job in tourism. And in the event that the family migrated to the United States, where she had relatives, Yanira felt that her daughter's English skills would give them a head start. Sex workers must and do carefully weigh their pressing needs for income in the short run with the need to establish a modicum of economic security and independence for their families in the long term in the face of rapidly changing local and global economies. Income, security, *and,* independence thus figure prominently in how these women lead their lives.

For example, many of the women I interviewed had previously worked in factories in the FTZs but reported that low wages, together with poor working conditions and workplace abuse, had forced them to leave—a pattern that is characteristic of FTZ-dependent economies (Ong 1991). Delia, a twenty-two-year-old masseuse, went to work in an apparel factory in the San Pedro FTZ at age eighteen to help support her parents, three younger siblings, and infant son. Her father, a worker in a state-owned sugar factory, had not been paid in nine months. Delia received about 3,000 pesos per month (U.S.$150) for a sixty-hour workweek—a sum that barely covered the family's food budget. Like her fellow workers, Delia was subjected to forced overtime and production quotas and sexual harassment from factory managers. After two years, she quit her job and began giving massages on the beach in Boca Chica. On a good day, Delia could earn 400 pesos for massages without sex, or roughly three times her daily wage at the factory.

Women pointed out to me that, since factory work did not provide a living wage, a viable household required a second wage earner, traditionally a spouse. For this reason, women viewed subproletarian factory work as presupposing a stable relationship with an employed man. Given the high rate of unemployment among Dominican men, this is not only a difficult condition to fulfill; it is also a domestic arrangement that binds a woman's future to a man's economic stability and, very often, control. "To survive in the factories," Delia told me, "you must have a husband. And I don't want one." Thus women often critically assessed the relative merits of domestic and paid-work arrangements in terms of the resulting control that men would hold over their lives whether as husbands, factory bosses, or as "boyfriends" (cf. Safa 1999).

Ivelisse, a twenty-eight-year-old hotel employee who does sex work, explained to me why she had begun an expensive cosmetology course at a private school in the capital:

> I am studying because I want to find a man. A man who is good, is intelligent and can help me make a future. . . . I'm not looking for a man to keep me because, at this point in life, women must have training [*preparación*]. They must have a profession; have their own businesses, their own lives. An ignorant woman thinks that if she finds a man with money she has everything; or, if she finds a foreign man. But that's ignorant because the man may give her nothing and, in that case, the woman must have her own life.

Like Ivelisse, many sex workers cultivate and sustain fluid and multiple links to both the formal and informal economies, which, to varying degrees of success, provide economic security through occupational flexibility. Some women pursue occasional sex work while employed full time in low-paying, service-sector jobs in Boca Chica. Others work in the FTZs surrounding the capital and San Pedro de Macorís and travel to Boca Chica on weekends to earn money to supplement their wages or, oftentimes, to address a financial calamity, such as a family illness, death, or job loss. For these reasons, the category "sex worker" fails to adequately capture the complexity of the relations of power that oppress them or, for that matter, the resourcefulness and fortitude with which they "struggle for life" in Boca Chica.

However, it would be wrong to reduce women's involvement in sex work to an economic survival strategy—to "merely the result of economic logic, rational choices, and free market mechanisms" (van der Veen 2001: 31). Involvement in sex work often enables women to exercise modes of agency and subjectivity, as well as patterns of consumption that they associate with middle-class urbanity and a cosmopolitan lifestyle (cf. Freeman 2000; Ebron 1996). For example, women take pride in having access to new technologies, such as cellular phones, pagers, and email accounts at local "cyber cafes." Exposure and access to current global trends in fashion and popular culture through cable TV stations (e.g., MTV and Spanish-language networks such as *Univisión*), the Internet, and women's magazines (such as *Essence* and *Latina*) were often described to me as important benefits associated with working in tourist areas. This concern with style is demonstrated by the considerable amount of attention and resources that many women devote to beauty products and services.[11] Yanira estimated that she spent on the average of $2,000 pesos (about U.S. $120) per month at the beauty parlor. More generally, women often described their work in the tourist sector as a process of "developing" themselves [*desarrollarse*], the implication being that of becoming modern, savvy, and cosmopolitan. For poor and, especially, racialized women, these cultural practices lay claim to prerogatives that are ordinarily reserved for middle-class women.

Equally significant, women involved in sex work challenge normative gender roles and forms of sexual regulation that enforce heteronormativity. Indeed, many women come to sex work only after having *already* rejected domestic and paid-work arrangements that are exploitative and subject them to abusive male authority, and heterosexual social arrangements that exclude or prohibit non-normative forms of sexuality. For this reason, it is impossible to disassociate the economic strategies pursued by sex workers from the cultural practices through which they contest and transgress heteronormative sex and gender identities. As Judith Butler put it, "both gender and sexuality become part of material life, not only because of the way in which they serve the sexual division of labor, but also because normative gender serves the reproduction of the normative family" (1997: 272).

To be sure, the success with which women are able to pursue these varied forms of struggle—at once economic, social, and semiotic—is conditioned by a wide variety of factors, including familial resources and responsibilities, education, and their perceived racial, class, and ethnic identities, which for sex workers as for others bear on their life chances. Ivelisse, for example, was from an economically stable urban family, a high school graduate, and light-skinned (*trigueña*) by Dominican standards of racial classification. Her life prospects contrasted sharply with those of Delia, born of a poor rural family, uneducated, and darker-skinned (*morena*). Moreover, for all women, sex work involves life-threatening risks of exposure to HIV-AIDS and other STDs, client and police violence, and powerful social stigmas. Nevertheless, women who participate in sex work do so with a critical and well-informed understanding of the interplay between political economy, gender, and sexuality.[12]

This claim contradicts male tourists' interpretations of how sex workers are negotiating their positions within the tourist sector. Many men maintain a dual and contradictory evaluation of women's identity and agency: they are either demonized as "whores," who care only about money, or romanticized as sensual and devoted partners who can be controlled and, for that reason, make ideal wives. The result is a Hegelian-like tension in their accounts between the desire to dominate, on the one hand, and on the other, a desire to sustain the fantasy that it is their masculinity and not their money that is the source of their power. In short, male tourists want women to affirm their desirability as *essentially* men.

A 1995 article published in TSM's Web-based newsletter, titled "White Sands, Blue Skies, Dark Women," wrestles with this seeming paradox:

> There are countries where the women are less expensive, and countries where the brothels are fancier or more conspicuous. . . . But I can't imagine that there are any countries where the women are better in bed than the women of the Dominican Republic. Perhaps it is as simple as this: Dominican women love sex and they love American men. Yes, you have to pay them. Everyone needs to make a living. But once you have paid them, you will begin to feel *as though they paid you* and that they are trying to get their money's worth by trying every possible position and configuration, by having you as many times as they can, and by begging for more. Don't be surprised if they ask you to stay and live with them. (TSM 1995: 5–6; emphasis added)

This fantastic reversal, mimicking the inverted logic of the rapist, denies the agentive quality of women's involvements with male tourists; instead, it argues that the latter's economic power over women is an effect of their *natural* appeal as men, on the one hand, and the unmediated sexual drives of Dominican women on the other. As one male tourist explained to me, "For Dominican women, sex is like breathing." By naturalizing their relationships with sex workers, male tourists deny their coercive character and, in the process, elide the gender, racial, and economic inequalities that make them possible.

Sex workers challenge this naturalization of sex work by insisting on a strict accounting of the value of their labor power and by disrupting the fantasies that tourists hold regarding their "natural" sexuality and the equally naturalized myth of male desirability. For example, Rachel, a part-time hotel employee, told me that she was once invited by a German tourist to spend a week with him at a luxury hotel in La Romana, a resort area east of Boca

Chica. Rachel told the tourist that, if she were to go, he would have to pay her the wages that she would lose from her job and pay her sister to take care of her two children during the trip. The tourist protested, she told me, maintaining that he was in love with her and that the trip itself would cost him a fortune. "I told him," she said, " 'the hotel is *your* business. But you must pay me for my time and for my children.' That is what I told him."

Conclusion

Boca Chica is a key site within a global tourism industry where regulatory norms regarding sex and gender differences are materialized through, as Butler put it, their "forcible reiteration . . . in the service of the consolidation of the heterosexual imperative" (1993: x). The reiterative practices through which these norms are exercised range from the mass-mediated discourses and images produced by men *for* men on the Internet, to the everyday performances of masculinity by men *with* men in the streets, bars, and hotel rooms of Boca Chica. These practices find their coercive force and conditions of possibility in a political economy that positions Dominican women as "natural" subjects of sexual subordination and labor discipline within a global and eminently patriarchal world order. It is the naturalizing function of this ideal of male sexual mastery that accounts for both its reiterative force and its capacity, as a discursive and institutional field, to articulate and lend stability to complex and, oftentimes, mutually antagonistic systems of social hierarchy. As Linda Singer has pointed out, "What increases the ideological potency of sexuality as a mechanism of social control is that regulation ultimately becomes translated into the currency of self-regulation, because sexuality has already been constructed as that which is or belongs to the realm of the private, i.e., as opposed to the social. The regulatory force is represented and enacted through a currency not of coercion but of desire, in a way that encourages its individuation or personalization" (1993: 59).

Nowhere is this power-evasive reduction of the social to the private, and of coercion to putatively self-regulated desire, more sordidly apparent than in the testimonies of sex tourists themselves. In a TSM travel report, a man claiming to have enlisted two women to act as procuresses, opines on this dialectic of power and desire:

> I don't think my two friends have a portfolio of girls—they just go out looking in their town of Andrés and when they see a good looking girl they ask her if she wants to make some pesos. Most times, I believe, they

say, "Sure, why not." Women in the Dominican Republic are very good at sex. It's as simple as that. From the highest born to the lowest, women are taught how to please a man. It's the only power that they have in this culture, so they learn it well. Mao said something like, "power springs from the barrel of a gun." He clearly never met a Dominican female. Of course, if he had, he would have just said to hell with the revolution and gotten a blow job. (TSM 1999: 2)

By obscuring political economy under the sign of the phallus, male sex tourists not only essentialize sex and gender identities; they also eroticize social hierarchy by imagining and experiencing its constituent forms of social power to be personal sources of pleasure. "Why," to paraphrase the writer, "fight a revolution when you can find pleasure dominating a woman?" It is in this sense that the practice of heteronormative masculinity serves at once to depoliticize and articulate hierarchy by actively imagining social inequalities to be *natural* sources of male power and pleasure, on the one hand, and of homosocial bonds and sentiments on the other.

Among white male sex tourists, racial, class, and ethnic distinctions are interpreted and negotiated through this lens of male power and desire. As we have seen, many men view dark skin color as a sign of pastoral simplicity, domesticity, and sensuality, and dark-skinned women are imagined to be uncorrupted by modernity and, above all, by feminism. For others, light skin tones evoke the trope of the exotic, Carmen Miranda-like *mulata,* a well-worn icon of licentious sexuality (see Kutzinski 1993). By contrast, Haitian women are reputed to be assertive and aggressive "professionals" and are viewed as threatening and lacking in feminine qualities. One Canadian man put it to me this way, "The Dominicans and the Haitians are completely different. The Haitians are all hardened pros, and they'll rip you off. The Dominican girls aren't like that. It's not in their culture." The lack of feminine subservience among Haitian women, imagined as a cultural trait, alters the significance of their racial identities, situating the trope of blackness within a symbolic field of danger and rebellion.[13]

Male sex tourism in Boca Chica provides insights into the role that heteronormative masculinity plays in constructing, naturalizing, and eroticizing social hierarchies grounded in a variety of claims about human differences. As a normative ideal and social practice, imperial masculinity transposes power differentials and social distinctions tied to race, class, ethnicity, as well as to gender into the symbolic economy of the heterosexual male body—a homoerotic economy of desire and consumption that finds its structuring principle in the real and imagined subordination of women. To be sure, heterosexual masculinity is neither stable nor monolithic. In the case of the Dominican Republic, it is the complicit exercise of disparate structures of male power by state authorities, global corporations, and foreign and Dominican men that situate Dominican women at the bottom of the global division of labor. Indeed, it is precisely the capacity of heteronormative masculinity to bond men across such differences and eroticize their power that accounts for its peculiar service in the structuring of the global economy.

Notes

I would like to thank the editors of this collection and the reviewers for Duke University Press for their insightful comments, which improved this essay considerably. I would also like to thank Sherry Ortner, Arlene Davila, and Marianell Belliard-Acosta for their helpful comments and suggestions on an earlier version of this essay. I would especially like to thank Milquella Reyes, my research assistant in the Dominican Republic during much of 2001, for her assistance, sharp insights, and support of this project.

1   Based on my experience, the percentage of men of African, Asian, or Hispanic descent participating in Boca Chica's sex tourist industry is relatively insignificant. During my stay in Boca Chica and Andrés, totaling fifteen months during four visits, I encountered no more than two dozen or so African American male tourists. Dominican men, other than those working in the tourist sector, do not frequent the bars, discos, and restaurants in tourist areas. There is, however, a nontourist sex industry that remains discrete from the tourist sector (see Cabezas 1999).

2   Marjolein van der Veen has recently pointed out that much of the literature on prostitution in the radical feminist tradition (e.g., Pateman 1988; Barry 1995) has tended to treat the selling of sexuality as the defining feature of persons engaged in sex work, which results in a reductionist view of the "self." "The selling of sexuality," van der Veen writes, "becomes the defining feature of that person: a sex worker is defined by that particular identity rather than by the multiple, other identities she may have as mother, sister, daughter, artist and so on" (2001:35). I share this view and, for that reason, reject the label "sex worker" as well as the tendency to view sex work either as essentially work or as essentially dehumanizing. See Overall 1992 for a review of the debate over prostitution in feminist theory.

3   See Pringle 1992 and Seidman 1996 for a discussion of the lack of attention given by social scientists to heteronormativity in lived, everyday experience.

4   For example, feminist writers have taken Foucault to task for not only overlooking feminist scholarship but also for failing to attend to the specificity of masculine power in his genealogical studies. Irene Diamond and Lee Quimby write, "Although his analyses remind us that in contemporary society power is not monolithically held by men, feminists have demonstrated that the kind of power that Foucault associates with the sovereign's rights of death—a power operating primarily within kinship systems that is 'essentially a right of seizure: of things, time, bodies, and ultimately life itself'—remains vested in individual men and men as a group" (1998: xiv).

5   Cabezas (1998; 1999) and Brennan (1998), working on the north coast of the Dominican Republic, provide accounts of heterosexual and bisexual male sex workers, popularly referred to as "Sanky-Pankies," a word play on hanky panky (see also de Moya et al. 1992). Male sex workers were probably more active in Boca Chica than it appeared to me as a heterosexual male researcher. Male "guides" with whom I spoke denied that they exchanged sex for money through their interactions with tourists but, nonetheless, took pride in the "gifts" (regalos) that they received from both women and men. See Kempadoo 1999: 24–25 for an excellent discussion of how constructions of gender in the Caribbean differentially figure the identities available to men and women engaged in sex work.

6   See Cabezas 1998; 1999 for a discussion of the complex and highly ambiguous legal status of prostitution in the Dominican Republic.

7   The editors of this volume alerted me to the potential for vignettes, such as this one, to incite a "voyeuristic complicity" between the reader's gaze and the gaze of male tourists. This is a very real possibility for those on the "constitutive inside" of heteronormativity, where I must position myself. In the spirit of this chapter I suggest that heteronormative males *are* complicit and, for that reason, the voyeur's position is potentially more reflexive and disruptive of the gaze than that of a more "detached [male] observer."

8   *Tigre* is a term used by Dominicans to refer to men who display a range of characteristics, such as womanizing, sexism, hustling, as well as criminal behavior. Although the meaning of the term varies by context, I most often heard it used to refer to men who abuse women or are involved in crime, and the word conveys the sense of predatory behavior.

9   O'Connell Davidson and Sanchez Taylor point out that sex tourists reproduce a Western travel discourse that imagines an opposition between a "civilized West" and "barbarous Other." They write: "In 'civilized' countries, only 'bad' women become prostitutes (they refuse the constraints civilization places upon 'good' women in favor of earning 'easy money'), but in the Third World (a corrupt and lawless place where people exist in a state of nature), 'nice girls' may be driven to prostitution in order to survive ('they have to do it because they've got kids' or 'they're doing it for their families'). In the West, 'nice girls' are protected and supported by their menfolk, but in the Third World, 'uncivilized' Other men allow (or even demand that) their womenfolk enter prostitution. In interviews, Western male sex tourists contrast their own generosity, humanity, and chivalry against the 'failings' of local men, who are imagined as feckless, faithless, wife beaters, and pimps. Even as prostitute users, Other men are fantasized as inferior moral beings who cheat and mistreat the 'girls' " (1999: 43–44).

10 Jonathan Rutherford, writing on the relationship between English masculinity and the culture of imperialism, described the upper-middle-class Victorian ideal male as a "perpetual adolescent." He writes, "The figure of the boy in all the great adventure stories of the era represented the repressed longing of these men for all they had been forced to renounce—maternal love, their own bodies, sexual desire" (1997: 27). Although this is a tenuous comparison, male tourists in Boca Chica do celebrate and describe their homosocial bonds and activities in ways that stress an adolescentlike freedom from responsibility (e.g., jobs, families, and ethical norms) as well as an unbridled pursuit of adventure and pleasure. I have heard more than one man describe being in Boca Chica as "like a kid in a candy store."

11 Beauty-parlor services that were very much in demand during my stay between December 2000 and August 2001 included hair braiding, extension weaving, color tinting and streaking, as well as manicures and fingernail decoration.

12 There is considerable HIV-AIDS awareness among both sex workers and tourists though it is difficult, of course, to determine the degree to which this awareness guides practice. On various occasions I have overheard sex workers discuss HIV-AIDS transmission with considerable sophistication. Condoms are prominently displayed in *colmados*, or general stores, as well as in street vendor stalls and, from what I gather, sex workers insist that they be used.

13 As noted above, white men constitute the overwhelming majority of sex tourists who visit Boca Chica. To be sure, the specific configuration of social distinctions and valences that adhere to constructions of white heteronormativity—a diverse category in and of itself—differ in significant ways from the masculine identities performed by say, African American or Puerto Rican tourists. Although a full treatment of this topic is beyond the scope of this chapter, I will provide one example that demonstrates how race inflects the heteronormative posture of male tourists. I spent one evening at the Zanzibar Cafe with three African American men from Chicago. They were all TSM members and, although they socialized occasionally with white American men at Jimmy's Bar and Grill, they tended to spend most of their time among themselves. Curtis, a forty-four-year-old police officer, had come to Boca Chica with his nephew and a friend from the job. Late in the evening, when his nephew asked whether he intended to take a hostess back to his hotel, Curtis replied, "Man, these girls are too dark for me. They're country broads who came over here from Haiti. I didn't come all the way here to bang no black chick." His words are disturbing but their meaning is clear. From Curtis's perspective, race and geography carry values different from those that they do for white men. Dark skin signals proximity, affiliation, and perhaps rural backwardness, rather than the idealized and eroticized landscape of *el campo*. Racial distinctions do figure in how African American sex tourists construct and exercise their masculinity, but they support it by different fantasies of sexual difference and control. White men wield a form of "epidermic capital," in their relations with Dominicans and Haitians that is unavailable, if not repugnant, to African American men.

11. Pulp Fictions of Indigenism

Alcida Rita Ramos

An American Orientalism

Were I to write in Portuguese (or in Spanish, had I the skills), I would be hard pressed to justify my use of the concept of indigenism. While in Latin American countries *indigenismo* invariably means state policy or indigenous organizing against national pressures (see, for instance, Jackson's 1989 characterization of "self-conscious indigenism"), what I wish to convey with indigenism is much more than this. The fact that the word in English has no such connotation helps me delimit my field of interest. As I interpret it, indigenism comes closer to being a sort of American orientalism, or, in Coronil's conception, "occidentalism," that is, "representational practices whose effect is to present non-Western peoples as the Other of a Western self" (Coronil 1997: xi). In the specific case of Brazil, indigenism is clearly an ideological apparatus that includes not only state policies but especially the vast repertoire of images, attitudes, and actions that both non-Indians and Indians have produced along the history of the country's interethnic front.

The present analysis is part of a larger project whose main purpose is to understand the Brazilian nation by means of the representations it has made of its Indians in the last 500 years. The multiplicity of these representations and of their authors renders the study of indigenism a very complex and seemingly unending enterprise, for wherever we turn, we stumble on its manifestations, be they capital events such as legislation declaring the In-

My thanks to Roberto Cardoso de Oliveira, Myriam Jimeno, Bill Fisher, and especially Donald Moore for their encouraging and valuable comments.

dian "relatively incapable," or quotidian, plain, and apparently inconsequential remarks such as that of an urban taxi driver confessing that his Indian grandmother had been "caught with a lasso." In short, "what the media write and broadcast, novelists create, missionaries reveal, human rights activists defend, anthropologists analyze, and Indians deny or corroborate about *the Indian* contributes to an ideological edifice that takes the 'Indian issue' as its building block" (Ramos 1998: 6). The country's kaleidoscopic capacity to produce new interethnic designs on a deep and lasting structure appears to be inexhaustible. Among the components of such a kaleidoscope is the widespread practice of essentialization both on the part of the majority population and of the Indians themselves. Culture, whether in its local manifestations or as a generic template for Indianness (or "indigenousness," as in Bowen 2000: 13) has wide currency in the fields of indigenism. I have selected four contexts in which the processes of naturalization of the Indians and essentialization of their "culture"—yes, in the singular!—are particularly evident, providing us with a suitable framework to discuss the theoretical and political implications of these processes.

The vignettes sketched below are taken from Brazil's civil life, some routine, others more spectacular, where Indians and non-Indians engage in capillary relations the content of which is rarely made explicit. The notion of capillarity is particularly apt to characterize the close encounters of protagonists who speak different ideological languages and yet engage in Leachian ritual situations in which tacit misunderstandings are shared by all participants to each one's benefit (Leach 1954: 102, 286). They are capillary relations also in Foucault's sense of power microphysics (1979b: 179–91) where blatant coercion is improper because it is superfluous. Another, but connected, sense of capillary relations can be glossed with the help of a dictionary definition: "of or pertaining to the apparent attraction or repulsion between a liquid and a solid, observed in capillarity" (*Webster's Encyclopedic Unabridged Dictionary of the English Language*).

What happens in the cracks of Western rationality is as revealing, or more, of the ways in which otherness is constructed and lived. The farcical dramas, wild mysticisms, and mixed-up ordeals focused on here are examples of phenomena pertaining to the tension generated by the attraction and repulsion of opposites that thrive at the margins of Western logic, and for this very reason, candidly reveal unexpected facets of interethnic relations that formal conventions are designed to conceal. In this sense, the pulp side of interethnicity is just another layer of bricks set on the extraordinary ideological edifice of indigenism. The material chosen for analysis evokes the subterranean, unconscious phenomena associated with Freudian slips whenever one says x while meaning y. Manifest as they are in collectivities rather than in individuals, such expressions of the national "unsaid" have an immense potential to unveil what might otherwise pass as mere *faits divers*, curiosities if not "infelicities" of the exotic (Mason 1998).

Episode 1

The material used here is drawn from nearly twenty newspaper clippings dating from 1988 to 1996. They display photographs of famous people in Brazil being "crowned" with feather headdresses by indigenous men and women. Among the celebrities are soccer players Romário and Ronaldo; the First Lady, Ruth Correa Leite Cardoso; former president Fernando Collor de Mello; presidential candidate Luiz Inácio Lula da Silva; an assortment of ministers, governors, and congressmen. In the 1980s and 1990s, practically anyone who aspired to be someone in Brazil was photographed either receiving or dodging an Indian headdress. So much public attention dispensed to an indigenous object is due to its reputation for bringing bad luck to non-Indian bearers. Associated with the item are macaw feathers, the macaw being an "ill omen in folk belief," according to a television newswoman (Marcia Peltier Pesquisa, *Rede Manchete*, 23 December 1997). The mass media may not have created this belief, but they have certainly amplified it, particularly at peaks of political effervescence. Taking no chances, public figures such as former President José Sarney admit their fear and never allowed any headdress to be placed on their heads. Some Indians and Indian sympathizers rebuff all this as "Whiteman's" superstition—"the whites always mix everything up," says Shavante leader Mário Juruna (*Correio Braziliense*, 12 June 1988: 5)—and respond by saying that it is the "Whiteman" himself who is the ill omen for the Indians (*Correio Braziliense*, 26 September 1988: 8). Pro-Indian Congressman Tadeu França repudiated the belief and added a possible explanation: "Throughout our history the Indians have become specialists in the art of losing. Perhaps for this reason, in the "Whiteman's" unconscious, the feather headdress represents the suffering of a race in extinction, and the whites fear the same destiny" (*Correio Braziliense*, 12 June 1988: 5).

Nevertheless, this has not deterred many an Indian from carrying on this newly invented interethnic tradition. Quite the opposite, they show themselves perfectly willing, in fact, rather eager to play the game of the "headdress curse." Adding fuel to the belief, a list of misfortunes that have beset famous heads is cited as evidence of the artifact's occult powers and, by extension, those of the Indians' themselves: Tancredo Neves, nominated president in 1985, died of septicemia just before his inauguration; Fernando Collor de Mello, elected president in 1989, was ousted two years later; Ulysses Guimarães, an immensely influential congressman, disappeared at sea in a helicopter crash on Columbus Day in 1992; Luiz Inácio Lula da Silva, several times presidential candidate, has never been elected. A 1995 cartoon depicts Luís Eduardo Magalhães, then president of the House of Representatives, wearing an indigenous necklace while turning away from a headdress. Says the caption: "Luís Eduardo Magalhães . . . did all he could to avoid having the headdress brought by a group of Indians put on his head. According to political folklore, it brings bad luck" (Folha de São Paulo, 8 April 1995, sec. 1, p. 4). A promising politician in his early forties, Magalhães died of a heart attack three years later. Even the statue of Justice that sits in front of the Supreme Court in Brasília was crowned by Indians during a demonstration for land demarcation in 1996 (Ramos 1998: 262). Nothing has yet happened to the statue, but it continues to be as blind as ever.

The self-fulfilling prophecy of the popular belief in the hidden powers of the Indians, reminiscent of the Putumayo historical miasmas described by Taussig (1987), is not limited to the fate of public people but can extend to their works as well. Let us see an example from Brasília.

Episode 2

In the 1980s, the Bank of Brazil provided funds for the construction of a monumental building to serve as the National Indian Museum, located in Brasília, the seat of the Federal District and the nation's capital. Oscar Niermeyer, the famous architect who had built Brasília and a myriad of modernist edifices the world over, was chosen for the job. He sought inspiration in the traditional round houses of various indigenous peoples and, turning thatch into concrete, erected the monument in the appropriate location known as the Monumental Axis. But, on gazing at his own achievement, even before completion, Niemeyer concluded that the construction was just too beautiful and large for the Indians. Together with the District's governor, Niemeyer then proclaimed his masterpiece as the future house of the city's Museum of Modern Art. Speaking for the Indians, the governor justified the move by saying that "the Indians don't want to be the object of folkloric contemplation, but rather of study and respect on the part of the community [i.e. the majority society]" (*Correio Braziliense,* 5 June 1988: 39). The consolation prize for the Indians was to have their museum built on the campus of the University of Brasília, "for the better knowledge of anthropology students" (Cunha 1988: 3). The timing was evocative, as the new constitution had just been approved and the Indians were in town celebrating their modest victories. A news item describes the occasion:

> The indigenous nations interrupted commemorations for their gains in the Constitution in order to register a loss. The Brasília Indian Museum, which was to be inaugurated on the 15th, will be transformed into the Brasília Museum of Modern Art by suggestion of architect Oscar Niemeyer, supported by the governor of the Federal District, José Aparecido de Oliveira. (*Jornal do Brasil,* 6 June 1988)

The initial reaction of a few Indians was somewhat fatalistic. The same newspaper added:

> Shaman Prepori Kajabi, who performed the shamanic ritual at the National Congress to insure that indigenous rights be recognized in the Constitution, repeated the ritual this weekend at the unfinished Indian Museum and concluded: "museum is a thing of the Whiteman and the Indians shouldn't fight for what has always been the Whiteman's." (*Jornal do Brasil,* 6 June 1988)

But then came the indigenous curse on Niemeyer's concrete fantasy. As a dismayed Indian sympathizer put it,

> Many artists swore never to set foot on the MAM [Museum of Modern Art] or have their works among its assets because the curse cast on it by the Indians Preporê and Sapain, when they evoked the Spirit of the Waters, is a permanent threat to both believers and non-believers and not yet undone. (Fonteles 1989: 6)

Ten years later, no significant art works, in number or quality, had been assembled to inhabit the new museum that is rapidly decaying under the relentless downpours of Brasília's rainy season. On the lawned expanses of the stately capital still stands Niemeyer's folly, a spellbound semiruin that is both an eyesore and "eyewitness" to yet another act of official disrespect for Brazilian Indians. Recently, in a true fit of absentmindedness, the government reverted its decision and gave the derelict museum back to the Indians.

So far we have seen how interethnic imagery is constructed and naturalized within the limits of a specific country. But what happens in Brazil is not so very different from the WASP variations on the Indian theme or the Western Apache variations on the "Whiteman" theme that Basso (1979), Stedman (1982), Strong (1996), and the authors in the collection suggestively titled *Dressing in Feathers* (Bird 1996) have described for the United States. But the process of essentialization is not confined to the nation-state. There is also a host of media-alluring indigenous prodigies catering to international audiences. The following episodes, although sharing features and protagonists, have different agendas, messages, and results. Both happened in Brazil, but part of their importance had to do with the massive presence of foreigners. As a matter of focus, I will not fully explore the institutional importance and consequences of these events but will limit myself to aspects directly relevant to the issue of essentialism.

Episode 3

In June 1989, the old town of Altamira in the northern state of Pará had its five days of fame. The occasion was a mammoth gathering called by members of nine Kayapó communities to protest against the Brazilian government's plans for the building of a series of hydroelectric dams along the Xingu River. This megaproject threatened to flood the lands of eleven indigenous peoples. Representatives of 24 indigenous groups, government officials, 300 environmentalists, members of nongovernmental organizations (NGOs), the Catholic Church, anthropologists, and other pro-Indian people flocked into humble Altamira. In all, about three thousand people attended the gigantic rally on the outskirts of town. In turn, a portion of the majority pro-dam population paraded on horseback, thus heightening the sense of nervousness that normally pervades interethnic relations in the region. On the first day, June 20, there were about 100 journalists from Brazil and abroad. On the last day, June 24, the foreign press alone included about 150 people.

Running parallel to the hard core political events involving Indian leaders and government officials, show business personalities, such as the English rock star Sting and Brazilian singer Milton Nascimento, added excitement to the already electrified atmosphere. Trying mimetically to mingle with Indian men and women in full ceremonial regalia, bands of ecstatic young women speaking an assortment of European languages, clad in minimal tropical outfits, body paint on face and limbs, danced and smiled at the cameras in a state of grace as though living some New Age energizing fantasy (O'Connor 1993).

Some momentous scenes were inscribed in word and image and widely circulated. The one that most impressed the public showed a middle-aged Kayapó woman in the act of waving a machete so as to touch the cheeks of the director of the state energy company. Captured from various angles, her gesture traveled around the world and fascinated TV watchers. Oblivious to ethnographic realities, some even suggested she should be elected the Woman of the Year for her courage in defying a powerful man. That, however, has more to do with culture than with courage:

> The first Meeting of the Xingu Indigenous Nations gained a dramatic dimension on the morning of the 21st when the Kayapó Indian, Tuira, rose from the audience and put her machete on the face of the Eletronorte director, José Antônio Muniz Lopes, who was trying to justify the construction of the Kararaô dam. Both the Eletronorte director and the emissary of the federal government, Fernando Cézar Mesquita, went pale the moment the machete cut the air a few inches from Muniz Lopes' face. Leader Paulinho Paiakan immediately explained that it wasn't a war motion, but simply a ritual gesture by means of which Kayapó women express indignation. (Centro de Documentação e Informação [CEDI] 1991: 335)

Equally spectacular was the arrival of Paiakan, the major promoter of the event:

> One hundred Brazilian and foreign journalists watched the majestic arrival of the Indian leader. Paiakan descended from the Bandeirante aircraft dressed in shorts and feather headdress, adorned with ritual paint and displaying the dressed wound on his belly [from recent appendicitis surgery]. He started crying as he stepped on the ground. Many of the warriors who protected him from the journalists' hysteria were also crying. Braced by leaders of the eleven Kayapó villages who came to meet him, the leader slowly crossed the lines of warriors greeting acquaintances. The scene left the foreigners spellbound. (CEDI 1991: 331)

For ethnographic clarification, ritual weeping is part of the arrival ceremonies in several indigenous societies in Central Brazil (see, for instance, Wagley 1977).

Another powerful incident occurred when the Eletronorte director announced that the name Kararaô would no longer be given to the dam because it meant an aggression to Kayapó culture. "Paiakan listened closely to his promise to change the name and also not to use indigenous names in his power plants. Then [Paiakan] asked the warriors to show him what Kararaô meant. A group of warriors got up and in the middle of the stadium started singing furiously and performing a war dance" (CEDI 1991: 335). The apotheotic closing session had a Kayapó leader displaying a copy of the Brazilian constitution, singer Milton Nascimento saluting the Indians, and Benedita da Silva, a popular black member of congress, wearing a feather headdress. The foreign journalists covering the event "seemed entranced" (CEDI 1991: 335).

With its manifold functions, the gathering highlighted the phenomenon of an international market of exoticism as manifested in the interplay between nonindigenous consumers and indigenous producers of cultural resources as commodities. It profusely displayed both sides of the same coin: on the one hand, avid white audiences whose close proximity with "real" Indians served either as inspiration for mystical pursuits or simply as cheap thrills; on the other, equally avid "real" Indians turning their cultural capital into political muscle against undesirable state policies. Both sides reinforced each other's cravings by parading their affected selves under the enthralled lenses of the media.

The Altamira event is one of those phenomena that, in unfolding their complexities, make social analysis both a delight and a challenge. One might dare call it a total social fact of interethnic politics. For there we find, on the non-Indian side, Altamira exposing the recurrent mixed messages: the Indians as obstacles to development who need to be fought back or persuaded to make room for progress, and the Indians as both nature keepers and virtuous victims of civilization, model cultures for a more enlightened West.

As for the Indians, we see their keen instrumentalization of cultural primordialities, their shrewd political sagacity, and their tremendous organizing drive. For instance, it was not by chance that the Kayapó chose the end of June to hold the meeting. As Terence Turner (1991a) explains, the Altamira gathering was planned to coincide with the final phase of the feast associated with the harvest of new maize, the most important intervillage ceremony. The Kayapó villagers, having already performed the first two phases of the ritual, were eager to assemble at Altamira as they would have done back home. That was the astute way the organizers found to motivate so many Indians, most of them monolingual, to come together for a series of political events that otherwise might not have caught their interest. On the other hand, the experience leaders like Paiakan had accumulated in their previous contacts with multilateral agencies such as the World Bank and various NGOs in Brazil and abroad was converted into financial aid to carry out the meeting. A well-regarded personality among environmentalists, Paiakan became known as a conservationist concerned with the future of the rain forest. After Altamira he was awarded the United Nations' Global 500 prize, the prize from the Society for a Better World, and was the subject of a *Parade* magazine 1992 cover story under the title "A Man Who Would Save the World." The irony of it is that Paiakan was one of the Kayapó who amassed substantial wealth with the selling of hardwood and royalties from gold miners who operated in their reservation. In the last episode we will see a dramatic reversal in Paiakan's fortunes. One year he was a hero; the next year he was a monster.

Episode 4

The 1992 United Nations Conference on Environment and Development, also known as the Rio Summit, congregated a significant number of indigenous representatives from many countries. On an improvised camping ground by the Guanabara Bay, they organized the Global Forum, a series of events independent of the official debates that went on at a posh hotel in an expensive part of Rio de Janeiro. As was the case in Altamira, the Indians, now from the world over, attracted the attention of cult followers, a multitude of journalists, and the public in general and stole the show from their official counterpart. What interests me here, however, is not the Summit per se but an occurrence that took place thousands of miles away in Amazonia, but which echoed stridently in Rio de Janeiro.

On the second day of the Summit, while Paiakan was being expected at the Global Forum, news broke that he had raped a non-Indian girl during a drinking spree on his ranch near the town of Redenção, adjacent to the Kayapó reservation. The case was immediately swept up in a wave of sensationalism that lasted for months. Accusations of savagery and cannibalism were hurled at Paiakan and his wife, who was reported as having inflicted severe physical harm on the girl. Paiakan became the object of pornographic jokes and his name turned into a household word overnight. *Veja,* one of Brazil's magazines of wide circulation, had a cover story with an enlarged photograph of Paiakan's face and the headline "The Savage: The Leader and Symbol of Environmental Purity Tortures and Rapes a White Student, and then Flees to his Tribe" (10 June 1992). *Veja* and most newspapers had no qualms in condemning Paiakan well before the trial. He was declared guilty until proved innocent. The case also raised a major polemic as to Paiakan's imputability. As an Indian he was legally deemed "relatively incapable" because indigenous people are legally presumed to be socially and culturally unequipped to operate in the national society as normal citizens. Hence, they are officially wards of the state. While his wife, who speaks no Portuguese, was considered to be unquestionably "primitive" (Ramos 1998: 54–55), opinions were divided about Paiakan: some charged him with full responsibility because he was de facto emancipated from indigenous special status—after all, he was a rich Indian who owned a ranch and a car. Others maintained that, as an Indian, he didn't know any better. On the one hand, although he knew what he was doing, he was driven by a "savage instinct," as *Veja* put it; on the other, he was a helpless example of indigenous ineptitude for civic life. In either case, public opinion divested Paiakan of human agency. Among the tangled arguments for and against Paiakan's imputability was the demand of a lawyer from the National Indian Foundation (Fundação Nacional do Índio, FUNAI) that only "an anthropological report showing that Paiakan was an Indian integrated into civilization [could] make him accountable to a penal process" (Ramos 1998: 54). Surprising as it may seem coming from a lawyer, this statement has no basis, considering that the Indians are as imputable as any Brazilian with regard to penal responsibility (Carneiro da Cunha 1992).

Paiakan was acquitted in 1994 on grounds of insufficient evidence. But a new trial in 1999 condemned him to six years in jail, after which his lawyers looked desperately for an anthropological expert willing to report on Paiakan's civil incapacity. In their view, there was no problem in trading his freedom for his agency.

This *cause célèbre* triggered a flood of arguments that went beyond the case itself. Anti-indigenous sectors exploited the unfairness of giving special treatment to members of minorities and thus creating a double standard among the citizenry. *Veja* magazine, for instance, complained that the environmentalists' "difficulty in accepting the criminal side of Paiakan comes from the recent mental habit according to which it is correct to always relativize the inconvenient behavior of minorities" (quoted in ISA 1996: 412). Journalist Janer Cristaldo "demanded that Paiakan be punished, and questioned what he calls juridical privileges of Brazilian Indians. According to Cristaldo, 'the Indian doesn't work, doesn't produce, he simply devastates'"

(ISA 1996: 417). Attorney Miguel Reale Júnior asserted that Paiakan was no longer unaccountable and should go on trial for rape and attempted murder. He added: "we must put a stop to the myth of the naturalist Indian; from the moment he left his tribe and became acculturated, he stopped being an Indian to become a civilized mixed blood" (quoted in ISA 1996: 413).

These opinions appeal to the feeble idea that democracy means equal treatment to all, regardless of whether all are seamlessly equal in a society as grossly unequal as in Brazil. Thus used, the concept of democracy enters the realm of those inexhaustible symbols that are always open to conflicting interpretations (Ricoeur 1978: 242–65), depending on the position being defended. Supporters of the indigenous cause were concerned that the negative repercussions of the scandal might be used by anti-Indian interests to undermine indigenous rights. The accusation against Paiakan could become a convenient argument for the " 'anti-environmentalist lobby' that opposes the demarcation of indigenous lands," feared Sydney Possuelo, FUNAI's president at the time (ISA 1996: 413). The minister of foreign affairs, Celso Lafer, stated that "the Brazilian government was worried about the publicity over the crime attributed to Paiakan and feared that the matter might be exploited to jeopardize the struggle of the Indians" (Folha de São Paulo, 10 June 1992, sec. 1, p. 14). From the Rio Summit, the environmentalist congressman Fábio Feldman declared: "At this moment when we are fighting for the rights of the Indians, doubt has been shed on the whole struggle for the preservation of Indian nations and the environment. I think journalism in Brazil should be more responsible" (Folha de São Paulo, 9 June 1992, sec. 1, p. 10). From London, Stephen Cory, director of Survival International, blamed Anita Roddick, the owner of the Body Shop cosmetic chain, for the Paiakan scandal. According to him, she "put too much power in the hands of a single individual" when she chose Paiakan's community as the center of her operations for collecting raw materials. Cory concluded that Paiakan's alleged crime was a "serious drawback" to the protection of indigenous rights (Seidl 1992, sec. 1, p. 10). Behind the common feeling of indignation over the treatment given to indigenous peoples, these testimonies, like their opponents, also expose the interests behind their authors: the FUNAI "guardian" of the Indians is anxious about having his role—demarcation of indigenous lands—undercut, the foreign office minister fears undue publicity, the environmentalist identifies defense of Indians with defense of environment, and the NGO director chides his old foe, the "green" entrepreneur. Thus brimming with intense meanings, the Paiakan case, particularly in its association with the environmentalist megaevent that was going on at the Rio Summit, becomes a veritable laboratory for observing the birth of what Latour (1993: 11) would call a hybrid or quasi-object, namely, the Indian as a combination of human-made and natural components. It is the naturalization of the Indian in its fullest expression.

What is there in common between episode 1 (in fact, an ongoing affair) where the Indians are extensions of spooky raw nature; episode 2 where Indians are carriers of evil forces; episode 3 where Indians cultivate exotic marvels; and episode 4 where Indians are unduly protected as wild creatures? Among other similarities, they all point in one direction: the fabrication of a metonymic bond between Indians and untamed nature.

The ambivalence that Brazilian society displays toward indigenous peoples is manifested in a recurrent pendular movement between distance and proximity. While there are national voices that claim that Brazilians are underdeveloped because we have Indians in our backyard, there are also those who affirm that we are a special nation precisely because we coexist with the Indians' wisdom and purity. These clashing conceptions bear, of course, no relationship to the realities of indigenous life. They are fabrications that serve different interests and apply only within certain conjunctures. In this sense the Indian is a product of non-Indian ideological engineering. Part nature, part artifact, the Indian provides the nation with a reservoir of arguments that justify positions as different as those just mentioned. As the Brazilians' privileged others, the Indians epitomize what Coronil attributes to occidentalism for bringing out "into the open their genesis in asymmetrical relations of power, including the power to obscure their genesis of inequality, to sever their historical connections, and thus to present as the internal and separate attributes of bounded entities what are in fact historical outcomes of connected peoples" (Coronil 1997: 14).

The metonymic association of Indians with nature is further motivated by another ambivalence—that of Brazil with its tropical geography. On the one hand, it is praised as the blessed land where anything grows without effort. On the other, it is an earthly inferno of pests and diseases, inappropriate for the blooming of a higher civilization. The country's sociohistorical record abounds in statements that defend either position (Leite 1992). No wonder the Indian-nature link is so strong in the minds of most Brazilians. While for some, Indians can be as unwieldy as the tropics, for others they are as indispensable as the proverbial "lungs of the world," an epithet the unpolished ecological imagination has attributed to the Amazon forest.

If Indians are partly nature, partly manmade, what does their culture consist of for themselves and for their alleged creators? Here we enter the realm of essentialism properly speaking.

Culture as Political Act

A 1995 issue of *Current Anthropology* (volume 39, number 1) was dedicated to the culture concept and problems of essentialism. Notable among the articles is Stolcke's analysis (1995) of what she calls "cultural fundamentalism," the truculent intolerance for different modes of life. Now rampant in Western Europe, this new form of social and political oppression of immigrants from poor countries has replaced the biological arguments of racism. By freezing alien cultures as immutable entities, cultural fundamentalism erects a barrier of incommensurability between the immigrants and the citizens of the receiving countries.

Stolcke's article is an excellent analysis of the new European ideology of inequality and very inspiring as a lead to examine other situations. I am inspired to follow a course that Stolcke did not take and cover ground that some of her commentators explicitly missed, that is, the view from the other side. One purpose of this essay is to show what this "other side" has to say and do about the intricate process of representations, misrepresentations, and counterrepresentations of itself. The very significant differences between immigrants in Western Europe and indigenous peoples in Brazil notwithstanding, a few lessons can be drawn from the case explored by Stolcke.

One of these lessons goes back to the polemic around the concept of culture. Culture as fixed essence has been the concern of many anthropologists in the past decade (Thomas 1991, Abu-Lughod 1991). Fearing the political consequences for minority groups, culture experts have even suggested the banning of the culture concept altogether. Two whole issues of *Current Anthropology* (the aforementioned volume 39, number 1, 1995, and the supplement of volume 40, 1999) are dedicated to scrutinizing the practical effects of the concept both on anthropology and on the world at large. One argument for abandoning the concept of culture is that it has been appropriated by the public at large and contaminated with political ingredients that are detrimental to the powerless. But, as Hannerz argues, to withdraw now from the century-long effort of propagating the ethical and political merits of the anthropological concept of culture and "dramatically turn around and attempt to persuade [our] audiences to reject it, too" would amount to, at the very least, a loss of credibility. If, for fear of unsuitable appropriation, we started eliminating concepts, soon we would be wordless, gagged hostages to whatever forces made use of our intellectual production. Furthermore, the conviction that anthropology turns natives into irrelevant exotica, forever caught in the prison house of frozen traditions, and thus hands them over to Western domination runs the risk of (a) attributing quasi-demiurge powers to the anthropologist, as if the natives had no will of their own; and (b) taking cultural differences to be political weaknesses in a globalized world.

On the basis of my experience with an indigenous inner world (Ramos 1995) and with the nationwide politics of contact in Brazil (Ramos 1998), I disagree with both implications. I also aspire to help deflate the anthropological ego and persuade the West that cultural diversity is not only good to think but, most importantly, indispensable for putting the West in proper perspective, and for the very sustainability of humankind. In this sense, I am still with Hannerz, who continues to be confident that the concept of culture allows anthropologists to transmit to lay audiences the opulence contained in "meanings and practices acquired (in varied ways) in social life," the "potential for human diversity," the value of contributing "to a public conversation," and the possibility of making "better use of such intellectual authority as we may have accumulated" (1999: 19).

The irony pointed out by Sahlins should not be lost on us: in the past, anthropologists bemoaned the vanishing of native cultures exactly when anthropology was ready to use the full potential of the culture concept. Now that the natives themselves seized culture as a political asset, anthropologists want to abandon it as a pernicious concept. Suffering from "epistemological hypochondria," anthropology, Sahlins argues, "has been seized by a post-modern panic about the very existence of the culture concept.... Everybody has a culture; only the anthropologists question it" (1997: 137; my translation). In indigenous hands, the culture concept, like the Latin alphabet, becomes an important tool to mark their differences from majority societies. Once in command of the technology of writing, the Indians use it to their own purposes. The same happens with culture (Turner 1991b). They have no qualms in instrumentalizing certain cultural features they know will impress the whites, regardless of whether such features are part of their own traditions, are borrowings from other peoples, or are newly created. Consider, for instance, the publicity that surrounded some Kayapó men during the big forest fires in the northern Brazilian state of Roraima in 1998. About half the state was on fire under the bewildered gaze of the world while the government was impotent to control the blaze. After weeks of near panic in the nation and beyond, two Kayapó men, stimulated by an official of the National Indian Foundation, flew to Roraima and performed shamanic rituals to induce rainfall. The next day a downpour began to extinguish the flames. The press wasted no time in promoting the supernatural powers of the Kayapó and, once again, the Indians were in the country's folkloric limelight. One interesting detail: shamanism is not a traditional feature of Kayapó culture. But who, apart from anthropologists and the Kayapó themselves, would doubt that *pajelança* (Portuguese for shamanism, derived from the Tupian word *payé*, usually translated as "shaman") is an Indian thing? Or take the megaevent into which the 1987–88 constitutional assembly was transformed when hundreds of Indians from various parts of the country descended on the National Congress in Brasília to influence the congressmen's decisions. Among them were groups of people from the Northeast, long ago stripped of traditional cultural diacritics and, in most cases, of their own languages. In an effort to affirm their Indianness not always evident from their physical appearance, they entered the capital city's political stage wearing a bricolage of feather skirts and headdresses of undefined cultural origin but fitting a popular stereotype. Thus clad, they made headlines about indigenous rights alongside the gorgeously attired Kayapó.

Strategic essentialism is not limited to matters related to collective empowerment and may not even be limited to the instrumentalization of one's own culture. It can also serve personal aspirations. Consider the following case, as it was described to me by a former employee of the National Indian Foundation, FUNAI. A woman from a highly mixed indigenous group in the Northeast married a Shavante man and planned to visit his family in the Center-West. In preparation to meet her in-laws, she went to the Indian art shop at the FUNAI headquarters in Brasilia. From the collection of artifacts on display she picked choice pieces of dress and adornment from various indigenous groups around the country. She then wrote a formal letter to FUNAI asking them to cover the cost of her "Indian Tribal Uniform." She justified her request with the following, to her, irrefutable argument: how could she present herself to her husband's obviously indigenous people dressed as she was in Western clothes? Short of mathematical formulae, practically any concept is open to different, even contradictory readings. As with the concept of democracy, essentialism, exoticism, and even incommensurability can be turned around to mean the exact opposite of what one might expect. Conflicting interpretations very often occur in a context of conflicting political or ethical positions when misunderstandings, either unintended or induced, fuel sometimes portentous wars of ideas. Take Lévy-Bruhl, the early French philosopher-anthropologist who was crucified by his peers and posterity for having proposed the near impossibility of Westerners to penetrate the cultural world of primitive peoples, as the mental principles in both types of society were so distinct that one should not assume that Western logic was adequate to apprehend other types of logic. In a world where being radically different has invariably meant being radically inferior, Lévy-Bruhl's theory was stamped as outright value-laden and ethnocentric nonsense. Actually, he was proposing a lesson of humility to anthropologists who took for granted that the human essence is the same everywhere, *ergo* perfectly grasped by Westerners, and that primitives were simply imperfect versions of Victorian society.

Introducing welcome inflections to the usually intransigent anti-essentialist position, some voices have reminded us that in human affairs absolute truths are neither appropriate nor desirable. "There may be possibilities of virtue in incommensurability," declares Fitzpatrick. "Not all notions of incommensurability are founded on the mutual hostility and oppression that typify cultural fundamentalism" (1995: 14). Debates around the evils of essentialism might be deflated with similar ponderings. Hale, for one, rejects the Manichean division between "essentialism" and "constructivism," which he regards as perhaps "useful to track theoretical allegiances within the academy, but . . . is insufficiently attentive to the range of ways that 'essentialist' precepts are woven into political consciousness and practice, and the highly variable material consequences that result" (1997: 578). In fact, he doubts that the constructivism-essentialism polarity will last much longer (1999: 492; see also Briggs 1996).

Applying this discussion to indigenous peoples, one may summarize the arguments by asking what would be worse, to be diluted into dominant societies, or fight to retain cultural distinctiveness at the cost of segregation. Of course, those in the position to best answer this question are the native peoples themselves. Before exploring this troubled ground of interethnic friction, to use a familiar concept in ethnic studies in Brazil and elsewhere in Latin America (Cardoso de Oliveira 1964), let us examine yet another bone of contention in the debate around the concept of culture, namely, exoticism.

"The Exotic Is Not at Home"

Although closely associated with essentialism, exoticism has a logic of its own. As with cholesterol, it is possible to identify negative and positive exoticism. Negative exoticism results from the political abuse that is made of alterity, be it directly extracted from native practices taken out of context or in distorted ethnographic descriptions (an icon of bad exoticism is the image of the Yanomami created by a host of authors that followed in Napoleon Chagnon's footsteps). Conversely, the positive side of exoticism asserts that cultural diversity is fundamental to deflate the bombastic *West* that poses as the winner, vis-à-vis the hopeless *Rest*, taken to be the loser. When promoting a movement toward constructive otherness, exoticism shakes off its *-ism* along with its ethical and political virulence and, as a banner of affirmative difference, becomes a legitimate tool to counteract the hegemonic affectation and superiority complex of majority societies.

Does exoticism exist at home, that is, involving national minorities, or does it occur only when there is a considerable physical distance between exoticiser and exoticized? I tend to agree with Peter Mason (1998: 148) when he maintains that "the exotic is not at home" because "the presentation of the exotic necessarily entails displacement and detachment." I would like, however, to add another layer of complexity to his argument. The historical coexistence of national societies with their internal others tends to erode the exotic flavor that cultural traits once had. The process of cognitive and affective metabolization of domestic differences wears out the sense of disengagement that characterizes the exotic gaze from afar. The curse of the feather headdress illustrates this point. Unlike the distant fascination or repulsion that characterizes the reaction of a distant observer of differences, Brazilians who either believe in or scoff at the occult powers of the artifact do so with a measure of involvement that can move them to participation. This process of engagement, whether intentional or not, would signal the passage from exoticism to essentialism.

Indeed, one can observe this process when a minority unrecognized as such, striving to affirm its cultural differences, hits the wall of national indifference. There is a moment when such a minority will have to artificially create displacement and detachment in order to be noticed. There are plenty of examples in the realm of so-called ethnogenesis where cultural traditions are revived or reinvented by minorities in search of ethnic recognition (Hill 1996; Oliveira 1999). Indigenous peoples in Northeast Brazil illustrate this mechanism. To resist the nation's indifference to and even denial of their ethnic singularity, these Indians have made a collective effort to distance themselves from the mass of the national population by displaying diacritics associated with Indianness in the popular imagination. Some, like the Pataxó in the eastern state of Bahia, in their quest for ethnic identity, sought to fill in the cultural gap left by the loss of their mother tongue by learning the related language of the Maxacali in the neighboring state of Minas Gerais. How could they claim to be different from Brazilians if the only language they could speak was Portuguese? How good can an official national language be as a vehicle for ethnic distinctness? Those who succeed in asserting their ethnic personae by exhibiting exotic traits are apt to join the chorus of authenticity be it real or constructed. If, as Rosaldo maintains, demanding authenticity from culturally despoiled minorities amounts to an act of "imperialist nostalgia" (Rosaldo 1989: 68–86), the cultural resurrection of peoples such as the Northeast Indians in Brazil could amount to an ironic relief from this malaise of the majority.

Once cultural differences are created and admitted by society at large— here the media play a major role—the artificiality of distancing is no longer necessary and exoticism makes way for essentialism. While exoticism at home may not last, it is precisely at home that essentialism qua political praxis prospers, as the European situation exemplifies.

The Essentialist Boomerang

In the complex interplay of interests, understandings and misunderstandings that are part and parcel of the interethnic "middle ground" (White 1991, Conklin and Graham 1995), the manipulation of primordialities (à la Geertz 1973, chapter 10) by means of overemphasized cultural diacritics or the emphasis on separateness via exclusive language and rituals indicates that indigenous peoples such as the Kayapó and Shavante, among others, insist on maintaining their specificities without, however, renouncing the possible benefits that the surrounding nation-state may offer. To this end, they don't hesitate in complying with some stereotypical expectations on the part of non-Indians. Under the guise of going along with what is expected of them, the Indians reinforce what they want the national society to see in them—if this brings them political benefits.

Two well-known concepts come to mind as I try to make sense of all this. One is Goffman's impression management: "The performer who is to be dramaturgically prudent will have to adapt his performance to the information conditions under which it must be staged" (1959: 222). The other is Bateson's schismogenesis: "a process of differentiation in the norms of individual behavior resulting from cumulative interaction between individuals" (1958: 175). Both concepts bring to the fore the mutuality of the parts involved in interaction, and their constant scrutiny of each other's actions and reactions. Goffman's concept emphasizes the minutiae of face-to-face interaction where the actors deliberately adjust their behavior according to their own reading of their interlocutor's reactions. In Bateson's schismogenesis, we have the factor of accumulated experience influencing an actor's predisposition toward another.

In the case of the feather headdress and the Indian Museum, Indians and non-Indians performed their respective roles in a rather hyperbolic fashion as a way to reinforce a context where otherness (of Indians to whites and vice-versa) had long been constructed. It also meant an ironic distance between the Indians and the powerful. In the case of the Altamira gathering, to many outsiders otherness meant proximity, a means to reach authenticity as if by osmosis, by contagion, following the assumption that Indianness is part of redeeming nature. In both cases, the Indians behaved as was expected of them by embroidering the outer layers of their Indianness. As each party acted out the other's expectations, Indians and non-Indians were together in the same grammatical mode of essentialization. Their tacit agreement to disagree in situations where antagonisms must give way to the maximization of social gains is, once again, reminiscent of Leach's operational definition of ritual and myth as applied to his Highland Burma data, "a language of argument, not a chorus of harmony" (Leach 1954: 278). Underneath the extravagant tales issued by the media, both sides were using culture as a productive political artifact for their own purposes.

It should be clear that the act of performing culture is not necessarily an act of essentialism. It would not be appropriate, for instance, to call essentialist the enactment of a rite of passage for the internal purposes of a given society. But whenever cultural traits are displayed out of their specific cultural contexts, one has at least potentially an act of instrumentalization.

Are indigenous peoples free to instrumentalize their cultures at will? Can they have the essentialist cake and eat it too? Given the fact that essentialization occurs in a context of political inequality in which the Indians are invariably placed on the weaker end of the power spectrum, invoking resonant symbols of alterity can bring about a boomerang effect like in the case of the Kayapó leader Paiakan. The ferocious response of the media to his alleged crime of rape paralleled the high praise he received as a genuine defender of indigenous and environmental integrity. On trial was the savage wearing feathers rather than the human male. Part of the outrage against him had to do with his economic success, which offended those people for whom real

Indians must be pure and poor. Paiakan's exercise in essentialism stumbled on the hurdle set up by the logic of interethnic politics.

Quasi-Objects or Full Subjects?

When it comes to visibility as an empowering mechanism, capitalizing on cultural traits in national arenas is one of the most effective resources at the disposal of indigenous peoples. But essentializing is not the only option that Indians have for claiming ethnic justice and recognition. We can detect at least two other courses of action taken by Brazilian Indians: one, clearly collective, is the appearance of indigenous and pro-indigenous organizations; the other, contingent on individual choice, is the pursuit of legitimacy from positions within the state apparatus such as ministries, the Indian agency, or party politics.

The first timid attempts at political organizing in the early 1970s (Ramos 1998, chapter 6) gathered momentum during the following decades and reached a pace of proliferation of indigenous organizations now on the order of 250 associations in the Amazon alone (Albert 2001). Most of these organizing efforts aim at amassing resources, both material and human, to carry out community projects such as economic production, education, and health assistance. They invariably come into existence as the result of the concerted action of nongovernmental organizations or the Catholic Church and indigenous leaders to meet demands that should be, but hardly ever are, fulfilled by the state as the legal guardian of the Indians. The outcome of these joint efforts has been dubbed "ethnopolitical hybridizations" and regarded as a mixed blessing (Albert 1997). With most indigenous lands in the Amazon legally demarcated, political claims that rallied around territorial issues have shifted to demands for development projects steered to the market economy with all the risks pertaining to commodification. A new style of indigenous awareness, more aligned with the rational standards of resource management, has replaced the charismatic era, when eloquent indigenous leaders exhorted nonindigenous audiences to recognize the legitimacy of their ethnic differences (Albert n.d., Ramos 1998, chapter 6).

Underlying this new ethnic managerial model is the relatively novel master narrative of the West that takes sustainable development as its banner. Indigenous peoples touched by contemporary concerns with nature conservation respond by organizing themselves in order to cope with the global market of sustainability. In the political economy of ecological wisdom it is not unusual to find expressions of essentialism when the Indians take on the role of guardians of nature as opposed to whites, destroyers of nature, either as an assertion of cultural autonomy or as a way to demonstrate their capacity as active producers in the land to which they have constitutional rights. The fact that a number of indigenous peoples are engaged in nonsustainable activities, such as lumbering and gold mining (see, for instance, the *Newsweek* article "Not as Green as They Seem," 27 March 2000: 10–14) does not seem to tarnish the Indians' more established reputation as natural environmentalists if for no other reason than the widespread belief that, after all, they are part of Mother Nature. A striking example of the influence of Western conservationist discourses on the assertion of ethnic pride is the blend of global environmental concerns with traditional beliefs formulated by Yanomami leader and winner of the Global 500 prize, Davi Kopenawa, for whom the "Whiteman's" demonstrations of ecological knowledge are an enormously impoverished and distorted version of shamanic wisdom. Westerners' failure to understand how nature really works in both its material and nonmaterial essence is, for Kopenawa, responsible for their ineptitude at preserving natural resources and their infinite proclivity for destruction (Albert 1993).

In a totally different key, other indigenous personages in the Brazilian ethnoscape have chosen a different path to ethnic politics. No longer taking collective decisions, these are individuals, usually urban dwellers, who have a good command of the Portuguese language, are thoroughly acquainted with the ways of national society, and have held posts in various public bureaucracies, such as the National Indian Foundation, the Ministry of Culture, or have engaged in party politics (Ramos 1988). While claiming full Indianness, these men and women have an overtly nonessentialist agenda in that they do not appeal to cultural diacritics to defend their ethnic identity. Their goal is to achieve ethnic justice by working from within the state system. There is, however, a category of indigenous "civil servants" who in no significant way distinguish themselves from any other civil servants who are more intent on keeping their jobs than on defending their fellow Indians if this involves challenging the powers that be. One of the best known urban leaders is Marcos Terena, who has been active in the Brazilian Indian movement since the early 1980s. An outspoken critic of attempts to essentialize the Indian, Terena defends equal rights for indigenous peoples, but with the preservation of ethnic differences. In other words, he advocates citizenship rights for Indians via integration without assimilation. Equality for him would be achieved through equivalence rather than similarity. In an interview just around the Brazilian quincentennial in April 2000, Terena stated: "My dream for this 500th anniversary is to establish an alliance of mutual respect so that we can transform this country into a place of good conviviality." Asked about the integration of indigenous peoples into the national society, he declared: "From the moment the Whiteman understood that he had to protect the Indian, another domination model was created around the idea that Indian is that who wears body paint, stays in his village, and engages in rituals. It is as though the Indian had no evolving dynamic of his own. Thus, the Indian was preserved and the consequence was the serious impoverishment of the original indigenous people. The Indian remained between two worlds. When some Indians jumped over the wall of that supposed protection, they discovered that there were people speaking in their name. Then another system of government domination emerged, paternalism" (Soares 2000).

Terena has often been criticized by both Indians and friends of the Indians for his gentle, apparently accommodating style. He has even been charged with co-optation for firmly keeping to his conviction that working from within the system can be as effective as frontal opposition. Like Terena, other Indians have been assailed with unfair legislation, unfair treatment at work, discrimination, prejudice, and all the barriers that meet individuals who challenge the deeply rooted stereotype that Indians should be relegated to the jungle, remain uneducated, forever captive of frozen quaint traditions.

Concluding Thoughts

Whether dressed in feathers, tee shirts, or executive suits, Brazilian Indians are a growing population that disclaims the pseudoprophecies that never tire of announcing their extinction. Among the heralds of doomsday, intellectuals of various persuasions have declared the end of indigenous peoples in Brazil by a specific date that never comes. The late anthropologist Darcy Ribeiro, who had forecast their disappearance by around the year 2000, reconsidered his prophecy when he realized that not only was the indigenous population recovering from one of its lowest points in the 1950s but the vitality of the Indian movement in the 1980s heralded a promising future. Indeed, under 100,000 in 1950, the indigenous population is now over 350,000, albeit still a fraction (0.2 percent) of the national population.

One might be tempted to generalize and state that the smaller the native population, the higher its visibility. However, potent counterexamples such as the indigenous peoples in the United States and, particularly, in Argentina quickly dispose of such a generalization. One is left with the conclusion that the Brazilian case is perhaps unique in the Americas. The *Indian* has inhabited the consciousness of the country's nonindigenous population since its early colonial days. Brazilian nationality has created indigenous imagery that suits its own claims that the Indians are the legitimate heirs to the land, a necessary cornerstone for its foundation as a unique society based on the myth of the three races (Indian, black, and white) and for its cry for cultural independence from European influences. Perhaps the novelty of contemporary indigenism is the active role Indians themselves play in the construction of this national imaginary.

The first two episodes discussed above exemplify the joint venture of Indians and non-Indians in the production of a pluriethnic scenario. Both episodes show how convoluted the process of forging otherness can be. The roundabout way in which some sectors of Brazilian urban society create an essential chasm between "civilized" and Indians discloses an interesting ambivalence regarding belief systems. Many cosmopolitan Brazilians are either unwilling or reluctant to admit their susceptibility to supernatural phenomena, particularly when these emanate from the mysterious indigenous world, so they transfer their metaphysical discomfort to the gullible populace: the macaw is a bird of ill omen in popular folk belief. Rarely confessing in public to be believers, these urbanites attempt to have the cake and eat it too: to play the folkloric game and keep their rational selves distanced from the "pre-logical" Indians. Their ignorance of indigenous lifeways, often tacitly nurtured, is convincing proof of this distance.

Once the great Indian/non-Indian divide is safely established, a whole range of symbolic possibilities opens up: indigenous diacritics become available for as much signification and resignification as needed to account for nonrational fissures in the allegedly rational world of civic affairs. Brightly colored feathers and esoteric shamanic seances are some of the most fitting items for this purpose both for their visual appeal and for the reassuring confidence that, thanks to protective ethnographic ignorance, social distance is comfortably preserved. Such are the ways of essentialization.

Oppression is hardly ever so complete as to leave no alternatives to the oppressed. In recent decades, particularly since the promulgation of the 1998 federal constitution, Brazilian Indians have been enlarging the number of their interethnic options to include courses of political action beyond catering to the essentialistic tastes of the majority society. Whereas "playing Indian" has been a very effective way to claim their rights and air their grievances, indigenous leaders are increasingly favoring other tactics of empowerment, either rejecting altogether the appeal to essentialization or invoking cultural primordialities not as bastions of incommensurable otherness but as an affirmation of equality within a regime of legitimate differences. On the long and winding road from quasi-objects to full subjects, Brazilian Indians, like so many native peoples the world over, have learned to value the concept of culture and, with remarkable sagacity, have taught the nonindigenous world, including anthropologists, how to critically absorb and reshape received ideas. Often acting as if in contradiction to good common sense, indigenous men and women have shown an extraordinary political wisdom behind what has appeared to many non-Indians as sheer naiveté. Well ahead of the critical capacity of their observers, Indian leaders have often surprised anthropologists with their novel tactics and strategic talents (Ramos 1998).

In the face of all this, we may well ask: how far does social theory help us understand the originality of the indigenous political imagination? Just to stay with the issue at hand, when theoreticians tell us that essentialism is bad politics, what they do is create a theoretical blind spot. As long as this blind spot persists we will always run the risk of colliding with reality.

12. *Masyarakat Adat*, Difference, and the Limits of Recognition in Indonesia's Forest Zone

Tania Murray Li

"We will not recognize the Nation, if the Nation does not recognize us."
This statement was made by AMAN (Aliansi Masyarakat Adat Nusantara), the Alliance of Indigenous People of the Archipelago, at their inaugural congress in Jakarta in March 1999. The congress was organized by a consortium of regionally based indigenous activists and Jakarta-based NGOs and funded by international donors (USAID, CUSO, and OXFAM, among others). Building on a process of mobilization that began with the International Year of Indigenous People in 1993, the congress marked the formal entry of *masyarakat adat* (literally, people who adhere to customary ways) as one of several groups staking claims and seeking to redefine its place in the Indonesian nation as the political scene opened up after Suharto's long and repressive rule. AMAN and its supporters assert cultural distinctiveness as the grounds for securing rights to territories and resources threatened by forestry, plantation, and mining interests backed by police and military intimidation. Their attempt to place the problems of masyarakat adat on the political agenda has been remarkably successful. While seven years ago the head of the national land agency declared that the category masyarakat adat, which had some significance in colonial law, was defunct or withering away (Kisbandono 1993), the term now appears ever more frequently in the discourse of activists, parliamentarians, media, and government officials dealing with forest and land issues.

The official view in Indonesia, at least until recently, was that the international legal category "indigenous people" did not fit Indonesia's situation: either all the people native to the archipelago are indigenous, or no one is

(Kusumatmadja 1993).[1] There is no colonial or postcolonial history of reserving land for particular ethnic or cultural groups, and such distinctions are not recorded in the census or used to differentiate citizens for the purpose of rule. Nor is race the usual idiom for understanding the differences between groups native to the archipelago. Folk concepts of difference focus rather on language and cultural practice, understood as mutable formations concentrated in particular ethnic groups (*suku*) but not inherent in them.[2] Nor is difference—whether cultural or ethnic—the primary liability of the people now demanding recognition as masyarakat adat. Although the numerically dominant Javanese are sometimes accused of ethnocentrism in their attitudes toward residents of the other islands (Dove 1985), all of Indonesia's rural villagers, regardless of physiognomy or cultural affiliation, were bullied in one way or another by the Suharto regime.[3] Their resource struggles are not, for the most part, horizontal ones that pit one cultural or ethnic group against another, although these can occur.[4] More centrally, it is the state apparatus, the military, and capitalists in varying combinations that form the constitutive outside, the "other" in relation to which the term *masyarakat adat* takes on its meaning and force. As one of the delegates to AMAN's congress stated, everyone "came with their own grievances about companies in their particular areas" (*Down to Earth*, Special Issue, October 1999; hereafter DTE). But there are other languages in which claims against the state could be made, the rights of citizenship being the most obvious. Why then do struggles over land and resources focus on difference?

To situate this question I need to explain the concerns, at once personal and political, that drive my inquiry. First there is a sense of puzzlement shared, I think, among many observers of the Indonesian scene, unclear about who exactly is encompassed by the term *masyarakat adat*. AMAN defines indigenous people as "communities which have ancestral lands in certain geographic locations and their own value systems, ideologies, economies, politics, cultures and societies in their respective homelands" (DTE: 4). But most Indonesians lay claim to a distinctive cultural heritage rooted in a particular region. While AMAN's focus is on people still residing on their ancestral land, it is not clear that the definition excludes the intellectuals and aristocrats who identify themselves as masyarakat adat but happen to live in cities, or people such as the Dayak who have been migrating out from the interior of Kalimantan toward the coast for the past century.[5] Neither does AMAN invoke the familiar contrast between intensively farmed, industrialized, and urbanized Java and the "outer islands" with their more extensive farming systems, lower population densities, and still-forested interiors. AMAN's elected assembly is to include fifty-four representatives, a man and a woman from each province *including* the four provinces of Java, with extras for West Papua because of its size. Nor, significantly, do AMAN's statements emphasize or limit masyarakat adat to a place in nature or a subsistence niche, although a general environmental conscience is implied (AMAN statements, AMAN's Explanatory Note on the Statutes of Masyarakat Adat, No. 1, 1999, cited in DTE: 4). AMAN considers masyarakat adat to number "tens of millions" (AMAN 10 September 1999; 25 May 1999) suggesting a definition of much broader scope than the government category of "isolated communities," one million overall (Social Affairs 1994/95). Consistent with International Labour Organization Convention 169's stress on self-identification as the key to indigeneity, AMAN does not seem concerned to draw a tight boundary: as more people see their struggles reflected in the concept of masyarakat adat, so the number will grow. But is this the scenario that the various parties now using the term so frequently and in apparently unproblematic ways have in mind?

My second concern is the danger I associate with a politics of difference in general, and the racialization of territory in particular. The essence of AMAN's demand is that the state acknowledge masyarakat adat as so many (thousand) sovereign communities with the right to govern themselves and the resources on which they depend. The basis for this claim is that they existed as organized collectivities with sovereign powers over their lives and living space "long before the nation-state." To make this argument, AMAN projects culturally distinctive, bounded, self-governing communities as Indonesia's aboriginal social form. It truncates history to occlude the colonial period, presenting adat as "the way resources were locally managed prior to the rise of foreign investment and forest industry in the 1960s" (Peluso 1995: 399). Thus the (assumed) autonomous social forms of the past, which are now to be reasserted, are not too far out of reach. AMAN's objection is to the way the New Order regime has unilaterally abrogated those rights, reallocated their resources, and dismantled their customary institutions and practices through various legal instruments, notoriously the Basic Forest Law of 1967 and the Village Government Law of 1979. AMAN thus reclaims the right to ways of life linked to the specific ancestral territories of distinctive cultural groups. But what about the people who find themselves out of place? How would territorial links be assessed in view of the centuries of migration that have occurred within and between the various islands of the archipelago, voluntarily or under duress? Images of minirepublics and ethnic cleansing come too readily to mind. Even if violent exclusions could be avoided, is there not a danger that defense of place would yield to a kind of social incarceration? This concern stems from my fieldwork among people who live in a remote corner of Sulawesi but have long been involved in commerce, admire urban consumer styles and desire to emulate them, and are busy commoditizing their ancestral land to that end (Li 1996; 1997; 2001). Their struggles, which center on transforming nature in order to claim a place in the modern world, have given me a general suspicion of platforms that would limit or consign them to ancestral territories and ways of life. For all the failure of the Indonesian state to deliver the promises of liberal citizenship, I worry too about a differentiated legal system in which recognition of customary law would subject people to local despotisms and the whims of "traditional" leaders who could monopolize or sell collective resources, or pass unreasonable judgments, substituting one tyranny for another (Cooper 1994: 1544).

Finally, I have the predictable, left-leaning concern that the politics of difference might be a distraction or mask for a struggle that is, or should be, about class-based inequalities and democracy.[6] I understand that a politics of difference may be unavoidable in nations where racial and cultural divisions are deeply inscribed both as the liabilities that must be contested and the framework within which mobilization most readily occurs. However, Indonesia has a history of popular struggles that were phrased in the early days of independence under Sukarno, and later under the influence of the Indonesian communist party, not as the claims of distinctive, culture-bound communities (*masyarakat adat*), but as struggles of "the people" (*rakyat*). Is the shift of focus from people to culture, which coincides with a shift of the site of struggle from agricultural land to forests and nature, the best approach to justice?

These concerns are still with me, but closer examination of the politics of difference being conducted by and on behalf of Indonesia's masyarakat adat has started to alleviate them. From all I have read and observed, nothing about the movement is exclusive or chauvinistic. Indeed, as I suspected, it is so inclusive that the boundaries are not coherent, but that is not the point. Rather, diverse parties are being drawn into a struggle for an imagined future that is inspired by the past but takes its shape from the injustices that need to be confronted in the present. As well as those who might claim the identity masyarakat adat as their own, the people caught up in this movement include government officials and parliamentarians, donors and activists, academics and the media. As populist sentiments silenced by Suharto are reawakened, I suspect there is broad support for the idea that people who live in "customary ways" should be allowed to continue to do so without having their resources stolen from them by greedy elites. AMAN's demands, far from being narrow or sectarian, continually blur the boundaries between rakyat and masyarakat adat to pose a fundamental challenge to what the state has become and argue for a comprehensive reevaluation of the meaning of citizenship. The goal at this point is to form alliances with other groups including those described as farmers or as other "local people," stressing common causes rather than dwelling on the details (about identities and resource entitlements) that could—but may not—divide them.

The category masyarakat adat and the social movement assembled around it has particular roots. It is not simply a replay of Amazonian econaturalism nor a continuation of the drama in which the Penan of Malaysia confronted bulldozers, although elements of these struggles are relevant here. Nor are the questions it raises exhausted by the issue of essentialism, its deconstruction by scholars, or its tactical deployment by indigenous people and their advocates. It is true that images of exotic tribes in tune with nature figure in AMAN's repertoire, as does a rather idealized "collective wish image" (Watts 1999: 88) of the past to be made future. But this is not surprising since I assume that "a touch of essentialism" (Hall 1996c: 472) is always needed to draw the boundaries that enable political mobilization. More significantly, my exploration of the fields of force within and against which this politics has emerged suggests the inadequacy of analytical models centered on sovereign subjects enacting strategies of their own choosing. The category masyarakat adat has not been conceptualized, constructed, selected, occupied, fought for, or manipulated as one option among others: the structures of recognition and identification in which it is embedded are much too broad and deep to sustain this kind of explanation.[7] Shorn of voluntarism, my concern over whether a politics of difference is "the best approach" also needs to be rethought. The analytical intervention that seems worthwhile, at this conjuncture, is the attempt to understand why politics is taking this form—its genealogy, and its limits, as far as these can be discerned. More specifically I ask: What are the fields of force, at once material and discursive, within and against which the category masyarakat adat has emerged and taken on political weight? Through what processes are demands for recognition made by or on behalf of masyarakat adat limited or contained?

Hegemony and the Limits of Recognition

The category masyarakat adat, the community it imagines, the problems that bind people and the ways they are addressed are configured by existing fields of force (Roseberry 1996: 80–81). This is the "contradictory complexity" of subaltern politics fully embraced by Gramsci in his account of hegemony but underestimated by those who imagine new social movements to operate in autonomous spaces outside of power.[8] Because subaltern subjectivities are formed within hegemonic relations, the process of ideological struggle seldom involves a "whole new alternative set of terms" but proceeds rather through the attempt to "win some new set of meanings for an existing term or category . . . dis-articulating it from its place in the signifying structure" and "re-articulating its associations" with other ideas and with particular social forces (Hall 1985: 112; Hall 1996a: 434). Hegemonic articulations secure at most the fragile and contingent *coordination* of "the interests of a dominant group with the general interests of other groups and the life of the state as a whole" (Gramsci, cited in Hall 1996a: 423).

In Indonesia as in other modern state systems, a "new terrain of politics [has been] created by the emerging forms of state and civil society, and new, more complex relations between them" (Hall 1996a: 427). As the boundaries between state and civil society become increasingly blurred, struggles must be "conducted in a protracted way, across many different and varying fronts" (426). The fields of force surrounding Indonesia's masyarakat adat are not concentrated in a singular class enemy or in the state apparatus but distributed across various institutional sites. To take just one example, while the kind of power Foucault (1991b) described as governmental, that which is concerned with regulating the "conduct of conduct," is concentrated in the apparatus we have come to call "the state," it is *also* a feature of many of the organizations we have come to call "nongovernmental." "N"-GOs and activists working on environment and development are often concerned with how people live their lives, and are exercising governmental power when they seek to reform them in an "improving direction."[9] Even NGOs dedicated to the restoration of the integrity of indigenous cultures and the preservation of traditional environmental knowledge imagine an ideal state (sometimes projected as a prior state) to which people should conform. Governmentality, as Foucault acknowledged, is always guided by a moral vision, and competing moral projects are central to the struggle for hegemony, especially for dominance in the configuration of what will count as everyday, popular, common sense (Hall 1996a: 431–32).

The fields of power surrounding recognition, AMAN's key demand, are especially complex. To open these up for scrutiny, it is useful to dwell for a moment on the word "recognition" itself, which in English elides a number of meanings. Detouring through the German language, Johannes Fabian (1999: 53) identifies three: *Erkennen*, meaning "I know these persons or objects when I see them" (an act of cognition); *Wiedererkennen*, "I know these persons or objects because I remember them" (an act of memory); and *Anerkennen* "I give these persons or objects the recognition they ask for and deserve" (an act of acknowledgment). Note that recognition in the first sense is about classification: an object or person is knowable because it meets the criteria of a preestablished cognitive slot, which could be an everyday "map of meaning" or a legal-bureaucratic category. Recognition as memory has an imaginative and emotional component, which draws variously on experience, projection, and déjà vu. The element of desire distinguishes it, sometimes only slightly, from recognition as classification. Recognition as acknowledgment has been, as Fabian points out, the focus of debates in political philosophy concerned with theories of the good life and the attempt to reconcile the interests of individuals and collectivities (Fabian 1999: 64; Taylor 1994). For Fabian recognition as acknowledgment is not something that can simply be granted by one party to another. It cannot be "doled out like political independence or development aid" (66), or it is merely "ethno-centric righteousness in the guise of supposedly universal principles" (65). Acknowledgment requires knowledge, and knowledge cannot be "brought along," as memory, projection, or classificatory schemes. It is the product of confrontation and struggle, of communicative exchanges between "coeval participants," with all their potentially upsetting consequences, including the unsettling of identities" (66). Knowledge changes people. Ideally, it is reciprocal.

AMAN's demand for recognition invokes each of these dimensions. The idea that masyarakat adat have special rights, or that resource access should be linked to cultural identity and "traditional" environmental knowledge, would mean nothing if the bearers of those rights and qualities could not be identified and rendered recognizable by legal and bureaucratic criteria. Supporters too need to be able to identify the subjects of their concern. If identification is power-laden so too is the way memory works to apprehend the present through an imagined or projected past. Recognition as memory depends on a repetition of what has been encountered before, if only as image or myth. To be recognized in this sense, masyarakat adat must fit into and build on images that are already available. The space they may fill is configured by national and transnational desires to retrieve a past of cooperative and autonomous village communities, subsistence security, abundant natural resources, and spiritual attachments to the land. Alternative memories of the past as a harsh and difficult struggle to overcome nature, attain a civilized state, and attract the attention of rulers bearing secular or spiritual powers— or development funds—are filtered out of this scenario. Finally, acknowledgment. AMAN makes the claim that masyarakat adat are sovereign groups that existed prior to the nation and whose legal systems are coequal with national laws, not subsumed within or subordinate to them. But there is a paradox here. Why should masyarakat adat demand recognition from a state whose claims to sovereignty they wish to challenge? The organization of AMAN by provinces, its adoption of notations that repeat those of the government (statutes, letters of clarification), and the demand for recognition itself acknowledge the legitimacy of the nation even as they challenge it. Notably, the group unwilling to compromise during the congress were the West Papuans: they refused to join the team drafting AMAN's political agenda on the grounds that their goal is not recognition but independence (DTE: 10). Implicitly, AMAN concedes to the power relations that frame and limit its most radical demand. Moreover, the assertion of a coequal—and coeval—presence is undermined by the very association of masyarakat adat with times past, making it more difficult for the surprises and shifts, the generation of new knowledge of self and other, on which acknowledgment depends.

Those who demand that their rights be acknowledged must fill the places of recognition that others provide, using dominant languages and demanding a voice in bureaucratic and other power-saturated encounters, even as they seek to stretch, reshape, or even invert the meanings implied (Rosenberry 1996: 81). Despite the countervailing dialectic implied in AMAN's threat to withhold recognition from the state, exposing the fragility of relations of rule, the surrounding field of force is too complex to be undone in such a binary fashion. The "others" with whom those who seek recognition must engage include government departments with diverse agendas; colonial and contemporary legal codes, subject to interpretation; individual politicians and bureaucrats with more or less populist inclinations; international donors; national and international "nongovernmental" organizations; and the media, which both form and respond to the commonsense understandings and sentiments of the "national-popular." By taking a lead from Roseberry (1996) and thinking of these as "fields" or concentrations of power or, as

Cooper (1994: 1533) puts it, arteries rather than capillaries, it is possible to investigate their characteristic configurations, as well as the ways they overlap and intersect.

Fields of Power and the Genealogy of Masyarakat Adat

Capitalist Accumulation and State Agendas

The New Order regime took power in 1965 after bloody massacres directed against alleged communists and Chinese. Popular mobilization to seize and redistribute colonial plantation land ended abruptly, and it became impossible to organize on the basis of class or the kinds of mass struggle implied by the term *rakyat*. The regime also declared race, ethnicity, regionalism, and religion illegitimate grounds for politics, as if these would unleash uncontrollable passions and more violence, a deeply cynical move in view of the evidence that the attacks on Chinese in 1965 (and again in 1997) had been instigated by the military itself. The regime began to refer to the citizenry as *masyarakat*, a term that emphasizes community and socialization, as part of a deliberate attempt to quell the disruptions of "politics" and to refocus rural energies on production and "development" (Langenberg 1990).

In 1967 the regime's attention shifted to Indonesia's outer islands with their extensive land and forest resources, and a forest law was passed declaring state ownership over all land not held under private title, the area amounting to 75 percent of the nation's territory. Forests were handed over for exploitation by national and transnational capitalists, military, and government officials in various combinations. The people inhabiting these forest areas, who considered themselves to have private, customary, communal, or individual land rights guaranteed by the 1945 constitution and by the 1960 Basic Agrarian Law (a product of Sukarno-era populism), were ignored. If recognized at all, it was not for their cultural diversity and particular territorial attachments but rather through the homogenized, negative, and acultural categories "isolated community" (*masyarakat terasing*), shifting cultivator, or forest squatter. Their forest uses were deemed illegal, and they were subject to harassment and displacement whenever they were found to be in the way.

Although I have used the past tense, this field of force still exists and in some areas it is out of control as military and government personnel take advantage of the post-Suharto vacuum to steal timber from reserved forests and national parks (Dursin 2000; Richardson 2000). Moreover, the monetary crisis of 1997 and IMF loan conditions have pressured the new regime to give priority to expanding exports (*Suara Pembaruan* 2000). The forests of Kalimantan—intact, logged over, or burned—are slated for conversion to massive palm-oil plantations, permanently appropriating them from local use, and West Papua faces an even greater onslaught. These "developments" continue to be backed by brute force, arrests, beatings, and harassment, although opposition by villagers, sometimes drawing on activist support and encouraged by sympathetic media coverage, is increasingly resilient (*Jakarta Post* 2000b). In March 2000 the press reported that fifty timber concessionaires holding ten million hectares throughout the country had been forced to cease their operations due to land conflicts with villagers (*Jakarta Post* 2000c). Some concessionaires have tried to buy peace by offering villagers cash compensation, while others call on the government to confirm the legal standing of their forest contracts in the face of overlapping claims (*Jakarta Post* 2000d).

This political-economic scenario accounts in part for the form taken by the movement for masyarakat adat and its emphasis on difference. Masyarakat adat assert what the New Order denied: the intrinsic value of diverse cultural forms; the capacity of villagers to organize themselves and garner livelihoods from existing resources without state direction or "development"; attachments to place that cannot be compensated by two-hectare allocations in new settlement schemes; and a vision of nature that resists its reduction to the monotones of timber or oil-palm and highlights various, sustainable, local uses. But difference as the converse of New Order (mal)development does not explain everything. Both under Suharto and subsequently, the media seem to report ordinary villagers contesting state appropriations just as sympathetically as masyarakat adat, so difference is not essential to attract their attention. And why did it take twenty-five years of forest exploitation for the emphasis on difference to emerge? Further, if the emphasis on culture and nature associated with masyarakat adat was so challenging to the regime, why was it permitted to gather momentum even while Suharto remained in power? It is possible that the regime missed its political charge, at least initially, allowing activists to mobilize people under the cover of apparently neutral labels such as biodiversity protection. Or there may have been a calculation that exotic difference was not a serious threat—recall the "discovery" of the "stone-age" Tasaday in the Philippines under Marcos. More likely, the regime was forced to pay attention to the conservation agendas of donors and show a progressive face by passing new environmental laws, participating at Rio, and—as I will later show—*agreeing* that some people have such unique and special environmental knowledge that it should indeed be protected. Here one field of force impinges on another, popular struggles and donor agendas helping to shape what the state becomes.

Donor Agendas, Nature Conservation, and Biodiversity

During the 1990s, nature conservation was a popular cause among donors because of its powerful international constituency and the legitimation it provided for their continuing involvement with the New Order regime. Biodiversity conservation, with its implied urgency (Brosius 1999b: 282 n.8), was an issue on which critics, donors, and government representatives could readily agree—at least so long as the divergent interests of the various "stakeholders" were not made too explicit. Under donor sponsorship, conservation became a site for the proliferation of managerial approaches that might be seen, perhaps too cynically, as institutionalized procedures for evading difficult political questions through "increased communication and understanding." The repertoire included seminars, training, collaborative research, participatory appraisal, adaptive management, consensus building, joint fact-finding, multistakeholder meetings, enhancing organizational capacity, community mapping, shuttle diplomacy, and so on.[10]

What are the places of recognition allocated to masyarakat adat in conservation agendas? For some of Indonesia's transnational and national conservation organizations, human activities have no place in the "natural" environment conceived as wilderness (Cronon 1996). Many, however, subscribe to the wish-laden "middle-ground . . . founded on the assertion that native peoples' views of nature and ways of using natural resources are consistent with Western conservationist principles" (Conklin and Graham 1995: 696). The compromise argument is that social groups that are unique or different should have their knowledge and rights respected *if* and *when* it is instrumental to conservation objectives. Thus only specific kinds of knowledge are relevant, and rights are conditional on performance. The International Convention on Biological Diversity obliges states, subject to their national legislation, "to respect, preserve and maintain knowledge, innovations and practices of indigenous and local communities embodying traditional lifestyles relevant for the conservation and sustainable use of biological resources." It also requires them to "protect and encourage customary use of biological resources in accordance with traditional cultural practices that are compatible with conservation or sustainable use requirements."[11] The niche opened up here is limited by these conditions, but for activists who assume that masyarakat adat do indeed manage their resources sustainably, there is little risked and much gained by framing arguments for masyarakat adat in terms of conservation benefits (Moniaga 1993).[12]

Indonesia's national strategy for implementing Agenda 21 (the outcome of the World Congress on Sustainable Development, held in Rio de Janeiro in 1992) was the outcome of extensive consultations involving government, donors, activists, and academics. It illustrates the limited gains that can be made by masyarakat adat through efforts to build "consensus" under the conservation banner. The document refers strongly and repeatedly to both the knowledge and the rights of people called, variously, indigenous, traditional, local, forest dwelling, and tribal. The argument moves from a recognition of indigenous knowledge and conservation-related practices to the need to "set-up a legal mechanism which protects traditional knowledge, territories, cultural practices and which also guarantees the genuine participation of traditional communities by recognizing their traditional laws and incorporating them into the national laws" (State Ministry for Environment and United Nations Development Program 1997: 401). Despite the rhetoric, the legal mechanisms proposed for forest-dwelling communities fall short of the recognition of their rights to occupy—still less to farm—state forest land. The emphasis is on conservation within a forestry framework, with traditional communities as participants. The "improving direction" anticipated in the document concerns the revival and transfer of traditional wisdom, again a paradox since it is only the prior possession of unique environmental knowledge that qualifies such people for a place in nature to begin with.

The Indigenous People's Movement and Legal Precedents

AMAN translates *masyarakat adat* as "indigenous people," directly linking its struggle to the international indigenous peoples' movement and claiming recognition under ILO convention 169. There is no doubt that the international movement has provided discursive and material resources for the mobilization of Indonesia's masyarakat adat, despite the lack of an obvious fit between a concept developed in the settler colonies and the Asian situation. Donor support for AMAN's inaugural congress can also be attributed to the international movement, since many donors have committed themselves to uphold the ILO convention. To meet this obligation, they need to have a "recognizable" and representative body that can be consulted when necessary, a position now filled by AMAN. But the term *adat* has a long and complex legal and political history in Indonesia, recalling configurations of population, territory, and sovereignty that diverge significantly from internationally circulating expectations about indigenous people, especially those relating to their existence as communities prior to the colonial encounter and their place in nature.

Originally Arabic, the term *adat* is usually translated as "custom" or "customary practice." It may include anything from specific rituals, to the character of everyday interactions, to the dispute-resolution mechanisms imposed on subordinate populations by precolonial chiefs (Li 2001). Thus it has variable significance in daily affairs, but no one is entirely without adat, hence the inclusiveness of the term. In some places, adat became fixed in the colonial period when Dutch legal scholars identified nineteen distinct cultural areas and codified customary practices to provide a basis for a native legal system. The areas subjected to this kind of colonial attention, with all its reifying, ethnicizing, and exoticizing effects, became highly invested in the idea of adat as a framework for regulating local affairs and relations with outsiders, not least the colonial power.[13] The Dutch fostered mediating institutions, adat chiefs, and adat councils, enhancing the position of elites in the process.[14] Villagers living within an adat law area were obliged to settle disputes through the relevant adat system, but the social and territorial boundaries were never fixed by means such as maps or identity cards, and many areas remained outside the adat-formalization process altogether. To this day, such places lack leaders prepared to pontificate on adat, and there are no rules or institutions of the kind expected by those familiar with the Dutch volumes on adat law in the recognized, adatized places (Li 2001; Ruwiastuti 1998; Tsing 1993). Generally remote and still forested, these areas have had less access to road links, schools, churches and mosques— elements of modernity introduced or consolidated together with adat in the colonial period.

By offering a truncated version of history that moves directly from sovereign communities of the mythic past to the New Order period, skipping over centuries of colonialism, AMAN is able to include both the groups that became orderly, adat law regimes under colonial tutelage and those that remained in the forests, filling the natural niche. I do not know whether this version of history was selected strategically or stems from a recognition that, whatever their diverse pasts, many or all of the people who are now coming to identify themselves as masyarakat adat have a shared memory of the New Order as a key point of rupture.

Activists, Media, and the National Popular

Debates about "the people" and the content of "the popular" are often conducted, as Watts (1999: 92) reminds us, primarily between intellectuals. Activists and academics based in Jakarta and other major cities, people who are not themselves masyarakat adat, have played an important role in the emergence of the category and the resulting mobilization. Combining the imagery and resources of the international indigenous peoples' movement with the populist orientation of Indonesia's independence struggle, they undertake the cultural-political labor of translating innumerable, particular instances of violation into a common language, assembling them so they can be understood and potentially resolved on a national scale. Although translation inevitably entails power, as the memories, images, and desires embedded in one idiom are subtly imposed on the other (Asad 1986), the activists do not see themselves as engaging in a process of transformation. Rather, they see themselves as affirming, and seeking to strengthen and preserve, what already exists: communities following customary ways that offer a healthy alternative to the kind of modernity offered by transnational capitalism and urban consumer culture in general, and the New Order regime in particular.

The activists who organized AMAN's inaugural congress must have had in mind the kinds of people that would be suitable as delegates, and hence some criteria for deciding who would, and who would not, qualify as masyarakat adat. The congress therefore had a somewhat tautological character: the people selected duly filled the slot, thus consolidating the category masyarakat adat as an embodied reality. Aware that they could be accused of "stage managing the whole event to fit their own agenda" (DTE: 15), the organizers were careful to take a back seat at the congress itself, giving the delegates as much time as possible to talk among themselves, discover commonalities, and constitute themselves as a united political force. Presumably, the activist organizers also learned something new while listening to the discussions, strengthening the grounds for acknowledgment.

The congress was surely designed, among other priorities, to have media appeal. There were photos, posters, and displays of handicrafts in the Jakarta hotel lobby. Delegates could be seen sitting in groups on the carpeted floor, smoking hand-rolled cigarettes and chewing betel nut—behavior common enough in villages but unusual for the venue. Some of them elected to wear traditional dress, especially for the street marches and rallies. *Down to Earth*, the newsletter of the International Campaign for Ecological Justice in

Indonesia, lamented in its coverage of the event that these choices had the effect of highlighting the exotic. "Journalists tended to focus on the plight of the Orang Rimba . . . forest peoples from central Sumatra, who—barefoot and clad in loin cloths—fit the popular stereotype of indigenous communities rather than the political message of the event and the Indigenous Alliance, AMAN" (DTE: 11). Instead of having masyarakat adat fill the primitive slot that already exists in the popular imagination, *Down to Earth* envisages the construction of a new niche that is recognizably "political." But understandings of what counts as politics may also diverge. *Down to Earth* notes that the delegates spent too much time in their sessions with government ministers and politicians pleading for fair compensation in cases affecting their own communities instead of making "full use of the opportunity to demand political reforms, make policy recommendations or call for greater consultation." It notes further that the indigenous delegates with their "lack of experience in confronting officialdom may have confirmed the Jakarta elite's prejudices that these were indeed 'primitive peoples' " (12). Thus some of their activist supporters, in this case *Down to Earth*, consider that Indonesia's masyarakat adat need some improvement: they should become more politically savvy, perhaps more like indigenous people of the Americas who have honed their skills and their media images through decades of campaigning. They should focus on the big picture.

Media appeal is a complex matter for Indonesia's masyarakat adat. People looking out from Java's crowded cities and villages toward the outer islands are fully primed for difference, expecting to encounter scenes of culture and nature that diverge from their experiences at home. But what kind of culture will this be? Cultural diversity as colorful song and dance, especially in the glittering forms associated with court traditions, saturated Indonesian TV in the New Order period, since this was the form in which difference could most readily be accommodated (Pemberton 1994). In the absence of a racial distinction, masyarakat adat must also emphasize cultural difference, since the claim that they follow "customary" ways of life is central to their argument for sovereignty and resource rights. At the congress, as noted earlier, it was the Orang Rimba who became the center of media attention, but there are risks in the identification of AMAN's platform with their plight. Outside activist circles, people who are seen as ill clad, ignorant, and forest dwelling are often despised and pitied, not admired, and there is support for government intervention to assist and transform them. As far as I can tell, the noble savage has not been a trope with a mass following in Indonesia, although this could be changing.

In other contexts where indigenous people have made claims on the grounds of difference, they have been confronted by suspicious journalists, hostile publics, and scholars anxious to expose a lack of authenticity, to deconstruct images, or to disprove claims. According to Sharp (1996: 91), indigenous minorities "*must* assert an identity of fundamental cultural difference, of absolute primordial continuity with the precolonial past. If they did not do this, their claims for restoration of their dignity, for social justice, and the restitution for past dispossession would simply not be seen as legitimate. The unspoken rule is that those who make claims and demands on the basis of difference had better be *really* different" (emphasis in original). But in Indonesia, as my case study will illustrate, the burden of establishing difference does not seem to lie primarily with masyarakat adat themselves. Expectations about masyarakat adat, reflected through the prism of memory and desire, seem to operate powerfully in both activist and media circles to identify and highlight difference, reframing in an exotic light cultural practices that, under other conditions, might be regarded as unremarkable.[15]

Limiting Recognition: Laws, Maps, and Exemplary Cases

Having outlined the fields of power within and through which the demands of masyarakat adat have taken shape, I now turn to the processes through which claims for recognition are being limited or contained. My goal is to highlight the ways in which the competing agendas of masyarakat adat, their activist supporters, conservationists, and various branches of the state-apparatus are caught up and coordinated into a revised—but never solid—hegemonic formation. Laws, maps, and their contestation figure centrally in this scenario. So too does the phenomenon I am calling "the exemplary case": a focus on unique and special places where difference takes on such spectacular proportions that all the contending parties can easily *recognize* and, indeed, affirm it, while leaving fundamental questions about the identity and rights of masyarakat adat unresolved. I use a case—the Orang Rimba we have already encountered—to illustrate.

Laws and Maps

A new forest law was passed in September 1999 by Habibie's interim reform cabinet amidst a storm of protest in which masyarakat adat figured prominently. The law contains many populist phrases about participation and forest access, adopting some of the language of activists and critics, but it stops far short of acknowledging the sovereignty of masyarakat adat or their right to manage their resources. The government is to decide whether or not masyarakat adat exist as a legally recognizable collectivity with a definite social organization, for which the law uses—tellingly—the Dutch term *Rechsgemeenschap*. The indicators include the presence of formal adat institution with recognized authority, a clearly defined territory, a body of customary laws that are still acknowledged and obeyed, and the dependence of people on the collection of forest products to meet their daily subsistence needs.[16] Thus, to qualify for forest licenses, masyarakat adat must have both the institutional formality of a colonial-era adat law regime and be embedded in nature, an unlikely combination for the reasons I indicated earlier. Even those that do qualify are treated under this law as another category of licensed user of the national forest estate, their practices to be "guided," monitored, and subject to regulation by the Forest Department. Moreover, the law limits them to forest-product collection, their projected "natural" niche, and sets steep fines for unlicensed uses including swidden farming and conversion to small-holder tree crops—the principal livelihoods of the tens of millions of forest villagers AMAN would include in its constituency.

Activists mobilized to oppose the forest law, taking strident positions against a clear foe, while also forming coalitions some of which crossed government/activist lines. Members of Riau's provincial parliament joined a protest delegation to bring the "people's aspirations" to Jakarta (FKKM 15 September 1999). The former ministers of forestry and of environment critiqued the law in a public statement, mentioning both environmental issues and the failure to acknowledge and protect the forest rights of masyarakat adat (Suryohadikusumo and Salim 1999). Such high-profile support indicates the increasing currency of the masyarakat adat concept as a vehicle for opposition politicians to express their populist concerns. AMAN warned of increased levels of conflict, national disintegration and civil disobedience (AMAN 1999a, 1999b). The Consortium for Agrarian Renewal (KPA) reiterated that there was no constitutional basis for the government's assertion of control over natural resources, and that nothing should take place within the sovereign domain of masyarakat adat without their informed consent (AMAN 1999b). The Forum for Communication on Community Forestry (FKKM) opposed the law for its continued neglect and repression of the people described, interchangeably, as rakyat and masyarakat adat (Simon and Awang 1999). It also expressed dismay at the process by which the new law was rammed through parliament, and at the content of the law, which bore little resemblance to the draft FFKM had prepared through protracted multistakeholder consultations with the Department of Forestry. A coalition of more than a hundred NGOS, which adopted the name KUDETA (Coalition for the Democratization of Natural Resources, also Coup d'Etat), petitioned against the law on the populist grounds that it favors the elite at the expense of the environment and "the people" (rakyat) who had managed resources sustainably for generations (KUDETA 1999). Green Robe of Kalimantan stressed the bond between masyarakat adat and nature: "The forest cannot be separated from the life of masyarakat adat. It is the center of their lives" (FKKM 1999).

In its limited way, the forest law accommodates popular demands for forest access through licensing schemes for customary (adat) forests and other programs (community forest, village forests), while advancing the governmental project of dividing and ordering population and resources according to bureaucratic imperatives (Vandergeest and Peluso 1995). Regardless of their label, these schemes have the same effect: to recognize peoples' presence in forested areas while conceding nothing on the issue of rights, and to enmesh them more securely in state regulatory regimes. Even when there is official acknowledgment of mistakes the Department of Forestry made in the (New Order) past (Kompas 1998), the governmental activity of reforming and improving the population continues under new rhetorics such as facilitation, participation, and the effort to increase *villagers'* understanding of forest matters (Suara Merdeka 2000). Indeed, if the experience of community forestry in India and Nepal is indicative, such programs greatly intensify the level of micromanagement of people and resources by government, while simultaneously invoking the effort of villagers to monitor and police themselves (Agrawal 2001; Shrestha 1999).

There are divergent interests at work in mapping. The World Bank has been involved in a long-term land-titling project intended to free up land for capitalist investment, which would also have the effect—conveniently enough—of fulfilling its more recent commitment to recognize and protect indigenous land rights. But there is a disadvantage to detailed maps, from a government perspective. They diminish the power of officials to assign vast concessions to capitalist interests on the basis of vague land classifications, or to resolve conflicts expediently, according to their own priorities. Thus the continued illegibility of forest spaces, the lack of official data about the numbers and locations of people living within "government forest" and the inadequacy of official forest maps (Peluso 1995: 390–91) gives the forest department room to maneuver.[17] Despite calls by activists and donors (Evers

1995) for a comprehensive inventory of forested areas and their users that identifies all the masyarakat adat and delimits their land, little progress is being made in this direction.

In a complex and perhaps ironic engagement with this field of force, it is masyarakat adat and their activist supporters who carry out the labor of documenting customary rules and regulations and preparing maps showing territorial boundaries and land-use zones. Although the energy of the countermapping movement is impressive, not enough land is covered by these maps to seriously impinge on state prerogatives. They are usually drawn up under the stimulus of a resource conflict in which social and territorial boundaries are clearly drawn, and activist supporters are in attendance. These are precisely the conjunctures at which government officials need to effect a resolution of a particular, problematic "case." Responding to popular pressure, officials find that carefully delimited and documented claims made by unique and special people to unique and special places are, sometimes at least, eminently recognizable. The accommodation of special "cases" demonstrates the Department of Forestry's receptiveness to "new" ideas, without opening the floodgates to the tens of millions of people—call them masyarakat adat or simply rakyat—who could seriously challenge the claim that so much of Indonesia's land mass is state-forest domain. Special cases of this kind also satisfy conservationists who are concerned about "ordinary villagers" invading protected areas but ready to concede ground in cases that exemplify traditional, sustainable resource management practices. Activists also need to be able to cite exemplary cases to support their more general claims. Unplanned but strategic nonetheless, special cases are conjunctural sites that condense and simplify the problematic of nature and culture and coordinate between diverse agendas, but only so long as the groups singled out for special treatment are—or can be construed as—very different. It is difference that supplies the logic of the case—focusing attention, delimiting categories, and reintegrating a hegemonic field frayed or rent by contestation.

Recognizing the Orang Rimba as an Exemplary Case

After the media drew attention to their sparsely clad bodies at AMAN's inaugural congress, the Orang Rimba of Sumatra were selected as one of five groups entitled to occupy places in the national assembly that had been designated—in response to popular pressure—for representatives of masyarakat adat.[18] Then in January 2000 they won the Kehati award, a prize for biodiversity conservation given by a prominent NGO headed by Emil Salim, former minister of state for the environment. How did activists, the media, government officials, and the public come to converge on the Rimba as an exemplary case?

According to a field study conducted by the NGO WARSI (Sandbukt and WARSI 1998), the Orang Rimba (people of the forest) comprise three groups. Those to the west have been severely affected by the Trans-Sumatran Highway, which has brought official transmigrants, voluntary migrants, and large-scale plantations to their lands. Mobile by tradition and also as a result of displacement, they live by some combination of rubber planting, share tapping, agricultural labor, swidden farming, forest-gathering, and begging at the roadside. A few have been allocated oil-palm plots, which they have leased out to Javanese settlers while they continue their own more diverse pursuits (Sandbukt and WARSI 1998: 6–15). Though still recognizably Orang Rimba, these people do not form the coherent stable communities envisaged in arguments for adat land rights, nor does the idea of "sustainable forest management" begin to capture the fast-changing and highly pressured resource scenario with which they must contend. They are obviously needy, but they do not easily fit places of recognition constructed in terms of sovereign customary communities or conservation agendas. WARSI recommends that their rights to their remaining land be secured and, where available, additional land be purchased for them (1998: 24–25). They are or should be on the way to becoming part of the "ordinary" village population.

The Orang Rimba of the Bukit Tiga Puluh area are similarly disorganized, many of them being outcasts or refugees from deforestation elsewhere (1998: 22). They inhabit the buffer area of a national park also threatened with plantation development. They collect forest products from an extensive tract of hilly land that WARSI argues is unsuitable for conversion to plantation uses but is of significant conservation value, notably as the habitat of elephants (1998: 27). Natives in nature, part of a park, seems to be the place of recognition available here. The argument WARSI makes is more about Orang Rimba needs than rights, and it hangs on a fortuitous coincidence with the conservation agenda. Depending on definitions, the masyarakat adat claim might indeed be harder for these people to make, since they lack the coherent social and institutional relations that masyarakat adat need to qualify for forest rights under the new forest law, and they have not been fixed for generations in their current locale.

WARSI is especially concerned about the fate of the Bukit Dua Belas groups, which maintain "an exceptionally integrated sociocultural system . . . elaborated upon in a complex cosmology and supported by a political and legal structure that emphasizes the separateness and autonomy of the Orang Rimba tradition" (1998: 16). Part of their land falls within a biosphere reserve, but much of their swidden area and the forests they have modified and nurtured over generations fall outside the reserve and are under threat. The Orang Rimba's "low intensity silviculture . . . makes them a very significant part of the forest ecosystem," as well as constituting "the basis for individual and collective claims to resources under traditional law" (1998: 16). In the effort to retain their traditions, some have withdrawn into the reserve, while others engage in limited ways with nearby transmigrant communities, selling them food produced in their swiddens. Two members of the group were killed as they tried to resist logging operations. Bukit Dua Belas is, according to WARSI, the Orang Rimba's cultural and demographic heartland. Thus "the dramatic marginalization of the Orang Rimba in other parts . . . makes it all the more significant that they be allowed to maintain this central enclave where their identity remains intact" and in which they can "adapt to a changing world at their chosen pace" (1998: 28). Once again the argument is framed in terms of need rather than rights and depends on a coincidence with a conservation agenda.

Media coverage of the NGO campaign to protect the forest of the Bukit Dua Belas has emphasized difference, sometimes against the odds. One reporter who went in search of Temenggung Tarib[19]—the figure already encountered in Jakarta—described his abode "on a hilltop in the middle of dense primary forest where the air is cool, far from city noise." The report later mentions the very loud noise of bulldozers and chainsaws clearing for a nearby plantation, and the actual location of his house, only five hundred meters from a transmigration settlement (Thahar 1999). "Orang Rimba: If the Forest Is Finished, We Will Die," stated another headline (Sumedi 1999). The article explains sympathetically that the Orang Rimba have been forced into nomadism because their forests have been taken from them by greedy entrepreneurs or for national parks and reserves. When the reserves are raided by illegal loggers, the authorities do nothing to stop them, then blame Orang Rimba for the resulting destruction. The article supports WARSI's plan to extend the biosphere reserve to protect Orang Rimba and the watershed. "What happens to the Orang Rimba is an indicator of changes in the environment: if the Orang Rimba disappear, the conservation area that helps protect other areas will also be gone. The Orang Rimba really care for the environment, so they should be left in place. Let them change naturally, without being forced." It continues, "they just want to be free to cultivate and hunt in their traditional ways, living peacefully in the middle of the forest."

When Temenggung Tarib went to Jakarta to receive the Kehati award, news coverage described his discomfort at wearing long pants and a batik shirt and his disorientation from flying, being above the sky instead of below it. It also described his problem with the hotel toilets—not because he did not know how to use them, the angle an unkind journalist might have highlighted, but because Orang Rimba have a taboo against soiling clean water—a lesson from which other Indonesians should learn (Julianto 2000). The report in the English *Jakarta Post* was especially colorful, describing Tarib as a "Tarzan . . . as innocent as fellow orang rimba (jungle people)" of the Kubu tribe who are nomads dependent on forest products like honey and resin. It adds, somewhat discordantly, that they also grow cassava, rubber, and rice (*Jakarta Post* 2000a)—much like other villagers.

Powerful images of Orang Rimba as unique and special people threatened by greed and destruction are ones to which government officials have been able to respond. According to the Forest Conservation Service of the Department of Forestry: "the Orang Rimba are very close to their environment and take care of it well. . . . The lifestyle of such people, who only wear loin cloths, is very modest but they remind us how important a modest lifestyle really is in the balance between people and nature" (Sumedi 1999). In recognition whereof, the minister of forests who visited the province and met with WARSI and other activists in August 1999 agreed to cancel a logging permit covering a significant part of their traditional lands, giving them some security, at least for the moment (*Jambi Express* 1999).

The Kehati award highlighted Temenggung Tarib's knowledge of medicinal plants and the contribution he and his group were making to the protection of neighboring forest threatened by small-holder expansion (*Kompas* 2000b, 2000a). Their technique, ironically enough, is to plant rubber trees of their own—a practice they consider taboo but which has enabled them to cordon off the forest from other villagers who would not bypass Orang Rimba out of respect for their place as the legitimate occupants of the forest frontier (*Kampas* 2000a; Thahar 1999). The field of force at work here is complex indeed. Note that the case Kehati presents does not highlight the state-sponsored forest and plantation corporations or the transmigration scheme, which have made the forest-frontier such a crowded place. For Kehati it is villagers and illegal loggers who threaten the forest, yet the villagers are described sympathetically, as people who also acknowledge the Orang Rim-ba's special place—even when they are directly in competition for the expansion of rubber small holdings. Combine this with the journalistic magic and WARSI's conservation-oriented campaign noted above, and it becomes clear why so many can agree on the Orang Rimba and Temenggung Tarib. The place of recognition is quite limited, however, absorbing surprises and contradictions rather than embracing them as the grounds for new knowledge. Meanwhile, thousands of western Orang Rimba and other, less "special" villagers struggle on, their needs and rights unrecognized and even their presence ignored.

Conclusions

Attention to the dire needs of people who seem to exemplify difference does not preclude attending to the needs of others, perhaps through alternative approaches. Any recognition of the presence and the capacities of "customary" communities by government departments is significant, in view of counterarguments that customary practices lack intrinsic value or legal relevance, or are simply trumped by other agendas pursued "in the national interest." The hegemonic field dominated by New Order ideologies has been significantly disassembled, and residual and emergent forces are being re-combined as NGOs, donors, the media, politicians, and bureaucrats, and those who consider themselves to be masyarakat adat reconfigure their identities, agendas, and mutual relations. Respect for cultural difference associated with nature conservation has become hegemonic, the kind of common sense on which many parties agree in principle, if not in detail.

The absence of clear boundaries to the category masyarakat adat provides the advocacy movement with important room for maneuvering, but it also permits a rather formidable array of forces to narrow and limit the places of recognition that masyarakat adat may fill. When the international environmental lobby and donors connect biodiversity with indigenous people, they probably have in mind some famous exemplars, such as the Kayapo of the Amazon (Conklin and Graham 1995; Stearman 1994). Their images and expectations resonate readily with support for especially remote and exotic people, assumed to have large and unique reservoirs of biodiversity knowledge. They resonate less readily with the tens of millions of rather ordinary farmers who also have "customary" resource-management practices and could well be considered masyarakat adat. Yet, so long as definitions remain vague and the compromise agenda focused on conservation can be invoked, support for the latter is not ruled out. Around the edges of consensus and compromise, struggles continue to be waged, often discretely, over the meaning of key terms as well as their applicability in particular contexts. Meanings are fixed, contingently, at the level of the "case."

Much less contentious than masyarakat adat and their demand for some kind of coequal sovereignty, the concept of natives attuned to nature is associated with an attractive set of images, the approval of the international environmental lobby, and donor support. The same features that make the image attractive and serve to coordinate diverse agendas also impose limits. There are still many who question the motives of activists who would leave fellow humans in a state of nature rather than help them out of it. The conservation alliance itself is precarious. Many of the complaints at AMAN's congress were against the appropriation of customary land for national parks. Exaggerated claims about the environmental wisdom of "indigenous people" are vulnerable to refutation by conservationists or by neighboring populations, if not now, when the challenge is limited to a few special "cases," then certainly in future as resource pressures increase. Such claims legitimate the restriction of rights to those who practice "traditional, sustainable" resource management. Government and conservation agencies can thus espouse the rhetoric but find very few "cases" that meet the criteria in practice. Even when special status is granted, the benefits are uncertain. The "traditional" fisheries management system sasi—one of the first "cases" to receive broad recognition—has been subjected to an array of new government regulations and reporting requirements (Zerner 1994). The celebrated damar (resin) gardens of Krui are still not secure from appropriation by government and private-sector interests despite their special legal status, and ninety Krui villages have been subjected to an "emptying" campaign (Safitri 1996).

Land and resource rights made contingent on stewardship are a pale version of the rights other citizens effectively enjoy. So are rights linked to demonstrated "difference." But this paradox cannot be avoided if the demand of masyarakat adat is for recognition, or some kind of nested sovereignty, rather than—as in the case of the West Papuans—independence. Difference both enables claims to be made and limits those claims by locating them within particular fields of power. This is the dilemma that, as Stuart Hall observes (1996b: 444), besets the attempt to construct a politics that works with and through difference, as the boundaries necessary for political mobilization risk becoming fixed. By drawing out the overlapping meanings of recognition, I have highlighted the ways in which boundaries become fixed not only by processes of political mobilization but by the places of recognition that others provide. In the generation of new knowledge, an openness to surprises, and the unsettling of limits lie prospects for acknowledgment.

Notes

Thanks to Marcus Colchester, Gillian Hart, Jake Kosek, Victor Li, Donald Moore, Anand Pandian, Nancy Peluso, Michael Watts, and participants at the UCB Workshop for critical comments on an earlier draft. I am indebted to many activists in Indonesia's indigenous rights movement who have shared materials and met with me to discuss these issues, without necessarily agreeing with my conclusions. My research in Indonesia from 1995 to 2000 was funded by Canada's Social Science and Humanities Research Council. This essay is a slightly edited version of an article previously published under the same title in *Modern Asian Studies* 35, no. 3: 645–76.

1 The term "native" (*asli*) excludes the few Dutch who stayed on after independence and the Chinese, still marked racially as well as culturally even after generations of residence and intermarriage. Gray (1995) and Kingsbury (1998) acknowledge the descriptive incoherence of the term "indigenous" in much of Asia, where it refers less to a fixed group of people than to a sentiment that emerges in the course of struggles over territories, resources, and cultural respect—rather like the "imagined community" of the nation (Anderson 1991). For reasons that have more to do with national laws than population composition, the International Working Group on Indigenous Affairs (IWGIA) registers only 1 percent of Indonesia's population as indigenous, compared to 16 percent in the Philippines, and 60 percent in Nepal (Erni 1996: 20).

2 Contrast the scenario in Europe described by Stolcke (1995), in which cultural fundamentalism is a polite reconstruction of enduring racism.

3 Colchester (1986a; 1986b) and personal communication, 25 January 2001, argues that cultural difference has been the grounds for particular viciousness and discrimination toward indigenous people on the part of the Suharto regime. I agree that the "isolated communities" resettlement program of the Department of Social Affairs was replete with demeaning stereotypes and had an overtly assimilationist intent. Its effects seem to have been culturally devastating in West Papua in the 1980s, the main focus of Colchester's analysis, but my research indicates the program did less damage in Sulawesi or Kalimantan (Li 1999). Mention of the resettlement program at AMAN's congress indicates that it has been, at the very least, a significant irritant to the people it labels "backward" and "estranged."

4 There have been bloody battles between Dayaks and immigrant Madurese in Kalimantan, and between Muslims and Christians in Maluku and Sulawesi, although there are reports that the latter were instigated by the military.

5 On the issue of migration from interiors to coasts see Li 2001.

6 Wilmsen (1996: ix, 5, 8) gives priority to class. See Watts 1999: 88, 101 on the dangers of racializing territory.

7 See Scott (1999: 125, 154). Contrast Wilmsen's (1996b: 7) account of Australian aboriginal

elites conceptualizing and constructing an identity-space and inviting rural aborigines to fill it, only to have it co-opted, manipulated, and contained by the European-dominated national government. The sequence is familiar enough, but the causal links inadequately explored.

8   On subaltern complexity see Mallon 1994: 1496, 1502 and Prakash 1994: 1480.

9   On governmentality as improvement, see Scott 1995. Here I diverge from Brosius, who sees governmentality as the activity of regulation and surveillance by states, and advocacy or "politics" as the domain of moral causes espoused by NGOs and social movements, "nonstate, nomadic . . . grassroots groups . . . outside the space of institutional sovereignty" (1999c: 50). Brosius argues that such groups should not be too closely studied lest the hidden transcripts of their rhizomatic practices be revealed (1999b: 288). But many rhizomes cross-cut government/nongovernment lines. See, for example, Hale's 1999b account of the convergence between Maya demands for cultural rights, exerting pressure from below, and new strategies of governance that adopt the language of multiculturalism to exclude activists who go "too far." Pieterse (1998) argues that mainstream development agencies have absorbed critiques to such an extent that the search for a development "alternative" is now incoherent, while the IMF conducts business as usual. Schild (1997) describes how Chile's new democratic government took on the rhetoric, practices, and personnel of the once-radical women's movement, deploying them to governmental ends. These processes of disassembly and reconstruction cannot be understood if the "N" in NGO is conceded without scrutiny.

10 NGOs and villagers understand endless negotiation to be a government ploy. See Fisher et al. (1998) on the limits to what can be achieved by increasing communication between stakeholders, and the compromised position of NGOs caught between the roles of advocate and mediator in conflicts over conservation.

11 In Article 8j and Article 10c, respectively.

12 See more generally Lynch and Talbot 1995, and my discussion of Lynch's work in Li (2002).

13 Dutch scholars disagreed on the nature of adat rights, their spatial extent, and their implications for sovereignty. The subtext was racializing and orientalist, based on an assumption of unalterable difference between East and West. Van Vollenhoven, the key figure, added to these premises a liberal respect for human rights, a concern for peasant welfare, and a respect for cultural diversity. He acknowledged native sovereignty but expected natives to consent to commercial uses of their traditional lands so long as they were consulted and given a token customary payment called—tellingly—*recognitie* (Burns 1989: 14). Opponents argued that the logical conclusion of Van Vollenhoven's approach would be the recognition of adat law areas as minirepublics, leaving the colonial power with an "inchoate claim to govern" (Burns 1989: 102). Such recognition would expose "the contradictions at the heart of colonialism" (104)—a contradiction that still besets both the successor "national" regime and contemporary adat activism. The problem has been more severe in Indonesia than elsewhere in Asia because the Dutch recognized that all natives had adat, making no sharp distinction between peasant masses and tribes. In contrast, the British in India made and marked the boundary by means of a "schedule" (Béteille 1998), while the United States in the Philippines quickly consolidated older distinctions with its mapping and listing of the "non-Christian tribes."

14 Hooe (1999) discusses the use of adat law to justify and maintain elite dominance in the Kei islands of Eastern Indonesia, and the increasing comfort of government officials with rule by and through these "traditional" elites. The presentation on Kei customary law at the IWGIA

did not discuss these embedded inequalities, focusing instead on harmony, mutual assistance, and consensus (Rahail 1996).

15 See Tsing 1999, Li 2000.

16 See clause 67 and its explanation.

17 Here and in Li 1999 and Li 2001 I argue, contra Scott 1998, that illegibility has an ongoing role in modern systems of rule.

18 The other four were from Irian, Kalimantan, Maluku, and Sulawesi, although the latter were apparently insulted by being placed in what they perceived as a primitive slot (*Kompas* 2000c).

19 *Temenggung* is a Malay title used by the Dutch in the context of indirect rule.

Bibliography

Abu-Lughod, Lila. 1991. "Writing Against Culture." In *Recapturing Anthropology: Working in the Present*, edited by Richard Fox. Santa Fe: School of American Research Press.

Adams, Buck. 1941. [1884]. *The Narrative of Private Buck Adams*. Reprint, with an introduction by Gordon A. Brown. Cape Town: Van Riebeeck Society.

Adorno, Theodor W. 1969 [1965]. "Auf die Frage: Was ist deutsch." In *Stichworte: Kritische Modelle* 2. Frankfurt/M: Suhrkamp Verlag. Reprinted from *Liberal* 7, no. 8.

——. 1974 [1961]. "Wörter aus der Fremde." In *Noten zur Literatur II*. Frankfurt/M: Suhrkamp Verlag. Reprinted in *Gesammelte Schriften*. Vol. 2. Frankfurt/M.: Suhrkamp Verlag.

——. 1974. "Über den Gebrauch von Fremdwörtern." In *Noten zur Literatur, Anhang. Gesammelte Schriften*. Vol. 2. Frankfurt/M: Suhrkamp Verlag.

——. 1980. [1951]. *Minima Moralia: Reflexionen aus dem beschädigten Leben*. Berlin: Suhrkamp Verlag. Reprinted in *Gesammelte Schriften*, edited by Rolf Tiedemann. Vol. 4 Frankfurt/M.: Suhrkamp.

——. 1985. "On the Question: 'What Is German?'" Translated by Thomas Y. Levin. *New German Critique* 36: 121–32.

——. 1991. "The Essay as Form." Translated by Sherry Weber Nicholson. In *Notes to Literature*. Vol. 1. New York: Columbia University Press.

——. 2000. [1951]. *Minima Moralia: Reflections from Damaged Life*. New York: Verso.

Agamben, Giorgio. 1998. *Homo Sacer: Sovereign Power and Bare Life*. Translated by Daniel Heller-Roazen. Stanford: Stanford University Press.

Agarwal, Bina. 1992. "The Gender and Environment Debate: Lessons from India." *Feminist Studies* 18, no. 1: 119–58.

Agrawal, Arun. 2001. "State Formation in Community Spaces?: Decentralization of Control over Forests in the Kumaon Himalaya, India." *Journal of Asian Studies* 60, no. 1: 9–40.

Agrawal, Arun, and Clark Gibson. 1999. "Enchantment and Disenchantment: The Role of Community in Natural Resource Conservation." *World Development* 27, no. 4: 629–49.

Albert, Bruce. 1993. "L'or cannibale et la chute du ciel: Une critique chamanique de l'économie politique de la nature (Yanomami, Brésil)." *L'Homme* 126–28, no. 33: 349–78.

—. 1997. Territorialité, ethnopolitique et développement: À propos du mouvement indien en Amazonie brésilienne. *Cahiers des Ameriques Latines* 23: 177–210.

—. 2001. Associações indígenas e desenvolvimento sustentável na Amazônia brasileira. *Povos Indígenas no Brasil 1996/2000*. São Paulo: Instituto Socioambiental.

Alcoff, Linda Martin. 1999. "Towards a Phenomenology of Racial Embodiment." *Radical Philosophy* 95 (May–June): 15–26.

Alexander, M. Jacqui, and Chandra Talpade Mohanty, eds. 1993. *Feminist Genealogies, Colonial Legacies, Democratic Futures*. New York: Routledge.

Allen, Anita. 1988. "Privacy. Surrogacy and the Baby M Case." *Georgetown Law Journal* 76:1759–92.

Allison, A. C. 1954. "Protection by the Sickle-Cell Trait Against Sub-Tertian Malaria Infection." *British Medical Journal* 1: 290.

—. 1956. "Sickle Cell Anemia and Evolution." *Scientific American* (August): 87–88.

Alonso, Ana Maria. 1995. *Thread of Blood*. Tucson: University of Arizona Press.

Althusser, Louis. 1971. [1969]. "Ideology and Ideological State Apparatuses." In *Lenin and Philosophy and Other Essays*. Translated by Ben Brewster. London: New Left Books.

—. 1977. *For Marx*. Translated by Ben Brewster. London: Verso.

Alvarez, Sonia, Evelina Dagnino, and Arturo Escobar, eds. 1998. *Cultures of Politics, Politics of Cultures: Re-visioning Latin American Social Movements*. Boulder: Westview Press.

AMAN (Aliansi Masyarakat Adat Nusantara). 1999a. "Rancangan Undang-Undang Kehutanan Versi Pemerintah Tidak Menghormati dan Melindungi Masyarakat Adat." 25 May. Available from fkkm@egroups.com.

—. 1999b. "Masyarakat Adat Nusantara Monolak Rancangan Undang-Undang Kehutanan (RUUK)." 10 September. Available from fkkm@egroups.com.

Amin, Samir. 1974. *Accumulation on a World Scale: A Critique of the Theory of Underdevelopment*. New York: Monthly Review Press.

Ammon, Ulrich. 1995. *Die deutsche Sprache in Deutschland, Österreich und der Schweiz. Das Problem der nationalen Varietäten*. Berlin: Walter de Gruyter.

—. 1996. "Die nationalen Varietäten des Deutschen im Spannungsfeld von Dialekt und gesamtsprachlichem Standard." *Muttersprache* 106, no. 3: 243–49.

—. 1997. "Schwierigkeiten bei der Verbreitung der deutschen Sprache heute." *Muttersprache* 107, no 1: 17–34.

Anderson, Benedict. 1991. [1983]. *Imagined Communities: Reflections on the Origin and Spread of Nationalism*. Revised and extended edition. London: Verso.

—. 1983. *Imagined Communities*. London: Verso.

Anderson, C., J. Allan, and P. Johansen. 1967. "Comments on the Possible Existence and Nature of a Heterozygote Advantage in Cystic Fibrosis." *Bibliotheca Paediatrica* 86: 381.

Anderson, Kay. 1991. *Vancouver's Chinatown*. Montreal: McGill-Queen's University Press.

Anderson, Warwick. 1995. "Excremental Colonialism, Public Health, and the Poetics of Pollution." *Critical Inquiry* 21, no. 3: 640–69.

—. 1996. "Immunities of Empire—Race, Disease, and the New Tropical Medicine, 1900–1920." *Bulletin of the History of Medicine* 70, no. 1: 94–118.

—. 2002. *The Cultivation of Whiteness: Science, Health, and Racial Diversity in Australia*. Melbourne: Melbourne University Press.

Ang, Ien. 2000. "Identity Blues." In *Without Guarantees*, edited by Paul Gilroy, Lawrence Grossberg, and Angela McRobbie. London: Verso.

Anhalt-Köthen, Fürst Ludwig von. 1622. *Kurtzer Bericht der Fruchtbringenden Gesellschafft Zweck und Vorhaben.* Gedruckt zu Cöthen.

—. 1971 [1646]. *Der Fruchtbringenden Geselschaft Nahmen, Vorhaben, Gemählde und Wörter: Nach jedes Einnahme ordentlich in Kupfer gestochen und in achtzeilige Reimgesetze verfasset. Das Erste [bis Viertes] Hundert.* Frankfurt/M.: Bey Mattheo Merian. Reprinted in *Die Fruchtbringende Gesellschaft,* edited by Martin Bircher. Vol. 1. Munich: Kösel-Verlag.

Anna J. v. Mark C. et al. (Cal. App. 1991) 286 Cal. Rptr. 372.

Anner, John, ed. 1996. *Beyond Identity Politics.* Boston: South End Press.

Anthony, Carl. 1995. "Ecopsychology and the Deconstruction of Whiteness: An Interview with Carl Anthony." Interview by Theodore Roszak. In *Ecopsychology: Restoring the Earth, Healing the Mind,* edited by T. Roszak, M. E. Gomes, and A. D. Kanner. San Francisco: Sierra Club Books.

Anzaldúa Gloria. 1987. *Borderlands/La Frontera: The New Mestiza.* San Francisco: Aunt Lute Books.

Appadurai, Arjun. 1993. "Number in the Colonial Imagination." In *Orientalism and the Postcolonial Predicament,* edited by Carol Breckenridge and Peter Van der Veer. Philadelphia: University of Pennsylvania Press.

—. 1996. *Modernity at Large: Cultural Dimensions of Globalization.* Minneapolis: University of Minnesota Press.

Appiah, Kwame Anthony. 1992. *In My Father's House: Africa in the Philosophy of Culture.* Oxford: Oxford University Press.

—. 2001. "Liberalism, Individuality, Identity." *Critical Inquiry* 27, no. 2 (winter): 305–32.

Aravamudan, Srinivas. 1999. *Tropicopolitans: Colonialism and Agency, 1688–1804.* Durham: Duke University Press.

Arenas Bianchi, Clara, Charles R. Hale, and Gustavo Palma Murga. 1999. *¿Racismo en Guatemala? Abriendo el Debate sobre un Tema Tabú.* Guatemala City: AVANCSO.

Arendt, Hannah. 1968. [1951]. "Imperialism." Part 2 of *The Origins of Totalitarianism.* New York: Harcourt Brace Jovanovich.

Aretxaga, Begoña. 1997. *Shattering Silence: Women, Nationalism, and Political Subjectivity in Northern Ireland.* Princeton: Princeton University Press.

Arizpe, Lourdes. 1996. *Culture and Global Change: Social Perceptions of Deforestation in the Lacandona Rain Forest in Mexico.* Ann Arbor: University of Michigan Press.

Arnold, David. 1996. *The Problem of Nature: Environment, Culture, and European Expansion.* Oxford: Blackwell.

Arnold, David, and Ramachandra Guha, eds. 1995. *Nature, Culture, Imperialism: Essays on the Environmental History of South Asia.* Delhi: Oxford University Press.

Asad, Talal. 1986. "The Concept of Cultural Translation in British Social Anthropology." In *Writing Culture: The Poetics and Politics of Ethnography,* edited by James Clifford and George Marcus. Berkeley: University of California Press.

Athanasiou, Tom. 1998. *Divided Planet: The Ecology of Rich and Poor.* Athens: University of Georgia Press.

Bacchetta, Paola, Tina Campt, Inderpal Grewal, Caren Kaplan, Minoo Moallem, and Jennifer Terry. 2001. *Transnational Feminist Practices Against War.* Available at http://home.earthlink.net/~jenniferterry/transnationalstatement.html.

Bachelard, Gaston. 1969. *The Poetics of Space.* Boston: Beacon.

Bacon, Francis. 1999. [1625]. *The Essays or Counsels Civil and Moral.* New York: Oxford University Press.

Bade, Klaus J. 1992. *Ausländer, Aussiedler, Asyl in der Bundesrepublik Deutschland.* Bonn: Bundeszentrale für politische Bildung.

Baines, Thomas. 1961. [1854]. *Journal of a Residence in South Africa, 1842–53.* Reprint, with an introduction by R. R. Kennedy. Cape Town: Van Riebeeck Society.

Baker, Houston, Manthia Diawara, and Ruth Lindeborg, eds. 1996. *Black British Cultural Studies: A Reader.* Chicago: University of Chicago Press.

Baker, Lee. 1998. *From Savage to Negro: Anthropology and the Construction of Race, 1896–1954.* Berkeley: University of California Press.

Balakrishnan, Gopal. 2000. *The Enemy.* London: Verso.

Balibar, Etienne. 1995. [1991]. "The Nation Form: History and Ideology." In *Race, Nation, and Class: Ambiguous Identities,* by Etienne Balibar and Immanuel Wallerstein. New York: Verso.

———. 1998. "Die Nation-Form: Geschichte und Ideologie." In *Rasse, Klasse, Nation,* by Etienne Balibar and Immanuel Wallerstein. Hamburg: Argument Verlag.

Ballhatchet, Kenneth. 1980. *Race, Sex, and Class under the Raj: Imperial Attitudes and Policies and Their Critics, 1793–1905.* London: Weidenfeld and Nicolson.

Bank, Andrew. 1996. "Of 'Native Skulls' and 'Noble Caucasians': Phrenology in Colonial South Africa." *Journal of Southern African Studies* 22, no. 3: 387–403.

Barkan, Elazar. 1992. *The Retreat of Scientific Racism.* Cambridge: Cambridge University Press.

Barker, Martin. 1981. *The New Racism: Conservatives and the Ideology of the Tribe.* London: Junction Books.

———. 1990. "Biology and the New Racism." In *Anatomy of Racism,* edited by David Theo Goldberg. Minneapolis: University of Minnesota Press.

Barrow, John. 1968. [1801]. *An Account of Travels into the Interior of Southern Africa in the Years 1797 and 1798.* Reprint. New York: Johnson Reprint Co.

Barry, Kathleen. 1995. *The Prostitution of Sexuality.* New York: New York University Press.

Barth, Fredrik, ed. 1998. [1969]. *Ethnic Groups and Boundaries.* Prospect Heights, Ill.: Waveland Press.

Barthes, Roland. 1972. [1957]. *Mythologies.* New York: Noonday Press.

Bartra, Roger. 1994. *Wild Men in the Looking Glass.* Translated by Carl T. Berrisford. Ann Arbor: University of Michigan Press.

Basch, Linda, Nina Glick-Schiller, and Christina B. Szanton. 1994. *Nations Unbound: Transnational Projects, Postcolonial Predicaments, and Deterritorialized Nation-States.* Basel, Switzerland: Gordon and Breach.

Bassin, Mark. 1987. "Imperialism and the Nation State in Friedrich Ratzel's Political Geography." *Progress in Human Geography* 11: 473–495.

Basso, Keith. 1979. *Portraits of "the Whiteman": Linguistic Play and Cultural Symbols among the Western Apache.* Cambridge: Cambridge University Press.

—. 1996. "Wisdom Sits in Places." In *Senses of Place*, edited by Steven Feld and Keith Basso. Santa Fe: School of American Research Press.

Bastide, Roger. 1968. "Color, Racism, and Christianity." In *Color and Race*, edited by John Hope Franklin. Boston: Houghton Mifflin.

Bastos, Santiago, and Manuela Camus. 1993. *Quebrando el Silencio: Organizaciones del Pueblo Maya y sus Demandas (1986–1992)*. Guatemala City: FLACSO.

—. 1995. *Abriendo Caminos: Las Organizaciones Mayas desde el Nobel hasta el Acuerdo de Derechos Indígenas*. Guatemala City: FLACSO.

Basu, Tapan, Pradip Datta, Sumit Sarkar, Tanika Sarkar, and Sambuddha Sen. 1993. *Khaki Shorts, Saffron Flags: A Critique of the Hindu Right*. Tracts for the Times, No. 1. New Delhi: Orient Longman.

Bates, Barbara. 1992. *Bargaining for Life: A Social History of Tuberculosis, 1876–1938*. Philadelphia: University of Pennsylvania Press.

Bateson, Gregory. 1958. *Naven*. Stanford: Stanford University Press.

Baudrillard, Jean. 1983. *Simulations*. New York: Semiotext(e).

Bauman, Zygmunt. 1989. *Modernity and the Holocaust*. Ithaca: Cornell University Press.

—. 1992. *Intimations of Postmodernity*. New York: Routledge.

Baviskar, Amita. 1997. "Tribal Politics and Discourses of Environmentalism." *Contributions to Indian Sociology* 31, no. 2: 195–223.

Bayer, Ronald. 1987. *Homosexuality and American Psychiatry: The Politics of Diagnosis*. Princeton: Princeton University Press.

Bayly, Susan. 1995. "Caste and 'Race' in the Colonial Ethnography of India." In *The Concept of Race in South Asia*, edited by Peter Robb. Delhi: Oxford University Press.

Bebbington, Anthony, and Simon Batterbury. 2001. "Transnational Livelihoods and Landscapes: Political Ecologies of Globalization." *Ecumene* 8, no. 4: 369–464.

Beck, Ulrich. 1991. *Risk Society*. London: Sage.

Beezer, Anne. 1993. "Women and Adventure Travel." *New Formations* 21: 119–30.

Belyaev, Dmitri K. 1969. "Domestication of Animals." *Science Journal* 5: 47–52.

Bendix, Reinhard. 1978. *Kings or People: Power and the Mandate to Rule*. Berkeley: University of California Press.

Benjamin, Walter. 1972. "Einbahnstraße." In *Gesammelte Schriften*, edited by Tillman Rexroth. Vol. 4, No. 1. Frankfurt/M: Suhrkamp Verlag.

—. 1998. *The Origin of German Tragic Drama*. Translated by John Osborne. New York: Verso.

Berenson, Laurien. 1995. *A Pedigree to Die For*. New York: Kennsington Publishing.

Berger, John. 1972. *Ways of Seeing*. London: Penguin.

Bergmann, Werner, and Rainer Erb, eds. 1994. *Neonazismus und rechte Subkultur*. Berlin: Metropol.

Berry, Mary Frances, and John Blassingame. 1982. "Military Service and the Paradox of Loyalty." In *Long Memory: The Black Experience in America*. New York: Oxford University Press.

Berry, Sara. 1993. *No Condition Is Permanent: The Social Dynamics of Agrarian Change in Sub-Saharan Africa*. Madison: University of Wisconsin Press.

Besteman, Catherine. 1999. *Unraveling Somalia: Race, Violence, and the Legacy of Slavery*. Philadelphia: University of Pennsylvania Press.

Béteille, Andre. 1991. "Race, Caste, and Gender." In *Society and Politics in India*. Oxford: Oxford University Press.

———. 1998. "The Idea of Indigenous People." *Current Anthropology* 39, no. 2: 187–92.

Bhabha, Homi. 1994. *The Location of Culture*. New York: Routledge.

———. 1999. "Staging the Politics of Difference: Homi Bhabha's Critical Literacy." Interview by Gary Olson and Lynn Worsham in *Race, Rhetoric, and the Postcolonial*, edited by Gary Olson and Lynn Worsham. Albany: SUNY Press.

Bhabha, Homi and John Comaroff. 2001. "Speaking of Postcoloniality, in the Continuous Present: A Conversation." In *Relocating Postcolonialism*, edited by David Theo Goldberg and Ato Quayson. Oxford: Blackwell.

Bhattacharyya, Gargi, John Gabriel, and Stephen Small. 2001. *Race and Power*. London: Routledge.

Biagioli, Mario, ed. 1999. *The Science Studies Reader*. New York: Routledge.

Biehl, Janet, and Peter Staudenmaier. 1995. *Ecofascism: Lessons from the German Experience*. Edinburgh: AK Press.

Bircher, Martin, ed. 1970. *Die Fruchtbringende Gesellschaft: Quellen und Dokumente in vier Bänden*. Vols. 2–4. Munich: Kösel-Verlag.

———, ed. 1971. *Die Fruchtbringende Gesellschaft*. Vol. 1. Munich: Kösel-Verlag.

Bird, S. Elizabeth, ed. 1996. *Dressing in Feathers: The Construction of the Indian in American Popular Culture*. Boulder: Westview Press.

Bischoff, Jörg. 1999. "Staatsbürgerschaft/Das FDP-Modell zum Doppel-Paß auf Zeit für junge Ausländer." *Schwäbische Tagblatt* (12 February): 2.

Blaikie, Piers. 1985. *The Political Economy of Soil Erosion*. London: Methuen.

Blaikie, Piers, and Harold Brookfield. 1987. *Land Degradation and Society*. London: Methuen.

Blakey, Michael L. 1999. "Scientific Racism and the Biological Concept of Race." *Literature and Psychology* 45, nos.1–2: 29–44.

Bliss, Eugene L., ed. 1962. *Roots of Behavior: Genetics, Instinct, and Socialization in Animal Behavior*. New York: Hoeber-Harper.

Bloch, Ernst. 1990. *Heritage of Our Times*. Cambridge: MIT Press.

Bloom, Lisa. 1993. *Gender on Ice*. Minneapolis: University of Minnesota Press.

Boas, Franz. 1945. *Race and Democratic Society*. New York: J. J. Augustin.

———. 1982. [1931]. "Race and Progress." In *Race, Language, and Culture*. Chicago: University of Chicago Press.

———. 1986. [1928]. *Anthropology and Modern Life*. New York: Dover Publications.

Böckelmann, Frank. 1998. "Bürgerrechte mit Rabatt. Verleugnete Fremdheit: blinde Flecken in der Debatte um das neue Staatsbürgerschaftsrecht." *Frankfurter Allgemeine Zeitung* 272 (23 November): 49.

Boelhower, William. 1981. "Open Secrets: African American Testimony and the Paradigm of the Camp." Working Papers in Cultural Studies, Ethnicity, and Race Relations, Department of Comparative American Cultures, Washington State University.

Böhm, Andrea. 1999. "Die Mischung macht's. Wer gehört dazu? Und wer nicht?" *Die Zeit* 8 (18 February): 13.

Boitani, L., F. Francisci, P. Ciucci, and G. Andreoli. 1995. "Population Biology and Ecology of Feral Dogs in Central Italy." In *The Domestic Dog: Its Evolution, Behaviour, and Interactions with People*, edited by James Serpell. Cambridge: Cambridge University Press.

Boltanski, Luc. 1999. *Distant Suffering: Morality, Media, and Politics.* Translated by Graham Burchell. Cambridge: Cambridge University Press.

Bookchin, Murray. 1990. *Remaking Society: Pathways to a Green Future.* Boston: South End Press.

Bosch, Daniel. 2002. *Crucible.* New York: The Other Press.

Bourdieu, Pierre. 1977. *Outline of a Theory of Practice.* Translated by Richard Nice. Cambridge: Cambridge University Press.

——. 1984. *Distinction.* London: Routledge and Kegan Paul.

——. 1991. *The Political Ontology of Martin Heidegger.* Cambridge: Polity Press.

Bowen, John R. 2000. "Should We Have a Universal Concept of 'Indigenous Peoples' Rights'?" *Anthropology Today* 16, no. 4: 12–16.

Bowker, John Mitford. 1962. [1864]. *Speeches, Letters, and Selections from Important Papers.* Reprint. Cape Town: C. Struik.

Bragg, Jeffrey. 1996. "Purebred Dogs into the Twenty-First Century: Achieving Genetic Health for Our Dogs." Canine Genetic Diversity Web Site, at www.magma.ca/~kaitlin/diverse.html.

Brandt, Allan. 1985. *No Magic Bullet: A Social History of Venereal Disease in the United States since 1880.* New York: Oxford University Press.

Brandt, Anthony. 1999. "Dodging Earl in the Ghost Islands." *National Geographic Adventure* 1 no. 2: 86–91.

——. 2001. "The Adventure Craze." *American Heritage* (December/January): 41–49.

Brasier, Mary. 1990. "Young Guardian: City of Terror Where the Wolf Packs Run Wild." *New York Times,* 22 August.

Braun, Bruce. 2002. *The Intemperate Rainforest: Nature, Culture, and Power on Canada's West Coast.* Minneapolis: University of Minnesota Press.

Braun, Bruce, and Noel Castree, eds. 1998. *Remaking Reality: Nature at the Millennium.* New York: Routledge.

Brecher, Jeremy, John Brown Childs, and Jill Cutler, eds. 1993. *Global Visions: Beyond the New World Order.* Boston: South End Press.

Brennan, Denise. 1998. "Everything Is for Sale Here: Sex Tourism in Sosua, the Dominican." Ph.D. diss., Department of Anthropology, Yale University.

Bridgman, Jon. 1981. *Revolt of the Hereros.* Berkeley: University of California Press.

Briggs, Charles. 1996. "The Politics of Discursive Authority in Research on the 'Invention of Tradition.'" *Cultural Anthropology* 11, no. 4: 435–69.

Brodkin, Karen. 2000. "Global Capitalism: What's Race Got to Do with It?" *American Ethnologist* 27, no. 2: 237–56.

Brosius, J. Peter. 1999a. "On the Practice of Transnational Cultural Critique." *Identities—Global Studies in Culture and Power* 6, nos. 2–3: 179–200.

——. 1999b. "Anthropological Engagements with Environmentalism." *Current Anthropology* 40, no. 3: 277–309.

——. 1999c. "Green Dots, Pink Hearts: Displacing Politics from the Malaysian Rain Forest." *American Anthropologist* 101, no. 1: 36–57.

Brosius, J. Peter, Anna Lowenhaupt Tsing, and Charles Zerner. 1998. "Representing Communities: Histories and Politics of Community-Based Natural Resource Management." *Society and Natural Resources* 11: 157–68.

Brown, George. 1855. *Personal Adventure in South Africa*. London: James Blackwood.

Brown, Jacqueline Nassy. 2000. "Enslaving History: Narratives on Local Whiteness in a Black Atlantic Port." *American Ethnologist* 27, no. 2: 340–70.

Brown, Wendy. 1995. *States of Injury*. Princeton: Princeton University Press.

——. 2001. *Politics Out of History*. Princeton: Princeton University Press.

Browne, Malcolm W. 1999. "New Breed of Fox as Tame as a Pussycat." *New York Times*, 30 March: D3.

Brownlee, Charles. 1977. [1896]. *Reminiscences of Kaffir Life and History*. Reprint. Pietermaritzburg, South Africa: University of Natal Press.

Brubaker, Rogers. 1992. *Citizenship and Nationhood in France and Germany*. Cambridge: Harvard University Press.

Brumberg, Joan. 1988. *Fasting Girls: The Emergence of Anorexia Nervosa as a Modern Disease*. Cambridge: Harvard University Press.

Bryant, Raymond. 1992. "Political Ecology." *Political Geography* 11: 12–36.

Buck-Morss, Susan. 1989. The *Dialectics of Seeing: Walter Benjamin and the Arcades Project*. Cambridge: MIT Press.

——. 2000. "Hegel and Haiti." *Critical Inquiry* 26, no. 4 (summer): 821–65.

Buffon, Georges Louis Leclerc, Comte de. 1997. "The Geographical and Cultural Distribution of Mankind." In *Race and the Enlightenment: A Reader*, edited by Emmanuel Chukwudi Eze. Oxford: Blackwell.

Bulkin, Elly, Minnie Bruce Pratt, and Barbara Smith. 1984. *Yours in Struggle: Three Feminist Perspectives on Anti-Semitism and Racism*. New York: Long Haul Press.

Bullard, Robert D. 1990. *Dumping in Dixie: Race, Class, and Environmental Quality*. Boulder: Westview Press.

——. 1993. "Race and Environmental Justice in the United States." *Yale Journal of International Law* 18 (winter): 319–35.

——. 1993. *Confronting Environmental Racism: Voices from the Grassroots*. Boston: South End Press.

——. 1994. *Unequal Protection: Environmental Justice and Communities of Color*. San Francisco: Sierra Club Books.

——. 1999. "Leveling the Playing Field Through Environmental Justice." *Vermont Law Review* 23: 453–78.

Bunche, Ralph J. 1968. [1936]. *A World View of Race*. Port Washington: Kennikat Press.

Bunzel, Ruth. 1986. [1962]. Introduction. In *Anthropology and Modern Life*, by Franz Boas. New York: Norton.

Burchell, William. 1953. [1822]. *Travels in the Interior of Southern Africa*. Reprint, with a foreword by Isaac Schapera. London: Batchworth Press.

Burns, Peter. 1989. "The Myth of *Adat*." *Journal of Legal Pluralism* 28: 1–127.

Burton, Richard D. E. 1997. *Afro-Creole*. Ithaca: Cornell University Press.

Butler, Judith. 1990. *Gender Trouble*. New York: Routledge.

——. 1993. *Bodies That Matter: On the Discursive Limits of Sex*. New York: Routledge.

——. 1997. *The Psychic Life of Power*. Stanford: Stanford University Press.

——. 1998. "Merely Cultural." *New Left Review* 227 (January-February): 33–44.

Buzard, James. 1993. *The Beaten Track: European Tourism, Literature, and the Ways to "Culture,"* *1800–1918*. Oxford: Oxford University Press.

Cabezas, Amalia. 1998. "Pleasure and Its Pain: Sex Tourism in Susua, the Dominican Republic." Ph.D. diss., University of California at Berkeley.

——. 1999. "Women's Work Is Never Done: Sex Tourism in Susua, the Dominican Republic." In *Sun, Sex, and Gold: Tourism and Sex Work in the Caribbean*, edited by Kamala Kempadoo. Lanham, Md.: Rowman and Littlefield.

Cabral, Amilcar. 1973. "National Liberation and Culture." In *Return to the Source*. New York: Monthly Review Press.

Cabrera, Federico. 2001. "La comunidad de Andrés: Una excursion al Lejano Oeste." *Listin Diario*, 3 June: 3.

Caldeira, Teresa. 2001. *City of Walls: Crime, Segregation, and Citizenship in Sao Paulo*. Berkeley: University of California Press.

Calderwood, Henry. 1858. *Caffres and Caffre Missions*. London: James Nisbet.

Camacho, David E., ed. 1998. *Environmental Injustices, Political Struggles: Race, Class, and the Environment*. Durham: Duke University Press.

Campbell, John. 1974. [1815]. *Travels in South Africa*. Cape Town: C. Struik.

Carby, Hazel. 1999. *Cultures in Babylon: Black Britain and African America*. New York: Verso.

Cardoso, Fernando, and Enzo Faletto. 1979. *Dependency and Development in Latin America*. Berkeley: University of California Press.

Cardoso de Oliveira, Roberto. 1964. *O Índio e o Mundo dos Brancos*. São Paulo: Difusão Européia do Livro.

Cargill, John C., and Susan Thorpe-Vargas. 1996. "A Genetic Primer for Breeders." *DogWorld* 81, no. 5.

——. 1998. "Devising a Genetics Game Plan." *DogWorld* 83, no. 9: 20–24.

——. 2000. "Seeing Double: The Future of Canine Cloning." *DogWorld* 85, no. 3: 20–26.

Carlson, Robert S. 1997. *The War for the Heart and Soul of a Highland Maya Town*. Austin: University of Texas Press.

Carneiro da Cunha, Manuela. 1992. "Justiça para Paiakan, justiça para os índios." *Folha de São Paulo*. 6 July: 1: 3.

Carney, Judith, and Michael Watts. 1990. "Manufacturing Dissent: Work, Gender, and the Politics of Meaning in Peasant Society." *Africa* 60, no. 1: 207–41.

Carruthers, Jane. 1995. *The Kruger National Park: A Social and Political History*. Pietermaritzburg, South Africa: University of Natal Press.

Carter, C. O. 1967. "Genetical Aspects of Cystic Fibrosis of the Pancreas." *Biblioteca Paediatrica* 10, no. 86: 374.

Carter, Paul. 1989. *The Road to Botany Bay: An Exploration of Landscape and History*. Chicago: University of Chicago Press.

Casaus Arzú, Marta. 1992. *Guatemala: Linaje y Racismo*. San José, Costa Rica: FLACSO.

Castoriadis, Cornelius. 1992. "Reflections on Racism." *Thesis* 11, no. 32: 1–12.

Cathcart, Brian. 1999. *The Case of Stephen Lawrence*. New York: Viking.

CEDI (Centro de Documentação e Informação). 1991. "O encontro de Altamira." *Povos Indígenas no Brasil 1987/88/89/90. Aconteceu Especial* 18: 329–35. São Paulo: Centro de Documentação e Informação.

CEH (Comisión de Esclarecimiento Histórico/Commission for Historical Clarification). 1999. *Guatemala Memory of Silence, Tz'inil Na'tab'al Conclusions and Recommendations.* Guatemala City: United Nations.

Cesaire, Aime. 1983. [1939]. *Notebook of a Return to the Native Land.* Translated by Clayton Eshleman and Annette Smith. Berkeley: University of California Press.

Chakrabarty, Dipesh. 1994. "The Difference-Deferral of a Colonial Modernity: Public Debates on Domesticity in British India." In *Subaltern Studies VIII,* edited by David Arnold and David Hardiman. Oxford: Oxford University Press.

—. 2000. *Provincializing Europe.* Princeton: Princeton University Press.

Chanock, Martin. 1985. *Law, Custom, and Social Order.* Cambridge: Cambridge University Press.

Chatterjee, Amal. 1998. *Across the Lakes.* New Delhi: Penguin.

Chatterjee, Partha. 1993. *The Nation and Its Fragments.* Delhi: Oxford University Press.

—. ed. 1998. *Wages of Freedom.* Delhi: Oxford University Press.

—. 2002. *A Princely Imposter? The Strange and Universal History of the Kumar of Bhawal.* Princeton: Princeton University Press.

Chatterjee, Pratap, and Matthias Finger. 1994. *The Earth Brokers: Power, Politics, and World Development.* London: Routledge.

Chavez, Leo R. 2001. *Covering Immigration: Popular Images and the Politics of the Nation.* Berkeley: University of California Press.

Cheng, Vincent. 1995. *Joyce, Race, and Empire.* Cambridge: Cambridge University Press.

Childs, John Brown. 1998. "Transcommunality: From the Politics of Conversion to the Ethics of Respect in the Context of Cultural Diversity—Learning from Native American Philosophies with a Focus on the Haudenosaunee." *Social Justice* 25, no. 4: 143–69.

Chomsky, Noam. 2001. "The New War Against Terror." Transcription of a talk delivered at the Technology and Culture Forum, Massachusetts Institute of Technology. Available at http://www.zmag.org/GlobalWatch/chomskymit.htm.

Churchill, Ward. 1992. *Struggle for the Land: Indigenous Resistance to Genocide, Ecocide, and Expropriation in Contemporary North America.* Toronto: Between the Lines.

Churchill, Ward, and Wadonna LaDuke. 1983. "Native America: The Political Economy of Radioactive Colonialism." *Insurgent Sociologist* 13 (spring): 51–63.

Clark, Timothy J. 1984. *The Painting of Modern Life.* Princeton: Princeton University Press.

Clarke, Adele. 1995. "Research Materials and Reproductive Science in the United States, 1910–1940." In *Ecologies of Knowledge: Work and Politics in Science and Technology,* edited by Susan Leigh Star. Albany: SUNY Press.

Clayton, Daniel. 1999. *Islands of Truth: The Imperial Fashioning of Vancouver Island.* Vancouver: University of British Columbia Press.

Clifford, James. 1997. *Routes: Travel and Translation in the Late Twentieth Century.* Cambridge: Harvard University Press.

Coates, Peter A., 1998. *Nature: Western Attitudes since Ancient Times.* Berkeley: University of California Press.

Cock, Jacklyn, and Eddie Koch. 1991. *Going Green: People, Politics, and the Environment in South Africa.* Cape Town: Oxford University Press.

Coetzee, J. M. 1988. *White Writing: On the Culture of Letters in South Africa.* New Haven: Yale University Press.

Cohen, Cathy. 1999. *The Boundaries of Blackness: AIDS and the Breakdown of Black Politics.* Chicago: University of Chicago Press.

Cohen, Phil, ed. 1999. *New Ethnicities, Old Racisms.* London: Zed Books.

Coile, D. Caroline. 1997. "Tipping the Genetic Scales." *DogWorld* 82, no. 10: 40–45.

Cojtí Cuxil, Demetrio. 1991. *Configuración del Pensamiento Maya.* Quetzaltenango, Guatemala: Academia de Escritores Mayas.

——. 1995. *Ub'anik Ri Una'ooj Uchomab'aal Ri Maya' Tinamit: Configuracion del Pensamiento Politico del Pueblo Maya.* Part 2. Guatemala City: Cholsamaj.

——. 1999. "Heterofobia y Racismo Guatemalteco." In *¡Racismo en Guatemala? Abriendo el Debate sobre un Tema Tabú,* edited by Clara Arenas Bianchi, Charles R. Hale, and Gustavo Palma Murga. Guatemala City: AVANCSO.

Colchester, Marcus. 1986a. "The Struggle for Land: Tribal Peoples in the Face of the Transmigration Program." *The Ecologist* 16, nos. 2–3: 99–110.

——. 1986b. "Unity and Diversity: Indonesian Policy Towards Tribal Peoples." *The Ecologist* 16, nos. 2–3: 89–98.

Cole, John, and Eric Wolf. 1974. *The Hidden Frontier.* New York: Academic Press.

Cole, Luke W., and Sheila Foster, eds. 2001. *From the Ground Up: Environmental Racism and the Rise of the Environmental Justice Movement.* New York: New York University Press.

Collier, Jane, and Michelle Rosaldo. 1981. "Politics and Gender in 'Simple' Societies." In *Sexual Meanings,* edited by Sherry Ortner and Harriet Whitehead. New York: Cambridge University Press.

Collingwood, Robin George. 1960. *The Idea of Nature.* New York: Galaxy.

Comacho, David E. 1998. *Environmental Injustices, Political Struggles: Race, Class, and the Environment.* Durham, N.C.: Duke University Press.

Comaroff, Jean, and John Comaroff. 1997. *Of Revelation and Revolution.* Vol. 2. Chicago: University of Chicago Press.

——, eds. 1999. *Civil Society and the Political Imagination in Africa.* Chicago: University of Chicago Press.

——. 2001. "Naturing the Nation: Aliens, the Apocalypse, and the Postcolonial State." *Social Identities* 7, no. 2: 233–65.

Comer, Krista. 1999. *Landscapes of the New West: Gender and Geography in Contemporary Women's Writing.* Chapel Hill: University of North Carolina Press.

Conca, Ken, and Geoffrey D. Dabelko, eds. 1998. *Green Planet Blues: Environmental Politics from Stockholm to Rio.* 2d ed. Boulder: Westview Press.

Conklin, Beth A. 1997. "Body Paint, Feathers, and VCRs: Aesthetics and Authenticity in Amazonian Activism." *American Ethnologist* 24, no. 4: 711–37.

Conklin, Beth, and Laura Graham. 1995. "The Shifting Middle Ground: Amazonian Indians and Eco-Politics." *American Anthropologist* 97, no. 4: 695–710.

Conneally, P. M., A. D. Merritt, and P. Yu. 1973. "Cystic Fibrosis: Population Genetics." *Texas Reports on Biology and Medicine* 31: 639.

Connolly, William. 1991. *Identity and Difference: Democratic Negotiations of Political Paradox.* Ithaca: Cornell University Press.

Conrad, Joseph. 1995. [1902]. *Heart of Darkness.* New York: Penguin.

Cooper, Frederick. 1994. "Conflict and Connection: Rethinking Colonial African History." *American Historical Review* 99, no. 5: 1516–45.

Cooper, Frederick, and Laura Ann Stoler, eds. 1997. *Tensions of Empire: Colonial Cultures in a Bourgeois World*. Berkeley: University of California Press.

Coppinger, R., and R. Schneider. 1995. "Evolution of Working Dogs." In *The Domestic Dog: Its Evolution, Behaviour, and Interactions with People*, edited by James Serpell. Cambridge: Cambridge University Press.

Corbin, Alain. 1994. *The Lure of the Sea: The Discovery of the Seaside in the Western World, 1750–1840*. Translated by Jocelyn Phelps. Berkeley: University of California Press.

Coronil, Fernando. 1997. *The Magical State: Nature, Money, and Modernity in Venezuela*. Chicago: University of Chicago Press.

———. 2000. "Towards a Critique of Globalcentrism: Speculations on Capitalism's Nature." *Public Culture* 12, no. 2: 351–74.

Cose, Ellis. 2001. "Getting Ready for the Fire Next Time." *Newsweek* (22 January): 29.

Cosgrove, Dennis. 1984. *Social Formation and Symbolic Landscape*. Madison: University of Wisconsin Press.

———. 1995. "Habitable Earth: Wilderness, Empire, and Race in America." In *Wild Ideas*, edited by David Rothenberg. Minneapolis: University of Minnesota Press.

Cosgrove, Dennis, and Stephen Daniels, eds. 1988. *The Iconography of Landscape*. Cambridge: Cambridge University Press.

Crawfurd, M. D. 1972. "A Genetic Study, Including Evidence for Heterosis, of Cystic Fibrosis of the Pancreas." *Heredity* 29: 126.

Crenshaw, Kimberle. 2000. "Were the Critics Right about Rights? Reassessing the American Debate about Rights in the Post-Reform Era." In *Beyond Rights Talk and Culture Talk*, edited by Mahmood Mamdani. New York: St. Martin's Press.

Crick, Malcolm. 1989. "Representations of International Tourism in the Social Sciences: Sun, Sex, Sights, Savings, and Servility." *Annual Review of Anthropology* 18: 307–44.

Croll, Elizabeth, and David Parkin. 1992. *Bush Base/Forest Farm: Culture, Environment, and Development*. New York: Routledge.

Cronon, William. 1983. *Changes in the Land: Indians, Colonists, and the Ecology of New England*. New York: Hill and Wang.

———. 1996. "The Trouble with Wilderness; or, Getting Back to the Wrong Nature." In *Uncommon Ground: Rethinking the Human Place in Nature*, edited by William Cronon. New York: Norton.

Cronon, William, George Miles, and Jay Gitlin. 1992. "Becoming West: Toward a New Meaning for Western History." In *Under an Open Sky: Rethinking America's Western Past*, edited by William Cronon, George Miles, and Jay Gitlin. New York: Norton.

Cross, Malcolm, and Michael Keith, eds. 1993. *Racism, the City, and the State*. London: Routledge.

Crumley, Carole L., ed. 2001. *New Directions in Anthropology and Environment*. New York: Altamira Press.

Cunha, Ari. 1988. "Museu do Índio vai para a Universidade." *Correio Braziliense*, 4 June.

Curtin, Philip. 1964. *The Image of Africa: British Ideas and Action, 1780–1850*. Madison: University of Wisconsin Press.

Curts, Perry. 1968. *Anglo-Saxons and Celts: A Study of Anti-Irish Prejudice in Victorian England.* Berkeley: University of California Press.

———. 1997. *Apes and Angels: The Irishman in Victorian Caricature.* Washington, D.C.: Smithsonian Press.

Cutter, Susan. 1995. "Green Rage, Social Change, and the New Environmentalism." *Progress in Human Geography* 18, no. 2: 217–26.

Daniels, Stephen. 1989. "Marxism, Culture, and the Duplicity of Landscape." In *New Models in Geography,* edited by Richard Peet and Nigel Thrift. Vol. 2. London: Unwin Hyman.

Darien-Smith, Kate, Liz Gunner, and Sarah Nuttall, eds. 1996. *Text, Theory, Space.* London: Routledge.

Darnstädt, Thomas. 1999. "Staatsbürgerschaft: Größter anzunehmender Unfug." *Der Spiegel* 7 (15 February): 30–32.

Darwin, Charles. 1981. [1871]. *The Descent of Man, and Selection in Relation to Sex.* Princeton: Princeton University Press.

Das, Veena. 1995. *Critical Events.* Delhi: Oxford University Press.

Davies, Hugh. 1990. "Wilding Gang Rapists Jailed." *The Times* (London), 12 September: 3.

Davies, Lincoln. 1999. "Working Toward a Common Goal? Three Case Studies of Brownfields in Environmental Justice Communities." *Stanford Environmental Law Journal* 18: 285–329.

Davin, Anna. 1978. "Imperialism and Motherhood." *History Workshop Journal* 5 (spring): 9–65.

Davis, Angela Yvonne. 1992. "Black Nationalism: The Sixties and the Nineties." In *Black Popular Culture,* edited by Gina Dent. Seattle: Bay Press.

———. 1998a. *The Angela Y. Davis Reader,* edited by Joy James. Oxford: Blackwell.

———. 1998b. *Blues Legacies and Black Feminism.* New York: Vintage.

Davis, Angela Yvonne, and Elizabeth Martinez. 1994. "Coalition Building among People of Color." *Inscriptions* 7: 42–53.

Davis, Mike. 1990. *City of Quartz.* London: Verso.

———. 1998. *Ecology of Fear.* New York: Metropolitan Books.

Davis, Susan. 1995. " 'Touch the Magic.' " In *Uncommon Ground: Rethinking the Human Place in Nature,* edited by William Cronon. New York: Norton.

de Araujo Castro, João Augusto. 1998. "Environment and Development: The Case of Developing Countries." In *Green Planet Blues: Environmental Politics from Stockholm to Rio,* edited by Ken Conca and Geoffrey D. Dabelko. 2d ed. Boulder: Westview Press.

De Beauvoir, Simone. 1953. [1952]. *The Second Sex.* Translated by H. M. Parshley. New York: Knopf.

de Certeau, Michel. 1984. *The Practice of Everyday Life.* Translated by Steven F. Rendall. Berkeley: University of California Press.

———. 1988 [1975]. *The Writing of History.* Translated by Tom Conley. New York: Columbia University Press.

de la Cadena, Marisol. 1996. "The Political Tensions of Representations and Misrepresentations: Intellectuals and Mestizas in Cuzco (1919–1990)." *Journal of Latin American Anthropology* 2, no. 1: 112–47.

———. 2000. *Indigenous Mestizos.* Durham, N.C.: Duke University Press.

De las Casas, Bartholome. 1992. [1552]. *In Defense of the Indians.* Translated by Safford Poole. DeKalb: Northern Illinois University Press.

Delgado, Richard, and Jean Stefancic. 2001. *Critical Race Theory*. New York: New York University Press.

DeLuca, Kevin. 1999. "In the Shadow of Whiteness: The Consequences of Constructions of Nature in Environmental Politics." In *Whiteness: The Communication of Social Identity*, edited by Thomas K. Nakayama and Judith N. Martin. London: Sage.

Demeritt, David. 1998. "Science, Social Constructivism, and Nature." In *Remaking Reality: Nature at the Millennium*, edited by Bruce Braun and Noel Castree. New York: Routledge.

De Moya, E. Antonio, Rafael García, Rosario Fadul, and Edward Herold. 1992. *Sosúa Sanky-Pankies and Female Sex Workers*. Santo Domingo: Instituto de Sexualidad Humana, Universidad Autónoma de Santo Domingo.

Dent, Gina, ed. 1992. *Black Popular Culture*. Seattle: Bay Press.

Dereuck, Anthony, and Julie Knight. 1967. *Caste and Race: Comparative Approaches*. Boston: Little, Brown.

Derr, Mark. 1997. *Dog's Best Friend: Annals of the Dog-Human Relationship*. New York: Holt.

—. 1998. "Missyplicity." *The Bark*. Volume 6: 11.

Derrida, Jacques. 1976. *Of Grammatology*. Translated by Gayatri Chakravorty Spivak. Baltimore: The Johns Hopkins University Press.

—. 1988. "Signature, Event, Context." In *Limited, Inc*, edited by Gerald Graff. Translated by Alan Bass. Evanston: Northwestern University Press.

—. 2000. *Of Hospitality*. Translated by Rachel Bowlby, edited by Anne Dufourmantelle. Stanford: Stanford University Press.

Descola, Philippe, and Gisli Palsson, eds. 1996. *Nature and Society: Anthropological Perspectives*. New York: Routledge.

DeSoto, Hermine, and Konstanze Plett. 1995. "Citizenship and Minorities in the Process of Nation Rebuilding in Germany." *PoLAr* 18, no. 1: 106–21.

Deutsch, Sarah. 1992. "Race Relations in the West, 1865–1990." In *Under an Open Sky: Rethinking America's Western Past*, edited by William Cronon, George Miles, and Jay Gitlin. New York: Norton.

Di Chiro, Giovanna. 1992. "Defining Environmental Justice: Women's Voices and Grassroots Politics." *Socialist Review* 22, no. 4: 93–130.

—. 1995. "Nature as Community: The Convergence of Environmental and Social Justice." In *Uncommon Ground: Rethinking the Human Place in Nature*, edited by William Cronon. New York: Norton.

—. 1997. "Local Actions, Global Visions: Remaking Environmental Expertise." *Frontiers* 18, no. 2: 203–31.

—. 2000. "Bearing Witness or Taking Action? Toxic Tourism and Environmental Justice." In *Reclaiming the Environmental Debate: The Politics of Health in a Toxic Culture*, edited by Richard Hofrichter. Cambridge: MIT Press.

di Sant Agnese, P. A. 1976. "Research in Cystic Fibrosis." *New England Journal of Medicine* 277: 481.

Diamond, Irene, and Lee Quinby. 1988. *Feminism and Foucault: Reflections on Resistance*. Boston: Northeastern University Press.

Diamond, Jared. 1991. "Curse and Blessing of the Ghetto." *Discover* (March): 60–65.

Diawara, Manthia. 1998. *In Search of Africa*. Cambridge: Harvard University Press.

Dirks, Nicholas. 1992. *Colonialism and Culture.* Princeton: Princeton University Press.

——. 2001. *Castes of Mind.* Princeton: Princeton University Press.

Dodman, Nicholas. 1996. *The Dog Who Loved Too Much.* New York: Bantam.

Donald, James, and Ali Rattansi, eds. 1992. *Race, Culture, and Difference.* Newbury Park: Sage Press.

Donzelot, Jacques. 1979. *The Policing of Families.* Translated by Robert Hurley. New York: Pantheon.

Douglas. Mary. 1966. *Purity and Danger: An Analysis of Concepts of Pollution and Taboo.* New York: Routledge.

Douglass, Frederick. 1992. [1889]. "The Nation's Problem." In *African-American Social and Political Thought, 1850–1920,* edited by Howard Brotz. Reprint. New York: Basic Books.

Dove, Michael. 1985. "The Agroecological Mythology of the Javanese and the Political Economy of Indonesia." *Indonesia* 39 (April): 1–35.

Dowling, Denise. 1998. "Let's Go on a Guilt Trip." *New York Times Magazine,* 7 June.

Down to Earth. 1999. Special Issue. Newsletter of the International Campaign for Ecological Justice in Indonesia. October.

Doyle, Laura. 1994. *Bordering on the Body: The Racial Matrix of Modern Fiction and Culture.* New York: Routledge.

Drayton, Richard. 2000. *Nature's Government: Science, Imperial Britain, and the "Improvement" of the World.* New Haven: Yale University Press.

D'Souza, Dinesh. 1995. *The End of Racism: Principles for a Multiracial Society.* New York: Free Press.

Du Bois, W. E. B. 1946. *The World and Africa.* New York: Viking.

——. 1986. [1897]. "The Conservation of the Races." In *W. E. B. Du Bois: Writings.* New York: Library of America.

——. 1986. [1940]. "Dusk of Dawn: An Essay Toward an Autobiography of a Race Concept." In *W. E. B. Du Bois: Writings.* New York: Library of America.

Dubow, Saul 1995. *Scientific Racism in Modern South Africa.* Cambridge: Cambridge University Press.

Dudley, Edward, and Maximillian Novak, eds. 1972. *The Wild Man Within.* Pittsburgh: University of Pittsburgh Press.

Dursin, Richel. 2000. "Illegal Loggers Now Bolder, Activists Say." *IPS,* 24 February. Jakarta.

Dussel, Enrique. 1995. *The Invention of the Americas: Eclipse of "The Other" and the Myth of Modernity.* New York: Continuum.

——. 1998. *The Underside of Modernity: Apel, Ricouer, Rorty, Taylor, and the Philosophy of Liberation.* Atlantic Highlands, N.J.: Humanities Press.

Dworkin, Andrea. 1981. *Pornography: Men Possessing Women.* New York: Perigree.

Dwyer, Daisy, and Judith Bruce. 1988. *A Home Divided: Women and Income in the Third World.* Stanford: Stanford University Press.

Ebron, Paula. 1996. "Traffic in Men." In *Gendered Encounters,* edited by Maria Grosz-Ngate and Omari Kokole. New York: Routledge.

The Ecologist. 1993. *Whose Common Future? Reclaiming the Commons.* Philadelphia: New Society Publishers.

Edwards, Jeanette, Sarah Franklin, Eric Hirsch, Frances Price, and Marilyn Strathern. 1999. [1993].

Technologies of Procreation: Kinship in the Age of Assisted Conception. 2d ed. London: Routledge.

Edwards, J. H. 1977. "Heterozygote Advantage." *Archives of Disease in Childhood.* 52: 344.

Eghigian, Greg, et al., eds. 2002. *Sacrifice and National Belonging.* College Station: Texas A&M University Press.

Eldridge, Colin C. 1996. *Disraeli and the Rise of a New Imperialism.* Cardiff: University of Wales Press.

Eley, George, and Ronald Grigor Suny, eds. 1996. *Becoming National.* New York: Oxford University Press.

Ellen, Roy, and Katsuyoshi Fukui. 1996. *Redefining Nature: Ecology, Culture, and Domestication.* Oxford: Berg.

Elliot, Dorinda, and Frisco Endt. 1995. "Twins—with Two Fathers; The Netherlands: A Fertility Clinic's Startling Error." *Newsweek* (3 July): 38.

Ellis, John. 1975. *The Social History of the Machine Gun.* London: Croom Helm.

Enloe, Cynthia. 1989. *Bananas, Beaches, and Bases: Making Feminist Sense of International Politics.* Berkeley: University of California Press.

Erb, Rainer. 1997. "Public Responses to Anti-Semitism and Right-Wing Extremism." In *Antisemitism and Xenophobia in Germany after Unification,* edited by Hermann Kurthen et al. New York: Oxford University Press.

Erni, Christian. 1996. "Indigenous Peoples in South and Southeast Asia: Between Twentieth-Century Capitalism and Oriental Despotism." In *Vines That Won't Bind: Indigenous Peoples in Asia,* edited by C. Erni. Copenhagen: International Working Group for Indigenous Affairs (IWGIA).

Escobar, Arturo. 1999. "After Nature: Steps to an Antiessentialist Political Ecology." *Current Anthropology* 40, no. 1: 1–30.

Escoffier, Jeffrey. 1991. "The Limits of Multiculturalism." *Socialist Review* 21, nos. 3–4: 61–73.

Essed, Philomena, and David Goldberg, eds. 2002. *Race Critical Theories.* Oxford: Blackwell.

Evans, P. R. 1987. "Tay-Sachs Disease: A Centennary." *Archives of Disease in Childhood* 62: 1056–59.

Evelegh, Robin. 1978. *Peace-Keeping in a Democratic Society: The Lessons of Northern Ireland.* London: Hurst and Co.

Evers, Pieter J. 1995. "Preliminary Policy and Legal Questions about Recognizing Traditional Land Rights in Indonesia." *Ekonesia* 3: 1–23.

Eze, Emmanuel Chukwudi, ed. 1997. *Race and the Enlightenment.* Oxford: Blackwell.

—. 2001. *Achieving Our Humanity: The Idea of a Postracial Future.* New York: Routledge.

Faber, Daniel. 1998. "The Political Ecology of American Capitalism: New Challenges for the Environmental Justice Movement." In *The Struggle for Ecological Democracy: Environmental Justice Movements in the United States,* edited by Daniel Faber. New York: Guilford.

Fabian, Johannes. 1983. *Time and the Other: How Anthropology Makes Its Object.* New York: Columbia University Press.

—. 1999. "Remembering the Other: Knowledge and Recognition in the Exploration of Central Africa." *Critical Inquiry* 26, no. 1: 49–69.

—. 2000. *Out of Our Minds.* Berkeley: University of California Press.

—. 2001. *Anthropology with an Attitude.* Stanford: Stanford University Press.

Fairhead, James, and Melissa Leach. 1995. "False Forest History, Complicit Social Analysis: Rethinking Some West African Environmental Narratives." *World Development* 23, no. 6: 1023–35.

——. 1996. *Misreading the African Landscape: Society and Ecology in a Forest-Savanna Mosaic.* Cambridge: Cambridge University Press.

Falla, Ricardo. 1984. "We Charge Genocide." In *Guatemala: Tyranny on Trial. Testimony of the Permanent People's Tribunal,* edited by Susanne Jonas, Ed McCaughan, and Elizabeth Sutherland Martínez. San Francisco: Synthesis Publications.

Fanon, Frantz. 1963. [1961]. *The Wretched of the Earth.* Translated by Constance Farrington. New York: Grove Press.

——. 1967. [1952]. *Black Skin, White Masks.* Translated by Charles Lam Markmann. New York: Grove Press.

——. 1967. [1956]. "Racism and Culture." In *Toward the African Revolution.* Translated by Haakon Chevalier. New York: Grove Press.

Faragher, John. 1992. "Americans, Mexicans, Métis: A Community Approach to the Comparative Study of North American Frontiers." In *Under an Open Sky: Rethinking America's Western Past,* edited by William Cronon, George Miles, and Jay Gitlin. New York: Norton.

Fauzi, Noer. 1999. "Eliminate the Concept of State Control: A Critique of the Forest Department's Version of the Forestry Bill." 10 September. Available at fkkm@egroups.com.

FAZ. 1999. "Vorschläge zur Reform des Staatsangehörigkeitsrechts." *Frankfurter Allgemeine Zeitung* 24 (29 January): 6.

Featherstone, Michael, ed. 1990. *Global Culture: Nationalism, Globalization, and Modernity.* London: Sage.

Fee, Elizabeth. 1979. "Nineteenth-Century Craniology: The Study of the Female Skull." *Bulletin of the History of Medicine* 53 (fall): 415–33.

Feld, Steven. 1996. "Waterfalls of Song: An Acoustemology of Place Resounding in Bosavi, Papua New Guinea." In *Senses of Place,* edited by Steven Feld and Keith Basso. Santa Fe: School of American Research Press.

Feld, Steven, and Keith Basso, eds. 1996. *Senses of Place.* Santa Fe: School of American Research Press.

Ferguson, James. 1990. *The Anti-Politics Machine: "Development," Depoliticization, and Bureaucratic Power in Lesotho.* Cambridge: Cambridge University Press.

Finger, Matthias. 1993. "Politics of the UNCED Process." In *Global Ecology: A New Arena of Political Conflict,* edited by Wolfgang Sachs. London: Zed Books.

Finke, Heinz-Peter. 1999. "Kommentar: Doppelter Ärger." *Schwäbisches Tagblatt* 54 (6 March): 1.

Finkler, Kaja. 2000. *Experiencing the New Genetics: Family and Kinship on the Medical Frontier.* Philadelphia: University of Pennsylvania Press.

Fischer, Edward F. 2001. *Cultural Logics and Global Economies: Maya Identity in Thought and Practice.* Austin: University of Texas Press.

Fischer, Edward F., and R. McKenna Brown, eds. 1996. *Maya Cultural Activism in Guatemala.* Austin: University of Texas Press.

Fisher, Larry, Ilya Moeliono, and Stefan Wodicka. 1998. "Cattle, Cockatoos, Chameleons, and Ninja Turtles: Seeking Sustainability in Forest Management and Conservation in Nusa Tenggara, Indonesia." Paper presented at the International Workshop on Community-Based Natural Resource Management, 10–14 May, Washington, D.C.

Fitzpatrick, Peter. 1995. Comment on "Talking Culture: New Boundaries, New Rhetoric of Exclusion in Europe," by Verena Stolcke. *Current Anthropology* 36, no. 1: 14–15.

FKKM (Forum Komunikasi Kehutanan Masyarakat). 1999. "The Riau Provincial Legislature Supports the Rejection of the Forestry Bill." 15 September. Available at fkkm@egroups.com.

Fleming, Peter. 1961. *Bayonets to Lhasa: The First Full Account of the British Invasion of Tibet in 1904*. New York: Harper.

Folbre, Nancy. 1994. *Who Pays for the Kids? Gender and the Structures of Constraint*. London: Routledge.

Fonteles, Bené. 1989. "Um museu para os deuses." *Correio Braziliense*, 21 April.

Forbes, Jack D. 1993. *Africans and Native Americans*. Urbana: University of Illinois Press.

Foster, Sheila. 1993. "Race(ial) Matters: The Quest for Environmental Justice." *Ecology Law Quarterly* 20: 721–53.

——. 1998. "Justice from the Ground Up: Distributive Inequities, Grassroots Resistance, and the Transformational Politics of the Environmental Justice Movement." *California Law Review* 86, no. 4: 775–841.

Foster-Carter, Aidan. 1978. "The Modes of Production Controversy." *New Left Review* 107: 47–77.

Foucault, Michel. 1979a. *Discipline and Punish: The Birth of the Prison*. Translated by Alan Sheridan. New York: Vintage.

——. 1979b. *Microfísica do Poder*. Rio de Janeiro: Graal.

——. 1981. "Omnes et Singulatim: Towards a Criticism of 'Political Reason.'" *The Tanner Lectures on Human Values, II*. Salt Lake City: University of Utah Press.

——. 1990. [1978]. *The History of Sexuality*. Vol. 1. Translated by Robert Hurley. New York: Random House.

——. 1991a. *Remarks on Marx*. Translated by R. James Goldstein and James Cascaito. New York: Semiotext(e).

——. 1991b. "Governmentality." In *The Foucault Effect: Studies in Governmentality*, edited by Graham Burchell, Colin Gordon, and Peter Miller. Chicago: University of Chicago Press.

——. 2000. *Power*. Edited by James Faubion. New York: New Press.

Fox, Daniel, and Elizabeth Fee, eds. 1990. *AIDS: The Burden of History*. Berkeley: University of California Press.

Fox-Keller, Evelyn. 1992. "Nature, Nurture, and the Human Genome Project." In *The Code of Codes*, edited by Daniel Kevles and LeRoy Hood. Cambridge: Harvard University Press.

Frankenberg, Günter. 1999. "Eine Rolle rückwärts: Streit um den Doppelpaß. Das FDP-Oppositionsmodell ist verfassungsrechtlich bedenklich." *Die Zeit* 8 (18 February): 11.

Frankenburg, Ruth. 1993. *White Women, Race Matters: The Social Construction of Whiteness*. Minneapolis: University of Minnesota Press.

Franklin, Sarah. 1995. "Romancing the Helix: Nature and Scientific Discovery." In *Romance Revisited*, edited by Lynne Pearce and Jackie Stacy. London: Lawrence and Wishart.

——. 1997. *Embodied Progress: A Cultural Account of Assisted Conception*. London: Routledge.

Franklin, Sarah, and Helen Ragone, eds. 1998. *Reproducing Reproduction: Kinship, Power, and Technological Innovation*. Philadelphia: University of Pennsylvania Press.

Fraser, Nancy. 1997. "Heterosexism, Misrecognition, and Capitalism: A Response to Judith Butler." *Social Text* 52-53: 279–89.

Frazier, Edward Franklin. 1957. *Race and Culture Contacts in the Modern World*. New York: Knopf.

Freeman, Carla. 2000. *High Tech and High Heels in the Global Economy*. Durham, N.C.: Duke University Press.

Freud, Sigmund. 1961. [1930]. *Civilization and Its Discontents*. Translated by James Strachey. New York: Norton.

Friede, Eva. 2000. "Made for Mambo: Colourful Feminine, Flirty, Latin Look Is Everywhere." *The Gazette* (Montreal), 13 June: C1.

Frost, April, and Randi Lightmark. 1997. *Beyond Obedience*. New York: Harmony Books.

Fuller, John L., and W. R. Thompson. 1960. *Behavioral Genetics*. New York: Wiley.

Fullwiley, Duana. 1998. "Race, biologie et maladie: La difficile organisation des patients atteints de drépanocytose aux États-Unis." *Sciences Sociales et Sante* 16, no. 3: 129–58.

Fusco, Coco. 1994. *English Is Broken Here*. New York: Free Press.

Fuss, Diana. 1989. *Essentially Speaking: Feminism, Nature, and Difference*. New York: Routledge.

Gadgil, Madhav, and Ramachandra Guha. 1993. *This Fissured Land: An Ecological History of India*. Berkeley: University of California Press.

Gairdner, D. 1975. "Heterozygote Advantage in Cystic Fibrosis." *Lancet* 1: 279.

Garzon, Susan, R. McKenna Brown, Julia Becker Richards, and Wuqu' Ajpub,' eds. 1998. *The Life of Our Language: Kaqchikel Maya Maintenance, Shift, and Revitalization*. Austin: University of Texas Press.

Gasman, Daniel. 1998. *Haeckel's Monism and the Birth of Fascist Ideology*. New York: P. Lang.

Geertz, Clifford. 1973. *The Interpretation of Culture*. New York: Basic Books.

Geiger, Klaus F. 1991. "Einstellungen zur multikulturellen Gesellschaft: Ergebnisse von Repräsentativbefragungen in der Bundesrepublik." *Migration* 9: 11–48.

Gelder, Ken, and Jane Jacobs. 1998. *Uncanny Australia: Sacredness and Identity in a Postcolonial Nation*. Carlton, South Australia: Melbourne University Press.

Gerhard, Ute. 1994. "Diskurstheoretische Überlegungen zu Strategien des Rassismus in Medien und Politik—Flüchtlinge und Zuwanderer in Deutschland als wiederkehrende Themen im 20. Jahrhundert." In *Überall, in den Köpfen und Fäusten*, edited by H. Tiersch, J. Wertheimer, and K. Grunwald. Darmstadt: Wissenschaftliche Buchgesellschaft.

Geschiere, Peter, and Francis Nyamnjoh. 2000. "Capitalism and Autochthony: The Seesaw of Mobility and Belonging." *Public Culture* 12, no. 2: 423–52.

Ghosh, Kaushik. 1999. "A Market for Aboriginality: Primitivism and Race Classification in the Indentured Labor Market of Colonial India." In *Subaltern Studies X*, edited by Guatam Bhadra, Gyan Prakash, and Susie Tharu. Delhi: Oxford University Press.

Giel, Klaus, and Philip Mattson. 1963. "Einführung in die sprachphilosophischen Schriften." In *Wilhelm von Humboldt: Schriften zur Sprachphilosophie*. Werke V. Reprint. Darmstadt: Wissenschaftliche Buchgesellschaft.

Gikandi, Simon. 1997. *Maps of Englishness*. New York: Columbia University Press.

Gilman, Sander. 1985. "Black Bodies, White Bodies: Towards an Iconography of Female Sexuality in Late Nineteenth-Century Art, Medicine, and Literature." In *"Race," Writing, and Difference*, edited by Henry Louis Gates Jr. Chicago: University of Chicago Press.

Gilroy, Paul. 1980. "Steppin' Out of Babylon: 'Race,' Class, and Autonomy." In *The Empire Strikes Back: Race and Racism in Seventies Britain*. Edited by the Centre for Contemporary Cultural Studies. London: Hutchinson and CCCS.

——. 1981. "You Can't Fool the Youths . . . Race and Class Formation in the 80s. *Race and Class* 13, nos. 2–3: 207–22.

——. 1990a. "One Nation under a Groove: The Cultural Politics of 'Race' and Racism in Britain." In

Anatomy of Racism, edited by David Theo Goldberg. Minneapolis: University of Minnesota Press.

———. 1990b. "Nationalism, History, and Ethnic Absolutism." *History Workshop Journal* 30: 114–20.

———. 1991. [1987]. *There Ain't No Black in the Union Jack: The Cultural Politics of Race and Nation*. Chicago: University of Chicago Press.

———. 1992. "It's a Family Affair." In *Black Popular Culture*, edited by Gina Dent. Seattle: Bay Press.

———. 1993. *The Black Atlantic: Modernity and Double Consciousness*. London: Verso.

———. 2000. *Against Race: Imagining Political Culture Beyond the Color Line*. Cambridge: Harvard University Press.

Gilroy, Paul, Lawrence Grossberg, and Angela McRobbie, eds. 2000. *Without Guarantees: In Honour of Stuart Hall*. London: Verso.

Giroux, Henry A., and Peter McLaren, eds. 1994. *Between Borders: Pedagogy and the Politics of Cultural Studies*. New York: Routledge.

Glacken, Clarence. 1967. *Traces on the Rhodian Shore*. Berkeley: University of California Press.

Glass, Bentley. 1956. "Malaria and Sickle Cell Anemia." *Science* (October): 473.

Glausiusz, Josie. 1995. "Unfortunate Drift." *Discover* (June): 34–35.

Glissant, Édouard. 1989. *Caribbean Discourse*. Translated by J. Michael Dash. Charlottesville: University Press of Virginia.

———. 1997. *Poetics of Relation*. Translated by Betsy Wing. Ann Arbor: University of Michigan Press.

Gobineau, Arthur. 1970. [1853–1855]. "Racial Inequality." In *Gobineau: Selected Political Writings*, edited and translated by M. D. Biddiss. New York: Harper and Row.

Godlonton, Robert. [1852] 1965. *Narrative of the Kaffir War, 1850–1852*. Reprint. Cape Town: C. Struik.

Goffman, Erving. 1959. *The Presentation of Self in Everyday Life*. Garden City: Doubleday.

Goldberg, David Theo, ed. 1990. *Anatomy of Racism*. Minneapolis: University of Minnesota Press.

———. 1993. *Racist Culture: Philosophy and the Politics of Meaning*. Oxford: Blackwell.

———, ed. 1994. *Multiculturalism: A Critical Reader*. Oxford: Blackwell.

———. 1997. *Racial Subjects*. New York: Routledge.

———. 2002. *The Racial State*. Oxford: Blackwell.

Goldman, James. 1989. " 'Wilding' Rape Shocks New Yorkers." *Toronto Star*, 24 April: A17.

Goldman, Michael, ed. 1998. *Privatizing Nature: Political Struggles for the Global Commons*. London: Pluto Press.

Goluboff, Sascha. 2001. " 'Race Places': Changing Locations of Jewish Identities." *Identities* 8, no. 2: 163–71.

Gonzalez, David. 2000. "Rights in Guatemala: At Risk Still." *New York Times*, 5 November.

González Ponciano, Jorge Ramon. 1991. *Guatemala, la civilizacion y el progreso: Notas sobre Indigenismo, Racismo, e Identidad Nacional, 1821–1954*. Anuario: Inst. Chiapaneco de Cultura. Tuxtla Gutierrez, México: Dept. de Patrimonio Cultura e Investigación.

———. 1997. *"Esas Sangres No Están Limpias": El Racismo, el Estado y la Nación en Guatemala* (1944–1997). Anuario Separata, San Cristóbal las Casas, Mexico: Centro de Estudios Superiores de México y Centroamérica.

Gordon, Avery F., and Christopher Newfield, eds. 1996. *Mapping Multiculturalism*. Minneapolis: University of Minnesota Press.

Gordon, Edmund T. 1998. *Disparate Diasporas: Identity and Politics in an African-Nicaraguan Community*. Austin: University of Texas Press.

Gordon, Robert. 1992. *The Bushman Myth: The Making of a Namibian Underclass*. Boulder: Westview Press.

Gould, Jeffrey L. 1998. *To Die in This Way: Nicaraguan Indians and the Myth of Mestizaje, 1880–1965*. Durham, N.C.: Duke University Press.

Gould, Stephen J. 1996. *The Mismeasure of Man*. New York: Norton.

Graeber, Charles. 2000. "How Much Is that Doggy in the Vitro?" *Wired* (March): 220–29.

Graham, Richard, ed. 1990. *The Idea of Race in Latin America, 1870–1940*. Austin: University of Texas Press.

Gramsci, Antonio. 1971. *Selections from the Prison Notebooks*. Translated by Quintin Hoare and Geoffrey Nowell Smith. London: Lawrence and Wishart.

—. 1990. [1920]. "Address to the Anarchists." Reprinted in *Selections from Political Writings: 1910–1920*. Selected and edited by Quintin Hoare. Translated by John Matthews. Minneapolis: University of Minnesota Press.

Grandin, Greg. 2000. *The Blood of Guatemala: A History of Race and Nation*. Durham, N.C.: Duke University Press.

Graphard, Allan G. 1994. "Geosophia, Geognosis, and Geopiety: Orders of Significance in Japanese Representations of Space." In *NowHere: Space, Time, and Modernity*, edited by Roger Friedland and Deirdre Boden. Berkeley: University of California Press.

Graves, Joseph. 2001. *The Emperor's New Clothes: Biological Theories of Race at the Millennium*. New Brunswick: Rutgers University Press.

Gray, Andrew. 1995. "The Indigenous Movement in Asia." In *Indigenous Peoples of Asia*, edited by Robert H. Barnes, Andrew Gray, and Benedict Kingsbury. Ann Arbor: The Association for Asian Studies.

Grayson, Deborah. 1998. "Mediating Intimacy: Black Surrogate Mothers and the Law," *Critical Inquiry* 24 (winter): 525–46.

Great Britain. 1851a. *Hansard Parliamentary Debates*, 3d ser., vol. 115.

Great Britain. 1851b. *Hansard Parliamentary Debates*. 3d ser., vol. 116.

Green, Linda. 1999. *Fear as a Way of Life: Mayan Widows in Rural Guatemala*. New York: Columbia University Press.

Green Robe. "Rejection of the Forestry Bill from West Kalimantan." 15 September. Available at fkkm@egroups.com.

Greenblatt, Stephen. 1991. *Marvelous Possessions: The Wonder of the New World*. Chicago: University of Chicago Press.

Greenfield, Karl Taro. 1999. "Under the Billboard Sky." *Outside* 24, no. 12: 104–06; 108; 110; 158–59.

Gregory, Derek. 1995. "Between the Book and the Lamp: Imaginative Geographies of Egypt, 1849–1860." *Transactions of the Institute of British Geographers* 20: 29–57.

Gregory, Steven. 1998. *Black Corona: Race and the Politics of Place in an Urban Community*. Princeton: Princeton University Press.

Grewal, Inderpal, and Caren Kaplan. 2001. *An Introduction to Women's Studies: Gender in a Transnational World*. New York: McGraw Hill.

Grewal, Shabnam, Jackie Kay, Liliane Landor, Gail Lewis, and Pratibha Parmar. 1988. *Charting the Journey: Writings by Black and Third World Women*. London: Sheba Feminist Publishers.

Griffin, Roger. 1995. *Fascism*. New York: Oxford University Press.

Grinde, Donald. 1995. *Ecocide of Native America*. Santa Fe: Clear Light.

Grove, Richard. 1995. *Green Imperialism.* Cambridge: Cambridge University Press.

Grunwald, Michael. 1999. "In Vitro, in Error—and Now, in Court: White Mother Given Black Couple's Embryos Will Give One 'Twin' Back." *Washington Post,* 31 March: A01.

Guha, Ramachandra, ed. 1994. *Social Ecology.* Delhi: Oxford University Press.

Guha, Ramachandra, and Juan Martinez-Alier. 1997. *Varieties of Environmentalism: Essays North and South.* London: Earthscan.

Guha, Sumit. 1998. "Lower Strata, Older Races, and Abriginal Peoples: Racial Anthropology and Mythical History Past and Present." *Journal of Asian Studies* 57, no. 2: 423–41.

Guillaumin, Colette. 1995. *Racism, Sexism, Power, and Ideology.* New York: Routledge.

Guinier, Lani, and Gerald Torres. 2002. *The Miner's Canary.* Cambridge: Harvard University Press.

Gunder Frank, Andre. 1967. *Capitalism and Underdevelopment in Latin America.* New York: Monthly Review Press.

Gupta, Akhil, and James Ferguson. 1992. "Beyond 'Culture': Space, Identity, and the Politics of Difference." *Cultural Anthropology* 7, no. 1: 6–23.

—. eds. 1997. *Culture, Power, and Place: Explorations in Critical Anthropology.* Durham, N.C.: Duke University Press.

Gutmann, Amy, ed. 1994. *Multiculturalism: Examining the Politics of Recognition.* Princeton: Princeton University Press.

Guyton, Patrick. 1999. "Staatsangehörigkeit: Massenweise Doppelstaatler durch die Hintertür." *Schwäbisches Tagblatt* 237 (13 October): 2.

Hacking, Ian. 1999. *The Social Construction of What?* Cambridge: Cambridge University Press.

Haden, Russell, and Ferris Evans. 1937. "Sickle Cell Anemias in the White Race." *Archives of Internal Medicine* 60 (July): 133–42.

Hale, Charles R. 1996a. "Introduction." *Journal of Latin American Anthropology* 2, no. 1: 2–3.

—. 1996b. "Mestizaje, Hybridity, and the Cultural Politics of Difference in Post-Revolutionary Central America." *Journal of Latin American Anthropology* 2, no. 1: 34–61.

—. 1997. "Cultural Politics of Identity in Latin America." *Annual Review of Anthropology* 26: 567–90.

—. 1999a. Comment on "Cultural Logic and Maya Identity," by Edward F. Fischer. *Current Anthropology* 40, no. 4: 491–92.

—. 1999b. "Does Multiculturalism Menace? Governance, Cultural Rights, and the Eclipse of 'Official Mestizaje' in Central America." Paper prepared for the session "Indigenismo/Mestizaje: New Views on Key Concepts in Latin American Cultural History." Annual meeting of the American Anthropological Association.

—. 1999c. "El Discurso Ladino del Racismo al Revés en Guatemala." In *¿Racismo en Guatemala? Abriendo el Debate sobre un Tema Tabú,* edited by Clara Arenas Bianchi, Charles R. Hale, and Gustavo Palma Murga. Guatemala City: AVANCSO.

Hall, Catherine. 1992. *White, Male, and Middle Class.* New York: Routledge.

Hall, Stuart. 1980. "Race, Articulation, and Societies Structured in Dominance." In *Sociological Theories: Racism and Colonialism.* Paris: UNESCO.

—. 1985. "Signification, Representation, Ideology: Althusser and the Post-Structuralist Debates." *Critical Studies in Mass Communication* 2, no. 2: 91–114.

—. 1986a. "Gramsci's Relevance for the Study of Race and Ethnicity." *Journal of Communication Inquiry* 10, no. 2: 5–27.

—. 1986b. "The Problem of Ideology: Marxism Without Guarantees." *Journal of Communication Inquiry* 10, no. 2: 28–43.

—. 1988a. *The Hard Road to Renewal.* London: Verso.

—. 1988b. "The Toad in the Garden: Thatcherism Among the Theorists." In *Marxism and the Interpretation of Culture,* edited by Cary Nelson and Lawrence Grossberg. Champaign-Urbana: University of Illinois Press.

—. 1990."Cultural Identity and Diaspora." In *Identity, Community, Culture, Difference,* edited by Jonathan Rutherford. London: Lawrence and Wishart.

—. 1991. "Old and New Identities, Old and New Ethnicities." In *Culture, Globalization, and the World-System,* edited by Anthony D. King. Binghamton: SUNY Press.

—. 1992. "The West and the Rest." In *Formations of Modernity,* edited by Stuart Hall and Bram Gieben. Oxford: Polity Press.

—. 1996a. "When Was the 'Post-Colonial'? Thinking at the Limit." In *The Post-Colonial Question,* edited by Ian Chambers and Lidia Curti. London: Routledge.

—. 1996b. "New Ethnicities." In *Stuart Hall: Critical Dialogues in Cultural Studies,* edited by David Morley and Kuan-Hsing Chen. London: Routledge.

—. 1996c. "What Is This 'Black' in Black Popular Culture?" In *Stuart Hall: Critical Dialogues in Cultural Studies,* edited by David Morley and Kuan-Hsing Chen. London: Routledge.

—. 1996d. "The After-Life of Frantz Fanon: Why Fanon? Why Now? Why *Black Skin, White Masks?"* In *The Fact of Blackness,* edited by Alan Read. London: Bay Press.

—. 1997a. "Culture and Power." *Radical Philosophy* 86 (November-December): 24–41.

—. 1997b. "The Spectacle of the Other." In *Representation,* edited by Stuart Hall. London: Sage.

—. 1999. "Cultural Composition: Stuart Hall on Ethnicity and the Discursive Turn." Interview by Julie Drew. In *Race, Rhetoric, and the Postcolonial,* edited by Gary A. Olson and Lynn Worsham. Albany: SUNY Press.

—. 2000. "Conclusion: The Multi-cultural Question." In *Un/Settled Multiculturalisms: Diasporas, Entanglements, Transruptions,* edited by Barnor Hesse. London: Zed Books.

—. 2002. "Reflections on 'Race, Articulation, and Societies Structured in Dominance.'" In *Race Critical Theories,* edited by Philomena Essed and David Theo Goldberg. Oxford: Blackwell.

Hall, Stuart, and Mark Sealy. 2001. *Different: A Historical Context.* London: Phaedon.

Hamburger, Viktor. 1980. "Embryology." In *The Evolutionary Synthesis,* edited by Ernst Mayr and William B. Provine. Cambridge: Harvard University Press.

Hamilton, Carolyn. 1998. *Terrific Majesty: The Powers of Shaka Zulu and the Limits of Historical Invention.* Cambridge: Harvard University Press.

Hanchard, Michael. 1999a. "Afro-Modernity: Temporality, Politics, and the African Diaspora." *Public Culture* 11, no. 1: 245–68.

—, ed. 1999b. *Racial Politics in Contemporary Brazil.* Durham, N.C.: Duke University Press.

Hannaford, Ivan. 1996. *Race: The History of an Idea in the West.* Baltimore: The Johns Hopkins University Press.

Hannah, Matthew G. 2000. *Governmentality and the Mastery of Territory in Nineteenth-Century America.* Cambridge: Cambridge University Press.

Hannerz, Ulf. 1999. Comment on "Writing for Culture: Why a Successful Concept Should Not Be Discarded," by Christoph Brumann. *Current Anthropology* 40: 18–19.

Haraway, Donna. 1988. "Situated Knowledges." *Feminist Studies* 14, no. 3: 575–99.

—. 1989. *Primate Visions: Gender, Race, and Nature in the World of Modern Science.* New York: Routledge.

—. 1991. *Simians, Cyborgs, and Women: The Reinvention of Nature.* London: Routledge.

1992. "The Promises of Monsters: A Regenerative Politics for Inappropriate/d Others." In *Cultural Studies,* edited by Lawrence Grossberg, Cary Nelson, and Paula Treichler. New York: Routledge.

—. 1996. "Universal Donors in a Vampire Culture." In *Uncommon Ground: Rethinking the Human Place in Nature,* edited by William Cronon. New York: Norton.

—. 1997. *Modest_Witness@Second_Millennium.* New York: Routledge.

Hardin, Garrett. 1968. "The Tragedy of the Commons." *Science* 162: 1243–48.

Harney, Corbin. 1995. *The Way It Is.* Nevada City, Calif.: Blue Dolphin Publishing.

Harrison, Faye. 1995. "The Persistent Power of 'Race' in the Cultural and Political Economy of Racism." *Annual Review of Anthropology* 24: 47–74.

—. 1998. "Introduction: Expanding the Discourse on 'Race.'" *American Anthropologist* 100, no. 3: 609–31.

Hart, Gillian. 2002. *Disabling Globalization: Places of Power in Post-Apartheid South Africa.* Berkeley: University of California Press.

Hartigan, John, Jr. 1999. *Racial Situations: Class Predicaments of Whiteness in Detroit.* Princeton: Princeton University Press.

Hartman, Saidiya. 1997. *Scenes of Subjection: Terror, Slavery, and Self-Making in Nineteenth-Century America.* New York: Oxford University Press.

Hartouni, Valerie. 1994. "Breached Birth: Reflections on Race, Gender, and Reproductive Discourse in the 1980s." *Configurations* 1: 73–88.

—. 1997. *Cultural Conceptions: On Reproductive Technologies and the Remaking of Life.* Minneapolis: University of Minnesota Press.

Harvey, David. 1989. *The Condition of Postmodernity.* Oxford: Blackwell.

—. 1996. *Justice, Nature, and the Geography of Difference.* Oxford: Blackwell.

Hawkins, John. 1984. *Inverse Images: The Meaning of Culture, Ethnicity, and Family in Postcolonial Guatemala.* Albuquerque: University of New Mexico Press.

Healy, M. J. 1997. "After They're Green: Brownfields Redevelopment and the New Environmental Wave." *Journal of Urban Technology* 4, no. 3: 83–96.

Hecht, Susana, and Alexander Cockburn. 1989. *The Fate of the Forest: Developers, Destroyers, and Defenders of the Amazon.* London: Verso.

Hegel, Georg Wilhelm. 1956. [1899]. *The Philosophy of History.* Translated by J. Sibree. New York: Dover.

—. 1997. "The Geographical Basis of World History." In *Race and the Enlightenment: A Reader,* edited by Emmanuel Chukwudi Eze. Oxford: Blackwell.

Hendley, Dave. 1978. "Black Disciple: An Interview with Winston Rodney—The Burning Spear," *Blues and Soul* (October): 239–40.

Herder, Johann Gottfried. 1772. [1975]. *Abhandlung über den Ursprung der Sprache.* Reprint. Stuttgart: Reclam.

—. 1778–79. *Stimmen der Völker in Liedern: Volkslieder.* 2 vols. Leipzig: In der Weygandschen Buchhandlung.

—. 1997. [1784]. "The Nature of the African Peoples." In *On World History,* edited by Hans Adler and Ernest A. Menze. Translated by Ernest A. Menze with Michael Palma. London: M. E. Sharpe.

—. 1999. [1784]. "Selections from Ideas for a Philosophy of the History of Mankind (1784–1791)." In *The Enlightenment*, edited by David Williams. Cambridge: Cambridge University Press.

Hernández, Lizette. 1999. *Building upon Our Strengths: A Community Guide to Brownfields Redevelopment*. San Francisco: Urban Habitat Program.

Hernon, Ian. 1998. *Massacre and Retribution: Forgotten Wars of the Nineteenth Century*. Stroud: Sutton.

Hesse, Barnor. 1997a. "It's Your World: Discrepant Multiculturalisms." *Social Identities* 3, no. 3: 375–94.

—. 1997b. "White Governmentality." In *Imagining Cities*, edited by Sallie Westwood and John Williams. New York: Routledge.

—, ed. 2000. *Un/Settled Multiculturalisms: Diasporas, Entanglements, Transruptions*. London: Zed Books.

Hexter, Alfred. 1968. "Selective Advantage of the Sickle-Cell Trait." *Science* 160 (26 April): 436.

Hildyard, Nicholas. 1993. "Foxes in Charge of the Chickens." In *Global Ecology: A New Arena of Political Conflict*, edited by Wolfgang Sachs. London: Zed Books.

Hill, Jonathan, ed. 1996. *History, Power, and Identity: Ethnogenesis in the Americas, 1492–1992*. Iowa City: University of Iowa Press.

Hille, Carl Gustav von. 1970. [1647]. *Der Teutsche Palmbaum: Das ist, Lobschrift Von der Hochlöblichen, Fruchtbringenden Gesellschaft Anfang, Satzungen, Vorhaben, Namen, Sprüchen, Gemählden, Schriften und unverwelklichem Tugendruhm*. Nürnberg: n.p. Reprinted in *Die Fruchtbringende Gesellschaft*, edited by Martin Bircher. Vol. 2. Munich: Kösel-Verlag.

Hintzen, Percy. 1999. "The Caribbean: Race and Creole Ethnicity." In *The Blackwell Companion to Racial and Ethnic Studies*, edited by David Goldberg and John Solomos. Oxford: Blackwell.

Hirsch, Eric, and Michael O'Hanlon, eds. 1995. *The Anthropology of Landscape*. Oxford: Clarendon.

Hitler, Adolf. 1943. [1927]. *Mein Kampf*. Translated by Ralph Manheim. Boston: Houghton Mifflin.

Hochschild, Adam. 1998. *King Leopold's Ghost: A Story of Greed, Terror, and Heroism in Colonial Africa*. Boston: Houghton Mifflin.

Hoffmann, Lutz. 1994. *Das deutsche Volk und seine Feinde: Die völkische Droge*. Cologne: PapyRossa.

Hofrichter, Richard. 1993. *Toxic Struggles: The Theory and Practice of Environmental Justice*. Philadelphia: New Society Publishers.

Hommel, Gaby. 1998. "Sturm im Wasserglas." *Konkret* 12: 24–26.

Hooe, Todd R. 1999. *Enduring Changing Currents: Adat Law and Social Hierarchy in the Kei Islands, Eastern Indonesia*. Chicago: American Anthropological Association.

hooks, bell. 1981. *Ain't I a Woman: Black Women and Feminism*. Boston: South End Press.

—. 1990. *Yearning: Race, Gender, and Cultural Politics*. Boston: South End Press.

—. 1992. *Black Looks: Race and Representation*. Boston: South End Press.

—. 1996. *Reel to Real: Race, Sex, and Class at the Movies*. New York: Routledge.

Howes David, ed. 1996. *Cross Cultural Consumption: Global Markets, Local Realities*. New York: Routledge.

Hull, Gloria T., Patricia Bell Scott, and Barbara Smith. 1982. *But Some of Us Are Brave: Black Women's Studies*. New York: The Feminist Press.

Hulme, Peter. 1986. *Colonial Encounters*. New York: Routledge.

Humboldt, Wilhelm von. 1963. [1818–35]. *Schriften zur Sprachphilosophie, Werke III*. Reprint. Darmstadt: Wissenschaftliche Buchgesellschaft.

———. 1995. [1834]. *Personal Narrative of a Journey to the Equinoctial Regions of the New Continent*. New York: Penguin.

Hume, David. 1997. [1748]. "Essays Moral and Political." In *Race and the Enlightenment*, edited by Emmanuel Chukwudi Eze. Oxford: Blackwell.

Humphrey, Elliot, and Lucien Hynes Warner. 1934. *Working Dogs*. Baltimore: The Johns Hopkins University Press.

Hunt, Nancy Rose. 1999. *A Colonial Lexicon of Birth Ritual, Medicalization, and Mobility in the Congo*. Durham: Duke University Press.

Huntington, Samuel. 1993. "Clash of Civilizations." *Foreign Affairs* 72, no. 3 (summer): 22–49.

Hurley, Andrew. 1995. *Environmental Inequalities: Class, Race, and Industrial Pollution*. Chapel Hill: University of North Carolina Press.

Hurston, Zora. 1995. *Folklore, Memoirs, and Other Writings*. Edited by Cheryl Wall. New York: Library of America.

Husbands, Christopher T. 1991. "Neo-Nazis in East Germany: The New Danger." *Patterns of Prejudice* 25, no. 1: 3–17.

Hutchins, Francis G. 1967. *The Illusion of Permanence*. Princeton: Princeton University Press.

Ifekwunigwe, Jane. 1999. *Scattered Belongings: Cultural Paradoxes of "Race," Nation, and Gender*. London: Routledge.

Iggers, Georg G. 1971. *Deutsche Geschichtswissenschaft: Eine Kritik der traditionellen Geschichtsauffassung von Herder bis zur Gegenwart*. Munich: Deutscher Taschenbuch Verlag.

Ignatiev, Noel. 1995. *How the Irish Became White*. New York: Routledge.

ISA (Instituto Socioambiental). 1996. *Povos Indígenas no Brasil 1991/1995*. São Paulo: Instituto Socioambiental.

Jackson, Jean. 1989. "Is There a Way to Talk about Making Culture without Making Enemies?" *Dialectical Anthropology* 14: 127–43.

———. 1999. "The Politics of Ethnographic Practice in the Colombian Vaupes." *Identities—Global Studies in Culture and Power* 6, nos. 2–3: 281–317.

Jackson, R. E. 1974. "A Perspective on the National Sickle Cell Disease Program." *Archives of Internal Medicine* 183 (April): 533.

Jacobs, Jane. 1994. "Earth Honoring: Western Desires and Indigenous Knowledges." In *Writing Women and Space*, edited by Alison Blunt and Gillian Rose. New York: Guilford.

Jacobson, Matthew Frye. 1998. *Whiteness of a Different Color*. Cambridge: Harvard University Press.

Jäger, Margret. 1993. "Sprache der Angst." *die tageszeitung* (24 March): 1.

Jakarta Post. 2000a. "Temenggung Tarib Wages Peaceful Resistance Against Loggers." 8 February.

———. 2000b. "Timber Firms Halt Work Due to Conflict with Locals." 4 March.

———. 2000c. "Conflicts Between Locals and Timber Companies to Grow." 9 March.

———. 2000d. "Logging Companies Ready to Share Revenues with Locals," 25 March.

Jambi Express. 1999. "Perjuangan WARSI Berhasil Inhutani Diminta Cabut IPK." 4 August.

James, C. L. R. 1963. [1938]. *The Black Jacobins*. Reprint. New York: Vintage.

———. 1994. [1939]. "Revolution and the Negro." In *C. L. R. James and Revolutionary Marxism*, edited by Scott McLemee and Paul LeBlanc. Atlantic Highlands: Humanities Press.

Jameson, Fredric. 1981. *The Political Unconscious: Narrative as a Socially Symbolic Act.* Ithaca: Cornell University Press.

Janich, Nina. 1997. "Sprachkultivierung—Aufgabe der Zukunft oder nur ein Generationenproblem?" *Muttersprache* 107, no. 1: 76–84.

Jaschke, Hans-Gerd. 1993. "Formiert sich eine neue soziale Bewegung von rechts?: Über die Ethnisierung sozialer und politischer Konflikte." *Institut für Sozialforschung,* Mitteilungen, no. 2: 28–44.

Jasen, Patricia. 1995. *Wild Things: Nature, Culture, and Tourism in Ontario, 1790–1914.* Toronto: University of Toronto Press.

Jelloun, Tahar Ben. 1999a. [1984]. *French Hospitality: Racism and North African Immigrants.* New York: Columbia University Press.

—. 1999b. *Racism Explained to My Daughter.* New York: The New Press.

John, Barbara. 1999. "Who Is German? The Debate over Citizenship and Germany's Immigration Policies." Paper presented at the American Institute for Contemporary German Studies, 28 January 1999, Washington, D.C.

Johnson v. Calvert (Cal. 1993) 19 Cal. Rptr. 2d 506–18, cert. denied (U.S. 1993) 113 S. Ct 206.

Jones, Andrew. 2001. *Yellow Music: Media Culture and Colonial Modernity in the Chinese Jazz Age.* Durham: Duke University Press.

Jones, LeRoi. 1966. *Home.* New York: William Morrow.

Jones, William Jervis. 1995. *Sprachhelden und Sprachverderber. Dokumente zur Erforschung des Fremdwortpurismus im Deutschen (1478–1750).* Studia Linguistica Germanica 38. Berlin: Walter de Gruyter.

Jordan, June. 1981. *Civil Wars.* Boston: Beacon.

Jordanova, Ludmilla. 1984. *Lamarck.* Oxford: Oxford University Press.

Julianto, Irwan. 2000. "Temenggung Tarib Digusur 'Rajo Godong.'" *Kompas,* 2 March. Jakarta edition.

Kabis-Alamba, Veronika. 1999. "Deutsch für alle—nein Danke?" *die tageszeitung* (1 November): 18.

Kandel, Randy Frances. 1994. "Which Came First: The Mother or the Egg? A Kinship Solution to Gestational Surrogacy." *Rutgers Law Review* 47 (fall): 165–239.

Kane, Joe. 1995. *Savages.* New York: Vintage.

Kant, Immanuel. 1978. [1798]. *Anthropology from a Pragmatic Point of View.* Translated by Victor Lyle Dowdell. Carbondale: Southern Illinois University Press.

—. 1983. [1795]. "An Answer to the Question: What Is Enlightenment?" In *Perpetual Peace and Other Essays.* Translated by Ted Humphrey. Indianapolis: Hackett Publishing.

—. 1997a. [1775]. "On the Different Races of Men." In *Race and the Enlightenment,* edited by Emmanuel Chukwudi Eze. Oxford: Blackwell.

—. 1997b. [1764]. "Observations on the Feeling of the Beautiful and Sublime." In *Race and the Enlightenment,* edited by Emmanuel Chukwudi Eze. Oxford: Blackwell.

Kaplan, Caren, Norma Alarcón, and Minoo Moallem, eds. 1999. *Between Woman and Nation.* Durham, N.C.: Duke University Press.

Karliner, Joshua. 1997. *The Corporate Planet: Ecology and Politics in the Age of Globalization.* San Francisco: Sierra Club Books.

Kathleen, Stewart. 1996. *A Space on the Side of the Road.* Princeton: Princeton University Press.

Katz, Cindi. 1998. "Whose Nature, Whose Culture?: Private Productions of Space and the 'Preservation' of Nature." In *Remaking Reality*, edited by Bruce Braun and Noel Castree. New York: Routledge.

Kautsky, Karl. 1972. [1926]. *Are the Jews a Race?* Westport: Greenwood Press.

Kaye, Sir John William. 1864. *A History of the Sepoy War in India: 1857–58*. Vols. 1 and 2. London: W. H. Allen and Company.

Keck, Margaret. 1995. "Social Equity and Environmental Politics in Brazil: Lessons from the Rubber Tappers of Acre." *Comparative Politics* 27, no. 4: 409–24.

Keegan, Timothy. 1996. *Colonial South Africa and the Origins of the Racial Order*. Cape Town: David Philip.

Kempadoo, Kamala. 1999. "Continuities and Change: Five Centuries of Prostitution in the Caribbean." In *Sun, Sex, and Gold: Tourism and Sex Work in the Caribbean*, edited by Kamala Kempadoo. Lanham, Md.: Rowman and Littlefield.

Kennedy, Reginald Frank, ed. 1961. *Thomas Baines' African Journal*. Cape Town: C. Struik.

Kenny, Judith. 1995. "Climate, Race, and Imperial Authority: The Symbolic Landscape of the British Hill Station." *Annals of the Association of American Geographers* 85, no. 4: 694–714.

Kenyatta, Jomo. 1962. [1938]. *Facing Mount Kenya: The Tribal Life of the Gikuyu*. New York: Vintage.

Kevles, Daniel. 1995. *In the Name of Eugenics*. Cambridge: Harvard University Press.

Kevles, Daniel, and Leroy Hood, eds. 1992. *The Code of Codes: Scientific and Social Issues in the Human Genome Project*. Cambridge: Harvard University Press.

Kiernan, Ben. 1998. "Genocide and 'Ethnic Cleansing.'" In *The Encyclopedia of Politics and Religion*, edited by Robert Wuthnow. Vol. 1. Washington, D.C.: Washington Quarterly.

Kingsbury, Benedict. 1998. "'Indigenous Peoples' in International Law: A Constructivist Approach to the Asian Controversy." *American Journal of International Law* 92, no. 3: 414–57.

Kinnaird, Vivian, Uma Kothari, and Derek Hall. 1994. "Tourism: Gender Perspectives." In *Tourism: A Gendered Analysis*, edited by Vivian Kinnaird and Derek Hall. New York: Wiley.

Kipling, Rudyard. 1971. [1899]. "The White Man's Burden." In *A Choice of Kipling's Verse*, edited by T. S. Eliot. London: Faber and Faber.

Kirshenblatt-Gimblett, Barbara. 1998. *Destination Culture: Tourism, Museums, and Heritage*. Berkeley: University of California Press.

Kisbandono, Heru. 1993. "The Head of the National Land Agency Will Eliminate Customary Law." *Forum Keadilan*, 18 February.

Klawiter, Maren. 1999. "Racing for the Cure, Walking Women, and Toxic Touring: Mapping Cultures of Action Within the Bay Area Terrain of Breast Cancer." *Social Problems* 46, no. 1: 104–23.

Klenk, E. 1939–1940. "Beitrage zur chemie der lipodosen (3 mitteilung). Niemann-Picksche krankheit und amaurotische idiote." *Hoppe-Seylers Z Physiol Chem* 262: 128–43.

—. 1942. "Uber die ganglioside des gehirns bei der infantilen amaurotischen idiotie vom typus Tay-Sachs," *Ber Dtsch Chem Ges* 75: 1632–36.

Klor de Alva, Jorge. 1995. "The Postcolonization of the (Latin) American Experience: A Reconsideration of 'Colonialism,' 'Postcolonialism,' and 'Mestizaje.'" In *After Colonialism: Imperial Histories and Postcolonial Displacements*, edited by Gyan Prakash. Princeton: Princeton University Press.

Knight, Alan. 1990. "Racism, Revolution, and Indigenismo: Mexico, 1910–1940." In *The Idea of*

Race in Latin America, 1870–1940, edited by Richard Graham. Cambridge: Cambridge University Press.

Knox, Robert. 1850. *The Races of Man: A Fragment.* Philadelphia: Lea and Blanchard.

Koerner, Lisbet. 1999. *Linneaus: Nature and Nation.* Cambridge: Harvard University Press.

Kolata, Gina. 1995. "Breast Cancer Gene in 1% of U.S. Jews." *New York Times,* 29 September.

Kompas. 1998. "Kembalikan Hutan Kepada Rakyat." 12 June. Jakarta edition.

———. 2000a. " 'Kehati Award' untuk Temenggung Tarib." 29 January. Jakarta edition.

———. 2000b. "Jaringan Kehidupan Ada Pada Hubungan Ketergantungan." 1 February.

———. 2000c. "Warga Sangir Tersinggung." 10 September. Manado edition.

Konotney-Ahulu, Felix I. D. 1972. "Sickle Cell Trait and Altitude." *British Medical Journal* 1: 177–78.

———. 1973. "Medical Considerations for Legalizing Voluntary Sterilization: Sickle Cell Disease as a Case in Point." *British Medical Journal.*

Kosek, Jake. 2002. "Deep Roots and Long Shadows: The Political Life of Forests in Northern New Mexico." Ph.D. diss., Department of Geography, University of California at Berkeley.

Krakauer, Jon. 1996. *Into the Wild.* New York: Villard.

Krech, Shepard. 1999. *The Ecological Indian: Myth and History.* New York: Norton.

Kristeva, Julia. 1982. *Powers of Horror: An Essay on Abjection.* New York: Columbia University Press.

Kroeber, Alfred Louis. 1939. *Cultural and Natural Areas of Native North America.* Berkeley: University of California Press.

———. 1969. [1939]. "Relations of Environment and Cultural Factors." In *Environment and Cultural Behavior: Ecological Studies in Cultural Anthropology,* edited by Andrew P. Vayda. Garden City: Natural History Press.

Kropotkin, Peter. 1955. [1902]. *Mutual Aid: A Factor of Evolution.* Reprinted, with a foreword by Ashley Montagu, along with "The Struggle for Existence" by Thomas H. Huxley. Boston: Extending Horizons Books.

KUDETA (Koalisi untuk Demokratisasi Sumberdaya Alam). 1999. "Petition to Reject the Bills on Forestry and Mining." 21 June. Available at fkkm@egroups.com.

Kulczycki, Lucas, and Victoria Schauf. 1974. "Cystic Fibrosis in Blacks in Washington, D.C." *American Journal of the Diseases of Children* 127 (January): 64.

Kulczycki, Guin, and Mann. 1964. "Cystic Fibrosis in Negro Children." *Clinical Pediatrics* 3: 692–705.

Kuletz, Valerie. 1998. *The Tainted Desert: Environmental and Social Ruin in the American West.* London: Routledge.

Kuper, Leo, ed. 1975. *Race, Science, and Society.* Paris: UNESCO.

Kurthen, Hermann, Werner Bergmann, and Rainer Erb. 1997. "Introduction: Postunification Challenges to German Democracy." In *Antisemitism and Xenophobia after Unification.* New York: Oxford University Press.

Kurthen, Hermann, and Michael Minkenberg. 1995. "Germany in Transition: Immigration, Racism, and the Extreme Right." *Nations and Nationalism* 1, no. 2: 175–96.

Kusumatmadja, Sarwono. 1993. "The Human Dimensions of Sustainable Development." In *Proceedings, Seminar on the Human Dimensions of Environmentally Sound Development,* edited by Arimbi Heroepoetri. Jakarta: WALHI and Friends of the Earth.

Kutzinski, Vera. 1993. *Sugar's Secrets: Race and the Erotics of Cuban Nationalism*. Charlottes-ville: University Press of Virginia.

Laclau, Ernesto. 1977. *Politics and Ideology in Marxist Theory: Capitalism, Fascism, Populism*. London: New Left Books.

LaDuke, Winona. 1999. *All Are Relations: Native Struggles for Land and Life*. Boston: South End Press.

Langen, August. 1952. "Deutsche Sprachgeschichte vom Barock bis zur Gegenwart." In *Deutsche Philologie im Aufriss*, edited by Wolfgang Stammler. Berlin: Erich Schmidt Verlag.

Langenberg, Michael Van. 1990. "The New Order State: Language, Hegemony, and Ideology." In *State and Civil Society in Indonesia*, edited by Arief Budiman. Monash Papers on Southeast Asia No. 22. Clayton, Victoria: Monash University Press.

Lansing, Michael. In press. "Different Methods, Different Places: Feminist Geography and New Directions in U.S. Western History." *Journal of Historical Geography*.

Lansing, J. Stephen. 1991. *Priests and Programmers*. Princeton: Princeton University Press.

Larson, Edward J. 1995. *Sex, Race, and Science: Eugenics in the Deep South*. Baltimore: The Johns Hopkins University Press.

Latour, Bruno. 1987. *Science in Action*. Cambridge: Harvard University Press.

—. 1993. *We Have Never Been Modern*. Cambridge: Harvard University Press.

—. 1999. *Pandora's Hope*. Cambridge: Harvard University Press.

Leach, Edmund. 1954. *Political Systems of Highland Burma*. Boston: Beacon.

Leach, Melissa. 1998. "Culture and Sustainability." In *Culture, Creativity, and Markets*, edited by Lourdes Arizpe. World Cultural Report. Geneva: UNESCO.

Leenhardt, Maurice. 1994. *Do Camo: Person and Myth in the Melanesian World*. Chicago: University of Chicago Press.

Le Goff, Jacques. 1992. *History and Memory*. New York: Columbia University Press.

Leiris, Michel. 1958. *Race and Culture*. Paris: UNESCO.

Leite, Dante Moreira. 1992. *O Caráter Nacional Brasileiro: História de uma Ideologia*. 5th ed. São Paulo: Editora Ática.

Lentin, Alana. 2000. " 'Race,' Racism, and Anti-Racism: Challenging Contemporary Classifica-tions." *Social Identities* 6, no. 1: 91–106.

Leps, Marie Christine. 1992. *Apprehending the Criminal: The Production of Deviance in the Nineteenth Century*. Durham, N.C.: Duke University Press.

Lerner, Steve. 1996. "Brownfields of Dreams." *The Amicus Journal* (winter): 15–21.

Levenstein, Charles, and John Wooding. 1998. "Dying for a Living: Workers, Production, and the Environment." In *The Struggle for Ecological Democracy: Environmental Justice Movements in the United States*, edited by Daniel Faber. New York: Guilford.

Levin, Thomas Y. 1985. "Nationalities of Language: Adorno's *Fremdwörter*." *New German Critique* 36: 111–19.

Lévi-Strauss, Claude. 1961. *Tristes Tropiques*. Translated by John Russell. New York: Criterion Books.

Lewis, Laura A. 2000. "Blacks, Black Indians, Afromexicans: The Dynamics of Race, Nation, and Identity in a Mexican *Moreno* Community (*Guerrero*)." *American Ethnologist* 27, no. 4: 898–926.

Lewontin, Richard C., Steven Rose, and Leon J. Kamin. 1984. *Not in Our Genes: Biology, Ideology, and Human Nature*. New York: Pantheon.

Li, Tania Murray. 1996. "Images of Community: Discourse and Strategy in Property Relations." *Development and Change* 27: 501–27.

———. 1997. "Producing Agrarian Transformation at the Indonesian Periphery." In *Economic Analysis Beyond the Local System,* edited by Richard E. Blanton, Peter N. Peregrine, D. Winslow, and T. D. Hall. Monographs in Economic Anthropology No. 13. Lanham, Md.: University Press of America.

———, ed. 1999a. *Transforming the Indonesian Uplands.* New York: Routledge.

———. 1999b. "Compromising Power: Development, Culture, and Rule in Indonesia." *Cultural Anthropology* 14, no. 3: 1–28.

———. 2000. "Articulating Indigenous Identity in Indonesia: Resource Politics and the Tribal Slot." *Comparative Studies in Society and History* 42, no. 1: 149–79.

———. 2001. "Relational Histories and the Production of Difference on Sulawesi's Upland Frontier." *Journal of Asian Studies* 60, no. 1: 41–66.

———. 2002. "Engaging Simplifications: Community-Based Resource Management, Market Processes and State Agendas in Upland Southeast Asia." *World Development* 30, no. 2: 265–83.

Lichtenstein, Hinrich. 1928. [1812]. *Travels in South Africa in the Years 1803, 1804, 1805, and 1806.* Reprint, with an introduction by Anne Plumptre. Cape Town: Van Riebeeck Society.

Light, Andrew. 1999. "Boyz in the Woods: Urban Wilderness in American Cinema." In *The Nature of Cities: Ecocriticism and Urban Environments,* edited by Michael Bennett and David W. Teague. Tucson: University of Arizona Press.

Limerick, Patricia, Clyde Milner II, and Charles Rankin, eds. 1991. *Trails: Toward a New Western History.* Lawrence: University Press of Kansas.

Lindee, Susan, and Dorothy Nelkin. 1995. *The DNA Mystique: The Gene as Cultural Icon.* New York: Freeman.

Lindqvist, Sven. 1996. [1992]. *Exterminate all the Brutes.* Translated by Joan Tate. New York: New Press.

———. 1997. *The Skull Measurer's Mistake and Other Portraits of Men and Women Who Spoke Out Against Racism.* Translated by Joan Tate. New York: New Press.

Linebaugh, Peter, and Marcus Rediker. 2000. *The Many-Headed Hydra.* Boston: Beacon.

Linke, Uli. 1995. "Murderous Fantasies: Violence, Memory, and Selfhood in Germany." *New German Critique* 64 (winter): 37–59.

———. 1997a. "Colonizing the National Imaginary: Folklore, Anthropology, and the Making of the Modern State." In *Cultures of Scholarship,* edited by Sally Humphreys. Ann Arbor: University of Michigan Press.

———. 1997b. "Gendered Difference, Violent Imagination: Blood, Race, Nation." *American Anthropologist* 99, no. 3: 559–73.

———. 1999a. *German Bodies: Race and Representation after Hitler.* New York: Routledge.

———. 1999b. *Blood and Nation: The European Aesthetics of Race.* Philadelphia: University of Pennsylvania Press.

———. 2001. "The Politics of Blood: Antisemitic Imaginaries after 1945." In *Das Flüstern eines leisen Wehens: Beiträge zu Kultur und Lebenswelt europäischer Juden,* edited by Freddy Raphael. Konstanz: UVK Verlagsgesellschaft.

Lipsitz, George. 1998. *The Possessive Investment in Whiteness: How White People Profit from Identity Politics.* Philadelphia: Temple University Press.

Litzinger, Ralph. 1999. *Other Chinas.* Durham, N.C.: Duke University Press.

Liu, Lydia. 1995. *Translingual Practice*. Stanford: Stanford University Press.

Livingstone, David N. 1994. "Climate's Moral Economy: Science, Race, and Place in Post-Darwinian British and American Geography." In *Geography and Empire*, edited by Anne Godlewska and Neil Smith. Oxford: Blackwell.

Livingstone, Frank. 1967. "The Origins of the Sickle-Cell Gene." In *Reconstructing African Culture History*, edited by Creighton Gabel and Norman Bennett. African Research Studies No. 8. Boston: African Studies Center, Boston University.

Locke, John. 1993. [1689]. *Two Treatises of Government*. London: J. M. Dent.

Lohmann, Larry. 1993. "Green Orientalism." *The Ecologist* 23, no. 6: 202–04.

—. 1999. "Forest Cleansing: Racial Oppression in Scientific Nature Conservation." Cornerhouse Briefing 13. Available at http://cornerhouse.icaap.org/briefings/13.html.

Lowe, Lisa. 1988. *Critical Terrains*. Ithaca: Cornell University Press.

—. 1996a. "Immigration, Racialization, Citizenship: Asian American Critique." In *Immigrant Acts*. Durham, N.C.: Duke University Press.

—. 1996b. *Immigrant Acts*. Durham, N.C.: Duke University Press.

—. 2001a. "Utopia and Modernity: Some Observations from the Border." *Rethinking Marxism* 13, no. 2: 10–18.

—. 2001b. "Epistemological Shifts: National Ontology and the New Asian Immigrant." In *Orientations*, edited by Kandice Chuh and Karen Shimakawa. Durham: Duke University Press.

Lowe, May, and Read. 1949. "Fibrosis of the Pancreas in Infants and Children." *American Journal of the Diseases of Children* 78: 349.

Lugard, Frederick. 1926. "The White Man's Task in Tropical Africa." *Foreign Affairs* 5, no. 1: 57–68.

Luke, Timothy. 1997. *Ecocritique: Contesting the Politics of Nature, Economy, and Culture*. Minneapolis: University of Minnesota Press.

Lynch, Owen J., and Kirk Talbott. 1995. *Balancing Acts: Community-Based Forest Management and National Law in Asia and the Pacific*. Washington, D.C.: World Resources Institute.

Macartney, H. E. 1840. *A Plain and Easy Way to Settle the Frontier Question*. London: Grahamstown.

MacCannell, Dean. 1989. *The Tourist: A New Theory of the Leisure Class*. New York: Schocken Books.

MacCormack, Carol, and Marilyn Strathern, eds. 1980. *Nature, Culture and Gender*. New York: Cambridge University Press.

MacKenzie, John M., ed. 1990. *Imperialism and the Natural World*. Manchester: Manchester University Press.

MacKinnon, Catharine. 1989. *Toward a Feminist Theory of the State*. Cambridge: Harvard University Press.

—. 1997. "Sexuality." In *The Second Wave*, edited by Linda Nicholson. New York: Routledge.

Macnaghten, Phil, and John Urry. 1998. *Contested Natures*. London: Sage.

Malinowski, Bronislaw. 1961. [1922]. *Argonauts of the Western Pacific*. Reprint. New York: Dutton.

Malkki, Liisa. 1992. "National Geographic—The Rooting of Peoples and the Territorialization of National Identity among Scholars and Refugees." *Cultural Anthropology* 7, no. 1: 24–44.

—. 1994. "Citizens of Humanity: Internationalism and the Imagined Community of Nations." *Diaspora* 3, no. 1: 41–69.

——. 1995. *Purity and Exile: Violence, Memory, and National Cosmology among Hutu Refugees in Tanzania.* Chicago: University of Chicago Press.

——. 1997. "National Geographic: The Rooting of Peoples and the Territorialization of National Identity among Scholars and Refugees." In *Culture, Power, Place: Explorations in Critical Anthropology,* edited by Akhil Gupta and James Ferguson. Durham, N.C.: Duke University Press.

Mallon, Florencia E. 1994. "The Promise and Dilemma of Subaltern Studies: Perspectives from Latin American History." *American Historical Review* 99, no. 5: 1491–515.

——. 1996. "Constructing Mestizaje in Latin America: Authenticity, Marginality, and Gender in the Claiming of National Identities." *Journal of Latin American Anthropology* 2, no. 1: 170–81.

Malthus, Thomas. 1985. [1798]. *An Essay on the Principle of Population.* New York: Penguin.

Mamdani, Mahmood. 1996. *Citizen and Subject.* Princeton: Princeton University Press.

——. 2001. *When Victims Become Killers: Colonialism, Nativism, and the Genocide in Rwanda.* Princeton: Princeton University Press.

Mandela, Nelson. 1965. [1959]. "Verwoerd's Tribalism." In *No Easy Walk to Freedom.* London: Heinemann.

Marcos, Subcomandate Insurgente. 2001. *Selected Writings.* Edited by Fuana Ponce de Leon. New York: Seven Stories Press.

Margolick, David. 2000. *Strange Fruit: Billie Holiday, Café Society, and an Early Cry for Civil Rights.* Philadelphia: Running Press.

Marks, Jonathan. 1995. *Human Biodiversity.* New York: Aldine de Gruyter.

Marsh, George Perkins. 1864. *Man and Nature.* New York: Scribner.

Martin, Emily. 1994. *Flexible Bodies.* Boston: Beacon.

Martin, Philip L. 1998. *Germany: Reluctant Land of Immigration.* German Issues 21. American Institute for Contemporary German Studies. Baltimore: The Johns Hopkins University.

Martinez, Elizabeth. 1991. "When People of Color Are an Endangered Species." *Z Magazine* 4: 61–65.

Martinez-Alier, Verena. 1974. *Marriage, Class, and Colour in Nineteenth-Century Cuba: A Study of Racial Attitudes and Sexual Values in a Slave Society.* Cambridge: Cambridge University Press.

Martínez Pelaez, Severo. 1985. *Motines de Indios.* Puebla, Mexico: Universidad Autónoma de Puebla.

——. 1990. [1970]. *La Patria del Criolla: Ensayo de Interpretación de la Realidad Colonial Guatemalteca.* Reprint. Mexico City: Ediciones en Marcha.

Marx, Karl. 1963. [1869]. *The Eighteenth Brumaire of Louis Bonaparte.* Translated by Clemens P. Dutt. New York: International Publishers.

——. 1967. [1867]. *Capital.* Vol. I. Translated by Samuel Moore and Edward Aveling. Reprint: New York: International Publishers.

——. 1975. "Debates on the Law on Thefts of Wood." In Karl Marx and Friedrich Engels, *Karl Marx and Friedrich Engels: Collected Works.* Vol. 1. New York: International Publishers.

——. 1977. [1867]. *Capital.* Vol. 1. Translated by Ben Fowkes. New York: Vintage.

Mason, Peter. 1998. *Infelicities: Representations of the Exotic.* Baltimore: The Johns Hopkins University Press.

Massey, Doreen. 1994. *Space, Place, and Gender.* Chapel Hill: University of North Carolina Press.

Matless, David. 1998. *Landscape and Englishness*. London: Reaktion.

Mattson, Michelle. 1995. "Refugees in Germany." *New German Critique* 64: 61–85.

Maurer, Trude. 1986. *Ostjuden in Deutschland, 1918–1933*. Hamburg: Christians.

Mbembe, Achille. 2001. *On the Postcolony*. Berkeley: University of California Press.

McClintock, Anne. 1995. *Imperial Leather: Race, Gender, and Sexuality in the Colonial Contest.* New York: Routledge.

McClure, Kirstie M. 1996. *Judging Rights: Lockean Politics and the Limits of Consent.* Ithaca: Cornell University Press.

McCulloch, Jock. 1995. *Colonial Psychiatry and the African Mind*. New York: Cambridge University Press.

———. 2000. *Black Peril White Virtue: Sexual Crime in Southern Rhodesia, 1902–1935*. Bloomington: Indiana University Press.

McFadden, Robert, and Susan Saulney. 2002. "DNA in Central Park Jogger Case Spurs Call for New Review." *New York Times*, 6 September: B1.

McNeil, Maureen, Ian Varcoc, and Steven Yearley, eds. 1990. *The New Reproductive Technologies.* London: Macmillan.

Mead, Margaret, and James Baldwin. 1971. *A Rap on Race*. New York: Dell.

Mehta, Uday Singh. 1992. *The Anxiety of Freedom: Imagination and Individuality in Locke's Political Thought*. Ithaca: Cornell University Press.

———. 1997. "Liberal Strategies of Exclusion." In *Tensions of Empire: Colonial Cultures in a Bourgeois World*, edited by Frederick Cooper and Ann Laura Stoler. Berkeley: University of California Press.

———. 1999. *Liberalism and Empire*. Chicago: University of Chicago Press.

Memmi, Albert. 2000. [1982]. *Racism*. Translated by Steve Martinot. Minneapolis: University of Minnesota Press.

Menchaca, Martha. 2001. *Recovering History, Constructing Race: The Indian, Black, and White Roots of Mexican Americans*. Austin: University of Texas Press.

Menchú Tum, Rigoberta. 1984. *I, Rigoberta Menchú: An Indian Woman in Guatemala*. Translated by Ann Wright. Edited by Elisabeth Burgos-Debray. London: Verso.

———. 1998. *Crossing Borders*. London: Verso.

Mercer, Kobena. 1994. *Welcome to the Jungle: New Positions in Black Cultural Studies*. New York: Routledge.

Merchant, Carolyn. 1980. *The Death of Nature: Women, Ecology, and the Scientific Revolution*. San Francisco: Harper and Row.

———. 1995. "Reinventing Eden: Western Culture as a Recovery Narrative." In *Uncommon Ground: Rethinking the Human Place in Nature*, edited by William Cronon. New York: Norton.

Meyer-Arendt, Klaus J., Richard A. Sambrook, and Brian M. Kermath. 1992. "Seaside Resorts in the Dominican Republic: A Typology." *Journal of Geography* 21, no. 5: 219–25.

Michaelis, Herbert, ed. 1964. *Ursachen und Folgen: Vom deutschen Zusammenbruch 1918 und 1945 bis zur staatlichen Neuordnung Deutschlands in der Gegenwart*. Vol. 9 of *Das Dritte Reich*. Berlin: Wendler.

Michaelsen, Scott. 1999. *The Limits of Multiculturalism: Interrogating the Origins of American Anthropology*. Minneapolis: University of Minnesota Press.

Michel, Hermann. 1911. "Bücheranzeigen: Friedrich Seiler. Die Entwicklung der deutschen Kultur im Spiegel des deutschen Lehnworts. Halle: Buchhandlung des Waisenhauses, 1910." *Zeitschrift des Vereins für Volkskunde* 21, no. 1: 431–32.

Mignolo, Walter. 1995. *The Darker Side of the Renaissance: Literacy, Territoriality, and Colonialization.* Ann Arbor: University of Michigan Press.

—. 2000. *Local Histories/Global Designs.* Princeton: Princeton University Press.

Milchman, Alan, and Alan Rosenberg. 1996. *Martin Heidegger and the Holocaust.* Atlantic Highlands, N.J.: Humanities Press.

Miller, Christopher. 1985. *Blank Darkness.* Chicago: University of Chicago Press.

Milton, Kay. 1996. *Environmentalism and Cultural Theory.* London: Routledge.

Mitchell, Don. 1996. *Lie of the Land: Migrant Workers and the California Landscape.* Minneapolis: University of Minnesota Press.

Mitchell, Katharyne. 1997. "Different Diasporas and the Hype of Hybridity." *Environment and Planning D: Society and Space* 15, no. 5: 533–53.

Mitchell, Timothy. 1991. [1988]. *Colonising Egypt.* Berkeley: University of California Press.

Mitchell, W. J. T., ed. 1994. *Landscape and Power.* Chicago: University of Chicago Press.

Mohanty, Chandra Talpade. 1992. "Feminist Encounters: Locating the Politics of Experience." In *Destabilizing Theory,* edited by Michele Barrett and Anne Phillips. Stanford: Stanford University Press.

Moodie, T. Dunbar, with Vivienne Ndatshe. 1994. *Going for Gold: Men, Mines, and Migration.* Berkeley: University of California Press.

Mohai, Paul, and Bunyan Bryant, eds. 1992. *Race and the Incidence of Environmental Hazards: A Time for Discourse.* Boulder: Westview Press.

Moniaga, Sandra. 1993. "Toward Community-Based Forestry and Recognition of *Adat* Property Rights in the Outer Islands of Indonesia." In *Legal Frameworks for Forest Management in Asia: Case Studies of Community/State Relations,* edited by Jefferson Fox. Honolulu: East-West Center Program on Environment.

Montagu, Ashley. 1972. *Statement on Race.* 3d ed. New York: Oxford University Press.

Montesquieu, Charles de Secondat. 1989. [1748]. *The Spirit of the Laws.* Translated and edited by Anne M. Cohler, Basia C. Miller, and Harold S. Stone. Cambridge: Cambridge University Press.

Moore, Donald S. 1993. "Contesting Terrain in Zimbabwe's Eastern Highlands: Political Ecology, Ethnography, and Peasant Resource Struggles." *Economic Geography* 69, no. 4: 380–401.

—. 1998a. "Subaltern Struggles and the Politics of Place: Remapping Resistance in Zimbabwe's Eastern Highlands." *Cultural Anthropology* 13, no. 3: 344–381.

—. 1998b. "Clear Waters and Muddied Histories: Environmental History and the Politics of Community in Zimbabwe's Eastern Highlands." *Journal of Southern African Studies* 24, no. 2: 377–403.

—. 1999. "The Crucible of Cultural Politics: Reworking 'Development' in Zimbabwe's Eastern Highlands." *American Ethnologist* 26, no. 3: 654–89.

Moore, Henrietta. 1988. *Gender, Text, and Space.* Cambridge: Cambridge University Press.

Moraga, Cherrie, and Gloria Anzaldúa. 1983. *This Bridge Called My Back: Writings by Radical Women of Color.* New York: Kitchen Table: Women of Color Press.

Morales, Mario Roberto. 1999. "Esencialismo 'Maya,' Mestizaje Ladino y Nación Intercultural." In *¡Racismo en Guatemala? Abriendo el Debate sobre un Tema Tabú,* edited by Clara Arenas Bianchi, Charles R. Hale, and Gustavo Palma Murga. Guatemala City: AVANCSO.

Moran, Daniel. 2000. *Wars of National Liberation*. London: Cassell.

Moser, Hugo. 1952. "Deutsche Sprachgeschichte der älteren Zeit." In *Deutsche Philologie im Aufriss*, edited by Wolfgang Stammler. Berlin: Erich Schmidt Verlag.

Mosse, George. 1985. *Nationalism and Sexuality*. New York: Howard Fertig.

—. 1996. *The Image of Man: The Creation of Modern Masculinity*. New York: Oxford University Press.

Mostert, Noel. 1992. *Frontiers*. London: Jonathan Cape.

Mudimbe, V. Y. 1988. *The Invention of Africa: Gnosis, Philosophy, and the Order of Knowledge*. Bloomington: Indiana University Press.

Mueggler, Erik. 2001. *The Age of Wild Ghosts*. Berkeley: University of California Press.

Muir, John. 1915. *Travels in Alaska*. Boston: Houghton Mifflin.

Mukerji, Chandra. 1997. *Territorial Ambitions and the Gardens of Versailles*. Cambridge: Cambridge University Press.

Mullings, Beverly. 1999. "Globalization, Tourism, and the International Sex Trade." In *Sun, Sex, and Gold: Tourism and Sex Work in the Caribbean*, edited by Kamala Kempadoo. Lanham, Md.: Rowman and Littlefield.

Nash, Catherine. 1994. "Remapping the Body/Land: New Cartographies of Identity, Gender, and Landscape in Ireland." In *Writing Women and Space*, edited by Alison Blunt and Gillian Rose. New York: Guilford.

The Nation. 2000. "The Century: An Alternative History." Special issue. 17 January.

Neel, James V. 1953. "Data Pertaining to Population Dynamics of Sickle Cell Disease." *American Journal of Human Genetics* 5: 154.

Nelson, Diane M. 1999a. *A Finger in the Wound*. Berkeley: University of California Press.

—. 1999b. "Perpetual Creation and Decomposition: Bodies, Gender, and Desire in the Assumptions of a Guatemalan Discourse of Mestizaje." *Journal of Latin American Anthropology* 4, no. 1: 74–111.

—. 2001. "Stumped Identities: Body Image, Body Politic, and the Mujer Maya as Prosthetic." *Cultural Anthropology* 16, no. 3: 314–53.

Neumann, Roderick. 1997. "Primitive Ideas: Protected Area Buffer Zones and the Politics of Land in Africa." *Development and Change* 28, no. 3: 559–82.

—. 1999. *Imposing Wilderness*. Berkeley: University of California Press.

Neumark, Georg. 1970. [1668]. *Der Neu-Sprossende Teutsche Palmbaum. Oder Ausführlicher Bericht, Von der Hochlöblichen Fruchtbringenden Gesellschaft Anfang, Absehn, Satzungen, Eigenschaft, und deroselben Fortpflanzung*. Nuremberg and Weimar: n.p. Reprinted in *Die Fruchtbringende Gesellschaft*, edited by Martin Bircher. Vol. 3. Munich: Kösel-Verlag.

Newmeyer, Frederick J. 1986. *The Politics of Linguistics*. Chicago: University of Chicago Press.

Newsweek. 2000. "Not as Green as They Seem." 27 March: 10–14.

Newton-King, Susan. 1980. "The Labour Market of the Cape Colony, 1807–28." In *Economy and Society in Pre-Industrial South Africa*, edited by Shula Marks and Anthony Atmore. London: Longman.

Nietzsche, Friedrich. 1967. [1887]. *On the Genealogy of Morals*. Translated by Walter Kaufmann and R. J. Hollingdale. New York: Random House.

Nixon, Rob. 1994. *Homelands, Harlem, and Hollywood: South African Culture and the World Beyond*. New York: Routledge.

Noakes, Jeremy, and Geoffrey Pridham, eds. 1974. *Documents on Nazism, 1919–1945*. New York: Viking.

Nölkensmeier, Petra. 1999. "Sprachpflege: Seltsamer Drang zu Konzernsprache." *Spiegel Online*, 21 April. Available at http:/www.spiegel.de/kultur/gesellschaft/0,1518,18793,00.html.

Noyes, John. 1992. *Colonial Space: Spatiality, Subjectivity, and Society in the Colonial Discourse of South West Africa, 1884–1915*. Chur, Switzerland: Harwood Academic Press.

Nussbaum, Paul. 1998. "On the Bus for an Eco-Tour of Chester." *Philadelphia Inquirer*, 28 July.

Oakes, Timothy. 2000. "China's Provincial Identities: Reviving Regionalism and Reinventing 'Chineseness.'" *Journal of Asian Studies* 59, no. 3: 667–92.

O'Connell Davidson, Julia, and Jacqueline Sanchez Taylor. 1999. "Fantasy Islands: Exploring the Demand for Sex Tourism." In *Sun, Sex, and Gold: Tourism and Sex Work in the Caribbean*, edited by Kamala Kempadoo. Lanham, Md.: Rowman and Littlefield.

O'Connor, Geoffrey. 1993. *Amazon Journal*. 60 min. New York: Realis Pictures Inc. Videocassette.

Okihiro, Gary. 2001. *Common Ground*. Princeton: Princeton University Press.

Oliveira, João Pacheco, ed. 1999. *A Viagem da Volta: Etnicidade, Política e Reelaboração Cultural no Nordeste Indígena*. Rio de Janeiro: Contra Capa.

Olson, Gary A., and Lynn Worsham, eds. 1999. *Race, Rhetoric, and the Postcolonial*. Albany: SUNY Press.

Olwig, Karen Fog, and Kirsten Hastrup, eds. 1997. *Siting Culture: The Shifting Anthropological Subject*. New York: Routledge.

Olwig, Kenneth. 1995. "Reinventing Common Nature: Yosemite and Mount Rushmore a Meandering Tale of Double Nature." In *Uncommon Ground: Rethinking the Human Place in Nature*, edited by William Cronon. New York: Norton.

———1996. "Recovering the Substantive Nature of Landscape." *Annals of the Association of American Geographers* 86, no. 4: 630–53.

Ong, Aihwa. 1987. *Spirits of Resistance and Capitalist Discipline: Factory Women in Malaysia*. Albany: SUNY Press.

———. 1991. "The Gender and Labor Politics of Postmodernity." *Annual Review of Anthropology* 20: 279–309.

———. 1999. *Flexible Citizenship*. Durham, N.C.: Duke University Press.

Orlove, Ben. 1993. "Putting Race in Its Place: Order in Colonial and Postcolonial Peruvian Geography." *Social Research* 60, no. 2: 301–36.

Ortiz, Fernando. 1990. [1947]. *Cuban Counterpoint*. Reprint. Durham: Duke University Press.

Ortner, Sherry, and Harriet Whitehead, eds. 1981. *Sexual Meanings: The Cultural Construction of Gender and Sexuality*. Cambridge: Cambridge University Press.

Ostrander, Elaine. 1992. "The Dog Genome Project." Paper read at Science Innovation 1992, New Techniques and Instruments in Biomedical Research, 23 July, San Francisco.

Otzoy, Irma. 1996. "Maya Clothing and Identity." In *Maya Cultural Activism in Guatemala*, edited by Edward F. Fischer and R. McKenna Brown. Austin: University of Texas Press.

Outlaw, Lucius T. Jr. 1996. *On Race and Philosophy*. New York: Routledge.

Overall, Christine. 1992. "What's Wrong with Prostitution? Evaluating Sex Work." *Signs* 17, no. 4: 705–24.

Packard, Randall. 1989. "The Healthy Reserve and the Dressed Native: Discourses on Black Health and the Language of Legitimization in South Africa." *American Ethnologist* 16, no. 4: 686–703.

Padgett, George A. 1996–97. "Canine Genetic Disease: Is the Situation Changing?" *DogWorld* 81, no. 12: 44–47; 82, no. 1: 26–29; 82, no. 3: 24–26; 82, no. 4: 36–39.

——. 1998. *Control of Canine Genetic Diseases.* New York: Howell.

Pandian, Anand S. 2001. "Predatory Care: The Imperial Hunt in Mughal and British India." *Journal of Historical Sociology* 14, no. 1: 79–107.

Pandolfo, Stefania. 1997. *Impasse of the Angels.* Chicago: University of Chicago Press.

Park, Robert Ezra. 1950. *Race and Culture.* Glencoe, Ill.: Free Press.

Parry, Benita. 1993. Review of *In Theory—Classes, Nations, Literatures,* by Aijaz Ahmad. *History Workshop Journal* 36 (fall): 323–42.

Pateman, Carol. 1998. *The Sexual Contract.* Stanford: Stanford University Press.

Paul, Diane. 1998. "The Rockefeller Foundation and the Origin of Behavior Genetics." In *The Politics of Heredity: Essays on Eugenics, Biomedicine, and the Nature-Nurture Debate.* Albany: SUNY Press.

Peet, Richard, and Michael Watts, eds. 1996. *Liberation Ecologies: Environment, Development, Social Movements.* New York: Routledge.

Peires, Jeffrey. 1989. *The Dead Will Arise.* Johannesburg: Raven.

Peitzman, Steven. 1992. "From Bright's Disease to End-Stage-Renal-Disease." In *Framing Disease,* edited by C. E. Rosenberg and J. Golden. New Brunswick: Rutgers University Press.

Pels, Peter. 1999. "The Rise and Fall of the Indian Aborigines: Orientalism, Anglicism, and the Emergence of an Ethnology of India, 1833–1869." In *Colonial Subjects: Essays on the Practical History of Anthropology,* edited by Peter Pels and Oscar Salemink. Ann Arbor: University of Michigan Press.

Peluso, Nancy. 1992. *Rich Forests, Poor People: Resource Control and Resistance in Java.* Berkeley: University of California Press.

——. 1993. "Coercing Conservation? The Politics of State Resource Control." *Global Environmental Change* 3, no. 2: 199–217.

——. 1995. "Whose Woods Are These? Counter-Mapping Forest Territories in Kalimantan, Indonesia." *Antipode* 27, no. 4: 383–406.

Peluso, Nancy Lee, and Michael Watts, eds. 2001, *Violent Environments.* Ithaca: Cornell University Press.

Pemberton, John. 1994. *On the Subject of Java.* Ithaca: Cornell University Press.

Peña, Devon. 1998. *Subversive Kin: Chicano Culture, Ecology, Politics.* Tucson: University of Arizona Press.

Penrose, Jan, and Peter Jackson, eds. 1994. *Constructions of Race, Place, and Nation.* Minneapolis: University of Minnesota Press.

Penrose, Lionel. 1959. *Outline of Human Genetics.* New York: Wiley.

Peters, Pauline. 1994. *Dividing the Commons: Politics, Policy, and Culture in Botswana.* Charlottesville: University Press of Virginia.

Phillips, Richard. 1997. *Mapping Men and Empire: A Geography of Adventure.* London: Routledge.

Pieterse, Jan Nederveen. 1992. *White on Black: Images of Africa and Blacks in Western Popular Culture.* New Haven: Yale University Press.

——. 1998. "My Paradigm or Yours? Alternative Development, Post-Development, Reflexive Development." *Development and Change* 29, no. 2: 343–73.

Pitt, David. 1989. "Gang Attack Unusual for Its Viciousness." *New York Times,* 25 April: B1.

Plough, Alonzo. 1986. *Borrowed Time: Artificial Organs and the Politics of Extending Lives.* Philadelphia: Temple University Press.

Polanyi, Karl. 1957. *The Great Transformation: The Political and Economic Origins of Our Time.* Boston: Beacon.

Pollan, Michael. 1991. *Second Nature: A Gardener's Education.* New York: Atlantic Monthly Press.

———. 2001. *The Botany of Desire.* New York: Random House.

Pollard, Ingrid. 1989. "Pastoral Interludes." *Third Text* 7 (summer): 41–46.

Polley, M. J., and Bearn, A. G. 1974. "Cystic Fibrosis: Current Concepts." *Journal of Medical Genetics* 11: 249.

Poole, Deborah. 1997. *Vision, Race, and Modernity: A Visual Economy of the Andean Image World.* Princeton: Princeton University Press.

Porch, Douglas. 2000. *Wars of Empire.* London: Cassell.

Portes, Alejandro, and Richard Schauffler. 1993. "Competing Perspectives on the Latin American Informal Sector." *Population and Development Review* 19, no. 1: 33–60.

Povinelli, Elizabeth A. 1999. "Settler Modernity and the Quest for an Indigenous Tradition." *Public Culture* 11, no. 1: 19–48.

———. 2002. *The Cunning of Recognition: Indigenous Alterities and the Making of Australian Multiculturalism.* Durham, N.C.: Duke University Press.

Prakash, Gyan. 1994. "Subaltern Studies as Postcolonial Criticism." *American Historical Review* 99, no. 5: 1475–90.

———. ed. 1995. *After Colonialism: Imperial Histories and Postcolonial Displacements.* Princeton: Princeton University Press.

———. 1999. *Another Reason: Science and the Imagination of Modern India.* Princeton: Princeton University Press.

Prashad, Vijay 1994. "Native Dirt/Imperial Ordure: The Cholera of 1832 and the Morbid Resolutions of Modernity." *Journal of Historical Sociology* 7, no. 3: 242–260.

———. 2000. *The Karma of Brown Folk.* Minneapolis: University of Minnesota Press.

Pratt, Mary Louise. 1985. "Scratches on the Face of the Country: Or, What Mr. Barrow Saw in the Land of the Bushmen." *Critical Inquiry* 12, no. 1: 119–43.

———. 1992. *Imperial Eyes: Travel Writing and Transculturation.* New York: Routledge.

Pred, Allan. 1998. "Memory and the Cultural Reworking of Crisis: Racisms and the Current Moment of Danger in Sweden, or Wanting It Like Before." *Environment and Planning D: Society and Space* 16, no. 6: 635–64.

———. 2000. *Even in Sweden.* Berkeley: University of California Press.

Price, Jennifer. 1999. *Flight Maps: Adventures with Nature in Modern America.* New York: Basic Books.

Pringle, Rosemary. 1992. "Absolute Sex? Unpacking the Sexuality/Gender Relationship." In *Rethinking Sex: Social Theory and Sexuality Research,* edited by R. W. Connell and G. W. Dowsett. Philadelphia: Temple University Press.

Pringle, Thomas. 1966. [1835]. *Narrative of a Residence in South Africa.* Reprint. Cape Town: C. Struik.

Proctor, Robert. 1988. "From *Anthropologie* to *Rassenkunde* in the German Anthropological Tradition." In *Bones, Bodies, Behavior: Essays on Biological Anthropology,* edited by George W. Stocking Jr. Madison: University of Wisconsin Press.

——. 1999. *The Nazi War on Cancer.* Princeton: Princeton University Press.

Pruitt, Deborah, and Suzanne Lafont. 1995. "For Love of Money: Romance Tourism in Jamaica." *Annals of Tourism Research* 22, no. 2: 422–40.

Pulido, Laura. 1996a. "A Critical Review of the Methodology of Environmental Racism Research." *Antipode* 28, no. 2: 142–49.

——. 1996b. "Development of 'People of Color' Identity in the Environmental Justice Movement." *Socialist Review* 26, nos. 3–4: 145–80.

——. 1996c. *Environmentalism and Economic Justice: Two Chicano Struggles in the Southwest.* Tucson: University of Arizona Press.

Pulido, Laura, Steve Sidawi, and Robert O. Vos. 1996. "An Archaeology of Environmental Racism in Los Angeles." *Urban Geography* 17, no. 5: 419–39.

Rabinow, Paul. 1989. *French Modern: Norms and Forms of the Social Environment.* Chicago: University of Chicago Press.

——. 1996. "Artificiality and Enlightenment: From Sociobiology to Biosociality." In *Essays on the Anthropology of Reason.* Princeton: Princeton University Press.

——. 1999. *French DNA: Trouble in Purgatory.* Chicago: University of Chicago Press.

Radhakrishnan, R. 2000. "Postmodernism and the Rest of the World." In *The Pre-Occupation of Postcolonial Studies,* edited by Fawzia Afzal-Khan and Kalpana Seshadri-Crooks. Durham, N.C.: Duke University Press.

Raffles, Hugh. 1999. " 'Local Theory': Nature and the Making of an Amazonian Place." *Cultural Anthropology* 14, no. 3: 323–60.

——. 2001. "The Uses of Butterflies." *American Ethnologist* 28, no. 3: 513–48.

——. 2002. *In Amazonia: A Natural History.* Princeton: Princeton University Press.

Rafinski, Karen. 1997. "Early Warning." *Chicago Tribune,* 5 June: 2.

Rahail, Johannes Paulus. 1996. "*Adat* Society in the Islands of Kei (Evav), South-East Maluku." In *Vines That Won't Bind: Indigenous Peoples of Asia,* edited by Christian Erni. Copenhagen: International Working Group on Indigenous Affairs (IWGIA).

Raloff, Janet. 1997. "Dying Breeds." *Science News* 152: 216–18.

Ramos, Alcida Rita. 1988. "Indian Voices: Contact Experienced and Expressed." In *Rethinking History and Myth: Indigenous South American Perspectives on the Past,* edited by Jonathan D. Hill. Urbana: University of Illinois Press.

——. 1995. *Sanumá Memories: Yanomami Ethnography in Times of Crisis.* Madison: University of Wisconsin Press.

——. 1998. *Indigenism: Ethnic Politics in Brazil.* Madison: University of Wisconsin Press.

Randall, Alice. 2001. *The Wind Done Gone.* Boston: Houghton Mifflin.

Randolph, Mike. 1999. "Things They'll Do for Fun." *National Post,* 29 December: B11.

Ranger, Terence. 1985. *The Invention of Tradition in Zimbabwe.* Gweru, Zimbabwe: Mambo Press.

——. 1999. *Voices from the Rocks: Nature, Culture, and History in the Matopos Hills of Zimbabwe.* Oxford: James Curry.

Ranney, Helen. 1972. "Editorial: Sickle Cell Disease." *Blood* 39 (March): 436.

Rattansi, Ali. 1994. " 'Western' Racisms, Ethnicities, and Identities in a 'Postmodern' Frame." In *Racism, Modernity, and Identity: On the Western Front,* edited by Ali Rattansi and Sallie Westwood. Cambridge: Polity Press.

Rattansi, Ali, and Sallie Westwood, eds. 1994. *Racism, Modernity, and Identity: On the Western Front*. Cambridge: Polity Press.

Ratzel, Friedrich. 1896. *The History of Mankind*. Translated by A. J. Butler. London: Macmillan.

—. 1988. [1876]. *Sketches of Urban and Cultural Life in North America*. Translated and edited by Stewart A. Stehlin. New Brunswick: Rutgers University Press.

Raxche' (Demetrio Rodriguez Guajan). 1996. "Maya Culture and the Politics of Development." In *Maya Cultural Activism in Guatemala*, edited by Edward F. Fischer and R. McKenna Brown. Austin: University of Texas Press.

Raynolds, Laura. 1998. "Harnessing Women's Work: Restructuring Agricultural and Industrial Labor Forces in the Dominican Republic." *Economic Geography* 74, no. 2: 149–69.

Reagon, Bernice Johnson. 1983. "Coalition Politics: Turning the Century." In *Home Girls*, edited by Barbara Smith. New York: Women of Color Press.

Rees, Ronald. 1996. "Under the Weather: Climate and Disease, 1700–1900." *History Today* 46, no. 1: 35–41.

Reiher, Ruth, and Rüdiger Läzer, eds. 1996. *Von "Buschzulage" bis "Ossinachweis": Ost-West Deutsch in der Diskussion*. Berlin: Taschenbuch Verlag.

Renan, Ernest. 1990. [1882]. "What Is a Nation?" Translated by Martin Thom. Reprinted in *Nation and Narration*, edited by Homi Bhabha. New York: Routledge.

Richardson, Michael. 2000. "Indonesia Faces Forest Dilemma." *International Herald Tribune*, 2 January, Jakarta edition.

Ricoeur, Paul. 1978. *O Conflito das Interpretações*. Rio de Janeiro: Imago.

Ritvo, Harriet. 1987. *The Animal Estate*. Cambridge: Harvard University Press.

Roberts, Dorothy. 1997. *Killing the Black Body: Race, Reproduction, and the Meaning of Liberty*. New York: Vintage.

Robinson, Jennifer. 1996. *The Power of Apartheid: State, Power, and Space in South African Cities*. Oxford: Butterworth-Heinemann.

Rocheleau, Diane, B. Thomas-Slayter, and E. Wangari, eds. 1996. *Feminist Political Ecology: Global Issues and Local Experiences*. New York: Routledge.

Rodriguez, Ileana. 1994. *House/Garden/Nation*. Durham, N.C.: Duke University Press.

Roediger, David R. 1991. *The Wages of Whiteness*. New York: Verso.

—. 1997. "White Looks: Hairy Apes, True Stories, and Limbaugh's Laughs." In *Whiteness: A Critical Reader*, edited by Mike Hill. New York: New York University Press.

Rohde, David. 1999. "Biological Parents Win in Implant Case." *New York Times*. Late edition, 17 July: B3.

Rojas Lima, Flavio. 1990. *Etnicidad: Teoría y Praxis. La Revolución Cultural de 1990*. Guatemala City: Serviprensa.

Rommelspacher, Birgit. 1997. "Fremd- und Selbstbilder in der Dominanzkultur." In *Projektionen: Rassismus und Sexismus in der visuellen Kultur*, edited by Annegret Friedrich et al. Marburg: Jonas-Verlag.

Rosada Granados, Hector Roberto. 1987. *Indios y Ladinos: Un estudio antropológico-sociológico*. Guatemala City: Editorial Universitaria.

Rosaldo, Michelle. 1974. "Woman, Culture, and Society: A Theoretical Overview." In *Woman, Culture, and Society*, edited by Michelle Rosaldo and Louise Lamphere. Stanford: Stanford University Press.

—. 1980. "The Use and Abuse of Anthropology: Reflections on Feminism and Cross-Cultural Understanding." *Signs* 5, no. 3: 389–417.

Rosaldo, Renato. 1989. *Culture and Truth: The Remaking of Social Analysis.* Boston: Beacon.

Rose, Mark. 1996. "Mothers and Authors: *Johnson v. Calvert* and the New Children of Our Imaginations." *Critical Inquiry* 22 (summer): 613–33.

Rose, Michael R. 1998. *Darwin's Spectre.* Princeton: Princeton University Press.

Rose, Nikolas. 1999. *Powers of Freedom.* Cambridge: Cambridge University Press.

Roseberry, William. 1996. "Hegemony, Power, and Languages of Contention." In *The Politics of Difference: Ethnic Premises in a World of Power,* edited by Edwin Wilmsen and Patrick McAllister. Chicago: University of Chicago Press.

Rosenberg, Charles, and Janet Golden, eds. 1992. *Framing Disease: Studies in Cultural History.* New Brunswick: Rutgers University Press.

Rosenfeld, S., and J. Pincus. 1932. "The Occurrence of Sicklemia in the White Race." *American Journal of Medical Science* 184, no. 9: 674–82.

Rosner, David, and Gerald Markowitz. 1991. *Deadly Dust: Silicosis and the Politics of Occupational Disease in Twentieth-Century America.* Princeton: Princeton University Press.

Rothenberg, David, ed. 1995. *Wild Ideas.* Minneapolis: University of Minnesota Press.

Roughgarden, Joan. In press. *Evolution's Rainbow: Gender and Sexuality in Nature and People.* Princeton: Princeton University Press.

Rubin, Gayle. 1975. "The Traffic in Women: Notes on the 'Political Economy' of Sex." In *Toward an Anthropology of Women,* edited by Rayna R. Reiter. New York: Monthly Review Press.

Rubin, Lionel F. 1989. *Inherited Eye Diseases in Purebred Dogs.* Baltimore: Williams and Wilkins.

Rubin, Lionel, Betty Nelson, and C. A. Sharp. 1991. "Collie Eye Anomaly in Australian Shepherd Dogs." *Progress in Veterinary and Comparative Ophthalmology* 1, no. 2: 105–08.

Ruf, Rainer. 2000. "Ausländer: Umstrittenes Integrationsgesetz. Vor der Einreise ein Deutschkurs." *Schwäbisches Tagblatt* (July 21); Südwestpresse, cover page.

Rumsfeld, Donald H. 2001. U.S. Defense Department News Briefing. 19 November.

Ruskin, John. 1897. "Of the Pathetic Fallacy." In *Modern Painters.* Vol. 3 Sunnyside: G. Allen.

Rutherford, Jonathan. 1997. *Forever England: Reflections on Masculinity and Empire.* London: Lawrence and Wishart.

Ruwiastuti, Maria R. 1998. "Menuju Pluralsime Hukum Agraria: Analisa dan Kritik terhadap Marginalisasi Posisi Hukum-hukum dan Hak-hak Adat Penduduk Asli atas Tanah dan Sumber-sumber Agraria oleh UUPA 1960." In *Usulan Revisi Undang-Undang Pokok Agraria: Menuju Penegakan Hak-Hak Rakyat atas Sumber-Sumber Agraria,* edited by KRHN and KPA. Jakarta: Kornsorsium Reformasi Hukum Negara and Konsorsium Pembaruan Agraria.

Ryan, James R. 1997. *Picturing Empire.* Chicago: University of Chicago Press.

Sachs, Bernard. 1896. "A Family Form of Idiocy, Generally Fatal, Associated with Early Blindness." *Journal of Nervous and Mental Diseases* 21: 475.

Safa, Helen. 1995. *The Myth of the Male Breadwinner: Women and Industrialization in the Caribbean.* Boulder: Westview Press.

—. 1999. "Free Markets and the Marriage Market: Structural Adjustment, Gender Relations, and Working Conditions among Women Workers." *Environment and Planning A,* no. 31: 291–304.

Safitri, Myrna. 1996. "Saresehan Tentang Akses Masyarakat Lokal Pada Sumberdaya Hutan Dalam Penerapan Peraturan Perundang-Undang." *Ekonesia* 4: 136–41.

Sagawe, Thorsten. 1996. "Industrial Free Zones in the Dominican Republic: National vs. Local Impact." *Journal of Geography* 95, no. 5: 203–10.

Sahlins, Marshall. 1997. "O 'pessimismo sentimental' e a experiência etnográfica: Por que a cultura não é um 'objeto' em via de extinção." *Mana* 3, no. 1: 41–73; *Mana* 3, no. 2: 103–50.

Said, Edward. 1979. *Orientalism.* New York: Vintage.

———. 1994. *Culture and Imperialism.* New York: Vintage.

———. 2001. "The Clash of Ignorance." *The Nation,* 22 October.

Salman, Michael. 2001. *The Embarrassment of Slavery.* Berkeley: University of California Press.

Sam Colop, Enrique. 1996. "The Discourse of Concealment and 1992." In *Maya Cultural Activism in Guatemala,* edited by Edward F. Fischer and R. McKenna Brown. Austin: University of Texas Press.

Sánchez-Eppler, Benigno. 1994. *"Por Causa Mecánica:* The Coupling of Bodies and Machines and the Production and Reproduction of Whiteness in Cecilia Valdés and Nineteenth-Century Cuba." In *Thinking Bodies,* edited by Juliet Flower MacCannell and Laura Zakarin. Stanford: Stanford University Press.

Sandbukt, Oyvind, and WARSI. 1998. *Orang Rimba: Needs Assessment for Resource Security and Development.* Final Report. Jakarta: The World Bank and the Government of Indonesia.

Sandoval, Chela. 2000. *Methodology of the Oppressed.* Minneapolis: University of Minnesota Press.

Saro-Wiwa, Ken. 1995. *A Month and a Day.* New York: Penguin.

Sartre, Jean-Paul. 1948. *The Emotions: Outline of a Theory.* New York: Philosophical Library.

———. 1976. [1948]. *Anti-Semite and Jew.* New York: Schocken Books.

———. 1988. [1949]. *Black Orpheus.* New York: Schocken Books.

———. 2001. [1956]. "Colonialism Is a System." In *Colonialism and Neocolonialism,* translated by Azzedine Haddour et al. New York: Routledge.

Sauer, Carl. 1952. *Agricultural Origins and Dispersal.* New York: American Geographical Society.

———. 1963 [1925]. *The Morphology of Landscape.* Berkeley: University of California Press.

Sawyer, Suzana, and Arun Agrawal. 2000. "Environmental Orientalisms." *Cultural Critique* 45, no. 7: 71–108.

Schaeffer, Robert K. 1997. *Understanding Globalization: The Social Consequences of Political, Economic, and Environmental Change.* New York: Rowman and Littlefield.

Schama, Simon. 1995. *Landscape and Memory.* New York: Knopf.

Schein, Louisa. 2000. *Minority Rules.* Durham, N.C.: Duke University Press.

Schiebinger, Londa. 1993. *Nature's Body: Gender in the Making of Modern Science.* Boston: Beacon.

Schild, Veronica. 1997. "New Subjects of Rights? Women's Movements and the Construction of Citizenship in the 'New Democracies.'" In *Cultures of Politics, Politics of Cultures: Re-visioning Latin American Social Movements,* edited by Sonia E. Alvarez, Evelina Dagnino, and Arturo Escobar. Boulder: Westview Press.

Schirmer, Jennifer. 1998. *The Guatemalan Military Project: A Violence Called Democracy.* Philadelphia: University of Pennsylvania Press.

Schirokauer, Arno. 1952. "Frühneuhochdeutsch." In *Deutsche Philologie im Aufriss,* edited by Wolfgang Stammler. Berlin: Erich Schmidt Verlag.

Schmidt Camacho, Alicia. 1999. "Migrant Subjects: Race, Labor, and Insurgency in the Mexico-

U.S. Borderlands." Ph.D. diss., Department of Modern Thought and Literature, Stanford University.

Schmidt, Elizabeth. 1992. *Peasants, Traders, and Wives: Shona Women in the History of Zimbabwe, 1870–1939*. Portsmouth, N.H.: Heinemann.

Schmidt, Heike. 1995. " 'Penetrating' Foreign Lands: Contestations over African Landscapes: A Case Study from Eastern Zimbabwe." *Environment and History* 1, no. 3: 335–50.

Schmitt, Carl. 1950. *Der Nomos der Erde im Völkerrecht des jus publicum Europaeum*. Koln: Greven.

——. 1996. *The Concept of the Political*. Chicago: University of Chicago Press.

——. 1997. *Land and Sea*. Washington, D.C.: Plutarch Press.

Schneider, David. 1968. *American Kinship: A Cultural Account*. Englewood Cliffs, N.J.: Prentice-Hall.

Schroeder, Richard. 1999. *Shady Practices: Agroforestry and Gender Politics in the Gambia*. Berkeley: University of California Press.

Scott, David. 1995. "Colonial Governmentality." *Social Text* 43: 191–220.

——. 1999. *Refashioning Futures: Criticism after Postcoloniality*. Princeton: Princeton University Press.

Scott, John Paul, ed. 1952. Minutes of the Conference on the Effects of Early Experiences on Mental Health. Bar Harbor, Maine: Roscoe B. Jackson Memorial Laboratory.

——. 1958. "Critical Periods in the Development of Social Behavior in Puppies." *Psychosomatic Medicine* 20: 878–93.

Scott, John Paul, and Frank A. Beach, eds. 1947. Minutes of the Conference on Genetics and Social Behavior. Bar Harbor, Maine: Roscoe B. Jackson Memorial Laboratory.

Scott, John Paul, and J. H. Fuller. 1956. "Heredity and the Social Behavior of Mammals." In *27th Annual Report*. Bar Harbor, Maine: Roscoe B. Jackson Memorial Laboratory.

——. 1965. *Genetics and the Social Behavior of the Dog*. Chicago: University of Chicago Press.

Scott, James C. 1998. *Seeing Like a State: How Certain Schemes to Improve the Human Condition Have Failed*. New Haven: Yale University Press.

Scott, Joan W. 1991. "The Evidence of Experience." *Critical Inquiry* 17, no. 4: 773–97.

Scott-Heron, Gil. 1994. *Spirits*. New York: TVT Records.

Sedgwick, Eve Kosofsky. 1985. *Between Men: English Literature and Homosocial Desire*. New York: Columbia University Press.

Seed, Patricia. 1995. *Ceremonies of Possession in Europe's Conquest of the New World*. Cambridge: Cambridge University Press.

Seidl, Antonio Carlos. 1992. "Entidade culpa comércio verde." *Folha de São Paulo*, 10 June: 1–14.

Seidman, Steven. 1996. *Queer Theory/Sociology*. Cambridge: Blackwell.

——. 1997. *Difference Troubles: Queering Social Theory and Sexual Politics*. Cambridge: Cambridge University Press.

Sekyi-Otu, Ato. 1996. *Fanon's Dialectic of Experience*. Cambridge: Harvard University Press.

Seltzer, Mark. 1992. *Bodies and Machines*. New York: Routledge.

Sen, Faruk. 1999. "Managing the Integration of Foreigners in Germany." Paper presented at the conference "Germany's Immigrants and the Debate over Citizenship," 31 March, Washington, D.C. Sponsored by The American Institute for Contemporary German Studies and the Washington Office of the Friedrich Ebert Foundation. Available at www.aicgs.org/events/99/sen.html.

Senders, Stefan. 1996. "Laws of Belonging: Legal Dimensions of National Inclusion in Germany." *New German Critique* 67 (winter): 147–76.

Senghor, Leopold. 1991. *The Collected Poetry*. Translated by Melvin Dixon. Charlottesville: University Press of Virginia.

Serpell, James, ed. 1995. *The Domestic Dog: Its Evolution, Behaviour, and Interactions with People*. Cambridge: Cambridge University Press.

Sharp, C. A. 1993. *Double Helix Network News*. Available via e-mail: helix@qnis.net.

———. 1998. *CEA and I*. Canine Diversity Project, available at www.magna.ca/~kaitlin/diverse.html.

Sharp, John. 1996. "Ethnogenesis and Ethnic Mobilization: A Comparative Perspective on a South African Dilemma." In *The Politics of Difference: Ethnic Premises in a World of Power*, edited by Edwin Wilmsen and Patrick McAllister. Chicago: University of Chicago Press.

Shier, W. T. 1979. "Increased Resistance to Influenza as a Possible Source of Heterozygote Advantage in Cystic Fibrosis." *Medical Hypotheses* 5: 661.

Shrestha, Neeru. 1999. "Forest Control, Development, and State Formation in Nepal." Ph.D. diss., Interdisciplinary Studies, Dalhousie University.

Sibley, David. 1995. *Geographies of Exclusion: Society and Difference in the West*. New York: Routledge.

"Sickle Cell Anemia, A Race Specific Disease." 1947. Editorial published in the *Journal of the American Medical Association* 133 (January): 33–34.

Simon, Hasanu, and San Afri Awang. 1999. "From Critique Towards an Alternative Natural Resource Management Law (RUU PSDH)." 12 May. Available at fkkm@egroups.com.

Simons, Lewis M. 1999. "Free Fire Zones." In *Crimes of War*, edited by Roy Gutman and David Rieff. New York: Norton.

Singer, Linda. 1993. *Erotic Welfare: Sexual Theory and Politics in the Age of Epidemic*, edited by Judith Butler and Maureen MacGrogan. New York: Routledge.

Skaria, Ajay. 1997. "Shades of Wildness: Tribe, Caste, and Gender in Western India." *Journal of Asian Studies* 56, no. 3: 726–45.

Skotnes, Pippa, ed. 1996. *Miscast: Negotiating the Presence of the Bushmen*. Cape Town: University of Cape Town Press.

Slater, Candace. 1995. "Reinventing Eden: Western Culture as a Recovery Narrative." In *Uncommon Ground: Rethinking the Human Place in Nature*, edited by William Cronon. New York: Norton.

———. 2001. *Entangled Edens: Visions of the Amazon*. Berkeley: University of California Press.

Slome, D. 1933. "The Genetic Basis of Amaurotic Family Idiocy." *Journal of Genetics* 27: 363–72.

Smith, Barbara, ed. 1983. *Home Girls: A Black Feminist Anthology*. New York: Kitchen Table: Women of Color Press.

Smith, Carol A. 1990. "Failed Nationalist Movements in Nineteenth-Century Guatemala: A Parable for the Third World." In *Nationalist Ideologies and the Production of National Cultures*, edited by Richard G. Fox. American Ethnological Society Monograph Series, No. 2. Washington, D.C.: American Anthropological Association.

———. 1992. "Marxists on Class and Culture in Guatemala." Paper presented at the Latin America Studies Association meetings, Los Angeles.

———. 1996. "Myths, Intellectuals, and Race/Class/Gender Distinctions in the Formation of Latin American Nations." *Journal of Latin American Anthropology* 2, no. 1: 148–69.

—. 1997. "The Symbolics of Blood: Mestizaje in the Americas." *Identities* 3, no. 4: 495–521.

—. 1999. "Interpretaciones Norteamericanas sobre la Raza y el Racismo en Guatemala: Una Genealogía Crítica." In *¿Racismo en Guatemala? Abriendo el Debate sobre un Tema Tabú*, edited by Clara Arenas Bianchi, Charles R. Hale, and Gustavo Palma Murga. Guatemala City: AVANCSO.

Smith, Henry Nash. 1950. *Virgin Land: The American West as Symbol and Myth*. Cambridge: Harvard University Press.

Smith, Neil. 1984. *Uneven Development: Nature, Capital, and the Production of Space*. Oxford: Blackwell.

—. 1996. *The New Urban Frontier: Gentrification and the Revanchist City*. New York: Routledge.

Soares, Ana. 2000. "A saga dos verdadeiros donos do Brasil. Interview with Marcos Terena." *Companhia*. Informativo do Centro Cultural de Brasília No. 5, p. 3. Available at www.ccbnet.org.br.

Social Affairs, Department of. 1994/95. *Isolated Community Development: Data and Information*. Jakarta: Directorate for Development of Isolated Communities.

Solnit, Rebecca. 1994. *Savage Dreams*. New York: Vintage.

—. 2001. *As Eve Said to the Serpent: On Landscape, Gender, and Art*. Athens: University of Georgia Press.

Solomos, John. 1986. "Varieties of Marxist Conceptions of 'Race,' Class and the State: A Critical Analysis." In *Theories of Race and Ethnic Relations*, edited by John Rex and David Mason. Cambridge: Harvard University Press.

Soper, Kate. 1995. *What Is Nature? Culture, Politics, and the Non-Human*. Oxford: Blackwell.

Spears, Ellen Griffith. 1998. *The Newtown Story: One Community's Fight for Environmental Justice*. Gainesville, Ga.: Center for Democratic Renewal and the Newtown Florist Club.

Spence, Mark David. 1999. *Dispossessing the Wilderness: Indian Removal and the Making of the National Parks*. New York: Oxford University Press.

Spencer, Herbert. 1965. [1892]. *The Man Versus the State*. Caldwell, Id.: Caxton Printers.

Spiers, Edward M. 1975. "The Use of the Dum Dum Bullet and Colonial Warfare." *Journal of Imperial and Commonwealth History* 4: 3–14.

Spillers, Hortense. 1987. "Mama's Baby, Papa's Maybe: An American Grammar Book." *Diacritics* (summer): 65–82.

Spivak, Gayatri Chakravorty. 1988. "Can the Subaltern Speak?" In *Marxism and the Interpretation of Culture*, edited by Cary Nelson and Lawrence Grossberg. Urbana: University of Illinois Press.

Spivak, Gayatri, and Gunew Sneja. 1993. "Questions of Multiculturalism." In *The Cultural Studies Reader*, edited by Simon During. London: Routledge.

Spurzheim, Johannes G. 1830. "On Phrenology." *Phrenological Journal* 6: 311–20.

Stammler, Wolfgang. 1954. "Sprachliche Beobachtungen an der Lutherbibel des 17. Jahrhunderts." In *Kleine Schriften zur Sprachgeschichte*, edited by W. Stammler. Berlin: Erich Schmidt Verlag.

Stansworth, Michelle, ed. 1987. *Reproductive Technologies: Gender, Motherhood, and Medicine*. Cambridge: Polity Press.

State Ministry for Environment and United Nations Development Program, KLH/UNDP. 1997. *Agenda 21-Indonesia: A National Strategy for Sustainable Development*. Jakarta: KLH/UNDP.

Stearman, Allyn MacLean. 1994. "Revisiting the Myth of the Ecologically Noble Savage in Amazonia: Implications for Indigenous Land Rights." *Culture and Agriculture* 49: 2–6.

Stedman, Raymond William. 1982. *Shadows of the Indian: Stereotypes in American Culture.* Norman: University of Oklahoma Press.

Steinhoff, Jürgen. 1999a. "Sprach-Störung." *Stern* 36 (2 September): 56–60.

———. 1999b. "Sprach-Störung." *Stern Online/Magazin/Archiv* (2 September): 1–6. Available in http://www.stern.de/servlet/stern/serv.

Stepan, Nancy Leys. 1990. "Race and Gender: The Role of Analogy in Science." In *Anatomy of Racism,* edited by David Theo Goldberg. Minneapolis: University of Minnesota Press.

———. 1991. *The Hour of Eugenics: Race, Gender, and Nation in Latin America.* Ithaca: Cornell University Press.

———. 1998. "Race, Gender, Science, and Citizenship." *Gender and History* 10, no. 1: 26–52.

———. 2001. *Picturing Tropical Nature.* Ithaca: Cornell University Press.

Stevens, Jacqueline. 1999. *Reproducing the State.* Princeton: Princeton University Press.

Steward, Julian Hayes. 1955. *Theory of Culture Change: The Method of Multilinear Evolution.* Urbana: University of Illinois Press.

Stewart, Kathleen. 1996. "An Occupied Place." In *Senses of Place,* edited by Steven Feld and Keith Basso. Santa Fe: School of American Research Press.

Stocking, George W., Jr. 1982. *Race, Culture, and Evolution: Essays in the History of Anthropology.* Chicago: University of Chicago Press.

Stolcke, Verena. 1995. "Talking Culture: New Boundaries, New Rhetorics of Exclusion in Europe." *Cultural Anthropology* 36, no. 1: 1–24.

Stoler, Ann Laura. 1991. "Carnal Knowledge and Imperial Power: Gender, Race, and Morality in Colonial Asia." In *Gender at the Crossroads of Knowledge: Feminist Anthropology in the Postmodern Era,* edited by Micaela di Leonardo. Berkeley: University of California Press.

———. 1995. *Race and the Education of Desire: Foucault's History of Sexuality and the Colonial Order of Things.* Durham, N.C.: Duke University Press.

———. 2002. "Racist Visions for the Twenty-First Century: On the Cultural Politics of the French Radical Right." In *Relocating Postcolonialism,* edited by David Theo Goldberg and Ato Quayson. Oxford: Blackwell.

Stoll, David. 1993. *Between Two Armies in the Ixil Towns of Guatemala.* New York: Columbia University Press.

———. 1999. *Rigoberta Menchú and the Story of All Poor Guatemalans.* Boulder: Westview Press.

Straßner, Erich. 1995. *Deutsche Sprachkultur. Von der Barbarensprache zur Weltsprache.* Tübingen: Niemeyer.

Strathern, Marilyn. 1988. *The Gender of the Gift.* Berkeley: University of California Press.

———. 1992a. *After Nature: English Kinship in the Late Twentieth Century.* Cambridge: Cambridge University Press.

———. 1992b. *Reproducing the Future: Anthropology, Kinship, and the New Reproductive Technologies.* London: Routledge.

———. 1999. *Property, Substance, and Effect: Anthropological Essays on Persons and Things.* London: Athlone Press.

Strong, Pauline Turner. 1996. "Animated Indians: Critique and Contradiction in Commodified Children's Culture." *Cultural Anthropology* 11, no. 3: 405–24.

Sturgeon, Noel. 1997. *Ecofeminist Natures: Race, Gender, Feminist Theory, and Political Action.* New York: Routledge.

Stutzman, Robert. 1981. "*El Mestizaje:* An All-Inclusive Ideology of Exclusion." In *Cultural Trans-*

formations and Ethnicity in Modern Ecuador, edited by Norman E. Whitten Jr. New York: Harper and Row.

Stuurman, Siep. 2001. "Francois Bernier and the Invention of Racial Classification." History Workshop Journal 51 (spring): 247–50.

Suara Merdeka. 2000. "Mengelola Hutan Bersama Masyarakat." 2 May.

Suara Pembaruan. 2000. "Pemberdayaan Hutan Dapat Kurangi Utang Negara." 1 May. Jakarta edition.

Sumedi T. P. 1999. "Orang Rimba: Jika Hutan Habis, Matilah Kita." Suara Pembaruan, 7 November. Jambi.

Super, M. 1977. "Letter: Heterozygote Disadvantage in Cystic Fibrosis." Lancet 2 (17 December): 1288.

Suryohadikusumo, Djamaludin, and Emil Salim. 1999. "Perlu Penundaan Pembicaraan RUU Kehutanan." 15 June. Available at fkkm@egroups.com.

Swarns, Rachel 2000. "Apartheid Still Burdens a Girl Who Didn't Fit." New York Times, 10 June: A4.

Tagblatt. 1999a. "Staatsbürgerschaft/Neuer Entwurf. Doppel-Paß für Jugendliche." 55/54 Schwäbisches Tagblatt (6 March): 1.

——. 1999b. "Staatsbürgerschaftsreform. Paß nur nach Sprachtest." Schwäbisches Tagblatt 55/13 (18 January): 2.

——. 1999c. "Doppelte Staatsangehörigkeit." Schwäbisches Tagblatt 55 (2 October): 1.

——. 1999d. "Doppelpaß für Kinder." Schwäbisches Tagblatt 55/105 (8 May): 1.

——. 1999e. "Sprache. Unwort 1999 gesucht." Schwäbisches Tagblatt 55/245 (22 October): 1.

——. 2000. "Shea bedauert 'Unwort.'" Schwäbisches Tagblatt 56/39 (17 February): 2.

Takaki, Ronald T. 1990. Iron Cages: Race and Culture in Nineteenth-Century America. New York: Oxford University Press.

Taussig, Michael. 1987. Shamanism, Colonialism, and the Wild Man: A Study in Terror and Healing. Chicago: University of Chicago Press.

Taylor, Charles. 1989. Sources of the Self: The Making of Modern Identity. Cambridge: Harvard University Press.

——. 1994. "The Politics of Recognition." In Multiculturalism: Examining the Politics of Recognition, edited by Amy Gutmann. Princeton: Princeton University Press.

Taylor, Diana. 1997. Disappearing Acts: Spectacles of Gender and Nationalism in Argentina's "Dirty War." Durham, N.C.: Duke University Press.

Taylor, Dorceta. 1997. "Women of Color, Environmental Justice, and Ecofeminism." In Ecofeminism: Women, Culture, Nature, edited by Karen J. Warren. Bloomington: Indiana University Press.

Taylor, Peter, and Frederick Buttel. 1992. "How Do We Know We Have Global Environmental Problems?" Geoforum 23, no. 3: 405–16.

Templeton, Alan R. 1999. "Human Race in the Context of Recent Human Evolution: A Molecular Perspective." Paper presented at the Wenner Gren Foundation Conference on Anthropology in the Age of Genetics, 11–19 June, Teresópolis, Brazil.

Terry, Jennifer. 1999. An American Obsession: Science, Medicine, and Homosexuality in Modern Society. Chicago: University of Chicago Press.

——. 2000. "'Unnatural Acts' in Nature: The Scientific Fascination with Queer Animals." GLQ 6, no. 2: 151–93.

Terry, Jennifer, and Jacqueline Urla, eds. 1995. *Deviant Bodies*. Bloomington: Indiana University Press.

Tesh, Sylvia N., and Bruce Williams. 1996. "Identity Politics, Disinterested Politics, and Environmental Justice." *Polity* 28, no. 3: 285–305.

Thahar, Nasrul. 1999. "Kami Orang Kubu." *Kompas*, 30 August, Jakarta edition.

Thomas, John, A. Merritt, and M. E. Hodes. 1977. "Electrophoretic Analysis of Serum Proteins in Cystic Fibrosis." *Pediatrics Research* 11:1148–54.

Thomas, Nicholas. 1991. "Against Ethnography." *Cultural Anthropology* 6, no. 3: 306–22.

Thompson, Edward P. 1975. *Whigs and Hunters: The Origin of the Black Act*. London: Penguin.

Thompson, George. 1827. *Travels and Adventures in Southern Africa*. London: Henry Colburn.

Thongchai Winichakul. 1994. *Siam Mapped: A History of the Geo-Body of a Nation*. Honolulu: University of Hawaii Press.

—. 2000. "The Quest for '*Siwilai*': A Geographical Discourse of Civilizational Thinking in the Late Nineteenth- and Early Twentieth-Century Siam." *Journal of Asian Studies* 59, no. 3: 528–49.

Tierney, Patrick. 2000. *Darkness in El Dorado: How Scientists and Journalists Devastated the Amazon*. New York: Norton.

Todorov, Tzvetan. 1993. *On Human Diversity*. Cambridge: Harvard University Press.

Trabant, Jürgen, ed. 1985. *Wilhelm von Humboldt: Über die Sprache*. Munich: Deutscher Taschenbuch Verlag.

Trabant, Jürgen. 1990. *Traditionen Humboldts*. Frankfurt/M: Suhrkamp Verlag.

Trabold, Annette. 1993. *Sprachpolitik, Sprachkritik und Öffentlichkeit*. Wiesbaden: Deutscher Universitätsverlag.

Treichler, Paula. 1999. *How to Have Theory in an Epidemic: The Cultural Chronicle of AIDS*. Durham, N.C.: Duke University Press.

Trinh T. Minh-Ha. 1989. *Woman, Native, Other: Writing Postcoloniality and Feminism*. Bloomington: Indiana University Press.

Trouillot, Michel-Rolph. 1991. "Anthropology and the Savage Slot: The Poetics and Politics of Otherness." In *Racapturing Anthropology*, edited by Richard Fox. Santa Fe: School of American Research Press.

Trut, Ludamilla N. 1999. "Early Canid Domestication: The Fox-Farm Experiment." *American Scientist* 87 (March-April): 160–69.

Tsing, Anna Lowenhaupt. 1993. *In the Realm of the Diamond Queen: Marginality in an Out-of-the-Way Place*. Princeton: Princeton University Press.

—. 1999. "Becoming a Tribal Elder, and Other Green Development Fantasies." In *Transforming the Indonesian Uplands: Marginality, Power, and Production*, edited by Tania Murray Li. Amsterdam: Harwood Academic.

TSM. 1995. "White Sands, Blue Skies, Dark Women." Available at http://www.tsmtravel.com.

—. 1999. "Boca Chica Postings." Available at http://www.tsmtravel.com.

Tucholsky, Kurt. 1989. *Sprache ist eine Waffe. Sprachglossen*. Reinbek/Hamburg: Rowohlt.

Tuhiwai Smith, Linda. 1999. *Decolonizing Methodologies: Research and Indigenous Peoples*. London: Zed Books.

Turnbull, Clive. 1948. *Black War: The Extermination of the Tasmanian Aborigines*. Melbourne: F. W. Cheshire.

Turner, Terence. 1991a. *Baridjumoko em Altamira*. In *Povos Indígenas no Brasil 1987/88/89/90*.

Aconteceu Especial 18. São Paulo: Centro Ecumênico de Documentação e Informação (CEDI), 337–338.

——. 1991b. "Representing, Resisting, Rethinking: Historical Transformations of Kayapo Culture and Anthropological Consciousness." In *Colonial Situations: Essays on the Contextualization of Ethnographic Knowledge,* edited by George W. Stocking Jr. Madison: University of Wisconsin Press.

Tylor, Edward B. 1896. Introduction to *The History of Mankind,* by Friedrich Ratzel. Translated by A. J. Butler. London: Macmillan.

Urry, John. 1990. *The Tourist Gaze: Leisure and Travel in Contemporary Societies.* London: Sage.

U.S. House. 1971. Statement of John Henry Johnson, former professional football player, in "Bills to provide for the prevention of sickle cell anemia." Committee on Interstate and Foreign Commerce. Subcommittee on Public Health and Environment. 92d Cong., 1st sess. 12 November. Serial no. 92–57.

Vandergeest, Peter, and Nancy Lee Peluso. 1995. "Territorialization and State Power in Thailand." *Theory and Society* 24: 385–426.

Van der Veen, Marjolein. 2001. "Rethinking Commodification and Prostitution: An Effort at Peacemaking in the Battles over Prostitution." *Rethinking Marxism* 13, no. 2: 30–51.

Vaughan, Megan. 1980. *Curing Their Ills.* Cambridge: Polity Press.

Velásquez Nimatuj, Irma. 1999a. "K'iche' Families: Race, Gender and Class in Guatemala." Paper presented at the Mayan Studies Conference, August 2000, Guatemala City.

——. 1999b. "Between the Body Politics and the Blood of Guatemala." Paper presented at the American Anthropology Association meetings, November, San Francisco.

Verein. 1999. "Verein zur Wahrung der deutschen Sprache. Bürger für die Erhaltung der sprachlichen und kulturellen Vielfalt Europas." Available at http://www.vwds/de.

——. 2001a. "Verein Deutsche Sprache e. V." Available at http://vds-ev.de.

——. 2001b. "Satzung: Verein Deutsche Sprache." Available at http://vds-ev.de/verein/satzung.php.

——. 2001c. "Pressespiegel: Verein Deutsche Sprache." Available at http://vds-ev.de/presse/index. php.

——. 2001d. "Sprachtest: Verein Deutsche Sprache." Available at http://vds-ev.de/denglisch/sprach test.php.

——. 2001e. "Sprachpanscher: Verein Deutsche Sprache." Available at http://vds-ev.de/denglisch/ sprachpanscher/sprachpanscher01.php.

Verges, Françoise. 1999. *Monsters and Revolutionaries: Colonial Family Romance and Métissage.* Durham, N.C.: Duke University Press.

Vilá, Carles, Jesús E. Maldonado, and Robert K. Wayne. 1999. "Phylogenetic Relationships, Evolution, and Genetic Diversity of the Domestic Dog." *The Journal of Heredity* 90, no. 1: 71–78.

Vilá, Carles, Peter Savolainen, Jesús E. Maldonado, Isabel R. Amorim, John E. Rice, Rodney L. Honeycutt, Keith A. Crandall, Joakim Lundeberg, and Robert K. Wayne. 1997. "Multiple and Ancient Origins of the Domestic Dog." *Science* 276 (13 June): 1687–89.

Virey, Julian-Joseph. 1837. *Natural History of the Negro Race.* Translated by J. H. Guenebault. Charlestown: D. J. Dowling.

Viswanathan, Gauri. 1993. "Raymond Williams and British Colonialism: The Limits of Metropolitan Cultural Theory." In *Views Beyond the Border Country,* edited by Dennis Dworkin and Leslie Roman. New York: Routledge.

Visweswaran, Kamala. 1998. "Race and the Culture of Anthropology." *American Anthropologist* 100, no. 1: 70–83.

Volpp, Leti. 1996. "Talking 'Culture': Gender, Race, Nation, and the Politics of Multiculturalism." *Columbia Law Review* 96, no. 6: 1573–617.

——. 2001. "Feminism Versus Multiculturalism." *Columbia Law Review* 101, no. 5: 1181–218.

Voltaire, François. 1961. [1759]. *Candide, Zadig and Selected Stories.* New York: New American Library.

Wacquant, Loic. 2001. "Deadly Symbiosis: When Ghetto and Prison Meet and Mesh." *Punishment and Society* 3, no. 1 (January): 95–133.

Wade, Peter. 1993a. "Race, Nature, and Culture." *Man* n.s. 28 (1): 17–34.

——. 1993b. *Blackness and Race Mixture: The Dynamics of Racial Identity in Colombia.* Baltimore: The Johns Hopkins University Press.

——. 1999. "Making Cultural Identities in Cali, Colombia." *Current Anthropology* 40, no. 4: 449–71.

Wagatsuma, Hiroshi. 1968. "The Social Perception of Skin Color in Japan." In *Color and Race,* edited by John Hope Franklin. Boston: Houghton Mifflin.

Wagley, Charles. 1977. *Welcome of Tears: The Tapirapé Indians of Central Brazil.* New York: Oxford University Press.

Wailoo, Keith. 1997. *Drawing Blood: Technology and Disease Identity in Twentieth-Century Medicine.* Baltimore: The Johns Hopkins University Press.

——. 2001. *Dying in the City of the Blues: Sickle Cell Anemia and the Politics of Race and Health.* Chapel Hill: University of North Carolina Press.

Walcott, Derek. 1998. *What the Twilight Says.* New York: Farrar, Straus and Giroux.

Waldman, Amy. 2001. "In Harlem, A Hero's Welcome for New Neighbor Clinton." *New York Times,* 31 July.

Wallace, Michele. 1990. *Invisibility Blues: From Pop to Theory.* London: Verso.

Walvin, James, ed. 1986. *A Testament of Hope: The Essential Writings and Speeches of Martin Luther King Jr.* San Francisco: Harper and Row.

Ward, Harriet. 1851. *The Cape and the Kaffirs.* London: Henry G. Bohn.

Ware, Vron. 1992. *Beyond the Pale: White Women, Racism, and History.* London: Verso.

——. 1997. "The White Issue." In *The Eight Technologies of Otherness,* edited by Sue Golding. London: Routledge.

Ware, Vron, and Les Back. 2001. *Out of Whiteness.* Chicago: University of Chicago Press.

Warren, Kay. 1998. *Indigenous Movements and Their Critics: Pan-Maya Activism in Guatemala.* Princeton: Princeton University Press.

——. 2002. "Voting Against Indigenous Rights in Guatemala: Lessons from the 1999 Referendum." In *Indigenous Movements, Self-Representation, and the State,* edited by Kay B. Warren and Jean Jackson. Austin: University of Texas Press.

Watanabe, John M. 1990. "Enduring Yet Ineffable Community." In *Guatemalan Indians and the State: 1540 to 1988,* edited by Carol Smith. Austin: University of Texas Press.

——. 1992. *Maya Saints and Souls in a Changing World.* Austin: University of Texas Press.

Watts, Michael. 1983. *Silent Violence.* Berkeley: University of California Press.

——. 1997. "Black Gold, White Heat: State Violence, Local Resistance and the National Question in Nigeria." In *Geographies of Resistance,* edited by Steve Pile and Michael Keith. New York: Routledge.

—. 1998. "Nature as Artifice and Artifact." In *Remaking Reality: Nature at the Millennium*, edited by Bruce Braun and Noel Castree. New York: Routledge.

—. 1999. "Collective Wish Images: Geographical Imaginaries and the Crisis of National Development." In *Human Geography Today*, edited by Doreen Massey, John Allen, and Philip Sarre. Cambridge: Polity Press.

Wayne, Robert K. 1993. "Molecular Evolution of the Dog Family." *Trends in Genetics* 9: 218–24.

Wehler, Hans-Ulrich. 1987. *Deutsche Gesellschaftsgeschichte*. Vol. 1, *Vom Feudalismus des Alten Reiches bis zur defensiven Modernisierung der Reformära 1700–1815*. Munich: C. H. Beck Verlag.

Weidensaul, Scott. 1999. "Tracking America's First Dogs." *Smithsonian Magazine*. 1 March.

Weisenfeld, Steven. 1967. "African Agricultural Patterns and Sickle Cell Anemia." *Science* 157: 1134.

Weiss, Rick. 1997. "Discovery of 'Jewish' Cancer Gene Raises Fears of More than Disease." *Washington Post*, 3 September: A1.

Weldon, Constance. 1984. "The Interaction Between the Missionaries of the Cape Eastern Frontier and the Colonial Authorities in the Era of Sir George Grey, 1854–1861." Master's thesis, University of Natal.

Werbner, Pnina, and Tariq Modood, eds. 1997. *Debating Cultural Hybridity*. London: Zed Books.

West, Cornel. 1990. "The New Cultural Politics of Difference." In *Out There*, edited by Russell Ferguson et al. Cambridge: MIT Press.

—. 1999. *The Cornel West Reader*. New York: Basic Books.

Westermann, Diedrich. 1949. [1937]. *The African To-Day and To-Morrow*. London: Oxford University Press.

Weston, Kath. 1998. *Long Slow Burn: Sexuality and Social Science*. New York: Routledge.

Westra, Laura. 1999. "Environmental Racism and the First Nations of Canada: Terrorism at Oka." *Journal of Social Philosophy* 30, no. 1: 103–24.

Westra, Laura, and Peter S. Wenz, eds. 1995. *Faces of Environmental Racism*. New York: Rowman and Littlefield.

White, Hayden. 1978. "Forms of Wildness: Archaeology of an Idea." In *Tropics of Discourse*. Baltimore: The Johns Hopkins University Press.

White, Lynn. 1967. "The Historical Roots of Our Ecological Crisis." *Science* 255: 1203–07.

White, Richard. 1991. *The Middle Ground: Indians, Empires, and Republics in the Great Lakes Region, 1650–1815*. Cambridge: Cambridge University Press.

—. 1995. *The Organic Machine: The Remaking of the Columbia River*. New York: Hill and Wang.

—. 1996. "Are You an Environmentalist or Do You Work for a Living? Work and Nature." In *Uncommon Ground: Rethinking the Human Place in Nature*, edited by William Cronon. New York: Norton.

Wiegman, Robyn. 1995. *American Anatomies: Theorizing Race and Gender*. Durham, N.C.: Duke University Press.

—. 1999. "Whiteness Studies and the Paradox of Particularity." *Boundary 2—An International Journal of Literature and Culture* 26, no. 3: 115–50.

Wigen, Karen. 1999. "Culture, Power, and Place: The New Landscape of East Asian Regionalism." *American Historical Review* 104, no. 4: 1183–201.

Wildenthal, Lora. 1994. "Colonizers and Citizens: Bourgeois Women and the Woman Question in the German Colonial Movement, 1886–1914." Ph.D. diss., Department of History, University of Michigan, Ann Arbor.

——. 1997. "Race, Gender, and Citizenship in the German Colonial Empire." In *Tensions of Empire,* edited by Frederick Cooper and Ann Stoler. Berkeley: University of California Press.

Wilkinson, Doris. 1974. "Politics and Sickle Cell Anemia." *Black Scholar* 5 (May): 26.

Will, George. 1990. "America's Slide into the Sewer." *Newsweek,* 30 July: 64.

Willems-Braun, Bruce. 1997. "Buried Epistemologies: The Politics of Nature in (Post) Colonial British Columbia." *Annals of the Association of American Geographers* 87, no. 1: 3–31.

Williams, Brackette F. 1989. "A Class Act—Anthropology and the Race to Nation Across Ethnic Terrain." *Annual Review of Anthropology* 18: 401–44.

——. 1995. "Classification Systems Revisited: The Flow of Blood and the Spread of Rights." In *Naturalizing Power,* edited by Sylvia Yanagisako and Carol Delaney. New York: Routledge.

Williams, Patricia J. 1991. *The Alchemy of Race and Rights.* Cambridge: Harvard University Press.

——. 1997. *Seeing a Color-Blind Future: The Paradox of Race.* New York: Noonday Press.

——. 1999. "Racism Explained to My Son." In *Racism Explained to My Daughter,* by Tahar Ben Jelloun. New York: The New Press.

Williams, Raymond. 1973. *The Country and the City.* New York: Oxford University Press.

——. 1976. *Keywords.* Oxford: Oxford University Press.

——. 1977. *Marxism and Literature.* Oxford: Oxford University Press.

——. 1980. [1972]. "Ideas of Nature." In *Problems in Materialism and Culture.* London: Verso.

——. 1989. *Resources of Hope: Culture, Democracy, Socialism.* New York: Verso.

Williams, Robert A., Jr. 1990. *The American Indian in Western Legal Thought.* New York: Oxford University Press.

Willis, Malcolm B. 1989. *Genetics of the Dog.* New York: Howell Book House.

Wilmsen, Edwin. 1989a. *Land Filled with Flies: A Political Economy of the Kalahari.* Chicago: University of Chicago Press.

——, ed. 1989b. *We Are Here: Politics of Aboriginal Land Tenure.* Berkeley: University of California Press.

——. 1996a. "Decolonising the Mind: Steps Toward Cleansing the Bushman Stain from Southern African History." In *Miscast,* edited by Pippa Skotnes. Cape Town: University of Cape Town Press.

——. 1996b. "Introduction: Premises of Power in Ethnic Politics." In *The Politics of Difference: Ethnic Premises in a World of Power,* edited by Edwin N. Wilmsen and Patrick McAllister. Chicago: University of Chicago Press.

Wilson, Alexander. 1991. *The Culture of Nature: Landscape from Disney to the Exxon Valdez.* Toronto: Between the Lines.

Wilson, Richard. 1995. *Maya Resurgence in Guatemala: Q'eqchi' Experience.* Norman: University of Oklahoma Press.

Winant, Howard. 2000. "Race and Race Theory." *Annual Review of Sociology* 26: 169–85.

Wolpe, Harold. 1986. "Class Concepts, Class Struggle, and Racism." In *Theories of Race and Ethnic Relations,* edited by John Rex and David Mason. Cambridge: Cambridge University Press.

Woods, Clyde. 1998. *Development Arrested: Race, Power, and the Blues in the Mississippi Delta.* New York: Verso.

Worster, Donald. 1977. *Nature's Economy: A History of Ecological Ideas.* Cambridge: Cambridge University Press.

Wright, Melissa W. 1997. "Crossing the Factory Frontier: Gender, Place, and Power in the Mexican Maquiladora." *Antipode* 29, no. 3: 278–302.

Wright, Winthrop R. 1990. *Café con Leche: Race, Class, and National Image in Venezuela.* Austin: University of Texas Press.

Yanagisako, Sylvia Junko. 1979. "Family and Household: The Analysis of Domestic Groups." *Annual Review of Anthropology* 8: 161–205.

Yanagisako, Sylvia, and Carol Delaney, eds. 1995. *Naturalizing Power: Essays in Feminist Cultural Analysis.* London: Routledge.

Yardley, Jim. 1999a. "Health Officials Investigating to Determine How Woman Got the Embryo of Another." *New York Times,* 31 March: B3.

——. 1999b. "Sharing Baby Proves Rough on 2 Mothers." *New York Times,* 30 June: B1.

Yoneyama, Lisa. 1999. *Hiroshima Traces.* Berkeley: University of California Press.

Young, Iris Marion. 1990. *Justice and the Politics of Difference.* Princeton: Princeton University Press.

——. 2000. *Inclusion and Democracy.* Oxford: Oxford University Press.

Young, Julian. 1997. *Heidegger, Philosophy, Nazism.* Cambridge: Harvard University Press.

Young, Lola, and Ingrid Pollard. 1995. "Environmental Images and Imaginary Landscapes." *Soundings* 1: 99–100.

Young, Robert J. C. 1995. *Colonial Desire: Hybridity in Theory, Culture, and Race.* New York: Routledge.

——. 2001a. *Postcolonialism: An Historical Introduction.* Oxford: Blackwell.

——. 2001b. Preface. In *Colonialism and Neocolonialism,* by Jean Paul Sartre. Translated by Azzedine Haddour et al. New York: Routledge.

Zammito, John H. 2002. *Kant, Herder, and the Birth of Anthropology.* Chicago: University of Chicago Press.

Zantrop, Susanne. 1997. *Colonial Fantasies.* Durham, N.C.: Duke University Press.

Zeitungsartikel. 1999. "Artikel über den Verein zur Wahrung der deutschen Sprache 1997–1999." Available at http://www.vwds.de/artikel.html.

Zerner, Charles. 1994. "Through a Green Lens: The Construction of Customary Environmental Law and Community in Indonesia's Maluku Island." *Law and Society Review* 28, no. 5: 1079–122.

——, ed. 2000. *People, Plants, and Justice.* New York: Columbia University Press.

Zimmerer, Karl. 1994. "Human Geography and the New Ecology." *Annals of the Association of American Geographers* 84, no. 1: 108–25.

——. 1996. *Changing Fortunes: Biodiversity and Peasant Livelihood in the Peruvian Andes.* Berkeley: University of California Press.

——. 2000. "The Reworking of Conservation Geographies: Nonequilibrium Landscapes and Nature-Society Hybrids." *Annals of the Association of American Geographers* 90, no. 2: 356–69.

Zur, Judith N. 1998. *Violent Memories: Mayan War Widows in Guatemala.* Boulder: Westview Press.

Contributors

Bruce Braun teaches geography at the University of Minnesota and works on the cultural politics of nature and First Nations land rights in the Canadian west. His research has appeared in *Annals of the Association of American Geographers, Ecumene,* and *Society and Space*. He is the author of *The Intemperate Rainforest: Nature, Culture, and Politics on Canada's West Coast* (Minnesota, 2002), and the coeditor, with Noel Castree, of *Remaking Reality: Nature at the Millennium* (Routledge, 1998) and *Social Nature: Theory, Practice, Politics* (Blackwell, 2001).

Giovanna Di Chiro teaches environmental studies and women's studies at Mount Holyoke College. She has published widely on the intersections of gender, race, and environmental justice. Her publications include contributions to the edited collections *Uncommon Ground* (Norton, 1996), *Reclaiming the Environmental Debate* (MIT, 2000), and *The Environmental Justice Reader* (Arizona, 2002), as well as *Socialist Review* and *Frontiers*. She is a coeditor of the forthcoming collection, *Appropriating Technology: Vernacular Science and Social Power* (Minnesota).

Paul Gilroy is professor of African American studies and sociology at Yale University. His books include *"There Ain't No Black in the Union Jack": The Cultural Politics of Race and Nation* (Chicago, 1987), *The Black Atlantic* (Harvard, 1993), *Small Acts* (Serpent's Tail, 1993), and *Against Race* (Harvard, 2000). He recently coedited *Without Guarantees* (Verso, 2000), a collection of essays in honor of Stuart Hall.

Steven Gregory teaches anthropology and African American studies at Columbia University. His books include *Black Corona: Race and the Politics of Place in an Urban Community* (Princeton, 1998), *Santeria in New York City: A Study in Cultural Resistance* (Garland, 2000), as well as the collection *Race* (Rutgers, 1994), coedited with Roger Sanjek. His articles on race, class, and the politics of difference have appeared in *Cultural Anthropology, American Ethnologist,* and *Social Text*. His recent work has focused on globalization, the state, and citizenship in the Dominican Republic.

Donna Haraway is a professor in the history of consciousness program at the University of California, Santa Cruz. Her books include *Crystals, Fabrics, and Fields: Metaphors of Organicism in*

Twentieth-Century Developmental Biology (Yale, 1976); *Primate Visions: Gender, Race, and Nature in the World of Modern Science* (Routledge, 1989); *Simians, Cyborgs, and Women: The Reinvention of Nature* (Routledge, 1991); *Modest Witness @ Second Millennium* (Routledge, 1997); and *How Like a Leaf* (Routledge, 2000). She is currently writing a sibling piece to her "Cyborg Manifesto," titled *The Companion Species Manifesto: Dogs, People, and Significant Otherness*, to be published by the University of Chicago Press in fall 2003.

Jake Kosek received his doctorate in geography at the University of California, Berkeley. He is presently the Lang Postdoctoral Fellow in the department of anthropological sciences at Stanford University as well as a visiting scholar in critical human geography at UC Berkeley. His dissertation research explored the cultural politics of nature, race, and locality amidst violent struggles over forest resources in Las Truchas, New Mexico. His current research examines how the eugenics movement linked nature to race in ways that haunt current debates over immigration, crime, and environmental conservation.

Tania Murray Li is associate professor in the department of sociology and social anthropology, Dalhousie University, Canada. Her work on urban cultural politics resulted in her book *Malays in Singapore* (Oxford, 1989). Since 1990, her research has focused on questions of culture, economy, environment, and development in Indonesia's upland regions. She edited the collection *Transforming the Indonesian Uplands* (Routledge, 1999).

Uli Linke is an associate professor in anthropology at Rutgers University. Her research explores issues of citizenship and sovereignty under globalization, with particular emphasis on discourses on blood, nature, and nation in postwar Germany. She is the author of *Blood and Nation: The European Aesthetics of Race* (Pennsylvania, 1999), and *German Bodies: Race and Representation after Hitler* (Routledge, 1999), as well as numerous chapters and articles on related themes about violence and modernity in Europe.

Zine Magubane teaches in the department of sociology at the University of Illinois, Urbana-Champaign. Her research explores the politics of race, imperial science, and colonial difference in nineteenth-century Britain and South Africa. She is the editor of *Postmodernism, Postcoloniality, and African Studies* (Africa World Press, 2002) and the author of *Bringing the Empire Home: Imagining Race, Class, and Gender in Britain and Colonial South Africa* (Chicago, forthcoming). Her articles have appeared in *Gender and Society, Socialist Review,* and the *South African Historical Journal,* among other journals.

Donald S. Moore teaches in the department of anthropology at the University of California, Berkeley. His ethnographic research has focused on the cultural politics of "race," governmentality, and landscape in Zimbabwe. His work has appeared in *American Ethnologist, Cultural Anthropology,* and *Transition,* among other journals, and in the edited collections *Liberation Ecologies* (Routledge, 1996) and *Geographies of Resistance* (Routledge, 1997).

Diane M. Nelson teaches in the department of cultural anthropology at Duke University. Her *A Finger in the Wound: Body Politics in Quincentennial Guatemala* (California, 1999) explores the biopolitics of race, nation, gender, and violence in contemporary Guatemala, where she has long been engaged in political and anthropological work. Her research has appeared in *American Ethnologist, Anthropology Today,* and *Cultural Anthropology,* among other journals. She is currently working on a project on duplicity and subject formation in postwar Guatemala. Her new research explores malaria eradication campaigns as a form of biopolitics in the milieu of neoliberal globalization.

Anand Pandian is a doctoral candidate in the department of anthropology at the University of California, Berkeley. His dissertation focuses on questions of cultivation and criminality in colonial and postcolonial south India. Prior work on imperial hunting rituals in India has appeared in the *Journal of Historical Sociology*.

Alcida Rita Ramos is a professor in the department of anthropology at the Universidade de Brasilia. Her work explores the cultural politics and anthropological representation of indigeneity in contemporary Brazil. She has long been active in the defense of indigenous rights, especially of the Yanomami. Her two most recent books are *Indigenism: Ethnic Politics in Brazil* (Wisconsin, 1998) and *Sanumá Memories: Yanomami Ethnography in Times of Crisis* (Wisconsin, 1995). Her work has appeared in *Critique of Anthropology* and *Cultural Anthropology*, among other journals, and edited collections in English, Portuguese, Spanish, and Polish.

Keith Wailoo is professor in the department of history and the Institute for Health, Health Care Policy, and Aging Research at Rutgers University. His research has explored the comparative history of disease. His writings include *Drawing Blood: Technology and Disease Identity in Twentieth-Century America* (Johns Hopkins, 1997) and *Dying in the City of the Blues: Sickle Cell Anemia and the Politics of Race and Health* (North Carolina, 2001). Both works place particular emphasis on the cultural role of biomedical technologies and the discourse of pathology in shaping identities, social relations, and ideologies of difference.

Robyn Wiegman is director of women's studies at Duke University. Her research in literary and cultural studies traverses the terrain of race, gender, and the cultural politics of difference in contemporary America as well as its historical precursors. She is the author of *American Anatomies: Theorizing Race and Gender* (Duke, 1995); *Literature and Gender,* with Elena Glasberg (Addison-Wesley, 1998); and coeditor of *Feminism Beside Itself,* with Diane Elam (Routledge, 1995), as well as *Who Can Speak? Authority and Critical Identity,* with Judith Roof (Illinois, 1995). She also edited a collection of essays by Thomas E. Yingling, *AIDS and the National Body* (Duke, 1997). Her work has appeared in *boundary 2, Critical Inquiry, Cultural Critique,* and the *Journal of the History of Sexuality,* among other locations.

Index

Environmental justice, 5, 15–16, 31, 50 n.19, 197, 206–7, 214–30

Environmental politics, 16, 31, 204–32, 361–67, 380–81, 395–402. *See also* Political ecology

Environmental racism, 15–16, 50 n.19, 215–16, 223

Environmental resources, 5, 11, 16, 23, 35, 205–6, 208–13, 329, 376, 395–98

Equality, 37, 366, 376–77. *See also* Inequality

Essentialism, 39, 41, 66 n.180, 96 n.5, 214, 350, 357, 361, 368–71, 373–75, 384. *See also* Exoticism

Ethics, 32, 81, 85, 179, 267, 349, 354 n.10. *See also* Selfhood; Sentiment; Soul

Ethnic absolutism, 24, 27, 88. *See also* Gilroy, Paul

Ethnic cleansing, 34, 383

Ethnicity, 35, 77, 156–58, 239, 357–58, 372, 376

Ethnology, 12, 28, 113. *See also* Anthropology

Eugenics, 21, 58 n.97, 129, 136, 237, 240, 243–46, 259–61. *See also* Breeding; Improvement

Europe: provincializing, 5, 85; racism in, 27, 60 n.122, 113–15, 149–74, 368. *See also* Fascism; Nazism

Evictions. *See* Forced removals

Evolution, 18, 19–21, 37, 242, 245, 265, 279–82. *See also* Darwin, Charles; Lamarck, Jean-Baptiste de

Exclusion, 6, 23, 28, 43, 46, 81, 112, 155, 157, 383

Exoticism, 358, 363, 371–73. *See also* Essentialism

Experience, 5, 63 n.143, 31–33, 89, 207, 217, 223–27, 238, 299–300, 307, 341

Exploitation, 38, 41, 74, 209, 328, 335–36, 388. *See also* Domination; Power

Exploration, 185–92

Fact, 24, 120–21, 286–87; race as a social and cultural, 43, 108. *See also* Truth

Family, 34, 37, 306, 309, 311, 319 n.33, 342. *See also* Kinship

Fanon, Frantz, 24, 26, 32, 44–45, 59 n.107, 62 n.141, 67 n.192, 73, 75, 76, 81, 83–85, 87, 92, 95, 96 n.11, 104, 115, 118, 248

Fascism, 18, 74, 152, 265. *See also* Nazism

Fear, 13, 19, 20, 21, 31, 77, 108, 149, 163, 184, 196, 262, 281–82, 358. *See also* Sentiment; Terror

Feld, Steven, 31

Femininity, 103, 108–12, 352. *See also* Gender; Masculinity

Feminism, 5, 16, 49, 50 n.22, 55 n.73, 300–304, 327, 342, 353 nn.2, 4

Ferguson, James, 23

Fertility, 297. *See also* Reproduction

Fetish, 358–59

Fixity, 4, 39, 42, 122–23, 127, 142, 198

Folk, 34, 128, 165, 359, 370

Forced removals, 13, 14, 22, 38, 106, 399

Forests, 9, 29, 367, 376, 380, 388–89, 391, 395–98. *See also* Conservation; Environmentalism

Formation: as analytical category, 3, 49 n.11, 395

Foucault, Michel, 8, 14, 37, 49 n.15, 56 n.75, 56 n.81, 78, 137, 141, 265–66, 328, 357, 385. *See also* Biopolitics; Biopower; Governmentality

France, 33, 39

Franklin, Sarah, 299, 301, 317 n.14

Freedom, 8, 44, 45, 74, 84, 89, 178, 229, 254, 265, 347. *See also* Liberalism; Liberation

Freud, Sigmund, 15, 358

Frontier: American, 30, 177, 190–96; colonial, 105; German linguistic, 159

Fuss, Diana, 39

Galton, Francis, 21

Gardens, 9, 39, 52 n.36, 170, 400. *See also* Cultivation

Gender, 5, 16, 34, 50 n.22, 55 n.73, 76, 101–2, 103, 108–11, 112, 194, 203 n.30, 323–55. *See also* Femininity; Heteronormativity; Masculinity; Sex: and sexuality

Gene, 11, 26, 35, 36, 299; as property, 304–6. *See also* DNA; Genetics; Genome

Genealogy, 5, 6, 49 n.15, 61 n.126, 73, 92, 152, 168–69, 384. *See also* History

Genetics, 26, 235–53, 296–99; canine, 254–95; folk, 128, 145 n.12; vs. gestation, 297–98, 301, 304, 314. *See also* DNA; Gene; Genome

Genocide, 13, 14, 25, 46, 78, 110, 122, 124, 126–28, 135, 141, 153, 241

Genome, 36–37, 76, 249, 254–55, 270, 293 n.3. *See also* DNA; Gene; Genetics

Geo-body, 63 n.149

"9/11," 20, 45–46, 68 n.197, 93–95, 144 n.9
Noble Savage, 1, 13, 39, 361–64, 394
Non-Governmental Organizations (NGOs),
126, 211–13, 380, 385, 397. *See also* Activists; Social movements
Normalization, 81, 167, 179, 300, 315. *See also*
Discipline
Nostalgia, 32, 190, 373. *See also* Melancholy;
Sentiment

Occupied Territories, 45
Oikos, 8, 18
Ong, Aihwa, 57 n.89, 59 n.110, 63 n.147, 154–
55, 328, 347
Organicism, 38, 64 n.151, 149, 153, 161–65,
170–72
Orientalism, 54 n.59, 356
Otherness, 128, 149, 162–63, 164–65, 249, 330,
357, 372. *See also* Alterity; Difference
Our Common Future, 204, 208–10

Palestine, 24, 45, 69 n.199
Pan-Africanism, 33, 92
Passionate attachment, 25, 31, 32, 36, 40, 62
n.141. *See also* Love; Sentiment
Pastoral care, 17, 22, 36, 136–37, 397. *See also*
Governmentality; Management
Pastoral imaginaries, 14, 342–43, 352
Paternity, 37, 298, 307–13
Patriotism, 45, 93, 162, 164, 166, 311. *See also*
Nationalism
Performance, 155, 165, 373–74; as performativity, 35, 185, 196
Personhood, 37, 109–10, 117; liberal, 297, 299,
302–5, 316. *See also* Property; Selfhood
Phillipines, 20
Phrenology, 104, 110
Place, 29, 32, 192, 219, 383, 402; and identity,
36, 178, 180, 181–82; sense of, 31, 62 n.137,
215, 229. *See also* Belonging: geography of;
Geography; Landscape; Landscapes of affect;
Spatial politics
Plants, 1, 170–72, 401. *See also* Environmental
resources; Forests
Pleasure, 19, 161, 196, 330, 332, 335, 352. *See
also* Desire; Sex: sexuality
Polanyi, Karl, 59 n.110
Political alliances, 31, 42–43, 45–47, 124, 128,
139, 143, 206–7, 211, 225–30, 384

Political ecology, 5, 8, 15–16, 23, 214. *See also*
Environmental politics
Political economy, 5, 15–16, 41, 105, 177–78,
210, 216, 312, 327–32, 345, 347–49, 351–52.
See also Class; Globalization; Neoliberalism
Politics, 25, 31, 37–47, 82, 227, 239. *See also*
Cultural politics
Politics of representation, 37–42, 177, 356,
368–79. *See also* Recognition
Pollard, Ingrid, 14
Pollution, 22, 29, 159, 171, 215, 217, 219–23,
228. *See also* Purity
Polyvalent mobility, 4, 49 n.15, 68 n.194, 138
Population, 11, 18, 79, 153, 240–44, 249, 255–
59, 261–62, 392, 397. *See also* Governmentality; Management
Positioning, 33, 40, 44. *See also* Cultural
politics
Postcoloniality, 5, 26–27, 73, 77, 81, 84, 90, 91
Poststructuralism, 27, 40
Power, 6, 14–17, 27, 206, 266, 327–28, 330,
339, 348, 357, 367, 385, 387. *See also* Discipline; Domination; Exploitation; Pastoral
care
Practice(s), 2, 3–4, 6, 8–11, 25–26, 32, 33, 42,
47, 48 n.10, 75, 79, 86, 104, 118, 120, 155,
165, 176, 178, 259, 263, 264, 283, 326, 336,
351, 371, 395. *See also* Cultural politics
Predation, 184, 342, 354 n.8
Primitivism, 12, 13, 23, 38, 39, 114, 192, 194–
95, 364–65, 394, 401. *See also* Essentialism;
Exoticism
Progress. *See* History; Improvement
Property, 92, 305; as basis of liberal personhood, 297, 300; and character, 199; contractual, 37; customary rights to, 11, 388, 390–
92; in land, 395–98; primitive accumulation
and, 107. *See also* Contract; Law(s); State
Protection, 22, 30, 377
Purity, 7, 27, 29, 30, 34, 130, 196–98, 203 n.24,
256–58, 342–43, 367; of language, 159–65,
169–70. *See also* Pollution

Queer theory, 29, 327. *See also*
Heteronormativity

Rabinow, Paul, 36, 49 n.11, 57 n.93, 250 n.4
Race: beyond, 74–75, 85–90; as biological, 175;
in the blood, 126–31, 132, 236, 302; catego-

Library of Congress Cataloging-in-Publication Data
Race, nature, and the politics of difference/edited by Donald S.
Moore, Jake Kosek, and Anand Pandian.
Includes bibliographical references and index.
ISBN 0-8223-3079-2 (alk. paper)
ISBN 0-8223-3091-1 (pbk. : alk. paper)
1. Race relations. 2. Ethnic relations. 3. Group identity.
4. Nature—Political aspects. 5. Power (Social sciences) I. Moore,
Donald S., 1963– II. Kosek, Jake. III. Pandian, Anand.
HT1521.R2355 2003   305.8—dc21   2002153599